Extravagance and Misery

OXFORD POLITICAL PHILOSOPHY

General Editor
Samuel Freeman, University of Pennsylvania

Oxford Political Philosophy publishes books on theoretical and applied political philosophy within the Anglo-American tradition. The series welcomes submissions on social, political, and global justice, individual rights, democracy, liberalism, socialism, and constitutionalism.

N. Scott Arnold
Imposing Values: An Essay on Liberalism and Regulation

Peter de Marneffe
Liberalism and Prostitution

William J. Talbott
Human Rights and Human Well-Being

Iris Marion Young
Responsibility for Justice

Paul Weithman
Why Political Liberalism? On John Rawls's Political Turn

Aaron James
Fairness in Practice: A Social Contract for a Global Economy

Margaret Moore
A Political Theory of Territory

Alan Thomas
Republic of Equals: Predistribution and Property-Owning Democracy

Dan Moller
Governing Least: A New England Libertarianism

Christian Schemmel
Justice and Egalitarian Relations

Waheed Hussain, edited by Arthur Ripstein and Nicholas Vrousalis
Living with the Invisible Hand: Markets, Corporations, and Human Freedom

Alan Thomas, Alfred Archer, and Bart Engelen
Extravagance and Misery: The Emotional Regime of Market Societies

Extravagance and Misery

The Emotional Regime of Market Societies

ALAN THOMAS, ALFRED ARCHER, AND
BART ENGELEN

OXFORD
UNIVERSITY PRESS

OXFORD
UNIVERSITY PRESS

Oxford University Press is a department of the University of Oxford. It furthers the University's objective of excellence in research, scholarship, and education by publishing worldwide. Oxford is a registered trade mark of Oxford University Press in the UK and certain other countries.

Published in the United States of America by Oxford University Press
198 Madison Avenue, New York, NY 10016, United States of America.

Library of Congress Cataloging-in-Publication Data
Names: Thomas, Alan, 1964- author. | Archer, Alfred, author. |
Engelen, Bart, 1980- author.
Title: Extravagance and misery : the emotional regime of market societies /
Alan Thomas, Alfred Archer and Bart Engelen.
Description: New York, NY : Oxford University Press, [2024] | Series: Oxford political philosophy |
Includes bibliographical references and index.
Identifiers: LCCN 2024023375 (print) | LCCN 2024023376 (ebook) |
ISBN 9780197781722 (hardback) | ISBN 9780197781746 (epub)
Subjects: LCSH: Income distribution—Psychological aspects. |
Income distribution—Social aspects. | Income distribution—Philosophy.
Classification: LCC HB523 .T46 2024 (print) | LCC HB523 (ebook) |
DDC 339.201—dc23/eng/20240729
LC record available at https://lccn.loc.gov/2024023375
LC ebook record available at https://lccn.loc.gov/2024023376

DOI: 10.1093/oso/9780197781722.001.0001

Printed by Marquis Book Printing, Canada

MIX
Paper | Supporting responsible forestry
FSC® C103567

In memoriam:
Waheed Hussain
1972–2021

Contents

Acknowledgements

The authors jointly acknowledge the support of the Sir John Templeton Foundation for funding the project "Inequality and Well-Being" from 2016 to 2018. The research conducted for this project forms the basis of much of the content of this book. We also thank Dan Haybron, the original grant recipient, for his support of this project at all stages.

Alan Thomas thanks the Independent Social Research Foundation for further financial support for the research contained in this book based on their project award "Plebeian Finance" for the calendar year 2019. He thanks Kathryn Brown for her constant love and support throughout the writing of this book. Writing this book with his co-authors has been a pleasure: it has been a lengthy but rewarding process.

Alfred Archer thanks Georgie Mills and Macky the Cat for their love and support during the writing of this book, his colleagues at Tilburg University for providing such a supportive and encouraging research environment, and the members of the European Philosophical Society for the Study of Emotions for the important role they have played in the development of his research on emotions. Finally, he is incredibly grateful to his two wonderful co-authors.

Bart Engelen thanks his co-authors for the long but gratifying journey, his colleagues at Tilburg University for the pleasant and supportive work environment, and his friends, family, partner, and dog for the support needed to keep him mentally sane throughout the entire process.

The authors would like to thank our series editor, Samuel Freeman, our editor Peter Ohlin, and project editor Meredith Taylor for their support and assistance. We are grateful to Joep de Groot, for his work on the index of terms. We would also like to thank Sara Protasi, editor, and Rowman and Littlefield for permission to reproduce material from 'The Politics of Envy, our contribution to *The Moral Psychology of Envy* (2021). We would also like to thank Leonie Smith, editor, and Springer for permission to reproduce material from 'The Shame of Living in Poverty in Capitalist Societies', our contribution to the edited volume *The Moral Psychology of Poverty: Reasoning, Agency, Emotions*. In addition, the table on page 8 is reproduced from Carter C. Price and Kathryn A. Edwards, *Trends in Income from 1975 to 2018,* RAND Corporation, WR-A516-1, 2020 with the permission of the RAND Corporation and the authors.

We have dedicated this book to Waheed Hussain, a brilliant philosopher who passed away in 2021. We hope that Waheed would have liked this book given that it deals with issues very close to his philosophical concerns (Hussain 2020, 2023).

While this book is a work of philosophy, it synthesizes results from other social scientific disciplines to develop its argument. We have attempted to make it accessible to readers from different disciplines. To this end, we signpost the different steps of the argument by including propositional summaries of the argument. The reader will find the argument of each chapter summarized at the start of each chapter.

Introduction

This book aims to explain the huge and often growing inequalities in our societies in the affluent West, to diagnose the impact that they have had on human well-being, and to propose more just alternatives. We use the empirical resources of the new science of happiness to diagnose what has gone wrong in our highly unequal and frequently unhappy societies. In assessing the consequences of the extensive economic inequalities of these societies, we specifically examine the role of key political emotions. This is one aspect of what French social scientist Thomas Piketty calls the study of "inequality regimes" (Piketty 2020, p.2).[1] We discuss which "dominant narratives" arise from the many putative justifications used to vindicate inequality in different societies and times.[2]

While much attention has been devoted to the concept of justice in Anglo-American philosophy over the last fifty years, we think one complementary issue has been comparatively neglected. That is the role played by political emotions in the stabilization of socio-economic regimes.[3] The issue of stability, canonically formulated by John Rawls, is whether a just society can command the allegiance of a sufficient number of its citizens. In his final monograph on domestic justice, Rawls prioritized this question of whether stability for "the right reasons" would be reinforced, or undermined, by a range of politically relevant emotions (Rawls 2001). Can a society well-ordered by justice withstand the fact that some citizens want to dominate others or that others are motivated by envy or spite?

[1] Piketty defines such regimes as "a set of discourses and institutional arrangements intended to justify and structure the economic, social and political inequalities of a given society" (Piketty 2020, p.2).

[2] He notes that current dominant narrative in the affluent West is meritocratic, in which "the poor [are] blamed for their own poverty" (Piketty 2020, p.2). In chapter 11 we argue that emotions are key to these putative meritocratic justifications that he argues "serve as a way for the winners . . . to justify any level of inequality whatsoever" (ibid.).

[3] An exception is Martha Nussbaum's work, to which we are indebted, particularly (Nussbaum 2015). She explicitly focuses on the role of love in fostering commitment to shared political goals that move us closer to justice.

Extravagance and Misery. Alan Thomas, Alfred Archer, and Bart Engelen, Oxford University Press.
 DOI: 10.1093/oso/9780197781722.003.0001

For example, Eric Lonergan and Mark Blyth detect a connection between patterns of socio-economic distribution, political instability, and the key emotion of anger in their book *Angrynomics* (Lonergan and Blyth 2020).[4] Why should this be the case? The Cold War has been over since 1989, and aside from major disruptions such as the global pandemic of 2020–22, our world is safer, more stable, and more prosperous than it has been for decades. Yet there is the looming threat of climate change and, across many societies in the affluent West, large-scale movements of social discontent. Why, when from a socio-economic point of view, one could echo Harold Macmillan's claim in 1957 that "you have never had it so good", do our affluent societies face a legitimation crisis?

Paradoxically, the lengthy period of comparative stability since the end of the Cold War and increasing affluence in the aggregate have caused this problem. In our view, that is because these material gains are not being shared fairly. Across countries, we are seeing what Christopher Lasch presciently called the "triumph of the elites" and that which Michael Lind has called a "new class war" (Lasch 1995; Lind 2020). The practical effects of that social conflict are manifold, but we think the key factor at play here is the extensive and ever-deepening inequality of income and wealth that characterizes our societies and how its (mal-)distribution is allegedly justified (Piketty 2014; Thomas 2017). Is this unrest motivated by the spiteful resentment of the group whom US presidential candidate Mitt Romney unwisely labelled as the "takers"—as opposed to the "makers" (Klein 2012)? Or do Romney's "takers" have reasonable grounds for their anger? (Note that this explanation already invokes an important, politically relevant emotion.)

When Romney divided the US electorate in this way, he tapped into a sense of entitlement on the part of the haves and identified what he took to be an insufficient degree of gratitude from the have-nots, who are supposedly "carried" by the efforts of "the 53%". As we will argue, this is one aspect of the fictional story of meritocracy that anyone in the United States can join the maker class if they exercise responsibility, initiative, and hard work. This narrative of social mobility invites scepticism in the light of the recent empirical data we will discuss in this book. Given the hegemonic cultural status

[4] The core of their argument is that our political life is dominated by the expression of public and private anger. The economic circumstances of the lives of many people across the affluent West have subjected them to uncertainty, which induces anxiety and a sense of unfairness that the gains from economic advance are distributed so unfairly that has produced anger (Lonergan and Blyth 2020).

of the United States, this "politics of aspiration" has spread more widely and sustains meritocratic narratives elsewhere, notably in the United Kingdom.

We are certainly not the first to draw on the empirical resources of economics, psychology, biology, health sciences, and sociology to address these issues (Payne 2017; Frank 1999/2010, 2007, 2016; Wilkinson and Pickett 2009, 2018). This is the body of work that we will refer to as the new science of happiness. Our book joins this plethora of books that have put this resource to productive use. Why add another? Because we think that our approach differs in two key respects from this existing literature.

First, we are political philosophers. We draw on the results of all these empirical sciences without contributing to those disciplines ourselves. But we frame these results, using our own discipline, to address this question: why, if a social system seems to have a wide-ranging, negative impact on well-being for so many people, is it not changed? The societies we focus on are, after all, social democracies. The views of the majority ought to hold sway. If extensive inequalities cause so many social ills, then why do we continue to tolerate them?

Our answer, foreshadowed in Piketty's work and our own earlier work, is "the drift to oligarchy" (Piketty 2014; Thomas 2017). First, a striking fact about inequality in, for example, the United States is how poorly informed the average citizen is about its extent. Secondly, the US political system seems to do a poor job of expressing the preferences of the average citizen unless those happen to coincide with those of the influential wealthy minority (especially its billionaire class) (Gilens and Page 2014).[5] Thirdly—and this will be our primary focus—these market societies embed an "emotional regime" that helps keep the system in place in a way that serves the interests of the wealthy.[6] These features, taken together, also explain why much of our argument focuses on the United States (a point to which we will return below).

This leads to our second difference from the existing literature. We formulate our explanations primarily in terms of what we call the "political emotions"—resentment, anger, envy, spite, admiration, and the desire for respect or esteem. We do not mean to imply that other political philosophers have ignored the topic. What they have not done is bring that discussion to

[5] This is not, however, another book on inequality that seeks to castigate the very rich, such as America's top 1% in the income and wealth distribution. The problem is more acute when we focus on the top 20% of the distribution and its relation to the lower 80% (Temin 2017).

[6] Our central thesis is complementary to Piketty's claim that traces of how pre-modern ternary societies organized and justified inequality carry over to the modern, "proprietarian" societies of our time (Piketty 2020, p.63).

bear on the topic of economic inequality to address Rawls's question about stability.[7] We argue that political emotions play a crucial role in the stabilization of inequality regimes. The question is whether they could play a different role in societies well-ordered by justice. Will the latter always be destabilized by envy, spite, or the will to dominate? That was Rawls's question, which we will answer using the new science of happiness (Rawls 2001). We will empirically support the claim that Rawls's conception of a just and stable society will require its institutions and policies to be complemented by a solidaristic political psychology.

[7] Except, notably, works by Kiran Bannerjee and Jeffrey Bercuson, that we discuss below (Bannerjee and Bercuson 2015; Bercuson 2014).

1
The Problem of Inequality

Propositional Summary

1. We set out the empirical data on the evolution of inequality globally and with a specific focus on the domestic economies of the United States and United Kingdom.
2. We synthesize four explanations of the substantial increase in income and wealth inequality over the last forty years: disproportionate returns to capital vis-à-vis income from labour; the politics of wage suppression; the rise of sectoral division; the expansion of policies of rent extraction.
3. We consider the explanation that our focus on the US economy is misleading because it is an outlier in recent development. While we note that the United States is exceptional in key respects, we still take it to be a bellwether for globalized changes across the affluent West.
4. We consider a challenge to our view, namely that it is Eurocentric and fails to consider a global process of globalization and free trade that will eventually bring hope to the global poor. This allows us to clarify our normative commitments: that inequality is inherently bad and that unjust inequalities, in particular, have further bad extrinsic effects.

Introduction

No one can decry the achievements of our affluent societies in providing an historically unprecedented standard of material well-being for their citizens. That can be true even if, historically, colonialism plays a larger role in this outcome than we are comfortable in acknowledging (Piketty 2020, pp.17–9). However, our societies are currently undergoing legitimation crises caused by persistent and growing inequality. In this chapter we first present the

Extravagance and Misery. Alan Thomas, Alfred Archer, and Bart Engelen, Oxford University Press.
 DOI: 10.1093/oso/9780197781722.003.0002

empirical data; after which we put in place the explanatory and normative frameworks that we believe explain this data.

1.1 The Facts of Inequality

The empirical evidence seems clear: inequality has deepened within a range of countries in the affluent West—even as it narrows internationally (Bourguignon 2012; Milanović 2016). There has been a striking increase in both income and wealth inequality in the United States, which is still the world's largest economy and the richest country ever to have existed with its annual GDP of $22.44 trillion in 2019 immediately before the COVID-19 global pandemic (Drennan 2015; Bourguignon 2012; Piketty 2014; Stiglitz 2012; Thomas 2017). The data on inequality in the United States between 1970 and the present are, by now, well known (Saez and Zucman 2016). François Bourguignon summarized it a decade ago as follows:

> The concentration of wealth far exceeds that of income. In the United States, the richest 10% receive 40% of total primary household income, but possess 71% of total wealth. For the richest 1%, the numbers are 15% and 35% respectively (. . .). (Wealth inequality) has risen quite significantly (. . .) and the richest 10% have seen their share increase from 64% to 71% between 1970 and 2010, a rise that is more or less equivalent to what happened with their share of income. (Bourguignon 2012, p.58)

The concentration of wealth is even more striking when you focus on the super-rich: "The top 1 percent own about 42 percent of the wealth, and the top 0.1 percent alone own 22 percent" (Stiglitz 2012, p.426).

There are different measures of inequality, but the results change only slightly using different measures. There is a distinction between wealth and income inequalities, with the former generally being much larger than the latter. Most data, however, concern the latter, which are easier to calculate. Often, disposable household income is measured: the sum of all monetary incomes a household receives minus taxes and social contributions. Also, different measures compare different groups. Not only can the focus be on inequalities within a region, a country or the world, the measure can define the rich and the poor differently or try and incorporate data from all groups.[1]

Overall, the top 0.1% now owns almost as much wealth as the bottom 90% of the population of the United States. The share of the bottom 90% is down from 35% in the mid-1980s to about 23% in 2012 (Saez and Zucman 2016). Of particular interest to us in this data is the steepness of the inequality gradient: over the last forty years, the top 10% have pulled away from the lower 90%; the 1% have pulled away from the remaining 9% of the top 10%; within the 1% the top 0.1% have pulled away from the 0.9%.

While the long-term effect of the coronavirus pandemic is unclear, in the short term its economic impact has been further to exacerbate these inequalities. Over the longer run, these developments have many complex explanations, some of which we will discuss in this book. Abstracting away from the truth of any single explanation, we can at least conclude that with the poor getting ever smaller slices of the pie it is evident that the (super-) rich are helping themselves to ever bigger slices (in both absolute and relative terms). The fundamental driver of our explanatory framework is the disproportionate political power that America's wealthiest citizens exert over the political process in the United States (Formisano 2015, 2017; Gilens 2012; Gilens and Page 2014; Page, Bartels, and Seawright 2013; Page and Gilens 2017).[2]

What actual figures, denominated in US dollar terms, are at issue here? The United States is, overall, a very wealthy society. We reproduce the following table from Carter C. Price and Kathryn Edwards's study for the RAND Corporation, omitting their "counterfactual" tracking of income trends that we will discuss below (Table 1.1; Price and Edwards 2020, p.10).

An overall aspect of these numbers may surprise non-Americans: strikingly, the United States is a comparatively low wage economy in aggregate. (Forty years of inflation suppression has had an effect.) An important qualification

[1] Some of the most widely used measures are the following. First, decile or quintile share ratios. The S80/S20 quintile share ratio, for example, refers to the ratio of average income received by the top quintile (S80: those 20% of the population with the highest income) to that received by the bottom quintile (S20: those 20% of the population with the lowest income). Another popular ratio is S90/S10 (average income of the 10% richest to the 10% poorest). Second, the Gini coefficient. This coefficient is derived from the Lorenz curve, which ranks households from the lowest to the highest income and plots the cumulative proportion of the population (horizontal axis) and their cumulative proportion of income (vertical axis). The Gini coefficient can range from 0 (perfect equality, straight Lorenz curve) to 1 (only one member of the population holds all its resources).

[2] As Christopher Hayes observes in the case of the United States "The 1 percent and the nation's governing class are more or less one and the same. If you are a member of the governing elite and aren't a millionaire you are doing something wrong" (Hayes 2012, p.154).

Table 1.1 Income Distribution for Adults with Income in 2018 Dollars

	1975	1979	1989	2000	2007	2018
25%	$9,000	$6,000	$9,000	$13,000	$14,000	$15,000
Median	$26,000	$23,000	$26,000	$32,000	$34,000	$36,000
75%	$46,000	$44,000	$48,000	$57,000	$59,000	$65,000
90th%	$65,000	$67,000	$73,000	$93,000	$98,000	$112,000
95th%	$80,000	$84,000	$95,000	$125,000	$138,000	$164,000
99th%	$162,000	$158,000	$222,000	$479,000	$371,000	$491,000
Top 1% Mean	$252,000	$272,000	$431,000	$1,009,000	$1,108,000	$1,160,000

that Price and Edwards note in the interpretation of this tabulated data is that "much of the movement at the bottom of the distribution is driven by an increase in hours not an increase in wages" (Price and Edwards 2020, p.11). Slumping real wages mean that people need to work longer hours for reasons we will explore later in this book. Conversely, at the top end of the range, it is worth bearing in mind on this point Piketty's observation that "income is often not a well-defined concept for very wealthy individuals" (Piketty 2014, p.525; Temin 2017, p.78).

These growing inequalities are mostly due to the rich and the super-rich getting richer at a much faster pace than the middle class and the poor, whose wealth is, by contrast, eroding. (That is if, in the case of the poor, they have any wealth to speak of at all as opposed to debt, fluctuating or precarious income, or a complete dependence on state benefits.) This rise in inequality represents a return to the vast inequalities witnessed in Europe and the United States at the end of the nineteenth century and the beginning of the twentieth century, reversing the post–World War II trend of declining intra-societal inequality. Piketty and Saez note, of income inequality alone, that "primary income concentration is currently higher than it has ever been in U.S. history" (Piketty and Saez 2014, p.839).

Income inequality can, and does, rapidly become wealth inequality given that the better off can more easily save. Saez and Zucman note an important factor they call the "snowball effect":

> Top incomes are being saved at high rates, pushing wealth concentration up; in turn, rising wealth inequality leads to rising capital income

concentration, which contributes to further increasing top income and wealth shares. (Saez and Zucman 2016, p.523)

In the aftermath of the 2008 financial crisis, income and wealth inequalities continued to grow. The benefits brought by whatever economic growth there has been since the recovery have gone disproportionately to the richest people. When we look at income, "the typical American didn't see any recovery even after the recession officially ended: 91% of all the increase in the first three years of the "recovery" went to the top 1%" (Stiglitz 2012, p.426).

Economist Pavlina Tcherneva has developed a data set that demonstrates the evolution of non-inclusive gains from growth for the United States for the entire period between 1970 and 2017 (Tcherneva 2014, 2017). Her data shows that from 1940 to 1970 the lowest 90% of the US population (by income) received between 80% down to 50% of income growth—at a steadily declining rate over these decades. But one might reasonably make the case that during these decades gains in prosperity were, to a degree, "shared". However, by the 1980s this had changed: from 1982 to 1990, the share of income growth going to the lowest 90% had dropped to 20% before it "rallied" between 1991 and 2000 to 27%.

At this point an even more striking change occurs: in the period immediately before the financial crisis (between 2000 and 2007) no less than 98% of income gains went to the upper decile. Yet, in the period immediately after the 2007–8 financial crisis, 116% of income gains went to the upper decile. In Tcherneva's words, this statistic is an "absurd result" which "is possible because the bottom 90 percent actually saw their incomes fall, on average, during this growth period" (Tcherneva 2014).

Clearly, the global financial crisis is a distorting factor here. Wealthy people lost money during the crisis but, as a class, they are better protected against economic downturns by professional investment advice and diversified and hedged portfolios, and are placed to recover from subsequent market gains (Malacrino 2020). They were, then, also comparatively well placed to weather the economic storm of the pandemic that shut down large parts of the global economy in 2020—an exogenous "biological shock", as Adam Tooze calls it (Tooze 2021, p.292).

Tcherneva documents how, since this post-crisis nadir, the weak "recovery" has seen the income gains from growth to the bottom 90% return to the range 18%–22% with the remainder going to the already wealthy.[3] However one explains the paradox of that which William Lazonick has called "profits without prosperity", it is clear that whatever prosperity exists, it is not shared, but monopolized by the already wealthy (Lazonick 2014; Lazonick and Shin 2019). That can be seen most clearly when Tcherneva further differentiates the gains from growth between the lowest 9% of the upper decile and the "1%". During the period 2009–12, 95% of all gains in income went to the top 1%. While academics and pundits used to discuss the "squeezed middle", the economic data shows why this discussion is rapidly evolving into one about the non-existent middle class in the United States (Temin 2017).

Other countries in the affluent West, notably the United Kingdom, exhibit the same tendency as the United States—but to a lesser degree.[4] The Institute for Public Policy Research, a UK-based think tank, issued a report in 2017, "Wealth in the Twenty First Century: Inequalities and Drivers", whose key finding was as follows:

> Between 2010–2012 and 2012–14, over half of the increase in personal wealth went to the top 10 per cent of households. . . . Wealth inequality is twice as great as income inequality. (Roberts and Lawrence 2017, p.2)

Equally significant as these figures on income and wealth are the figures for what is euphemistically called "negative wealth" in the United Kingdom: "one third of adults in the poorest fifth of households have no savings at all . . . half of the adults in this group have debts that are at least 83 percent of their annual income" (Roberts and Lawrence 2017, p.13). We will discuss this extensive personal indebtedness, specifically in the case of the United States, when we discuss the evolution of its "debtfare" state in chapter 8.

As in the United States, the gap between the rich and the poor has been on the rise in most OECD countries ever since the 1970s and 1980s.[5] However,

[3] In her 2017 update for the United States, which takes into account data available until 2015, Tcherneva notes that "The growing economy continues to deliver the most benefits to the wealthiest families" (Tcherneva 2017).

[4] Piketty observes that "[W]hile inequality has indeed increased since 1980, the magnitude of the increase varies widely from country to country. . . . For example, the trajectory of the United Kingdom is closest to that of the United States while income inequality in Sweden remains the lowest on the continent; Germany and France fall between these two extremes" (Piketty, 2020, p.419).

[5] "Wealth inequality is high among all developed economies. The UK sits somewhere in the middle of comparable countries, with a Gini coefficient for wealth inequality lower than that for Germany, the US and France, but higher than Spain, Italy and Australia" (Roberts and Lawrence 2017, p.14).

in most European countries, the gap is not yet as big as it was before the World Wars and the increase in inequality is somewhat less pronounced:

> In Europe, the top decile income share fell sharply, from 45 to 50% to about 30%, between 1914 and the 1950s–1960s. It has been rising somewhat since the 1970s–1980s, and it is now close to 35% (somewhat less in continental Europe and somewhat more in the United Kingdom, which has experienced an evolution closer to that of the United States). (Piketty and Saez 2014, p.839)

Yet when we scale up, global inequalities are, unsurprisingly, even more staggering in their extent. In 2017, Oxfam calculated that the richest eight people—all men—possess the same wealth as the poorest half of the world. In 2010, you still needed the richest 388 people to generate the same result (Oxfam 2017). The same report provides another striking observation about the extreme wealth concentration at the top: "Since 2015, the richest 1% has owned more wealth than the rest of the planet." Or, when we look at the ten largest corporations, it turns out that together they own more revenue than the combined government revenue of the poorest 180 countries.

François Bourguignon and Branko Milanović have documented how global inequality between countries is reducing just as inequality within countries in the affluent West is increasing (Bourguignon 2012; Milanović 2016). That note of optimism apart, for now, we argue simply that the statistics that we have cited reveal the extent to which those with capital easily gain more capital. As we have noted, Robert M. Solow famously called this the "rich get richer" dynamic as a specific instance of the "snowball effect" (Solow 2014). Oxfam put a figure on it:

> The wealth of the richest 62 people has risen by 44% in the five years since 2010—that's an increase of more than half a trillion dollars ($542 bn), to $1.76 trillion. Meanwhile, the wealth of the bottom half fell by just over a trillion dollars in the same period—a drop of 41%. (Oxfam 2016, p.2)

With the rich getting richer at a much quicker pace than everyone else, inequalities between individuals across the world are increasing since the last three or four decades as well. That is a countertrend to the convergence of inter-country averages (Bourguignon 2012).

> All these figures basically falsify optimistic models that predict the trickling-down of wealth: While most serious economists have always been sceptical of notions of trickle down economics—that if the top does well, so does the rest of society—what has happened in the last third of a century bears testimony to just how wrong that theory is. (Stiglitz 2012, p.427)

On the one hand, taking into account Piketty's point that capital accumulation is only significantly disrupted by war (and we would add pandemic disease), we should collectively congratulate ourselves that relative peace has seen such a massive global accumulation of wealth (Piketty 2014). On the other hand, how this accumulated wealth is distributed is seriously unjust. Many people in poverty, in both global and national comparisons—such as within the United States—have seen their incomes stagnate, and have been unable to accrue any wealth, while the already rich have rapidly grown even richer.

These vast and growing economic inequalities have raised worries amongst economists, psychologists, sociologists, philosophers, and policy makers. As the phenomenon becomes too striking to ignore, there has been a succession of books on the subject, both academic and non-academic—including one by one of the authors of the current study (Thomas 2017). Yet, it seems to us, no one is putting the pieces together to identify, explain, and theorize the ways in which inequality harms well-being in what we will call "market societies".

1.2 The Structural Basis of the "New" Inequality

All these data prove that we are currently living under "the New Inequality" (Freeman 1996; Thomas 2017, p.xv). There is some good news in this data: inequalities between countries have been narrowing globally (Bourguignon 20015; Milanović 2016). The main reason is that highly populated countries, such as Brazil, China, and India, have narrowed the gap with the affluent West. However, this positive news is balanced by further negative news: within both the rising economies and the already affluent countries, intra-societal inequality is increasing. In some cases—the United Kingdom and United States in particular—this trend has intensified.[6]

[6] Branko Milanović detects a Eurocentric bias in work whose focus on intra-societal inequality takes the affluent West as its starting point and does not, therefore, place sufficient emphasis on the

A sequence of political events in the 1970s, from the Nixon Shock of America's abandonment of the gold standard on August 15, 1971, to OPEC's oil shock price rises of 1973, to fears of economic stagnation, hyperinflation and a crisis of competitiveness—these led to a radically changed macro-economic course for the United Kingdom and the United States (Fazi and Mitchell 2017). Other countries in the affluent West, though less extreme than the United States and the United Kingdom, have followed a broadly similar pattern of development.

According to Piketty, we are witnessing a return to normal in the sense that a capitalism unrestrained by social democratic politics will always produce increasing intra-societal inequality given how returns to capital exceed returns to labour over the long run (Piketty 2014, 2020). Other economists, such as James K. Galbraith, offer a more detailed analysis that we think is fully compatible with Piketty's "big picture": that a macro-economic course was selected in the United States that has led to increased inequality and increased macro-economic instability—where those two phenomena are connected (Galbraith 1998, 2008, 2014, 2012). We think this analysis can be extended to the United Kingdom (not directly Galbraith's topic). These are the two countries of the Reagan/Thatcher revolutions (Prasad 2006).[7] As historian Adam Tooze notes:

> The war on inflation waged by Thatcher and Reagan was a comprehensive campaign against a threat of social upheaval, which they saw as coming from without and from within. It had the ferocity that it did because in the 1970s and early 1980s, class conflict in Europe, Asia and the United States was still framed by the global struggles of decolonization and the Cold War. (Tooze 2021b, p.15)

With the goal of full employment abandoned, the wage structure has been allowed to erode from below (Galbraith 1998). For the most vulnerable

material gains on what count as, in context, the "middle classes" of South-East Asia (Milanović 2016, p.19). However, as he points out, this shift is largely explained by the rise of China (Milanović, p.24; see also Therborn 2017). Egalitarians ought to be concerned about *how* China has achieved this rapid development (Klein and Pettis 2020, pp.107–19). Klein and Pettis describe China's development model as an instance of a type "naturally suited to authoritarian regimes that do not need to be held accountable to their voters" (Klein and Pettis 2020, p.107).

[7] Prasad's thesis is that these were the countries where social democracy had made the greatest gains, so represented the most serious threat to the capitalist order.

workers, the underpinnings of the wage structure are politically determined: minimum wage policy, unionization, and support (or neglect) of the goal of full employment (Galbraith 1998).

Moreover, two other factors explain inequality in the United States and the United Kingdom (our primary focus in this book). Piketty's thesis is a generalization over all capitalist societies over the long run; Galbraith's explanation is also a general model of the role played by monopoly rents in generating sectoral inequalities. We think we need further to supplement Galbraith's thesis with a claim defended by Lance Taylor and Özlem Ömer, namely, that even if firms in a dynamic sector of the economy with high productivity and profitability are forced to share rents with those employees that add value to a high degree, that wage is lower than it would have been absent generalized wage suppression across the whole economy (Taylor and Ömer 2020, p.83).

Furthermore, inequality in the United States has yet another, distinctive, explanation. Dean Baker emphasizes the extraordinary success of America's wealthiest citizens in politically structuring markets to lock in place their rent-extracting opportunities.[8] As Baker puts it in his critical comments on Piketty's first book:

> To find the origins of rising inequality in the United States, we have to look to the factors that led to huge paychecks for CEOs, Wall Street traders, and other high-end earners, and it is not a story of corporate profits rising at the expense of wages. (Baker 2016, p.17)

While Piketty does note the rise of the American "supermanager", we accept that his general explanation needs supplementation in the case of the United States.[9]

In our view we have complementary explanations here that are mutually reinforcing. A complete explanation will cite all four: Piketty's long-run generalization about the evolution of capitalist societies; Galbraith's neo-Schumpeterian model based on sectoral rents; Taylor and Ömer's

[8] Schwartz notes that "the US state undertook a concerted, 40-year campaign to create and extend US IPR [intellectual property rights] law globally in order to secure revenue streams for the US firms concentrating on production of information-rich goods while offshoring production" (Schwartz 2021, p.254).

[9] The point is even clearer in the later *Capital and Inequality* (Piketty 2020, pp.421–2, p.525, pp.530–4). Galbraith, too, is sensitive to the political factors on which Baker concentrates his focus (Galbraith 2008).

neo-Keynesian focus on wage suppression; Baker's explanation in terms of rent-extraction-cum-predation.[10] (The latter, we think, needs to be supplemented by Schwartz's account of the institutional transformation of the US economy, which we will describe below.)

We should, at this point, immediately forestall an objection: if we accept the Schumpeterian account of the dynamic efficiency of capitalism, how can we be critics of all forms of economic rent? In Schumpeter's explanation, every firm competes for a monopolistic edge, even if that edge is rapidly "competed away" by competitors. The whole point of that edge is to extract rent above the normal level of profit in a zero-sum game.

To explain the form of rent that we take to be objectionable, we appeal to Rawls's account of "pure ownership" (Rawls 2007). Bill Edmundson explains Rawls's use of that term:[11]

> Rawls conceived the entrepreneurial or control aspects of ownership as inhering not in capital assets, but in the acquired skills and "natural assets" exercised in marshalling and managing capital assets. To say that a doctor has a basic right to own a stethoscope is to obscure what is important, namely, the excellence that a competent doctor manifests in skilfully making use of a stethoscope and other tools of the trade. A right to have use of a stethoscope in this sense is an aspect of the basic right to occupational choice, which choosers in the original position already recognize as a basic liberty. The right to profit from the sale or lease of medical instruments is another matter.[12] (Edmundson 2017, p.27)

We can only hope that this point was familiar to the writers of the film *Wall Street* (Oliver Stone and Stanley Weiser) given that its anti-hero, Gordon Gecko, states emphatically that "I create nothing, I own".

State policy—whether by act or omission—is central to all these explanations of the structural basis of inequality. The state has not, as neoliberal rhetoric would suggest, been "rolled back" during this forty-year period; it has, rather, been selective in the interests that it has advanced, and which it has impeded (or abandoned) (Galbraith 2008; Thomas 2020b).

[10] A parallel analysis to Baker's for the United Kingdom is (Christophers 2020).

[11] Rawls takes the phrase "pure ownership" from Joan Robinson (1966).

[12] According to Edmundson, Rawls construed the point of Marx's labour theory of value to be a critique of "liberal and right-wing libertarian conceptions which regard pure ownership as making a tangible contribution to production" (Edmundson, 2017, p.27, fn. 5).

Galbraith argues, that the United States has not been governed by the signature neo-liberal policies of "monetarism, supply side economics, balanced budgets, free trade, and deregulation":

> [E]ach one of [these ideas] was tried, and then discarded as unworkable, ineffective, or actually destructive. What remained was rule by predators, and in particular the transfer of the power of supervision, of regulation, to the organized business and banking lobbies. (Galbraith 2008, p.xiv)[13]

The question is whether this brand of capitalism has itself run its course—whether it has proven to be no more stable than the socio-economic system it has displaced (Galbraith 2014; Gamble 2014).

We should, at this point, explain how we are going to use the term "neo-liberal" given the broad concern that the term has outlived its usefulness. We prefer a term introduced by George Soros: "market fundamentalism" (Soros 1998). The latter is a utopian ideal: the ideal of restructuring as many of our social institutions as possible on the model of an ideal market. We will go into the motivations for market fundamentalism later in the book: markets are valued for their function of price discovery, the elicitation of private knowledge to determine publicly specifiable values, to encode convergent predictions about future values, but above all for the dispersal of power across all market agents.

It is the latter point about power that makes the view different from neo-liberalism, which is the result, either intentional or unintentional, of implementing the marketization strategy selectively at the service of some social interests—those with prior power over others—as opposed to others. Market fundamentalism sees markets as avenues of emancipation; neo-liberalism sees markets as instruments of power. Tooze notes that:

> As a practice of power, neoliberalism had always been radically pragmatic. Its real history was that of a series of state interventions in the interests of capital accumulation, including the forceful deployment of state violence to bulldoze opposition . . . the social realities with which the market revolution had been entwined since the 1970s—the entrenched influence

[13] For how a corporate ethos of extractive capitalism became the American norm, see William Lazonick's discussion of "predatory value extraction" (in joint work with Jang-Sup Shin) (Lazonick and Shin 2019).

of wealth over politics, the law and the media, the disempowerment of workers—all perdured. (Tooze, 2021b)[14]

Further problems arise when unrealistically utopian attempts to implement market fundamentalism produce a damaging politics of the "second best". Intellectuals who sincerely believe that marketization will be emancipatory discover that the implementation of their ideas has produced perverse policy outcomes. These outcomes advantage some market actors over others, usually because of prior inequalities in power that cannot be overcome—even by the utopian market fundamentalist.

These distinctions explain why even canonical "neo-liberals" express frustration and disappointment with the evolution of our affluent societies over the last forty years—even though it is commonly believed that their side won. We prefer to identify them as frustrated market fundamentalists. If we have, instead, a form of pragmatic, neo-liberal, socialism for corporations then the market fundamentalist can be as unhappy with this outcome as the progressive.[15]

We can see this process of contestation at work when market fundamentalism seeks to re-make our social reality in what it takes to be progressive ways. The line between what counts as a morally blocked exchange and a gain in economic efficiency is frequently contested. Ought there to be a market in derivatives, or are futures markets for securities unethical gambling (Mackenzie 2006)? Is buying life insurance a morally outrageous profiting from death or the mark of rational prudence that manifests care towards one's dependents (Zelizer 1979)? Should care workers accept low pay symbolically to acknowledge that their service is a form of gift exchange and display the moral quality of their motivation? Examples such as these show how "marketization"—a process justified in terms of economic efficiency—requires transformations in social relations and within the self.

In calling the United States and the United Kingdom neo-liberal societies, then, we mean that the last forty years of their development has been determined by class-based power. Primarily, it is the rentier/investor class that has benefitted from this new political and economic regime. After the inflation shocks of the 1970s, the last forty years of policy has prioritized their

[14] See also (Thomas 2017, pp.65–6) and (Fazi and Mitchell 2017).

[15] A key inflection point, to which we will return, is the Chicago School's shift towards tolerating a high degree of corporate monopoly as the price of efficiency (and low prices) as opposed to a focus on inter-firm competitiveness (Crouch 2011, chapter 3).

interests through inflation targeting, appreciation in the value of core assets (notably housing), and—particularly in the United States—a form of corporate socialism.[16] Inflation targeting suppresses real wages while asset inflation builds a middle-class coalition around asset ownership, thereby splitting the majority of citizens into essentially opposed interest groups with further implications for inter-generational justice. Yakov Feygin has helpfully called this politico-economic constellation the "deflationary bloc" (Feygin 2021). The story of the last forty years is, to use Adam Tooze's word, the "perdurance" of this bloc.

Corporate socialism takes many forms: the state puts in place a wide range of guarantees. It guarantees private profits as captured in the famous Kalecki-Levy profits equation (Levy, Farnham, and Rajan 2008). It can underwrite innovation at scale and then guarantee extractive rents by placing the state's own spending power at the service of key sectors (Janeway 2018).[17] Domestic industries may be subsidized or protected by tariffs. The state guarantees patent protections and vocational licensing requirements that, for example, create rent-seeking monopolies in America's healthcare and pharmaceutical sectors (Baker 2016, chapter 7). Corporate socialism allows lobbyists to write the laws that "regulate" their clients, to change crucial laws in favour of business or the financial sector, and to preserve legal loopholes that favour them.[18] The state turns a blind eye to tax evasion on a vast scale (Zucman 2015).[19] Most strikingly, in 2007–8, it was conclusively demonstrated that the

[16] In the words of neo-Keynesian economist Hyman Minsky: "In truth, corporate America pays lip service to free enterprise and extols the tenets of Adam Smith, while striving to sustain and legitimize the very thing that Smith abhorred—state-mandated market power" (Minsky 1986/2008, p.322). For similar analyses from across the political spectrum see (Galbraith 2008); (Lindsey and Teles 2017); (Philippon 2019).

[17] As Joan Robinson argued, the post–World War II American state learned to love massive deficits, but the beneficiary of that state largesse was to be military spending (Robinson 1972). We return to this issue in chapter 13.

[18] An incomplete list of such changes in the United States includes: permitting trade in financial futures via a changed understanding of the Commodities Exchange Act in 1973 (MacKenzie, 2006, p.150); repealing the Glass-Steagall Act (which separated commercial and investment banking) in 1999; the deregulation of derivatives trading in 2000; the exemption of repurchase agreement collateral (securities) from the "automatic stay" provision of bankruptcy law in 2005; the rewriting of SEC rule 10b-18 which permitted the extensive use of share buybacks; probably the most famous legal loophole is the "carried interest rule"—the foundational basis of the private equity industry—where the gains of private equity firms are taxed as if they were capital gains and not personal income. (A 2020 estimate puts these comparative figures as a tax rate of 23.8% versus 37%, respectively, in the United States.)

[19] As Piketty succinctly puts it, "today's hypercapitalism is an outgrowth of the era of the digital revolution and tax havens" (Piketty 2020, p.154). The tech sector has been at the forefront of new codifications of capital assets "to protect ownership claims as long as possible while concealing those activities from those who might want to challenge those claims" (ibid.). This pushes the "frontiers and forms of property to the maximum possible extent" (Piketty 2020, p.154). He cites (Pistor 2019).

financial sector, a key component of both the US and the global economy, essentially depends on the capacities of what Daniela Gabor calls "the derisking state" (Gabor 2020). The United States underwrites global capitalism by supplying dollars to the international financial system and creating the system's default safe assets in the form of US Treasury bonds. The Federal Reserve banking system of the United States is the core of a deeply globalized, tightly connected, set of financial institutions whose influence is global (Tooze 2018). In the 2007–8 financial crisis the Federal Reserve provided "swap lines" to other central banks, thereby backstopping the global financial system. These lines of credit allow central banks in other countries to draw down US dollars to pass on to banks or firms in their own jurisdictions, or for US-based firms to have access to foreign currencies.

Corporate socialism builds a political coalition between these selective exercises of state power or tactical state withdrawal. These policies have advanced the interests of the already wealthy: executives of large corporations, those who work in finance, and the rentier-investor class more generally. At the global level, these domestic elites coalesce into that which Michael Lind has called "a transatlantic elite" that is "based in the corporate, financial, government, media, and educational sectors" and which has engaged in a forty-year class war—very successfully (Lind 2020, p.1).[20] Warren Buffett famously remarked that "there's class warfare, all right, but it's my class, the rich class, that's making war and we're winning" (Stein 2006).

How has corporate socialism re-made the institutions and structures of the US economy in particular? We already noted the neo-Schumpeterian analysis of Minsky, James Galbraith, and others; yet it may seem limited to the capital goods–creating sector of the US economy. It seems that only there are firms forced to share their monopoly rents with indispensable employees.

However, this thesis generalizes to explain the comparative sectoral development of the whole US economy, which explains the emergence of the United States' "fissured" or "franchise" economy and its evolution (Thomas 2020b; Schwartz 2021). Recent developments must be put in a longer historical framework.

Minsky argued that US economic and industrial policy in the post-war period put in place the structural conditions for the inflationary problems of the United States in the 1970s (Minsky 1975). The "big government capitalism"

[20] Michael Lind acknowledges the indebtedness of his analysis to earlier work by John Kenneth Galbraith and Christopher Lasch (Galbraith 1967/2007; Lasch 1995). See also Temin (2017).

Minsky described had, in his view, misunderstood Keynes (Minsky 1975). It forced overinvestment in those sectors deemed strategically important during the Cold War. These were the "good jobs" in capital-intensive sectors which created surplus income, in turn spent on consumer goods produced by sectors that, comparatively, were under-invested. Wage inequality between sectors produced industrial conflict, which was resolved, piecemeal, by wage concessions to those workers already earning a premium—not to all workers. Capital did not flow into the consumer goods–producing sectors, where returns were comparatively low: the general level of prices rose as a result in an inflationary way.

Keynes's demand for the planning of overall investment was ignored, and this maldistribution of investment put in place structural tensions in the US economy. The predictable results were that aggregate demand was boosted only via a privileged sector of the economy; investment in producing consumer goods lagged; the spiral between prices and wages occurred because of this underlying sectoral imbalance.

According to this neo-Keynesian analysis, the inflation of the 1970s was inevitable given these structural causes: yet the political solution was to bring the power of the state to bear on the aspirations of "greedy workers" who were blamed for generating this "wage price spiral" (which, Minsky argued, was sectorally local). Inflation, on this rival monetarist story, is not a fundamentally political phenomenon as it is in the neo-Keynesian explanation: it appeals to Milton Friedman's formulation of "too much money chasing too few goods".[21] This allegedly justified the political solution of the Volcker Shock, where the cost of borrowing money (the central bank interest rate) briefly rose in the United States to 19% (Sonti 2018). This intentionally destroyed parts of the real economy, caused mass unemployment, and created the political conditions for the political emergence and then dominance of the deflationary bloc (Feygin 2021).[22]

This is the context that shapes the neo-Schumpeterian analysis of the US economy as it is now configured. First, the capital goods–producing sector

[21] The alternative approach to inflation treats it as the outcome of political contest over the productive surplus (Hirschman, 1985). We know, as a matter of historical fact, what caused inflation in the 1970s, and it was not the factors cited by Friedman. Alan S. Blinder explains it in terms of rising food and energy prices combined with Nixon's wage controls (1982).

[22] One of Feygin's insights is to connect Minsky's early work on the misinterpretation of Keynes to his later work on financial crises: "propping up private profits would do nothing to help rectify these [sectoral] imbalances and instead only create financial instability, driving markups by capitalists realizing their investments" (Feygin, 2021). See also Galbraith (1998).

creates monopoly rents that have to be shared with key categories of employee (Galbraith 1998; Thomas 2020b).[23] This is partially reproduced by the capital goods–using sector—manufacturing—but it is largely absent from the "low end" service sector (Galbraith 1998).[24] The most vulnerable service workers do not get a share of their firms' rents. They are precariously employed, poorly paid, with stagnant real wages and with diminished protection from trade unions. Nor has this "precariat" been protected by the state, given its weak employment and minimum wage policies and complicity with political attacks on unionization (Standing 2011).

As Herman Mark Schwartz has argued, we need to track through these sectoral changes to the micro-structure of the organization of the institutions in an economy (Schwartz 2021).[25] We have to do this to understand how firms put in place differing profit-seeking strategies and, in so doing, transform their own institutional structures. In the background is the insistence that the profit-maximizing firm is answerable solely to its equity holders and must focus on its "core competence". The result is the fissuring of the economy via the fissuring of the firm (Thomas 2020b; Schwartz 2021).

Firms always aspire to be price-setting oligopolists. But Schwartz argues that under "Fordism", the large-scale industrial organization of the firm was at the service of the domination of competitors via control of large-scale physical assets in vertically integrated firms. Stable firms shared their rents with unionized labour. Inter-firm competition was suppressed because the scale of capital investment created barriers to entry. Firms re-invested retained earnings and the wages they paid supported aggregate demand (Schwartz 2021). These were the firms on the commanding heights of the US economy during that which, in France, are called the "trentes glorieuses" (1945–1975).

The rise of technology firms has both facilitated and, in the case of the handful of Big Tech monopolies exemplified, radical changes in firm structure.[26] The post-Fordist monopolist seeks primarily to control intellectual

[23] This neo-Schumpeterian diagnosis is shared with the work of Lazonick and Shin noted above (Lazonick and Shin 2019; Schumpeter 1942).

[24] By contrast, some members of the high-end service sector—law, finance, and accounting—have seen significant income gains over the last forty years. The financial sector is, technically, a "service sector".

[25] See also Schwartz (2017, 2019). For a complementary discussion see Furman and Orszag (2018).

[26] As an example of facilitation: "the communications revolution . . . allowed firms to relocate factories to distant countries where they could take advantage of cheap labour without relinquishing control" (Milanović, 2016, p.18).

property rights. Combined with the financial sector's promotion of the doctrine of shareholder value, the production chain has been disintegrated as firms seek to divest themselves of fixed investments and a large labour force. Schwarz identifies three "ideal typical" post-Fordist firms:

> [H]uman capital-intensive, low headcount firms whose high profitability stems from robust IPRs [intellectual property rights]; physical capital-intensive firms whose moderate profitability stems from investment barriers to entry or tacit knowledge production; and labor-intensive, high headcount firms producing undifferentiated services and commodities with low volumes of profit. (Schwartz 2021, p.248)

A firm can either exemplify a type or some combination of these ideal types to varying degrees. But the primary impact of this more refined sectoral analysis is on income and wealth inequality.

The most highly profitable firms employ very few people. Those employees share in excessive rents—but their numbers are limited. Investment, for these firms, means hiring more highly paid professionals—so investment does not produce the Keynesian multiplier effect, as the already wealthy have a lower marginal propensity to consume (Schwartz 2021, p.249). Traditional, physical capital-intensive firms who have survived into this new eco-system fear an unstable environment in which they may over-produce and are hesitant further to invest. Finally, firms at the apex of the pyramid have proven to be adept at tax evasion because intellectual property can easily be located overseas.

As Schwartz notes, these developments were the result of active lobbying. We have already itemized the legal achievements of the neo-liberal order. Schwartz adds to the list crucial changes to the franchisor–franchisee relationship (Schwartz 2021).[27] Firms actively sought to shed staff while keeping overall control of production: franchise arrangements, outsourcing, offshoring, and jurisdiction shopping between US states have all played this role. Manufacturing firms have exploited these methods too. Finally, on the commanding heights of the US economy, are the "superstar firms" of Big Tech who are highly profitable, employ few people, and utilize all the above strategies—combined with tax evasion.

[27] Representative, here, in the US case is "a twenty year legal campaign to remove anti-trust laws banning vertical constraints and to establish that franchisees, not franchisors, were the legal employer of the growing pool of low wage labor" (Schwartz, 2021, p. 253).

This whole process has created a hierarchy of firms: the bottom of the pyramid is occupied by firms with very tight margins, low investment, and low productivity—mostly in the service sector. (A reminder that monopolistic competition is zero sum.) Yet they are bound into multi-firm structures—for example, by supplying cleaners for an auto factory or making cheap mobile phone cases. This represents a major challenge to anti-monopoly or antitrust policy: if the target is a superstar firm at the apex of the pyramid, what happens to the peripheral firms that constitute the eco-system in which the monopoly operates (Blyth 2023)?

Our interpretation of Schwartz's important arguments is this: in the past, even if the commanding heights of the economy were dominated by large Chandlerian firms that constituted a set of interlocking monopolies, overall there was this side-benefit: economic stability. In our financialized "franchise economies", by contrast, we have the worst of both worlds: large-scale monopoly and macro-economic instability. Whereas stable monopolies offered partial protection to the worst-off workers—if, for example, they were in a sectoral union with their demands bundled with those of more skilled workers—this unstable structure disadvantages them in every way. Financial instability is routinized, destabilizes the business cycle, and sees the worst-off rotate between poorly paid jobs and unemployment.[28]

The state, lobbied by private interests, has been—both by omission and commission—the facilitator of wage suppression across the whole economy and a major cause of inequality. It is a general truth that there is a structural consumption deficit in highly unequal societies (Palley 2012). As Baker notes, we can accurately quantify the extent to which the New Inequality has exacerbated this consumption deficit in the United States, namely, to the tune of a 3.5% reduction in aggregate consumption (Baker 2016, p.29; Alichi et al., 2016).

So-called privatized Keynesianism steps in, supplying extensive private credit for the poor, and increasing the scale and importance of financialization in these economies (Crouch 2011; Deutschmann 2012; Palley 2013). As Minsky also identified, a deregulated "money manager capitalism" formed part of the political solution to inflation: stabilizing consumer prices while shifting inflation to the value of assets (Minsky 1986/2008). Private

[28] Hyman Minsky also explains how financial crises have become routinized; their resolution continually inflationary; their destabilizing of the business cycle underwritten by central bank "puts" (the promise to put a floor under asset prices). See Beggs (2018).

credit creation expanded credit which was not directed to investment in the real economy, but to ever inflating asset values in a financial sector prone to frequent crises. At the other end of the income scale: those on stagnant wages—both the very worst off and the so-called squeezed middle—become excessively dependent on credit to compensate for this shortfall in income from labour and their frequent unemployment. For this broad class of citizens, private credit is treated like a supplementary form of income.

The United States and the United Kingdom may be outliers, but other societies are following these trends. All these previous factors have combined in a damaging way: inequality, financialization, selective intervention by the state at the service of rentier/investment class interests, and the assault on organized labour. Wage suppression exacerbates a structural deficit in consumption. This adds up to macro-economic instability for the whole system, that, in turn, makes recessions more frequent, longer lasting, and more damaging than they need to be (Galbraith 1998).[29]

If you are an advocate of "free enterprise", you will also note with concern the emergence of a conflict between the investor class and entrepreneurs in an economy dominated by the large, monopolistic, corporation and financial firms of all kinds (Deutschmann 2012; Philippon 2019). When Lazonick and Shin complain of predatory value extraction from the US corporation, that is money diverted away from the firm's own investment in innovation and growth (Lazonick and Shin 2019). Rent extractors not only hoard equal opportunity goods, but also sacrifice future market innovation, growth, and profit for excessive rent, that is, for short-term benefit in the present.

Our conclusion is that this policy-induced macro-economic instability entrenches the political power of the rentier class. Members of this elite are better protected against economic downturns; they are better placed to take advantage of any eventual recovery, and they are less exposed to unemployment (the whole point of being a rentier is not to depend on wage income). That is why recoveries are always "for the rich": and why the whole political dynamic of inequality and instability is further entrenched—and the cycle repeated. The watershed financial crisis of 2007–8, far from breaking this cycle, further entrenched it, although its long-run political consequences remain unclear (Tooze 2018). Forty years after the Reagan/Thatcher revolutions, the upshot is a deeply unstable rentier capitalism prone to serious financial crises and rapidly losing political legitimacy. Margaret Thatcher's famous

[29] For the idea that financial crises represent a form of domination, see (Bryan 2019).

claim that "there is no alternative" no longer carries conviction. A crisis of legitimacy is forcing the development of alternatives.

1.3 Is America an "Outlier"?

Our discussion so far has taken changes in the US economy over the last forty years to be trend setting: further along a path of development that other affluent countries will follow. As three Europeans, we seem to be following de Tocqueville in taking the United States to be an experimental laboratory of a social democratic society implementing a capitalist market society in a political context without prior aristocratic institutions. Suppose that we have established that the United States did indeed break with a putatively "Keynesian" consensus of democratically constrained growth and this has led to widening intra-societal inequality.[30] What if the United State is an exceptional outlier?

There are certainly respects in which the United States is exceptional; we will now consider their bearing on our argument. There is a persistent strand of racism that arguably continues a legacy of slavery that keeps Black Americans poor and politically dominated to the present day (Temin 2017). The importance of race to the evolution of US welfare provision—or lack of it—has been documented in a classic book by Alesina and Glaeser amongst others (Alesina and Glaeser 2004, chapter 6). As one recent commentator notes of the post–World War II US political settlement:

> Levels of political polarization were then significantly lower than at any other time in American history. . . . But this was made possible by the fact that the really momentous conflicts—over the basic structure of the domestic economy, the distribution of income and wealth, and the racial makeup of the electorate—had been taken off the table, either through local violence and federal indifference (in the question of race) or by the force of overwhelming numbers (in the question of social democracy). (Thompson 2019)

[30] In Piketty's longer view, it was the emergence of a propertied middle class that radically changed the fundamental wealth distribution. As ternary societies became the ownership societies of the nineteenth century, they produced extraordinary wealth concentrations up to 1914 exclusively in the hands of a "financial, capitalist, and industrial elite" (Piketty 2020, p.136).

It is hardly surprising, then, that post–World War II embedded liberalism in the United States offered prosperity, but not to all. We will not fall into the trap of idealizing this post-war consensus: while it was marked by a stable structure of institutions and regulations that made a more inclusive capitalism possible, certain groups were nevertheless excluded.

Secondly, throughout much of its history the United States was largely unconstrained in its supply of capital and human labour, the latter originally provided by slavery, but also later powered by mass migration (Piketty 2014). The prospect of continual economic growth may seem more plausible in this historical context—even as exogenous constraints suggest that it is no longer sustainable (Galbraith 2014; Gamble 2014).

Thirdly, another form of US exceptionalism is the role played by employers in funding social insurance for their employees in America's unique form of corporatist welfare state capitalism. It expressed a putatively paternalistic outlook that showed that American workers did not need unionization—or socialism—even when major sectoral unions were part of this social settlement. It exacerbated the fact that the New Deal settlement was, itself, focused on citizens who work. (For example, Social Security in the United States is funded via a dedicated payroll tax.) The removal of the goodwill of the US corporate sector towards this social settlement led to it unwinding rapidly (Hacker 2006). The US welfare state is based on corporate paternalism to avoid the spectre of "socialism"; we have endorsed Minsky's claim that investment planning in the United States saw the state play a subordinated role to the underwriting of private profit—again to avoid the taint of "socialism" (Barker 2020). As Mark Blyth has summarized recent research: "the US welfare state is really about middle-class redistribution rather than tail risk insurance" (Blyth 2023).

The United States occupies an exceptional position as a global political hegemon and controller of the world's currency of last resort, the US dollar, the currency of choice for international trade (Eichengreen 2011). The United States is so large that it is a mostly self-contained economy dominated by an extensive service sector and by its own domestic consumption: oddly enough, for these reasons trade is not a major factor in the workings of the US economy. But this is not the case when it comes to international finance, where the United States is uniquely dominant. The overseas demand for US government assets, denominated in dollars, produces capital flow into the United States, keeping interest rates low, fuelling domestic consumer debt, and weakening the power of the US Federal Reserve to constrain the economy via its alleged "control" of the interest rate (Thomas 2023).

We do not deny that these facts inform a specific thesis about globalization: "market fundamentalism" and its illusory promise of continual growth require both domestic change and the furthering of a trans-national project. That project aimed at increasing convergence between developed and developing economies based on "free trade" and unlimited capital mobility (Fazi and Mitchell 2017; Rodrik 2011). We have expressed our scepticism about the former point, and capital mobility has played a major role in the structural transformations we have described. However, we simply note that as the world's remaining hegemon and custodian of its currency of last resort, the United States is uniquely unconstrained by this allegedly irresistible force of globalization (Thomas 2017, p.350). Not only is it monetarily sovereign—the monopoly supplier of new US dollars—it enjoys that sovereignty over the global reserve currency.

Globalization, in its American variant, is a political project driven by specific political interests that police new entrants to the international market order without imposing the same discipline on themselves. We have already argued that the claim that domestic inequality is the inevitable corollary of an increasingly globalizing economy is, in this specific case, an instance of bad faith (Baker 2016). These "constraining" circumstances reflect a set of economic and political choices by America's political elite often in coordination with elites in countries in its hegemonic periphery (Klein and Pettis 2020).

We concede that firms in other countries have rarely captured the state as successfully as in America's corporate socialism. Controlling the prices of part of the domestic basket of consumer goods with cheap imports from Mexico and China caused disastrous costs for American domestic workers because the US welfare state is so weak. Small economies, if "open" to globalization, typically offer domestic compensation via a strong welfare state. The large US economy is selectively "open" in some sectors combined with a weak and inefficient domestic welfare state. The American welfare state offers scant compensation for the loss of jobs through offshoring or through the structural transformation in the US economy.

However, overall, our response to the challenge that we ought not to take the United States as exceptional is basically that of Herman Mark Schwartz: "the US economy looks different because, relatively speaking, it has a larger proportion of 'apex' firms, a harsher labor relations system, and a stratified welfare state. But *it is not unique in terms of general trends*"

(Schwarz 2021, p.267, emphasis added). Implicit in this response is another issue: is the United States at the global apex of capitalist countries such that these changes we are deprecating are forced on it by globalization?

1.4 Inequality and Globalization

An important response to the concerns we have expressed is this: if we take an aggregative view of outcomes, the data is less troubling (Milanović 2016). We are—explicitly—merely documenting a "first world" problem. Intra-societal inequality is a pseudo-problem of the affluent West because the very same process that made our affluent Western societies so rich, in global terms, is producing the same effect for some of the world's poorest people during the episode of "high globalization" (Milanović 2016, p.11).

If a rising tide is lifting all boats globally, then we ought accept some comparatively highly placed vessels dropping while some lower placed vessels rise. Why worry that "lower half of the US income distribution" is in comparative decline if the "emerging global middle class" is rising (Milanović 2016, p.19, p.20)? This view exemplifies a form of "trickle down" economics, a view that may have been discredited within each domestic jurisdiction, but which continues to live on in justifications for a globalized capitalism.[31] Indeed, there is a major cause for celebration here: the optimistic take is that we have empirical proof that the global poor do not have to "remain mired in perpetual poverty" (Milanović 2016, p.21).

This concern allows us further to articulate our own normative perspective. The challenge posed here is that we are mistaken to think that inequality raises any distinctive problem at all. As Thomas Scanlon Jr. puts the point:

> One reason for wanting to redistribute resources from the rich to the poor is simply that this is a way of making the poor better off, at comparatively small cost to the welfare of the rich. This . . . is not, at base, an objection to *inequality* . . . it is simply a reason . . . for increasing the well-being of the poor. The fact that some people are much better off than the poor is relevant to this rationale for redistribution only because, as Willie Sutton, a

[31] Milanović's views these changes in income and wealth attributable to globalization as "fundamentally ambivalent" because the process itself is "a force both for good and bad" (Milanović, 2016, p.30).

famous American bank robber, is said to have remarked when asked why he robbed banks: "That's where the money is." (Scanlon 2018, p.1)

Throughout this book we will distinguish this kind of argument from those that do invoke the value of equality. We will appeal to two different kinds of egalitarian arguments. The first begins from the premise that while some inequality may be permissible, inequality can also be normatively impermissible and intrinsically wrong. The second kind of argument notes that inequality can have further bad effects and hence be extrinsically wrong.

The argument to which Milanović adverts (without endorsing) is supposed to be reassuring: inequality in the United States (for example) is a by-product of a process that is justified overall if we widen our approach globally. Drops in aggregate welfare, because workers formerly employed in the manufacturing sector are laid off in rust belt America, are compensated for by gains for the Vietnamese middle class even if this phrase—"middle class"—must be relativized to context. This process has led to a decrease of the amount of people living in extreme poverty ($1.90 per day) from 1.9 billion in 1990 to 650 million in 2018 and to a near eradication of extreme poverty in East Asia and the Pacific. Despite the recent pandemic-related spike, this process if allowed to work its way through, the argument goes, will eventually alleviate global poverty—it is tempting to add "in the long run". It is equally tempting then to add John Maynard Keynes acerbic remark that in the long run "we are all dead" (Keynes 1923, p.80).[32] Throughout this book we will explain why we are unconvinced by this putatively reassuring argument. We will now explain why we believe it is unconvincing.

Our interlocutor is not offering an argument based on inequality, but well-being. The globalizer's version of the "Willie Sutton" argument is that moving resources from the affluent West to, for example, sub-Saharan Africa will improve the well-being of individuals there while reducing the comparatively high well-being of WEIRD (Western, Educated, Industrialized, Rich, and Democratic) people (Henrich 2020). Point taken. But this is simply an argument about how to improve the well-being of people living in sub-Saharan Africa. It is not about inequality at all. Notably, this argument says nothing

[32] Piketty briefly discusses the argument that the socially democratically constrained inequalities of the "trentes glorieuses" were too equal, obstructing more inequality "for the sake of the poor", but notes the weak factual premises of this argument. Levels of growth were higher under these inclusive forms of capitalism than during the successive period of "hypercapitalism" (Piketty 2020, p.24). He notes that "the countries where top earners gained the most are not those where the poor reaped the largest benefits" (Piketty 2020, p.27).

about history: if sub-Saharan Africans were poor because of the legacy of colonial oppression, and the affluent West owed them compensation, then this would be a different argument—one based on egalitarian reasons.

Furthermore, suppose the globalization argument is enthymematic: there is a hidden premise that can be inferred: we are supposed to infer the presence of "one and the same process" that makes poorer Vietnamese more affluent, and middle-class Americans poorer.[33] What institutional or relational setting places poor Vietnamese and middle-class Americans in "the same process" and whose interests does this process serve?

This leads directly to our next point: the putative answer is capitalism and "free trade" at the service of globalization. But the inter-connected policies pursued by the affluent West in trade and finance have, once again, been an expression of the policy interests of the rentier-investor class and not free trade. We cannot assume the truth of the laissez-faire claim that free markets enable poor people in developing countries to become prosperous by selling goods and services to the affluent West. That is false both as an account of development as it should occur and as it has occurred (Baker 2016, pp.5–13; Chang 2007; Fazi and Mitchell 2017, pp.123–4; Galbraith 1998).[34] The path of development for societies that are already affluent involved colonialism, domestic protectionism, and tariffs.[35]

Why is it so unthinkable that people in developing countries might produce goods and services for each other in their domestic economies (Baker 2016, p.2; Fazi and Mitchell 2017, p.123)? Why cannot they be agents of their own economic fate? Perhaps, as the orthodox economics textbooks tell us, capital could flow from the affluent West where it enjoys a lower return to developing countries, where its scarcity would find higher returns to enhance that process (Baker 2016, pp.4–5; Fazi and Mitchell 2017, p.123)? Yet by the

[33] See Scanlon's remark that "Inequality is relevant only insofar as it figures in what is objectionable about the institutions or other factors that produce these differences" (Scanlon 2018, p.13). Milanović poses it as an open question (Milanović, 2016, p.21).

[34] Fazi and Mitchell observe that "[A]s noted by Ha-Joon Chang, 'export success does not require free trade': since the late 1970s, China and other developing countries have been characterised by a dualistic trade regime in which a strong export-oriented economy coexists with a highly protected domestic economy" (Fazi and Mitchell 2017, p.124). The quotation is from (Chang 2007).

[35] Keynes, and Keynesians, do not deny that in fact colonialism was used to sustain capitalist development in the West, but they argue that domestic justice in colonizing states would have removed this spurious justification of colonialism as the only way to address a domestic crisis of accumulation. Ha-Joon Chang argues that the affluent societies of the West did not develop by following the policy advice of the "Washington consensus" imposed on developing countries via the US-dominated international market order (Chang 2007).

time of the global financial crisis, capital was flowing "uphill" from developing to developed nations. The reassuring narrative is bogus:

> [T]here is no truth to the story that the job loss and wage stagnation faced by manufacturing workers in the United States and other wealthy countries was a necessary price for reducing poverty in the developing world. This is a fiction that is used to justify the upward redistribution of income in rich countries. (Baker 2016, p.7)

The trans-national version of trickle-down economics is no more successful than its domestic counterpart. The last forty years of global trade has involved the same class war we have already identified under a different aspect (Klein and Pettis 2020).[36]

Indeed, as Dean Baker points out, the crucial policy shift that reversed the flow of capital from developed to developing nations was the IMF's insistence that debt repayment take priority for the latter—a policy instigated by the "Clinton administration Treasury Department" (Baker 2016, p.4). He also notes that much of this trade flow involves developing countries paying rent on intellectual property protections that the United States includes in its trade deals: "paying [these] fees, especially for prescription drugs, is a huge burden on the developing world" (Baker 2016, p.5). This is another manifestation of the domestic changes to the American economy we have already noted: the political importance and power of firms who are monopolists over intellectual property rights.

Those who laud what they take to be encouraging figures about free trade ought to look behind the statistics to the underlying realities.[37] While the rising tide has lifted some boats, it has done so in a haphazard way, swamping others, leaving some in the mud and ensuring that those in the first-class cabins of luxury liners have risen a very long way. The real issue here is that the gains to the best off in this scenario have been at the expense

[36] Thomas (2017, pp.357–9). As Baker notes, if the offshoring of economic activity is inevitable on the grounds of economic efficiency, it is hard to explain the differential impact of this on sectors of American society with differing degrees of political power. It was workers in the manufacturing sector in the United States who were deemed to be demanding "too much" of the productive surplus and it is their work that has been replaced by cheap labour overseas (and automation domestically).

[37] These include the fact that much "trade" is actually the internal movement of factors of production within the "black box" of the multinational company (Fazi and Mitchell 2017, p.125); that a significant proportion of this trade is rent extraction via, for example, patent protections for technology, pharmaceuticals, and other high-value-added products (Baker 2016); and that, in any case, trade flow is both limited and declining.

of those placed below them in the income and wealth distribution domestically. It is a contingent by-product of this process—unintended and perhaps not even foreseen by globalizers—that trans-nationally this has improved the prospects of the emerging global middle class in Asia.

Yes, says our critic, but I am an aggregationist about outcomes! When America's comparatively (globally) affluent lower 50% of workers lose out, the proportionate gains to the global emerging middle class in Asia generate far more well-being or utility because the latter started from so low a baseline. The poorest Americans remain comparatively (globally) affluent. That is true, but, as Milanović further notes, "44 per cent of absolute gain has gone into the hands of the richest 5 per cent . . . the 'emerging global middle class' have only received between 2 and 4 per cent of the increase in the global pie" (Milanović 2016, p.24). Furthermore, for the globally worst off, the standard of living of the global poor has barely shifted over this time in real terms.[38] This is particularly so given that we have to factor in finance policy to trade policy when it comes to the refusal to forgive developing world debts (Varoufakis 2011, p.125).

The aggregationist's putative "gains" from globalization are a chimera because of the "enormous gaps", as Milanović puts it, in the global income and wealth distribution (Milanović 2016, p.25). When a crumb drops from the rich person's table, misses the poorest in their own society, and ends up in the hands of the emerging global middle class, there are "disproportionate" utility gains because even the latter are, in global terms, absolutely badly off even if they are not the worst off (Milanović 2016, p.25). We will focus on this book on a key corollary: the diminished well-being of those deemed "disposable" to the domestic part of the globalizer's trans-national project. We will also, later in this book, discuss the terms of moral address: is a wealthy American really proposing to justify economic changes that enrich her, and impoverish industrial workers in the United States, by pointing out that it has made a poor person in Vietnam less poor and, in any case, her fellow citizen is not living in as much poverty as a subsistence farmer in Bangladesh?

Most problematic is that the fact that in the affluent West there is currently a crisis of political legitimacy that we view as primarily driven by inequality (and a related process of "globalization as class war" by other means). The

[38] As Varoufakis notes: "[I]n and around 1980, for every $100 of world growth, the poorest 20% of people received $2.20. . . . By 2001 . . . an additional $100 of world growth translated into a measly extra 60 cents for the poorest 20 per cent. . . . [T]here appears to be very little cause for celebration" (Varoufakis 2011, p.125).

question we put to our critic is this: if capitalism loses whatever legitimacy it possesses in those societies in which it has allegedly succeeded, what hope is there for a humane and democratically constrained capitalism in those societies it is currently "lifting from poverty", if that is, indeed, what is happening?

The Willie Sutton argument invites us to take a certain view of the world as an ocean of individual preferences. Clusters of preference satisfactions rise and fall; but the connection is actually invisible in a globalization framework. It matters, as Milanović notes, that the bearers of those preferences have individual political identities (Milanović 2016, pp.1–2). They are members of some polity or other, and each political unit sees both internal arguments as to how best to organize its economic order, and external arguments as to how it engages with an international market order governing trade, finance, and migration.

Our own view is that internally just societies will engage with other societies, via a system of trans-national public goods, so as to produce a globally just world—a collection of states each of which is internally just (Rawls 1999b; Thomas 2017, pp. 343–50). The globalization project has to secure internal legitimacy within a society before it can begin to address the legitimacy and justification of a trans-national market order. The questions of who decided to reduce the well-being of rust belt Americans and increase the well-being of middle-class Vietnamese—and why—are political questions not addressed by the kind of aggregationist argument under scrutiny here, as some economists have noted (Milanović 2016; Rodrik 2011).

Fifth and finally, we argue that our critics' claim rests on a false dichotomy: to use Phil Parvin's useful distinction, we do not have to choose between solving the problem of poverty and solving the problem of inequality (Parvin 2017). Unjust inequality in our own societies, and political corruption, are not bitter pills we have to swallow because of our concern for the global poor's absolute levels of wealth. We argue that the reverse is the truth: just societies that are both affluent and fair will be responsible partners in a globalization process that steers developing economies along the same path of legitimacy, fairness, and increasing comparative affluence and prosperity. The climate crisis strengthens, and does not weaken, that argument.

2
Empirical Data on Inequality and the Dual Economy

Propositional Summary

1. We expand on our hypotheses about how economic inequalities in the affluent societies arise. Empirical data is brought to bear on sectoral inequalities in different economic sectors in the US economy and their explanation in terms of rent-seeking opportunities. Rent extraction and wage suppression go hand in hand, presided over the ideological dominance of the "Samuelson Keynesians".
2. Econometric data quantifies the rent-seeking hypothesis; we describe the application of the Lewis model from development economics to identify the United States as a regressing, financializing and de-industrializing society. Peter Temin's argument is evaluated, namely, that the upper 20% have an interest in wage suppression for the 80%. Workers are displaced into a low-productivity, under-capitalized, large service sector where employer practices adapt to this pool of cheap labour.
3. These developments are underpinned by an ideology of meritocracy; the question is raised of whether elite rent extraction will itself prove to be unstable because of an elite reproduction problem.

Introduction

In this chapter we expand on our hypotheses about how current levels of inequality in the affluent West have arisen. The rent-seeking hypothesis, which we set out in the previous chapter, does not explain inequality by appealing to ineluctable forces of economic growth, nor globalization, nor technological change, nor its corollary in a skills bias towards skilled employees who

Extravagance and Misery. Alan Thomas, Alfred Archer, and Bart Engelen, Oxford University Press.
 DOI: 10.1093/oso/9780197781722.003.0003

have successfully adapted to technological change. Nor does it accept that a rising tide lifts all boats, with high inequality being the price (possibly regrettable, even to its defenders) for some boats rising at different rates. Nor does it run the same argument internationally, claiming that high levels of inequality in the affluent West is the (maybe equally regrettable) price to pay for helping the global poor.

Our preferred hypothesis, the rent-seeking hypothesis, sees citizens in our societies as locked into zero-sum competitions with class-based elites in those societies who have extracted resources that ought to have been more widely (pre-)distributed for the benefit of all. It is this aspect of specifically capitalist forms of market society that we seek to explain in this book.

2.1 The Critique of Rent Seeking

We canvased this general explanation in the previous chapter; here we go into more detail. It seems to us obviously true that the political framework within which economic institutions operate has seen them generate unfair rewards for different classes of employee (Piketty 2020, pp.421–2). As we will see in the next chapter, philosopher Thomas Scanlon is as sceptical as Piketty towards the claim that the high pay (and other rewards) of America's supermanagers is justified by individual productive contributions (Scanlon 2018).

Scanlon concedes that there *can* be "inequalities . . . justified by the fact that they arise from the exercise of rights and powers that are required for economic productivity" (Scanlon 2018, p.140). However, any proposed inequality should also pass this test:

> it must be true either that these inequalities could not be eliminated without infringing important personal liberties, or that they are required in order for the economic system to function in a way that benefits all. (Scanlon 2018, p.141)

Scanlon believes that many economic institutions in the recent history of the United States have spectacularly failed this test. We agree. We also think it is easy to generalize from this jurisdiction to the managers of other transnational corporations or those who work in banking and finance across the affluent West. This is so, even if the US corporate class is an outlier on corporate executive pay.

Taking executive remuneration as an exemplary issue, the grotesque ratios between the pay of US executives and average pay in their own companies is frequently justified by appeal to the "global" competition for top management talent. However, senior executives in Japan and Germany do not pay themselves the same kind of outlandish salaries and executive share awards/options as their counterparts in the United States. Scanlon notes that arguments of this kind must be empirically informed:

> Unlike alternative conceptions that identify fairness or justice with some particular pattern of outcomes, this conception makes conclusions about fairness depend on complex empirical questions about how economic institutions do function and how they could function if arranged differently. (Scanlon 2018, p.142)

The research we have already cited provides relevant data in the case of the United States that evidence demonstrates that the primary explanation for high levels of inequality is rent-seeking behaviour by advantaged social classes (Baker 2016; Lazonick and Shin 2019; Price and Edwards 2020; Taylor and Ömer 2020). It is a natural extension of Scanlon's critique to examine unjust rent seeking. Rent seeking, of its nature, involves inequalities that can be eliminated *without* infringing anyone's "important personal liberties" and that are *not* required for "the economic system to function in a way that benefits all".

Dean Baker emphasizes that Piketty's general thesis of increased returns to capital as opposed to labour over the long run requires an important supplementary hypothesis in the case of the United States (Baker 2016). Policy after the Reagan Revolution has suppressed real wages. There has not been a shift from wage income to profits with a disproportionate amount of those profits going to America's wealthy citizens. America's wealthiest citizens have not achieved their comparative gains as fair returns on commercial activity that has proved to be highly profitable.

That this explanation is wrong is obscured, Baker argues, by the rapid rise of Big Tech. In the technology sector, relatively new companies have become massively profitable, but those profits "have come at the expense of older more established companies, not from workers' wages" (Baker 2016, p.16). It is also true that intense competition has driven down not only wages, but also prices—that is the point of targeting inflation. Consumption inequality is not as bad as income inequality (Thomas 2017, p.53, fn. 27). That leaves the mystery: where has the substantial increase in the income and wealth of America's richest citizens come from?

The richest Americans do, of course, own far more capital assets, shares, bonds, and parts of the public debt than other citizens. That fact will be important in chapter 8 of this book. But that simply pushes the question one stage further back: where did the money come from to enable this dominance? Baker's answer is straightforward: out of the pockets of other citizens. Not everything that the higher earner does is economically unproductive, but part of their remuneration is excessive rent generated by an artificial monopoly. This is a cost to the rest of us. Rent seeking, in other words, is an extractive zero-sum game (Baker 2016, pp.18–21).

In Taylor and Ömer's (2020) analysis of sixteen sectors of the US economy, the seven sectors with the lowest productivity and lowest real wages increased their share of total employment from 47% in 1990 to 61% in 2016 while their share of total wages went down from 57% to 56%. The real output of these sectors also went down from 48% to 41% (Taylor and Ömer 2020, pp.59–61). They estimate that one out of three employed Americans work in these stagnant sectors with wages topped up by state transfers (Taylor and Ömer 2020, p.64). Employers in these stagnant sectors offer lower working hours; 5% of Americans have two jobs to compensate for this (Taylor and Ömer 2020, p.72).

This is the practical effect of rent extraction, wage suppression, suppressed consumer demand, and structural unemployment. Unemployment, combined with political assault on organized labour, has disciplined worker power in the United States. Scale matters here: wage suppression has had an impact on the great majority of American workers (with parallel explanations for other countries) (Taylor and Ömer 2020).

This critique of rent seeking serves three important purposes for us. First, it conforms with Scanlon's test by identifying an unjustifiable inequality. This is important, because it gives our arguments here an irenic basis: a wide range of political outlooks, from the Left to the Right of the political spectrum, are critics of "crony capitalism" and of a rent-seeking society that drains off resources from genuine productive investment in a way that contributes to economic stagnation.

Secondly, egalitarians always face the "levelling down" objection and the jibe from Harvard economist Martin Feldstein that only "spiteful egalitarians" would reject improvement to the well-being of the better off that leave the worst off in an unchanged position (Thomas 2017, p.38). This is part of a general, trickle down, conception where the wealth creators must be liberated to grow the economy for everyone. That the last forty years have seem income and wealth fail to trickle down but rather gush upwards, into the bank accounts of wealthy people across the globe (and into tax havens, shell companies, and freeports) is illustrated by the data that shows this competition is zero sum (Shaxson 2011; Zucman 2015).

In our view, this is illustrative of how an emotional logic is used to frame an issue as part of an ideological "war of position" over inequality. Baker notes that it can be obscure to a low-paid worker why taxing the rent extractor benefits the low paid as a whole: "they may see such efforts as vindictive, rather than as an essential part of a policy to reduce inequality" (Baker 2016, p.20). That is correct, but it is the beneficiary from rent extraction who seeks to frame this reaction as "vindictive", grounded on spite, and as the gratuitous punishment of society's "winners".

That is why the ideology of meritocracy is not an optional way of legitimating what is, in fact, a rent extractors' paradise. If it is emotive to accuse the egalitarian of spite, then it is equally emotive to apply the language of theft to rent extraction; yet that seems to us a helpful reframing of the issue. "Kleptocracy" is a word we are happier applying to countries with extensive overt corruption and failures in the rule of law. However, we are now accustomed to a beaten-down state, with its learned helplessness, standing by while private agents engage in the looting of their own corporation, or the evasion of taxes, or rigging each others' remuneration by sitting on remuneration committees. Even worse, the state becomes an enabler of these strategies (Galbraith 2008). Finally, these points have political consequences: the politics of the situation are that the wealthy are not living separate lives in a separate sphere. They are extracting income and wealth from their "fellow citizens" while, in the process, showing their contempt for that very idea of a fate shared with others (Lasch 1995).

Baker's important work is representative of a recent cluster of books and papers on the topic of rent-extracting corporate socialism in the United States (Baker 2016; Galbraith 2008; Lindsey and Teles 2017; Posner and Weyl 2018; Price and Edwards 2020; Taylor and Ömer 2020). It is an important part of this critique to detail the ways in which institutional and ethical barriers to rent seeking have been removed by political action. Both Baker and Scanlon note the importance of the sustained political and ideological attack on trade unionism in the United States as an important factor explaining why supermanagers and the rentier-investor class have had their own way on this issue.

What kind of rent-extractive activities become possible when political opposition to rent seeking has been eliminated? Historian Adam Tooze has recently contested explanations of capitalist inequality, like ours, that appeal to Kalecki's idea that unemployment is a class-based disciplinary device. He does so on the grounds that organized capital in the United States has so completely won the class war that the US elite can do what it likes (Tooze 2021a).[1] From Tooze's perspective our argument in this book is naive. We are overlooking the fact that the class war has been over for some time with decisive victory for one side. What the victors, the US elite, like to do, it seems, is extract rent—without limit. As we will see in chapter 6, Hegel presciently identified this sense of impunity on the part of the rich. If poverty is shameful in capitalist society, by way of contrast, becoming rich is, it seems, admirable without limit.

Baker tracks this theme across the American industrial sectors of finance, technology, pharmaceuticals, and copyright protection for intellectual property. He examines trade policy and CEO remuneration and helpfully extends his treatment from the high end of supermanagers to the protected status of "high end" professionals such as doctors, dentists, accountants, lawyers—although perhaps mercifully he does not extend his account to academics.[2] Like others working on US inequality, such as Peter Temin, he helpfully turns the focus away from the 0.1% or the 1.0% to the split between the upper 20% of the American income and wealth distribution and the remaining 80%.[3]

The rent-seeking diagnosis is compelling: the turn to market fundamentalism may have been motivated in the 1970s by a belief that there was a crisis of profitability in the US economy. Unfortunately, the policy response to a self-generated problem produced an entrenched form of rentier capitalism

[1] "The Kaleckian scenario, from today's point of view, presumed too much countervailing force from the left and by the same token too many constraints on active economic policy. Trump opened a new era of voluntarism in economic policy. You really could do what you liked" (Tooze 2021a).

[2] But he does extend it to university presidents, pointing out that alongside ballooning CEO pay in the United States is a substantial increase (if lower in absolute terms than the corporate case) in the remuneration of the top managers/administrators of universities and non-profits that are, as he notes, beneficiaries of tax exemption of donations to them (Baker 2016, pp.210–1).

[3] Thus we agree with Richard Reeves that "this obsession with the upper class allows the upper middle class to convince ourselves that we are in the same boat as the rest of America; but it is not true" (Reeves 2017, pp.3–4).

that proceeded to stabilize itself over a forty-year period—both politically and culturally (Feygin 2021).

However one interprets what has happened in the meantime, America's "superstar" firms over the last fifty years have seen high levels of profit produce issues of their own. For example, how much cheaper it is to lobby for the protection of one's rent-extracting niche rather than actually to invest and innovate? Far from needing external financing from the financial sector, firms with excess retained earnings were lending that cash out on the "repurchase" (or "repo") market to a significant extent in the run up to the financial crisis of 2007–8.

The rent-seeking hypothesis also provides an explanation of why an economy dominated by financialization and oligopolistic firms is showing a lack of innovation and a tendency to stagnation. These firms were put in a guaranteed, protected, position to succeed by the US developmental state. Yet they not only claim the credit for their own super-profits, but refuse to honour their part of the social contract by evading both their corporation tax and, for their senior executives, lobbying to reduce their personal tax "burden".

As Lazonick points out, we no longer hear about the "corporate raiders" or hostile takeovers of the 1980s because chief executives, activist institutional shareholders, hedge fund managers, and a slew of financiers, lawyers, and accountants are all on the same page when it comes to the "looting" of the US business corporation (Lazonick and Shin 2019).[4] But the key point, which follows from Baker's analysis and which we will further develop by looking at the econometric data compiled by Taylor and Ömer, is that the primary explanatory factor here is wage suppression (Taylor and Ömer 2020). Superstar firms, the growth of monopoly, slowing overall productivity and innovation, and the risk of secular stagnation are all downstream from that fundamental development. We do not take the current inflationary turn in our economies in the immediate aftermath of a global pandemic—via supply chain shocks—to have fundamentally changed this picture.

Which ideas legitimized these changes? There are specific theses, such as the doctrine of the primacy of shareholder value, which have been trenchantly criticized (Lazonick and Shin 2019, chapter 7; Stout 2012).[5] More generally,

[4] Lazonick does believe this is a case of American exceptionalism: corporate governance regimes elsewhere have prevented similar developments.

[5] The view's proponents were Milton Friedman, William Meckling, Michael Jensen, and Kevin J. Murphy (Friedman 2002; Jensen and Meckling 1976; Jensen and Murphy 1990).

however, we side with Robinson and Minsky in their diagnosis that the culprit here is the synthesis of Keynesianism and neo-classicism represented quintessentially by Paul Samuelson's work. Robinson, famously impolitely, called it "bastardised Keynesianism" because it bore no relation to Keynes's own work. If, in the 1970s and 1980s, "neo-liberalism" meant the work of Milton Friedman, the Chicago School, the Mount Pelerin Society, and the historical influence of German ordoliberalism, the "Great Moderation" of the 1990s and early 2000s was, as Adam Tooze points out, legitimated by the technocratic elite educated in the Samuelson school (Tooze 2021a).[6]

Moreover, it was the Samuelson "Keynesians" who presided over the changes in the US economy that led to the financial crisis (Tooze 2018, 2021a). They did not pay attention to the deliberate paradox in the title of Minsky's magnum opus—*Stabilizing an Unstable Economy* (Minsky 1986/2008). It is by those very measures assumed to be "stabilizing" that you hasten the next Minskyan institutional super-cycle to its disastrous conclusion, in this case, the global crisis of 2007–8 (Dafermos, Gabor, and Michell 2020; Tooze 2018; Palley 2011).

Even by the Samuelson School's standards, the post-crisis stimulus of the US economy was too little, too late. It produced the post-2008 perfect storm of economic and political instability. Indeed, the only constant during this period was the inexorable rise in inequality—and public anger. Following a brief interlude during which the leading lights of the Samuelson school wondered aloud whether the major economies in the affluent West were in a state of secular stagnation, the pandemic of 2020 produced another shock—this time a truly exogenous one—forcing elites across the world into crisis management mode again.

The working ideology of America's economic elite did no harm to the prospects of its rent-extracting elites in finance and business who have benefitted from a form of corporate socialism (Hayek calls it "syndicalism"). Furthermore, there is plenty of blame to go around; a focus on the "1%" or top "0.1%" is misleading. A much broader class of citizens form part of this rent-extracting elite and not just in the United States. America's wealthiest citizens may be at the apex of a pyramid, but that structure has a broader base. The United States is at the centre of a trans-national group of elites who

[6] Tooze labels this school "actually existing neoliberalism" noting that the monetarist ideology of Friedman et al. "serve[d] more and more as an alibi" for this group and that the foundational works of neoliberalism "had been consigned to the fringes" of economic ideology (Tooze 2021a).

have convergent interests with no overt coordination between them (Klein and Pettis 2020).

2.2 Wage Suppression and the Dual Economy

One helpful way to understand the data we marshalled in the previous chapter and the critique of rent seeking in the previous section is to ask this question: if the embedded prosperity of the period 1945–70 had continued until 2010, what would the upshot have been for all citizens across the whole income and wealth distribution?

In the case of the United States, two macroeconomists have developed a model of how one might calculate the path of its economy had this rent extraction not taken place. One needs to make some supplementary assumptions, namely, that a more embedded economic system would have been more resilient and less financially fragile. Price and Edwards demonstrated the result of assuming that income growth had "kept pace with the real per capita growth rate of 118 percent" (Price and Edwards 2020, p.10). Their conclusion was striking: they calculate that $47 trillion has been extracted in rent by the top 1% of US citizens from the bottom 90% between 1975 and 2018 (Price and Edwards 2020, p.12). That is equivalent to nearly two and a half years of total GDP at pre-2020 pandemic levels.

Price and Edwards may be under-estimating the cost to growth if a fairer distribution of this $47 trillion had redressed the structural deficit in consumption and itself stimulated more investment and growth to meet this increased consumer demand—the Keynesian multiplier effect.[7] The "lost" $47 trillion, if put to the right uses, could have generated a far higher dollar value of shared prosperity. This counterfactual scenario needs not only to assume that financial crises would not have happened, but also to factor in what they cost, both to private households and the cost of state interventions.[8] This massive rent extraction has harmed everyone—possibly even many of the wealthy, for whom a loss of social and political power might have been compensated for with stable and sustainable wealth. In assessing this tally, then, it is worth building in the estimated cost of $15 trillion dollars, in the form of credit guarantees, that the US state was forced to issue after the

[7] A point we owe to Stefan Sciaraffa (personal communication).
[8] Price and Edwards's model does factor in business cycles.

financial crisis of 2007–8 which was, in turn, the culmination of a series of crises (Tooze 2018).

Taylor and Ömer's data shows how far, during this period, the US economy departed from the Keynesian ideal of a full employment/mass consumption economy and has financialized, de-industrialized, and in every way generated a structural deficit in aggregate demand. They provide a comprehensive econometric analysis for the US economy from 1970–2020 that is consistent with Baker's analysis, taking the main explanation for inequality to be wage suppression. While this suppression increased profit share overall by "only" 0.43% a year, that accumulated over five decades to 27% of real productivity growth. That is an immense shift in the composition of income share (Taylor and Ömer 2020, p.5). An important fact when writing about inequality in the United States is that it is always misleading to discuss averages because of the "ski jump" distribution of income and wealth, with the top 1% and 0.1% having a distorting effect on averages. More important, then, is to look at the rise in the "Palma ratios" that relate the mean incomes of the United States' top 1% with the mean incomes of its "middle class" (from the 61st—99th percentile of the income distribution) and lower class (up to 60th percentile).

These ratios grew at 2% annually (Taylor and Ömer 2020, p.17) over this fifty-year period.[9] This accumulates into a significant advantage for the better off produced by the policy of wage suppression in aggregate. While the existence of "superstar firms", for example, forms a derivative part of the explanation of current inequality, this follows on from wage suppression—it is an opportunity for super-profit that takes advantage of wage suppression for the majority of workers.[10] But the latter is the more explanatorily fundamental, as it is in Baker's analysis, where the wage suppression of the many is the policy outcome of the action of the few. This data reinforces Baker's argument that we are dealing here with a rent-extractive economy.

[9] In 2014, pre-tax mean income for the "middle class" was $130,000; for the lower class, annual wage income was $30,000 with state transfer support of $25,000. Income data is not very helpful for the 1%, as they have a variety of non-income sources: the most insightful metric is that the top 1% in 2014 took 15% of total GDP made up of $2.7 trillion of income and $0.3 trillion of capital gains (total $3tn of a total of $17.4tn). Clearly, in this analysis the phrase "middle class" is no longer particularly helpful; "upper middle class" is better, but obscures the steep drop-off at the lower point of this distribution.

[10] This sector exhibits a high degree of "churn" because the productivity growth that powers superstar firms cannot be sustained and individual corporations fall out of this classification (Taylor and Ömer 2020, p.8).

Productivity increases in some sectors, then, have been combined with wage suppression and hence increased profitability overall. Wages from labour only went up for the 1% in the United States (Taylor and Ömer 2020, p.2). As workers transitioned into the service sectors, where significant productivity gains cannot be made, productivity slowed in aggregate. In the only dynamic sectors of the economy, increased demand is met with increased productivity, so while wages are high in those areas it is for a substantially reduced number of workers while those sectors lose jobs overall. Businesses change their modus operandi once a large pool of surplus labour is created who will take poor-quality, poorly remunerated work in low-end services: firms take advantage of it.

At the top end, America's wealthiest citizens pay more, but also take a disproportionate share of the "profit growth"—actually rent extraction—caused primarily by wage suppression (Taylor and Ömer 2020, pp.2–3). That is channelled through returns on bonds and equities and capital gains on business assets. These citizens were, as we will see in chapter 8, in a position to save and disproportionately did so. That explains their increased wealth: "the share of wealth in the total held by rich households was around 25 percent in the 1960s; now it is in the vicinity of 40%" (Taylor and Ömer 2020, p.3). In their view the primary causes of inequality were the following:

> Higher capital gains were stimulated by wage repression in two ways. Businesses enjoyed rising profits and falling interest rates, the latter due to slower inflation because there was no wage-driven cost push. Insofar as asset price increases are driven by capitalization of higher profit rates as interest rates declined, they basically result from lagging wages.[11] (Taylor and Ömer 2020, p.3)

This is a difference of emphasis from that of Baker, but these two explanations are complementary. Like economist Peter Temin, Taylor invokes the ideas of pioneering development economist Sir Arthur Lewis, who postulated,

[11] They explain the impact of the changed position of the wealth in the overall distribution on other groups as follows: first, the worst off—"Households at the bottom of the income distribution received modestly increasing government transfers. They apparently have negative savings rates, which supported their consumption spending" (Taylor and Ömer 2020, p.3). Secondly, the "squeezed middle": "Income of middle-class households, which principally rely on labor earnings, was squeezed from above and below; their share of total income went down" (Taylor and Ömer 2020, p.3). This picture of the squeezed middle is basically that of Galbraith (Galbraith 1998/2000) but with updated econometric evidence.

as Taylor puts it, "a natural transition of employment from a low-wage, low productivity stagnant or subsistence zone to higher productivity industries or sectors"—but in this case operating in reverse (Lewis, 1954; Taylor and Ömer 2020, p.7, p.58, chapter 4).

In the United States this "natural" process is headed in the opposite direction from the original Lewis hypothesis: "employment and the structure of production have shifted towards sectors with low growth and levels of real wages and productivity" (Taylor and Ömer 2020, p.7). Lewis's "dual economy" diagnosis usually applies prospectively, to a developing society, whereas the United States is a regressing, de-industrializing, and financializing society. Alarmingly, Temin argues that the Lewis model is the most descriptively adequate model for the description of the world's largest and most sophisticated economy (Temin 2017; Storm 2017a). From a developmental perspective, rent seeking is producing economic regression—even as some sectors do staggeringly well.

Temin's descriptors of his two sectors are "the finance, technology and electronics" ("FTE") sector and the "low wage" ("LW") sector: 20% of American citizens occupy the former sector while 80% occupy the latter (Temin 2017, p.4, p.9, pp.77–8). He elucidates his distinction as follows:

> The first sector consists of skilled workers and managers who have college degrees and command good and even very high salaries in our technological economy. I call this the FTE sector to highlight the roles of finance, technology and electronics in this part of the economy. The other group consists of low-skilled workers who are suffering some of the ills of globalization. I call this the low-wage sector to highlight *the role of politics* and technology in reducing the demand for semi-skilled workers. (Temin 2017, p.8, emphasis added)

Temin's core claim is that "one implication of the Lewis model is that the upper sector *tries to keep wages low in the lower sector*" (Temin 2017, p.xiv, emphasis added, see also pp.6–7). This is not, then, a "win/win" competition in which a rising tide lifts all boats.

> Rural people sold food to cities in the Lewis model; members of the low wage sector typically sell services to the FTE sector in this modern reincarnation of the model. They work in fast-food restaurants and clean hospitals and hotels. They drive people around as needed, transport items in factories

> and stores, work in nonunionized industries and engage in other similar activities that vary too much for robots to take over. (Temin 2017, p.28)

This is, as we have noted, a shift to a zero-sum contest where the few extract resources at the expense of the many. In this restructured economy, whole categories of jobs are disappearing. The two sectors are disconnected: "the low wage sector has very little impact on the progress of the FTE sector" (Temin 2017, p.29).

Both Dutch economist Servaas Storm and Taylor and Ömer hypothesize that in a society like the United States, where the support for the unemployed is so weak, workers are displaced from a narrow range of dynamic sectors into stagnant sectors of employment where more workers are used to maintain the same (low) level of productivity (Storm 2017a; Taylor and Ömer 2020, pp.78–9). This relationship between the sectors accelerates an overall structural deficit in consumption and is one cause of so-called secular stagnation (Storm 2017b). It furthers the material interests of the wealthy, who already derive most of their income from the expanded profit share produced by wage suppression—which we have diagnosed as largely made up of rent extraction—to have the costs of many basic services driven down in exactly the way Lewis predicted.

We have already described Schwartz's model of the franchise economy; Temin also notes the flourishing of an outsourcing model that sees shareholder value maximized by concentration on core business while other service functions are "contracted out". LW workers often work for subcontractors who compete to be hired by the various businesses who specialize in their core competencies alone. This is one, important, aspect of the "fissured economy" we described above.[12] Cost cutting, precariousness, and increased monitoring are the realities of life for employees in the LW sector:

> The shift from paying wages to hiring subcontractors is a momentous change in the place of workers in a business enterprise. When workers were wage earners, there was a social component to their work. Workers saw themselves as a group, and being a member of a stable group fostered morale.... When workers are hired instead by a competitive service company, they have no identification with the parent firm. They have low morale

[12] This is not happenstance, but an example of "divide and rule employer tactics" (Taylor and Ömer 2020, p.8), with macro policy producing a reserve pool of cheap labour. The rise of the "gig economy" which employs 8%–10% of the US workforce, is another effect of these tactics (ibid, p.80).

> and will not exert any extra effort for the parent firm's benefit. Intrusive monitoring replaces morale, and antagonism replaces cooperation. (Temin 2017, p.31)

In addition to poor working conditions—including insecurity—the increasingly monopolistic character of US business, with monopoly rent extraction, leads both to increasing consumer prices and to the de facto collusion between employers who seek to keep wages low (Temin 2017, pp.32–3).

Meanwhile, public sector services are, where possible, privatized and then cut: "The Lewis model asserts that the FTE sector wants to keep incomes low in the low wage sector, and that includes lowering the quality of public services in the low-wage sector" (Temin 2017).[13] The poor, then, work longer hours, with worse pay and conditions, increased close supervision and monitoring, no job security, little access to pensions or employer healthcare, and ever reduced public services alongside increased consumer prices.[14] They are also deterred from union representation. Perhaps the development of "angrynomics", which we discuss in the next section, is not so hard to understand.

A further important aspect of the dual economy is the disparity between educational outcomes in each sector:

> Government decisions over the past generation have constructed a bifurcated school system, one for prosperous suburban whites who go on to college and one for urban black and brown people who are preoccupied by the threat of jail. (Temin 2017, p.xvi)

As Temin notes, laconically, "the FTE sector has made this transition increasingly costly over time" (Temin 2017, p.41). This obstacle race places more and higher obstacles in the path of children whose parents are in the LW sector, and even those who complete the course find that other factors—notably

[13] A notable redirection of public funds has been from investment in communities to funding mass incarceration, predominantly for Black Americans, which Temin describes as "a form of social control" (Temin 2017, p.38).

[14] For the record, we accept that in the high-end services sector, employment can be precarious and monitored. However, that precarity is reflected in the remuneration packages of these workers. We will discuss Claudia Goldin's idea that the high-end professional services employer, for example in banking and law, has come to presume the existence of the 24/7, always available, committed employee in Temin's FTE sector (Goldin 2021). In the LW sector, the problem is that employers assume constant availability while hiring and firing on an "as and when" basis; offering so-called zero hours or precarious contracts.

social capital—are involved in landing a job in the FTE sector. By contrast, "members of the FTE sector are not aware of the social capital that surrounds and sustains them" (Temin 2017, p.42). When it comes to education, the very real "rolling back" of state funding has slammed shut the gates of social mobility via the publicly funded sector.[15] This reinforces the point that the putatively neo-liberal commitment to rolling back the state only rolls public provision back selectively—when it suits the class interest of the managerial overclass to restrict access to educational opportunity so that they may selectively advantage their own offspring via a process of elite credentialing.

These arguments about rent seeking suggest the importance of internally disaggregating the effects of inequality. Elites in the United States, like elites in other countries, are benefitting from these changes while most citizens are not. It also suggests it is naive to ignore the United States' role as the remaining global hegemon at the centre of the international monetary order and capable of running an extensive trade deficit "recycled" into the holding of US Treasuries by its "in surplus" trading partners. This makes America's comparatively wealthy people, its upper 20%, the world's consumers of last resort (Varoufakis 2011).[16]

The only policy solution, as Baker, Taylor and Ömer all conclude, is curtailing top end income and wealth (Baker 2016; Taylor and Ömer 2020, p.4). Given that this is rent extraction, you cannot "grow your way" out of this kind of inequality by expanding the pie for all via "inclusive growth". We will return to this important point in our Conclusion.[17] While we are, then, pre-distributivists about a just society, the transition to such a society is going to require a massive curtailment of the wealth of the richest citizens under the current distribution in societies such as the United States and the United Kingdom before that becomes a realistically utopian aspiration. For

[15] "Student loans are now held by more than 40 million people who owe more than $1.2 trillion in student-loan debt" (Temin 2017, p.44). Temin notes the macroeconomic effect: debt depresses spending, which lowers demand for labour in the LW sector and helps to depress wages (Temin 2017, p.46).

[16] Again, it is necessary to disaggregate: "exorbitant privilege" makes the dollar-centric global monetary order sound like an unqualified benison to US citizens. But in their role as consumers of last resort these citizens are supporting producers in other countries. The flow of capital into the United States is good news for Wall Street and other intermediaries in the insurance and real estate sectors, but less good news for ordinary US citizens. See (Pettis 2001, chapters 7 and 8).

[17] That this is the lesson of the past can be inferred from the title Piketty gives to his section "Liquidating the Past, Building Justice: Exceptional Taxes on Private Capital" (Piketty 2020, pp.441–5).

example, Taylor and Ömer suggest a capital gains tax that funds a wealth fund paying a social dividend for all (Taylor and Ömer 2020, p.4).[18]

2.3 Rent Seeking, Resentment, and Angrynomics

Defenders of inequality are obviously keen to deny the rent-seeking hypothesis. From their perspective, their core value is truthfulness: the market simply is, unfortunately, the bearer of bad news about the differential value of different citizen's capacities to make an economically valuable contribution. This is the basis of Mitt Romney's "makers versus takers" narrative: don't shoot the messenger! From the market's perspective, some people are simply worth less than others—if only from an economic point of view.

You might suspect that nearly all who put this explanation forward view their own economic contribution as substantial and, for that matter, not a candidate for offshoring, outsourcing, or automation any time soon. The official ruling ideology of the technocratic elites is meritocracy—a view we will examine in detail in chapter 12. The market supposedly tells the truth about market-based merits—the kinds of individual capacities that bring an individual an entitlement to a certain level of material reward. We will explain in chapter 12 both why it is not surprising that highly unequal societies see a wider uptake and belief of meritocratic discourse and why we think this particular legitimation narrative is false (Mijs 2021).

If anything, our class-based, sectoral explanation of inequality in terms of rent extraction views our elites as victims of their own success. Their predatory value extraction, with its proceeds recycled into political lobbying to perpetuate it, or diverted into tax havens, or invested in high-end art works stashed in global freeports to avoid any form of taxation, has become too conspicuous—too flagrant (Mayer 2017; Thompson 2018; Shaxson 2011). Across jurisdictions, stagnant wages for the many, combined with high levels of private debt, are perpetuating that which Galbraith memorably called "an economy of tax slaves and debt peons . . . an economy of frightened and frustrated people" (Galbraith 1998, p.16). Fear and frustration have since

[18] A similar policy proposal is made by (Lonergan and Blyth 2020). It is a standard part of the approach of the pre-distributivist egalitarian going back to James Meade (Thomas 2017; Meade 1964; Atkinson 2015).

become anger. It seems to us that the range of political responses to the crisis of 2007–8 marked a turning point in the development of this legitimation crisis.

In context, Galbraith was describing America's squeezed middle class—soon effectively to go extinct—since the burden of tax and transfer for the nation's poor fell on them given the capacity of America's very wealthy to evade their fair share of taxation. This was, however, a prescient explanation that we can now generalize beyond the United States. High private indebtedness, with no inflation to reduce the real burden of debt, stagnant wages, and a state-backed financial sector making easy credit available, creates societies with a high private debt burden that is constantly re-structured and rolled over. Even in our post-pandemic world of transitory inflation, the alleged "control" of inflation by central bank increases in interest rates hits a political constraint. It is hard to envisage those rates going particularly high in a world with so much private indebtedness.

It is not surprising that the generalization of this model produces Blyth and Lonergan's "angrynomics" (Lonergan and Blyth 2020). Watching others enrich themselves, without restraint, from an allegedly shared economy produces first resentment and then anger. We are certainly not, as we increasingly realize, "all in this together".

Another way in which the wealthy are victims of their own success is that it is difficult to maintain the meritocratic narrative when, in the light of ever-increasing standards of merit, the number of elite positions available fails to increase. To succeed as a form of legitimation, meritocracy would have to see the competition it generates also generate a commensurate extension in the range of rewards: as the competitors "up their game", so prizes must be more widely distributed. However, it is clear to many of the hard-working, elite-credentialed, children of the middle class that their likely economic fate is downward, and not upward, social mobility.

It seems, in fact, that breaking into the elite requires an insider status whose criteria are obscure. As the prizes to be won increase in size, but not in extent, and as the capacity for achieving them via merit yields dwindling returns, so there is the "democratization" of what social theorist César Rendueles calls "the possibility of a collapsing life" (Rendueles 2017, p.143).[19] The sphere

[19] Rendueles argues that this is the return to the core capitalist countries of an experience all too familiar in the periphery: "The idea that something exceptional happened in 2008 must seem strange to the hundreds of millions of people for whom financial shocks and the delegitimizing of democratic institutions have been their daily experience for decades. Mexicans and Colombians under

of education is a microcosm for Rendueles's more ambitious thesis that the attack on organized labour is, as Polanyi argued before him, an attack on working-class culture as a basis of social solidarity:

> In contrast, the upper classes managed to shield themselves from post-modern individualization by preserving their social capital—for example, through elite educational establishments or affinity networks bound up with lifestyle—a simulacrum of a cultural project, based on sophisticated consumption. (Rendueles 2017, p.150)

The social bases of countervailing power have been fractured by policy. By contrast, the interests of the rentier-investor class are naturally convergent—capital is self-organizing, while the forces opposed to it are not.

There is, however, a looming problem of so-called elite reproduction when the meritocratic narrative becomes too obviously false: when working hard and playing by the rules doesn't cut it. Rendueles finds hope in the thought that, as Marx put it, political change is driven primarily by those who lose out under capitalism (Rendueles 2017). Those numbers are growing—even in the heartland. As political economist Helen Thompson has remarked, immediately after the financial crisis there was an academic and semi-popular literature on why this "crisis in the heartland" seemed only to have strengthened capitalism (Gowan 2010). Yet post-2016 that narrative has gone out of business. The language of the "1%", of generationally privileged "baby boomers", and "frustrated and angry Millennials" is now common currency. Emotions play a key role in explaining this transformation. The importance of such emotions in the stabilization of political order is the theme we will now start to develop. We will begin by clarifying the normative framework that we have already put to use.

forty have literally known nothing other than economic crisis and political decomposition. And something similar is happening to broad sectors in the rich countries" (Rendueles 2017, p.144).

3

Addressing Inequality

A Normative Framework

Propositional Summary

1. Scanlon's "narrow" reasons for objecting to the badness of inequality are described. We focus on domination as manifested by the drift to oligarchy in our political institutions. Scanlon's parallel concerns are inappropriate control and the unfair outputs from our socio-economic institutions. We set out the sceptical case against the intrinsic, as opposed to extrinsic, badness of inequality.
2. Scanlon takes as his baseline assumption the moral equality of all. In the case of distinctions of caste and class, the inegalitarian does try to re-introduce categorical distinctions into the moral equality of persons. Scanlon relates this to the false evaluative belief held by many people that our social world should be structured by status distinctions. He attributes to Rousseau the insight that eliminating this false belief harms no one.
3. We distinguish different vectors of poverty. Rawls argues that domination can arise either from egotism or from social anxiety. The will to dominate can be a defensive measure arising from anticipatory anxiety of possible domination by others. In this way anxiety can produce domination, produced by anxiety, without anyone actually seeking to dominate others.
4. A distinction is introduced between the strong egalitarianism of Rawls's conception of justice as reciprocal fairness and the weak egalitarianism of the Roman republican tradition epitomized by Pettit's work. This distinction acts as a touchstone for competing conceptions of the egalitarian policies demanded in response to inequality.

Extravagance and Misery. Alan Thomas, Alfred Archer, and Bart Engelen, Oxford University Press.
 DOI: 10.1093/oso/9780197781722.003.0004

Introduction

Our first two chapters have been diagnostic: we hope we have convinced you that extensive income and wealth inequality is real and in large part due to extractive rent seeking by elites. The implicit claim is that our most affluent and economically developed societies are regressing. They are financializing, de-industrializing, and levels of innovation and productivity are dwindling. Wages, in real terms, stagnate for the great majority of citizens while a transnational cohort of the super-rich consolidate their gains, jurisdiction by jurisdiction.

In chapter 1 we addressed the challenge of the "Willie Sutton" argument: the sceptical claim that inequality is not bad, per se. It is bad only if it has bad effects. Our response to that argument may have given a misleading impression that we are anxious to correct in this chapter: it is not that there is one set of arguments exclusively about well-being and a different set exclusively about the intrinsic or extrinsic badness of inequality. That would, in fact, misunderstand our central claim, which is that the intrinsic badness of inequality ramifies through its well-being effects. The well-being of an individual suffers particularly badly when he or she believes that they are living under unjust inequalities. We will develop that theme in this chapter after we have set out our general normative orientation. We hope to reach readers from several disciplines and being explicit about this framework may help to frame the discussion to come.

3.1 The Badness of Inequality

The normative framework for this book is a synthesis of ideas drawn from both the liberal and republican traditions set out in previous work (Thomas 2017). The liberal-republican embeds Rawls's conception of justice as reciprocal fairness in a general account of non-domination. This view expands Rawls's conception of the basic structure of society to develop a conception of an expanded basic structure: a basic structure in which the domination of one citizen by another is made structurally impossible (Thomas 2017). Within this framework, what is bad about inequality?

We are influenced by Scanlon's cataloguing of the six reasons for objecting to inequality: objectionable inequalities of status; violations of procedural fairness; unfairness in the allocation of valued social roles and the failure to ensure that there are enough such roles; the excessive control that the social power of the wealthy gives them over others; the unfair political influence of the wealthy; the output of unjust economic rewards from unfair economic institutions (Scanlon 2018).[1] In what follows we treat Scanlon's ideas as elements that egalitarians can dis/assemble in different ways. It is a question of what, in a specific context of explanation, you view as primary.

As liberal-republicans, we take domination to be the most fundamental orienting concept to explain the failures of equality in capitalist market societies (Thomas 2017). This unjustified, excessive control over the lives of others, which Scanlon rightly identifies as one of the reasons to object to inequality, is expressed by our unfair political institutions. The failure of those institutions is, in turn, transmitted to their failure to constrain unequal outcomes from our socio-economic institutions. In an instance of what Piketty calls the "drift to oligarchy", unfair economic outcomes enrich those who use their social and political power to perpetuate the very unfair political outcomes that confer that power on them (Piketty 2014). That is how, as liberal-republicans, we will combine and explain the distinct elements of Scanlon's reasons for objecting to inequality.

This analysis explains how the emancipatory ideal of a market society is distorted under rentier capitalism. The rentier-investor class introduces various disciplinary measures into economic life that impact on the well-being of others directly and indirectly. Directly, we will describe mechanisms of both domination and opportunity hoarding and the role they play in creating a "money society". In such a society you must take an interest in money whatever your prior ethical or political orientation. That is because our institutions pit people against each other (Hussain 2023). Money is made important for a broader range of societal institutions that impact everyone's life chances.

Indirectly, these disciplinary measures undermine the necessary background for the implementation of a fair equality of opportunity principle. Once again, we will describe a self-reinforcing process in which the wealthy, with undue control over the lives of others, shape both culture and institutions in their own image. This leads both to false claims about meritocracy (to justify the social standing of themselves as wealthy and successful)

[1] There are seven items on our list, as we split out two aspects of fair equality of opportunity—items three and four on our list—that Scanlon treats as a composite.

and to status discrimination against the worst off. The reduced agency for the poor, we will argue, significantly harms their well-being.

Further, their inferior status plays the kind of disciplinary role that loops back into the undermining of fair equality of opportunity: we so organize work that some social positions of advantage are well remunerated, meaningful, with considerable autonomy; while other positions at the opposite end are menial, degrading, of low social status, and closely supervised (Gomberg 2007).[2] The mere existence of the latter kind of jobs is an instrument of social discipline: they are jobs to be avoided. If Gomberg is correct that as early as the school system children are sorted, in a class-based way, towards these different categories of job, then the associated emotions, for those destined for the "worst" jobs, are shame, despair, or the cultivation of counter-cultural values that shield a person from those emotions (Gomberg 2007).

The foregoing account faces another challenge: the objection that these are not objections to inequality, but other issues closely related to inequality that are, nevertheless, distinct from it. This is the foundational question Scanlon addresses. He notes that, prima facie, the case against the existence of a special class of narrowly egalitarian reasons—reasons for objecting to the intrinsic badness of inequality—seems a strong one. Each of us has our own life to lead and wants the liberty to direct our life's course and be free from domination or interference by others. From that starting point and our republican focus on domination, there seem to be materials for a critique of one kind of egalitarianism that targets certain patterned outcomes that arise from our institutions and their shaping of market transactions.

For example, suppose that we have our current system of rights and private property and that we all follow "the rules of the game". Why, then, does the egalitarian insist that any end result of free voluntary transactions must exemplify some pattern of "correct" distribution of resources (Nozick 1974)? Conversely: if we aim at the pattern, then we seem forced to interfere with the freedom of individuals to enter into the transactions they choose—whether commercial transactions, or gifts?

Furthermore, if narrow egalitarian reasons did have independent force, then there would be prima facie reason to prefer an outcome in which all were more equal, but all were less well off, compared to an outcome where

[2] We owe to Dan Hind the observation that the classification of much of this labour as "unskilled" itself involves class prejudice: these jobs can involve complex skills, simply not skills valued by the "exam-passing classes" (as Oxford political scientist Vernon Bogdanor once labelled them).

there was more inequality, but at a higher level of well-being for all (not merely for the better off). The economic concept of Pareto optimality adds that this "levelling down" argument (Parfit 1991) is not merely objectionable: it is irrational.

A natural conclusion, is that the concern of egalitarianism is exhausted when we have brought the worst off to a decent minimal standard (Frankfurt 2015). There are, of course, many other moral reasons bearing on the question of distribution, but Frankfurt argues that this conclusion blunts the force of those narrowly egalitarian reasons that identify its intrinsic wrongness. His view is that if there are objections to a situation where no one falls below that standard, but some are much better off, then those can only be broad, instrumental, reasons for objecting to the further bad effects of that distribution.

Scanlon adds yet another hurdle for the egalitarian: even if there are narrowly egalitarian reasons for more equal outcomes, we need to observe constraints on the means used to bring them about. To use a familiar libertarian trope: if redistributive taxation were theft, then the reasons we have to use it, guided by our narrow egalitarian reasons, have to be traded off against its wrongness as theft—the answer to that trade-off is not obvious.[3] Scanlon concludes that, in spite of these obstacles, there is a wide class of both narrow and broad egalitarian reasons that are not undermined by Nozick's, Parfit's, and Frankfurt's arguments. We agree, and think it is helpful to review some of his arguments to clarify our own position.

3.2 Distinctions of Caste and Class

Scanlon's discussion begins by establishing the moral "baseline" in this debate: we can exclude people who simply do not believe in the moral equality of persons. The question, for him, is how from that shared starting point we can acknowledge further objections to inequality (Scanlon 2018, pp.4–5; see also Thomas 2018). This first class of "baseline" reasons is grounded on social status: there is a narrowly egalitarian objection to some people in a political community being treated as socially inferior to others:

[3] This concern is not, of course, one that the pre-distributive egalitarians (such as ourselves) have to address.

> [E]xtreme inequality in income and wealth can mean that the poor must live in a way that is reasonably seen as humiliating. . . . The evil here is . . . comparative . . . economic inequalities have these effects only given certain prevailing attitudes about what is necessary for someone to be socially acceptable. (Scanlon 2018, p.5)

This first class of reasons will be important to the argument of this book because we will highlight the way in which class stratification in a putatively meritocratic society works to stigmatize the poor. Our argument applies even to these basic baseline assumptions about moral equality.

In some cases, this is stigmatization imposed on the poor, while in others the poor identify with their own stigmatization by internalizing the very values that justify that judgement.[4] The disciplinary mechanisms of a capitalist society do not merely apply to some citizens dominating others. A poor person, for example, might appeal to shared values around the shame of poverty to stigmatize another poor person. Even as a young boy, heavyweight boxer George Foreman was physically imposing. That did not protect him from the fear of poverty stigma. When he pretended that he could afford to take lunch to school by smearing grease on an empty paper bag he was trying to avoid being ashamed not in the eyes of the wealthy, but from the gaze of other children as poor as him.

In societies structured by what Scanlon calls "caste and class distinctions" the accident of one's birth determines one's access to certain kinds of jobs, political participation, and in some cases whether one receives equal concern from the state or other public bodies.

Scanlon also notes that the peers of the poor may deny them "associational goods": the poor are not people you want as your "co-workers, potential friends, potential marriage partners, or even neighbors" (Scanlon 2018, p.26). He also notes that this is a loss to both sides: to those who discriminate and those discriminated against (Scanlon 2018, p.28). Being ascribed an inferior status may be connected to harmful social stereotyping: that people of this sort deserve to be treated this way because of their "typical" characteristics. As Scanlon points out, not only is the stereotyping harmful; deriving conclusions about individuals from putative generalizations is unfair in any case (even if the generalizations were true).

[4] These are values that paradigmatically would fail that which Bernard Williams called the "critical theory test" (Williams 2002, p.221).

Two particularly damaging further effects are the interiorization of these judgements by those subject to them (with or without their endorsement of their validity). Feeling oneself inferior is damaging to a person's self-respect and sense of their own worth (Scanlon 2018, p.27; Rawls 1971/1999, p.386). Yet, as Scanlon often notes, the positive endorsement of these norms—by a person content to "know their place"—does not legitimate them even if the norms do not, for that person, represent a humiliation. For example, a butler in Edwardian England who takes himself to be the social inferior of his gentlemanly master may not find his job humiliating because he accepts his social place. He may, indeed, feel superior to others because he shares in the reflected social status of his important employer. But these feelings depend on what Scanlon calls "false evaluative beliefs": it is false that this is a good way to structure our social world. This putative hierarchy of social status has no evaluative basis.

Nevertheless, history tells us that such attitudes can structure a social hierarchy in which the sense of social superiority on the part of one group is important to their self-respect and esteem, just as it is ambivalent on its effects on those deemed to be "inferior" (in the latter case it may be positive or negative). Scanlon attributes this insight to Rousseau:

> [T]here is likely to be a pathology of attitudes on both sides, the pathology of valuing or disvaluing one's life and activities for inappropriate reasons, and governing one's attitudes and behavior toward others by these mistaken reasons. (Scanlon 2018, p.28)

Scanlon notes how the elimination of this class of reasons is not vulnerable to any accusation of levelling down. This false sense of social superiority is not something to which anyone is morally entitled. The entire class of false beliefs about social superiority and inferiority concern values: how it is appropriate to lead one's life. Scanlon, like other pioneering analysts of positional goods like Adam Swift and Harry Brighouse, focuses on this class of goods precisely because there can be no "levelling down" objection to the egalitarian project to eliminate unnecessary positional competitions, something we will analyse further in chapter 9.

3.3 Domination, Wealth, and Anxiety

We agree with Scanlon that there is a connection between a narrow egalitarian reason, connected to unequal status, and a wider set of evaluative beliefs. Scanlon argues that one's material status impacts on which "status projecting" positional goods one can own and control. From his perspective, if you believe that social status makes you a better or worse person than another, such that your inferiors belong to a lower class or type, then you have a false set of values where those false values are not, per se, about equality,[5] though these reasons may be a powerful factor in understanding our social world.

The relationship between this specific kind of belief and inequality has been insightfully mapped out by Jiwei Ci as the distinction between subsistence, status, and agency poverty (Ci 2013). Comparative poverty can lead to a life below subsistence level, or a life without the respect of others, or a life where one cannot be a "normal functioning agent" (Ci 2013). Ci argues that these are three separable vectors of poverty: a person may vary in which form of poverty they exemplify. The relationship between these components clearly varies from society to society and their prevailing social norms.

While agency poverty does not depend on the attitudes of others; status poverty does, though, "poverty can interfere with agency *by* marking a person as of low social status" (Scanlon 2018, p.31). For us the crucial point is one that Ci and Scanlon both make, namely, that socio-economic inequality is translated into status hierarchy only if certain social attitudes are presupposed. We argue that capitalist market societies have a vested interest in developing an emotional logic that establishes and entrenches these bridging attitudes between socio-economic standing and social status. If poverty is a mark of failure, then low social status, and its impact on a person's sphere of agency, can play its disciplinary role. The emotional regime we will criticize frames the issue in precisely this way.

It follows that if people seek disproportionate wealth to feel socially superior to others, then the eradication of these attitudes would be no loss to them. This is the inverse of the envy objection to others having more than you: it is not that the worse off want the better off to have less grounded on

[5] Technically, Scanlon thinks that false evaluative beliefs about the intrinsic superiority or inferiority of classes of people fall outside his taxonomy of "narrow" reasons. Furthermore, throughout his book he attaches little weight to the social power of the wealthy (Scanlon 2018, pp.36–7).

envy. It is that a certain kind of attitude for resisting greater equality has no moral standing: the desire for wealth *so as to have more than others*. In a society where people are pitted against each other wealth is sought not for its own sake, but to achieve and consolidate a position of domination over others.

The motivations of the dominator, if eliminated, would be a social good not only for those they seek to dominate but also for those who structure their life projects around the aim of dominating others. Once again, Scanlon traces these anti-social attitudes to an evaluative error: the claim that these differences play an ethically important role, when they do not. But our argument is that, for a certain kind of society that we call a capitalist form of market society, its internal dynamics produce a legitimating ideology that does entrench social attitudes whereby the desire for wealth is legitimated. This evaluative error has a functional explanation.

Rawls recognizes this desire to be *wealthier than other people* and charitably interprets it as produced by "insecurity and anxiety":

> [A]s a general psychological fact . . . strong or inordinate desires for more primary goods on the part of individuals and groups, particularly a desire for greater income and wealth and prerogatives of position, spring from insecurity and anxiety. And the same is true of the desire to be wealthy (to have more wealth than others). (Rawls 1999a, p.277)

The desire to have more than others is motivated by anxiety about one's own comparative position. Throughout this book we will note the importance of this argument to the form that Rawls's egalitarianism takes and the political psychology it presupposes. In a more sinister, and less charitable, interpretation of the desire for wealth, Rawls arguably connects it to an egoistic desire to dominate others. Rawls draws on Philip Leon's distinction between "egotism" and "egoism": the former is a biological striving, the latter is a social pathology of craving objects "as symbols for his superiority and for the sake of his superiority" (Rawls 2009, p.150).

The key point, as Edmundson also points out, is that Rawls's original position rules out the pursuit of wealth—as opposed to the fair distribution of primary goods (Edmundson 2017). Parties in that situation express no interest in the interests of others, so the model cannot even represent the motivations of those who seek to dominate, those who are spiteful, or even the motives of those who seek wealth defensively out of anxiety.

The issue *for us* is whether Rawls's conception of justice is stable. Is it stable, given that we know people in our own societies *actually are* fearful and anxious, or spiteful and dominating? We know that Rawls was a keen student of Thomas Hobbes, for whom the destabilizing political emotion above all was prideful "vainglory"—the emotion which political society cannot subdue but only protect itself against. Even if, charitably, we take this desire rashly to start conflicts with others as resting on anxiety, then how is it to be contained in a society well-ordered by justice?

We can formulate an explanation of why, in capitalist market societies, there is a circular logic of the creation of anxiety and fear about one's social position, which produces a desire for more wealth than others as a "defensive necessity" (to use Hirsch's phrase) which in turn creates a social world structured by false evaluative beliefs that status matters. A notable aspect of this particular suboptimal equilibrium is that, on Rawls's explanation, it could be true that, in fact, no one in this scenario seeks to dominate anyone else. Domination paradoxically arises when one fears becoming the victim of domination by others. This can be true whether or not that anxiety is grounded on a true belief. Groundless anxiety, then, can lead a group to coordinate on a low trust, low cooperation equilibrium where everyone takes pre-emptive defensive measures against threats of domination that never actually materialize.

For us, this explains some, but not all, of the data. An additional component is explained by the will to dominate itself: plausibly, one can abandon Rawls's charitable assumption and assume that some people want more wealth than others because they believe that this grounds a superior social status for themselves. That fact is important to them. Scanlon thinks they are evaluatively in error; we diagnose this belief as legitimated by the emotional regime of the society in which we live. Either way, the status-conscious person is a catalyst for a suboptimal equilibrium for us all.

The presence of a few "would be" dominators is enough to make the creation of anxiety about their comparative social position rational from other citizens' point of view. This triggers a competitive arms race in the sphere of the positional, that we document in chapter 9, and the marketization of the goods of opportunity and mobility (education and healthcare). A few bad actors can be the catalyst for a suboptimal equilibrium that cascades through an ever-expanding set of social practices.[6] Solidaristic mutual trust, once lost, is difficult to recover.

[6] There is no need to assume that, in any particular case, these two kinds of explanation are mutually exclusive. As we will see later in our argument, we can recognize the figure of the successful

In Maupassant's *Bel-Ami* (1885), George Duroy is clearly motivated to dominate others, in every respect and in every domain: he seeks status to deny it to others, and he extends the same zero-sum logic to wealth and to power.[7] By the end of the novel he "has it all"—wealth, political power, and social status. That makes him, for us, the quintessential modern anti-hero of commercial society. Nothing, for Duroy, is ever enough. But there do not need to be many Duroys in society for their cumulative social effects to ramify damagingly. Their existence precipitates everyone into a wasteful and mutually damaging equilibrium.

In this book we will be placing equal emphasis on the two other points we have emphasized: our focus will be less on a small group of dominators, but a much wider set of practices whereby people seek pre-emptively to protect themselves from domination. There might be practices that a small dominating class tolerates as convergent with their own interests—that is the basis for our discussion of opportunity hoarding in chapter 9. Furthermore, we will take seriously Rawls's point that anxiety may provoke pre-emptive action which lacks any rationale. We will also, in our last chapter, focus on the stabilizing role of solidaristic institutions that reinforce a high trust environment. This explains our focus on the kinds of institutions that pre-empt oligarchic threats—notably, by dispersing holdings of capital. Rawls, rightly in our view, connects concentrations of capital with concentrations of both economic and social power.

Scanlon also points out the tension between high economic inequality and reasons of status: "extreme inequality in income and wealth can mean that the poor must live in a way that is reasonably seen as humiliating" (Scanlon 2018, p.5). Poor people cannot avoid appearing in public in a way deemed by others to be stigmatizing. Here, inequality interacts with prevailing social norms to generate social exclusion. The key word here is "must": it is beyond individual choice to have to meet Smith's "prevailing standard" for appearing in public without shame.

dominator of others in commercial life who is made miserable by her status failures in the eyes of those who occupy her elevated social tier.

[7] As we will see in chapter 6, this pathological, insatiable, nature of desire in commercial society was of particular interest to Hegel. In his memoir, Stephen King recounts the anecdote of a friend with a drinking problem seeking therapeutic help. When the counsellor asked how much he drank, the friend looked momentarily puzzled before answering, "all of it" (King 2000, p.95). Duroy exhibits the same insatiable ambition.

Scanlon emphasizes that none of the narrow egalitarian reasons that he identifies are grounded on unreasonable envy; nor do they demand "pointless levelling down" (Scanlon 2018, p.6). The worst off can want to be treated fairly, even if doing so contributes nothing to their well-being. A sense of unjustified inferiority can prompt envy, but in the cases we have described envy would be well-motivated and reasonable. If you look at the relative position of a putative social "superior" from your position of undeserved inferiority, and think that the claim to superiority is bogus, you may well be reasonably envious—and also angry. Channel these reasons via ascriptive identities, and the potential for an antagonistic toxic brew of political emotions—predominantly anger—is there. Add social media to the mix as a form of what Quinn Slobodian has called "incitement capitalism" and you can see why anger is so prevalent (Slobodian 2019).

As we have noted, Scanlon's project is to anatomize all the "narrow" egalitarian reasons, but not all of them are relevant to our project in this book. Further, he sometimes uses a less familiar terminology than we will: our concern with domination is tangential to his concept of "control". Control, for Scanlon, is where a person has control over the freedom of another that is inappropriate either in its extent or its scope. This is a more nuanced idea than domination: for example, Scanlon's example of a wealthy uncle who promises his nephew a car if he marries is not a case of domination (Scanlon 2018, p.100). It is, however, intrusive and inappropriate. Yet control intersects with domination in its political dimension. Scanlon assembles the components for a critique of the inequalities we are now witnessing across the affluent West without, as it were, actually putting them together. Control, as Scanlon uses the term in its political dimension, can easily be related to two of his other concerns: the undue political influence of the wealthy and the distorted, unjust, output from economic institutions.

It is by extension, then, that we combine his emphasis on control with his radical discussion of inequality of income from work. There seems to be a natural way to put these ideas together: the disproportionate political power of the wealthy has seen them steer the political process in their favour in various ways. Unlike control, narrowly conceived, Scanlon contends that this process raises broader issues because "undermining the fairness of the political system is morally significant in other ways, for example, because it affects the legitimacy of laws and policies" (Scanlon 2018, p.6).

3.4 A Distinction Within Egalitarianism

How does the foregoing discussion contribute to a systematic approach to inequality? Here we must say more about the convergence between the conception of fairness articulated by John Rawls and the conception of domination articulated by republicans. We aim to advance the understanding of the relationship between the two views by distinguishing weak and strong forms of egalitarianism.

Rawls famously defended both the individual liberties of the classical liberal tradition, plus fair (and not merely formal) equality of opportunity and a socio-economic principle that argues that permissible inequality requires a distribution that maximally advantages the representative worst-off person (the "difference principle") (Rawls 1971/1999). In the decades following the publication of *A Theory of Justice*, conceptions of justice from other political traditions were also articulated, notably the conception of justice as non-domination defended by Philip Pettit and Ian Shapiro (Pettit 1997, 2012; Shapiro 2016). While Pettit represents his project as essentially opposed to Rawls, on the grounds that they have irreconcilable conceptions of liberty, other political philosophers—including one of the current authors—have argued that there is actually notable convergence between the two views such that we ought to speak of a "republican liberalism" or "liberal republicanism" (Thomas 2017; Larmore 2004; Dagger 1997).

That said, there is a substantive difference between Rawls's and Pettit's conceptions of fairness. We will take each view as representative of a family of views: the strongly, and the weakly, egalitarian. Rawls explains this distinction as follows:.

> The difference principle is a strongly egalitarian conception in the sense that unless there is a distribution that makes both (the more advantaged and the less advantaged) person better off . . . an equal distribution is to be preferred. (Rawls 1971/1999, pp.65–6)

Weakly egalitarian views do not accept this constraint. Under this broad heading we will discuss the view that, when it comes to justifying inequalities, only aggregate well-being matters; the view that Paretian improvements are mandatory and, finally, the view that society should aim solely to enable the representative worst-off person to participate in public life without shame (a form of sufficientarianism). Our central thesis is that only a strongly egalitarian view can stabilize a market society and that weakly egalitarian views are unable to resist the destabilizing social mechanisms that we describe.

While we want to convince readers of this book to be strong egalitarians, there is a much broader group of political philosophers who can see the appeal of a more minimal, weakly egalitarian view. This distinction is helpfully formulated by Scanlon (2018). He evaluates institutions in terms of human well-being and fundamental interests in the light of his contractualist standard of right and wrong:

> [I]nstitutions must be justified to those who are asked to accept them in a way that takes all their interests seriously and gives them equal weight. (Scanlon 2018, p.158)

A set of principles, or an institutional set-up that incorporates them, is justified if it is not wrong and it is wrong if it can be the subject of a reasonable individual complaint.[8] In politics, Scanlon argues, two questions arise. Can the individual object that the prevailing distribution of burdens and benefits is too burdensome for her? Can others raise similar objections to variations in that institutional set-up that redistribute those benefits and burdens (Scanlon 2018, p.41)? Scanlon contrasts a more minimal egalitarian standard with Rawls's difference principle, treating the former as a necessary condition for justified inequalities:

> [To] generate significant inequalities [. . .] it must be true either that these inequalities could not be eliminated without infringing important personal liberties, or that they are required in order for the economic system to function in a way that benefits all. (Scanlon 2018, p.141)

This offers an irenic basis for the egalitarian arguments of this book. Scanlon then contrasts it with Rawls's difference principle:

[8] Scanlon makes a further important Rawlsian point, which is that justice as fairness is not merely allocative and we are not distributing manna from heaven that is ex ante given. The productive surplus is, indeed, the upshot of productive activity and that introduces constraints on the process that may generate "inequalities . . . justified by the fact that they arise from the exercise of rights and powers that are required for economic productivity" (Scanlon 2018, p.140).

> This disjunctive condition is a relatively weak interpretation of Rawls's idea that a system that generates inequalities must be "to everyone's advantage". Rawls's preferred interpretation of this idea, the Difference Principle, is stronger. It requires that a system that generates inequalities must not only benefit all, but must benefit those who have less as much as possible. The inequalities that a system generates are "excessive" if they could be reduced in a way that would benefit those who have less. (Scanlon 2018, p.142)[9]

We are also drawn to his framework because we share other of Scanlon's central assumptions, such as that egalitarian views ought to be relational, institutional, and pre-distributive (Thomas 2017).[10] But how does Scanlon's distinction map on to the prior distinction between strong and weak egalitarianism as Rawls and Pettit defend those claims? The more minimal standard seems to point to a welfare state capitalism of the kind shared by Scanlon and Pettit. Pettit is a consequentialist, so justice is not for him a fundamental concept but rather a derived one. The more maximal standard seems to suggest a break with capitalism and hence a break with welfare state capitalism—as one of the current authors has already argued (Thomas 2017). This is, then, a significant distinction, and we hope, by the end of the book, to have made the case for strong egalitarianism. This is an argument that has surprisingly radical consequences in mandating a break with capitalist forms of social organization (just as Rawls argued).

When it comes to applying Scanlon's test, we think it is important to add a point made by Samuel Freeman (2020). He is sceptical about the idea, defended by classical liberal John Tomasi, that there is a special class of economic liberties that ought to be elevated to the constitutional level of protection that Rawls gave to his basic liberties (Tomasi 2012). Freeman stresses the basic liberty to form associations; however, qua basic liberty, this applies primarily to personal and political associations. Economic associations are different. The right to form, or join, any given economic association is not a basic liberty but covered by Rawls's second principle that conjoins fair equality of opportunity and the difference principle (Freeman 2020, p.218).

[9] Later, he narrows the gap between the two formulations (Scanlon 2018, pp.150–1).

[10] He notes that "the objections to inequality that I have listed all presuppose some form of relationship or interaction between the unequal parties" (Scanlon 2018, p.9); he defends his pre-distributionism as follows "whether a distribution . . . is just depends on the nature of the institutions that produce [a pattern] and inequalities in income and wealth are fair if the institutions that produce them can be justified in the proper way" (Scanlon 2018, p.156, see also p.102 ff). For a recent defence of the distinctiveness of a pre-distributive strategy, see (Thomas 2020a).

There is no more basic robust economic liberty that can trump these derivative principles. Therefore, economic associations must pass Scanlon's disjunctive test before they can be associations that a liberal-egalitarian would view as permissible to join.

Consider a putative right to work for a firm that is part of a cartel sustaining unfair prices: this violates no one's rights, but it is impermissible as such a company is undermining the difference principle (Freeman 2020, p.220). These kinds of legal restrictions on permissible forms of corporations are not violations of anyone's basic liberties: that policy could not be the subject of anyone's reasonable complaint that their basic economic liberties had been restricted.

Qua institutional designers, then, our task is to devise institutions of economic life guided by Rawls's three principles, or Scanlon's summative pair of principles. Freeman's point is that the end result cannot be overturned by arguing that they interfere with basic economic liberties. The latter would be modelled on Rawlsian basic liberties: they would trump any subordinated principles and would be constitutionally entrenched with any threats to them assessed by the Supreme Court. Like Freeman, we do not believe that there are any robust economic liberties in this special sense. On his view, and ours, economic freedoms are regulated by the correct principles of justice.

Throughout our argument we will apply both Scanlon's minimal and maximal tests to our societal institutions. In many cases, these two tests will give the same verdict. For example, the extractive rent seeking that characterizes our rentier societies have been criticized from across the political spectrum from a variety of normative perspectives. In other parts of this book there will be a more fine-grained comparison between the less committal view of the weak egalitarian and the more committal, Rawlsian, view of the strong egalitarian. Similarly, there can be sharp divergences between the two views, too: Philip Pettit has gone to some lengths to distance himself from what he calls the "moral fantasy" of Rawls's difference principle (Pettit 2014, p.107; Thomas 2017, p.374, fn. 19). Our aim, at the end of this book, is to have deepened the case for strong egalitarianism. However, pointfully to organize this contrast, we will always contrast these two ways of interpreting unjust inequalities.

4

Recruiting the Science of Happiness

Propositional Summary

1. In addition to the intrinsic badness of inequality we want to draw on the science of happiness to show that unjust inequalities lead to particularly bad well-being effects. We note how paradoxes can arise when trying to argue from inequality data to diminished well-being.
2. Instead of generalizing from the science of happiness, we focus on the notion of an emotional regime. Emotional regimes serve to stabilize the ideological underpinnings of market societies. Class stratification, the increased importance of positional goods, and opportunity hoarding explain the form that inequality has taken in our own societies and its well-being effects. Together these mechanisms vindicate a refined version of the so-called Easterlin paradox.
3. We contrast our approach to others in the literature, notably the work of Wilkinson and Pickett. We focus on market societies specifically and the specific role that emotional regimes play when it comes to well-being.

Introduction

With our normative assumptions clarified, we can now introduce the distinctive resources that we will draw on to develop our argument. Based on Scanlon's "narrow" egalitarian reasons, we think we have established that the empirical data in our opening two chapters prove that we live under intrinsically bad forms of inequality. But we also believe that people chafe under unjust levels of inequality. Impermissible inequality has particularly harmful extrinsic effects that compound. It is because it is intrinsically bad that inequality is justifiably resented, exacerbating its negative extrinsic effects. The

Extravagance and Misery. Alan Thomas, Alfred Archer, and Bart Engelen, Oxford University Press.
 DOI: 10.1093/oso/9780197781722.003.0005

unfair inequalities that characterize our societies reduce well-being and do so because they are (perceived to be) unfair.

Here is where the new science of happiness can help our argument. Let us note, however, at the outset, that the egalitarian finds it hard to establish a direct argument from unjust inequality to low levels of well-being. One of the leading experts in the field, Carol Graham, outlines the pitfalls in such arguments. In her work she has mapped out the tortuous path from results in the science of happiness to the determination of public policy (Graham 2009, 2011, 2017). We begin by documenting some of these well-known complications.

4.1 Problematic Correlations

To begin, Graham notes that sometimes inequality, per se, is perceived as a side effect of a breakdown in social structures that, in turn, reflect economic progress. Here, inequality can rightly be perceived by the currently disadvantaged as a sign of new opportunities and upward mobility. We noted, in chapter 2, Milanović's data about the rising global middle class (Milanović 2016, p.24). To people entering this class, "inequality can be a signal of future opportunity and mobility as much as it can be a sign of injustice" (Graham 2009, p.17). If, for example, you live in a society dominated by corporatism, corruption, and state-sanctioned monopolies, the market fundamentalist's appeal to a "free market" may well be welcomed as bringing a new avenue for social mobility even if an inevitable side-effect is more inequality, too.

Unfortunately, for the societies that are our primary concern here, there is no evidence that current inequality trends reflect the breaking up of corporate socialism, no matter how many times people use the word "disruption" in business schools. In the affluent, developed, societies of the West, our current levels of inequality are not a portent of more social mobility: on the contrary, this process has gone into reverse. For example, the late Alan Krueger's "Great Gatsby Curve" charts how increased inequality correlates with diminished, not increased, social mobility in the recent history of the United States (Krueger 2012).[1] We will identify the social mechanisms that

[1] See also (Chetty et al. 2016; Chetty et al. 2017). Obviously relevant here is what Piketty calls America's "significant inequality of access to education", for which he provides empirical evidence (including Chetty's work) (Piketty 2020, pp.34–5).

turn this ostensible correlation between inequality and diminished social mobility into a claim about causation. Crucially, there is no unambiguous message to be read off from the empirical results of the science of happiness. Context dependence is needed for interpreting these results.

Graham gives more examples: the global financial crisis of 2007–8 impacted the well-being of Americans seriously, but not for long (Graham 2011, p.22). After the initial uncertainty, Americans reconciled themselves to an overall lower level of wealth, and their well-being rebounded to a reduced but relatively good overall level. This may suggest that we ought not to be so concerned with the most serious crisis in capitalism since the Great Depression of the 1930s, given its negative impact on people's well-being was so short-lived.[2] There would seem to be a serious disconnect between the ramified damage that this crisis caused for millions of people and its arguably small and temporary effects on well-being.

Consider another case Graham discusses: unemployed people feel less bad about their status in society if a significant number of other people are also unemployed; this makes the employed in that same society feel better too (Graham 2009, pp.218–9).[3] Does this imply that, when we have some unemployment in an advanced economy, we should mitigate its impact on well-being by having even more?

More directly relevant to our concern with inequality: nearly every philosopher, psychologist, or economist who writes about inequality notes that one reason for its entrenchment is that people are psychologically so configured as to compare themselves with members of their immediate peer group, no matter how the boundaries of that latter group are determined (Dawtry, Sutton, and Sibley 2015; Graham 2009, p.158; Irwin 2018; Lockwood 1966; Luttmer 2005; Rawls 1971/1999, p.388, p.470; Scanlon 2018, pp.36–7; Minkoff and Lyons 2019). One way, then, to reconcile people to the psychological harms of inequality is to divide society into strictly stratified groups that make only comparisons inter se, and never across strata. This psychological tendency to make only intra-group comparisons of inequality is merely one aspect of what Graham calls "adaptation": that people

[2] Graham concludes this reflects the more general finding that "people seem to be better at adapting to unpleasant certainty than they are to uncertainty" (Graham 2011, p.23).

[3] The suppressed part of the explanation here is the role played by social norms, such as norms stigmatizing the unemployed (Graham 2011, p.46). We noted above Scanlon's parallel argument that issues of status poverty can depend on the widespread prevalence of false evaluative beliefs in a society—an issue, then, that goes beyond justice narrowly conceived (Scanlon 2018).

can adjust, over the longer term, even to serious changes in their material circumstances (Graham 2009, chapter 7; 2011, chapter 4).[4]

This has been an entrenched strategy for legitimating inequality. Piketty notes how, in the ternary societies of the past, extensive inequality was legitimated by an ideology which taught everyone that their social standing in the various strata of society was fixed by that society's internal organization (Piketty 2020, pp.60–1, pp.66–7). Is this part of the explanation of why these societies persisted for as long as they did?

Does this also explain why, at a time when the United States is developing levels of inequality comparable to Mexico or Turkey, the level of political resistance to this change is blunted by the fact that Americans have also increasingly sorted themselves into non-comparing groups via residential zip code? Deep cleavages in our unequal societies are organized by geography: cities, suburbs, exurbs, and the rural; coastal elites versus flyover states. Private choice has seen Americans choose to live only with those significantly like themselves—unless, that is, they have no choice about where to live (Payne 2017, pp.52–3). These facts might also explain why wealthy, white, Americans are so optimistic about the lives of poor Black Americans—a group with whom they have scant social contact (Jan 2017).

Overall, then, when egalitarians turn to the new science of happiness to find an explanation of the badness of inequality, they find instead a series of paradoxes. This is not good news for egalitarians! Perhaps it helps to explain, as Pierre Rosanvallon noted, that we are unprecedentedly concerned with increasing inequality, but practically paralysed when it comes to political action to address it (Rosanvallon 2013, p.6).[5] A first possible conclusion to draw, then, is that the science of happiness can play only the limited role, for the egalitarian, of identifying the psychological obstacles to political action to counter unjust inequality. Perhaps the best it can do is explain why inequality does not cause the drops in well-being that it ought to and how, on that basis, political action to counter inequality is obstructed.

[4] Graham notes that adaptation is itself quite well understood: "[I]ndividuals are much more able to adapt to unpleasant certainties such as mobility problems, low levels of income, and high levels of crime and corruption than they are to uncertainty—pain and anxiety, rapid or unstable economic growth, and rapid changes in the crime rate" (Graham 2011, p.114).

[5] As Carol Graham notes, in the United States "the only cohort that seems bothered by income inequality is that of left-leaning rich people!" (Graham 2011, p.112). She adds that this may be partly explained by the firm belief many Americans have that they live in a land of "exceptional opportunity", despite the lack of evidence for this belief (Graham 2011, p.112). See also (Graham and Young 2003).

While we think that this is part of the correct explanation, it is not the whole story. We advise egalitarians to proceed with caution. What these examples show is that the generalizations in the social sciences that the egalitarian wants to deploy all come with significant "ceteris paribus"—all other things being equal—clauses. Trimming those hedging clauses is difficult—but not, we hope to show, impossible.

4.2 A Positive Role for the Science of Happiness?

Our view is that the egalitarian ought not to give up on the science of happiness just yet: the connection between inequality, its psychological harms, and the policies needed to address it require only a new approach, which we develop in this book.

Unjust societies ought to be conceptualized as imposing different kinds of emotional regimes on the citizens who live under them. We take the idea of an emotional regime in this context—if not the exact phrase—from a paper by Earl Gammon titled "Affect and the Rise of the Self-Regulating Market" (Gammon 2008).[6] Adopting a psychoanalytic approach, Gammon explains the origins of market society by appealing to the functional roles of the emotions of anxiety and aggression. In Gammon's narrative, the Victorian middle class in England, when confronted with a crisis of social order, reacted with a specific "economy of affect": aggression towards the poor motivated by societal anxiety. "Specifically, the market increasingly became conceived of as a mechanism of rewards and punishments" and the motivation for this remaking of the market were emotional and not solely a matter of rational interests (Gammon 2008, p.273).

Our aim is not specifically to evaluate Gammon's ambitious thesis, rather to emulate his project of analysing which emotional rules and expectations govern market societies.[7] While we agree with Gammon that anxiety and anger are also key explanatory emotions, we develop a broader methodological idea of an emotional regime.

Such regimes appeal to specific emotions both in their justification and their reflexive accounts of what Rawls calls their own "stability". Conceptions

[6] Gammon's own preference is for the phrase "economy of affect", that he takes from Sara Ahmed (2004a). We discuss Ahmed's views below.

[7] For an exceptional, and insightful, account of a Rawlsian "emotional regime", see (Bannerjee and Bercuson 2015). We discuss this in chapter 5.

of justice recruit emotions for this process of stabilization in various ways: to reinforce an individual's sense of justice, to explain why justice is compatible with individual emotional self-regulation, and to explain the goodness of social relations of mutual reciprocity. There is also a defensive aspect of this project: to demonstrate that a conception of justice (or other core political values) can remain stable in the face of various emotions that threaten to destabilize it.

We explained, in the previous chapter, why we are concerned in this book solely with two generic conceptions of justice: the republican conception advanced by Philip Pettit and the liberal conception defended by John Rawls (Pettit 1997, 2012; Rawls 1971/1999, 2001). We have taken them to be representative of what we have called weakly and strongly egalitarian views of justice (Thomas 2017). We will focus, in the arguments to come, on the emotions that each recruits in its favour. This is a project anticipated and developed by both Pettit and Rawls, each of whom has an extensively developed moral psychology in which affect figures significantly. Curiously, there is scant focus in the literature on assessing these two views as competing emotional regimes.

That is the task we undertake here: to ask whether the inequalities of our societies are unjust and, if they are, how that is reflected in its emotional regime. To make this project manageable we will restrict ourselves to one kind of society: a market society. What we mean by this, and develop further in chapter 8, is a society that makes extensive use of markets and promises continual growth with the overall aim of securing the good of its citizens (typically understood in welfarist terms). The one step we do not take is to identify market societies with all and only capitalist societies for reasons that will become apparent as our argument develops.

Our argument is that market societies, which promise both affluence through continual growth and social mobility, fail to deliver on those promises for predictable reasons. Our own societies do not begin from a political tabula rasa; market societies originate against a background of preestablished patterns of inequality in wealth and power. Their early promise of rising standards of living meets a threshold at which, from that point on, further material gains seem no longer to yield increased well-being, but increasingly disappointing and frustrating social outcomes in exactly the way described in the famous, yet controversial, "Easterlin paradox" formulated by economist Richard Easterlin (1974, 1995, 2005a, 2005b, 2017; Easterlin et al. 2010).

That echoes the claim of Wilkinson and Pickett's first book, *The Spirit Level*, that there is a correlation, sufficiently robust to support a claim of causation, between relative (income) inequality in affluent societies and a range of social indicators of bad outcomes across health, education, and social problems such as crime (Wilkinson and Pickett 2009).[8] To control for cross-country variations, they established exactly the same claim for different states in the United States. We stereotypically expect these problems to be associated with poverty, but these social outcomes are worse even adjusting for income levels—that is their point. No one is denying that it is an achievement to have lifted citizens of affluent societies to a point where they do not have to worry about the material basis of their lives. But affluence brings a new range of problems of its own that, according to Wilkinson and Pickett's later book, are centred on "self-worth and social comparisons", fuelled by growing (perceived) inequality (Wilkinson and Pickett 2018, p.10). There is little point sneering at these issues as "first world problems" or "affluenza" if this is all that citizens of currently developing societies can look forward to when they become more affluent in the future.

In our view, the increasing importance over time of positional goods and deepening class stratification are key to explaining this development. As those with a capacity to dominate exercise that power, class structure hardens, and the most powerful tolerate "opportunity hoarding" by a broader class of the comparatively affluent (Reeves 2017; Stewart 2018b; Tilly 1998). Such practices directly thwart fair equality of opportunity. These groups colonize the goods of social mobility, turning them into positional goods, absent any effective political opposition to their doing so. A logic of marketization sees the comparative retreat of the provision of public goods by the state and the colonization of education, healthcare, and housing as private goods subject to positional competition. State provision becomes, in James Galbraith's memorable phrase, the provision of "shabby amenities" to avoid, and that increases the pressure of the more affluent to seek private, market-based alternatives (Galbraith 1998, p.16).

This self-reinforcing structure explains the phenomenon described by the Great Gatsby Curve as increasing inequality causes diminishing social mobility via these mechanisms of domination, opportunity hoarding, and the absorption of social mobility goods into the sphere of the positional. The

[8] "They included homicides and violent crime, school achievement and dropout rates, teenage births, life expectancy and infant mortality, obesity, mental illness and more—exactly the kinds of issues that are worse among the poor" (Payne 2017, p.48).

emancipatory promise of market societies dissipates as they become class stratified societies with chronic and unjust inequality, low or non-existent social mobility, and an unhappy similarity to the rigidly class-structured societies from which capitalism promised to be a liberation.

This social structure produces a distorted emotional regime that does not fall on all members of society equally. Positional competition clearly has its winners given that, if the appropriate analogy is a casino, they dictate the "house rules", making it difficult for them to lose. These winners invoke capitalism's risk taking in theory to explain their own success, but actual risk taking seems to be reserved for the poor. Our societies are certainly divided into winners and losers but not, as many of the winners claim, on the basis of merit. While winning is emotionally rewarding, other citizens in the same society experience status anxiety, generalized frustration, and for the worst off both inescapable poverty and its stigmatization as a shameful condition. It is shameful because, ostensibly, market societies enable social mobility when, as we shall demonstrate, they typically do not.

We thereby give an institutional account of the social mechanisms that make Easterlin's diagnosis more plausible. Above a certain threshold of affluence, positional goods become increasingly important and come to encompass the category of "merely material" goods in a way anticipated by social theorists (Bourdieu 1985; Hirsch 1976; Veblen 1899/2009). We diagnose this development as an undermining of the conditions necessary for the full realization of the principle of fair equality of opportunity (Fishkin 2014a; Gomberg 2007; Scanlon 2018). If we are to take a step beyond the identification of correlations, we need to identify underlying social mechanisms, and for that, put these classics of social theory at the service of the liberal-egalitarian political philosopher. We describe the interaction of prior inequality, positionality, and opportunity hoarding with our particular focus on the emotions that drive, sustain, and are produced by these processes and mechanisms (Robin 2013). That market societies become not only unfair but also rife with anxiety, frustration, and aggression is, then, explicable by drawing on a range of classical social thinkers. We add, to the foregoing, the complementary explanation in terms of rent seeking that refines and deepens the Easterlin paradox and determines the form it takes in our societies (Buttrick, Heintzelman, and Oishi 2017).

In this way we hope to put a slew of recent writing on the nature of inequality in the United States by Elizabeth Currid-Halkett, Robert Frank, Carol Graham, and Robert Reeves in a wider historical frame (Currid-Halkett

2017; Frank 2007, 2011, 2016; Graham 2009, 2011, 2017; Graham and Pinto 2018; Reeves 2017). We think each of them has developed important insights into the nature of equality in the United States over the last forty years and the emotional regime that it has brought about. But these insights can be strengthened and deepened by setting them in a broader explanatory model in which Currid-Halkett builds on Veblen, Frank on Hirsch, and Reeves on Tilly—while Carol Graham synthesizes complementary work in the science of happiness.

Our model, then, is a dynamic one, but one that builds into its assumptions a background of prior inequality. Could we dispense with that assumption? We believe that the answer is "yes". If, as Piketty claims, returns to capital outstrip returns to labour over the very long run, this has the effect that a background of wealth inequality, were it not assumed, would arise endogenously in a market society in any case (Piketty 2014, 2020; Thomas 2017). But we do not need that assumption for our main argument here. Rather than assume that capitalism tends to capital accumulation, we will operate with the less controversial starting point that, as a matter of historical fact, the market societies with which we were concerned evolved from a starting point of preexisting inequality.

4.3 Going Beyond the Spirit Level

How does our argument relate to the existing literature? The closest studies to our own are the two well-known works by Richard Wilkinson and Kate Pickett (Wilkinson and Pickett 2009, 2018). *The Spirit Level* was a deservedly influential trans-national study of the correlation between income inequality and a variety of social indicators. We will discuss its findings in more detail in the chapters to come, but here we note that our work is in one respect less ambitious than that of Wilkinson and Pickett, in one other respect more ambitious, and in a third respect simply different.

As we will reiterate throughout this book, the established findings in the science of happiness, to which Wilkinson and Pickett have made substantial contributions, are, to date, robust but localized and hedged with "ceteris paribus" conditions.[9] By localized, we mean local to social groups, classes, or

[9] Conversely: the robust international generalizations are, indeed, very general: "In all countries, income clearly mattered to happiness, but other key variables such as age, marital and employment status, and health, mattered as much if not more in some instances" (Graham 2011, p.63).

geographies. This makes generalization over these results hazardous: if each individual case study has a set of hedged provisos, then the generalization over all of them cannot simply disjoin all of these in a list.

A further point of concern is that some of these "ceteris paribus" conditions are themselves normative, such as corruption and the rule of law.[10] Corruption is bad for people's well-being unless they adapt themselves to it; at which point it is relegated to a "ceteris paribus" condition. It may be a locally suboptimal state, but for the agents concerned who are powerless to change it, their adaptation to its bad effects reduces it from an explanatory factor to a taken-for-granted background condition.[11] Yet, clearly, it is a normatively contested condition: this group of people, in spite of a high level of well-being, would (we hope) have an even higher level of well-being if they politically organized to eliminate corruption and restore the rule of law. They have adapted to something to which they ought not—ethically—to have adapted. But these counterfactuals are difficult to evaluate.

Wilkinson and Pickett were open about these methodological issues, but scepticism remains as to whether they were fully able to overcome them. In one respect we aim to do less than they do. Instead of drawing together comparative data for many different kinds of society and trying to establish correlations between social indicators and levels of inequality, as Wilkinson and Pickett do, we construct a model of one particular kind of society, market societies, theorize connections between inequality and well-being for societies of this type, and extend that analysis from our base case to the key variation on it: capitalist societies.

Yet there is another respect in which our goal is more ambitious than Wilkinson and Pickett's: relative to our limited focus, we make claims about specific social mechanisms that exhibit how societies of this kind will generate unfair inequalities (in not only income but also wealth) and the impact that these will have on the emotional life of those who live in societies of this kind. We claim to have moved from correlations to causation and, importantly, to the identification of specific social mechanisms.[12]

[10] "The well-being effects of corruption seem to be lower for those living in countries where corruption is a long-established feature of the status quo and people have become accustomed to it" (Graham 2011, p.94).

[11] Graham notes that individual adaptation may lead to a collectively self-defeating toleration of bad equilibria that ought, instead, politically to be resisted (Graham 2009, p.211).

[12] Wilkinson and Pickett also take themselves to have moved beyond correlations to the identification of a causal claim; but they do not, as we do, break down that causal claim into the operation of specific social mechanisms (Wilkinson and Pickett 2018, pp.xix–xx).

There are two key insights to Wilkinson and Pickett's work. First, various problems have a "social gradient": "In other words, those [problems] which become more common with each step down the social ladder" (Wilkinson and Pickett 2018, p.xx). What social scientific research exposes is a macro-level truth that is not discernible from a micro-level perspective: for example, that the gradient for health outcomes is made more steep by inequality.[13] For example, a comfortably off middle-class person in a highly unequal society may not realize that his or her health outcomes are worse than they would be in a more equal society, but it is still true.

Their second major insight is that each of these gradients is made steeper by the same thing. Given their background in public health, a good analogy for their argument about inequality is finding a contaminant in the water supply with a range of bad effects: you are puzzled as to why a certain group of people have worse health, or worse learning outcomes, and discover that this group (as opposed to others) has been drinking contaminated water. For Wilkinson and Pickett, inequality is like a generalized social pollutant that harms everyone and contaminates many areas of our social life.

We hope to add a third insight, and here is why: unlike the case of polluted water, and pace Wilkinson and Pickett, inequality does not seem to harm everyone. Wilkinson and Pickett, like Keith Payne, are right to focus on social-evaluative threat: inequality worsens people's well-being because we are such status-conscious animals (Payne 2017).[14] But if this is the primary way in which inequality causes harm, those of robustly high status should be immune to this threat. We will also note later (in chapter 9) that if the gaps between social groups are extensive, many putative competitors for esteem may simply give up—if the Joneses are out of reach, why try to keep up with them?

Suppose people are made worse off by polluted water because their municipality subcontracted an evil capitalist to replace the water pipes. Commissioned to supply copper pipes, the evil capitalist supplied lead pipes,

[13] Implicit in this macro-perspective is Wilkinson and Pickett's institutionalism; in a manner congenial to our relational egalitarianism, they note that these are not issues of individual psychology, but products of socially constituted contexts where explanatory patterns emerge that transcend the robustness or fragility of an individual's reaction to a social-evaluative threat (Wilkinson and Pickett 2018, pp.2–4).

[14] "[M]any seemingly distinct problems which we know are related to social status (whether measured by income, education or occupation) within our societies, get worse when bigger income differences make the status differences larger and more important. Position in the pecking order and the scale of status differences—inequality—play a causal role in problems with social gradients" (Wilkinson and Pickett 2018, p.xx).

but is so rich as a consequence that she and her family all drink imported French mineral water and never drink from the tap. Not only is she immune from the pollutant; her imposing it on others helps to explain her immunity. Switching back to inequality, one should ask: does everyone lose, including the super-rich, from extensive inequality? It seems to us that the answer is, plausibly, no.

Wilkinson and Pickett should, in fact, be happy with the claim that most—instead of all—people's lives are damaged by inequality. That is surely reasonable—in societies that are liberal democracies, that ought to be enough! The median voter theorem would suggest that if a substantial majority in a democracy is harmed by and wants to restrict inequality, then the democratic process should convert those preferences into policy: unfortunately, current research on the political impact on inequality is problematizing the median voter theorem. Wilkinson and Pickett claim specifically that:

> *Inequality affects the vast majority of the population*, not only a poor minority. Although its severest effects are on those nearer the bottom of the social ladder, the vast majority are also affected to a lesser extent . . . larger income differences immerse everyone more deeply in issues of status competition and insecurity. (Wilkinson and Pickett 2018, p.xxi, emphasis in original)

From the fact that everyone is more "immersed" in status competition does not mean that everyone is negatively affected by it.[15] While Wilkinson and Pickett claim that "inequality makes everyone more worried about status and how they are judged by others" (Wilkinson and Pickett 2018, p.34), we believe not everyone converts this worry into elevated stress levels produced by social-evaluative threat.[16]

The main difference between them and us is over the identification of the underlying social mechanisms and what purports to justify them. Wilkinson and Pickett, from their social scientific perspective, and Robert H. Frank,

[15] We will return to this point throughout the book. For example, Rousseau thinks that participation in status competition is, in itself, degrading for everyone—win or lose. ("Master and Slave Degrade Each Other", Rousseau, *Emile*, 1762/1964, Book 2, p.70; Thomas 2017, p.379, note 24). He also thought that the very currency of status depends on retrograde capacities of ours that we would be better off without, collectively and individually (Scanlon 2018, p.34).

[16] As, for example, they later note that "the higher the rank that people held and the more power and control they had, the less stressed they were", citing (Sherman et al. 2012).

from the perspective of economics, argue that inequality is both wasteful and damaging—so self-evidently pointless.[17] Veblen, by contrast, takes the waste to be the point. A panoply of liveried servants in the retinue of a wealthy man, most of whom stand around idly, certainly makes no economic sense, unless we embed economics in a broader cultural context—now it makes perfect sense. While Wilkinson and Pickett, and Frank, consider inequality powered by positional competition as obviously irrational, unreasonable, and something we ought simply to eliminate, Veblen's deeper account of why this mechanism operates as it does asks what alternative, normative conception of society is involved in removing what we have called a "social pollutant" (Veblen 1899/2009).

As Rawls stressed, actual markets contain agents who take an interest in the interests of others in order to dominate them, exploit them, and otherwise to exhibit the personal vices of envy, malice, and spite. We see our view of the emotional regimes of market societies as part of an alternative, cultural explanation of economic life—pioneered by Veblen—where these emotions are central. Such emotions are central to an emotional regime that justifies hierarchical social structures: primarily class.

This has a direct bearing, of course, on the politics of inequality. Pickett, Wilkinson, and Frank think it suffices to show that inequality is all downside, and no upside: to continue the metaphor, it is like a negative social externality that we all have a reason to eliminate, just like pollution. (We should simply impose what economists call a "Pigouvian tax" on it.[18]) But if the diminished well-being of most is not only accompanied by the heightened well-being of some, but actually a causal result of the latter, then the politics looks very different. Only in an oligarchy, you might think, would the benefits to the few so outweigh the well-being of the many, and this, indeed, seems to be the case.

If the social power of the wealthy co-opts the democratic state to "lock in" their class-based dominance, then we can explain the failure of social democratic politics to defend the interests of the average citizen. That leads to the final, major point of difference between our project and Wilkinson and

[17] As Geoffrey Brennan and Philip Pettit note, what they call "mainstream economics", with its assumption that individual preferences are exogenously given, thereby assumes a "thin theory" of the good in Rawls's sense of that term. From that minimal perspective one can judge of positional contests for esteem that: "There is a powerful case to be made, just on the basis of a thin theory of the good, for discouraging this form of wasteful competition" (Brennan and Pettit 2004, p.252).

[18] Just as we set carbon emissions targets for the environment, perhaps we should index the taxation of the wealth to a society's Gini coefficient (Golden 2020).

Pickett's project: our engagement with theories of justice. The touchstone of our discussion throughout is the normative issue of justifying particular schemes of justice and the emotional regimes each brings in its train. Here, too, we see a difference of degree, not kind.

At one point, Wilkinson and Pickett's psychological explanation in terms of social-evaluative stress resorts to a more fundamental explanation. That further explanation cites "processes of dominance and subordination" as crucial, later adding that "aspects of the cultural differences between classes seem to exist *primarily* to provide test of status, almost for the purpose of identifying those who can be devalued and excluded" (Wilkinson and Pickett 2018, p.4, p.29, emphasis added). They also offer a theory of the function of systems of social status: "ranking systems are fundamentally about gaining access to resources . . . power matters because it ensures privileged access to all the necessities, pleasures and comforts of life" (Wilkinson and Pickett 2018, p.23). As the latter are our primary focus here, we take our project in this book to be complementary to theirs: a deepening of this range of explanations connecting social-evaluative status to the elite's control of key resources. This motivates our extended consideration to Tilly's account of opportunity hoarding (Tilly 1998). Tilly anticipated Wilkinson and Pickett's connection between rank and control of resources. He also, we will argue, developed a powerful tool of social criticism when he widened his focus from a comparatively narrow class of dominators to a broader class of "opportunity hoarders" whose rent-extracting activities are tolerated by the former.

5

Emotions, Explanations, and Emotional Regimes

Propositional Summary

1. We distinguish emotions, sensations, moods, drives, and propositional attitudes. We note the internal complexity of pleasure, the importance of flow experiences, and the connection between depressed mood and self-worth.
2. Consideration of the various ways in which one can change an emotional state requires the introduction of the idea of an interest. Avowable interests, as thematized by the republican tradition, play an important role in Bernard Williams's "critical theory test".
3. We discuss the relevant notion of a ceteris paribus law, Elster's distinction between two forms of social mechanism in explanations, and the distinctive roles played by genetic inheritance and environment.
4. We compare and contrast universalist and constructivist conceptions of emotions.
5. We describe Reddy's conception of an emotional regime as a set of norms that regulate the expression of emotions in a specific political culture. A universal core of emotions has culturally specific forms of articulation.
6. Other aspects of emotional regimes are introduced: Reddy's views are compared to Hochschild's view of emotional labour, Jaggar's view of emotional hegemony; Burkitt's view of decentred emotional regulation; Ahmad's view of the connection between emotion, signification, and social relationships; Scheer's account of the embedding of emotions in practices.
7. We set out the existing literature on the deep emotional appeal of market fundamentalism. Successive spirits of capitalism valorize work in different ways, but in each case it is an avenue of personal

Extravagance and Misery. Alan Thomas, Alfred Archer, and Bart Engelen, Oxford University Press.
 DOI: 10.1093/oso/9780197781722.003.0006

emancipation and emotional fulfilment. Boltanski and Chiapello's account of these spirits of capitalism is combined with Koning's account of the moralized, financialized self, and Illouz's account of the therapeutic self and the democratization of trauma and psychic injury.

Introduction

Relatively early in our discussion we must address scepticism as to whether any approach to an issue such as inequality can be grounded on something as amorphous and fleeting as the emotions. Such scepticism is understandable. Throughout the history of Western political philosophy, rationality has been elevated in importance and the emotions downgraded by comparison. It can be difficult to separate out whether we are understanding the mind via metaphors drawn from political philosophy or understanding politics via models of the mind. On the one hand, "Sovereign Reason" is taken rightly to govern over our other mental capacities; on the other hand, democracy is consistently denigrated because, like the emotions, it is a source of unstable change not guided by principle. The mob, like the tyrant, is capricious—as are fleeting emotions that buffet a person like a ship on the open sea. Conceptions of the political and conceptions of the mental both supply metaphors for the understanding of each other. These are "metaphors we live by": it can be difficult to disentangle the directions of influence.

We associate the idea of authoritative justification of policies with the idea of impartiality in justification. Legislation, we think, must be presented from a general point of view. The emotions are too partial—too tied to the specifics of individual idiosyncrasy—to supply an impartial and hence public basis for the justification of policies. Such policies must be public to act as a stable basis for social coordination via mutual, reflexive, acceptance: a citizen undertakes allegiance to these public principles because she is assured other citizens have done the same. There is a problem of inter-personal assurance that any conception of the just arrangement of society must address. How could the emotions figure in any such principled justifications guided by the ideal of impartiality (Krause 2008)?

In addition, consider the possibility of abnegation. We will, throughout this book, treat the emotions as intentional, rationally guided propositional attitudes rationalized by their subject. If a mental state is rationally justified, then one can seek to satisfy it via the realization of its proper object. But suppose you cannot realize the object because it is out of your control; now the emotional state persists, unsatisfied, in a way that can reduce your well-being. Yet there is another way to rid yourself of the state: abnegation. Make it the case that you no longer experience that emotion. The marathon runner, experiencing pain, fatigue, and a sense of hopelessness about completing the course may decide to focus her thoughts elsewhere or that negative thinking may become self-fulfilling.

Here, too, the possibilities divide: adaptive preference formation sees you adjust your emotions to the circumstances you cannot change so that they now "fit" once more. The concern here is that this might be a form of *ex post facto* rationalization. Alternatively, you can work indirectly on the state to rid yourself of it in a way that undercuts its standing as a rational response: it becomes a therapeutic problem to be managed away. That is the problem of states that persist as you cannot change your condition to satisfy them; what of states that persist when they are simply inappropriate? The claustrophobic who is in no danger in an elevator (lift) nevertheless feels anxious, with a dry mouth, sweaty palms, and quickened breathing. Stepping out of the lift would be to "give in" to one's anxiety; how does one "manage" the occurrence of the state not rationalized by an appropriate object at all?

Moral psychologists have distinguished "object directed" from "state directed" justification: a person suffering from paranoia who has feelings of persecution has no reason to make the persecution stop, as it does not exist (Greenspan 1988). They do have reason to make an appointment to see their therapist. That is a "state directed" reason; the occurrence of the underlying state conveys information independently of the way in which it is rationalized by its proper object. By contrast, the persecuted person who feels persecuted when they are, has a reason to want to it to stop that is grounded on the proper object of the emotion. They should not call their therapist—perhaps they should call the police (Hornsby 2008).

These complications problematize the idea that political justification can appeal to the emotions. Our limited aim in this chapter is to explain why we believe this scepticism is mistaken. We can, at least, point to precedent—we will note throughout this book how some of the most influential political philosophers appeal to key emotions as part of the justifications for their views. But we will also add a systematic, as well as an historical, justification for proceeding as we do—with the history following in chapter 6.

5.1 A General Conception of Emotions

From the substantial literature on the emotions we endorse a widely held conception of them as propositional attitudes, directed to a proper object, that include an evaluative component such that it is good for the agent for that emotion to be satisfied by that object. To develop this account, we need to say more about the distinction between emotions, sensations, drives, and moods. Emotions are central to this cluster of mental states, but they share family resemblances with both sensations and moods.

The key distinction here is intentionality: the directedness of certain mental states on objects that rationalize them. Propositional attitudes are ascribed with complementary "that" clauses that explicitly flag their intentionality: Susan hopes *that* her team will win the trophy tonight. The mental ascription here indicates that her propositional attitude—hoping—is directed to a truth-evaluable proposition. (Brentano famously took intentionality to be the "mark" of the mental (Brentano 1874/1995).)

Sensations, on the other hand, lack this feature of intentionality: you feel cold, which is distinct from your belief that you are cold. There is no role here for a complementary "that" clause. Sensations are not intentionally directed to anything beyond themselves. They have an impact on our concept-using and inference-making psychological systems, but in themselves they lack conceptual structure (which is not to say that they are "simply given"). They are better theorized as "self-presenting" as Christopher Hill and Brian McLaughlin explain that phrase:

> The experiences that guide and justify one in applying the concept are always identical with the experiences to which the concept is applied. Sensory states are self-presenting states: we experience them, but we do not have sensory experiences of them. We experience them simply by virtue of being in them. Sensory concepts are recognitional concepts: deploying such concepts, we can introspectively recognize when we are in sensory states simply by focusing our attention directly on them. (Hill and McLaughlin 1999, p.448)

They place special demands on the concepts that we use to describe them; such concepts are best thought of as "recognitional-demonstrative hybrids" (Thomas 2008, pp.68–9).

In the interest of completeness, we should take note of the historically important category of "drives": from Hobbesian motives to Freudian drives, these simple mental states share a feature with sensations, namely, lacking a content. They cannot, therefore, engage with the inferential capacities of reason: they have neither internal structure nor any analogue of syntax. That which is distinctive of them is their putative special tie to motivation. To borrow a joke from Jonathan Dancy, if beliefs are intrinsically inert these states are intrinsically "ert" (Dancy 1993). They have long attracted suspicion on three grounds.

First, as Dancy complains, they are introduced as a dependent complement for the idea of belief states as not motivational at all (Dancy 1993). Secondly, the sense in which they are motivating is given a Molière-style explanation (in his play *The Involuntary Invalid*) of a sleep potion as possessing "dormitive virtue" (Norman 2001). In other words, it is a sleep potion because it puts you to sleep. Motives, or drives, motivate because that is simply what they do. Thirdly, this seems to form part of what John McDowell called a "hydraulic" theory of motivation—an expression in the theory of practice of an inner analogue of a "myth of the given" (McDowell 1982).

In addition to emotions, sensations, and drives/motives it is important to include the fourth category of moods. When it comes to the well-being of individuals, an important concern in this book, this class of states is of particular interest. Moods, like sensations, lack intentional objects. Yet they are not simple sensations: they are complex forms of affect that interact with both emotions and beliefs. Before we can explain their complex nature, however, we need as a necessary preliminary to say more about the nature of emotions to show how moods are intertwined with them.

Emotions may be viewed in one aspect as propositional attitudes; in another aspect, as realized in complex multi-track dispositions. The enamoured may sigh for his beloved, write lyric poetry about his adored object, and gaze wistfully out of the window; these are all manifestations of an underlying disposition that is multi-tracked as opposed to single-tracked (Vetter 2013). A multi-track disposition is: "a disposition which cannot be characterized adequately in terms of a single conditional" (Vetter 2013, p.334). Vetter further explains:

> A fragile glass may manifest its fragility in breaking upon being hit with a spoon, being dropped on the floor, being sung to by a soprano, or being subjected to pressure over a period of time. . . . Irascible people may

> manifest their irascibility by becoming angry upon being yelled at, being politely told to wait, or being disagreed with. (Vetter 2013, p.335)

As Ryle pointed out, most of our characteriological ascriptions are multi-track dispositions (Ryle 1949/2000). Emotions, construed as complex propositional attitudes, do not differ in this respect. Yet do emotions not additionally require some conscious manifestation? To focus the question precisely: on which side of the emotion/sensation boundary does pleasure fall?

Ryle considers this question—mischievously—in his neo-Aristotelian treatment of pleasure in his essay of that title (Ryle 1954). Ryle avers that when he is playing a pleasant round of golf, nothing distracts him—not even his pleasure. In this neo-Aristotelian conception, in engaging in a complex, intentionally directed, range of activities requiring concentration, planning, execution, and, indeed, creative imagination and problem solving, Ryle the golfer experiences absorption in these high-level mental accomplishments. Perhaps the only emotions he consciously experiences are frustration and anger (as anyone who has ever played golf will attest). Yet, three and a half hours after starting his round of golf, Ryle avows that he has played a pleasant round of golf.

Indeed, we can go a step further. Psychologist Mihaly Csikszentmihalyi has identified the kind of rapt absorption that Ryle describes as a "flow state" (Csikszentmihalyi 1991). In his view it represents one of the most fulfilling subjective states that a person can experience. It involves an appropriate matching of the person's competencies and the degree of difficulty of the task in which he or she is engaged. If Ryle were attempting to play on a professional standard course, where the individual holes are very long, and the putting green is so flat it has been described as like trying to putt on a mirror, then his round of golf would be a disaster. Ryle's frustration and anger would boil over—given his inability to get the ball in any hole under twelve shots, he would quickly give up. Yet if there is an appropriate matching of competence and challenge, then a person enters into a state of relaxed achievement in which complex goals are attained apparently effortlessly.

Some high-performance athletes report going into a trance-like state in which their complex achievements seemed effortless; indeed, they later report being unable to recall their actions. This seems to capture part of Ryle's neo-Aristotelian conception: a degree of absorption in the complex achievement of a challenging task that excludes distraction—even distraction by pleasure or, for that matter, a process that excludes the weaving together of experiences into memory.

Clearly, however, this depends on one's conception of what pleasure is: the hedonist will protest that the hedonist tradition in ethics—a long and internally complex tradition—cannot accept Ryle's description wholly at face value. Pleasure is a multi-track disposition, but a capacity to enjoy pleasant experiences will, the hedonist insists, have to be at its core. Simple hedonic experiences include the pleasures of the senses that have a consciously experienced sensational aspect; yet we also speak of taking pleasure in complex aesthetic appreciation. The pleasures of a fine wine or tasty snack do not seem comparable to taking pleasure in appreciating a Chopin Prelude. Where, then, in the categories of the propositionally directed (intentional), the non-intentional sensation or the complex multi-track disposition is the concept of pleasure best located?

In our view, the proper response to this complexity is to embrace it: pleasure is an internally complex hybrid concept. Yet it also seems to us that an easily available compromise can solve the dispute between Ryle and his hedonist critics: in the exercise of our complex capacities, absorbed flow can give rise to supervenient, but irreducible, occurrent states including those with a hedonic aspect. It would, indeed, be curious if Ryle at no point in his round of golf experienced a sensation of pleasure as a tricky putt falls into the hole; yet we can reconcile this with his intellectualist conception if we note that these sensations supervene on this more complex exercise of his capacities. Given that he is absorbed in the exercise of his complex capacities to a high degree, then we might expect him periodically to experience occurrent states of satisfaction, or pleasure—but not to experience the latter without the underlying achievement that grounds and justifies them.

This has a direct bearing on whether it makes sense to set pleasure as the goal of one's action; as Hume remarked, there is a major difference between exercising virtue for the sake of pleasure and taking pleasure in the exercise of virtue, as Hume believed that virtuous people typically do. Supervenient ends are the reliable side effect of that at which one intentionally aims, but cannot be set as the aim of action itself. In an overall economy of pleasure, a person may seek pleasure directly via a glass of fine wine, seek it indirectly via choosing a hobby that matches competence to challenge in the right kind of way (as we have seen from Csikszentmihalyi's examples), but would be foolhardy to decide late in life to take up golf professionally (or playing Chopin Preludes to a comparable professional standard).

All of this has formed a lengthy prolegomenon to the introduction of the separate category of moods. While moral philosophy has had a good deal to say about pleasure, achievement, or the satisfactions of virtue, it has had less to say about depression, ennui, anomie, accidie, or other instances of low mood. Yet these mood states clearly have a bearing on an individual's well-being. A person may have a wide range of opportunities for realizing goods in her life; she may have a subjective set of capacities that allow her to do so. Yet if such a person is depressed, and unable to value either those goods or herself, then her well-being will be seriously impaired.

Carol Graham contrasts the impact of chronic non-psychological health conditions with depression, noting of the former that people adapt their expectations downwards and accommodate their long-term condition such that they return to their pre-illness level of happiness. For depression, however, this is not so: "perhaps because coping mechanisms are weakened by the lower happiness levels that characterize depression" (Graham 2009, p.123):

> [T]he well-being costs associated with mental illness . . . are much greater than those associated with physical problems . . . suggesting it is more difficult to adapt to psychological than to physical conditions. (Graham 2009, p.124)

In particular, uncertainty and anxiety have a strikingly negative effect on long-term well-being (Graham 2009, p.133, pp.139–40). She suggests a key role is played in explaining these facts by false beliefs: in advance of actually experiencing a condition, people fear that physical illness will be worse than it proves to be, but that mental illness will be less serious than it proves to be, with a subsequent impact on adaptation to each type of condition (Graham 2009, p.138).

It follows, then, that this class of states is crucial for one of the arguments of this book, as a failure to value oneself adequately may lie at the basis of this failure of evaluation of other goods in one's life. Rawls, as we will see, is particularly concerned with a state of alienation in which citizens fail to value their projects because of an underlying failure to value themselves. That is why, in our terms, he focuses not solely on reciprocal investment as a form of mutual assurance, but also as the grounds for a psychology of boldness.

Each of these mood states can be characterized functionally in terms of their typical causes: ennui is caused by a lack of challenge, producing listlessness, or torpor (where both of the latter are synonyms for "accidie"). The person's context may actually be challenging; he is simply unable to set himself any goals in response to them. Anomie is produced by a sense of isolation and the loss of orienting social norms and a sense of purpose. The depressed person cannot "see the point" to anything; he or she experiences fatigue, irritability, listlessness, discouragement, impaired rationality, and impaired decision making caused by an overly pessimistic ranking of options.

Mood states, then, do not in themselves have a propositional object; in that respect they are like sensations. Yet they are clearly complex functional states because of the way in which they impair the exercise of a wide range of our mental capacities: evaluation, planning, self-control, and an appropriate sense of self-worth. One way to appreciate the significance of depression, for example, is to consider the range of mental functions that it impairs. We will treat mood as an important part of individual well-being, and will treat it as "higher order", not in the special sense in which that term is used in theories of consciousness, but to indicate how mood is manifested in its impact on a wide range of mental functions while lacking any distinctive phenomenology of its own.

As we will develop our argument, it will focus on Rawls's account of the relationships between being valued, valuing oneself, having confidence in one's own projects, and societal recognition. One aetiology for depressed mood is social exclusion, feeling devalued by others, and being repeatedly "silenced": a reaction of withdrawal, depression, and a failure to act even on the options open to one are intelligible responses to being treated in this range of ways. The experience of poverty may indeed lead to feelings of loss of control and hopelessness. Without adequate material resources, the sphere of what you control does shrink, as Ci pointed out (Ci 2013). Easily overlooked, however, is the subjective component in being able to value the options that are open to one even if they are comparatively restricted. The depressed person can attach value to nothing.

With this outline of how we will understand emotions, sensations, drives, and moods in place, we turn now to the question of the canonical form of psychological explanations.

5.2 The Justificatory Role of Emotions

As Bernard Williams famously argued, beliefs are not subject to the will. The way to rid yourself of a belief is to discover that it is false; as Williams put it later in his work, falsity is a "fatal defect" in a belief (Williams 2002, 1973a). Our beliefs are, then, answerable to evidence. But are emotions, similarly, only answerable to evidence? No, for several reasons: a supporting belief may be undercut, yet an emotion persist, or an emotion may arise from non-standard causes.

It seems that there are five ways to change an emotional state. In the first, simplest case, you act to align your emotion to its proper object. Secondly, you can change an emotion by convincing yourself that, qua merited response, the emotion is not merited in this case. Thirdly, you can undermine an emotion by changing its object via the process of adaptive preference formation. Fourthly, you can act directly on the emotion by simply ridding yourself of it—the strategy of abnegation that we have already described. Fifthly, you can rid yourself of the emotion by manipulation that undercuts its standing as a merited response. We will now give examples of each of these cases.

The first case is simplest: you experience fear when you hear a fire alarm and see smoke billowing from under a nearby door. You flee the building; your fear subsides as it has done its functional job. It motivated you to seek safety—and you have. With its object satisfied, the emotion is removed because it has manifested its satisfaction condition.

In the second case, you work on an emotion indirectly; given that it is a reason-sensitive state, you can change an emotion by working on the underlying belief. Suppose a foreigner finds herself in rural Australia, and is presented with a bowl of witchetty grub soup. Her initial response is one of disgust: yet she informs herself further about how aboriginal culture values this food and has eaten it for many centuries; how many people of many different cultures have come to value it as a delicacy, and so on. As she amasses evidence, and changes her belief in the object of her disgust, so she removes the feelings of disgust: this is a food like any other (which, in fact, it is). The work of reason undermines her initial response, and she no longer experiences the emotion of disgust. She cognitively endorses the belief that the object concerned does not merit the response, so she abandons the response.

In the third case, in Aesop's famous fable of the fox that could not reach a bundle of grapes just and so formed the belief that they were sour, we can see the process of adaptive preference formation: the fox no longer wants what it now considers to be undesirable.

In the fourth case, self-abnegation, you decide to stop experiencing a particular emotion. You do not work indirectly on it; you simply decide to stop experiencing it. Perhaps you have decided that, overall, your life will go better if you do not experience it anymore. You do not try to undermine it via the evidence for it, via its proper object. You simply rid yourself of it. Turgenev suffered from unrequited love, to the point where he actually lived with the object of his unrequited affection—and her husband. Would his torments have been eased if he had simply rid himself of the emotion? Plausibly, the (unromantic) answer to that question is "yes".

In the fifth case, you put in place an indirect strategy to remove an emotion. A prisoner of war, waiting to be liberated at the end of the Second World War, experienced daily hunger as his rations had been cut to subsistence. Kept awake by hunger, the prisoner discovers that by pressing his fist hard into his abdomen, the hunger pangs go away. This is bypassing the standing of the emotion as a reason-sensitive state. To adapt an example of Wittgenstein's, if your hunger can be assuaged by food or a punch in the stomach, what makes us say that you want the former and not the latter (Wittgenstein 1979)? Wittgenstein's point is that not any termination of a reason-sensitive state terminates it by meeting its satisfaction condition in the right way; yet we can rid ourselves of mental states in this way. The hungry prisoner avails himself of this fact in removing his hunger pangs.

If belief revision is a relatively straightforward issue, emotional revision has some further complications. But do those complications disqualify emotions from playing any role in political justification? Why would anyone think that it did? Primarily because propaganda, and other forms of manipulation, target the emotional framing of an issue and exploit known biases to drive political choice through emotion rather than from the impartial consideration of evidence. Beliefs are, constitutively, sensitive solely to evidence, but evidence is mediated via epistemic policies, and those policies can be subverted by a framing that appeals to the emotions.

Inquirers make investments in which they trade off the importance of answers to the costs of inquiry. Emotional framing can influence those choices. A person who does not want to believe that his partner is unfaithful may, it seems to you qua impartial observer, be strangely incurious about whole classes of evidence because he fears what he may discover—better not to look. Anyone who is not naive can see that political campaigning in our own democracies has learned a great deal from the techniques of successful commercial marketing: the emotional framing of complex issues via "bumper sticker" slogans is one explanatory component of the political polarization of our own societies. If a political proposal is to be grounded on an essentially justificatory role for the emotions, then an objection to this approach is that emotions are too unstable to play this role. How can a justification be grounded on the kind of mental state that is, itself, so blatantly open to manipulation by oneself or others?

Our answer is to emphasize that emotions are reason-sensitive states. Throughout this book, when we discuss (for example) envy (in chapter 11), we are concerned with whether it is reasonable envy. For any emotional justification, we take it to be criterial for the presence of an underlying belief. That is why emotions can be included into a general account of that which Gilbert Harman calls reasoned changes of view (Harman 1986). In any such process, we can accept an inferred conclusion or use its obvious unacceptability to reject a premise of the argument. If the premise of a political argument rationalizes an emotion, it is not, in any relevant respect, materially different from this case.

Consider Feldstein's claim that anyone opposed to Paretianism is motivated solely by spite (Feldstein 2005). Presumably we can infer this conclusion: if your irrational policy is motivated by spite, then you ought to engage in self-abnegation and stop feeling spiteful. But the structure here is no different from any other reasoned change in view: spite can be a rationally grounded emotion, even if an unlovely one. Feldstein is appealing to nothing more than the claim that a conclusion can discredit the premises from which it is inferred: something we knew generally to be the case.

More problematic, from our point of view, is the class of "sour grapes" cases and the dangers of *ex post facto* rationalization. To resolve the problems posed by adaptive preference formation—a kind of self-manipulation—we need to develop our overall argument in two ways. First, the problem demonstrates that we cannot remain non-committal on the issue of political freedom. Secondly, any political theory of emotional justification must incorporate what Bernard Williams called the "critical theory test" (Williams 2002, p.221). We will now develop this argument in two stages.

For current purposes, we will not exposit at length the controversy between negative, positive, and republican theories of liberty. The theorist of negative liberty identifies it with an absence of coercion or constraint (internal or external); the theorist of positive liberty views these conditions as necessary, but not sufficient, as "freedom from" ignores the dimension of "freedom to"—the freedom to realize one's essential human capacities in a flourishing life. Finally, the republican theorist identifies freedom with the controlled absence of interference not simply in actual cases, but in counterfactual cases (Pettit 1997). The example of the freed slave in ancient Rome, who enjoyed a third-class citizen status and was free "on license" at the whim of his Master, illustrates the modally robust nature of liberty. He is negatively free, but does not meet the modally robust criterion for liberty.

We are committed to this republican conception of liberty (Thomas 2017). The issue that we have identified as potentially problematic for any attempt to justify a political practice or policy via an emotion is identified by Philip Pettit, the leading exponent of the republican view, as a decisive argument against the negative conception of liberty. Hobbes takes it to be an advantage of his view that, if I reduce or inhibit the range of free actions available to you, then you can still be free if I do not obstruct the one option you want. Pettit takes this to be a reductio ad absurdum of the view—and we agree—as it has the consequences that my actions can reduce your options to one, but you can make yourself free by the simple expedient of forming a desire for that option (Pettit 2012). Adaptive preference formation of this kind is for us, given our view on liberty, a problem for any associated conception of freedom. Actual choice is not the issue; the quality of choice and the set of options from which you choose are the important factors.

The republican plausibly insists that your liberty depends on more than Hobbes's reduced conception; that it involves an appropriate range of choice-worthy options. Your freedom can be diminished in a restriction of the range of options available to you even if, on reflection, you most wanted to do one of the remaining eligible candidates. Consider this example from Joseph Fishkin:

> In a patriarchal society, a woman might grow up in modest circumstances and marry into wealth, achieving great success in class terms. Her trajectory exemplifies class mobility; the more there are like her, the weaker the relationship between class origins and class destinations. Yet at the same time, she might never have had more than the most constrained range of paths open to her to pursue other, different kinds of roles in her life, offering different forms of human flourishing. (Fishkin 2014, p.4)

Fishkin is committed not merely to reasonable moral pluralism, but also to opportunity structures that realize what we would identify as freedom as non-domination: as broad an opportunity set as is practically realizable. In his example, the person who has "married well" may be happy and her story exemplified the value of social mobility. But, just as Thomas Piketty worries that inequality is returning us all to the world of Balzac and Jane Austen, where patrimonial capitalism makes marrying well a securer path to wealth than income from work, Fishkin is concerned about the background opportunity structures within which choices are made (Piketty 2014). The republican also has to say more to explain why some forms of interference with your action are restrictions on liberty, while those that you author yourself, either directly or indirectly, are not. For that reason Pettit introduces the idea of an avowable interest, and an interest is another element of a person's well-being that we have not, as yet, considered (Pettit 1997).

The idea of an interest is an evaluatively committed notion, which is why it inherits its essential contestability from the values with which it is associated. An interest identifies that which is objectively good for a person, thus it is essentially linked to a conception of a person's well-being. The simplest examples to illustrate an interest involve health: if you are a diabetic, then taking your insulin when your blood sugar level drops is in your objective interest. This is true even if the only available means of taking it is via a hypodermic syringe and you are phobic about needles. You do not want to inject yourself, but it is in your interest; to that extent, an interest involves a degree of objective authority over your more immediate desires.

If we can vindicate an appeal to a person's interests, then we can explain the existence of "happy slaves". It is a trivial truth about domination that a person, A, may dominate another, B, but B can be better off in some respect as a result; for example, if B were not employed as A's slave, then B would starve. Both benefit from the relation of domination, but A far more than B. In this case, A is interfering with B's essential liberty interests. But what if B not only accepts his or her reduced benefit, but avows satisfaction with their lot in life? Now we have a further resource we can draw upon; the happy slave may avow their life satisfaction, but their objective interests are compromised.

Furthermore, with the concept of an interest in play, we can draw upon it for the next part of our view: Williams's "critical theory test". We want, minimally, to be able to say of a certain set of social arrangements that they pass this test:

> Suppose that of two parties in the society, one is advantaged over the other, in particular with respect to power; and suppose that there is a story which is taken to legitimate this distribution, a story which is at least professed by the advantaged party and is generally accepted by the disadvantaged; and suppose the basic cause of the fact that the disadvantaged accept the story, and hence the system, is the power of the advantaged party: then the fact that they accept the system does not actually legitimate it, and *pro tanto* the distribution is unjust. (Williams 2002, p.221)

This test requires some elucidation: in terms of the power of the advantaged being the "basic cause" for a false legitimation story being accepted by the disadvantaged we would elucidate this claim in terms of counterfactual insensitivity to evidence. Belief in the false legitimation is held in place no matter what, as it were; the complication that rational justifications can be causes of true beliefs is dealt with by noting that the "basic cause" here is not appropriately counterfactually sensitive to the usual process by which we critically assess beliefs in the light of further evidence (Thomas 2006, pp.258–64).

Putting the pieces together: the happy slave engages in adaptive preference formation. How might they be open to rational criticism? A person, or group, can be subject to disadvantage, and part of that disadvantage is their manipulation so that they accept justifications held in place solely by their relative power disadvantage and not because those justifications have any rational force. Particularly important, amongst this general class of cases, is the disadvantage as regards one's core interests—those aspects of one's personal good that are central to one's life going well. These include effective agency, a sense of control, and an adequate sense of self-worth to ground a related sense of the worthwhileness of one's own projects.

We have contrasted various respects in which the justification of belief contrasts with the justification of emotion. We have narrowed our focus to reasonable emotions; the emotions that a reasonable person who is in good mental health has reason to welcome. Because of this intrinsic tie to reasonableness, emotions can feature in the justification of reasoned changes in views. More needs to be said about the problematic case of adaptive preference formation and we have extended our account in two directions to address it: to our explicit commitments in the theory of freedom and the idea of an objective interest, and to the explicit incorporation of Williams's critical theory test.

We note, without wishing to enter too deeply into the methodological debate, that economists and psychologists interested in the science of happiness have had to address similar issues. Carol Graham, for example, to whose work we will advert repeatedly as she is the pioneer in this field, notes that one of the motivations for moving away from the orthodox economist's approach of examining preference as revealed in choice was that actual choices can be misleading in two ways (Graham 2009, pp.8–9). She echoes our concerns when she notes that actual choices may be the product of pathological addiction (Graham 2009, p.8). We have tried to capture this point in our criterion that a reasonable emotion be one that a reasonable person in good mental health has reason to welcome: this would rule out the attitudes of the addict who has no second-order control over what she desires.

Secondly, Graham also cites Amartya Sen's work on capability theory (on which we will also draw) as making the point that the range of options a person is capable of achieving may be more important than their actual choice (Graham 2009, p.9). We made the same point for a different reason; adapting Pettit's critique of Hobbes, the defect of adaptive preference formation is that free choice cannot involve your changing your desires to the only option that is, de facto, open to you. Influenced by Fishkin, Gombrich, and Tilly, we will be placing particular emphasis in this book on background structures of opportunity that are, in turn, shaped by a background ethical pluralism—multiple visions of the good life. We turn now to an associated question: if emotions can play a role in justification, can they also play a role in social explanation? If so, how can they do so?

5.3 Emotions in Social Explanations

In his own enquiry into the role of emotions in social and political life, Jon Elster begins with this question: "are there lawlike generalizations in the social sciences? If not, are we thrown back on mere description and narrative? In my opinion, the answer to both questions is no" (Elster 1999, p.1). We agree, and we share Elster's more specific conception of how emotions can figure in genuine social scientific explanations. Like Elster, we develop this conception from the work of Nancy Cartwright. Elster quotes the following passage from Cartwright's work:

> I know that camellias like rich soil, so I planted them in composted manure. On the other hand, the manure was still warm, and I also know camellia roots cannot take high temperatures. So I did not know what to expect. But when many of my camellias died, despite otherwise perfect care, I knew what went wrong. The camellias died because they were planted in hot soil. . . . So we have an explanation for the death of my camellias. But it is not an explanation from any true covering law. . . . We may insist that there may be some differentiating factor which brings the case under a covering law: in soil which is rich and hot, camellias of one kind die; those of another thrive. I will not deny that there may be such a covering law. I merely repeat that our ability to give this humdrum explanation precedes our knowledge of that law. (Cartwright 1983, pp.51–2)

Cartwright is here being concessive and counselling epistemic humility: there may well be, as the *Encyclopaedia of Unified Science* insisted, a single directory of fundamental laws that underpin all "lower level" explanatory generalizations. If we know the background law, then particular instances are explained via a hypothetic-deductive inference. But, here in the sublunary, the knowledge of those laws seems a long way off. In the meantime, we have to make sense of our explanatory practices which seem to get along just fine without the covering law model of explanation in most cases.

However, Cartwright's thesis could be formulated in a less concessive way to her opponent, for example, by noting that the fewer the items in our ultimate directory, the more ad hoc adjustments have to be made to make the "laws" pragmatically useful in the context of our actual explanatory practices. Helen Longino comments: "Cartwright has argued that the laws of physics, strictly construed, are false. In order to make something like Snell's law, or Boyle's law, true, an indefinite number of qualifying clauses, what Cartwright calls ceteris paribus clauses, must be added" (Longino 2001, p.110). But Longino continues:

> [T]he role of laws in physics, and hence their utility . . . lies in covering a range of related phenomena in which a similar principle is operating, *but the cost of the range is expression of the principle for ideal and unrealized rather than actual situations.* . . . Not only are laws, strictly speaking, false, but they are more useful in their false versions than in their indefinitely qualified, but true, versions. (Longino 2001, p.112, emphasis added)

Longino's point is that even if we can, in principle, know the final compact directory of laws we are always trading off compactness of formulation against breadth of coverage. You can have few laws, and many ceteris paribus clauses to buy coverage, or many suitably qualified laws where coverage is bought by a significant expansion in the number of laws each of which is internally hedged. The trade-off is inescapable. So, on this re-formulated view, perhaps Cartwright's concession is not that concessive after all; we are never going to do better than to accept the irreducible plurality of a patchwork of context-specific laws.

We do not have to come to some final determination of that issue when it comes to, say, physics; we need to acknowledge the point only for the case that concerns us, namely, explanations in the social sciences and psychology. Taking Cartwright's and Longino's points on board, we are not dealing here with a second grade class of explanations: the hedged explanations of the social sciences differ in kind from the covering law explanations of the physical sciences, but are none the worse for that difference. Such social scientific explanations, as Elster claims, can involve two kinds of mechanism that he labels "Type A" and "Type B" mechanisms. They involve neither strict, exceptionless, covering laws nor are they mere case studies or narrative descriptions; they are explanatory, but of little use in making predictions for the reasons Cartwright identifies.

In Elster's typology of social explanations Type A mechanisms are indeterminate as to which of several causal patterns will be triggered and the patterns are mutually exclusive (Elster 1999, p.7). Type B mechanisms involve one of two causal patterns, each of which would have a reverse effect on an independent variable—leaving it indeterminate what the net output will be, as they may operate together. They go beyond correlations, but they require explicit specification of context.

For Elster, the paradigmatic theorist of such mechanisms is de Tocqueville. He discusses some of the puzzling claims of *Democracy in America* where de Tocqueville repeatedly appears to contradict himself. How can an ethos of democracy lead, as Tocqueville seems to claim, *both* to increased religiosity and the rejection of religion? Because, Elster argues, we need a further specification of context and a description of the mechanism as either a compensation effect or a spill over effect.

Take the compensation effect first: if we do not find the authority we seek in politics we turn to religion. Or the context may differ and there is a spill-over effect: if democratic authority rests with each individual, they will tend to be anti-authoritarian in religious beliefs. How can the same cause (democracy) produce two incompatible effects?

> *If* the influence of democracy on religion is mediated by the compensation effect rather than the spill over effect (a Type A mechanism), democratic societies will be religious. *If* the negative effect of democracy on desires (mediated by religion) is strong enough to offset the positive effect of democracy on opportunities (a type B mechanism), democratic citizens will behave moderately. (Elster 1999, p.20)

The relevance of these methodological issues is that—complementing the general truth of a posteriori functionalism in the philosophy of mind—Elster believes that folk psychology is a repository of such incomplete, mechanism-based, explanations of the role played by the emotions. Thus our evidence base in the social sciences can include proverbs and works of literature where such schematic descriptions of explanatory mechanisms are compiled.

To take the case we have just considered in the previous section: if some of your options become unavailable, will you either value the deleted option less ("sour grapes"; adaptive preference formation) or more ("forbidden fruit"; counteradaptive preference formation) (Elster 1999, pp.21–2)? Proverbs often formulate apparently contradictory predictions, but this is an interpretation that follows only if they are understood as failed attempts to formulate exceptionless laws. Interpreted as incomplete explanation sketches that require contextualization, they are an important part of our folk psychological understanding of the emotions. We will draw on such mechanism-based explanations when we claim, for example, that the emotion of shame leads to a desire for social withdrawal. This is not to cite an exceptionless law, but the hedged generalizations typical of the social sciences that are also drawn on in folk psychological generalizations.

We will also work with Elster's more general conception of the role of the identification of robust causal patterns in social explanation. A typical example is when, in chapter 9, we discuss Charles Tilly's explanations of what he called "durable inequality" and its production of "socially organized differences in well-being" (Tilly 1998, p.6). Examples are the differential access to nutrition, in different social contexts and times, between men and women, or civilians and soldiers. Tilly's explanations of what he calls "categorical inequality" mediated by ascriptive identities (black/white, old/young, male/female) are mid-level causal generalizations inevitably hedged by ceteris paribus clauses: "social mechanisms—recurrent causal sequences of general scope—that actually lock categorical inequality into place" (Tilly 1998, p.7). Rawls called these the "laws and tendencies of the social world" and we will draw on such evidentially grounded "tendencies" throughout the argument that follows. Our methodological presupposition is that the new science of happiness formulates mid-level, ceteris paribus, generalizations of this kind, including Elster's Type A and Type B mechanisms.

It is also significant here that we are dealing with human subjects. As Joseph Fishkin has argued, in the context of his assessment of the issue of equal opportunities, philosophers do not have to skirt round or hand off the issue of whether human development is determined either by heredity or the environment. The answer is that the contribution is 100% heredity, 100% environment as they are inextricably linked (Fishkin 2014, pp.99–100). Furthermore, the relevant sense of the environment is manipulable and there is no such thing as a "normal" or "typical" environment. All these generalizations are restricted to a specified environment—specified for measuring the particular effect to be measured. He cites the geneticist Theodosius Dobzhansky:

> The norm of reaction of a genotype is at best only incompletely known. Complete knowledge of a norm of reaction would require placing the carriers of a given genotype in all possible environments, and observing the phenotypes that develop. This is a practical impossibility. The existing variety of environments is immense, and new environments are constantly produced. Invention of a new drug, a new diet, a new type of housing, a new educational system, a new political regime introduces new environments. (Dobzhansky 1955, pp.74–5)

Fishkin puts this argument to use to rebut the claim that inequalities result from natural differences between individuals: the "intrinsic difference" argument (Fishkin 2014, pp.89–90). That argument is committed to a generalization over all environments and ignores the fact, as Dobzhansky's capacious list illustrates, that the relevant sense of an environment is manipulable. It also, as Fishkin diagnoses, slides from the "intrinsic difference" to the "irremediable difference" claim that there is nothing we can do to redress these intrinsic differences. It is, as Fishkin notes, implausible to claim that there is no possible environmental change that could eliminate the intrinsic difference in question (Fishkin 2014, p.102).

This argument crops up in the science of happiness literature, too, in the figure of the "natural curmudgeon" whose low level of happiness is putatively genetically determined by some determinate amount—such as 33% (Neve et al. 2012). We agree with Fishkin that the scientist of happiness should be wary of such claims because of the "Flynn effect". The Flynn effect is the hypothesis that, in spite of very small changes to the genetic profiles of whole populations over the span of a century, environmental changes have transformed IQ scores radically over the course of a single century (from 1877 to 1977) (Flynn 1987). What we can learn from Flynn's study is that environmental manipulation can, as Fishkin puts it, "utterly dwarf the variance among individuals in the present population" (Fishkin 2014, p.103). As we will indicate in chapter 13, we share Fishkin's optimism about the plasticity of human psychology and hence the availability of the strategy of changing our political institutions to enhance well-being. Even the "natural curmudgeon" can see his or her well-being enhanced by these institutional and societal changes.

5.4 Universalism or Constructivism About Emotions?

We will be relying heavily on the idea of an emotional regime in this book, and the idea requires further clarification. This concept was first outlined by William Reddy in his book *The Navigation of Feeling* (Reddy 2001). Reddy argues that the concept of an emotional regime allows those studying emotions to bridge a gap between two incompatible views of emotion dominant in different academic fields. According to Reddy, the basic issue that these views are trying to address is, "how much influence to attribute to culture, how much to attribute to underlying universal psychic factors" (Reddy 2001, p.37).

According to universalist views, which traditionally have dominated psychology and the life sciences (Reddy 2001, chapter 3; Plamper 2012, chapter 3), emotional experience is universal.[1] In other words, human experience of emotions will be the same regardless of the time and place a particular person is living in. A prominent example of universalist thinking can be found in Paul Ekman's view that there are a set of emotions that are common to people from all cultures and that are accompanied by a corresponding

[1] See Plamper (2012, chapter 3) for an excellent overview of universalism in the life sciences.

universal form of facial expression (Ekman 1992). According to this view, these basic emotions include happiness, anger, disgust, fear, sadness, and surprise and potentially also contempt, shame, guilt, embarrassment, and awe.[2] Other emotions may be formed from a combination of these more basic ones. (Ekman understands smugness, for example, as a mixture of happiness and contempt (Ekman 1994, p.19).)

Universalist views such as this tend to focus on the biological phenomena underlying emotions and the evolutionary processes that give rise to them. As this suggests that the proper study of emotions will involve the tools of psychologists and life scientists, rather than cultural studies, anthropology, sociology, or history, it is perhaps unsurprising that such views have seemed appealing to psychologists and life scientists studying emotions.

However, such views face problems when we consider the extent to which emotions can vary across culture. Take, for example, the emotion *gham*, a kind of sadness, which according to Benedicte Grima is the most intense and significant emotion that Paxtun women in Pakistan are encouraged to express in public (Grima 1992). Although *gham* is similar to sadness, the way this emotion is expressed varies significantly from how we might expect someone to express sadness in a Western society. For example, a woman is expected to publicly express *gham* during her wedding ceremony. In addition, Paxtun women may get together to express *gham* to each other over an injury to a loved one, rather than attending to the needs of the injured person. The contrast with how we would expect women to express their sadness in Western societies puts pressure on the idea that emotional experience is universal. It suggests that culture has a large role to play in determining emotional experience. It is not just the occasions on which an emotion is expressed that will vary, the emotions themselves also vary between different cultures. Similarly, there is no perfect English translation for the Ilongot people's (a tribe who live in the Philippines) emotion *liget* which, according to Reddy (discussing work by Rosaldo 1980), "encompasses a number of English notions, including anger, energy, envy, heat" (Reddy 2001, p.36). Even within the same culture an emotion may vary over time. For example, Eva Illouz claims that the American ideal of love has been changed dramatically since the beginning of the twentieth century due to the influence on people's behaviour of advertising (Illouz 1997).

[2] Two years later, Ekman relegated surprise to the potentially basic category (Ekman and Davidson 1994, p.413).

If we reject the universalist approach for failing to appreciate the influence of culture in emotional experience, should we become social constructivists about emotions instead? According to this view, emotions are a product of culture. It appears to be advocated by the anthropologists discussed in the previous paragraph. According to these theorists, emotions are intimately related to culture. It follows that we cannot understand emotional experience without looking at how it relates to the social world in which it is a part. This approach fits comfortably with the observation that emotional expression and experience varies between different cultures, as this variation is what we would expect if emotions are socially constructed. Societies will construct emotions differently and so we should expect this kind of variation. What counts as a normal and expected emotional expression in one culture, *gham* at a wedding, would be unexpected and perhaps even shocking in another. As Grima puts the point, "emotion is culture" (Grima 1992, p.6).

Grima is far from alone in this assessment. For example, fellow anthropologist Michelle Rosaldo claims that, "what individuals can think and feel is overwhelmingly a product of socially organized modes of action and of talk" (Rosaldo 1984, p.147). Similarly, anthropologist Lila Abu-Lughod describes as "nonsensical" the assumption that, "emotions could be detached in meaning and consequence from the flow of social life" (Abu-Lughod 1990, pp.24–5). More recently, psychologist Lisa Feldman Barrett has defended a constructivist view of emotions according to which we categorize and interpret our basic affective experiences using the emotion concepts we have in our possession (Barrett 2017). Emotion concepts are the products of culture and will largely be drawn from people's cultural background: the society they grew up in, the social roles they have occupied and other features of their identity. If we accept this kind of view then the cross-cultural variation in emotional experience should not be surprising. Different cultures developed different emotional categories and so interpret their affective lives differently.

However, Reddy claims that strong social constructivist approaches face major problems (Reddy 2001, pp.43–4). First, being unable to analyse an emotion outside of the social and cultural context in which it occurs may make it difficult to engage in any normative evaluation of a society's emotional life. If we cannot abstract our emotions from their cultural context, then how can we find a point of view from which to assess emotional life? If no such viewpoint can be found, then it seems that there is no way to engage in praise or criticism for a society's emotional practices. As Reddy notes, anthropologists such as Abu-Lughod, Lutz, and Rosaldo were reluctant to criticize the cultures they were studying but happy to criticize Western culture. This is incoherent according to Reddy:

> Even if the Western view was "wrong" because it "constructed" the domain of emotion as a "natural" one, and women as especially emotional, this could not change the fact that, for Westerners, it thereby *became* a natural domain. If it made no sense for Rosaldo to criticize her Ilongot informants for feeling grief over the end of headhunting, then it made no sense for Lutz or Abu-Lughod to criticize Western social science for being male-centered and for seeing emotions as natural and peculiarly female. (Reddy 2001, p.42)

In other words, once we have accepted a form of cultural relativism about emotions then we are left without a point of view to make value judgments about any culture's emotional practices—notably, one's own (Plamper 2012, p.252).

The second objection that Reddy raises against social constructivism is that it assumes there is some culturally uniform account of culture (Reddy 2001, p.45). To see the problem here, consider the following example from Anna Welpinghus: "Bobby and Jean live in a society in which monogamy is a well-established social institution. Bobby and Jean, however, live in an open marriage—they have allowed each other to sleep with other people" (Welpinghus 2018, p.76). How should we understand Bobby and Jean's love? If we accept a social constructivist approach, then the emotion of love that they experience has been constructed by the social context they find themselves in. But how should we understand this social context? Their love does not conform to their culture's dominant understanding of what romantic love is. Perhaps then we should understand it as constructed by polyamorous subculture present in their society. Alternatively, we could understand their love as a construct of the micro-community consisting of only Bobby and Jean. This gives us at least three different socially constructed accounts of love, and it is far from clear how we should determine which one is interpretatively correct.

Thirdly, Reddy claims that a social constructivist approach to emotion is unable to make sense of the ways in which emotions can change over time. Discussing the absence, as he saw it, of an account of how the emotional life of the Ilongot people may have changed over time in the work of Michelle

Rosaldo, he argued that this was not simply the result of a lack of source material. Instead he claims:

> The problem arose because it is impossible to account for emotional change unless one can draw on some conception of the universal features of emotional life. If emotional change is to be something other than random drift, it must result from interaction between our emotional capacities and the unfolding of historical circumstances. (Reddy 2001, p.45)

If emotions cannot be detached from a cultural context then there is no way to analyse how they have changed over time, as all we have are two different emotions operating in different cultural contexts. As Plamper explains the problem:

> In this view, the floods of tears accompanying a medieval act of subordination (*deditio*), such as the Walk to Canossa, are just as radically culturally-contingent as the tears of a young hopeful auditioning for a casting show in the twenty-first century; one would only be able to talk of change if these tears had the same emotional core. (Plamper 2012, p.256)

In other words, given the different social contexts in which these tears take place, we will be unable to understand the twenty-first-century tears as being emotionally connected to the medieval tears unless we accept that they are both connected to some core emotional response. We should, according to Reddy, reject a view of emotions that prevents us from analysing the historical development of emotions in this way. A culturally invariant core must, instead, be subject to culturally and historically variable articulations.

5.5 Reddy's Conception of Emotional Regimes

In response to the problems facing both universalism and social constructivism, Reddy offers an alternative view designed to capture the attractive features of both views. According to Reddy, there is a universally applicable core biological foundation for emotions, but they are nevertheless culturally flexible. In Reddy's view then, "Emotions are largely (but not entirely) learned" (Reddy 2001, p.xi). Key to his account is the concept of *emotives* (Reddy 2001, p.105).

Emotives, according to Reddy, are expressions, usually verbal expressions, of emotions: for example, "I am happy", "I am sad", "I admire you". It is tempting to think that these speech acts are simply descriptive. There is a pre-existing emotion that we are experiencing (e.g. fear) and these speech acts simply express that emotion. According to Reddy, however, these speech acts do not only describe the world; they also change it (Reddy 2001, p.105). Emotives are, in the terms of speech act theorist J. L. Austin, both *constative*, in that they declare something to be the case, and *performative*, in that they change the world in some way (Austin 1962). This observation is in line with a point recognized by a number of emotion theorists, namely, that in choosing to label emotions in a certain way, we change our own affective experience.[3] As Margaret Clark puts the point: "There is [...] some clear evidence that choosing to express an emotion or to cognitively rehearse it may intensify or even create the actual experience of that emotion while choosing to suppress it or not think about it may have the opposite effect" (Clark 1989, p.266). The way in which people label and express their emotions then will play an important role in determining their affective experience.

Importantly for Reddy, the culture in which people live will have a major influence in shaping their emotional labelling and expression. Emotions are also of great political significance. In order to ensure a stable political order it is essential that emotions are managed and guided in the right way. Reddy introduces the idea of an emotional regime to describe this normative process of shaping people's emotional experiences. He defines an emotional regime as:

> The set of normative emotions and the official rituals, practices, and emotives that express and inculcate them; a necessary underpinning of any stable political regime. (Reddy 2001, p.129)

These regimes may vary in the amount of emotional liberty they afford people. Strict regimes will demand people to express a range of normative emotions and prohibit a wide range of other emotions. Such regimes may require people to express, "respect for a father, love for a god or a king, or loyalty to an army," and severely punish those who do not comply (Reddy 2001, p.125). Other emotional regimes may involve strict regulation but only within certain institutions such as the military, religious institutions,

[3] See, for example, (Campbell 1997), (Ellsworth 1994), and (Kagan 1984).

schools, or the law courts, while placing fewer restrictions and demands on emotional navigation outside of these institutions.

The advantage of this account of emotions is that it is able to account for the importance of culture in influencing emotional experience without facing the problematic implications of social constructivism. The cultural variation of emotional experience can be at least partially explained by the varying emotional regimes that exist in different societies. However, because this account is not committed to the claim that emotions are entirely socially constructed, it allows room for the normative evaluation of different emotional practices. For example, Reddy discusses the ways in which overly restrictive emotional regimes that have "an incomplete account of human nature and human possibilities" can impose emotional suffering on people (Reddy 2001, p.126). This kind of critique is open to Reddy because his account holds that there is a shared universalist core of emotional experience. Reddy can also avoid the objection of assuming a uniform account of culture, as he is not committed to defining emotions in terms of a dominant social understanding of that emotion. Finally, by including a biological core of emotional experience, Reddy's view is able to make sense of the way in which emotions may change over time. While the tears accompanying a medieval act of subordination will differ in cultural context from the tears of a talent show contestant, there may nevertheless be enough of a shared biological core of these emotional expressions for it to make sense to talk about how this emotional expression has changed over time.

5.6 Other Aspects of Emotional Regimes

Reddy's conception of emotional regimes also fits well with a number of other views about the way in which emotions function. First, an important predecessor of Reddy's account is Arlie Russell Hochschild's concept of feeling rules (Hochschild 1979, 1983). Hochschild begins with the question: why is our emotional experience as well ordered as it is (Hochschild 1979, p.552)? The starting point for Hochschild's response is Erving Goffman's (1961) claim that the display or suppression of certain emotions is an important part of the way we present ourselves in the social world. Hochschild went beyond this to claim that people do not just make an effort to present certain emotions to the world, they also attempt to actually feel certain emotions (Hochschild 1979; Hochschild 1983). For example, for flight attendants to maintain a cheerful demeanour, it is important that they actually feel cheerful. This involves a form of what Hochschild calls "deep acting", in which the flight attendant has to engage in emotional labour to ensure that she is able to feel cheerful (Hochschild 1979, p.563). This kind of deep acting will often be a response to what Hochschild calls "feeling rules"—the norms that tell us how we should feel in particular situations (Hochschild 1979, p.564).

Reddy's account of an emotional regime can be seen to extend the concept of a feeling rule to the wider range of emotion practices that operate within society and that are essential for a stable political regime. In doing so, Reddy's account provides an analysis that is similar to Alison Jaggar's account of emotional hegemony (Jaggar 1989). Jaggar, like Reddy, holds that our emotional reactions are partially socially constructed. According to Jaggar, because of the fundamental connection between emotions and values, learning the language of emotion involves absorbing the values of one's society (Jaggar 1989, p.165). As Jaggar points out, in an unequal society, these values are likely to support the continuation of inequality within that society:

> Within a hierarchical society, the norms and values that predominate tend to serve the interests of the dominant groups. Within a capitalist, white supremacist, and male-dominant society, the predominant values will tend to be those that serve the interests of rich white men. (Jaggar 1989, p.165)

As a reaction against such an emotional hegemony, people may experience what Jaggar calls "outlaw emotions", which are emotions that are forbidden by the emotional conventions, or feeling rules, of that society (Jaggar 1989, p.166). As we will emphasize later in the book, part of our project here is to re-frame justified anger at rent extraction as no longer an "outlaw" emotion—as in Feldstein's jibe at "spiteful egalitarians".

Another important predecessor of Reddy's view is the view defended by many feminist philosophers of emotion that that the emotions people experience and the way in which they are experienced are influenced by the emotions they are enabled to express (Scheman 1980; Spelman 1989; Campbell 1997). Certain groups of people are more enabled to express certain emotions than others. Men for example may be more enabled in their expression of anger than women (Spelman 1989), though we should also be aware of the influence that other sources of oppression, such as race, may have on who is enabled to express anger. Similarly, women may be better enabled to express emotions such as sadness, love, and compassion than are men. These differences in the emotions men and women are enabled to express will impact upon the emotions they are able to experience. The fact that women are not supported in the expression of anger can result in women being less likely to be angry. Similarly, the fact that men are not supported in the expression of love or compassion can result in men being less likely to feel love or compassion.

This point is not simply the epistemic claim that it would be more difficult for women to *know* they are angry and men to *know* they are experiencing love or compassion. It is the stronger, ontological claim that how people are supported in the expression of certain emotions will influence what emotions *exist* (Harbin 2014, p.484). Not being enabled to express anger may influence someone's ability actually to be angry. Not being supported in the expression of love may influence someone's ability actually to have this emotion. Hochschild pointed out that the commercialized "emotional labour" of workers in the service economy can alienate them from their own emotional lives as the line between their managed emotional presentation and the reality of their emotional life becomes blurred.

This view about the way in which social support in the expression of emotions can influence what emotions exist provides support for Reddy's claim that a society's emotional regime can shape the emotional life of the people living in it. The support and encouragement offered for the expression of some emotions and the discouragement of the expression of other emotions will not just change what emotions people feel able to express, it will also alter what emotions they actually have.

Related to this point is Ian Burkitt's (2018) claim that emotional regulation should be understood in a decentred way. Emotional regulation refers to the management of emotional experience and expression. According to James Gross's influential definition of emotional regulation, it "refers to the processes *by which individuals influence which emotions they have*, when they have them, and how they experience and express these emotions" (Gross 1998, p.275 emphasis added). As is clear from this quote, traditional accounts of emotional regulation refer to an individual's ability to manage her own emotions. Burkitt (2018, p.169) argues that this individualistic approach fails to adequately account for the ways in which people manage and influence each other's emotions. Nor can they account for the way in which emotions are regulated by culture. For example, different cultures may have different normative emotions associated with funeral rituals. A culture in which funerals are viewed as sombre situations will regulate for different emotions than a culture in which funerals are seen as a celebration of life (Burkitt 2018, p.170). However, Burkitt argues that even allowing a role for culture in emotion regulation, as defended by Mesquita et al. (2014), does not go far enough, as it fails to do justice to the way in which the *generation* of emotions is also influenced by culture (Burkitt 2018, p.171). Rather, Burkitt argues that we should accept that "emotion generation and regulation occur in patterns of relations involving embodied dialogical selves in a social cultural world" (Burkitt 2018, p.173).

The claim that social and cultural factors impact the generation and regulation of emotion helps to support Reddy's claim about the ability of an emotional regime to shape the emotional life of the people living there. This is the case regardless of whether or not we accept Burkitt's specific account.

Another relevant view about the way in which emotions function can be found in Sara Ahmed's *The Cultural Politics of Emotion* (Ahmed 2004b). Ahmed argues that we should view emotions as cultural practices that serve to bind us together with some people and move us away from others. Emotions become attached to certain people through the use of emotion-laden or "sticky" signifiers. For example, the word "P*ki", a derogatory term for people from Pakistan, "might then stick to other words that are not spoken: immigrant, outsider, dirty, and so on" (Ahmed 2004b, p.92). Emotions have a key role to play in making these signs sticky. The speech act of naming something as "disgusting" may have the effect of attaching the term to the object so that it comes to be seen as disgusting. Whether or not it has this effect will depend at least in part upon whether that object has a history of being associated with that sign. This serves to bind together one group of people ("the disgusted") and cast-out another ("the disgusting") (Ahmed 2004b, p.98). This attaching of signs to particular people then, plays a role in drawing the boundaries of who is seen as belonging together and who is seen as an outsider. In doing so they also serve to bind us to some ways of life and not other ways. This view fits well with Reddy's claim that a society's emotional regime can shape the emotional life of the people living there. However, it also makes the further point that the emotional labels attached to people serve to draw boundaries that draw certain groups of people together whilst casting other groups out. Throughout our argument we will focus on this politically important process known somewhat dryly in the social policy literature as "social exclusion".

Another important extension of Reddy's view can be found in Monique Scheer's account of emotional practices (Scheer 2012). Scheer draws on Pierre Bourdieu's (1990) practice theory to provide an account of emotional practices and to argue that emotions are themselves a form of practice. The two important points we wish to draw on for our purposes are Scheer's account of an emotional practice and the four kinds of emotional practices she identifies. According to Scheer, emotional practices are "manipulations of body and mind to evoke feelings where there are none, to focus diffuse arousals and give them an intelligible shape, or to change or remove emotions already there" (Scheer 2012, p.209). The first kind are mobilizing practices which involve "habits, rituals, and everyday pastimes that aid us in achieving a certain emotional state" (Scheer 2012, p.209). These often involve the use of media or rituals to try and bring about the desired state. For example, someone might listen to a song to try and achieve a certain emotional state. Similarly, informal rituals like those involved in courtship or formal rituals like those involved in Christian penance, may be intended to bring about the right emotions in their participants (love in the case of courtship and regret or guilt in the case of penance). The second kind are naming practices, which involve putting a name to our emotional experience, either alone or in company (Scheer 2012, p.212). Like Reddy, Scheer views these practices as not simply describing a pre-existing feeling but also influencing what it is that we feel. The third example of emotional practices are communicating practices which involve exchanging emotions with others (Scheer 2012, p.214). For example, a politician may wish publicly to communicate sadness to his constituency via television after a tragic event. The final kind of emotional practices are regulating practices. These involve emotional norms or feeling rules and the accompanying punishment for transgressing these norms.

5.7 The Emotional Appeal of Market Fundamentalism

Drawing on Reddy's account of an emotional regime and the related work we have discussed in the previous sections, we will now explain how we will be using the term for the remainder of the book. To recap, Reddy defined emotional regimes as, "the set of normative emotions and the official rituals, practices, and emotives that express and inculcate them; a necessary underpinning of any stable political regime" (Reddy 2001, p.129). Following Hochschild, we will understand these to involve feeling rules that proscribe certain emotions in certain contexts. As Jaggar points out, in unequal societies these regimes will tend to serve the interests of those in a position of power and dominance, though they may also be subject to resistance and the development of counter-cultural norms. In addition to feeling rules, there will also be cultural narratives and practices that attach certain emotions to some people rather than others and that create boundaries that draw certain groups of people together whilst casting other groups out. Finally, following Scheer, we will understand the emotional practices involved in emotional regimes as involving mobilizing, naming, communicating, and regulating practices. With this working definition in place, we will apply the idea of an emotional regime to the particular kind of society we are concerned with: a market society.

We are certainly not the first to concern ourselves with this theme: something like our working definition is evident in the accounts of the emotional regime of capitalist market societies in the work of Eva Illouz in *Cold Intimacies* (Illouz 2007) and Martijn Konings in *The Emotional Logic of Capitalism* (Konings 2015). An important part of the motivation for this literature is captured by Koning's subtitle, "What Progressives Have Missed". Also important to our argument is a book that is not about capitalist societies in general, but a changing emotional regime that has emerged over the last forty years of "neo-liberalism" or, as we have preferred to call it, "market fundamentalism". (We explained why we prefer this term in our opening chapter.) That book is Luc Boltanski and Ève Chiapello's *The New Spirit of Capitalism* (Boltanski and Chiapello 2005).

The general theme of all these books is that progressive critics seriously underestimate the deep ethical and emotional appeal of the market fundamentalist revolution.[4] All their authors agree with the late Rawls that an economic system will need to be emotionally appealing to people if it is to be stable. As Boltanski and Chiapello point out, in the case of capitalism, such an appeal will need to be powerful enough to overcome the inherently unattractive features of the system:

> In many respects, capitalism is an absurd system: in it, wage earners have lost ownership of the fruits of their labour and the possibility of pursuing a working life free of subordination. As for capitalists, they find themselves

[4] As Illouz puts it, the social critic has to "develop strategies of interpretation that are as cunning as the market forces we want to oppose" (Illouz 2007, p.94).

> yoked to an interminable, insatiable process, which is utterly abstract and dissociated from the satisfaction of consumption needs, even of a luxury kind. For two such protagonists, integration into the capitalist process is singularly lacking in justifications. (Boltanski and Chiapello 2005, p.7)

Material incentives and the threat of unemployment and poverty may be able to explain some engagement in the labour force. However, these incentives by themselves will not be able to generate the kind of active engagement and voluntary sacrifices that are increasingly required from all wage earners (Boltanski and Chiapello 2005, p.8). Moreover, appeals to economic self-interest by themselves will be unlikely to be enough to generate sufficient active engagement.

In order to generate the right level of commitment what is needed is a "spirit of capitalism"—a set of ideals that present a vision of capitalism as serving the common good and which provides a means for fulfilment and self-realization (Boltanski and Chiapello 2005, p.16). These ideals will have to generate enthusiasm for engaging in the process of accumulation distinctive of capitalism whilst also providing people with a sense of security and a sense that this accumulative activity is morally justified. Moreover, these ideals will have to be reasonably effective in capturing people's imagination and allowing them to make their lives liveable. We should not then view such ideals simply as the views the strong force upon the weak. Rather these ideals need to have broad appeal to people throughout different levels of society. If critics of capitalism view citizens of our affluent societies as hapless dupes of a social system that was always designed to make them physically and mentally ill, then this emotional regime is not well understood in the first place. (Mark Fisher's essay *Capitalist Realism* seems to us to make precisely this mistake (Fisher 2009).)

It would equally be a mistake to view the spirit of capitalism as static and unchanging. One of the core insights of Boltanksi and Chiapello's work is that this legitimation narrative is capable of adapting in response to anti-capitalist critiques of it. They sketch three distinct spirits of capitalism, spanning three historical periods. The first spirit, articulated around the end of the nineteenth century, generated enthusiasm through the figure of the heroic entrepreneur engaging in innovation and courageous acts of risk to generate profit (Boltanski and Chiapello 2005, p.17). This provided an ideal of liberation from the traditional constraints of dependence on the land and local communities. As we will see in chapter 6, the tradition that justifies market society stemming from Adam Smith places emphasis on how the new commercial society created opportunities for the working poor through industrialization.

Boltanksi and Chiapello emphasize how bourgeois morality, emphasizing the family, a patriarchal benevolence from an employer towards one's employees, and the importance of charity to relieve the sufferings of the poor, provided a sense of security and moral justification for entrepreneurs. A broader moral justification was provided by a belief in scientific progress and the benefits of industry. These, combined with a crude form of utilitarianism, were used to justify the sacrifices that needed to be made for those benefits from industry. This spirit of capitalism contained clear internal conflicts between a celebration of profit seeking, greed, and scientism on the one hand and paternalistic moralism, family values, and charity on the other. These internal conflicts led to criticisms of hypocrisy at the core of this justificatory narrative—so it evolved and adapted.

The second spirit of capitalism emerged between the 1930s and 1960s and involved a change of focus away from individual entrepreneurs and towards large, hierarchically structured, bureaucratic organizations. We will refer to this as the age of the Chandlerian firm (Chandler 1962). Here, enthusiasm was generated for the heroic figure of the salaried company director, appointed not through family connections but through merit. These directors did not own these large organizations but were responsible for developing methods of mass production, for expanding the reach of the company, and for exercising power over large workforces. These firms also provided a sense of security for their employees, offering long-term career prospects and opportunities for promotion. The moral justification was provided by an emphasis on "institutional solidarity", in which large firms were seen as collaborating with the state to produce a better life for all (Boltanski and Chiapello 2005, p.18). However, by the 1980s, this spirit of capitalism came under criticism for its celebration of large, inhuman, bureaucracies: their capacity for emancipation, it was argued, had been stifled.

In response, a third spirit of capitalism emerged which represented the ideal firm as a flexible, non-hierarchical network. Within these companies, managers should not seek to exert technocratic control over their workforce. Rather they should try to motivate their teams by articulating an inspiring vision to which their workers will subscribe. This commitment to their manager's vision and the self-satisfaction they will take in doing their work well means workers will no longer need to be motivated by the threat of external sanctions. The motivating figure in this spirit of capitalism is that of the charismatic leader who is "proficient at numerous tasks, constantly educating themselves, adaptable, with a capacity of self-organization and working with very different people" (Boltanski and Chiapello 2005, p.76).

These new heroic figures are highly flexible both in terms of their skill set and in their lack of rootedness to any particular place. They have excellent communication skills, which enable them to draw on a large network to address whichever project they are working on. In this third spirit of capitalism, the security of the large firm has been replaced by the freedom of moving from one project to the next. Security of a sort is found through constantly developing one's skills to maximize one's employment prospects. The moral justification for this spirit of capitalism is that it offers a more humane and personal form of organization than the hierarchical firms of the past. More flexible, less bureaucratic firms are also better able to meet genuine human needs, both of employees and consumers. In our view, if anything epitomizes this final spiritual ideal of capital it is the Silicon Valley start-up, at least in its romanticized manifestations, as a place of both commercial "disruption" and personal fulfilment through identification with a project that transcends the self.[5]

However, this new spirit of capitalism is also open to new forms of critique. First, by dealing with people as complete human beings rather than simply as workers, these new forms of management create possibilities for a more expansive form of exploitation. It is no longer enough for workers to treat their work simply as work. Rather, "people are expected to 'give' themselves to their work" (Boltanski and Chiapello 2005, p.96). They must constantly be developing their skill set and engaging in meaningful activity, even in their leisure time. This leads to an instrumentalization of human beings in their totality, rather than simply during working hours. This spirit of capitalism emphasizes the importance of activity whether it be in one's personal or professional life, "To be doing something, to move to change—this is what enjoys prestige" (Boltanski and Chiapello 2005, p.155).

Secondly, the focus on individual skills and performance leads to increased competition and decreased solidarity between workers. The linking of wages

[5] In a parody of shortened time horizons and faster gratification, the heroic entrepreneur has been replaced by the heroic founder, whose aim is to bring a start-up to its initial public offering, sell his stake, and move on to repeat the process. There is to be no long-term stewardship of a commercial enterprise; the aim is to "move fast and break things" (Taplin 2017). (Taplin is a scathing critic of this ideology and its social effects.)

to individual performance, for example, leads to a situation where workers are continually appraising the performance of both their colleagues and themselves. This reduces solidarity, as "wage-earners obliged to appraise one another can also find it more difficult to forge a common front against central management" (Boltanski and Chiapello 2005, p.284). Finally, the emphasis on flexibility, mobility, and constant skill development "went together with the exclusion of those individuals or groups that did not possess the requisite resources to seize those opportunities and, consequently, with an increase in poverty and inequality" (Boltanski and Chiapello 2005, p.324). In other words, this ideology subtly interacts with that of meritocracy: those who cannot muster the appropriate skill set can expect only downward mobility.

We will be drawing on Boltanski and Chiapello's insights in our own argument, particularly the way in which work is associated, in market fundamentalism, with a new emancipatory individualism where the focus for the individual is on "self-discipline" as well as self-development. Their work in sociology complements the more psychologically oriented approaches of both Illouz and Konings. They are equally concerned to distance themselves from one strand of Frankfurt School critical theory that diagnoses the ills of capitalist society as arising from the "totalizing" administration of life, the degeneration of reasonableness into a merely instrumental conception of rationality, and the undermining of the organic ties of traditional society by the alien logic of the market.

Konings argues that this style of critique makes the error of portraying capitalism as a cold, emotionless, machine-like social system that represents an external threat to our lived experience. Capitalism is conceptualized in this framework as anonymous, systemic, universalizing, "alien", and corrosive of the social order. Konings, by contrast, views capitalist economies as themselves articulations of an ethical and social outlook that has succeeded in generating a deep emotional identification from those who live under it in ways similar to those identified by Boltanski and Chiapello.

In the process, capitalism forms a new, taken for granted, way of negotiating our social world that is neither reducible to social atomism, nor to an instrumental conception of rationality, nor to an ethos of possessive individualism, nor to the fetishizing of commodities. Konings claims that the capitalist economy is not the displacement of a religious impulse, but an expression of it (Konings 2015, pp.5–6). In that respect, as he notes, he is updating Weber's core thesis in *The Protestant Ethic and the Spirit of Capitalism.*

> The discursive force of neoliberalism was anchored in the emotional needs of the social self as it has evolved by the 1970s: neoliberalism was synched to the affective economy of the capitalist subject in a way that progressive discourses were not. (Konings 2015, p.91)

One interpretation of the triumph of market fundamentalism was that it did not win any arguments, but was useful to a convergent set of powerful interests so that it triumphed anyway, with no regard to its intellectual merits. By contrast, Konings thinks that line of critique ignores market fundamentalism's ethical, religious, and emotional appeal. What, then, does he view as this core emotional appeal that has proven to be so enduringly successful?

Those whom Konings portrays as the moral scolds of late twentieth-century American progressivism targeted, in their social critiques, the degeneration of the republican citizen into the narcissistic consumer. Yet such narcissism was interpreted by David Riesman, in 1950, as an expression of anxiety and insecurity derived from "a heightening of awareness of the self in relation to others"—a remark that, as we will see in the next chapter, is familiar from Rousseau (Riesman 1950, p.49, quoted in Konings 2015, p.93).[6] Furthermore, in the subsequent chapter, we will expand upon the point already noted, namely, that Rawls also argued that the will to dominate is a product of anxiety. We have our own explanation of this point: we will repeatedly draw on Waheed Hussain's suggestion that to replace solidaristic with non-solidaristic institutions is politically to choose to "pit people against each other" (Hussain 2020). He illustrates the point with this example:

> When I take my daughter to the local park, I am often aware that the other parents are diligently hiring tutors and saving money to help their kids go to better high schools and colleges and eventually beat my daughter (or anyone else) out for a decent job. And I will have to do some of the same things to help my daughter eventually to beat these kids (or anyone else) out for a decent job. We may not know all of the other individuals involved, people in distant cities and towns, but given the character of our background

[6] Konings echoes Hegel when he writes that "we can have a better version of our current self, our present attachments and identity, without the anxiety. The logic is epitomized by money, which is almost always a problem and almost always itself the solution to the problem, iconically representing both lack and saturation: there is nothing money cannot buy and for that very reason no amount of money is ever enough" (Konings 2015, pp.94–5).

> institutions, we must act with disregard for all of these individuals, abstractly conceived—if we do not, we will get pushed in the dirt ourselves. (Hussain 2020, p.94)

If one lives in such a society, heightened anxiety would seem to be inevitable. A common thread running throughout the argument of this book is that if people are increasingly anxious, and concerned both with social evaluative threats to their status and with defensive actions to pre-empt those threats, then that anxiety can be traced back to the institutional set-up of our societies.

Riesman argued that this anxiety, combined with a lack of self-knowledge, produces the external management of the individual's symptoms as a form of displacement activity.[7] Meanwhile the citizen reinvests in the promise of a more authentic, better, version of oneself (Konings 2015, p.95). The upshot, Konings claims, is the "logic described by Veblen: an anxious pattern of competitive emulation revolving around standards that hold out tremendous promise yet never fail to disappoint" (Konings 2015, p.96). In the next chapter we will look at this originating idea in the work of Adam Smith and focus, specifically, on the emulation of the rich in chapter 11. Self-realization needs a template—an exemplar—and for many people the wealthy are living emblematic lives that a culture of celebrity presents as worthy of emulation. This overlaps with the presentation of the heroic Silicon Valley entrepreneur as a cultural icon.

Similarly, Veblen's thesis is at the core of this book's argument: competitive emulation in the light of an unattainable ideal is a potent source of anxiety. We add to it Fred Hirsch's point—implicit also in Hussain's argument—that certain societies set up positional competition as the motor for competition-driven growth. Now participation in institutions where people are pitted against each other becomes a "defensive necessity". Opting out is no longer an option. This may be a suboptimal equilibrium from the general point of view, but not one that anyone can change.

Konings also interprets Erich Fromm as arguing that capitalism encourages the management of an individual's anxiety by another form of displacement: by seeking to manipulate others via an ethos of competitiveness

[7] Eva Illouz notes the centrality of anxiety to Weber's account of the Protestant ethic's *indirect* connection to early capitalism: "it is the anxiety provoked by an inscrutable divinity which is at the heart of the capitalist entrepreneur's frantic activity" (Illouz 2007, p.1).

(Fromm 1973; Konings 2015, pp.101–2). Self-management can manifest itself in anti-social, hostile, behaviour. Anxiety may be a forgivable fault, but some of its modes of expression are less forgivable. Perhaps we can see Hussain's point as a specific expression of Fromm's diagnosis of the way in which the emotional regime of capitalism encourages socially destructive behaviour.[8] Yet, once again, we focus on the institutional background that fosters such behaviour: a background that reflects the controlling interest of money in structuring the field of opportunity with a deep impact on the sort of people individuals feel compelled to be (Fishkin 2014). A society which holds up the wealthy as exemplars, where they constitute an unattainable ideal, and where money is vital for the goods necessary for anyone to lead a good life represents one guise of republican domination.

Konings is an historian of American finance, and his particular concern is with the way in which Weber's account of the relation between the Protestant ethic and capitalist motivations—the way in which the mundane activity in the economy can glorify god—was transformed by its reception in America. Konings claims that there was always more emphasis, in American Protestantism, on ethical satisfactions in the here and now and that the American version of the Protestant ethic had a therapeutic dimension (Konings 2015). Part of the appeal of market fundamentalism is the way in which Americans changed their behaviour in the light of "financial principles" woven into "the texture of everyday life and the American psyche" (Konings 2015, p.115). Market fundamentalism creates a character based on economic faith: to make investments, to take on liabilities, in the hope of future redemption—a narrative of faith and redemption transposed into a secular idiom. The progressive critic emerges, by contrast, as the false prophet of free lunches, bailouts, and handouts for the undeserving. The Volcker Shock emerges, in this accounting, as a moral purgation for America: "what capitalism demanded was not the extinction of debts but an intensification of Americans' commitment to their indebtedness" (Konings 2015).

One guise of the rent-extraction regime that we described in chapter 2 is the extent to which the institutional and "high net worth" investors in money manager capitalism have succeeded in extracting a steady flow of income from America's increasingly indebted middle and lower classes (Dymski 2010; Gowan 2010; Montgomerie 2010). As Susanne Soederberg has

[8] As Konings puts it: "Capitalism's therapies, then, are not innocent, neutral or benevolent: they typically allow us to solve our own problems by causing trouble for others" (Konings 2015, pp.102–3).

argued, for the poorest Americans, credit card debt replaces the lack of state-based social insurance creating a "debtfare state": given their precarious circumstances, they can be charged extraordinarily high rates of interest (Soederberg 2013). For the less poor, credit is treated as a complement to stagnant income (Hockett and Dillon 2019a, 2019b; Montgomerie 2009). As we have noted, the rentier-investor class wants a zero- or low-inflation environment except for inflation in the value of their own assets; inflation control requires the financial disciplining of the population. It is, in Konings word, a form of "governance" in a rent-extracting form of capitalism (Konings 2015, p.114). The financial interests of the wealthy, then, shape the institutional structures and fields of opportunities within which other citizens must live their lives. The payment of one's debts to the rentier class is, at its core, an ethical commitment and an ideal of citizenship.[9]

We have noted, in disparate reactions to the financial crisis, how the American Right mobilized a moral hazard narrative to critique both the reckless borrowers who had loaded up on unsustainable credit and the corrupt institutions that facilitated this—the "Wall Street versus Main Street" narrative. We take Konings's basic point to be that progressives would do well not to ignore the deep entrenchment of ideals of self-sufficiency and personal responsibility at the heart of this critique. The moralizing of debt and the undercurrent of the desire to punish reckless borrowers and lenders is part of the moral core of this ideal: it is crucial to financialization as a form of individual governance.

He is also anxious to position the philosophical republican in the right place in this argument: some republican writing does have a moralizing tone when it comes to excessive consumerism, the rise of private despotism, and the turning away from the common good. But we are more confident than Konings that the liberal-republican can get this right: we have emphasized the detachment of issues of access to credit from issues of personal responsibility by pointing out that in the circumstances of late twentieth-century American capitalism access to credit was a "defensive necessity". The problem was not solipsistic consumerism, but genuine threats to one's prospects and those of one's children in a society with a diminishing sphere of (non-marketized provision of) public goods. People did not over-extend their indebtedness

[9] With its mirror image as the social parasite, the freeloader, the "welfare queen" or the "benefits cheat", all of whom expect "something for nothing".

from vanity, but because they had no choice if they wanted to secure key life goods: stable housing, access to education, and access to healthcare.

Nevertheless, we do think it is an insight of Koning's account to trace out the dual aspect of America's conception of economic life as a form of civic religion: it plays this role for a "populist-republican subject . . . forever dissatisfied with existing institutions but maintain[ing] an unwavering belief in their redemptive promise" (Konings 2015, p.8). Charitably interpreted, Konings's complaint is that civic republicanism became, because it mistakenly (in his view) set itself up in competition with capitalist motivations, forced into the role of the moral scold. By contrast, the "neoliberal" offers an authentic relationship to money and the market:

> Neoliberal discourses manifest a fully secularized Protestant spirit: acutely aware that money is a "mere" convention, they insist that we not fetishise it, not expect proceeds without *making investments and honoring our debts.* (Konings 2015, p.11, emphasis added)

There is, certainly, a stand of Protestant rigorism about truth telling in connection with the market as we have already noted. For the market fundamentalist it is a context that is hostile to illusions and supplies hard truths that only the strongest of character can deal with. As we will see in chapter 12, it is central to the ideology of meritocracy that the "big sort" of individuals into their respective market based merits is a harsh truth teller about people's characters—with many found wanting. The market economy, like a competitive sport, is grounded on a notion of success that requires personal discipline, dedication, and a "work ethic"—"making investments", as Konings puts it. And "honoring our debts" directly relates money, as one form of promissory obligation, to an ethic of gifts given and appropriately reciprocated. Konings interprets neo-liberalism as offering a path to the "realization of an authentic, republican self", but it is not entirely clear why he is so specific as to which conception of civic virtue is particularly to be aligned with neo-liberal truth telling.

Konings emphasizes that the emotional regime of market fundamentalism is not a straightforward one of individualized responsibility. Financial crises are normal occurrences in such an unstable system, and someone has always been irresponsible in explaining how they came about. The resilience of this emotional regime is that it absorbs and copes with failure and disappointment in the light of its promise of future redemption. Furthermore, the complement to the focus on responsibility is the punitive, cleansing, emotion of anger towards the irresponsible—a wave of populist sentiment that rises, abates, leaving financialization and its structural preconditions more entrenched than before the last crisis (Konings 2015, p.122). This reflects the general truth that the emotional logic of capitalism binds people even to that which damages their interests. Trials and tribulations reflect the depth of one's commitment and allow one to measure one's emotional investment. The religious overtones of such narratives of trials and eventual redemption are obvious.

Market fundamentalism, for Konings, offered a simplistic but compelling diagnosis for the anxieties surrounding the financialization of everyday life for many Americans: the appeal to self-sufficiency and the critique of dependency went together.[10] Life is hard, and that fact must be truthfully faced. The foundation of the American republic is a "responsible and accountable" citizenship (Konings 2015, pp.108–9). When, in the face of rising inequality and stagnant wages, financialization rises from mortgage repayments to managing credit card debt, the emphasis is on creditworthiness and taking responsibility for one's personal "financialization". This is the origin of what James K. Galbraith called American "debt peonage", namely, the rise of revolving debt that is indefinitely rolled over.[11] The re-moralizing of the issue of debt as a question of character is fully embraced by market fundamentalism as a judgement passed on individual character. One strand of therapy also emphasizes empowerment through tough love, both towards oneself and, importantly, others. It is the inability of progressives to come to terms with this emotional appeal that leaves them on the outside, baffled by the ease with which ordinary people have fallen prey to propaganda—as Konings notes, Thomas Frank's book *What's the Matter with Kansas?* is the apogee of such baffled liberal despair (Konings 2015, p.113; Frank 2005).

Konings is right that the economy is the home of "highly emotionally charged discourses" and that point had already been developed by Eva Illouz, who focuses, more than Konings, on the reciprocal influence here between economic and intimate life. Not only does the capitalist market justify itself via the emotions; it starts to colonize intimate life so that it, too,

[10] We would emphasize, more than Konings, the racial encoding of this distinction in American politics. When Ronald Reagan and Bill Clinton referred to "welfare queens", the ethnicity of the stereotype did not have to spelled out to their respective audiences.

[11] The suppression of inflation for forty years means that the real value of debts has never been decreased so that debt burdens are never reduced; but they can be rolled over (Blyth 2015).

is "marketized" (Illouz 2007, p.4). Affect becomes central to the economy, while in emotional life "market repertoires become intertwined with the language of psychology and . . . offer new techniques and meanings to forge new forms of sociability" (Illouz 2007, p.5).[12] For her, the problem is that in true intimacy, people come together in virtue of their idiosyncrasies, while the invasion of a therapeutic terminology produces a mutually alienating commonality of expression. Marketizing, here, practically means standardization and commensuration in the terms on which people relate to each other (Illouz 2007, p.112). This is an unanticipated side effect of putative "emancipation through marketization".

The "primary commodity circulated" is that of "mental and emotional health"—a new form of capital "on the seam line between cultural and social capital" (Illouz 2007, p.62, p.66):

> In the culture of emotional capitalism, emotions have become entities to be evaluated, inspected, discussed, bargained, quantified, and commodified . . . they have also contributed to creating a suffering self, that is, an identity organized and defined by its psychic lacks and deficiencies, which is incorporated back into the market through incessant injunctions to self-change and self-realization. Conversely, emotional capitalism has imbued economic transactions . . . with an unprecedented cultural attention to the linguistic management of emotions, making them the focus of strategies of dialogue, recognition, intimacy, and self-emancipation. (Illouz 2007, p.109)

A wide range of social agencies and interests have supported the development of this cultural field: government, academia, mass based social movements (particularly, in Illouz's narrative, second wave feminism), civil society associations, accredited professionals, the medical professions, and the pharmaceutical industry. "Self-help" is itself a massive industry. The goal is the development of an "emotional competence" that allows quick translation into social capital and personal and professional advancement (Illouz 2007, p.63). When science journalist Daniel Goleman documented the phrase "emotional intelligence" he was putting a name to a cultural phenomenon

[12] In an ironic reversal, Illouz believes that second wave feminism succeeded in importing Weberian rationalization into the intimate life of the bourgeois family via "the rise of egalitarian norms within marriage" while stereotypically feminine traits of empathy and care are being instilled into the "empathetic" relationships between managers and workers in the workplace (Illouz 2007, p.31).

that already existed and, like IQ measurement, is put to use in business organizations to sort its workers into the productive and unproductive.

Illouz diagnosed the rise of a "private" self that is publicly performative "which combines the aspiration to self-realization with the claim to emotional suffering" (Illouz 2007, p.63), connecting it to the rise of the politics of recognition (Illouz 2007, p.4). She presciently describes how the rise of the internet has both facilitated and accelerated this transformation, although her book pre-dates the way in which social media achieved extraordinary dominance in many people's lives.[13] Like Konings, Illouz emphasizes how, from the time of Freud's famous lecture series in the United States, the "therapeutic emotional style" took hold in America—both Illouz and Konings take *The Oprah Winfrey Show* to be emblematic in this regard as the historical successor to 1920s "advice literature" (Illouz 2007, p.51; Konings 2015). Psychoanalysis made the mundane life of the bourgeois family replete with drama and interest.

The workplace becomes an important location for the development of interpersonal relations. Like Lazonick and Shin, Illouz notes the importance of the separation of ownership from control in enabling the rise of the large Chandlerian firm with an extensive internal administration. This administration needed a source of cultural authority in the firm and found it in the language of management theory. The strand of Taylorist engineering of the production process was complemented by the professional advice of the psychologist concerning "the irrational dimension of work relationships and . . . workers' emotions" (Illouz 2007, p.14). Internal administration started to use a therapeutic and emotional register in the context of its concern with worker productivity: the workplace became the worker's second family in the process subtly redefining stereotypically gendered emotional repertoires. Monitoring was replaced by—or at least morphed into—empathetic understanding that seemed to soften conflicts of interest between workers and managers. Illouz believes that the success of this transformation was partly because—although she does not use this word—it has a "meritocratic" character—"one's personality—independent of social status—was the key to social and managerial success" (Illouz 2007). The worker was being

[13] Illouz notes how digital technology facilitates the idea that authenticity is more purely realized between disembodied selves (p.75) and intensifies the sense in which the "private psychological self becomes a public performance" (Illouz 2007, p.78). Admittedly this self now performs not for a specific other, but for "a generalized and abstract audience" (p.80). In the process, specifically when it comes to the presentation of the self on the internet and on dating sites, Illouz believes (unlike in her previous book) that commodification and marketizing is destructive of intimacy (Illouz 2007, p.91).

respected as an individual: taken seriously as a person with an individual voice. Paradoxically, as the worker is invited to express his or her authentic self via the communication of emotions and needs, so the precarious self is shielded via a "mechanism of social recognition" (Illouz 2007, p.21).

Relations of hierarchy within the firm had become "democratized" as rule by mutual recognition, while also being professionalized via procedural rules; high-end work became both more complex and collaborative—above all, workers and managers must be "good communicators" in just the way that Boltanksi and Chiapello emphasize (Illouz 2007, pp.18–23). The triumph of the rhetoric of recognition, however, has in Illouz's view produced only a splitting of the self: between an "intense subjective life" expressed via an "intensely subjectivist way of legitimating one's sentiments. . . . 'I feel that . . .' implies not only that one has the right to feel that way, but also that such right entitles one to be accepted and recognized simply by virtue of feeling a certain way" (Illouz 2007, p.39).[14] The complementary dynamic sees how we speak about emotions, in a therapeutic or managerial context, as disengaged—as "bracket[-ing] the emotional glue that binds us to others" (Illouz 2007, p.38).

We interpret Illouz as postulating both an intensely expressive, fragile, private self, prone to fantasy, combined with a (hypocritical?) ironized workplace personality—striving for self-realization—that has been commodified (Illouz 2007, p.113). Illouz argues that if the practical wisdom of a Machiavelli is to know when to present one's private or one's public self, or how best to juxtapose them, that is a form of practical wisdom that the emotional regime of capitalism takes from us. There is no switching between registers, as these two aspects of self-hood are two facets of the same process (Illouz 2007, pp.112–4).

In the process, Illouz also argues that what has been successfully democratized is "psychic injury". Illouz juxtaposes Samuel Smiles's Victorian optimism that the cultivation of virtue could lead any man (the gendering was deliberate) to success, with Freud's belief that only the socially privileged could heal their psychic wounds—the poor, in his view, being beyond help. America's democratization of both self-help and psychoanalysis has seen Americans of all social classes view themselves as mentally suffering. It follows, then, that "recovery has strangely become an enormously lucrative

[14] Illouz continues, "To say 'I feel hurt' allows little discussion and in fact demands immediate recognition of that hurt" (Illouz 2007).

business and a flourishing industry" (Illouz 2007, p.42). Internal changes in psychoanalysis aligned it not with Freudian pessimism, but with Smiles's optimistic views of self-improvement. The mass consumption of paperback books from the late 1930s spread the Gospel that is now delivered across multiple media: self-realization has become a right, and those who lack it are psychologically unhealthy and in need of therapeutic (or pharmacological) intervention.[15]

Illouz identifies an equivocation here between lack of health consisting in an incapacity and its consisting in a normal human capacity, but one that is not exercised well. It became a moral failing not to be happy or not to be successful qua person. These failures are medicalized: Illouz notes that given the vagueness of the ideal aspired to, all we have are the multitudes of ways in which people fall away from the ideal—a rapid multiplication of the field of sick people requiring intervention (Illouz 2007, p.48). As Illouz also notes, this also creates multiple, overlapping niches of consumers of therapeutic services (Illouz 2007, p.52). Rooted in trauma, therapeutic recovery has to "paradoxically privilege suffering and trauma" as it regresses to an originating traumatic event as part of the process of realizing an implicit future redemption (Illouz 2007, p.52). One can be responsible for trying to change, but not for the original psychic wound (that lies in early life and can not be avoided).

> [M]ost crucially, the therapeutic narrative emerges from the fact that the individual has become embedded in the culture saturated with the notion of rights. Both individuals and groups have increasingly made claims to "recognition", that is, demanded that one's suffering be acknowledged and remedied by institutions. (Illouz 2007, p.56)

Illouz believes that the scaffolding for the self is provided by social institutions: the American state played its role in the rise of a culture of both personal self-affirmation and the narration of victimhood. The National Institute of Public Health was founded in 1946 and the therapeutic narrative was advanced by the state through its social agencies. This therapeutic agenda was also developed by other associations in civil society, including the

[15] "[T]he very idea of self-realization . . . was central to the deployment of psychology as an authoritarian knowledge system and to the penetration of market repertoires inside the private sphere" (Illouz 2007, pp.109–10).

broad-based social movement of feminism (Illouz 2007, pp.58–9). The rise of private health insurance demanded the codification of pathologies and the still widely used DSM was the result, used by medical professionals, insurance companies, and the pharmaceutical industry. By the time of DSM-III the range of potential mental pathologies had significantly expanded: these became "mental and consumer" territories that attracted the profit motive of pharmaceutical companies (Illouz 2007, p.61).

But it is the profession of psychology, above all, that has codified emotional intelligence and put this new cultural tool at the disposal of the professional managerial class "responsible for the management of emotions" (Illouz 2007). This "middle rank" of the professional-managerial class has to manage both "up" and "down", work collaboratively, and must carefully manage their self-presentation in the workplace. Illouz thinks that this resource has become particularly important in the changed form of capitalism described by Boltanski and Chiapello. Their "connexionist capitalism" is particularly focused on "mobility, switching projects, versatility, ability to communicate during training courses" (Boltanski and Chiapello 2005, p.345).

These cultural resources are vindicated because, in their own terms, Illouz believes they work—even in the sphere of intimate life the educated professional versed in the language of emotional intelligence can put these concepts and techniques to use. Positives are intertwined with negatives: the very ways in which people make themselves accountable to each other rationalize and commodify the self (Illouz 2007, p.109). It is a pragmatically successful organizational model, but, as Freud intimated, not for every social group:

> [H]aving become the property of the middle class workplace, the therapeutic ethos makes men and women far more ready and able to cope with the tensions, contradictions and uncertainties that have become intrinsic to and embedded in contemporary biographies and identities. (Illouz 2007, p.73)

Just because the demands of the organization of capitalist production creates new forms of capital does not mean that it will be equally distributed. In our view it is the professional managerial class that has, above all, learned these techniques and puts them to use both professionally and personally. They are, above all, the articulate class: able to articulate the very skills that play into their own sense of entitlement.

At this point we are going to take a step back with the aim of drawing out the connection between the idea of an emotional regime of capitalism, how that regime was transformed by market fundamentalism, and competing philosophical conceptions of a just society. To develop our project of identifying and assessing the emotional logic of market societies in general, and capitalist societies in particular, we will turn now to the classic roots of this debate. Jean-Jacques Rousseau, Adam Smith, and Georg Wilhelm Friedrich Hegel all produced visions of the emerging commercial societies of their time that were so radical, insightful, and fruitfully engaged each with the other (apart from Rousseau's characteristic solitariness) that they have dominated philosophical discussion ever since. One of our questions in this book will be: which of their rivalrous visions is confirmed or refuted by the latest empirical work on the science of happiness? We will begin this task, in the next chapter, by outlining their respective visions of the emotional regimes of commercial society.

6

Rousseau, Smith, and Hegel on the Emotional Regimes of Commercial Society

Propositional Summary

1. Rousseau's critique of emerging commercial society is expounded. Under commercial institutions our self-love is inflamed and we are tyrannized by the good opinion of others. Our lives are consumed by self-defeating positional competition.
2. Smith counters that we are not naturally good, but the hybrid natural-cum-conventional device of market society can correct us.
3. Hegel's political psychology describes a path of emancipation through the right kind of work—an emancipation mediated by the corporations and cut off from the poor rabble and the rich rabble alike. But his realistic account of actually existing capitalist societies emphasizes their chaos, dysfunction, and lack of rationality, as they are scenes of extravagance and misery. He is concerned, in particular, with their failure to provide employment to all.
4. We examine recent works by historians such as Boucoyannis and Rasmussen and political economists such as Preiss which develop a Smithian diagnosis of what is involved in the New Inequality of our own time. They ask whether Smith's work offers a resource for a more just and inclusive form of economic development.
5. Rousseau, Smith, and Hegel agree on the main failure of commercial society: it inflames positional competition and a pathological and insatiable desire for wealth and distinction.

Introduction

This chapter offers an historical perspective on the argument to come. The topics of the next chapter are the emotional regimes developed by

Extravagance and Misery. Alan Thomas, Alfred Archer, and Bart Engelen, Oxford University Press.
 DOI: 10.1093/oso/9780197781722.003.0007

Pettit, as part of his Roman republicanism, and Rawls, as part of his liberalism (Rawls 2001; Brennan and Pettit 2004). Here we frame that discussion in history: the classical sources upon which Pettit and Rawls draw, namely, the works of Jean-Jacques Rousseau, Adam Smith, and Georg Wilhelm Friedrich Hegel. Each of these three authors takes emotional regimes to be essential to the workings of emergent capitalist societies.

The relationships between Rousseau, Smith, and Hegel produce a crucible of ideas, as each reacted to the other. Smith was the first Enlightenment philosopher to respond to Rousseau's "Counter-Enlightenment" views (Rasmussen 2008, 2013). The young Hegel was also obsessed with Rousseau (Church 2010, p.125). Each of them debates the prospects and threats posed by the new "commercial society". This is a term we take from Adam Smith in this famous passage from *The Wealth of Nations* (1776):

> When the division of labour has once been thoroughly established, it is but a small part of a man's wants which his labour can supply. He supplies the far greater part of them by exchanging that surplus part of the produce of his own labour, which is over and above his own consumption, for such parts of the produce of other men's labour as he has occasion for. Every man thus lives by exchanging, or becomes in some measure a merchant, and the society itself grows to be what is properly a commercial society. (Smith 1776/1981, I.IV.I.37)

This passage insightfully makes the division of labour central to the emergence of this new form of society positioned between a largely agrarian society with roots in feudalism, but not yet the modern industrial capitalism of mass industrialization and monopolistic corporations. That Smith and Hegel are on the cusp of that transition gives their work significant contemporary resonance (Herzog 2013; Rasmussen 2016; Pippin 2020). By the close of this chapter, we identify Hegel as the most prescient interpreter of the political psychology of commercial societies (Church 2010; Pippin 2020; Herzog 2013).

We are not historians of philosophy; our aim, similar to that of Lisa Herzog in her book *The Invention of the Market* is to mine these debates for resources to allow us to thematize the emotional regimes of commercial societies of our own times (Herzog 2013). It takes an act of historical imagination to recover just how different the political and economic circumstances were when Rousseau, Smith, and Hegel discussed commercial society. They all wrote their books before the Industrial Revolution, in the context of largely agrarian societies which offered few opportunities for social mobility.[1] (Although Smith, in particular, was impressed by the potential that commercial society offers for greatly enhanced social mobility.)

However, in explaining the potential of commercial society for the advancement of human freedom, and in identifying its characteristic pathologies, all three of these philosophers note the role played by emotions in stabilizing, or destabilizing its social order. The key emotions of recognition, esteem, amour de soi, amour-propre, and desire are crucial to their respective accounts—the simplest explanation being that Smith and Hegel are responding to Rousseau's trenchant critique of commercial society. Their treatment of the emotions, in turn, is rooted in sophisticated psychological theories focused on identity, recognition, and the formation of the self.

Independently of the classic studies of the emotional regimes of modern capitalism developed by Weber, or Hirschman, our limited focus here is on these foundational discussions of the political psychology of the market in these classic philosophical sources. They anticipate the project we are undertaking here, even if the commercial societies that they examine are very different from our affluent capitalist societies—after two and a half centuries of further development and the global spread of capitalism. We identify the crucial issues that have a bearing on our theme: the relationship between emotional regimes, inequality, and the stabilization of a commercial order.

6.1 Rousseau's Originating Critique

The puzzle over the Rousseau/Smith connection is that they both seem to agree on the threats incipient in commercial society to political order: why, then, is Rousseau critical of it while Smith endorses it (Schwarze and Scott 2019)? Rousseau certainly seems to be what we would now call a "total" critic

[1] Herzog does note that "While Smith wrote before the first great wave of industrialization in Great Britain, Hegel received the news about the development of the United Kingdom through newspapers and magazines", though adding that "the Germany of his day was still largely pre-industrial" (Herzog 2013, pp.7–8).

of the emerging commercial societies of his time (Yack 1986). Rousseau's critique, as Rasmussen summarizes it, has three main strands: the effect of commercial society on the quality of the citizens that live in it; the tyranny in their lives of the good opinion of others; the ceaseless toil brought on by what we would now call "status evaluative" competition for relative position (Rasmussen 2008, chapter 1).

Central to this analysis is Rousseau's famous account of amour-propre, usually translated into English as "self-love". The solitary creatures in his idealized state of nature exemplify an appropriate degree of love of self: they care for their own interests (*amour de soi*). It is only in the debased condition of society and its corrupting interdependencies that this becomes the problem of self-love (*amour-propre*), which now can be either inflamed or healthy. While healthy amour-propre envisages us as seeking appropriate esteem and recognition from others, inflamed amour-propre motivates us to seek superiority over others (Kolodny 2010). *Amour de soi* seeks out goods that are non-comparative while inflamed *amour-propre* is assuaged only if one wins the competition for goods that are positional through and through.

In Niko Kolodny's detailed explanation, amour-propre only becomes inflamed when combined with a specific set of beliefs. Kolodny begins from the reasonable points that it is wholly appropriate both to be concerned with one's own well-being (*amour de soi*) and to want to be held in an appropriate regard by others (*amour-propre*). Rousseau is not holding out the fantasy that to be good, people ought to withdraw wholly from sociality—fortunately, given that this is neither possible nor desirable. Kolodny thinks that *amour-propre* originates not simply in a comparative concern that others rank one highly; it has a non-comparative dimension that includes one's own value, as well as how one is valued by others. The dimension of assessment here is "'equality/superiority of *basic worth or standing*' or 'equal/superior *entitlement to respect*'" (Kolodny 2010, p.170) It is because one wants to be superior to others *without limit* that, relative to a given society, the currency of competition is positional goods that exist only in the space of comparative ranking. This is the core explanation: a range of other vices radiate from this core.[2]

Which beliefs does Rousseau believe lead to inflamed amour-propre, such that changed beliefs would produce its healthy variant? Desire,

[2] "We refuse to accept moral equality or to moderate our claims accordingly... we are locked into zero-sum Competition for Social Advantage, where our gain must be another's loss and another's gain must be our loss" (Kolodny 2010, p.172).

Rousseau stresses, for creatures with imagination who can project themselves into the future, can easily degenerate into fantasy or wish (Williams 2002). As Kolodny notes, Rousseau's conception of desire "encourage[s] wishful thinking" (Kolodny 2010, p.175). Kolodny argues that the relevant beliefs are that one ought never to be thought less of than anyone else, from which it follows that one must seek out "first position". Under current social conditions, *amour-propre* becomes inflamed by false evaluative beliefs: that one's value lies in how others value one. Further, the only path to good opinion, we come to believe, is through social advantage.

We will devote some attention to Joshua Cohen's slightly different account of *amour-propre* as it is closest to Rawls's views (Cohen 1997). (Furthermore, his argument will be important for our own.) In Cohen's explanation it is important for the development of the pathological version of *amour-propre* that we collectively live under institutions that do not offer us any institutional affirmation of our equal worth as citizens. Only then do we collectively replace it with a concern for social advantage instead. If we lived under a stable, publicly affirmed, conception of our equal worth as citizens then we could channel our energies in this healthier dimension for the expression of legitimate *amour-propre*. The competition for social advantage will then become, as it were, optional as the concern to be evaluated as morally superior to others would be assuaged. As Frederick Neuhouser puts it:

> [T]he economic features of society affect the consequences amour propre will have in it by structuring the field of possibilities within which social recognition can be pursued. . . . A society that limits disparities in wealth generates different recognitive aspirations in its members from one whose economic system feeds on and celebrates the desire to be "filthy rich". (Neuhouser 2013, p.206)

It is in such a context that inflamed *amour-propre*, on Cohen's account, is precisely to believe that, given one's sincere belief that one is superior to others, that they truthfully evaluate you as such (Cohen 1997, p.109; Neuhouser 2013, p.206). We will examine Rawls's similar account in the next chapter.

We will not try to resolve the exegetical controversy between the different views of amour-propre defended by Cohen and Neuhouser on the onc hand and by Kolodny on the other. However, we note the key issue: can the desire for comparative standing be satisfied by my comparing myself to you and our finding ourselves to be equals? As Neuhouser puts it, "the standing I seek is comparative but not superior; equal standing is still comparative standing" (Neuhouser 2013, p.214; Cohen 2010, pp.101–4); Kolodny contests this claim (Kolodny 2010, p.178). Neuhouser makes the complementary suggestion that, with civic equality in place, the desire to be evaluated as superior can be localized to particular aspects of social competition. We will see below that Rawls seems to share a similar dual strategy of equalizing status as citizens, but re-channelling competition for status to other aspects of our social life (Rawls 1971/1999, §79).

Rousseau argues that the pathology of inflamed amour-propre emerges in the state of nature when people no longer act directly on their desires with no need for imagination or foresight. In their natural condition they have no need of the good opinions of others. Their basic desires are limited to the core needs of their animal-like life (Rasmussen 2008, p.22). In this idealized narrative, the burden of survival is lessened given the adaptation of these people to their environment, so they are leisured and happy. Happiness here is, in Rousseau's conception, the self-sufficient tranquillity of the Stoics—*ataraxia*. This natural goodness of human life is distorted by our mutual interdependence in commercial society.

In Rousseau's speculative genealogy, sociality is forced on the human species, but the degree of material inter-dependence involved is compatible with relative self-sufficiency and hence happiness. The multiple falls from grace of the invention of tools, the practice of agriculture, land scarcity, and the emergence of private property leads to the miseries of commercial society as we know it.[3] People had to change in these new circumstances, notably via the development of imagination and foresight, so that they started to "live in the future". This is a future of prospective esteem and consumption. Commercial society arrived on the scene to exacerbate all the ills of our newly interdependent condition:

> [D]eveloped faculties and moral corruption are both a cause and consequence of commercial society and its attendant division of labor, superfluous commodities, technology, acquisitiveness, interdependence, mobility, and cosmopolitanism. (Rasmussen 2008, p.25)

[3] Rasmussen notes that Smith fully concurred that government was instituted only to preserve the socio-economic inequality produced by the institution of private property—instituted by the rich for their own protection (Rasmussen 2008, p.72; Smith 1776/1981, V.i.b.12).

This lengthy charge sheet against commercial society is explained by Rousseau's more specific critiques that, as we have noted, Rasmussen helpfully separates into three strands.[4]

The idea that citizens in commercial society are divided from themselves in a way exacerbated by the division of labour is the origin of one strand of modern social thought that would become the mainstream of Left Hegelianism (Yack 1986). Our inner capacities for being free cannot be reconciled with the contingency of our social world unless we re-make the latter via a complete emancipatory transformation in social relations. In doing so, we make the individual whole again via re-making society (Yack 1986).

For Rousseau, the division of labour starts not with any analogue of Adam Smith's pin factory, but when people engage in the limited inter-dependence of life in small groups and begin to work the land. Self-sufficiency is lost, interdependence becomes a curse, and the very existence of a productive surplus becomes the problem. We have the original form of what we would now call the rent-seeking critique: "there are poor people only because there are rich ones" (Fragments, 48. *Inequality*). According to Rousseau then, there is a zero-sum competition between social classes. The social power of the wealthy is in inverse proportion to the misery of the poor ground down as they are by the rich. That the rich delight in flaunting their wealth to humiliate the poor is the origin of the kind of critique of capitalism discernible in recent works like Jerry Cohen's *Why Not Socialism?* where the origin of capitalism is traced to the twin motivations of "greed and fear" (Cohen 2009, pp.41–4). Rousseau certainly thinks that the poor have reason to fear the greed of the rich given that all are locked into a zero-sum competition.

Positionality is central to this zero-sum game and explains Rousseau's claim that "master and slave degrade each other". This positional competition, then, has no winners: the putative winners are as psychologically damaged as the losers. As Scanlon sums up Rousseau's position, these are false evaluative beliefs that everyone would be better off without.

Rousseau argues that technology, and luxury, create false needs in us and this leads to a degeneration of character and to physical and mental weakness and ignorance. Characters like these cannot be the kind of citizens that a republic demands. Commercial society expands political boundaries,

[4] He follows Smith's anatomization of Rousseau's arguments in his famous review of the *Discourse On Inequality* in the *Edinburgh Review* in March 1756 and the three lengthy passages Smith chose to translate (Rasmussen 2018, p.68). That review is the explicit focus of (Schwarze and Scott 2019).

weakening attachment to any specific republic. This entire critique is framed in terms of happiness: the citizens of commercial societies may have more commodities at their (collective) disposal, but they are unhappy. Stoic tranquillity is impossible in these conditions.

Rasmussen's second theme in his interpretation of Rousseau focuses on the tyranny of opinion. The famous paragraph we quoted from Smith to introduce the very idea of a commercial society centred on the fact that the division of labour means that we are dependent on society for nearly all our needs. In Rousseau's diagnosis, our dependence on others becomes total (Rasmussen 2008, p.30). This weakness means that you must take an interest in how others view you, until this becomes an all-embracing concern. The individual lives wholly in the eyes of the other and sociality hollows out individuality. Rasmussen focuses on the phrase from the *Letter to M. d'Alembert on the Theatre* where Rousseau speaks of the "empire of opinion". Character dissolves into personality: our multiple social masks that, in each case, seek to please and flatter our audience. The dominators, as much as the dominated, are in the grip of their audience: the rhetorician who seeks to move an audience in the light of their prejudices must assume those very prejudices to do so.

In another argument that will deeply influence Smith and Hegel, Rousseau argues that the desire for wealth is deceptive: it is actually a desire to be esteemed for being wealthy—not quite the same thing. That is why, for the wealthy, there seems to be no stopping point. If you need to stand out, then you need to stand out even amongst the other wealthy people against whom one wants to be measured. Typically, Rousseau goes one step further: the point of flaunting one's wealth is, as we would say, to "rub the noses" of the poor in their comparative poverty (*Discourses*, p.63).

We turn to commercial society to meet our desires and needs; we are, therefore, dependent on others and must cultivate their interest in our interests via commercial exchange. For Rousseau, this suggests that we care about others, when we do not, and under the surface everyone is in competition with everyone else. Commercial society is, then, a collection of practiced hypocrites who feign a concern with others while being wholly self-interested. Rousseau's particular target is what we would now call the Mandevillean strategy of institutionally channelling selfishness for the public good: Rousseau thinks that project is doomed, and that must have shaped Smith's insistence that self-interest and selfishness are distinct.[5] If two parties

[5] The connection between Rousseau and Mandeville was the focus of Smith's earliest known engagement with the former's work in his "Review" [1756] (Rasmussen 2008, pp.62–5). However, as

are motivated to competition by selfishness as opposed to self-interest, then the better outcome is spitefully to harm the interests of the other, to free ride, or to cheat, rather than to sign up for a Mandevillean institution that will transform this contest into a win-win competition.

Third, Rasmussen notes that Rousseau's critique is, once again, cast in terms of tranquil happiness. Commercial societies have an internal motor: the endless multiplication of human desires. The desire for wealth, acting as a covert surrogate for the desire for distinction, puts us all on a treadmill of desire satisfaction where no amount is ever enough. The ceaseless striving makes happiness impossible for us. In an early identification of the endowment effect, Rousseau observes that losing objects of satisfaction is painful, while enjoying them is only a matter of momentary respite (Rasmussen 2008, p.66). The activity of achieving material satisfaction is displaced on to the limitless demand for money.

Can we weave all these threads together into a unified critique that is centred on the idea of inequality? Frederick Neuhouser argues that we ought to: Rousseau wants severely to limit the degree of inequality not for its own sake, but for our freedom, and to enable a mutual recognition that is key to our well-being.[6] As Neuhouser puts it:

> [T]he relation economic inequality has to unhappiness is weaker than its relation to domination, but the connection—and the danger it poses—is real nonetheless. (Neuhouser 2013, p.206)

Rasmussen points out, Smith does not explicitly note the deepest similarity between Mandeville and Rousseau, namely, "that commercial society is based on vice" (Rasmussen 2008, p.63). Michelle Schwarze and John Scott note that Smith treats Rousseau's moral psychology as "essentially egoistic" (Schwarze and Scott 2019, p.67). As they note, one issue is whether Smith got Rousseau right, while another issue is what Smith thought whether or not he was right on the exegetical question. He certainly believed, rightly or wrongly, that there was a significant distance between Rousseau's account of pity and his own account of mutual sympathy. The key point is whether, in pitying another, we seek their good (happiness) or are merely avoiding our own pain in sympathizing with the pain of the other.

[6] More precisely, Neuhouser argues plausibly that it can only be the business of the state to promote what one might call a person's fundamental well-being interests rather than the vagaries and inconsistencies of individual happiness. "I believe it is plausible to attribute to Rousseau the view that finding satisfaction of one's amour propre . . . counts as a fundamental interest of human beings (an essential part of their well-being) . . . social and political institutions play a significant role in shaping and satisfying individuals' recognitive desires" (Neuhouser 2013).

This threat to our well-being depends on a society electing to channel its opportunities to be recognized, via the achievement of wealth, through its own conception of social mobility.[7]

Wealth inequality in particular is objectionable. Rousseau's goal is not strict material inequality in that dimension, but a limitation that prevents inequality of wealth from undermining the republican values of freedom, mutual recognition, and happiness (Neuhouser 2013, p.207 ff). Freedom is threatened when economic interdependence is corrupted into republican domination, and the economic power that comes with excessive wealth creates this threat.[8] Neuhouser formulates Rousseau's position as follows:

> [D]isparities in wealth are permissible only when they do not pose systematic obstacles to the freedom of any individual, especially the freedom of the less well off; economic inequality is permissible only to the extent that it is compatible with the absence of domination amongst social members. (Neuhouser 2013, p.209)

We would make three points about Rousseau's criterion. First, we endorse it, with one amendment, and will take it as the normative orientation of this book. Secondly, the amendment is that we would tighten up the formulation by making the domination of one citizen by another structurally impossible (Thomas 2017). Thirdly, endorsing this criterion does nothing to separate the strong egalitarianism of Rawls from the weak egalitarianism of Pettit—at least in theory—because both of them endorse it. Our argument is, rather, that when it comes to the realization of this shared ideal the strong egalitarian has the more finally defensible position, as we will explain in our concluding chapter.

Neuhouser identifies two ways to proceed—two ways that Rousseau also distinguishes. The first is the reform of society to eliminate class difference to eliminate the fundamental cause of inequality. The second accepts class

[7] It must make sense to aspire to "rise" via one's wealth, and Rousseau notes that highly stratified societies may block this channel for self "improvement". There is no point seeking out distinction via wealth if social stratification traps you in your class with its fixed position in a hierarchy. Neuhouser comments that this proposal "stands in great tension with Rousseau's commitment to avoiding arbitrary distinctions in basic social or political status" (Neuhouser 2013, p.206).

[8] This is not quite, as Neuhouser emphasizes, the conception of freedom as non-domination one finds in Pettit or, for that matter, (Thomas 2017). For Rousseau, it is not a matter of the tracking of a person's interests; rather, his concern is with free self-determination of one's actions (Neuhouser 2013, p.198): "You are treating me like a child" can be a reasonable complaint even to a well-intentioned interference with one's interests which promotes them.

difference and inequality but puts in place safeguards protective of freedom (Neuhouser 2013, p.210).[9] The latter takes steps to balance power imbalances between competing social interests: examples would be trade union legislation, legislation for worker representation, and so on. Insightfully, Neuhouser notes that what pushes Rousseau in the former, more radical direction is "a fundamental pessimism about the power of purely political measures to correct imbalances residing in a society's economic structure" (Neuhouser 2013, p.210).

In Rawlsian terms, this is the question of how we are to react to the historical record of what Bill Edmundson has called "the fact of domination"—the Machiavellian and Rousseauian argument that the rich do not pursue their own concerns and leave other citizens in peace, but actively take steps politically to promote their sectional interests. (This makes sense if Rousseau is correct that this is a zero-sum game.)[10] We will return to this crucial issue in our final chapter, but we here note our agreement with Neuhouser (and Rousseau) that the focal point is "the division of society into propertied and non-propertied classes" (Neuhouser 2013, p.210). The weak egalitarian, by contrast, may be more willing to accept this basic distinction between the propertied and the non-propertied provided that it is complemented by the politics of redress—for example, redistributive tax and transfer. By contrast, in our view, and Rawls's, it is the capitalization of each citizen that is crucial.

Rousseau also has an explanation of the way in which poverty impacts on unhappiness; obviously, even under a limited degree of inequality, some are worse off than others in that they have less all-purpose control over resources. A distinctive problem for the worst off is that they are cut off from recognitional goods. In societies where wealth tracks social status, the poor are not simply humiliated, but unable to be recognized as equals in the eyes of others. Furthermore, even the poor are victims of inflamed amour-propre and seek superiority over others in a collectively self-stultifying competition. In summary, "desires become boundless in a way that is inimical to genuine happiness" for the poor as much as the rich (Neuhouser 2013, p.206).

[9] Neuhouser notes that Pettit records the same distinction between two strategies and explicitly opts for the latter (Neuhouser 2013, p.210; Pettit 1997, p.67, p.85).

[10] This point about zero-sum competition also helps with another point Neuhouser considers: is Rousseau's critique of absolute poverty, or of relative poverty? As he points out, the correct answer is "both", but for different reasons. Being absolutely poor makes it more likely that a person will enter into relations in which they are dominated. However, being relatively poor, in the context of a zero-sum game, is to be the wrong end of a relation in which some are "privileged" vis-à-vis others (Neuhouser 2013, pp.211–2).

A crucial transition point here is not simply that the concept of needs is relative to economic development, but also that false needs can do the same functional job as true ones. In this book we will be placing particular emphasis on this Rousseauian insight that:

> [T]he needs invoked in explaining the connections among dependence, inequality, and domination do not have to be "true" but only perceived needs, since the latter, too, provide dependent individuals with an incentive to obey others in order to secure their cooperation: the danger of domination raises whenever the worse off perceive themselves as needing something that cooperation with the better off could give them. (Neuhouser 2013, pp.212–3)

Rousseau's point, as Neuhouser details, is that, in a society where our social institutions make the only channel for recognition the acquisition of positional goods (as the only way to satisfy inflamed amour-propre), desires will be transformed into needs. But this is correct for both actual and false needs alike. What we feel we must have, in order to be recognized by others as worthy, will in an unjustly unequal society make us more dependent on others as that category of needs expands (Neuhouser 2013, p.213). When the sole motive for production is anticipated profit, this could be promoted as much by false needs as true needs. In the process—as a side effect as it were—the scope of domination is expanded.

What, then, is to be done? Rousseau's imagined genealogy cannot simply be reversed: we must design institutions that transform our social relations to make us truly free.[11] Yet in Rousseau's own telling, it takes a deus ex machina—the Legislator—to put us on the true path of austere republican virtue. Rousseau thought that the prospects for success in this endeavour were low. For him, then, commercial society is—in Rasmussen's memorable phrase—"an unmitigated disaster" from the point of view of human happiness construed as a self-sufficient tranquillity (Rasmussen 2008, p.40). Both Smith and Hegel were centrally concerned to address this critique and assess its fairness as an estimation of the potential of commercial society.

[11] According to Kolodny, the point of Rousseau's fictional genealogies is to address the objection that all the socialized human beings in our actual historical experience are corrupted by the "wrong" institutions; so the residual optimism that we could be better off under a different institutional set up requires a sketch of a different path of human development (Kolodny 2010, p.166 ff).

6.2 From Rousseau to Smith

Smith sees the dangers of the emerging commercial order but believes they can be overcome in his "system of natural liberty" (Smith 1776/1981, IV.ix.51, 687). It is, as Rasmussen puts it, the "central puzzle" of Smith's thought that he believes this, notwithstanding his agreement with Rousseau's critique of commercial society. The point of agreement is that:

> [C]ommercial society necessarily produces great inequalities; that an extensive division of labor can exact an immense cost in human dignity by rendering people feeble and ignorant; that an emphasis on wealth and material goods can encourage moral corruption; and that the desire for wealth often leads people to submit to endless toil and anxiety in the pursuit of frivolous material goods.[12] (Rasmussen 2008, p.7)

In taking the first steps to resolve this puzzle, Lisa Herzog makes a convincing case that any complete account of Smith's theory of the market must include his metaphysical and religious assumptions.

> [If] there are natural moral sentiments, and nature has a normative status as created by God, then men should indeed follow these sentiments. (Herzog 2013, p.24)

It does not follow that everything natural is automatically good; the market is exemplary in this respect as being a hybrid of nature shaped by institutions.[13] For Smith, the market is part "natural"—he calls it a "contrivance of nature"—and part conventional in that it requires institutional contextualizing under the watchful guardianship of a wise, impartial, legislator.[14] Furthermore, he makes the point that Mill later emphasized—that

[12] This puzzle is also the starting point for the discussion of (Schwarze and Scott 2019).

[13] Emotion, in the guise of natural sentiment, plays a critical role in Smith's account of moral philosophy: as the circles of sentiment expand, and as we reach the key stabilizing idea of justice, that sentiment reinforces reason (Smith 1776/1981, II.I.1.5.10). We are to attend to our own interests, because nature and society work best as an overall design when we fulfil the allotted role best suited to us given our cognitive limitations.

[14] Deborah Boucoyannis notes that, for Smith, "politics and legislation have a central role in the economy: the 'invisible hand' is a minor mechanism, not a guiding economic principle of his theory" (Boucoyannis 2013, p.1052). Overall, Smith believes that the individual is often a better judge of their own economic prospects than the state, but the context is free choice of occupation. No liberal is defending state control of occupational choice today—it is derivable from the basic liberty of free association (Boucoyannis 2013, p.1058).

convention, or artifice, is natural to humans. Humans may need to "correct" nature via artifice. The same is true for the evolution of artifice and nature into historically established institutions: in the form we inherit them, they may need revision (Herzog 2013, p.27). This point is key to understanding Smith's fundamental dissent from Rousseau's belief in the natural goodness of humanity (Rasmussen 2008). It is because we are not naturally good that our nature stands in need of correction. Commercial society represents such a correction.

The correction comes from the standpoint of the impartial spectator concerned with the general good. Competition in the market presupposes an ethos of "fair play" (Smith 1776/1981, II.II.2.1). The whole system must be guarded by virtuous state actors, both judges and politicians, who must in particular be wary of the activities of cartels and the "merchants and manufacturers" who try to impose rent-seeking practices that hinder the market as much as feudalism did.[15] That is why Smith can come to his nuanced verdict that, in assessing what Rawls calls our "realistically utopian" options, the system of natural liberty wins out over realistic alternatives with remnants of feudal dependence, mercantilism, and widespread poverty.[16]

Smith is equally clear that commercial society has its own emotional regime: we will draw extensively upon his account of admiration for the rich in chapter 11. Each of us has a natural capacity for sympathy with others based on imaginative identification with the other's point of view (Smith 1776/1981, I.I.1.3). It is identification with others which is activated by our interactions with them (Schwarze and Scott 2019). As Michelle Schwarze and John Scott emphasize:

> Sympathy rightly understood thus motivates us to be mutually accommodating and to recognize others as equals instead of inferiors, rendering the moral economy positive-sum overall. (Schwarze and Scott 2019, p.72)

[15] Herzog suggests that we read *The Wealth of Nations* as a practical manual of statecraft (Herzog 2013). Rasmussen notes the depth and intensity of Smith's critique of "the malicious activities of rich and powerful merchants", whom he views as extractive rent seekers not because of their personal deficiencies of character but because of the economic structures within which they operate (Rasmussen 2008, p.80).

[16] Contrary to stereotype, Smith is no anti-statist and his ideal legislator has a complex tax policy that always favours the productive use of capital over the rent seeker and seeks to deter frivolous luxury consumption. While it is a defeasible presumption that the individual knows his or her economic interests, the tax system incentivizes the productive virtues and everyone's long-term interests, but as determined by the ideal legislator (Boucoyannis 2013, pp.1058–60).

We take pleasure in the happiness of others—even if only as its passive witness (Smith 1776/1981, I.I.1.1). Smith is one of the earliest formulators of the idea that self-consciousness constitutively depends on a person's capacity to think of herself as others view her (Herzog 2013, p.73). However, while Rousseau can see only the damage from living "in the eyes of others", for Smith that psychological datum has, itself, to be morally neutral given that concern for how others esteem oneself can also be a positive reinforcement for moral conduct (Rasmussen 2008, pp.12–3).[17]

A characteristic difference between Rousseau and Smith concerns the necessity, in commercial society, of requiring other people to take an interest in one's own interests—the corollary of our mutual dependence. Rousseau, as we have seen, thinks this opens the door to extensive hypocrisy. Smith, perhaps with a clearer eye, views such appeals to the interests of others as usually honest and not fraudulent—his two signal exceptions being his *bêtes noires* of merchants and manufacturers who are always malicious and hypocritical (Rasmussen 2008, pp.79–80). The institutional set-up puts these merchants and manufacturers in a position of power over others that enables them to lie and to cheat. That is not, for Smith, the situation of most people in a commercial society who do not hold power over others so must appeal to their interests—just as they take an interest in their own interests.

In the most famous passage *in The Wealth of Nations* this mutual regard for each other's interests is contrasted with fawning and flattery:

> It is not from the benevolence of the butcher, the brewer, or the baker, that we expect our dinner, but from their regard to their own interest. We address ourselves, not to their humanity, but to their self-love. . . . Nobody but a beggar chuses to depend chiefly upon the benevolence of his fellow-citizens. (Smith 1776, I.ii.2, quoted in Anderson 2017, p.2)

Revealingly, Elizabeth Anderson includes this passage in a section of her book titled "When the Market Was Left" (Anderson 2017). We also think she was right to contextualize this famous passage at the end of the discussion that immediately precedes it:

[17] Rasmussen notes that: "For Rousseau this tendency arises only with the development of amour-propre. For Smith, by contrast, it is a natural phenomenon: the concern for the opinions of others has its basis in human nature and not an artificial faculty" (Rasmussen 2008, p.76).

> When an animal wants to obtain something either of a man or of another animal, it has no other means of persuasion but to gain the favour of those whose services it requires. A. . .spaniel endeavours by a thousand attractions to engage the attention of its master who is at dinner, when it wants to be fed by him. Man sometimes uses the same arts with his brethren, and . . . endeavours by every servile and fawning attention to obtain their good will. (Smith 1776/1981, I.II.2)

For Smith, the "prospective purchaser" gives equal consideration to the interests of the butcher, the brewer, and the banker, just as they do when they enter into commercial relations with him (Smith 1776/1981, I.II.2). That represents a substantive egalitarian commitment. As Stephen Darwall puts it, such sympathetic understanding of each other's interests "implicitly recognizes the other as having an independent [and as such an equal] perspective" (Darwall 2004, p.131).

While Rousseau objects to commercial society as it turns us all into fawning spaniels; Smith thinks that this point can be addressed and that commercial society, correctly institutionally configured, supports republican independence and makes it newly available to the working poor.

It is hard to underestimate the importance of this argument for Smith. It is crucial to his view that while modern commercial society can, and will, produce great inequality the working poor have reached what we would now call a "sufficient standard" of independence from domination by any specific individual (Rasmussen 2008, p.12). This answers one of Rousseau's critiques: that extensive inequality produces psychological harms, including dependence. Smith clearly believes that socio-economic independence in his sense protects the individual from the psychological harms of extensive inequality—of seeing other people's economic contribution valued far more highly than one's own. Clearly this argument founders if any group of citizens can co-ordinate to introduce dependence into the wage relationship or if, for that matter, commercial society simply cannot offer this avenue to independence through the right kind of employment to all (as Hegel feared).[18]

For Smith, once the worker in commercial society can no longer meet his or her immediate needs, the impact of our mutual dependence for that person

[18] Both points combine if a distinct capitalist class uses unemployment as a class-based weapon to discipline workers—a prospect that would have horrified Smith. That is even worse than Hegel's view that commercial society is constitutively unable to employ everyone without producing either deflationary stagnation or colonial exploitation.

is far more serious. The institutions of private property motivate production and the generation of a surplus but also intensify our mutual dependence. The commercial worker has lost self-sufficiency given that they do not work directly on the land. Fichte, one of Smith's most insightful critics, remarks that in commercial society it is not enough that one "merely *may* exchange", rather, "one *must* do so" and, Fichte added, on fair terms (Fichte 1800/2012, Pt. I, 2, p.96). Republican values are preserved if the exchange nexus does not introduce dependence on any other agent in particular. Hence Smith's sensitivity to cartels or monopolists who reintroduce systemic power imbalances to the nexus of exchange. It is Fichte who notes the flaw in this argument: you are not dependent on any particular agent, but you are dependent on the aggregate of agents who constitute the sphere of private governance.[19]

This is the first glimmering of an argument for the market as an emancipatory ideal because all market agents are price takers, not price makers, and power is dispersed between them (Arrow and Debreu 1954). Does Smith not pay the price of commodifying labour in this optimistic account of the potential fate of the working poor? Patricia Werhane and others argue not: to sell one's labour is not to sell one's person (Werhane 1991, p.132). Yet it remains true, as Herzog notes, that Smith conceives of the labour market as "flexible"—that labourers should relatively easily re-train themselves so as to re-deploy their "human capital" as the market requires (Herzog 2013, p.72). In that respect, the self is to some extent "dis-embedded": a person is not wholly defined by their economic role.[20]

For Smith, bargaining is the exercise of our capacity for reasonableness, trade is a stand-in for dialogic communication itself, and emotion plays as important a role in commercial life as our capacity to reason. The universal desire to better oneself is not limited to the acquisition of material goods alone (Herzog 2013, p.31). Acquisitions can bring the attention of others because each of us deeply desires "[t]o be observed, to be attended to, to be taken notice of with sympathy, complacency and approbation" (Smith 1776/1981, I.III.2.1). Conversely, what we want to avoid, above all, is to be nobody.

[19] You cannot exit a market—sell—if no one is buying. That's why we have state lenders of last resort for capital markets; Fichte infers, in our view correctly, that we need a labour market employer of last resort and it, too, should be a public agency outside the sphere of private governance. See (Hockett 2019; Thomas 2021).

[20] As Herzog notes, costless entry and exit from the labour market are crucial to Smith's subtle view that labour market outcomes reflect patterns of deserving behaviour, that is, the virtues as assessed and rewarded by the ideal spectator (Herzog 2013, pp.95–6). Smith seems to anticipate the Rawlsian claim that in a society well-ordered by justice, labour market incentives will be wholly compensatory (Smith 1776/1981, I.X.1).

Like Thorstein Veblen, Smith acknowledges that many market agents are not motivated by material goods alone, but by "vanity" (Smith 1776/1981, I.III.II.1). This fits our twenty-first-century notion of the "attention economy": attention is finite, and it is exemplary individuals whose fortunes are attended to, while the ordinary run of people do not draw such attention. Furthermore, we presuppose that wealthy celebrities must be happy in virtue of their wealth. For that reason, Smith agrees with Rousseau that people also particularly value the esteem of the rich if it can be directed to themselves.

This explains the motivation for a life of wealth and power for oneself that, in Griswold's severe judgment, puts a false evaluative belief (as Scanlon might phrase it) at the core of Smithian system: that our search for happiness is marred by a "deception" (Griswold 1999, p.222) or a "comic irony":

> First, we yearn for the harmony or beauty of a correspondence of sentiments with spectators that we (rightly) imagine is the good fortune of the wealthy and powerful. Second, the spectators' approval of the wealthy and powerful is "disinterested" (I.iii.3.2.), . . . Both levels of aesthetic appreciation are the work of the imagination, yet the association of happiness with that seemingly beautiful life is fallacious . . .we are plunged into the world of unceasing work, of "bettering our condition" and therefore of unhappiness. Bettering our condition leaves us "constantly dissatisfied" (VI.iii.51). . . . The comic irony of this general picture of human life is unmistakable.[21] (Griswold 1999, pp.221–2)

This Smithian explanation of the impulse to Veblen's conspicuous consumption—the source of this comic irony—is grounded on our fear of being a "nobody" in the eyes of others. How strong is this impulse?

Phillip Pettit and Geoffrey Brennan, in their Smith-inspired account of the economy of esteem that we will consider below, cite John Adams:

> He feels himself out of the light of others, groping in the dark. Mankind takes no notice of him; he rambles and wanders unheeded. . . . He is not disapproved of, censured or reproached: he is only not seen. This total

[21] This comic irony undermines Smith's otherwise optimistic account of how the new egalitarian economic order produces better forms of governance bringing societal standards in line with the perspective of the ideal observer (Herzog 2013, p.135). Herzog notes that Smith is saved from inconsistency by his belief that moral education "direct[s] vanity to its proper objects' (Smith 1776/1981, VI.III.46). A correct moral education guides citizens to respect the different logics of agency of life's different spheres governed by the master virtue of "self-command" (Herzog 2013, p.132).

> inattention to him mortifying, painful and cruel. . . . To feel ourselves unheeded chills the most pleasing hope—damps the most fond desire—checks the most agreeable wish—disappoints the most ardent expectations of human nature. (Adams 1790/1973, no.5)

Adams's example is of an overlooked performer, for whom the pains of not being recognized are particularly a blow. But we can infer that for Adams, and for Smith, in the commercial realm all of us seek the limelight. Darwall argues that this is because attention is accompanied by sympathy—and hence approbation (Darwall 2010). The desire for wealth, then, is the desire for distinction (as Rousseau insisted) but with a typical twist Smith argues that the wealthy of the previous social system, feudalism, brought about their own downfall by indulging in a taste for "trinkets and baubles". In commercial society, too, the Smithian view is that we can expect the wealthy to dissipate their wealth quite rapidly over a generation or so through reckless consumption. Piketty has observed Condorcet's parallel observation that:

> It is easy to prove that fortunes tend naturally toward equality, and their excessive disproportion either cannot exist or must promptly cease if civil laws do not establish artificial means of perpetuating and combining them, and if freedom of commerce and industry eliminate the advantages that any prohibitive law or fiscal right gives to acquired wealth. (Condorcet 1794, p.380; Piketty 2020, cited at pp.117–8).

As Herzog rightly notes, Smith is explicit about the psychological costs of stepping on to the treadmill of positional competition (Herzog 2013, p.127). In *The Theory of Moral Sentiments*, he tells the tale of a poor man's son whose life is wholly consumed by emulation of the rich and successful at the cost of any reasonable conception of his own happiness (Smith 1776/1981, IV.I.8, 181).

For Smith, only the correct formation of character in private education can avoid this disastrous outcome, where the approval of those whom one imagines to be the rich and powerful substitutes in a person's moral judgement for the approval of the impartial spectator. Admiration and emulation of the rich, then, can be a source of moral corruption in a way we will discuss in more detail in chapter 11 (Smith 1776/1981, I.iii.3.i). Rasmussen argues that this, in fact, is why Smith is concerned with extreme inequality: our attention is caught by the spectacularly rich, but this leads to our comparative lack of sympathy for the poor (Rasmussen 2016). The rich themselves spurn moral standards, because they are admired anyway; it is the middling sort who are led astray by the antics of the rich because they anticipate their own success in becoming wealthy and feel able to act with impunity (Rasmussen 2016, p.349). They suffer from what one might call "Colonel Tom Parker Syndrome" given that Elvis's notorious manager apocryphally claimed that "you don't have to be nice to people you meet on the way up if you're not coming down again".

Once again, this seems to be a substantive concession to Rousseau's critique that the nascent commercial society sets up a concern with status evaluation that is degrading to all and, in the meantime, puts us all on the treadmill of positional competition with no real winners. Yet Rasmussen claims that this concession needs to go into the overall assessment of both the merits and defects of commercial society: "doux commerce" sees the standard-setting behaviour of the impartial spectator spread throughout society, radiating from its commercial life to its legal and political institutions.[22] Poverty, dependence, and fear are removed by impartial justice and governance in addition to the removal of economic dependence (in Smith's special sense) (Rasmussen 2008, p.13). The overall reckoning, once more, favours the system of natural liberty.

However, historical perspective matters here: there is nothing like the Easterlin hypothesis in Smith's worldview—how could there be, when the path of future economic development was so uncertain? And no one troubled by the Easterlin paradox is denying that it was an achievement to raise everyone in an affluent society of our time to the point where they do not have to worry about material needs. The point is simply that this achievement was the necessary presupposition of a new set of problems.

Another subtlety lies in Smith's account of the division of labour. Geoffrey Brennan has suggested that the thematization of this is the signature achievement of *The Wealth of Nations*—and we agree (Thomas 2017, p.164 ff). This system of commercial society works best if each of us takes a primary interest

[22] Rasmussen notes that Smith's close friend David Hume had a conception of happiness more tied to action than tranquillity and Smith could have contested Rousseau's critique of commercial society by contesting his view of happiness as tranquillity. But, in fact, Smith shares Rousseau's view of happiness as largely consisting in tranquil self-sufficiency—Stoic *ataraxia*—to which Smith adds enjoyment or pleasure (Rasmussen 2008, pp.83–4). Smith's conception of the ingredients of happiness is centred on loving relationships and taking pleasure in having acted virtuously (Rasmussen 2008, pp.83–4). Material prosperity matters up to a point, but the enjoyment of luxuries adds little to happiness.

in our own case and is motivated to better ourselves. The main educative effect of the market is that it makes it advantageous to develop self-control and cultivate the virtue of prudential long-term planning (Herzog 2013, chapter 5.2). It is the division of labour that facilitates each of these goals. Each of us can specialize in improving ourselves in key respects relevant to our market entitlements. That, of course, means that unlike the self-sufficient small farmer, we produce (one aspect of) only one product so we must take our wages to the market to satisfy our other desires. Markets are there to overcome our cognitive limitations, and Smith pioneers this crucial, epistemic, case for markets (Thomas 2017). However, while this diremption in human nature became central to the Marxist critique of capitalism, concerns over the psychological effect of the division of labour also originate with Smith.[23]

Smith's particular concern, writing for his time, is with what we would now call "the working poor"—those for whom the new commercial society creates new opportunities to better themselves and their dependents. But the first theorizer of the division of labour also saw the potentially damaging effect on workers' minds of repetitive specialized labour (Smith 1776/1981, V.I.Conc.5). This requires redress from a publicly funded education system (Smith 1776/1981, V.I.III.II,50).[24] In other respects, however, the independent worker, even if a specialist, exhibits the master virtue of self-command while also being more enterprising and engaged than the slave or feudal labourer (Herzog 2013, pp.121–2). (We can see here the origins of the worker as engaged "entrepreneur of the self" described by Boltanski and Chiapello.)

For those familiar with Sartre's brilliant account of the relationship between shame, the gaze of the other, and the very idea of the self as existing "for another", all of these ideas are foreshadowed in Smith (Smith 1776/1981, III.III.38; Thomas 2010).[25] The presence of another, in the guise of a "spectator", triggers the moral sentiments. Smith combines this psychological observation with the sociological observation that the rural worker, moving from the village to the newly industrializing city, loses the context

[23] Rasmussen makes a plausible case that Smith's critique of the psychological effect of the division of labour is even harsher than Rousseau's (Rasmussen 2008, p.72).

[24] This inability to develop the full range of one's mental capacities is psychologically damaging, producing an incapacity to sympathize with others, and hence a political immaturity in which a person of limited horizons is prey to religious fanaticism or political factionalism. The effect, in either case, is social instability (Smith 1776/1981, V).

[25] As Herzog notes, "'[L]iving only in the opinion of others', which Rousseau had decried as an aspect of the moral corruption of modern society, is for Smith the very condition of being human" (Herzog 2013, pp.65–6).

in which their character is constituted by their circle of acquaintance. They have a character only as known by others. In the obscurity and anonymity of the city these newly urbanized poor lose their characters, in this sense, and become vicious. They lack the corrective gaze of those who take an interest in them in the narrower circles of acquaintance in rural life (Smith 1776/1981, V.I.III.III.1.2). In other words, they risk becoming a "nobody" in a way that leads to their degradation. Conversely, for the sake of one's own prosperity in the market, a person's character ought to matter to him and her as a matter of commercial probity—at least with those they deal with regularly.

For Smith, our capacity for "truck, barter and exchange" underpins the division of labour whereby the productive surplus turns "as it were, into a common stock" (Smith 1776/1981, I.II.2). Mutual exchange places people in relations that benefit each and avoids the domination of any citizen by any other. In commercial society, republican independence becomes accessible to all, as much through the wage labour relationship as via capital holding. The key idea is that, via the division of labour in commercial society, one is not beholden to any person in particular for one's livelihood (Smith 1776/1981, III.IV.11 ff; Herzog 2013, p.70). Smith is an opponent of the power of monopolies that undermine this capacity for commercial society to liberate the individual.

6.3 From Smith to Hegel

Hegel's account of commercial society is indebted to his engagement with both Rousseau and Smith. In her comparative study of Smith and Hegel, Herzog notes that Smith's conception of the individual is not as embedded in the roles specific to commercial society as Hegel's conception of membership in a corporation. It is through identification with a role in market society and its attendant duties that a man—Hegel's conception is gendered—finds a path to self-realization through work and the establishing of one's "individuality" in Hegel's technical sense of that word.[26]

The mutual dependence that so alarmed Rousseau, and which framed Hegel's conception of the problem, is finally understood "not as limiting, but

[26] "Individuality [is the] mediation of universal and particular. . . . The one principal of civil society is the 'concrete' person, *das Besondere*, someone who has her own particular ends, unique to her" (Pippin 2020, p.578).

as self-realizing for each" (Pippin 2020, p.579).[27] The move from individuality to sociality is a problem in Rousseau; Smith qualifies it via his careful distinction between selfishness and interest; Hegel's argument is the culmination of this progression given that the right kind of social relation is the *only* way to realize the true freedom of the individual. Sociality is not the problem, it is the solution, and indeed the solution *for* each individual. It is a solution both for any and for all.

Hegel was more aware than Smith of the ugly realities of the English Industrial Revolution. Perhaps that acquaintance underlies the fact that his account of the market is, as Herzog puts it, more "chaotic and Dionysian than the Smithian market" (Herzog 2013, p.43). In the background is Hegel's claim that only through inter-subjectivity can we jointly realize each other's freedom and equality through recognition. We find ourselves in a pre-given social order that is the trace of such joint self-constitution as norm-responsive creatures.

Writing the philosophy "for his time", which Hegel understood as the mission of the philosopher, he took the relevant "Sitten" (customs) of his time to be those of the constitutional state, family, and the economy. The free self aims to find these social structures as the realization of their individual freedom together with the freedom of others (Herzog 2013, p.49). As Pippin puts it:

> We would normally think that in order for all and each to be free, a particular subject must sacrifice a full realization of freedom in consideration of the other. That is what Hegel wants to avoid.... He thinks the right sort of institutions would make it possible to experience the other and objective institutions as the full realization of freedom rather than its sacrifice. (Pippin 2020, pp.572–3)

It is, to use a form of words that was appealing to Rawls, a project of "reconciliation"—of either recognizing or creating a social world that is hospitable to the expression of one's moral powers (in Rawls's conception) of rationality and reasonableness (Thomas 2017, p.30). The question, then, is how this

[27] This "mediated" universality in commercial society is, as it were, a way station to our full joint realization of our freedom in the state. Pippin is careful to separate this final form from the sectoral representation of the state in the regulation of commercial society, the *Rechtspflege* in charge of the state regulation of commerce (Pippin 2020, p.580).

general frame is applied to Hegel's conception of the market—via his intellectual engagement with the nascent science of political economy.

The location of the market in "civil society" draws on Hegel's technical use of that phrase in his system—not our modern sense of the associational space between family and the state. Importantly for Hegel—as it was for Smith and will be for Rawls—the market also plays an educative role in character formation (Herzog 2013, p.123).[28] The individuals in civil society are "particular" subjects who are drawn together into a system of mutual dependence. To preserve their standing to achieve the status of "individuals", this association must be underpinned by rights, notably the right to private property and the coercive legal institutions correlated with it. Only with this context in place can the individual pursue his or her interests, which are psychologically complex phenomena. Following fashion, or the desire to be esteemed, can be a person's "interest" in this broad sense of the term (Herzog 2013, p.54). Yet from this chaos of competing interests a stable form of social order emerges that, as Herzog notes, certainly has Smithian overtones: mutual dependence, reciprocity, and the advanced form of the division of labour emergent in industrial society.

Nevertheless, Hegel is more attuned than Smith to the chaos within this order if one focuses not on the macro-level system, but on its micro-level interactions. It is a "battlefield" of each competitor against every other and, indeed, against the state. Limited information, shifting preferences, unclear lines of mutual dependence, and caprice make the market inscrutable and the system inherently unstable. In this battle, both the winners and the losers actually lose out: civil society is "a spectacle of extravagance and misery"—the insightful phrase we have taken as our title—where the winners are equally degraded. They share with the losers, in Hegel's words, "the physical and ethical degeneration common to them both" (Herzog 2013, p.55; Hegel 1820/1991, §185). That seems a direct echo of Rousseau's claim that "master and slave degrade each other" (Rousseau 1762/1964, Bk 2, p.70).

Compared to Smith, then, Hegel's conception of the market is more plagued by instability and dysfunction. Caprice and emotion play a crucial part in generating this instability (Herzog 2013, p.88). As Herzog notes, Hegel is sceptical about the very idea that a person could deserve any market entitlements. In a market driven by fashion, need the manufacturer or merchant whose goods are now "passé" be any less deserving than when

[28] A concern originating with Rousseau's *Emile*.

their goods were in fashion (Herzog 2013, p.88)? This is an important contrast with Smith, for whom "the basic argument is that in markets the free decisions by a large number of individuals result in patterns that resemble the judgements of an impartial spectator, and this impartial spectator makes judgements based on an idea of desert" (Herzog 2013, pp.89–90). For Smith, an appropriate degree of everyday virtue (not perfection) must find its reward—at least for the limited class of "bourgeois virtues" (Herzog 2013, p.91). This is, indeed, a matter of desert and not entitlement, as this is the moral ideal that generally useful actions would attract the gratitude of the impartial spectator and hence society as a whole, but the virtuous person has no right to this approbation.

This partly explains the important macro-level dysfunctions that Hegel emphasizes: structural unemployment, a dangerous underclass—and overclass—and a lack of any systemic mechanisms to overcome them. Herzog suggests that it is because Hegel lacked a full appreciation of the resources of market societies to overcome these limitations that he is driven to emphasize the mechanisms for the containment of market society and its inherent dangers (Herzog 2013, p.56). However, perhaps a deeper appreciation of the nature of emergent modern capitalism might lead one to share Hegel's belief in the necessity for such containment mechanisms.

As Pippin notes, Hegel is sceptical about particular emergent commercial practices. Given the interest of factory owners in simplifying and then mechanizing work, there is a potent threat to workers' desire to be recognized as having individual worth. Factory owners actively seek to "de-skill" workers in this way, and deaden their sensibilities, because of the profit motive (Pippin 2020, p.580). The concern is that this is paradigmatic of processes that are essential to capitalism and hence cannot be addressed by state regulation. There is, as it were, no way back from the destruction of a person's dignity and self-worth involved in nascent industrial capitalism and the way in which it interprets the division of labour.

Consider Hegel's conception of the emotional regime of market societies. Hegel noted that Rousseau's diagnosis of the pathologies of commercial society involves the claim that apparently simple drives can be conceptually structured by reason and imagination. Hegel agreed that this sharply separated the "desires" of animals from the complex structure of desire in rational animals such as ourselves. Rousseauian amour-propre becomes, for Hegel, the desire for recognition—recognition from others on the terms dictated by the commonly established norms. This explains the centrality in Hegel's conception of the overriding aim of being recognized as a "somebody" that is also at the core of Smith's system (Hegel 1820/1991, §207Z). The problem is, as Herzog notes, that:

> Although . . . for Hegel the liberating from purely biological needs is an aspect of the development towards freedom in human history, it can lead to psychological afflictions. Men want to be equal with others (preferably with those who have more), but they also wish to be different . . . which is another source of the "multiplication of needs and their expansion".[29] (Herzog 2013, p.128)

This is recognition in the light of prevailing norms as expressed by the institutional structure one shares with those who will appraise you. A presupposition of this is that the sphere of work is a way to detach oneself from one's immediate impulses, control and regulate them, and relate to the similarly objective interests of others. Herzog notes the importance to Hegel of this "moment of liberation intrinsic to work" (Hegel 1820/1991, §194; Herzog 2013, p.123). This character formation is a "necessity" of participation in the marketplace (Hegel 1820/1991, §186).

For Hegel, commercial society, driven by the Smithian division of labour, leads to our material inter-dependence and the proliferation of desire. We seek to be idiosyncratic individuals in a community governed by shared norms of recognition. Each of us needs to conform, and to stand out, or at least to pretend to stand out—and this latter element introduces competition. Money is, in this respect uniquely damaging as it offers a means of commensurating all comparisons.[30] However, commercial society also introduces the capacity for limitless accumulation. It accelerates the process of detaching a person from the communal roles and norms that set the terms of recognition, while offering a channel for competition in which desire can never be satisfied. As Jeffrey Church puts it:

> [I]ndividuals in a "false infinite" can never find satisfaction, because they do not belong to a concrete community that can provide them with recognition. Rather, they find themselves competing with a faceless crowd

[29] The interpolated final quotation is from (Hegel 1820/1991, §193).

[30] Herzog makes a convincing case that both Smith and Hegel's views can be interpreted using Walzer's theory of justice (Herzog 2013, p.134; Walzer, 1983). See also (Pippin 2020, p.573).

> of selfish individuals who will never offer recognition but only will defeat every effort of the individual to find completeness—the "false infinite" appears as an infinite series of desires without an internal principle of satisfaction. (Church 2010, p.132)

The Hobbesian view of negative freedom and the nature of desire go hand in hand: given that desires are simple, non-conceptualized, impulses, freedom consists in their untrammelled exercise. However, Hegel believes that as complex states mediated by social norms, human desires can be caught up in false conceptualizations that make them insatiable in the way that Hobbesian desires are intrinsically insatiable. The modern market brings about this dangerous transformation of desire into a pathological form. In the latter setting, Hegel fears that desire can become un-anchored, "arbitrary", and placed beyond the social contexts that are the only possible location for the genuine satisfaction of desire. For Hegel, true freedom is within a self-determined sphere: a social context freely chosen. The market is a profound threat to this ideal as it sets up a new sphere in which desire may be unleashed, made insatiable, while also splitting society into those who may gain from the new social order and those permanently excluded from it. Whatever the benefits of market society, Hegel clearly thinks that it will never offer those benefits to all.

This political psychology is the philosophical basis for Hegel's account of the mediating institutions of civil society rooted in economic life. Crucial here is the emancipatory effect of work of the right kind. Through work the individual can achieve personal freedom while also being recognized in the light of established social norms attaching to roles. Hegel acknowledges that private interests are inescapable under modern conditions. The question is which institutions stabilize them and channel such interests for the common good. Hegel answers that question by appealing to the corporations.[31] These are voluntary associations which reflect the individual's desire to control one's own economic fate:

> This is one reason the modern phenomenon of "the rabble" is so problematic, according to Hegel—the class of the poor are systematically disadvantaged by the modern market such that they perceive themselves as "infinite,

[31] By contrast, Adam Smith was suspicious of the guild system as "favoring employers and workers at the expense of apprentices and the public" (Boucoyannis 2013, p.1060).

> free" beings yet as utterly without control of their own destiny. (Church 2010, p.133)

It is the role of the intermediate corporations of the three estates of economic life to ground recognition in one's economic role as judged by one's peers in the relevant corporation. They solve the recognition problem and stop it being pathologically converted into the desire for money via the establishment of common norms that supply the terms for recognition. Once again, the contrast is with the fate of the "rabble":

> The poor person cannot feel honor in his situation as he is not recognised as "somebody". He does not enjoy the dignity of recognizing the success of his own agency in the fruits of his efforts. He does not feel a sense of belongingness with others in working for this common effort and shared good to which they are jointly tending. He feels himself to be a "nobody". (Church 2010, p.135)

In a series of concentric circles, the peer groups of the corporations embed the individual in the Estates and mediate a psychological identification with the State as a whole being the fundamental enabling condition of individual freedom.[32] They also stand as a check against centralized state power impinging on the freedom of the individual. Again, by contrast, the rabble stand outside political society, impotently raging against it.

It is a short step to connect this Hegelian idea with Rawls's conception of the worst off to highlight the very features that the latter do not share with Hegel's rabble. Rawls's worst off citizens are "working members of society" doing meaningful work (Freeman 2013, p.22). They are capable of "doing their full share" of handicap-adjusted economic reciprocity and are able to "manage their own affairs" (Rawls 2001, p.131). As we will see below, Rawls's critique of welfare state capitalism focuses precisely on the exclusion and alienation of those who feel socially excluded. Church continues his exposition of Hegel's view:

[32] Pippin explains why he finds Hegel's appeal to corporations to redress the inescapable problems of commercial society wholly unconvincing: "Corporations that are organized around the interests of different worker groups cannot be the basis of any true universal equal standing among all" (Pippin 2020, p.584). Hegel stressed how even the citizen who finds the good fortune of extravagant wealth or poverty and social exclusion are still redeemed by corporation membership. Pippin thinks that claim is strained too, particularly in the latter case: that group solidarity would not be sustainable if it had to "carry" the claims of its unemployed members.

> Instead, the poor need to depend on the "contingency" of goodwill and charity, which does not encourage an ethic of self-determination, but dependence, passivity and "laziness". . . . Such a cycle makes the poor increasingly unfit for membership in a community by rendering each individual with an ever more attenuated sense of one's "self-dependence" and of "the feeling of standing on [one's] own feet". (Church 2010, p.135)

Our modern idiom, in an attempt to avoid stigmatizing the poor, prefers to speak of "social exclusion". Hegel is explicit that the element of exclusion is caused by poverty and that the poor suffer distinctive psychological harms. Their desires are unlimited, but they are cut off from the only means of satisfying them. This discussion of the rabble evolves into Marx and Engel's description of the lumpenproletariat in the *Communist Manifesto* as "the dangerous class, the social scum, that passively rotting mass thrown off by the lowest layers of the old society" (Marx and Engels 1848/2011, p.76).

It follows, then, that inescapable involuntary unemployment and the consequence of what we now call "social exclusion" is one of Hegel's main concerns (Hegel 1820/1991, §240 ff). Hegel feared that commercial society would simply not have the capacity to generate paid employment for all and those trapped in unemployment would become angry and resentful of their lot forming an underclass. The precarity of employment would also fail to allow even the working poor to rely on improved prospects. If the market is a scene of competitive struggle, and if it is underpinned by a life of destitution, then life within it will become even more competitive as the stakes of employment are higher. As Herzog notes:

> The Smithian vision that economic growth would expand the cake for all is absent from Hegel's view of the modern economy. He also lacks any discussion of the role of capital accumulation for economic growth. (Herzog 2013, p.56)

Hence Hegel's emphasis on extensive regulation of what seemed to him a highly dysfunctional system: public authority extends not only to the regulation of the market and the protection of property but also to guarantee a right to a livelihood. Core commodities were to have their prices regulated by the state—as they still are (Hockett 2019).

The corporations also take advantage of a fact we have emphasized: the importance to welfare of peer group comparison. Here, in the corporations,

Hegel finds terms of social engagement between peers that can act as a stable support for recognition and respect in one's "second family" (Hegel 1820/1991, §238, §252; Herzog 2013, p.57). Notably, these corporations offer social insurance to their members. Once again, we see the origins of the evolution of work in the twentieth century as a place where conflict between social classes is softened, the idiom of management is inflected with therapeutic valence, and a person finds his or her workplace to be a second family.

Putting these pieces together, Herzog suggests that Hegel wants production to be organized by the corporations, while it is unclear whether there could be other producers on the market too (Herzog 2013, p.58). Hegel does not fully theorize or explain the nexus between producers and consumers: he certainly does not have the modern Walrasian notion of a market being cleared by price.

In the background lies the Hegelian state: not the public or public-private supervision of the market, but the sovereign power of the state itself. Given Hegel's ambivalence about the impact of the market on social relations, it is a good question why the state tolerates its destabilizing influence. Herzog gives the answer: Hegel's primary concern is freedom, and commercial society is one social sphere in which a modern society enables a new form of commercial freedom compared to its feudal antecedents (Herzog 2013, pp.59–60). Since, however, for Hegel, both commercial society, organized by the corporations, and civil society are essentially incomplete, they must be complemented by the state that meets the Aristotelian standard of self-sufficiency for a political unit. This dimension of citizenship is where particular citizens accept the authority of the social order over their private ends so that the co-instantiation of everyone's freedom can be achieved.[33] This is, for Herzog, where Smith's and Hegel's visions converge:

> The Smithian legislator who embodies the perspective of the impartial spectator corresponds to the "universal sphere" of the Hegelian state that stands above private interests and impartially serves the common good. (Herzog 2013, p.138)

[33] Herzog also notes the missing element of this conception from our perspective: our answer to the question of "who guards the guardians" is democratic oversight, a notion "present only in rudiments in Smith and Hegel" (Herzog 2013, p.145).

As Rasmussen notes, Smith's stringent critique of aspects of commercial society leads to his ultimate endorsement of the system of natural liberty as he calculates the various trade-offs that this new social system highlights. We can now enumerate the primary risks that Hegel identifies in the commercial sphere of a modern society.

Commercial society, according to Hegel, threatens to expand the realm of desire and, in the process, threatens to make it insatiable. Hegel fears that individuals may be corrupted towards a pure selfishness that cuts them off from the very institutional norm setting that is the only way for the desire for recognition legitimately to be satisfied. The individual ends up atomized, and alone, living solely at the mercy of the good judgement of others, but lacking the shared normative terms on which this recognition could take place. The endpoint of this process is individual "misery" in a social order that exhibits, for different classes of people, both "extravagance and misery" (Hegel 1820/1991, §185).[34]

The parallelism here is important: the excluded poor do not feel themselves to be part of society leading to Hegel's account of the "rabble". But it is important to emphasize that, for Hegel, neither do the rich feel themselves part of society. He also refers to the "rich rabble" ("reiche Pöbel") (Pippin 2020, p.581). Key to this explanation is the educative effect of work and the self-realization that it affords people. Hegel thought it was inevitable that commercial society would produce both great wealth for some and poverty for many. But both groups are cut off from work:

> The premise for both accounts is that labor is essential in any scheme of actualized freedom. . . . This educative benefit *does not happen through exchange but through work and the positive, educative experience of a vital dependence on others.* (Pippin 2020, p.581, emphasis added)

It is this experience that is unavailable to the socially excluded, poor rabble at the bottom end of the distribution and to the rich rabble at the top. They either do not work at all, or, if they do, they do not experience it as a necessity. Their sole relation to the economy is as consumers.

[34] Quoted also by Herzog, who notes that she has altered the standard translation of that phrase which we have taken as the title for this book (Herzog 2013, p.106). She also notes, later, the clear implication that the wealthy are just as corrupted by economic competition as the poor in Hegel's critique (Herzog 2013, p.138).

They also have, Hegel predicts, deeply anti-social attitudes of thinking they are above respecting other people's rights and feel they can act with impunity (Pippin 2020, p.581). They are, in that sense, "above" the very idea of a societal good:

> Hegel thus anticipates the paradoxical phenomenon of ludicrously wealthy and privileged burghers who feel constantly aggrieved about state "seizure" of their money in taxes, and who spend a great deal of money corrupting the political process to prevent such seizures and who often form common cause with the equally disenfranchised poor, who can easily be manipulated by populist and nationalist sentiment. (Pippin 2020, p.581)

The problem is even worse, from Hegel's own perspective, as there cannot be a Smithian "trade-off" here in the sense of modern commercial society making the rich and poor psychologically distressed while improving human well-being in the aggregate. That is because market society, mediated via the corporations, is fundamental to the realization of the right kind of freedom-in-dependence (Pippin 2020, p.583).

If Smith and Hegel are responding to a problem set for them by Rousseau, the Hegelian answer, unlike Smith's, cannot be a balancing of advantages and disadvantages. Emancipation must be emancipation for all, not merely for some. We cannot simply add a separate calculation of the balance of overall well-being between three groups: first, those emancipated through work via the corporations; second, the rich rabble; third, the poor rabble. For Hegel, freedom is too essential to a person's core interests for that to be a realistic method of tallying up the advantages and disadvantages of commercial society. Hence, as Bernard Yack noted, the rationale for the development of Hegel's ideas towards the demand for a total transformation of social relations—and hence society—typical of Left Hegelianism (Yack 1986).

Pippin adds a further consideration to Hegel's argument: that as capitalism develops, "modern commodity production" depends on the creation of "values distinct to a market economy, well beyond the general commitment to the value of freedom" (Pippin 2020). If we are tolerant of commercial society, in spite of serious and ineradicable problems, because it can contribute to the egalitarian aim of mutual recognition via work, then it matters if the profit motive takes on an intrinsic value of its own. (Admittedly, later in its historical development.) That is because:

> Capital for Hegel is just accumulated wealth: it does not become a value in itself. And it obviously does in capitalism, inverting Hegel's treatment of money as a mere means, as the ends of capitalism subordinate all human value, including the human value most important for Hegel, equality as mutuality of recognition. Anyone who ignores the value of maximizing profit for some such human end insures their competitive disadvantage and eventual ruin. (Pippin 2020, p.582)

This argument develops Hegel's concerns about market society into the view that Pippin thinks he ought to have held: that the emergent features of capitalism that Hegel has identified are simply, in his own terms, "unreasonable" as a social form. Forming a bridge to Marxism, Pippin suggests that Hegel ought to have concluded that only a radical historical transition could lead to the realization of his central values given that they could not be realized in commercial society. There is no avoiding:

> [T]he incompatibility of a productive system in which the constraints of competitiveness require the maximization of profit and the minimization of the cost of labour, with the real social bases of self-respect and the achievement of standing in the eyes of others. (Pippin 2020)

For Pippin, then, Hegel's pessimism about the market is not thoroughgoing enough. However, even his moderate pessimism clashes with Smithian optimism.

Herzog is right that their respective views of the nature of employment are central to this difference. For Hegel, recognition requires that a person be embedded in the life of a corporation: that they occupy a specific professional role from which it is hard to extract oneself. Complementarily, Hegel's incomplete conception of the market means that he never thinks that full employment for all is a realistic goal. Smith's people of "middling rank" and the emergent working class looking to improve their lot can find an economic niche, free from domination, where marketing their labour in a flexible labour market with a high degree of free opportunities does offer the prospect of long-term improvement for all. Those markets need to be freed of the vestiges of cartels and monopolies. Underpinning this specific conflict is a clash of visions.

A crucial demarcation line between Smith and Hegel, then, is over the long-term problem of poverty. As Herzog points out, both take rights as prior to market participation and constrained by the substantive constraint of the co-realizability of these rights for all. Market transactions, then, cannot undo these protections. However, even Smith was aware that the emancipatory potential of the market could be undermined if, as in his example of a group of colliers and salters in Scotland for whom higher pay was combined with restricted liberties, an employer has what we would call an "expensive taste" for dominating others (LJ(A) 92; Herzog 2013, p.102).[35] He was also aware of the problem of oligarchy: we have noted his pathological dislike of rent-seeking merchants and manufacturers. He also drew attention to the leveraging of economic success into political influence, not least for the aim of perpetuating one's economic advantages (Thomas 2017). Herzog argues that the design of the market is innocent here—it is the anti-social preferences for discrimination and domination that agents bring to the market that is the issue. Conversely, Rasmussen argues it is one of Smith's insights that it is the structure of the market that affords these merchants and manufacturers the rent-seeking opportunities that they seize (Rasmussen 2008, p.80; Smith 1776/1981, I.VI.8, 67).

Smith retains an optimism that markets sustain growth that can be inclusive in a way that potentially makes this process "win/win" for everyone. If everyone wins, then the poor win too, even if not as handsomely as those above them in the distributive order. Smith gives particular priority to the opportunities and well-being of the working poor in justifying market society overall. He thinks that Rousseau neglects that point: the worst off would be even worse off without commercial society (Rasmussen 2008). Hegel thinks the opposite: that there is no realistic prospect of inclusive growth. Furthermore, commercial society induces immiseration. Conversely, then, the worst off are worse off for the existence of commercial society than they would have been without it.

One explanation for this divergence is that, on the chaotic battlefield of the competitive market, Hegel notices a true generalization that those with prior advantages leverage them to generate increased advantage. (We would

[35] Following an Act of Parliament of 1806, employed colliers and salters in Scotland were, in effect, bonded workers—they could legally only be offered new employment if their current employer would supply them with a testimonial. The payment of a token gift recruited the worker's children into the same arrangement (which involved, for example, a six-day working week). An individual worker could not be sold, but the sale of a colliery would include the sale of its workers (Weinstein, 2019). The example is discussed in both versions of Smith's "Lectures on Jurisprudence" compiled from students' lecture notes, namely, the "Report of 1762–3" and the "Report of 1766", conventionally referred to as LJ(A) and LJ(B), respectively.

now call this "cumulative advantage" (Salganik, Dodds, and Watts 2006).) In particular, and anticipating Marx, those with large holdings of capital have a bargaining advantage over labour. In markets driven by caprice and accident, involuntary unemployment is a frequent occurrence. Given his conception of what markets are, Hegel simply does not envisage them expanding to provide commercial opportunities for all. This focus on the necessity of involuntary employment is crucial (Hegel 1820/1991; Herzog 2013). There is money enough for the poor, mediated by private charity, but not the creation of jobs that would provide a path to mutual recognition and self-respect. Hegel actually offers a sophisticated objection to state mandated full employment: that the creation of "make work" would lead to over-production and, we would say, generate deflationary pressures (Herzog 2013, pp.106–7). The problem of poverty would not have been solved in one's own country leading, in Hegel's view, to the project of colonization.

The increasing sophistication of economic theory means that we can formulate rejoinders to these concerns. John Hobson agreed with Hegel that the imperial impulse had a macro-economic cause in domestic inequality (Hobson 1902). The plutocracies of Edwardian England and elsewhere hoarded surplus capital while a structural deficit in consumption—produced by inequality—saw capitalist elites look for returns on their investments in colonial markets.[36] Hobson's solution was simple: a project of domestic justice and equality and the elimination of this structural deficit in consumption.[37] This reflects a non-Hegelian understanding of the scope of commercial society. That full employment is an achievable policy goal and not inflationary is the central claim of Keynesianism and its more recent descendant, post-Keynesian "modern monetary theory" (Tcherneva 2013; Keynes 1936/1964; Thomas 2020b).[38] That Hegel's critique has convincing

[36] Piketty supplies the empirical data: at the time Hobson wrote, the wealthy of France and the United Kingdom held foreign investments of "immense (and to this day unequalled) scope ... in 1914, on the eve of World War I, the UK's net foreign assets ... amounted to 190 percent (or nearly two year's worth) of the country's national income. French investors were not far behind, with net foreign assets worth more than 120 percent of French national income in 1914" (Piketty 2020). By comparison, mercantilists of recent history—countries with deliberately engineered trade surpluses then reinvested overseas—have foreign investments representing 60%–80% of national income (Germany and Japan) and 20% in China (as of 2018) (Piketty 2020, p.279).

[37] Hobson's basis thesis has been endorsed, and his arguments updated, for our post-colonial world in (Klein and Pettis 2020). They argue that co-ordination between elites across various jurisdictions is a reflection of, and deepens, intra-societal inequality at the service of global inequality. Endorsement of Hobson's explanation of the causes of imperialism is not to endorse the racism and anti-semitism that are also present in his book.

[38] As we have noted, this position was anticipated by Fichte.

answers does not detract from his prescience and insight in framing the issue this way.

Herzog also notes that, while Smith and Hegel differ over the eradicability of poverty, they share an explanation of its psychological harms by drawing on their respective emotional regimes. It is not simply that a person drops below a certain relative material threshold: it is really about what this means in emotional terms. Smith emphasizes the shame of poverty, hence his famous requirement that we will examine in detail in chapter 11 that everyone ought to have the material means to appear in public without shame. The long-run working of society will tend, in his view, to ameliorate the structural sources of inequality, produce a tendency to reduced inequality, and in the process enhance mutual respect and sympathy.

Hegel argues that the poor compare themselves to those above them in their own society and are scarcely comforted by the thought that they are better off than the poor in less developed countries. The poor have had desires instilled in them by commercial society that they can never realize. Their anger and resentment sees them drop to the level of the "rabble". As Herzog points out, this is even more problematic in Hegel's scheme as not merely economic participation but also political participation is mediated by the estates and corporations (Herzog 2013, p.115). Those who have fallen into the rabble lack political representation, too.

We can hope to be doing better in our own affluent societies, and to emphasize that even the worst off have a vote. However, to the extent that associational social capital, the reach of political parties and trade unions and other civil society organizations are weakest in the case of the worst off, here too, the "fair value" of the political liberties of the worst off is not realized. As Jeffrey Edward Green puts it, in a political society organized around extremes of material inequality an oligarchic politics divides us into "the Many" and "the Few" reducing the former to passivity, resentment, and what he calls a "plebeian condition" comparable to the plebeians of ancient Rome (Green 2016). However, the latter at least had their own forms of recognition in an agonistic political system that offered them the means of surveilling and addressing the rich; in our own putatively "classless" societies these mechanisms are unavailable.

From this summary it seems that the worst possible combination would be for a system of natural liberty to be corrupted by the drift to oligarchy. In such a case, the small group of merchants and industrialists whom Smith cautioned against would induce structural inequality via their oligarchic influence on state policy. At least, in Hegel, the failure to provide employment for all is a structural flaw in the system; post-Keynes and Kalecki we have a deeper economic understanding of Marx's argument that the creation of involuntary unemployment was a disciplinary measure to control workers. This undermines the free exit and flexibility of re-deployed labour that Smith sees as essential to market societies' potential emancipation of all workers from dependence on any particular "other"—his vision of a society without domination. Finally, the psychological effects on the worst off in a society with enforced involuntary unemployment will be exactly as Smith and Hegel feared: shame, stigmatization, and social exclusion. This depressing narrative is, needless to say, central to the argument of this book 250 years after these arguments were formulated: Hegel's worst fears have been realized in our capitalist market societies that are, indeed, scenes of both extravagance and misery.

6.4 The New Inequality in a Classical Frame

To summarize, then: Rousseau is condemnatory of market society; Smith guardedly optimistic; Hegel falls somewhere between the two while Robert B. Pippin argues this is not the view Hegel ought to have held. Clearly, it takes some interpretative work to leap across two and a half centuries and apply these ideas to critiques of the New Inequality of the present. However, in the case of Adam Smith, that is precisely what Dennis C. Rasmussen, Deborah Boucoyannis, and Joshua Preiss have attempted (Boucoyannis 2013; Rasmussen 2016; Preiss 2021). What would it be to imagine a commercial society designed according to the intelligent plan of the ideal spectator? What verdict would that plan deliver for our own societies in the affluent West, particularly the United States and the United Kingdom? Boucoyannis argues that the system of natural liberty, thus imagined, would contain multiple devices to limit the extent of inequality.

According to Boucoyannis, Smith's concession that there will be inequality in a market society has led to the assumption—mistaken in her view—that it will be of an unjust and extreme extent as opposed to the kind of permissible inequalities found in alternative social systems (such as in a Rawlsian society well ordered by justice).[39] Boucoyannis is even prepared to align Smith's views with those of recent pre-distributivists such as Jacob Hacker (and by

[39] Samuel Fleischacker offers precisely such an interpretation of Smithian inequality (Fleischacker 2004, p.225).

extension one of the authors of this book) (Thomas 2017; Hacker 2011).[40] Given her aims, she does not devote much attention to what one might call Smith's "pro-inequality" arguments—as Rasmussen notes, Smith argues that political stability depends on a prior "evident distinction of ranks" of society (Rasmussen 2016, p.344). In fairness to Boucoyannis, however, she does identify the main cause of inequality even in an ideal system of natural liberty, namely, that the division of labour itself makes some occupations far better remunerated than others.

Smith's treatment of this issue is remarkably sophisticated. Unlike Rawls, he does not believe in the "natural lottery" of talents—for Smith, market entitlements are grounded on talents that are wholly social and the result of education. And the differential reward he notes includes, prominently, what Rawls would call compensatory incentives—for difficult jobs, jobs that need lengthy training, are precarious, require high trust, or are unlikely to succeed in their goals (Smith 1776/1981, I.X.b.1, 116–7). Paul Smith notes that Rawls is also committed to the view that, in a market pre-structured to be fair and with full equality of opportunity, incentives will only be compensatory and wage differentials radically compressed (Smith 1998). That argument is not in (Adam) Smith, but its preconditions certainly are.

The pre-emptive dispersal of wealth, Boucoyannis claims, will occur in a society well-ordered as a Smithian system of natural liberty. Smith's critique of the mercantilism of his time can be extended to any special interest group that creates and sustains rent-seeking niches. Furthermore, the economic design (not moral design) of Smith's proposed institutional set-up aims to keep profits low, thereby limiting capital accumulation, forcing the "man of business" to remain actively engaged in productive activity. Wages ought to be high, to promote a productive workforce with a high level of well-being, meeting Smith's criterion of at least living at a standard that allows participation in society without shame (Boucoyannis 2013, p.1054). Smith was a stringent critic, on productivity grounds, of excessive concentrations of land holding and favoured high inheritance taxes. However, as Boucoyannis notes, in Smith's ideal pre-distributive scheme such concentrations of capital

[40] Boucoyannis notes that Smith does not go as far as Thomas Paine in demanding demogrants to ground a basic income or pensions (Boucoyannis 2013, p.1062). However, she does note that the bargaining advantage that employers always have over labourers must be redressed by state action and one could reasonably interpret that as a high minimum wage policy that includes at least an element of politically determined uplift in wages.

would be pre-empted by the normal operation of the market as he conceived it (Boucoyannis 2013, p.1062).

From our perspective, we would say that this kind of hyper-competitive market has pre-emptively eliminated a rentier-investor class. If there are high returns on offer in this Smithian economy, that is an accurate measure of the risks involved in that investment—high returns must track high risks. Our recent outbreak of "predatory value extraction" would be, for Smith, evidence of excessive profits whereby manufacturers and merchants act against the general interest. Monopoly and exploitation are the generators of excess profit (Boucoyannis 2013, pp.1053–4). Overall, Smith has no hesitation in blaming market distortions on what Bill Edmundson calls the "fact of domination". This is the fact that the wealthy take advantage of their economic power (their "information and bargaining asymmetries", as Boucoyannis puts it) to advantage their own interests at the expense of the common good (Boucoyannis 2013, p.1055). Smith is only consistently a critic of government when it produces bad legislation, corrupted by private interests, as the outcome of what we would now call lobbying. Employers will always seek to drive down wages because the capital-holding asymmetries between the two sides give excessive bargaining power to the employer (Smith 1776/1981, I.VIII.12). The only redress Smith envisages is state action on the side of the worker (Boucoyannis 2013, pp.1056–7). We have proposed the supplementation of this policy with Fichte's more radical policy of the state functioning as employer of last resort (in spite of Hegel's misgivings); Rawls embraced that policy, too (Thomas 2020b).

In a discussion complementary to Boucoyannis's, Rasmussen also focuses on the difference between the inequality that Smith thinks is the motor of progress and the extreme inequality that is corrupting, with the clear implication that the New Inequality falls under the latter category. Smith's wise, impartial, legislator will have found a solution to the multiple problems of actual commercial society as Smith was acquainted with it. Smith's balance of advantages and disadvantages will be replaced by a realistically utopian system of natural liberty that will have ameliorated the disadvantages as far as possible. Perhaps it is unrealistic to hope, in a mass industrialized society, that the private sphere of education will teach people the key virtue of self-command so that our vanity will be directed to its "proper objects". This could, however, be the goal of the free, high-quality, public education system that Smith believed was necessary to redress the stultifying effects of the division of labour on human development. Perhaps we can, taking heed of Rousseau's observation that automation turns the people working with machines into automata too, use automation to free people to do only meaningful work and eliminate the worst drudge work completely. Once again, Rawls concurs by envisaging a society with only meaningful work (Moriarty 2009).

Joshua Preiss's approach is the most historically distanced from Smith's project: his conception of a "Smithian well-ordered society" is of a socio-economic system where any American who elects to work hard will be entitled (as we noted earlier) to a "middle class" standard of life (Preiss 2021). Preiss identifies a crucial strategic aspect of any neo-Smithian argument: we need what economist Arthur Okun called a "high-pressure economy" (Okun 1973, p.207).[41] In such an economy there is a rising tide lifting all boats, but so far and so fast that the rent-extracting proclivities of the rich are, to continue the metaphor, swamped. There is "government policy in favour of the worker" that makes the demand for labour tight with a continually rising level of wages as workers receive their fair share of the productive surplus (Preiss 2021, p.60). The state acts as the employer of last resort—in a way Adam Smith did not envisage—and individual security is advanced by the provision of key public goods such as healthcare and housing. Ultimately, the political agency to realize this Smithian ideal lies in a "large, inter-racial coalition of working Americans" (Preiss 2021, p.174). We have two general doubts about Preiss's optimistic picture: the first is where the political agency to put together such a large coalition will come from. (Alternatively: how it will be self-constituting?) The second is whether we can step into the same river twice—whether we can simply go back to an era of comparatively inclusive growth given what has happened in the meantime. If Price, Edwards, and others are right that trillions of dollars of rent have been extracted by America's wealthiest citizens, does that not put an obstacle in the path of Preiss's hoped-for pattern of development (Price and Edwards 2020)? We fully accept that this is a question for us as much as for Preiss. We will return to it in our Conclusion.

The sophistication of more recent economic theory might give us a realistic hope that the further development of commercial society will provide full employment, thereby guaranteeing exit rights from employment (Thomas 2020b). The worker, with meaningful exit rights, can participate in the labour

[41] To be clear: the connection between Preiss's ideas and Okun's paper is our interpretation of Preiss's strategy.

market without being dominated by any specific other, with social mobility, life-long training, and the capacity to improve her material condition. The impartial legislator will have crafted an institutional scheme that eliminates the rent-extracting power of the merchants and manufacturers or any other minority of citizens who attempt to re-introduce domination over other citizens in the workplace. We will also discuss our version of this ideal in chapter 13.

Can we interpret Smith as anticipating the modern welfare state—taking Hegel's model of the insurance of members of the corporation by other members and putting that in the hands of a public administration? Probably not, although Deborah Boucoyannis makes the interesting point (from our pre-distributive perspective) that if the impartial legislator implements the system of natural liberty correctly, there will be no inequalities to redress via welfare in the first place (Boucoyannis 2013). We take that to be an important part of Rawls's pre-distributivist critique of welfare state capitalism, too (Thomas 2017).

We have to judge the Smithian system to be incomplete, as he was not writing about our modern, inter-connected, industrialized economies. However, his outlook can provide the basis for an attractive, realistically utopian, social system which is not, as every commentator on Smith notes, the system of laissez-faire. The state is involved in the regulation of trusts and monopolies, in supplying the legal framework for economic transactions and in public education. However, unlike Hegel and Fichte, Smith does not even raise the question of whether the state could guarantee full employment as Hegel believed it ought to do (but could not) while Fichte insisted that it must as a logical extension of any republican conception of freedom as non-domination. Only that policy avoids the pitfall that other people can engage in commercial transactions with you, via an anonymous and emancipatory nexus of exchange that eliminates domination by any specific other, but that is insufficient unless someone must trade with you. That "market maker" of last resort must be the state. Financial markets dramatize the point, given the frequency of crises in such markets, given that they are micro-liquid but macro-illiquid. But that is true of any market: you need at least two agents to transact and only the state can be the transactor of last resort.

6.5 Rousseau's, Smith's, and Hegel's Emotional Regimes

In conclusion, then, we can see how central key emotions are to Rousseau's critique of commercial society and to its partial redemption in Smith and the tempered diagnosis in Hegel. All three can agree on a paradigmatic form of failure in such a society: it inflames positional competition and a desire for wealth that is actually a desire for distinction. These pathologies trigger desires that are insatiable. They inform the desires of those cut off from access to commercial society, who impotently rage against it from below, and those cut off from commercial society from above—the idle rich rabble. That, then, is the outcome that must above all be avoided. However, we will argue in chapters 8, 9, 10, and 11 that these classic sources help us to identify the way in which the New Inequality of our time is so damaging to human well-being. Even Smith would join in this chorus of disapproval when some of our affluent societies have gone down the very paths he cautioned against. Smith could not, of course, have foreseen the Easterlin paradox or the reformulation of this thesis for highly unequal societies by Nicholas Buttrick, Samantha J. Heintzelman, and Shigehiro Oishi that we will examine in some detail in chapter 10 below (Buttrick, Heintzelman, and Oishi 2017). There, we will take the insights of these classic theorists of the emotional regimes of commercial society and relate them to the science of happiness. In the next chapter we will turn to the work of their immediate successors: recent philosophers who have been openly inspired by Rousseau and Smith in particular.

7

The Emotional Regimes of Roman Republicanism and Political Liberalism

Propositional Summary

1. We set out the political psychology expressed by Philip Pettit's version of republicanism. We focus less on freedom than on the psychology of the undominated and the nature of what Pettit calls an "economy of esteem". We set out the Smith-inspired account of this economy which Pettit developed with Geoffrey Brennan.
2. Rawls's concern with political psychology throughout his work is set out, and, in particular, the very strong connection he saw between the defensibility of a conception of justice, its stability, and its connection to the destabilizing social attitudes. We describe the centrality of self-respect in Rawls's overall conception of political psychology.
3. A point of contrast emerges between the boldness that Pettit expects from his ideal of the free person and Rawls's focus on mutual investments. We see a connection between their respective weak and strong forms of egalitarianism and the political psychology of Rawls's (Rousseau-inspired) republic of equals.

Introduction

As we noted in the previous chapter, it is not merely an academic exercise to contextualize Geoffrey Brennan's, Philip Pettit's, and John Rawls's political psychologies in the context of Rousseau's, Smith's, and Hegel's works: the line of influence is avowedly direct (Brennan and Pettit 2004; Rawls 2007). In this chapter we set out the emotional regimes that each of them develops in the course of either a general description of an "economy of esteem", or specifically the political psychology of Roman republicanism, or of justice

Extravagance and Misery. Alan Thomas, Alfred Archer, and Bart Engelen, Oxford University Press.
© Oxford University Press 2024. DOI: 10.1093/oso/9780197781722.003.0008

as fairness.[1] We will begin with the jointly authored work by Brennan and Pettit before engaging in a more detailed consideration of Rawls's views. We will, in each case, contextualize these recent discussions in the light of the historical issues discussed in the previous chapter. We will refer back to these competing accounts when we subject them both to empirical scrutiny from the perspective of the science of happiness in chapter 10.

7.1 Republicanism's Economy of Esteem

We are going to focus on the political psychology of the leading republican philosopher in recent political philosophy: Philip Pettit (1997, 2012, 2014). We are going to be selective: in so far as the concept of freedom is a psychological concept we will, ironically, not be engaging directly with Pettit's account of it in spite of its centrality to his republicanism. We are, instead, interested in his account of esteem, recognition, and the psychology of being dominated, as those are, it seems to us, the key ideas we need to explain the stability of his conception of justice. It is worth bearing in mind here that Pettit is a consequentialist and justice is not, for him, a basic justificatory concept.

We will begin our excavation of his extended political psychology in one of his many jointly authored works. The most extended consideration he gives to issues of recognition and esteem is his essay on "kudonomics" co-authored with economist Geoffrey Brennan (Brennan and Pettit 2004, p.2). Kudonomics, they explain, is the systematic study of one of the three fundamental desires of human life: "the study of the laws governing the system of kudos or renown" (Brennan and Pettit 2004, p.2).[2] What justifies their use of the metaphor of an "economy"? They are appealing here to an older sense of the word that, as Michelle Schwartze and John T. Scott put it:

[1] We should note, at the outset, that we will not be discussing that strand of the republican tradition—one particularly associated with Charles Taylor—that looks back to the "Athenian" conception of political participation as itself an essential component of the good life. Our focus here is on the contrasting Roman tradition in which political virtue is a matter of prudence: of protecting the presuppositions of each citizen's deepest interest in effective political agency (Thomas 2017).

[2] By contrast, conventional economics studies the desire for property and political science the desire for power (ibid.).

> [B]uilds on the usage of the term . . . in the eighteenth century . . . to refer to the structure of a complex system, as seen, for example, in Smith's terminology of "the oeconomy of nature". (Schwarze and Scott 2019, p.67)[3]

Brennan and Pettit's idea is that while dis/esteem cannot literally be bought or sold, there is a systematic pattern to its allocation that can be studied at two levels, the micro and the macro, with a reflexive loop from the micro *to* the macro. That, for them, justifies the analogy with an "economic" analysis of a phenomenon (Brennan and Pettit 2004, p.81).

The analogy is sustained because they detect an emergent pattern in how we esteem or disesteem each other. As befits its Smithian antecedents, their question is whether this pattern can be reformed by institutional engineering to enhance the general good (Brennan and Pettit 2004, p.3, p.5). The economy of esteem will prove to be an autonomous domain, for the purposes of social explanation, it gives rise to "some distinctive laws of its own" within the domain of informal social norms (Brennan and Pettit 2004, p.31). They characterize this domain as follows:

> Norms materialise as regularities in social life, because there is general approval for the pattern of behaviour involved, disapproval for the failure to elicit that behaviour, or the expectation of such general approval or disapproval. In this respect norms contrast with market regularities, which do not need to be approved—at least not as a matter of logic—in order to materialise. (Brennan and Pettit 2004, p.267)[4]

Within this general class of social norms, the specific domain of the economy of esteem is paradigmatically that of civil society, as opposed to the locations of the "invisible hand" of the market and the "iron hand" of the law.[5]

This economy of esteem regulates both attitudes and dispositions of character (Brennan and Pettit 2004, pp.7–8). The content of an ethos of esteem is whether an individual is dis/esteemed for having or lacking certain qualities

[3] The reference is to (Smith 1776/1981, II.i.5.10).

[4] They add an important caveat: "a norm obtains in a society only if it is generally complied with; only if people generally approve of others complying with it and/or disapprove of their not complying, or are at least expected to do so; and only if this pattern of approval, real or imputed, is not incidental to the compliance: it is required in some part to explain the compliance, presumably because compliance is relatively burdensome" (Brennan and Pettit 2004, p.270).

[5] The legal system itself, as they point out, relies as much on informal sanctions as it does on the "iron hand" of punishment (Brennan and Pettit 2004, p.250, p.269).

as measured by an ideal standard. That directly makes a connection with Smith's views, as discussed in the previous chapter, where the ideal standard is determined by the ideal observer, institutional designer, or legislator. Further, Smith originated the economist's interest in the desire for esteem as prior to, and explanatory of, the desire for wealth. This is a theme that Brennan and Pettit view as neglected in mainstream economics apart from "the odd renegade like Thorstein Veblen" (Brennan and Pettit 2004, p.7).[6]

Reasons for the neglect of esteem, they surmise, are its contingent—and mistaken—connection with an aristocratic ethos of honour, or a belief that a desire for esteem must be inherently hypocritical. The latter seems to be manifested in the fact that we do not trust the motivations of an agent who explicitly avows a desire to be esteemed. Better simply to be virtuous than seek to be esteemed for seeming to be so? By contrast, the preferences of the market, while less reputable per se, have a blunt honesty about them. However, Brennan and Pettit conclude that, if your aim is to explain social life, then you cannot omit the desire to be esteemed on the basis of its ambivalent moral standing because too much of our social life is explained by it (Brennan and Pettit 2004, p.10).

Although esteem is an attitude, and not an action, it must be something that a person can intentionally control and for which he or she can take responsibility. An individual must be able to influence whether it is to their "credit" or not to possess the properties in question (Brennan and Pettit 2004, p.21). Esteem must also be something that can be reciprocally exchanged even if, as we shall see, it makes no sense to treat it as literally a tradable commodity.

What, then, is "esteem" in this Smithian sense? To esteem is to form an evaluative attitude that ranks people according to a standard. It is explicitly comparative and "directive", given that individuals can make an effort to change their ranking given its connection to voluntariness (Brennan and Pettit 2004, p.16). It is indexed, implicitly or explicitly, to a comparison class—to a relevant peer group (Brennan and Pettit 2004, p.18). Therefore, there are two parameters for the assessment: the implicit ideal and the "prevailing practice" where the latter operates contextually to adjust a context-relative evaluation (Brennan and Pettit 2004, p.19). An important corollary is that:

[6] They cite his remark that "the struggle is substantially a race for reputability on the basis of invidious comparison" (Veblen 1899/2009, p.32).

> Being comparative, esteem involves the grading of people against one another on a more or less continuous scale. And it contrasts in this way with recognition. (Brennan and Pettit 2004, p.20)

Recognition lacks the scalar dimension of esteem as, in another contrast, does the attitude of love which is not directed to a person in virtue of their attributes. There is a deformation of the attitudes when recognition is actively sought—even at the cost of being disesteemed. Yet recognition and dis/esteem are distinct. To round out the analysis, we think it is also helpful to take into account the appraiser group—which group of agents is assigning dis/esteem.

Given the importance of recognition in Rousseau and Hegel, we think it is helpful to demarcate it as clearly from esteem as do Brennan and Pettit. We have already taken note of their reference to John Adams and to his claim that not to be attended to—to be of no interest to anyone—is a deeply felt injury. (Brennan and Pettit note that Adams viewed it as "worse than censure" (Brennan and Pettit 2004, p.186).) Their point is that neither esteem nor its opposite presupposes recognition. This is not wholly a binary status: some may recognize you, others not, and in some spheres and not others. This is why people seek notoriety, or disesteem—better that than to be a "nobody". The other key aspect of recognition is that it is an unlimited good: recognizing others "is a matter of attitude and not action and we do not think that scarcity applies in this domain" (Brennan and Pettit 2004, p.189). There is no point constructing an analogy of an economy for such an unlimited good.

There is, by contrast, competition over esteem. We think it is a real insight of Brennan and Pettit's account accurately to identify the competitive element in dis/esteem: the extent to which it shares some, but not all, of the features of a positional good. Prima facie, this seems in tension with another basic idea about esteem: that if it is an evaluative attitude directed to real achievement then it is as unlimited as achievement itself. Paul Gomberg, for example, argues that:

> If opportunity is to be unlimited, the goods have to be ones that can be expanded indefinitely. Luckily, there are important goods with that characteristic: social esteem and self-esteem. (Gomberg 2007, p.57)

Gomberg's (Hegelian) view is that esteem norms are bound up with specific social identities and scripts that tell one, for example, what it is to be a good teacher (Gomberg 2007, p.58). He adds a further distinction: these identities differ from social positions some of which are high-status and some of which are low-status: in the former case, what is on offer is not simply esteem but prestige.

> In societies with limited positions of prestige, prestige is a positional good in limited supply; in contrast, esteem grounded in norms of identity is not a limited or positional good, for there is no limit to the number who can be esteemed for doing what they do well. (Gomberg 2007, p.59)

We will return to Gomberg's views later. Here, we note the convergence between his ideas and Brennan and Pettit's identification of the aspect of dis/esteem that typically involves competition:

> [E]steem is scarce, not just in the familiar, economic sense that it is costly to earn—it doesn't fall like manna from heaven—but also in the more specific sense that there is an element of interpersonal competition in people's attempt to acquire it. This competitive scarcity has an important impact on the nature of the economy of esteem. (Brennan and Pettit 2004, pp.20–1)

We see no inconsistency here: Gomberg, Brennan, and Pettit agree we need to separate out the evaluative attitude of, say, admiring the exercise of virtue from the separate question of esteeming the virtuous. The former is fitness to a proper object; it is potentially unlimited. Gomberg's point, one from which Brennan or Pettit need not dissent, is that the way in which we assemble tasks into "jobs"—distinct social role types with different individual occupants—moves from token instances of admirable achievement to status types in a contestable way.

For example, if there are a limited number of surgeons in a particular hospital, then the high status of that position of advantage has been made scarce by our political decisions about how work ought to be organized. Gomberg contrasts that way of limiting avenues of esteem of handing out drivers' licenses to all qualified drivers: you have to qualify, but then we do not view the number of those who qualify as limited. There is no social point to putting a quota on drivers' licenses, but we have so arranged work that only some avenues of esteem are open and only some social roles carry prestige. There is "competitive scarcity" in esteem because this reflects competitive scarcity in access to it. We will not withhold from you esteem for the exercise of your talents across many domains, but we may well, as a society, limit your access to the development and expression of talent.

What, exactly, is the mechanism of evaluation in terms of esteem? Brennan and Pettit give a helpful example: recycling by domestic consumers. While it is now ubiquitous, the early pioneers who recycled, given the lack of social and infrastructural support for doing so, ought to have been highly esteemed for their conscientious care for the environment. They set an ideal, but in the process, via emulation, a high-esteem activity has become commonplace such that the average level of achievement has substantially increased. Now recycling does not attract much esteem because the contextual standard has risen; it is disesteem that has increased. Obeying the norm now attracts little esteem, while violating it is now strongly disesteemed. By setting a good example, pioneers of recycling aimed to shift attitudes in this way even at the "cost" of their own esteem. There is no inconsistency, then, between being an object of esteem—an indefinite good—and an economy of esteem where agents try to shift the levels of esteem upwards at their own "cost". The "meriting" relation—for example, that a virtuous action merits admiration—is as unlimited as the number of occasions for virtue. Being esteemed, however, has a competitive dimension that agents can take voluntary actions toward re-shaping. If the tidal estuary of social norms shifts, such that your esteem-worthy behaviour is now commonplace, if you still want to be esteemed you will have to take action to secure that standing in the eyes of others.

We can use this model to interpret, for example, the Smithian concern for the emulation of the rich. As we have noted, what attracts people to the rich, in Smith's account, is their distinction—they are far above the common run of people. However, suppose that a "rising tide does lift all boats": if that happens, the wealthy exemplar ought to welcome her good example allowing the general standard to rise even as she loses her distinction in the process. Not all competitive losses in the economy of esteem are regrettable. Recruiting the motivational pressure of social norms can improve the general standard of achievement. However, whether a particular wealthy person welcomes the contribution of her example to the general good, or re-doubles her effort to achieve distinction at a new level, is an open question. This will come up later when we discuss the unhappiness of the wealthy, either because they fear losing their wealth, or because they no longer attract distinction in the class of wealthy people.

Brennan and Pettit's analysis further allows us to identify the ways in which competition bears on esteem: being esteemed is not simply a matter of individual effort. The social context is a competitive one and the actions of others may make esteem harder to achieve. There are two sources of competitive pressure, not one: there is the positional aspect of the good of esteem and there is the pressure from the implied contextual standard of customary practice. If conventional expectations rise and fall, then dis/esteem can be harder or easier to achieve relative to conventional expectation. If the ideal of presenting a respectable appearance of your home to passers-by is operative in your neighbourhood, then esteem is more easily achieved if your neighbours all have untidy front lawns and yours is tidy. But if everyone's lawn is tidy, then the competitive pressure becomes more demanding.

So why do people care so deeply about being esteemed? Brennan and Pettit argue that people care about it for a range of reasons. They begin with a simple case of prudential reasons: social life runs more smoothly if a person is esteemed or disesteemed particularly given the connection between esteem and trustworthiness. Secondly, the esteem of others is defeasible evidence that a person should esteem him- or herself for living up to the ideal standard shared between them and the community of esteem. These pragmatic reasons ground a concern for scale: to be widely esteemed by many, or conversely to be disesteemed only by a few (Brennan and Pettit 2004, p.27; Williams 1993, ch.4).

These features do not exhaust the evaluative basis of esteem because these are only instrumental reasons to value esteem. We can also want to be thought well of by posterity or by people whom we will never meet: both of these facts suggest that esteem has an intrinsic value. For all these reasons, Brennan and Pettit argue, esteem fits the profile of a Rawlsian primary good (Brennan and Pettit 2004, p.29). The economy of esteem rests on "a substructure of widely acknowledged values and ideals . . . [it] is evaluatively charged in a manner that the economy of goods is not" (Brennan and Pettit 2004, p.93).

To vindicate the language of an "economy" of esteem, what constitutes its "demand" and "supply"? Demand, in this economic sense, implies a good that is actively sought. Since this is a competitive context, the parallel motivations of others matter, too. Is this analogy undermined by what Brennan and Pettit call the "teleological paradox"? There are desirable ends that would be thwarted if one sets them as intentional goals of action: falling asleep, for example, or pleasure seeking. You can control the presuppositions of achieving these ends—a relaxing bath before bedtime, perhaps—but the wrong kind of control subverts them. Jon Elster has argued that esteem has this character of being essentially a by-product: "nothing is so unimpressive as behaviour designed to impress" (Elster 1983, p.66).

However, Brennan and Pettit dispute this: rarely is behaviour exclusively designed to impress because that would, indeed, be self-stultifying. When it is so motivated, we do indeed judge that the person is vain or hypocritical and lacks the putative virtue that was supposed to impress us. But the field of such cases is narrow—that of virtue. Achievement more broadly is esteemed, however motivated. The motivations of a talented pianist or golfer are not even relevant—"are they in it just for the money?" It does not matter: we are admiring what the performer achieves. And Brennan and Pettit argue that even the imitation of virtue is better—and exhibits a better character—than displays of vice.

They have an ingenious account of what they call the "virtual control" of behaviour: the desire for esteem functions as a standby cause that counterfactually regulates behaviour that goes "off track" without its being the direct cause of that behaviour. The agent is not, then, directly motivated by the desire for esteem in the way that would trigger the paradox of teleology. But nor is esteem simply something that happens, or not, to a wholly passive agent. It can reinforce an Aristotelian "second nature" by keeping the manifestation of an action on track and by acting as a functional constraint on the field of permissible actions in a given context. The desire for esteem and to avoid disesteem plays a virtually controlling role; it may be both "silent" yet "enormously powerful" (Brennan and Pettit 2004, p.44). This resolves the paradox that we criticize both the hypocrite, but also the person who could not care less what others think of them. People *ought* to care about what others think of them. No one wants to be the slave of common opinion, but a complete disregard for the judgement of society is not an admirable trait either. Therefore, they conclude that, like any virtually controlling meta-disposition, the desire for esteem figures not in the direct explanation of how an individual behaves, but in the meta-explanation of the robust stability of her actual dispositions.[7]

How, then—to sustain the economic analogy—is esteem supplied? The very idea seems to face an analogue of the problem of teleology: but it cuts

[7] This is not to rule out atypical cases where a desire to be well thought of is a manifest motivation of the agent. Explanations of this general form are less prominent in folk psychological explanations because of our misleading bias towards the "fundamental attribution error" (Brennan and Pettit 2004, pp.74–5).

deeper. Being an esteem "supplier" is incoherent: it is an attitude rationalized by all and only its proper objects. I cannot "gift" it to you if it is not a merited response to the facts about what you have done. Then it follows that, if it cannot be gifted, neither can it be traded nor passed from one person to another. We are all forced by these commonly known facts to be "parametric suppliers": we "cannot help what we do and cannot seek strategic advantage from it" (Brennan and Pettit 2004, p.53).

I can choose to attend, or not, to what you do; I can seek your company or shun it. But if I know what I know, then dis/esteem simply cannot be withheld at will. If you have just given a brilliant piano recital, then I cannot withhold my esteem from you. But, to blunt the force of this paradox once again, there are things a person can voluntarily do that "raise the probability" that another person will be esteemed (Brennan and Pettit 2004, p.55). Appraiser and appraisee can agree on what the scope is of the performance to be attended to; evaluations can be expressed, or not; I may contribute to common knowledge of your esteem—to your good reputation or infamy. Further, I can choose to associate or disassociate with you and that will allow my reputation to impact on yours, for good or ill.

How do supply and demand for esteem come together to form an "economy" for it? Economic goods must be "attractive and scarce" and the product of competitive effort (Brennan and Pettit 2004). This competition has an aggregative feedback effect of which the most salient is price itself. This is an economy of esteem because:

> [R]ational individuals will control the things that they do, and the relationships they form—in particular, the esteem services they offer to one other—with a view to promoting the esteem in which they are individually held. (Brennan and Pettit 2004, p.66)

This will produce a set of "self-organizing" patterns that, in turn, ground distinct laws for this domain and thereby vindicate the assumption that this is a distinctive domain for the purposes of social explanation. So what are the behaviours open to agents who seek to take responsibility for how they are esteemed? Brennan and Pettit compile the following list:

Location: people will specialise in those areas where they can expect to do best in esteem terms.

Level: they will seek that level of performance there that promises to maximise their esteem at acceptable cost.
Dimensions: they will highlight the dimensions on which they score well and downplay the dimensions on which they do badly.
Ideals: and they will push the case for the importance of those ideals or desiderata that they satisfy in best measure.
Public: they will select audiences from whom the esteem supplied is likely to be large and of most evidentiary, pragmatic, or inherent value.
Comparators: they will frame their performance so as to ensure comparison with a maximally flattering reference group.
Average: they will propagate favourable information—or perhaps misinformation—about the statistical norms among comparators.
Access: they will control the access that the relevant public has to their performance—say, increasing or decreasing those who will form an audience—so as to increase their expected esteem. (Brennan and Pettit 2004, p.69)

This is an exhaustive list of what certainly looks like a calculated set of strategies, but this is the theorist's list, not that of the ordinary person seeking to be well thought of. But in each case the control by the desire for esteem is merely virtual. Exchange features here, too, where there is a "trade" of attention, good testimony, and mutual association.

As institutional engineers, Brennan and Pettit ask what policy interventions might shift equilibria—for example, transform recycling from an activity highly esteemed and practiced by the virtuous few to being the new regularized norm of the many (thus attracting little esteem, but where noncompliance is strongly disesteemed). Increased publicity via audience size might be such a trigger; so might increased accuracy about what compliance levels actually are. A subtlety of their analysis is that a policy maker may choose to take advantage of esteem effects or not: consider simply passing a law that makes recycling mandatory. Now compliance attracts no esteem at all; it has been "crowded out" by legislation (Brennan and Pettit 2004, p.138). Publicity, they conclude, is "the chief means by which the forces of esteem can be channelled and directed" (Brennan and Pettit 2004, p.141).[8] Policy

[8] They add "observer attention is a scarce resource . . . policy actions that serve to make some performances more conspicuous will usually serve simultaneously to make others less so" (Brennan and Pettit 2004, p.142).

interventions take advantage of the fact that more information, appropriately targeted, can influence both standards and prevailing practice.

A crucial component of their final view is how dis/esteem is influenced by the fundamental social fact of human association—both voluntary and involuntary. In voluntary associations, "esteem services" are enabled even though literal trade in esteem is impossible.[9] Those were recall, "attention, testimony, and association", and their particular focus is on the clustering, macro-effect of that which James Buchanan called "club goods" (Buchanan 1965). Such clubs, from an esteem perspective, are a local form of "economy of scale" where "reputation pooling" confers benefits on members (Brennan and Pettit 2004, p.196). Further, members of such clubs reciprocally enforce each other's esteem. Club members show in-group loyalty and correctly esteem each other's achievements. This leads to Robert Frank's idea of "choosing the right pond". Frank applies this to intra-firm compensation dynamics: wage compression occurs because the high performing in a firm are partly compensated by esteem and not income while the low performing are compensated financially for being disesteemed (Frank 1985, pp.41–43).

How does one choose the right pond? By trading off the esteem of the club to external appraisers; the individual's likely place in the hierarchy; the internal levels of mutual esteem versus expected performance; the average performance standard. If you do choose the right pond, then you will receive a reputational boost without having to "blow your own trumpet"; but you will be expected to show in-group loyalty at the risk of exclusion if you do not.

The complementary aspect of such associations is that, if a person lacks the capacity to earn esteem and many others feel the same way then countercultural groups may form to challenge the dominant values. Here the only esteem on offer is "in group" (Brennan and Pettit 2004, p.226) so these groups will be tightly bonded forms of association.

When it comes to involuntary associations, the major change is that individuals are assigned to their metaphorical "pond" with no say in the matter: society does it for you. Ascriptive identities are the basis of dis/esteem from "outsiders" or society as a whole, and it is beyond the power of the individual to change these imposed categories. (Complementarily, the

[9] "Exchange in esteem is a barely coherent idea: B cannot offer some of her surplus esteem to A, either in exchange for goods or in exchange for some of A's esteem in another domain of activity. Nor can A add to his esteem just by buying approval from observers: any esteem that A derives is grounded in a belief that A is estimable, and that belief cannot be for sale" (Brennan and Pettit 2004, pp.196–7).

group cannot police its boundaries either by inclusion or exclusion.) There is no meaningful "exit". On the positive side, if the group is widely esteemed, then every member, simply by involuntary inclusion, will enjoy higher esteem. Conversely, however, the demarcation of such groups via ascriptive identities can work to perpetuate disesteem or stigma. The pressure here for the formation of counter-cultural groups is very strong: the perception that one is unfairly stigmatized for one's identity creates a strong incentive for a counter-culture. In this new association the disesteem of outsiders is shunned for the esteem of fellow group members.

Like those with not much to contribute on the esteem scale, the discriminated against are excluded—but in the latter case this in spite of their capacity or actual achievement level. Here, Brennan and Pettit claim that "separate but equal" makes institutional sense as parallel domains are set up where prejudice is neutralized. Mobilization is forced upon the marginalized group by the fact of their exclusion. While free riding, in the voluntary case, is suppressed by loyalty, in a marginalized group advocacy is demanded in the light of a shared fate. Both the active and the passive benefit equally. Yet the fact that individual and group esteem are so tightly linked motivates individual action to benefit the group.

How does all of this culminate in choices for institutional design and policy? In line with its Smithian antecedents, Brennan and Pettit's goal is the regulation of the "intangible hand" of civil society. This steers between overt legislation and market regularities: its domain is informal social norms and the sanctions of dis/esteem. At the outset, Pettit and Brennan note that the intangible hand can be recruited to bad ends: for example, a particular sports franchise may come to esteem cheating, in its internal culture, as part of a "win at all costs" mentality. This pattern may spread, just as a previous honour code believed that the only remedy for personal slights was duelling (Brennan and Pettit 2004, p.247). A particularly interesting case is "pluralistic ignorance", where a breakdown in common knowledge leads to the emergence of large-scale patterns that everyone disfavours—they simply don't know enough about the attitudes of others. That seems to us a plausible explanation of one aspect of the persistence of inequality: surveys of attitudes to inequality show remarkable levels of ignorance about its true extent. Many of us, it seems, are in a suboptimal equilibrium that we would have the power to change if we were not subject to such pluralistic ignorance.

To improve levels of esteem, the target must be underlying performance and the important levers influencing performance are publicity and "presentation". By the latter, Brennan and Pettit mean the ideals that set a standard for judgement, the appraiser group (its size and composition) and the comparison class (Brennan and Pettit 2004, p.249). Each of these can be, and regularly are, objects of policy (Brennan and Pettit 2004, p.249):

> The intangible hand . . . represents a social pattern that can to some extent be brought under intentional influence and that can be reoriented with a view to securing yet greater social benefit. (Brennan and Pettit 2004, p.250)

This institutional engineering interacts with a general predisposition in society to be motivated to virtue and to want to be esteemed. They conclude that one object of policy is to remove inhibitors of those generalized dispositions.

Institutional engineering needs to be evaluatively committed: it is good that a society exhibits some evaluative patterns while others are to be avoided. Given this inevitability of "thick" evaluation, to which values will the institutional engineer appeal? Brennan and Pettit argue that we can explicate those values immanent in the economy of esteem itself: how people dis/esteem each other, in specific contexts, displays their values. These values ground preferences so they are not reducible to the latter. In particular, these are not the "taste-based" preferences of mainstream economics where it makes sense to imagine the frustration of preferences in return for monetary compensation (Brennan and Pettit 2004, p.254). I cannot betray an ideal in a way that leads you to disesteem me and try to ameliorate the situation by paying you compensation—indeed, that would make the situation worse.

Brennan and Pettit take a particular interest in the sphere of "quasi autonomous" organizations at arm's length from but funded by the state, and therefore candidates either for intrusive monitoring and regulation or for "marketization".[10] If the intangible hand is the preferred model, then the desired results—accountability and successful performance—can be achieved cheaply, effectively and in a "virtue-compatible" way (Brennan and Pettit 2004, p.258).

It costs nothing to encourage a culture of self-reinforcing dis/esteem: no more than "start up costs" to encourage the salient facts to be mutually known.

[10] Examples are "hospitals, schools, universities, research institutes, broadcasting stations, public utilities, women's refuges, consumer bodies, indigenous people's commissions, and the like" (Brennan and Pettit 2004, p.257).

In addition, attempts to escape the regime of the intangible hand are self-frustrating. If you dodge a legal penalty concealing your behaviour, then good for you, and perhaps we will admire your ingenuity. But it will lead us to disesteem you even more. Similarly, estimable behaviour that a person tries to hide is even further esteemed. And there is an answer to the question of "who guards the guardians": we all check each other's behaviour without a central source of authority (Brennan and Pettit 2004, p.260). This approach supports virtue, and creating an economy of esteem does not "crowd out" virtue in a way that legal or monetary incentives do.

Dual control systems that try to reinforce virtue with self-interest have an empirical track record of failure (Brennan and Pettit 2004, p.261). The intangible hand respects the autonomy of the virtuous agent and does not reduce her self-esteem; it is not a competitor motivation supplanting the desire for virtue. It encourages the development of an Aristotelian "second nature":

> If the intangible hand is compatible with the presence of virtue . . . then it can be productive of ever more independent habits of virtue; it can constitute a support for virtue that gradually renders itself less and less necessary: a ladder to virtue that can be kicked away at a certain level of habituation. (Brennan and Pettit 2004, p.263)

Is the intangible hand the invocation of social forces that are still a form of control of the individual by the invidious forces of public opinion? Brennan and Pettit concede the threat, but think that our shared ethical consciousness is too internally diverse for the intangible hand to become oppressive.

We detect here the influence of Hegel as much as Smith: Hegel's corporations were part of "civil society" in his extended sense of that latter term. Brennan and Pettit hope that a broad range of intermediary social institutions can be internally regulated primarily by esteem, controlled neither by law nor by internal marketization. We agree with them that, for example, collective guidance by an explicit esteem of public service is a better regulatory regime than public sector management based on artificial marketization, performance targets, and the rise of the culture of audit.

Brennan and Pettit's project is an updating of Smith's account of the centrality in human motivation of the (virtual) motive of being esteemed. People want to be well thought of, and we will focus in particular in this book on the connection that Gomberg draws out between the ways in which we choose to organize work and the possibility of esteem-worthy achievement. Work ought to be a sphere of social life where all can achieve, relative to a pertinent social standard, so that they can be mutually esteemed (Taylor 2004). However, we will go into some detail into Gomberg's argument that this is not, in fact, how capitalist societies organize employments that also carry social advantage in our concluding chapter 13. The economy of esteem also reinforces the Smithian point that the poor are further harmed by their social invisibility (bearing in mind the clear distinction Brennan and Pettit draw between esteem and recognition).

Furthermore, this pioneering discussion of the economy of esteem is of considerable importance when we come to compare and contrast this neo-Smithian view with Rawls's views on respect and self-respect. In particular, as we will indicate, Brennan and Pettit's idea of "virtual control" will help to exonerate Rawls from the charge that he was merely confused about his subject matter. However, there is one other aspect of Pettit's political psychology on which we want to focus here and that occurs later in his work, notably in *On the People's Terms* (Pettit 2012). For our purposes we want to isolate his comments on the psychology of justice and, specifically, on his "eyeball test" and what it is to fail to meet it because of a lack of boldness.

Pettit's later extended discussion of political psychology is in his book *On the People's Terms*, which goes into more detail about what it is for an individual to achieve the ideal of the republican status of being a *liber* or free person. It is one thing to secure the status of the *liber*, or free person, and another thing to assure that a person who enjoys this status will boldly assert his or her projects:

> The eyeball test does not require that people should be able to look one another in the eye, regardless of their personal lack of nerve. It requires that they have this capacity in the absence of what would count, even by the most demanding standards of their society, as mere timidity or cowardice. The reference to timidity is essential, since *no public safeguards can compensate for differences between individual personalities and for variations in people's capacity to deal with the overbearing assumptions of others.* (Pettit 2012, pp.84–5, emphasis added)

It seems to us that there are three key points in this passage: a distinction between a status and the exercise of those capacities that it makes possible; the cultural relativity of the relevant standards; and how there can be no "public safeguards" for republican boldness in a context where liberty will see citizens of many different psychological profiles interact in social life: the mutually sympathetic, the antagonistic, and those who seek to belittle or otherwise dominate others.

The passage suggests that if citizens lack this kind of boldness, or confidence, to stand up to the would-be dominator, then it is difficult to see how state action in a republican polity can bring it about. Pettit argues that those who are dominated are craven, deferential and manipulative towards those upon whose quality of will they depend for the satisfaction of their own needs and interests. Of particular interest to our argument is something Pettit says about the undominated: that they must possess a certain boldness or self-confidence. We have picked out this later passage because it is central to our concerns here. Our aim is to counter Pettit's pessimism and to argue that it does fall within state action, broadly conceived, to make people bold and give them confidence in their projects.

Overall, then, generalizing over both the economy of esteem and the status of the *liber*, we can say that in Pettit's republican political economy there is a useful contrast to be drawn between recognition and esteem. Recognition is an unlimited good and it operates in a binary way: you are recognized or not (relative to particular contexts and appraisers). A particularly important way to structure our social world recruits the motivational force of informal social norms that lie in a hinterland between the ethical and the legal. In the light of governing ideals, social norms can be engineered to drive standards of compliance with ideals upwards. Sometimes external agency is required—such as when a group occupies a suboptimal equilibrium as no one knows what the collectively held ideal standard actually is.

Certainly, we share Brennan and Pettit's aim of preserving the autonomy of a domain: that of civil society, spanning the space between the family and the state, and where quasi-autonomous bodies can, we hope, be motivated to serve the public good (if that is their explicit aim) by recruiting esteem, ideals, and an ethos—not by being closely monitored nor marketized. However, to some extent our ambitions are broader than theirs as we want to pick up on Gomberg's suggestion that an account of this kind can be extended to economic organizations and, in particular, to how we structure work. Work is, undeniably, primarily a source of labour market income. However, as we organize economic organizations by importing structures from social life more generally, so we may be able to treat workplaces as microcosms of the economy of esteem. We will turn to that specific project in chapter 13. Our next task is to compare this approach to that of John Rawls and the development of his political psychology for justice at the service of what he calls the theory of stability.

7.2 Political Liberalism's Emotional Regime

We know that John Rawls was an insightful interpreter of the historical traditions of political philosophy (Rawls 2007). We also know that a great deal of reflection went into the revision of his annual "primer" for his graduate teaching assistants for publication as his last summative statement of domestic theory of justice as fairness in *Justice as Fairness: a Re-Statement* (Rawls 2001). The latter book is organized around our question of the psychological propensities that either stabilize or destabilize a society well-ordered by justice. It is the leitmotif that structures his whole discussion.[11] The importance of this issue to Rawls can be inferred from its prominence in this letter he sent to James Buchanan in 1975:

> I also found your Hobbesian analysis as to how one might arrive at the DP [Difference Principle] very illuminating. . . . The kind of argument you are making is closely related to what I call the problem of stability. . . . I introduced this problem by saying that I would divide the argument for the two principles into two stages (pp.144, 530f): at the *first* stage one would choose principles without worrying about the question of stability and psychological feasibility. At the second stage, we take the principles adopted at the 1st stage and see whether they are stable, that is, whether people, or *enough* people, *can* live by them without resentment, hostility, envy, etc. If they *can* then the argument is complete; if not, then we have to begin again at step one, and revise the initial choice of principles. (Rawls, Letter to James Buchanan, February 25, 1975)

This is, as we have noted, a recurrent concern for Rawls. It shapes the entire argument structure of *Justice as Fairness* that was published in 2001—twenty-six years after that letter to Buchanan.[12] It seems, then, that Rawls took this

[11] As Bannerjee and Bercuson observe, "choosing a conception of justice that is not stable is *not* justice" (Bannerjee and Bercuson 2015, p.215). They cite in support Rawls's discussion at (Rawls 1971/1999, p.454).

[12] We take this to be a specific instance—one of particular importance to our project—of the more general truth that "the emotions always play a central role in providing the motivational resources necessary in any stable, legitimate political community" (Bannerjee and Bercuson 2015, p.214).

aspect of the stability test—the stabilization (or destabilization) of justice as fairness by the political emotions—seriously and this was a constant preoccupation even though other parts of his overall view changed significantly.

Rawls was concerned with explaining how we can put in place social conditions that stabilize a society well ordered by justice by removing what he takes to be the proximate cause of instability, namely, anxiety. This is an argument that Rawls could not have given in Part I of the original position because of the nature of that artificial justificatory device. The parties behind the veil of ignorance draw from a list of "primary goods" that are "socially strategic": "if these goods are justly distributed, then other injustices are unlikely to occur" (Rawls 1999a, p.276). However, the goods cannot violate the restriction imposed on the choice situation represented by the original position taken as a whole: that the parties are mutually disinterested. Therefore, the psychology of the dominator—a person who wants more explicitly at the expense of others—is not even represented in this situation (Edmundson 2017). As Bill Edmundson puts it, wealth is not a maximand (Edmundson 2017, pp.24–25). For the limited purposes of this "device of representation" Rawls assumes that the parties in the original position lack the "strong will to dominate and exercise power over others" (Rawls 2001, p.87). Whatever results the use of that device produces, then, they must still be subject to the test of stability. The results must be assessed to determine if they still hold true when the will to dominate turns out to motivate (at least some) actual people.

This corresponds to the distinction that we have drawn between two kinds of egalitarian concern, and hence two distinct arguments, in Rawls's work. One concern is with what Piketty has called the "drift to oligarchy": the concern that the inequalities permitted under Rawls's overall scheme will see the better off and the best off combine their interests to dominate others. This is what Bill Edmundson calls the "fact of domination" and it is of central concern to numerous recent philosophers working in the Machiavellian republican tradition (Edmundson 2017; Green 2016; McCormick 2011; Vergara 2020). This is Rawls's concern with the "fair value" of the political liberties, but they are the "gatekeepers" to all the basic liberties (Thomas 2017, p.103 ff).

Wholly separate, however, is Rawls's second argument, grounded on his further concern with whether his overall view will be destabilized once it takes into account the "destabilizing special attitudes" of citizens, such as the will to dominate. This problem arises not simply for the basic liberties, and the fair value of the political liberties amongst them, but for the entire conception of justice as fairness.

Ordinary citizens possess such "special psychologies": for example, the fact that some of them may "be envious or spiteful, or have a will to dominate or a tendency to be submissive, or to be peculiarly averse to uncertainty and risk" (Rawls 2001, p.180). There is also the negative special psychology of "attitudes of domination and submission" to be considered (Rawls 1971/1999, pp.80–81, pp.468–74). The same topics come up in Rawls's lectures on the history of political philosophy in his accounts of Hobbes and Rousseau (Rawls 2007). By the time of *Justice as Fairness* all these issues are deemed crucial to what, in Part V, is called the "Question of Stability" (Rawls 2001, p.185, pp.196–7). It is in the context of stability that these problematic attitudes are involved in "put[-ting] to the test" candidate conceptions of justice.

Given that, in our role as democratic citizens, we construct a model of justice to give us insight into it and then draw surprising consequences from it, it is up to us how that model is constructed (Thomas 2017, p.33). We have a free hand in stipulating that, in the derivation of the principles in the original position, these special psychologies are to be omitted (Rawls 2001, §25.5, §54). That reflects the limited purposes to which the different stages of Rawls's construction procedure correspond. But with the informational restrictions lifted, and all the "thick" claims about human well-being in Part III of *A Theory of Justice* available for reflection, wide reflective equilibrium takes into account data from the social sciences. That must include the critical reflections embodied in the new science of happiness. That broader test, as we have indicated, comes to the fore in Rawls's culminating discussion of the stability of justice as fairness.

That is why, given that our focus in this book is on justifications for inequality that appeal to well-being and to key emotions, it is Rawls's second argument that is our concern here: how the stability of justice is undermined by the destabilizing special attitudes.[13] Some people do exhibit such attitudes: they are prone to anxiety, envy, and the will to dominate just as they experience pride, satisfaction, and taking pleasure in things going well for other people. As we have noted, Rawls speculates that the will to dominate

[13] Whereas the "fact of domination" and Rawls's resources in dealing with it were central to (Thomas 2017).

itself rests on specific emotions, namely, "insecurity and anxiety". Rawls considers it

> a general psychological fact, that strong or inordinate desires for more primary goods on the part of individuals and groups, particularly a desire for greater income and wealth and prerogatives of position, spring from insecurity and anxiety. And the same is true of the desire to be wealthy (to have more wealth than others). (Rawls 1999, p.277)

This is a relatively charitable interpretation for at least some of the destabilizing special attitudes exemplified by particular citizens. Rawls does not assume, for example, that on the whole people are incorrigibly malicious or spiteful towards others even if his "general psychological fact" could accommodate specific instances of this.[14] If we can redress people's anxiety, then "one who is confident in himself is not grudging in the appreciation of others" (Rawls 1971/1999, p.387). But if we fail to do so, then corrosive envy is the cause of spite: "the spiteful man is willing to give up something to maintain the distance between himself and others" (Rawls 1971/1999, p.468).

This account also points towards Rawls's positive proposals for containing the potentially destabilizing effect of the special psychologies of the people represented in the original position (bearing in mind that those attitudes themselves cannot be so represented because of the inherently limited purpose of the model). They are not fundamentally malicious: they are insecure and hence anxious and, as a reaction to their own anxiety they seek to dominate others—pre-emptively, as it were. Later on, we will argue that the psychology of positional goods fits this specific Rawlsian explanation of the psychological origins of the will to dominate very well. We will also be putting to use Brennan and Pettit's point that lack of shared knowledge can lead suboptimal equilibria to persist that no one wants, but where shared ignorance leads to lack of effective action to counter them.

[14] Bill Edmundson comments that "it may be that Rawls accepted Kant's view that 'radical evil', that is, the desire to dominate others, is simply a metaphysical fact about human beings (see *A Brief Inquiry Into Sin and Faith*, passim)". However, he continues, "But Rawls has not said that it is a fact of moral psychology that people inevitably try to dominate each other". He mentions instead "moral faults", epistemic limitations such as the burdens of judgement, but also the crucial interaction of limited perspectives and anxiety (Edmundson, 2017, p.144). Edmundson cites, as evidence, Rawls's statement that "judgement is likely to be distorted by anxiety, bias, and a preoccupation with their own affairs" (Rawls 1971/1999, p.110) see also (Rawls 1999, p.277).

Crucial to Rawls's account is his theory of a citizen's self-respect and its basis. Has our topic changed when we switch from Brennan and Pettit's economy of esteem (and self-esteem) to Rawls's views? This is an important interpretative controversy: several commentators have argued that while Rawls intended to theorize the nature of self-respect, he actually—inadvertently—wrote about self-esteem instead. This is so, even if Rawls himself later clarified that his intention was to theorize self-respect. We aim here to do three things: set out what Rawls actually said and explain why there seems to be the risk of ambivalence here, before following Jeffrey Moriarty's lead and taking the interpretatively charitable line that given his goals Rawls ought to be interpreted to be theorizing self-respect just as he claimed to do (Moriarty 2009, p.445).[15] Grounds for this charitable reading are the obvious importance to his overall project of the influence of both Rousseau and Hegel (Bercuson 2014; Neuhouser 2008).

In the overall argument of this book, we will be placing further emphasis on another point made by Moriarty, namely that with the benefit of hindsight, the overall structure of Rawls's position is clearer. It begins with relational egalitarianism and runs, via the importance of self-respect to Rawls's political psychology, to its social ground in meaningful work (Moriarty 2009). As we saw in the previous chapter, Hegel was concerned that the emerging commercial society of his time would fail to provide employment for all. We noted, in passing, Fichte's insightful critique of Adam Smith's vision of commercial society as non-dominating. Fichte responded that it may well be true that, in a commercial society "well ordered" in a Smithian sense, you do not have to contract with anyone in particular nor anyone in particular contract with you. (This point has been central to the "doux commerce" tradition.) However, the problem Fichte identified was that the institution of private property requires more than a negative duty of non-interference; it also required a positive obligation to engage in market exchange (Fichte 1800/2012, Pt I, 2, p.96).[16] We will return to the importance of this point in our concluding chapter 13. We note it here because Moriarty is right that this

[15] "It is easy to see why a state should seek, as a Rawlsian state would, to ensure that people think of themselves as having full moral status. It is less easy to see why a state should seek to ensure that people think positively of themselves" (Moriarty 2009, p.455).

[16] Re-defining a right to private property as the right to exclude others from an activity, Fichte demanded that the state act as guarantor of a sufficiently good ("agreeable") life for all by guaranteeing the right to work, not simply the right to (compensatory) transfer payments (Fichte 1800/2012, chapter 7).

commitment, which is also in Rawls, originates from the requirements of his relational egalitarianism.

The origin of this complex argument, then, is Rawls's relational egalitarianism that seeks to assure for each the status of citizen. The role of the state is to underpin each citizen's self-respect, a complex idea that for Rawls has dual elements. There is, first, a sense of one's own "value"/"worth" (Rawls 1971/1999, p.256, p.440). Secondly, there is a further belief that one's "conception of the good . . . is worth carrying out" (Rawls 1971/1999, p.440). This is also expressed as "a confidence in one's ability, so far as it is within one's power, to fulfil one's intentions" (Rawls 1971/1999, p.440). In this book we will refer to these, respectively, as the *value dimension* and the *confidence dimension* of self-respect.

Robert S. Taylor insightfully relates the centrality to Rawls of a rational life plan—and the fundamental capacity to revise such plans—to the idea of both internal and external resources. Taylor puts the point as follows:

> Rationality's task of designing and implementing a plan of life requires the utilization of external resources, including especially the generic, liquid form of such resources—money. But there is a middle term, so to speak, between a plan of life and the external resources needed for its realization: *internal* resources, including skills, drive and self-discipline. As we noted above, self-realization is solely concerned with cultivating such resources, just as rationality is focused on organizing and culling desires. Moreover, like rationality, self-realization may be impeded by refractory animal impulses.[17] (Taylor 2004, p.344)

We will be placing a great deal of emphasis in this book on these "internal resources". In assessing the value dimension of self-respect Rawls drew on his central principle of well-being, the Aristotelian principle. In language reminiscent of the views of Csikszentmihalyi discussed in chapter 5, Rawls claimed that people "enjoy the exercise of their realized capacities (their innate or trained abilities), and this enjoyment increases the more the capacity is realized, or the greater its complexity" (Rawls 1971/1999, p.426). Again, in

[17] In support of this interpretation Taylor cites (Rawls 1971/1999, pp.376–7). Our focus, then, is closer to Sen's capability approach (Sen 1985b). Sen focuses on the conversion of resources (such as primary goods) into welfare. We continue to endorse the Rawlsian objection that personal conversion rates are too variable, and too subject to privacy constraints, to play the public role of a conception of justice (Thomas 2017, p.50). However, between primary goods (as input) and well-being (as output) we share Rawls's focus on the "internal resources" Taylor describes.

terms similar to Csikszentmihalyi, Rawls argues that the relevant notion of complexity here is a person-relativized one: for example, a challenging chess problem for an international master is not appropriate for the amateur chess player.

From the outset, Rawls combined these claims about individual well-being with his account of free associations and his Humboldtian conception of society as a social union of social unions. The evaluative dimension of well-being is reinforced in associations: "unless our endeavors are appreciated by our associates it is impossible for us to maintain the conviction that they are worthwhile" (Rawls 1971/1999, p.387). The modality here is a strong one: in order to value oneself, you need social endorsement of the value of your projects. Unsurprisingly, then, associations also figure in Rawls's account of the self-confidence dimension of assessment: one's confidence is sustained by sociality as others provide a social support that "reduce[s] the likelihood of failure and . . . provide support against the self-doubt when mishaps occur" (Rawls 1971/1999, p.387). As we will emphasize throughout this book, Rawls's associational pluralism converges with his normative pluralism and his account of equal opportunity.

People have varied evaluative interests, which ground distinct projects, and each of us might "find the right pond" for ourselves—as Robert Frank puts it—by finding separate spheres of association each grounded on that distinct combination of interests and projects. Yet within those spheres we are held to certain standards and it may be shameful not to live up to them (Rawls 1971/1999, pp.443–4). Bannerjee and Bercuson interpret this emphasis on the social supports for self-respect as another aspect of the desire for recognition:

> Rawls regards . . . selves as deeply affective, as desirous of a certain kind of recognition from the institutions that coerce them and from the fellows with whom they are engaged in social cooperation. . . . Self-respect is not just a quality of individuals, it is a quality of the configuration of societies. (Bannerjee and Bercuson 2015, p.217)[18]

[18] They take this to reflect Hegel's influence on Rawls, not simply his institutionalism, but also the extent to which life under institutions plays an educative role for individuals in Rawls's developmental psychological perspective (Bannerjee and Bercuson 2015, p.218). They cite, in particular, (Rawls 1993, §I.7.1).

We would complement this point with Brennan and Pettit's distinction between dis/esteem and recognition: the former presupposes the (unlimited) domain of the latter. Rawls takes mutual recognition for granted; the importance of self-respect is that one seeks to be rightfully esteemed for those projects that are authentically one's own. That, to use Taylor's terminology, involves the overcoming of both internal and external obstacles. A marketized society that places too much importance on money sets up external obstacles; a society that demoralizes and stigmatizes the poor sets up internal obstacles. A just society removes both kinds of obstacle. We agree with Bannerjee and Bercuson that "*the* political problem is the institutional support for salutary inter-subjective relations" (Bannerjee and Bercuson 2015, p.219). That which is a primary good in Rawls's scheme is the social *basis* of self-respect, not self-respect itself, given that this basis is the only plausible candidate to be a distribuendum in the original position.[19]

We will place a great deal of emphasis on this point about the symbolic role of jointly acknowledged investments:

> [T]he social bases of self-respect are those aspects of basic institutions that are normally essential if citizens are to have a lively sense of their worth as moral persons." (Rawls 1999, p.366)

Rawls discusses the point further in the important section 82 of *A Theory of Justice*:

> [T]he basis for self-esteem in a just society is not . . . one's income share but the publicly affirmed distribution of fundamental rights and liberties. (Rawls 1971/1999, p.477)

This seems to us very close to Joshua Cohen's emphasis, that we noted in the previous chapter, on the primacy of mutual respect for each other's status as citizen over any interest in each other's unequal share of income, particularly given that the latter is a justified inequality. Furthermore, the reason Rawls gives for this concern is a solidaristic one: were income the basis of self-respect we would be "pitted against each other" (to use Hussain's phrase) or, in Rawls phrase "set at odds with one another" as we seek "self-esteem"

[19] *Justice as Fairness* is explicit that the state distributes "not self-respect as an attitude toward oneself but the social bases of self-respect" (Rawls 2001, p.60).

(self-respect) in a way that would make "the good of social union difficult if not impossible to achieve" (Rawls 1971/1999, p.478).

Mutual respect, then, never has to be a zero sum game: "the best solution is to support the primary good of self-respect as far as possible by the assignment of the basic liberties that can indeed be made equal, defining the same status for all" (Rawls 1971/1999, p.478). It matters here that Rawls, like Fishkin, is a moral pluralist and that even ideal opportunity structures offer many different pathways for a good life—so many, in fact, that choices must be made and you cannot realize all such values in your own life. But you do not have to, because if you can enter into society with your fellow citizens on the basis of mutual assurance, then you will participate in the social union of social unions. As Robert Taylor puts it, in his sympathetic exposition of Rawls's views:

> [I]ndividual men and women have neither the time nor the requisite inborn potentials to achieve all the forms of human excellence. They are forced to *specialize*, choosing to develop some skills and allowing others to lie fallow. Fortunately, however, they can participate in and enjoy the complementary excellences of their fellow citizens through social cooperation in the pursuit of shared ends. (Taylor 2004, p.341)

Because we are not just citizens, but free and equal citizens, this guarantees the social bases of self-respect by making possible those shared communities of interest in which our particular projects will be affirmed. However, we do so in a social context in which the projects of others are affirmed, too, in a mutually reinforcing way. This is a more local form of publicity, but it is shared knowledge nonetheless: it "normally suffices that for each person there is some association (one or more) to which he belongs and within which the activities that are rational for him are *publicly affirmed by others*" (Rawls 1971/1999, p.441, emphasis added). Furthermore, as the gatekeeper to the other liberties, the fair value of political liberty sets a higher bar for what counts as sufficient to resource these relationships. Jeff Moriarty draws attention to the discussion in *Political Liberalism* where the equal political liberties are to be "fair valued" (Rawls 1993, p.318): in the "competitive space" of the political, people's basic political liberties must be fair valued and secured in the context of justified inequality (Moriarty 2009).

Overall, then, it is significant that the basic liberties apply not just to individuals but also to their capacity to participate in associations in civil society, because we can anticipate that any inequality—even justified inequality—runs the risks of fanning the flames of positional competition. That is inevitable for any view, like Rawls's, that takes valuing to involve the exercise of our higher psychological capacities: if we value achievement, some will achieve more than others in some respects. Hence we have his "safety valve" argument: that diverse associations mitigate the threats of status competition leading to status anxiety and hence the will to dominate. With your status assured, you need not fear the justified inequality between you and others grounded as it is on wholly compensatory work incentives (Smith 1998). Each of us will find the right pond in which our own commitment to the Aristotelian principle finds affirmation from some contextual appraiser group or other thereby undermining the sense that justified inequality can lead to "social evaluative threat" and the need pre-emptively to dominate others.

7.3 Rawlsian Stability in a Rousseauian Frame

Relating the current discussion to the insights from the previous chapter, it seems to us that the influence of Rousseau on this Rawlsian concern about anxiety leading to "pre-emptive" defensive action is evident. We drew on Frederick Neuhouser's work in the previous chapter, specifically, his argument that:

> [A] well-ordered state can go a long way toward satisfying its members' needs for recognition by creating political institutions that guarantee citizens equal respect. . . . [T]he legitimate republic accommodates citizens' fundamental interests in finding recognition, for the core ideal of its principle of legitimacy is the moral equality of all, as embodied, for example, in the ideal of equality before the law. In realizing this ideal in a variety of ways, the legitimate republic provides a stable source of public recognition of (one significant dimension of) the worth of all individuals. (Neuhouser 2013, pp.214–5)

This might as well be a description of Rawls's view. However, the convergence extends to a deeper underlying issue:

> *To the extent that economic inequalities built into the basic structure of . . . social spheres generate inflamed desires for recognition*, a political philosophy

> committed to securing the fundamental interest of all its members must be concerned with regulating those inequalities. (Neuhouser 2013, p.215)[20]

As we have noted in the previous chapter, Neuhouser also agrees with Joshua Cohen that under the right kind of social institutions, the desire for superior status can be addressed by finding oneself to be an equal political citizen in a republic of equals. Yet that leaves a desire for social comparison that needs to be channelled via the safety valve of social comparison: this is one aspect of Rawls's non-comparing groups in his social union of social unions.

It is hardly surprising, then, when Neuhouser describes Rawls as "the most prominent of contemporary Rousseauians" (he lists Elizabeth Anderson, Joshua Cohen, and Samuel Scheffler as well) (Neuhouser 2013). He places particular importance on Rawls's strategy of prioritizing the social bases of self-respect as the most important primary good. He stresses how the difference principle requires the restriction on wealth inequality "for the purpose of preventing the rise of inflamed passions—most prominently envy" that would otherwise lead to the "pathologies of recognition" (Neuhouser 2013).[21] As Bannerjee and Bercuson put the same point:

> How are these destructive emotions mediated or prevented? On Rawls's view, the solution to the lack of recognition . . . is to institutionalize political and relative economic inequality in the basic structure of society . . . to be a citizen is to be secure about one's place in society . . . he gives us an institutional-basic structure solution to the problem of socially destructive envy. (Bannerjee and Bercuson 2015, p.220)

We not only agree, but would go further than Neuhouser, Bannerjee, and Bercuson in three respects. The first is to note, as one of the current authors already has, that all three of Rawls's principles have significant egalitarian implications—it is not as if securing the basic liberties and fair equality of

[20] Earlier in his argument Neuhouser drew a moral from Marx's "On the Jewish Question" (Marx 1994). "[T]he aims of politics cannot be much out of line with the pattern of interests in the economic sphere is the former is to remedy the problems generated by the latter: a harmony of interests 'at the top' (in politics) requires some basis for the harmony 'below' (in the economy)" (Neuhouser 2013, p.210).

[21] Noting Rawls's claim that our self-respect is reinforced by "finding our deeds appreciated and confirmed by others" (Rawls 1971/1999, p.440).

opportunity does not require a major transformation in our institutions and the constitutional securing of a right to access productive capital (Thomas 2017).

Secondly, we agree with Neuhouser's implication that Rousseau presents, in an acute form, the "fact of domination" and that focus on who holds private property and capital in any given society is the primary way to address it. Our own view is that Rawls's preferred social system of a property-owning democracy is justified by each of Rawls's principles, cumulatively, and also is his primary guarantee of the fair value of the political liberties (Thomas 2017). Neuhouser notes that:

> Property-owning democracy is an "alternative to capitalism" because it ensures "widespread ownership of productive assets," thereby obliterating (or reducing) the class distinctions (*Justice as Fairness*, 139) on which capitalism depends. Whatever property-owning democracy might look like when fleshed out in more detail than Rawls provides, it is surely not remote from the kind of society Rousseau, if writing in the twentieth century, might have endorsed.[22] (Neuhouser 2013, p.218)

We are happy to accept Neuhouser's expert opinion that Rousseau was a property-owning democrat *avant la lettre*. In our final chapter 13 we will continue to "flesh out the details" of the entire approach to which Rawls's anti-capitalist, yet non-Marxist, alternative is paradigmatic.

Thirdly, and most centrally, we will be putting to use the empirical results of the new science of happiness to vindicate Rawls's account of the importance, to citizenship, of feeling "secure". We apply this, in particular, to Taylor's idea of the overcoming of internal obstacles. This is an amplification of the previous point: the emotional logic of capitalist societies works to ease the internal obstacles of the wealthy to their self-realization, while undermining the path to self-realization of those positioned lower in the social hierarchy. Unjust inequality is, demonstrably, most harmful to the (stigmatized) poor.

[22] Neuhouser has legitimate worries that Rawls and Rousseau end up in the same place, but from different starting points (Neuhouser 2013, pp.219–21). The former is concerned primarily with fairness, but only derivatively with domination, whereas Rousseau's starting point is domination. One of the current authors has defended the view that it is a substantive and interesting discovery that an extended basic economic structure of society that makes domination structurally impossible is also one that is fair by the lights of justice as fairness (Thomas 2017).

Chapter 13 of this book will return to the question of which of these two conceptions of justice, republicanism or political liberalism, is the more realistically utopian way of addressing the problems we will identify in implementing the ideal of a market society. At this point we will simply note that there is one issue where we suspect—this is yet to be proven—that the more demanding egalitarianism of the strong egalitarian has the upper hand in this comparison. We turn, now, to our next task: that of describing the emotional regime of market societies as a whole, and capitalist market societies in particular, related as genus to species. We will place particular emphasis on the positive ways in which people have conceptualized the market fundamentalist form of capitalism prominent across the affluent West over the last forty years.

8

The Promises and Failures of Capitalist Market Societies

Propositional Summary

1. Adam Smith's vision has continuing appeal: of the organization of society under the aegis of the wise legislator to offer prosperity to all and freedom from domination by any specific individual. This vision has been taken up and developed in the classically liberal tradition allied to a conception of the free market as a liberty-preserving form of social order.
2. The central theorem of welfare economics, the Arrow-Debreu theorem, can be extended through time in the theory of finance to the idea of an Arrow-Debreu security whereby future contingent claims on income are priced. This completion of the model has an egalitarian point: the societal management of how we allocate risk in the interests of justice—via financialization.
3. Veblen cautions against confusing the technician designing an economy to maximize well-being with the capitalist whose sole motive in a monetary production economy is the profit motive. Capitalism is rescued from a crisis of over-production by the nuisance value that attaches to liberal rights of private property ownership. The capitalist tactically underproduces, or otherwise exploits market inefficiencies, in the name of profit.
4. Involuntary, structurally determined unemployment is the core disciplinary mechanism of capitalism; the Phillips Curve myth underpins the illusion of a trade-off between price control and full employment. In fact, it is an ex post facto justification for the class interests of the rentier-investor class.
5. The fear of unemployment permits the structuring of work so as to generate rents attaching to the most desirable occupations just as a

Extravagance and Misery. Alan Thomas, Alfred Archer, and Bart Engelen, Oxford University Press.
 DOI: 10.1093/oso/9780197781722.003.0009

disciplinary role is played by the worst occupations. Capitalist societies thus transform the field of opportunities in a way dictated by the social power of the wealthy.

6. Our financialized societies are structured by the interests of wealthy asset holders. Galbraith identifies a form of middle-class debt peonage; at the bottom end of the income distribution indebtedness is the effect of stagnant real wages and an inefficient welfare state.
7. Proponents of an updated version of Smith's ideal hope that a high-pressure economy of high and rising wages and tight labour markets will allow a society to grow its way out of inequality. We question whether the rent-extracting elite will permit, politically, the kind of political coalition that would already have to be in place to make these policies realistic.

Introduction

In this chapter we will distinguish the generic idea of a market society from the specific idea of a capitalist market society. Each constitutes a "social system" in Rawls's sense when he formulated his choice of systems from a closed list (Rawls 2001). They are abstract, schematic, descriptions akin to Weberian ideal types which isolate explanatorily fundamental features of socio-economic structures (Thomas 2020c). They function as templates, that need to be filled in, but that does not make them indeterminate in their content (Thomas 2015). We have, to this point, identified an ideal conception of a Smithian commercial society marked by a potential harmony of interests. In this chapter we will set out the continuing appeal of this Smithian ideal of a market society and contrast it with the problems inherent in a capitalist version of this generic type.

8.1 The Continuing Appeal of Smith's Ideal

We have already drawn on Lisa Herzog's book *Inventing the Market*; she opens her discussion by identifying that which Smith and Hegel could be taken to mean by a "market society":

> Our societies have, to a greater or lesser degree, become "market societies": they are differentiated societies whose economic sphere is characterized by individual property rights, the pursuit of self-interest, highly divided labour, and complex mutual interdependencies. Their economic sphere is a "market economy" functioning according to its own laws and principles, rather than supervening on other social relations. (Herzog 2013, p.1)

Key to this interpretation is the functional differentiation of an autonomous social sphere. It is this context that determines the relevant sense of "self-interest": it implies neither selfishness nor egoism. For Smith, these interests taken as a whole, may reasonably be combined via the correct institutions. The designer of those institutions is an impartial spectator with a benevolent concern for the interests of all. The other notable aspect of Herzog's list is that she does not mention capital—correctly, in our view. In that respect, at least, it is reasonable to conclude that Smith's vision is radically incomplete because he does not have a complete account of capital.[1] Smith's vision is of a market society, but not a fully capitalist market society which, in our sense, is a financialized society.

What, then, are market societies in this generic form—of which, as we shall see, capitalist societies are a species? Such societies attach importance to the institution of the market as a way of coordinating joint action for mutual advantage, for stabilizing mutual expectations, and for the generation, transfer, and accumulation of value.

We accept Polanyi's point that no society can be "fully marketised" (Polanyi 1944). In *The Great Transformation*, he focused on the "transformation of society into a market economy" that occurred since the Industrial Revolution (Polanyi 1944, p.101). Polanyi argued that once markets—construed as organized institutions of exchange on the basis of the prices produced by a supply-demand system—started to dominate the production, distribution, and the consumption of goods and services, this transformed people's motives from "subsistence" to "gain" and to "truck and barter". This also transformed their social relations after this revolution (Hodgson 2017). While market patterns existed before this, a market society is a society in

[1] Herzog develops an insightful account of Smith's explanation of the role of capital in commercial society and his proposal that the investment priority be—at the time of writing—the labour intensive domain of agriculture first, followed then by manufacturing and finally trade (Herzog 2013, p.33; Smith 1776/1981, IV.VII.III.35).

which markets take centre stage in their autonomized form where that is, itself, a product of political action.

Polanyi contests the way in which this process was falsely naturalized—via the postulation of a "natural" tendency to truck and barter, for example, which he argued was only one aspect of gift exchange with no natural priority over any other such system. He also emphasized how national markets were originally projects of the centralized state and how much force and violence went into introducing and policing them. A parallel account applied to the forced enclosure of the commons.

For these reasons, he drew an illuminating comparison between the way in which colonialism strips peoples of their culture and the way in which, domestically, state action on behalf of capitalism robs working people of their culture, too.

> Instead of economy being embedded in social relations, social relations are embedded in the economic system. . . . For once the economic system is organized in separate institutions, based on specific motives and conferring a special status, society must be shaped in such a manner as to allow that system to function according to *its own laws.* (Polanyi 1944, p.60, emphasis added)

We have already noted Konings's objection that this Polanyian account represents marketization as an alien, corrosive, force dissolving non-market relations—an account that makes it unclear why so many citizens across the affluent West find this so compelling because they are ethically identified with it (Konings 2015). That point is apposite and we will return to it later in this book. At this stage we will simply ask: what is it about this process of marketization that might sustains Smithian optimism as opposed to Polanyian scepticism about the outcomes from this process?

A good place to start is with "Econ 101": what do economists find valuable in a market society? A typical Cold War textbook from 1945 was appropriately optimistic about market societies interpreted as implementing the "free economy":

> The theory of a free economy, in which the consumer is "boss," would indicate that the proper balance is that which maximizes the satisfactions of the individuals who make up the economy. Moreover, the theory would indicate that this balance should be attained through a market process which

> reflects the free decisions of those individuals. (Van Sickle and Rogge 1954, p. 163)

Revealingly, priority is placed here on the citizen not just as consumer but as "the boss" via consumer sovereignty. We have noted how this fatefully shaped the later Chicago School's toleration of monopolies on the grounds that they lower prices for consumers—as envisioned in Robert Bork's *The Antitrust Paradox* that revolutionized US anti-trust law by making a putative "consumer welfare" standard dominant (Bork 1978/1993).[2]

For Van Sickle and Rogge, "being the boss" expresses our fundamental liberty interests. They assume that such interests are protected by markets as morally privileged institutions. They do so for Smith's reasons: markets are modelled, in classical political economy, as idealized entities that generate stable and mutually beneficial equilibria. They generate spontaneous social order based purely on participants doing what they want or, in the language of economics, trying to satisfy their preferences as "given".

On this conception, it is not the job of the economist to make evaluatively engaged judgements about the content of such preferences—that would violate the scientific norm of value neutrality. Elizabeth Anderson helpfully highlights in this context Marx's remark that, in market societies, liberty rules "because both buyer and seller of a commodity, say of labour-power, are constrained only by their own free will" (Anderson 2015, p.63). Market agents putatively freely and voluntarily consent to being bound by the terms of commercial contracts (which Marx took to be an illusion).

Thus the explanatory core of the conventional view lies in the coordination of mutual interests. Robert Sugden goes back to John Stuart Mill in describing the market as a "community of advantage" (Sugden 2018, p.1).[3] Markets provide participants with opportunities for mutually beneficial interactions. In competitive markets:

> [E]ach consumer is able to get whatever he wants and is willing to pay for, when he wants it and is willing to pay for it. The idea that profit-seeking traders might provide this kind of opportunity is hardly mysterious. (Sugden 2018, p.137)

[2] Extraordinarily, this intellectual dominance has only recently been challenged by the "neo-Brandeisian" School in US competition law, e.g. (Khan 2017) or (Wu 2020).

[3] Sugden cites, in particular, Mill (1871/1909, Book 3, Chapter 25, § 1).

Sugden's contractarian approach stresses exactly this: the core of what markets do is to provide opportunities for consumers to get whatever they want and for producers and arbitrageurs to benefit from that. Again, like Van Sickle and Rogge, Sugden here prioritizes the interests of the citizen-consumer.

Hayek, too, focused on market opportunities: "opportunities" and the "arbitrageurs" that take advantage of them are central to "The Use of Knowledge in Society" (Hayek 1945). In Hayek's view, markets are decentralized systems of self-organization, voluntary cooperation, and spontaneous order. Hayek understood the market order to be a "catallaxy": a spontaneous order that is the unintended outcome from the free interaction of different individuals with separate goals and dispersed information and knowledge (Hayek 2012, chapter 10). The price mechanism plays a pivotal role in mutually coordinating those interactions: this is its crucial price discovery function which is a macro-level, systemic, feature of markets.

Many of the strongest proponents of markets are, not coincidentally, amongst the fiercest critics of states, which they argue inevitably make use of, or end up with, coercion and violations of people's liberties. For example, Milton Friedman argued that decentralized markets are prerequisites for freedom. A centralized state ought to provide national defence, and a monetary system, and enforce the rule of law—especially property rights. But any attempt to overstep these boundaries leads to infringements of freedom and ultimately to dictatorship (Friedman 1962/1982/2002).

> Economic arrangements play a dual role in the promotion of a free society. On the one hand, freedom in economic arrangements is itself a component of freedom broadly understood, so economic freedom is an end in itself. In the second place, economic freedom is also an indispensable means toward the achievement of political freedom. (Friedman 2002, p.8)

Friedman praises societies with strong market economies for the ways in which they decentralize and diversify power and steer it away from the state. According to him, this provides a necessary and integral ingredient for a robust set of political and civil freedoms. This view sees an intrinsic connection between robust economic liberties and classically liberal basic liberties more generally.

Another version of this argument thinks that it ought to be reformulated: markets maximize real freedom through the wealth they generate such that they are instrumentally justified. (Of course, the two arguments are often combined.) Market societies have proven to be efficient in generating wealth and this in turn increases the real freedom of their members (McCloskey 2016). Just compare, so the argument goes, the possibilities of a twenty-year-old person now to those of a twenty-year-old person in the early nineteenth century. Due to increased societal wealth, people now have more resources, which increase their opportunities and enable them to pursue more (different kinds of) life paths.

While that argument is undoubtedly true, and we would not contest it, it is an ambivalent argument: there have been many varieties of capitalism, including such historical practices as mercantilism and colonialism, that have played a causal role in explaining the extraordinary wealth of the average person's collective "inheritance" from the past (Thomas 2017; Piketty 2020). It is not true that this affluence is the result solely of the operation of the kind of market centred, anti-statist, classically liberal vision that Friedman, Hayek, and McCloskey favour. It would be a selective reading of history to defend that claim, as Piketty makes clear in his history of inequality regimes (Piketty 2020).

The more formalized version of these pro-market arguments from Hayek and Friedman focus on what Debra Satz calls their "welfare Paretianism"—an aspect of their concern with efficiency (Satz 2010). Markets are instrumentally good at achieving a specific goal, which is often defined in welfarist terms and can thus refer to the generation of wealth or to the satisfaction of actual preferences. If the first advantage that the proponents of markets envisage is that it ensures that people are free to prefer what they want, the second advantage is that markets promote the satisfaction of whatever people freely choose to prefer. Whatever the motivations for economic competition—ethically admirable or not—the outcome is promised to be the aggregate good of all.

Whatever the outcome is, markets ensure that it is Pareto optimal: a distribution of resources such that no resource can be transferred from one agent to another to make him or her better off without making some other agent worse off. While individual economic agents are in competition with each other, the competitive system as a whole produces Pareto optimal outcomes. In that sense, everyone wins from this social system and all win-win opportunities are exhausted in a clearing market. The connection with the concerns of this book ought to be clear: markets ideally respect both individual liberty and the good of all—construed as welfare or preference satisfaction.

This ideal is most clearly expressed in the Arrow-Debreu theorem—the foundational theorem of welfare economics (Arrow and Debreu 1954). This theorem states that, under ideal conditions, there is a general (Walrasian) equilibrium such that the market will clear in a way that optimizes welfare. Under the appropriate conditions, a decentralized market economy, with perfect competition and suitably defined property rights, will generate economically efficient equilibria.

At the core of this justification for marketization, then, is the ideal of individual liberty. Every agent in the Arrow-Debreu model is equally *powerless*: both consumers and firms. Market power is fully dispersed when every agent is a price taker and not a price maker. Here we loop back to Smith's ideal of non-domination: market exchange is unlike hierarchical relations in which some outrank others because market exchange occurs amongst equal, not subordinate parties and thus avoids servility, subordination, deference, and dependence on any other particular agent. Consider, by analogy, a traffic jam: a multiplicity of private decisions have obstructed your freedom if you also intended to drive to work. But there is no dominating agent in this case, either individually or collectively, so on this view you are not dominated.

This ideal seems confirmed by the historical record of the emergence of markets: when societies slowly turned into market societies, a plurality of actors combined to roll back privileges, such as state-enforced monopolies, in a way that would prove beneficial to all in the long run as part of a process of marketization.[4] That is why, faced with high levels of inequality, economic liberals argue that our response ought to be more marketization, not less. When states move beyond their minimal role and "interfere" in otherwise "autonomous" markets, they inevitably over-step their boundaries and tip the balance of power, which makes for hierarchy and subordination.

Hayek makes the strongest claim that equality in power relations protects liberty in *The Road to Serfdom* (Hayek 1945/2007). Hayek there argues that whenever politics intervenes in the economy, and central government planning replaces free markets, individual freedoms are lost and bureaucracy

[4] However, we do think it is necessary to balance this observation with a sensitivity to the historical evolution of the different cultures of capitalism. The United States, for example, has risen from being a British colony to superpower status largely because of the role played by the American developmental state (Levy 2021).

incrementally gains power. The inevitable result is similar to the relation between feudal lords and their serfs—hence his title.[5]

Hayek's view of markets as systems of voluntary exchange, and not socially engineered technologies aimed at maximizing welfare, plays directly into this argument. Markets with private property are to be preferred because they maximize freedom and minimize mutual dependency. They are not directly justified in terms of economic efficiency. Even if such an arrangement is not fully economically efficient (why does each family have its own lawnmower?), this form of market order reduces mutual dependency and decentralizes power. For this classically liberal tradition, by far the best way to let people's non-admirable motivations, such as self-interest, greed, and thirst for status and power, to reign freely is to allow them to interact in markets.

In other circumstances, these motivations inevitably lead to hierarchies and relations of domination and servility. In markets, they disperse power and stimulate mutually beneficial interactions between agents of equal standing. It is unusual to find Keynes echoing the same theme, but he also believed that economic competition was a channel for less than admirable human propensities that would be even more damaging if employed elsewhere. The obvious question, however, is what this liberty first approach, focused on non-domination and robust economic liberty, implies for equality.

The mainstream of the classically liberal tradition certainly aspires to vindicate many principles to which we are also committed: fair equality of opportunity, social mobility, and the value of market-based merits (taken as admirable forms of achievement). In the ideal of a fully marketized society, social mobility is enabled by economic opportunity and material advancement. It is natural for market-based societies to attach a great deal of importance to market-based merits. As in the original Smithian ideal, markets require investments of human capital in the sense that the division of labour requires the "all purpose" farm labourer to become as skilled in specialized tasks as an industrial labourer. On this view, markets and meritocracy go

[5] Hayek argues that the case against "central planning" has been won: the problem he faced (as he penned prefaces to later editions) was the rise of welfare state capitalism. This is an invalid slippery slope argument: Hayek argues that if a welfare state ever plans, in a domain where it should marketize, then it will find itself planning all aspects of economic life and suppressing political liberty. However, we agree with Hayek that the kind of rent-extracting halfway house where uncoordinated planning is carried out by private capitalists who have subordinated the state to their private interests is equally undesirable—Hayek calls this "syndicalism".

hand in hand.[6] Markets reward individual productive contribution: the marginal addition that each employee makes to the overall productive surplus.

However, the promise to which this tradition attaches the highest importance is of a higher standard of living. Arguments for the dynamic efficiency of capitalism point to its constant innovation that, once again, creates an opportunity for anyone to come up with a "disruptive innovation" producing both wealth and social advancement.

However, there would seem to be one, very important, omission from the basic concerns of the classical liberal. The leading such liberal in recent philosophy, John Tomasi, explains that he is a classical liberal and not a libertarian because his view—free market fairness—has an intrinsic concern for justice (and does not make a fetish of property rights) (Tomasi 2012). He criticizes Hayek's rhetoric directed against the "mirage" of social justice, although it is worth bearing in mind here Hayek's specific target, namely, redistributive "interference" with patterned outcomes (Meshelski 2019). The views of Hayek and Friedman that we have set out to this point may well have a concern with the worst off, but the risk in their views is that those concerns will be extrinsic to justice.

The worst off may be taken into account because their low level of welfare impacts aggregate welfare, or they may be appropriate subjects for a duty of charity, but we think that Tomasi is right to suspect that market-friendly classical liberalism has no intrinsic concern with justice. In particular, the premises we have set out for the classical liberal do not rule out economic inequality in outcomes. If they are to be avoided, it can only be a contingent side effect of respecting people's free choices. Alternatively, it accompanies the desirable consequences generated by markets (efficiency, productivity, wealth maximization, and maximal satisfaction of preference, power dispersal, and equal standing). One of our major claims in this book is that there is no way of evading the question of the intrinsic value of justice. We will turn to that point after discussing in more detail the canonical formulation, within economic theory, of these desirable features of markets: the Arrow-Debreu theorem.

[6] Yet we will note in chapter 12 that both Nozick and Hayek deny that the market is "for" the reward of personal merit because in that sense the market is not "for" anything: it is a matter of procedurally respecting just entitlements, or following the pre-distributed "rules of the game". (There is no equivalent of the Smithian ideal legislator adjusting outcomes to merit in their systems.)

8.2 Extending the Model to Financialized Capitalism

We have stressed that, in our view, the major break between the commercial society of Smith's day, the market society Hegel critiqued, and our own sophisticated capitalist economies is that the latter are financialized through-and-through. Finance is not some "veil" over the real economy: it is the real economy. The theory of finance is a natural extension of the most developed justification of markets in welfarist terms, namely, the Arrow-Debreu theorem.

What is being maximized in these abstract models—with highly idealized assumptions of perfect competition and fully rational market agents—is social welfare. This is understood to be the satisfaction of preferences of all the parties involved. This welfarist goal can be equated with well-being, at least on the latter's preferentist view according to which people are better off the more of their highly ranked preferences they satisfy. More technically, the convex indifference curves that model consumer preferences and that make up aggregate demand and the convex production sets for firms that make up aggregate supply together result—under conditions of perfect competition—in prices that generate Pareto efficient equilibria. In that set of equilibria every consumer finds the good that she is willing to pay for and vice versa. (Informally, you could put it this way: the utility-maximizing consumer meets the profit-maximizing firm.)

This ideal market setting is maximally deep, efficient, and it attaches prices to all commodities both now and into the future. Such markets are *complete* and *perfectly competitive*. It is the ideal of market completeness that forms of the basis for the extension of the view for all possible future states of the economy.

We have stressed Schumpeter's point that the superiority of capitalism over other forms of economic organization depends on its dynamic and not its static efficiency. When we turn to this dynamic, through time, model we can introduce a derived theorem that expands the basic Arrow-Debreu model into the future via an Arrow-Debreu *security* (Hockett 2014). That is a means of pricing a contingent future claim on income—it is an extension and completion of the model. It also, in theory, offers a rational basis for the theory of external financing—how a future return on an asset can be priced. If we can price risk, then we can also spread and channel risk to those best placed to be the risk bearers. Adam Smith, once again, was aware of the point:

> The trade of insurance gives great security to the fortunes of private people, and by dividing among a great many that loss which would ruin an individual, makes it fall light and easy upon the whole society.[7] (Smith 1776/1981, V.I.3.821)

If the concerns of insuring future claims seem, on the face of it, to have nothing to do with justice, Robert Hockett explains how both Rawlsians and luck egalitarians can be interpreted as taking justice to involve:

> [A] kind of ongoing, life-long market in goods, services and insurance, the participants in which market are equally endowed with knowledge and control over future contingencies. (Hockett 2014, p.627)[8]

Thus we can see Smith as anticipating a financialized society. His wise legislators, armed with the Arrow-Debreu theorem, will take note of such facts as the fact that a citizen can exhibit all the bourgeois virtues and yet find themselves ruined either by involuntary unemployment, or finding their house in "negative equity", as a result of macro-level contingencies wholly outside of their control (Hockett 2014).[9] The answer is market completion via insurance.

Hockett argues, compellingly from our perspective, that to address problems such as these we need more financialization of risk, not less (Hockett 2014). Financialization, and the finance sector, certainly play a key explanatory role in explaining the rent seeking and inequality we have documented. But that is not because we can live without finance, but because the financial system we have is undemocratic, and has been distorted to serve the interests only of the wealthy and those who work in the financial sector (where those two groups substantially overlap). Hockett describes his alternative radical vision for a "capital commons":

[7] Or, as Hockett puts it: "Insurance is a means of pooling, generally through market exchange, broad classes of risk, the eventuation of which, in relation to the pool's risk-bearers as a whole, are reasonably affordable, while in relation to all or most risk-bearers taken as individuals, are not. Herewith . . . is the source of insurance's capacity to both effectuate and allocate risk-bearing more efficiently" (Hockett 2014, p.629).

[8] In Hockett's responsibility-sensitive egalitarianism, parties start from an initially equal set of endogenous endowments and make trades for which they can be held responsible, where those trades include taking out insurance contracts. In this way current consumption is foregone to insure against future contingencies: this constitutes market completion.

[9] That is the point of Hockett's parable of Bill and Barbara, the small-town lawyer and business owner, respectively, who exhibit all the Smithian commercial virtues but find themselves ruined by risks they could not have foreseen and not insured themselves against (Hockett 2014, pp.617–21).

> The process of financialization begins when private managers of public capital attempt to re-socialize the investment risk attendant on decentralized privately ordered production. Offloading risk in this way quickly turns capital markets into sites of individually rational, collectively irrational "feedback" dynamics at which capital managers find greater profit in *gambling* on price movements in "capital *markets*" than in *investing* in productive capital *projects.* (Financialization is in this sense the "foam" of which Keynes speaks in the justly celebrated twelfth Chapter of the *General Theory.*) (Hockett 2020a)

If a company seeks to fund investment by going to the capital markets, that is, in Hockett's terms, a primary market: speculation emerges when claims in the market are reflexively traded on meta-markets of every kind. These bets on bets, iterated into different levels, are the speculative "foam" that dominates our financial sector.

That is our current reality—largely the product of successful Wall Street lobbying—but the Arrow-Debreu theorem and its extension and completion seem important to the development of the idea of a just society as progressive economists (not merely Arrow and Debreu themselves) have concluded.[10] We ought to allow all citizens to insure themselves against life's key risks and such core assets as their future income stream qua return on their labour and their housing assets (Hockett 2014).[11] Actually existing financial markets may be dysfunctional for the reasons Hockett indicates, but we actually need more such markets, not fewer, as at present we leave most citizens uninsured against some of life's gravest risks (Schiller 1993). A democratized "capital commons", as Hockett calls it, is the necessary precondition for an extension of insurance markets along the lines suggested by Hockett and Schiller—and anticipated by Smith. It is the completion of the Smithian ideal. As we will discuss in our concluding chapter, insurance of this scope and scale requires the insurer of last resort and the monopolist of money, namely, the monetarily sovereign state.

[10] See, for example, in the work of William Baumol, Robert Schiller, Hal Varian, and Bill Vickrey (Baumol 1986; Schiller 1993; Varian 1976; Vickrey 1960).

[11] Any egalitarian who thinks either that it is a matter of basic well-being that people ought to own a primary housing asset, or who is more generally committed to widening access to capital, has to worry that she is simply spreading more uninsurable risks to more citizens (Hockett 2014; Thomas 2017). That will be true unless we make our financial system serve the interests of justice—as in Abba Lerner's "functional finance" (Lerner, 1943).

We have, then, the theoretical tools to formulate what is attractive about the classically liberal market ideal—but it has no intrinsic concern with justice. When we seek to complete it for all possible states of the economy, we have to theorize the nature of a financialized economy. Again, it seems we can hardly do so without introducing the concept of justice.

What, then, explains the gap between these ideal models of the economy and actually existing capitalism? Why did Keynes, the greatest of all economists, view our capitalist societies as merely an historical stage that ought to be overcome—via the "euthanizing" of the rentier (Keyes 1936)? Why have we not, in fact, succeeded in moving beyond this historical stage and seem, in fact, to be trapped in it? We next examine one famous diagnosis: that we have been working in the utopian sphere of the theorist—the technician—who seeks to design an economic system (or explain how it spontaneously arises) to maximize the human good, or justice, or hopefully both. The reason we cannot understand actual economies is because their fate is determined by a different kind of animal—the capitalist!

8.3 Veblen: The Engineer Versus the Capitalist

Veblen argued in "The Engineers and the Price System" that the classical liberal arguments which we have just explored were written from the point of view of one kind of engineer, namely, the institutional engineer (Veblen 1921/2019).[12] The economist plays this role when she explains how to design markets for the general good armed, for example, with technical results like the Arrow-Debreu theorem. But this engineer, whose revolutionary goals are oriented to an end state—the utility-maximizing consumer meeting the ideally competitive firm—is not the capitalist. Capitalist economies, Veblen is reminding us, are monetary production economies. The sole motive for commercial activity, for the capitalist, is anticipated profit. The search for technical efficiency may serve that purpose; equally, in some cases, it may not. Indeed, the capitalist, unlike the engineer, may seek out systemic design flaws (or, indeed, try to generate them) because they are a source of profit.

Veblen opens his essay with the etymology of "sabotage": it is taken from the French word, "sabot", for an uncomfortable wooden shoe in which one

[12] With one important caveat: Hayek's caution against taking up precisely this perspective of the "engineer" of socially desirable economic outcomes.

can only walk with effort. It slows you down, just as the saboteur seeks to undermine a productive process. Veblen's point is that the owners of a business, as much as an employee who "owns" his or her productive capacity, has the right to withdraw it. Both Amartya Sen and Thomas Scanlon have noted that merely allowing someone to use your property can be a productive contribution in this technical sense of "contribution (Sen 1982; Scanlon 2018, p132, fn. 16).[13] In their treatment, that forms part of (in our view) a well-motivated critique of the idea that we can isolate an individual's marginal contribution to production. But the flipside of that idea is of interest to Veblen: if I can grant you permission to use a resource of mine (whether my land or my labour or my capital) equally I have a right to withdraw it. That is because the legal right to private property also generates the permission to generate that which, in legal terms, is called "nuisance". If business owners did not have this right over their productive resources, then they could not limit supply to sustain profit.

If that seems perverse, then Veblen points out that without this way of supporting profit, recessions would be more frequent. More generally, optimal sustained profit may require regulation of supply below optimal levels of output even if the latter is technically productively efficient. Veblen asks for parity of reasoning: if you are in favour of the right to strike then you need to note the symmetry here. The withdrawal of labour via a strike is of the same category as lockouts by employers: the withdrawal, for a temporary period, of a factor of production to defend an established interest.

The ordinary working of the economy, then, is a product of the dynamic interaction of the interests of owners of "factors of production" working within the sphere of their rights and entitlements and the only true, general, explanation overall that explains the working of the whole system is the profit motive. The aim of the business owner is not to maximize Kaldor-Hicks efficiency, but to sustain profits over the long-run.

> In any community that is organized on the price system, with investment and business enterprise, habitual unemployment of the available industrial plant and workmen, in whole or in part, appears to be the indispensable condition without which tolerable conditions of life cannot be maintained . . .

[13] We will discuss Sen's ideas in more detail in chapter 12 in the context of a critique of meritocracy. Sen (1985) is a general treatment of the idea that we can isolate an individual's marginal contribution to production; he calls it "the personal production view" in (Sen 1982). One obstacle to that—the one relevant here—is the necessity of "owned impersonal resources" to production.

> in no such community can the industrial system be allowed to work at full capacity for any appreciable interval of time, on pain of business stagnation and consequent privation for all classes of men. The requirements of profitable business will not tolerate it. (Veblen 1921/2019, p.13)

The way to avoid the Marxist crisis of over-production is to allow capitalists to judge, within their rights, when it is prudent to restrict output. That, in turn, requires discretionary market power—hence we have an over-determined case for the Schumpeterian argument that every firm seeks a monopolistic edge, no matter how temporary. Monopoly control gives the capitalist "elbow room" to increase or decrease production as she sees fit.

As Veblen points out, this is not a point made in the literature that celebrates the heroic exploits of the entrepreneur: that the routine management of commercial enterprise involves the judicious use of self-sabotage in the form of tactical under-production influenced by prior investment decisions—fixed costs of debt repayment to the rentier class. If you financed your factory with a loan or by issuing bonds, repaying the interest is a fixed cost. While Schumpeter celebrates the entrepreneur who pushes forward the production frontier, temporarily giving a firm a monopolistic "edge", Veblen focuses on under-use of the production capacity there is already to hand in the interests of sustaining profit. Veblen's explanation is similar to Marx's in that he takes this to be a systemic feature of capitalism and no individual business owner could depart from the norm without risking bankruptcy (Veblen 1921/2019, p.15).

There is also a nod to Marx in the implicit argument that if capitalist over-production would lead to crisis, then the capitalist class does not over-produce. Veblen also traces the emergence of this issue to the rise of financialization: when technological problems of production had been solved, external financing of the corporation became the norm and—as Minsky also later noted—external financiers (both investors and bankers) want to invest in firms that are price makers and not price takers (Veblen 1921/2019, pp.20–1; Minsky 1986/2008).

As Veblen shrewdly observed, those at the top of such firms carry the title "captains of industry" when actually their putative knowledge of the technologies of production they control is lacking; they are, instead, "captains of finance" (Veblen 1921/2019, p.21). Below them in the corporate hierarchy are the real experts concerning production whom Veblen memorably calls, in an illuminating military metaphor, the "general staff" of the large firm (Veblen 1921/2019, p.25). His revolutionary "soviet of engineers" would see industrial capacity placed wholly under the supervision of this class freed from the "sabotage" of managers or politicians. The goal of this soviet would be maximal productive efficiency for the common good. You could conceptualize this as the implementation of the Arrow-Debreu vision by, as it were, fiat. Veblen's point is that this is not the form of capitalism that we have. The gap between the intellectual justifications for capitalism we discussed in the previous section and the realities of monetary production economies is significant.

We can now update Veblen's critique: the work of Bill Lazonick and Jang-Sup Shin documents the struggle, in the Chandlerian firm, between the large-scale professional managerial class who constitute a "general staff" with detailed knowledge of the productive process, and the emergent all-purpose "executive" who moves freely between the different departments of the large-scale industrial conglomerate without that repository of local knowledge (Lazonick and Shin 2019). Finally, above the general staff, we have the executives of the C-suite who are as much financial engineers as executives and whose rent-extracting activities in the US context—which Lazonick and Shin call in many cases "looting"—have seen them promoted from Veblen's "captains" of finance to an even higher rank (Lazonick and Shin 2019).[14]

There is one aspect of Veblen's argument that we focus on here: the pre-eminent systemic form of "underproduction" in an economy directed by private investors and managers motivated solely by profit is involuntary unemployment. If there is one resource, above all, that capitalism does not employ with maximal efficiency it is labour. As we noted, Robert Pippin has argued that Hegel's optimism about commercial society as an avenue for emancipation ought to have been derailed by the observation that it was a monetary production economy (in Veblen's sense) focused primarily on profit (Pippin 2020). Furthermore, Hegel ought to have connected that point to his concern that commercial societies would not provide employment, and hence not provide this avenue to emancipation, to all.

[14] So named because the occupants of the C-suite have job titles that begin with "c", usually the word, "chief": chief executive officer, chief financial officer, and the like.

8.4 Kalecki: The Disciplinary Role of Unemployment

Hegel's concern anticipates the twentieth century's most famous nine pages of political economy: Michael Kalecki's "Political Aspects of Full Employment" (Kalecki 1943). If Keynes was correct to identify structural unemployment as the single most important indicting feature of capitalism, then it is Kalecki who identifies it as capitalism's most important disciplinary device (Keynes 1936/1964; Kalecki 1943).

The paper poses this puzzle: suppose we have, for the sake of argument, discovered the true economic theory. We can use the monopoly powers of the monetarily sovereign state to smooth out the business cycle through the state's capacity to go into deficit, put in place artificial buffers and stabilizers, and the other policy resources of Keynesian demand management. The result is good for all sections of society: under full employment, with mass consumption, we can envisage what we would call a "Taylorist-Fordist" model for capitalism with prosperity for all—including the capitalist class. Profits, underwritten by the state, will be consistently and sustainably high (Levy, Farnham, and Rajan 2008).[15] Why, then, is the capitalist class not as willing to embrace this option as the others who stand to gain from it—such as the working class?

Kalecki's answer is straightforward: such a concession would be to call a truce in a class war where the rentier-investor class claims its excessive share of the productive surplus. This class would lose its authority over the workplace where discipline over workers is at the service of suppressing the workers' share. This diagnosis echoes Marx and Engels's sardonic comment that "the executive of the modern state is but a committee for managing the common affairs of the whole bourgeoisie" (Marx and Engels 1848/2011). The monetarily sovereign state could exercise its monopoly powers to underwrite full employment, just as Keynes, neo-Keynesians and more recent "modern monetary theorists" insist, yet on the contrary it exercises its monopoly powers selectively to further some social interests as opposed to others (Hockett 2019; Tcherneva 2013; Thomas 2020b).

This is, obviously, not the form of capitalism we have; the rentier-investor class has captured the state in the political development of the "deflationary

[15] Kalecki and Jerome Levy are the eponymous originators of the Levy-Kalecki profits equation (Levy, Farnham, and Rajan 2008).

bloc". As we diagnosed in our opening chapters, the last forty years has seen the entrenching of what Mark Blyth has called the "creditors' paradise":

> [P]ositive real interest rates, low inflation, open markets, beaten-down unions, and a retreating state—all policed by unelected economic officials in central banks and other unelected institutions that have only one target: to keep such a creditor's paradise going. (Blyth 2015)

The rentier-investor class has, it seems, exerted extraordinary political power and has successfully resisted being "euthanized".

One of its central achievements has been to elevate a local econometric generalization—the Philips Curve—to the status of the founding myth of the macroeconomic organization of our societies. That myth claims that we can desire both full employment and low inflation but we cannot achieve both in practice: the politics of the deflationary bloc dictates that the trade-off must be made at the expense of full employment. The Phillips Curve arrives on the scene to offer an economic rationalization for this political demand.

The best we can manage under these constraints, it seems, is "active labour market policy" where, in the Nordic welfare state model, private capitalists drive the cycle of investment, business, and employment, with the state in the role of trying to guess which sector the next downturn will affect in its generation of cyclical unemployment. Under such a policy, the state continually retrains the unemployed for jobs that, as Hyman Minsky drily put it, don't yet exist and probably never will (Minsky 2013; Thomas 2020b).

The politics of the deflationary bloc "naturalizes", in Polanyi's sense, permanent, structural unemployment as a means of inflation "control" such that the only realistic effect of state action can be to spread unemployment more "fairly" amongst the involuntarily unemployed (Minsky 2013; Thomas 2023). A failure to supply work for all who want to work is, on the contrary, a paradigm of unfairness. It invites a supplementary narrative, notably that of the meritocrat, whose incipient social Darwinism is brought out in the observation that the market flags up who is entitled to a job and who is not. As Scanlon notes, this also invites a subsequent moralization of the defects of those who could have been amongst those fortunate to be employed—had they only tried harder (Scanlon 2018, p.60). This stigmatization acts as an ideological cover for the fact that this unemployment was structural and hence involuntary.

As the argument of this book unfolds we take this issue—the disciplinary role of involuntary unemployment—to be the central defect of capitalist market societies that leads to the distortion and failure of the Smithian ideal. The open question, then, is whether the wise Smithian legislator, having read Michael Kalecki (and Fichte) can simply add a policy of full employment to the Smithian design of the ideal economy. We discuss that option in our final chapter.

The Philips Curve is a myth amongst myths: another aspect of the "learned helplessness" of the state is that, if it is construed as redistributive tax and transfer state to produce desirable social outcomes, it putatively becomes structurally dependent on the wealth-creating activities of private capitalists. As the directors of the overall flow of capital investment, their rights over their productive property allows them to generate the underuse of resources in the interests of maximizing private profit, as Veblen argued. Specifically, it allows them (as a class) to under-use people in a way that preserves their disciplinary control of the workplace, as Kalecki argued. The negative impact of this structurally generated unemployment on human well-being is profound.

The defender of capitalism might shrug: have we not witnessed, under recent capitalism, the end of joblessness? It is, indeed, of structural interest that in particular capitalist societies at particular times, the elite-driven projects of specific states have seen many people employed—recent examples would be the United Kingdom and Germany (before the global pandemic of 2020–1). However, behind those numbers are the facts of poverty in work and the capacity of employers to adapt (to put it politely) to taking advantage of the payment of welfare to those in work to generate a substantial category of low-paid and precarious employees.

In these societies, labour market participation rates are low, not least because of the structural perpetuation of poverty traps. Even when levels of employment are high, the threat of unemployment performs its disciplinary role in influencing the quality of available work. Poorly paid and precarious workers, non-unionized, have virtually no bargaining power and are individually subject to the disciplinary threat of unemployment even if the productive process could not dispense with them as a class. Once again, as part of its learned helplessness, the state is not playing the role it ought to play as the employer of last resort which would serve to drive up the standards for the employed in the private sector in terms of both pay and working conditions. A state acting as employer of last resort can drive up employment standards such that private employers are forced to raise their own standards—unless they want no workers at all.

8.5 The Proliferation of Capitalist Discipline

From this core disciplinary mechanism others are generated: there is a damaging derivative effect from structural unemployment on the implementation of fair equality of opportunity. Veblen's contrast between the engineer and the capitalist can be extended to the very idea of a Smithian division of labour. That is our interpretation of Paul Gomberg's important work: work is currently organized not to promote efficiency, but to establish inefficient rents used to generate a conception of "prize" jobs and those jobs at the other end of the spectrum that function more like punishment (Gomberg 2007).

The putative rationale for the Smithian division of labour is productive efficiency: it shares the justification that Scanlon endorses in Marx—some inequalities are necessities of the productive process. However, Gomberg's point is that in our actually existing capitalism a different organization of work exists that we will call the "rent enhancing division of labour". It, too, functions as a disciplinary device within the field of employment, just as involuntary unemployment functions as a disciplinary device in society as a whole. It is the fear of involuntary unemployment that forces people to accept work organized as it is currently organized. It is not Veblen's engineer who has organized work; it is the capitalist, motivated solely by profit.

Gomberg diagnoses a clustering of the best work—the most meaningful, autonomous, prestigious, and highly remunerated work—at one end of the spectrum of positions of advantage. If unemployment is the stick, these attractive jobs at the apex of the pyramid are the carrot. At the other end of the spectrum is the worst work—drudge labour, closely supervised, low status or stigmatized, poorly paid, and, or, precarious. Most jobs lie somewhere on the range between these two end points. Feminists point out that a great deal of domestic labour, tending as it does to be at the lower end of this spectrum, is not even on the market and not acknowledged to be work at all (Fraser 2014, 2016).[16]

[16] As Joshua Preiss notes, "the majority of the remaining gender pay gap is due to intra-occupational inequalities, which vary widely by occupation" (Preiss 2021, p.12). Gomberg's point is that it is this individuation of occupations that is open to challenge (Gomberg 2007).

Rent seeking attaches to the best jobs because the bundling of these features constitutes the generation of rents attaching to positions of advantage. The rent-enhancing division of labour is a violation of another principle that Scanlon cites, namely, that:

> If an institution is organized in a way that requires those occupying a certain role to have a certain ability, but could serve its purposes equally well if it were organized in a different way that did not require this ability, then equality requires that it make this change, because giving preference to candidates who have this ability is unjustified.... [T]he values that are relevant for institutional justification... are not limited to what might be called values of output efficiency, but also include the value, for individuals, of the opportunities for productive work that an institution provides. (Scanlon 2018, p.46)

Involuntary unemployment grounds a derivative way in which people are pitted against each other that both Gomberg and Fishkin highlight: within jobs, the competition is intense for the "best jobs": this "pits people against each other".

The way in which a society structures its opportunities is a matter of common knowledge; its members decide to be the kinds of person they have to be in order to compete—or not—within the field of the rent-enhancing division of labour. The more de facto exclusion from the field of opportunity there is, the stronger the development of counter-cultural norms.[17]

This explains, for example, the derivative importance of elite credentialling via education as marking a person off as the possessor of the right kind of market-relevant merits. While we may want to pretend that our societies offer equal opportunity for the full development of the talents of all young people, Gomberg points out that we actually organize educational opportunity by reverse engineering it from the field of opportunity as a whole. Work is organized via the "socialization principle":

> Societies such as ours limit opportunities to contribute complex abilities through a lifetime of labor. They train the young so that aspirations

[17] Gomberg develops his account, in particular, in the context of his approach to racial justice. We do not discuss this aspect of his views here, not because it is not important, and Gomberg's approach to it insightful, but because a full consideration of the issue would require more extended treatment than we can give it.

> correspond to what will exist. . . . The alternative would be the social unrest arising from the frustration of not being able to do what one has spent years training to do. (Gomberg 2007, p.36)[18]

Young people receive education correlated with their social class and its expectations, or their gender or race, with children streamed from a young age into those intended for closely supervised, menial work and those intended for high-status, autonomous work.[19] The alternative, it seems, from a societal point of view, is the waste of social resources and the education of young people for jobs they cannot hope to attain. Given the Veblen point that the rationale for positional competition is social waste, it seems there are some forms of waste that we are, as a society, prepared to tolerate and some we are not.

It may well be an improvement on the existing state of affairs if these fixed, and limited in number, positions were actually assigned on the basis of merit in a procedurally fair competition. We will return to why this is not the case in our own societies and how this myth of meritocracy damages human well-being. However, Gomberg's and Fishkin's fundamental point, independently developed, is that this entire way of organizing the field of opportunity is an extensive waste of human potential and constitutes a form of political domination. Being forced, by the social power of others, to organize your life and character around the centrality of money is to have your choices dominated by others (Fishkin 2014, p.5).

Daniel Markovits offers the complementary insight that a meritocratic ideology also damages the well-being of the ostensible "winners"—an immense expenditure of resources on elite credentialling, and the acceptance of gruelling and stressful workplace conditions as evidence of one's rightful place amongst the chosen (Markovits 2019). Since our interest in this book is well-being, it is important to note that domination by money damages the well-being of society's "winners" as much as its ostensible "losers". Winners of the prize jobs may well be handsomely remunerated, but the hundred hours a week you have to put in to display your market-relevant merits has well-being costs of its own.

[18] Compare Fishkin's conception of the "unitary model": "In this unitary model, all of those desired jobs and roles are competitive positions with a fixed number of slots. . . . The opportunity structure is, from the perspective of any individual, wholly external and fixed" (Fishkin 2014, p.15).

[19] In addition to class and race, Gomberg notes the relevance of citizenship status, with the worst work often performed disproportionately by people of certain ethnic categories, and/or illegal migrants or those with precarious migrant status.

We have, at various points in this book, appealed to Fishkin's central argument that we ought to implement a reasonable ethical pluralism in an opportunity rich environment for all (Fishkin 2014). This is a point that both the republican and the liberal can endorse: the republican, because a choice rich environment is an enhancement of individual liberty via the expansion of one's option set (even the unchosen options). The liberal, because it is part of Rawls's defence of fair equality of opportunity—a point brought out explicitly by Thomas Scanlon and Norman Daniels—that in addition to "top down" procedural fairness in job allocation, there must be substantive equality of opportunity throughout a society well ordered by justice.

Our aim here, is to put Fishkin's argument in a more general frame—we interpret his focus on the structural basis of the distribution of opportunities such that this structure is non-dominating over individual choice as a particular instance of Tilly's "opportunity hoarding". In the specific case of positions of advantage, centrally jobs, Fishkin notes that if the wealthy succeed in marketizing positional goods, this has a deep impact on the life choices of those forced to compete with them (Fishkin 2014, p.14):

> [T]he *instrumental good bottleneck*, exists when people who may have widely varying conceptions of the good, who may be seeking quite different goals, nonetheless find that they all need the same instrumental good—the paradigm case is money—in order to achieve their goals. (Fishkin 2014, p.14)

This is one, particularly subtle, way in which the social power of the wealthy dominates the free choices of the non-wealthy: the former make some putatively free choices excessively costly to the latter by imposing a penalty on certain options thereby reducing the available set. Fishkin also notes that if the main components of a good life become expensive and the number of positions of advantage that pay highly becomes restricted, then a person ought rationally to increase their efforts to get through that key bottleneck. The stakes have been raised. Once again, if the spillover effect of the actions of the wealthy is demand pull inflation for core goods, combined with the narrowing of opportunity, then higher stakes mean more intense competition.[20]

20 "Demand pull inflation" is, simply, "too much money chasing too few goods"—a spike in demand when supply is restricted.

Fishkin is equally insightful about how the structure of opportunities known to be available in a society constrain people's expectations: if money narrows that field of possibilities to the necessity of "playing the game" of getting ahead then it is one form of social conformism. Further, he shares Mill's view that this leads to a stunting of the self: a failure to cultivate one's capacities that sees those capacities lost (Mill 1869/2006) . Fishkin quotes Mill's remark that: "by dint of not following their own nature, they have no nature to follow" (Mill 1869/2006, p.58).[21]

Fishkin operates with a stylized contrast between a society that is conformist in its social attitudes, hence is organized around a unitary model of the good life and whose citizens have unitary preferences about which jobs are desirable, and a non-conformist, pluralist society with diverse preferences about desirable jobs (Fishkin 2014, p.15). As he notes, the dominance of money forces the latter kind of society into the mould of the first kind. Our interpretation of his claim is this: you can lead whatever kind of life you want, provided you make enough money to make it a viable choice—and as the stakes of positional competition rise, so does that threshold.[22]

We would add another distinctive feature of US inequality that reinforces this point: stagnant wages mean that one can only increase one's relative economic standing by working longer hours (apart from drawing down more debt). It is obviously true that the default of capitalist organization is longer hours because greater productivity offers greater opportunity for profit. There must be some pushback against this tendency, such as legally mandated limits to working weeks, or countervailing power in the workplace, or the default will operate unimpeded. However, there are various biases in the US economy that work to reinforce employer power to extract as many working hours from employees as possible.

Crucial here is the fact that America's private healthcare system operates as a de facto poll tax, as Dean Baker notes. Employers reluctant to pay this head tax on new employees would rather see their existing employees work longer hours.[23] As the Rand Corporation report that we cited in chapter 2 noted, the

[21] (Fishkin 2014, p.44).

[22] Conversely, as Fishkin puts it, in a pluralist society with many different templates for a successful life, "many of the goods that people value are non-positional, that is, one's enjoyment of the good is unaffected by who else also has it" (Fishkin 2014, pp.15–6).

[23] From the employee's point of view, this head tax creates a "job lock", making it excessively costly to risk even transitory unemployment. Fishkin notes the damaging effect of such locks on the structure of opportunities (Fishkin 2014, p.221). Joshua Preiss notes the effects on well-being: in the United States "More than 80% of those who work more than 50 hours per week would prefer to work

divergence between productivity per worker and real wages has increased, with the primary compensation effect being in number of hours worked. The main constraint that money imposes on conceptions of the good life is on the number of hours spent at work. The main "instrumental good bottleneck" connected to money is time in the workplace, bearing in mind that the latter has been radically expanded in scope by new technology to wherever you and your smartphone are co-located. There is a significant impact for well-being derived from the social norm that one ought to spend over sixty hours a week, or more, in one's workplace (even a virtual workplace).

Claudia Goldin has described the rise of "greedy" jobs (Goldin 2021, pp. 10–3). As the competition intensifies not only for top jobs, but also within jobs, it is the worker who puts in the extra time—evenings, weekends, foregoing holidays—who takes the prizes in an (internal) winner takes all market that is the contest for promotion and status within workplaces. The implications for gender injustice, in a society where informal social norms pressurize women to play a disproportionate role in childcare, are obvious. Women may now have access to a much wider range of job opportunities than in the past. However, once in these careers, they face the realities of employer expectations structured around the permanently "on call" employee, tethered via technology, and locked in to a job for multiple reasons. "At will" employment is the legal norm in the United States, and a large pool of unemployed people plays its disciplinary role, particularly in an economy with unionization at a record low.

We conclude that the disciplinary actuality of market societies is, for the most part, structured around the creation of bottlenecks. A key theme in all these different ways in which market societies ossify and become unstable is the denial of access to the goods of social mobility—education and healthcare. If, then, structural unemployment is capitalism's primary disciplinary mechanism, it grounds a further such mechanism, namely a field of opportunities structured in terms of artificial bottlenecks. Access to positions of advantages is both curtailed and, as we will argue in the next chapter, subject to "opportunity hoarding" by the already advantaged, who create these artificial bottlenecks in access to education, or to the "best" jobs, or the most prestigious credentials (Reeves 2017; Tilly 1998).

less, with 20–30% of those 'overemployed workers' preferring to do so even with a corresponding reduction in pay" (Preiss 2021, p.31).

Why, then, is our society organized this way if it violates the principle that Scanlon cites—that if justice demands that we reduce false "necessities" of the production process it compels us to do so? Our explanation is the social power of the wealthy. In the next section we focus on a more direct way in which wealthy people in the United States, and to a lesser extent the United Kingdom, dominate the life choices of other citizens via the rise of the "debtfare state". It is another blow to the view that the success and good fortune of the wealthy is independent of the struggles of the majority. The rent-seeking hypothesis explains how the wealth of the few is at the expense of the many in the very sense Rousseau identified.

8.6 Financialization and the Disciplinary Role of Debt

In his insightful interpretative essay on Hegel, we have already singled out Robert Pippin's comment on the "rich rabble" that they constantly complain, in spite of their personal wealth, of the oppression they face from the taxation system. Why should they be forced to pay for a society of which they do not view themselves as a part? In our own, connected, globalized world they can relocate to a tax haven, or to a country with low progressive taxation, or zero progressive taxation (such as the United Arab Emirates or the US state of Florida, both of which have zero personal income tax).

However, the alternative is to remain in one's "home" jurisdiction, avail oneself of the income defence industry, and campaign politically for a low effective tax rate or for a taxation system that is so byzantine that the income defence industry can put itself to work exploiting numerous loopholes for its clients (Winters 2011). If successful in these endeavours, then the wealthy will have an extensive capacity to save, and that is indeed a major cause of the structural deficit in consumption in highly unequal societies (Palley 2012). However, this has been complemented by the rise of what Susanne Soederberg calls the "debtfare" state for those who—and we noted this euphemism earlier—have "negative savings" (Soederberg 2013).

This is the logic traced out by James Galbraith: the emergence of "debt peonage" places economic stress on America's "middle class", charged with carrying a disproportionate burden of tax and transfer for an ageing population, for a growing segment of poor people, with a significant proportion of America's wealthy de facto opting out from paying their fair share of taxation (Galbraith 1998). America's richest citizens have successfully won the

Gramscian "war of position" on the issue of taxation, making the argument that as society's wealth creators, they ought not to be taxed "excessively"—for example, progressively. Regressive, flat rate, taxes may be marginally acceptable even though the ideal (as we have noted represented currently by the state of Florida) is no personal income tax at all. (Why penalize success?)

America's wealthiest citizens have succeeded most in eliminating estate/inheritance (or "death") taxes. They have nearly been as successful in undermining the rate of capital gains tax. When it comes to progressivity, the wealthiest Americans consistently pay federal taxes at a lower effective rate than those below them in the income distribution. As Jeffrey Winters explains, amongst the class of the wealthy income tax is regressive because it as a lower effective rate as one moves up the income scale (Winters 2011). Winters argues that the tax system is "essentially flat, rather than progressive," because the putatively "progressive" part of the system is offset by payroll and consumption taxes. Both of the latter are regressive (Winters 2011). To top it off, social security funding is "the most regressive tax in the U.S." because the level of income to which it is applied is capped. If wealthy people in America, unlike their European counterparts, avail themselves less of tax havens and outright tax evasion that is because their political control of the tax system means they do not have to do so.

Part of the collapse of America's inefficient, racialized, welfare state is to be explained not only by its focus on those in work (or retired from it), but also by the political withdrawal from it of America's corporations and wealthy people—a process traced out in Jacob S. Hacker's *The Great Risk Shift* (Hacker 2006). The message, as Hacker puts it, is that every American citizen "is on their own". In practice, that means finding an elite job that recovers the cost of student debt, funds housing debt, with a sufficiently generous employer-provided health insurance scheme that allows remaining disposable income to go towards one's personal 401k retirement account while also funding the provision for, and education of, one's children via tax advantaged 529 college savings plans and funding the rest of a "middle-class lifestyle". For an increasing number of US citizens, those numbers just do not add up. However, this leads to the question of how the marketization of social provision, from the privatization of pensions to other forms of social insurance, places more resources at the disposal of the financial sector.

The more punitive debt peonage is at the other end of the wealth and income distribution: those with no wealth, only debts, and with stagnant real wages cross-subsidized by unsecured credit (Soederberg 2013). Susanne

Soederberg takes credit cards as paradigmatic for her analysis: it is the poor, especially members of minorities, who "carry" high levels of credit card indebtedness that is continually "rolled over".[24] In making only minimal repayments, America's poorly paid, unemployed, or precariously employed workers are exposed to significant risk taking with their future well-being. This borrowing is a substitute for social insurance. As we will see, just as a rhetoric of democratization was exploited by proponents of the "maximizing shareholder value" thesis to lobby the SEC to force shareholders to be "active", so the extension of credit to subprime borrowers is valorized as "democratizing" access to credit. On the debtor's side, the rhetoric is of "consumer protection", as though access to credit were itself the purchase of a consumer good (Soederberg 2013, p.500). Soederberg comments:

> It is important to highlight that this expansion of credit took place alongside the ongoing dismantling of the social welfare state and the disappearance of secure, high-wage jobs in the productive realm, producing a social reality that dragged poorer workers into a growing reliance on private financing (e.g. credit cards) to augment or replace not only their social wages and subsistence needs, but also essential welfare services. (Soederberg 2013, p.501)

Soederberg observes that, in search of yield, the debtfare industry has successively worked its way through the precariously employed, the unemployed, and migrant labour in the United States, including illegal labour. The latter are particularly attractive, as unscrupulous brokers can invent a credit score out of thin air for a "non-citizen". The overall effect is not simply a maldistribution of capital away from its productive to its unproductive use; it is also a maldistribution of exposure to risk away from those most able to sustain exposure to risk to those least able to do so.

We have already set out Robert Hockett's explanation of the convergence between justice and insurance. Universal and solidaristic pooled risks marry justice to efficiency (Hockett 2014). The unravelling of social insurance begins when one party, citing its class grievance, withdraws from the collective agreement citing either the irresponsibility (moral hazard) of a minority of other users (Ronald Reagan's "welfare queens") or the monitoring

[24] Although credit cards are complemented by many other forms of predatory lending from loan sharks, to payday loans, pawnbrokers, and the misleading marketing of many debt instruments (e.g. "teaser rates").

costs of controlling the latter (Hockett 2014). Once collective insurance has dissolved in this way, then different regimes of risk apply to different classes of society ranging from the hedged and protected investments of the rich, down to the social policing (in some cases literal policing) of the worst off in America's debtfare state. The problem is not really the conspicuous consumption of the rich viewed as a form of economic activity: that is, at least, activity (Stropoli 2021). Someone needs to manufacture and retail those yachts, supercars, and wristwatches.

The deeper problem is that the state, with its learned helplessness, has been politically captured by the deflationary bloc and has abdicated its responsibility of stabilizing the macro-economy (Galbraith 1998). No one seriously believes that, in the fissured economy, the superstar firms on the commanding heights of the US economy depend on the savings of the rich in order to make the productive investments they choose to make. (If any, perhaps the money is better spent on lobbyists who will preserve a rent-seeking niche that the firm currently occupies.) They have extensive retained earnings and direct access to capital markets if needed, but the most successful of such firms are lending to the market, not borrowing from it.

Foreign investors, companies, and the wealthy hold their respective shares of US savings; the wealthiest citizens, in search of "safety" have purchased extensive amounts of public debt (Treasury bonds and mortgages held by Government Sponsored Enterprises).[25] Rent-extracting activities grow, at the expense of the productive use of capital, with a stifling effect on the latter. Social structure hardens and social mobility stagnates as society becomes divided into rent-extracting insiders and the rest of us. While Keynes sought the euthanasia of the rentier class, it seems to be enjoying a renaissance, to the point where Javier Moreno Zacarés thought it was more pertinent to title his recent analysis of developments within capitalism, "Euphoria of the Rentier?" (Zacarés 2021).

This is a deepening, accelerating, and reflexive cycle of inequality, a structural deficit in consumption, financialization, and increased private debt, leading to periodic Minskyan cycles of financial instability and eventually the culmination of the kind of multi-decade super-cycle represented by the

[25] The two major GSEs, "Fannie Mae" and "Freddie Mac" are distinctively US institutions, respectively, the Federal National Mortgage Association and Federal Home Loan Mortgage Association, both originating from the New Deal and intended to broaden the basis of home ownership in the United States by creating a liquid "secondary market" for mortgage loans, primarily those insured by another branch of the US state, the Federal Housing Administration.

global financial crisis (Dafermos, Gabor, and Michell 2020; Minsky 1986/2008; Palley 2011). We need to recall, as Benjamin Braun notes, just how unequal the initial set up of the financial system is:

> [T]he top 1 per cent of the wealth distribution own 50 per cent of the corporate equity and mutual fund shares (versus 35 per cent of total wealth), while the top 10 per cent own 86 per cent. . . . [S]hareholders may be fully diversified, but only half the population owns any shares at all. (Braun 2021, p.21)

The contribution of the financial sector to our rent-seeking explanation of current levels of income and wealth inequality in chapters 1 and 2 is succinctly captured by Braun in one sentence: "Wage stagnation for the bottom 50 per cent of the wealth distribution . . . certainly has some negative externalities for the economy as a whole . . . for shareholders . . . these externalities may be outweighed by higher corporate profits and thus higher returns" (Braun 2021, p.22).

It is the business of the state to address the macro-effects of a structural deficit in consumption, but a state that is so beholden to the interests of the rentier-investor class is hardly well placed to do so. It really is far from clear how we collectively break free of these suboptimal equilibria that are worsening over time, driven by underlying shifts in the tectonic plates of the economy that the short-termist vision of democratic politics seems unable, or unwilling, to address. What does this imply for our aspirations to implement an updated version of Smith's ideal?

8.7 Can Smith's Ideal Survive in the Twenty-First Century?

Smith's ideal is historically anachronistic: we live in a totally financialized version of capitalism. Yet the appeal of this Smithian vision endures. It combines an ideal of the market nexus as potentially non-dominating with a conception of it as offering significant opportunities for prosperity for all. It is a virtue-centred approach that seeks to cultivate responsibility, self-sufficiency, and commercial virtues in citizens. It also adopts a sufficientarian criterion for justice: justice requires that every citizen can live at a material level where he or she can appear in public without shame. It is the ideal constitutional-cum-legislative designer who adjusts market-friendly virtues to just market outcomes.

This is an incomplete theory sketch of what has become a modern industrial society. But in filling in this sketch two important points can act as a guide. First, we have noted the strength of Smith's feelings against the instigators of monopolies and cartels. Secondly, we have also noted his focus on the important role of the state in keeping markets competitive so that they serve the common good. If this new form of commercial society offers a particularly significant expansion of the opportunities for the working poor, then it also holds out the prospect of social mobility.

It is reasonable to ask how one might adjust Smith's model to our changed historical circumstances. Joshua Preiss's *Just Work* is invaluable in this regard (Preiss 2021). It is an avowed updating of the Smithian ideal so that, for example, "individuals should be able to exchange hard work for at least a middle-class quality of life for themselves and their families" (Preiss 2021, p.3). For Preiss, then, the Smithian ideal is not so much a narrative of rural labourers moving to urban factories, becoming absorbed into the division of labour, and enjoying far higher material standards. Following two centuries of economic development, we can adjust that ideal so that those who exercise the bourgeois virtues can live a "middle-class quality of life".[26]

Preiss echoes Smith when he calls this "a context-relative standard of quality of life" that includes "one's share of the benefits of economic growth" as well as secure employment and, further, what he calls "access to 'basic' services such as health care and education" (Preiss 2021, p.3, p.73). Why shouldn't ordinary Americans, with a strong work ethic who take responsibility for their own economic fate, live a "middle-class" lifestyle? Concern with their own economic fate is not selfishness, but includes a concern for the interests of family, friends, neighbours, and communities.

Our answer in this book is simple: they cannot live this lifestyle because they share their society with a predatory, rent-extracting, elite. This elite would prefer that the majority of Americans pay fees to debt merchants and generate the rental income for its corporate monopolies (particularly in, but not restricted to, the sectors of healthcare and education). The importance of

[26] Peter Temin, similarly, writes of "a high enough income"—he identifies it as annual individual income in the United States of $100, 000 or more—"to live in a good school district, own your house, and drive a new car. It is what we used to call a good middle-class living" (Temin 2017, p.24).

those latter two sectors is that they allow the top 20% of US society to pull up the ladder of social mobility up behind them to consolidate their advantages.

Higher up the income and wealth scale, the already wealthy are objects of emulation and admiration in Smith's narrative, but not directly for their wealth—rather, for their social distinction. We surmise that, like the virtuous pioneering environmentalists in Pettit and Brennan's narrative, as they drive up the general standard of prosperity, via their exemplary conduct, Smith's wealthy people ought to welcome no longer being distinguished in this way. As a driving force for economic betterment, they can happily relinquish that role when they have more than others, but are no longer comparatively rich. Yet, in the next chapter, we will document how an obsession with positionality interferes with this rosy vision.

Will the rich always be with us? On the Smithian scheme, the answer may well be "no"—although we will see later that Hayek takes a different view. It has also been surmised that the reasons Americans are relaxed about inequality is that they believe that fortunes quickly dissipate: there are always rich people, but the composition of this group constantly changes. Wealth does not, on this view, tend to become "dynastic". Piketty's diagnosis of the emergence and consolidation of "patrimonial capitalism" in the United States is, then, a wake-up call for such complacency (Piketty 2014). As Richard Reeves points out, in the United States the opposite is true: it is the wealthiest class that puts in place mechanisms for sustaining its position far more than any other social class in America (Reeves 2017, p.9). If a person lives the rags-to-riches plot line of a Horatio Alger novel, he or she can now expect their descendants to stay in the wealthy elite. The crucial disciplinary role in a capitalist market society of positional concerns—a core argument of this book—is the subject of our next chapter.

9
Positional Goods and Opportunity Hoarding

Propositional Summary

1. Hirsch is the pre-eminent theorist of positional goods. His account is embedded in a schematic account of capitalist development. We supplement his arguments by noting that what he calls oligarchic wealth can wholly supplant the claims of democratic wealth.
2. We supplement Hirsch's account via Tilly's theory of opportunity hoarding. Existing alongside open domination, the rent-extracting hoarding of opportunities is tolerated by dominators as action by a much larger social group who have come to have a stake in social structures which serve domination.
3. Corey Robin's important arguments offer a cultural explanation for why oligarchic wealth encompasses democratic wealth. The wealthy are construed as cultural legislators who, in virtue of their wealth, constitute a cultural avant-garde who legislate the nature of value. The market is re-conceptualized as analogous to a battlefield where glory may be won, or failure is shameful.
4. One important strategy for countering the spread of positionality is de-marketization via public goods. We explain how this strategy works in the case of education and healthcare.

Introduction

We are certainly not the first to take positional goods to be central to the failings of capitalist market societies. Even if economic competition could be win/win for all concerned this is not true of positional goods (Brighouse and Swift 2006). Positional competition, of its essence, either involves

Extravagance and Misery. Alan Thomas, Alfred Archer, and Bart Engelen, Oxford University Press.
 DOI: 10.1093/oso/9780197781722.003.0010

some people winning and others inevitably losing or everyone losing. For Brighouse, Swift, and Scanlon, this suggests an argument from a prioritarian concern for the worst off to a strong egalitarianism for the domain of positional goods because there is no pertinent "levelling down" objection here (Scanlon 2003). Levelling down is, in fact, the only way to produce a fair outcome in any positional domain.

In a complementary set of arguments from the social sciences, economist Robert Frank has pointed out—for decades—that positional competition is both collectively self-defeating and economically wasteful (Frank 1985, 2007, 2011). As Wilkinson and Pickett further point out, it stands in a damaging and circular relationship to inequality: positional competition is a powerful motivation that, when aggregated across society, deepens inequality. Yet inequality intensifies status evaluative threats; threats from which people feel the need pre-emptively to protect themselves against where this feeling is grounded on their own anxiety (Payne 2017; Wilkinson and Pickett 2009, 2018). As we have seen, Rawls offered a more general diagnosis along the same lines. It is this circular logic that ends up exacerbating reduced well-being across a range of indicators.

We also noted the conclusion that Frank, Pickett, and Wilkinson draw: as social scientists it seems to them obvious that we should seek policies that eliminate such self-defeating and collectively irrational attitudes that are no loss to us. By contrast, we agree with Veblen's more cynical view that were this class of attitudes eliminated, an important part of the motor of capitalist commercial society would be removed. In this chapter we will begin to expand on Veblen's point by connecting positionality to class stratification. We will emphasize that this was part of Fred Hirsch's original account of positionality in his book *Social Limits to Growth*, a classic that has largely defined this field (Hirsch 1976).

9.1 Hirsch on Positional Goods

Hirsch's monograph focuses on positional goods which are "limited in absolute supply" (Hirsch 1976, p.19). This limitation implies that we cannot argue that a person possessing less of such a good is a side-effect of a process that increases the stock of such goods as a whole. Hirsch anchors his discussion in an historical thesis: that there has been an historic inflection point within the history of capitalism:

> The contemporary impasse on who gets what and the associated impediments in the operation of the market economy can be seen as the surfacing of an embedded historical process. A long latent conflict is coming to a head. (Hirsch 1976, p.161)

With the benefit of hindsight that looks like a prescient comment; Hirsch was writing on the cusp of the Reagan/Thatcher revolutions. He was also interested in developing the long view of this conflict by analysing class stratification in capitalist societies and how it interacts with positional competition.

Hirsch argued that the problem of positionality emerges only under conditions of relative affluence. It is generated by the tension between "material" and "positional" goods. Revealingly, for our purposes, Hirsch switches between these terms and another pair of terms he takes from Roy Harrod: "democratic" versus "oligarchic" goods (Harrod 1958):

> Democratic wealth . . . comprises such command over resources as is available at a particular moment in time to everyone. It is limited by, and can rise only with, the average level of productivity. Oligarchic wealth (or income) is what is possible for the few but never—whatever the level of average productivity—for all. (Hirsch 1976, p.23)

Hirsch is interested in Harrod's apparent paradox: that the existence of some very rich people in a society is prima facie evidence that future economic growth will see everyone lifted to the same bracket as the currently rich. (Just as Smith hoped.) Yet Harrod notes that the historical record seems to point to the opposite: as standards rise, there is always a gap between the wealthy few and the democratic many. It is not true, then, that the wealth of the few is an indicator of higher material prospects for all. It seems that Smith's class of exemplary rich people, distinguished by their wealth, will always be with us. Hirsch thinks that positionality explains away Harrod's paradox.[1] Some kinds of consumption are oligarchic with a threshold of satiety far higher than the consumption needs of the many. There is always, then, a vector with two components in any distribution.

[1] As Hirsch mentions, Keynes noted in passing in his 'Economic Possibilities for Our Grandchildren', (Keynes 1930/1932), the distinction between "the needs that are absolute in the sense that we feel them whatever the situation of our fellow human beings may be, and those which are relative in the sense that we feel them only if their satisfaction lifts us above, makes us feel superior to, our fellows" (Hirsch 1976, p.25, fn.13).

In defence of this thesis, Harrod drew a further distinction between the command of a wide range of goods and services and more limited forms of luxury goods. Examples of the former are a rich person's retinue of advisers, personal assistants, domestic servants, and therapists. This is the possession of the same kinds of goods as many, more numerous, ordinary people, but possessed to a far greater degree. Then there are goods that are absolutely scarce such as $25,000 wristwatches or luxury sports cars: "If an unequal distribution prevails, the richer people will price these rare things beyond the pocket of the average man" (Harrod 1958, p.209). More limited material goods are, as it were, a residual category of things that have not been bid up by the wealthy to prices far beyond ordinary consumption.

This distinction, while it originates in Harrod, runs throughout Hirsch's discussion. Our aim here is to make explicit a feature of his discussion that remains mostly implicit: the connection between positionality and historically prior inequality. This goes beyond Hirsch by developing an argument that Harrod's category of "oligarchic wealth" always, systematically, puts pressure on "democratic wealth". We also want to address the counter-argument that any citizen has the option of opting out from status competition by living with democratic wealth alone. Once positional competition becomes entrenched as a defensive necessity there is a high price to be paid by anyone who wants to, as Timothy Leary once put it, "turn on, tune in, drop out".

Hirsch's basic idea is that in our conditions of relative material affluence people place disproportionate value on a class of positional goods for which competition is a zero-sum game. Yet individuals willingly enter the game for two reasons: there is no a priori reason why they might not be the winner, yet it is overwhelmingly probable that they will not win. Secondly, not participating is not an option because it has become a "defensive necessity". It is a classic form of irrational collective self-defeat yet one that, up to the point where Hirsch examined it, had been neglected in behavioural economics.

Hirsch argues that the importance of positionality varies from society to society and from epoch to epoch. Our argument is that there is a developmental dynamic in the affluent societies of the West that sees the aspiration for "distinction" become more intense. More importantly, it extends to the goods of social mobility and at that point entering into the competition is definitely no longer an option. To draw on Waheed Hussain's ideas: whether you are "pitted against" your fellow citizens is a suboptimal equilibrium that you do not choose, but which in a society oriented around money is chosen for you (Hussain 2020). It only takes a minority of "bad actors" to precipitate everyone into pre-emptive defensive action. We have noted the potency in this context of false beliefs—your belief that other people are seeking to disadvantage the educational prospects of your children, for example, do not even have to be true. This is, at least, the case in low-trust environments where mutual assurance has broken down.

Hirsch's analysis is not, in his original discussion, embedded in a history of distribution under capitalism. But that background can easily be reconstructed from what he does say. This game that each of us must play is systematically rigged as a result of its historic evolution through the operation of a mechanism of cumulative advantage. It is rigged in favour of those who have inherited from the past systemic advantages based on being the first entrant or from playing the same game when the relative stakes were lower. In the case of positional competition, the cost of a stake is only ever relative.

This is the theoretical underpinning for our refinement to the Easterlin paradox in this book: the workings of a social system as a whole, with its specific history, explain why increasing material prosperity may no longer translate into well-being. Capitalist societies undoubtedly deliver high levels of material prosperity only, at an inflection point, to shift the focus of most of its citizens to positional goods. The logic of frustration in the achievement of such goods is inherent to the system, and that is why affluent societies can, paradoxically, see stagnant and even falling levels of well-being.

In our interpretation of Hirsh's conclusion it was (non-exclusively) disjunctive: the paradox of collective action that he identifies either produces social waste or exacerbates inequality—but it usually does both. When you book your vacation at an exclusive resort of your own choice you are strongly motivated by the word "exclusive". Yet, once you are at the resort, then you discover that while that may have been a true description last year it is no longer true this year—all your neighbours are at the same resort as you. This reflects your limited situation of choice in any conventional market.

Hirsch's point is that the individual economic actor is never given the opportunity to select between total social states that are determined by the collective decisions of all the disparate actors who produce the outcome. Therefore, you have no reason to regret the choice you made relative to your restricted informational situation. This is a market failure explained by the mismatch between individual choice and desired social outcome that cannot be coordinated:

> The choice facing the individual in a market or market-type transaction in the positional sector, in a context of material growth, always appears more attractive than it turns out to be after others have exercised their choice. (Hirsch 1976, p.52)

These unplanned private choices by individuals aggregate to produce "system externalities" which are so "broad ranging" that they resist the standard measures for dealing with them such as "taxes and subsidies" (Hirsch 1976, p.53).[2] There are also systemic incentives for persisting in this behaviour: while not everyone seeking what he calls oligarchic wealth can achieve it, you cannot know a priori that it will not be you who does so:

> The social constraints imposed by absolute scarcities are imperfectly transmitted to the individual—no single individual is confronted with the limitations that confine society as a whole. However small the favored minority, no individual knows that he will be excluded from it; all can therefore set their sights on participating in it. (Hirsch 1976, p.26)

The risk averse can avoid entering any lottery. But the social nature of positional goods is a case where the actions of others, in aggregate, force the individual to participate in a lottery under duress.

Hirsch describes two kinds of allocation processes to "contain" excessive demand. The first is the auction as a form of rationing by price (Hirsch 1976, p.31). Its point is to "anticipate (in the sense of forestall) deterioration in quality through crowding" (Hirsch 1976, p.31). If we use the simple device of the Dutch auction we can guarantee that the market will clear. In a Dutch auction the price of a good is reduced, step-by-step, until it is taken by a buyer or—at the limit—the good becomes free.

If we do not use an auction, then we must accept the "potential social waste" of unrelieved congestion in the demand for a good. Consider the money we invest in a new highway that promises faster commuter times for all until it attracts more congestion; such that we now have two roads, the old and the new, each just as slow as the other. Our investment has been wasted.

Hirsch notes that we can turn to two further methods: setting up an extended obstacle course to reach the scarce good by "screening" or relieving

[2] As we have noted, this distinguishes Hirsch's view from Frank's, as the latter believes we can throw sand in the gears of positional competition by taxing away most of the social waste.

the congestion by taxation. An example of "screening" might be introducing a licensing requirement tied to higher educational attainment for certain classes of jobs.

Punitive taxes may literally take the form of a "congestion charge" for the crowded roads in our example: users of one road may be required to pay a toll for its use to reduce the demand. But it will, of course, displace drivers onto the free road, making the latter so unendurable that paying the toll becomes more attractive to those who can afford it—the tax structure will change the incentive structure.

From our perspective, it is important to note that there is an unhappy disjunction throughout Hirsch's discussion. In each case, prior inequality plays an important role in his analysis:

> [O]f the three basic mechanisms . . . potential social waste is therefore associated with two—crowding and screening to avoid crowding. (Hirsch 1976, p 31)

If we do not bother to relieve crowding we have social waste; if we lengthen the obstacle course to achieve a scarce good we commit people to wasting resources to ensure that they can still achieve a good, but at greater cost than previously. But that makes it look as if we should prioritize, instead, auctioning as a means of avoiding social waste entirely. The economically efficient way to deal with positional goods is auctioning them off.

It now makes a difference what class of good is under discussion. For example, to become a barrister who can appear in court in England and Wales, one must complete one's training pupillage for twelve months at a London chambers. This apprenticeship requires living in central London for a year—with no pay. If one has graduated with student debt it looks as though that form of "screening" favours the children of the wealthy and it would be more honest to announce that pupillages would be sold at auction. However, given the kind of good that this is, this marketization would be outrageous so it represents a form of "blocked exchange": you cannot literally buy a pupillage.

That seems to leave only screening: the creation of an artificial bottleneck, in Fishkin's sense. Perhaps barristers' chambers could announce that they will consider only graduates in law from the United Kingdom's ancient universities, Oxford and Cambridge. That would, from a political point of view, be as outrageous as the auction proposal. Fishkin's point, however, is that if one examines who actually receives these training places, the children of the already wealthy and those of a certain educational "pedigree" are already systematically advantaged. We are simply not honest about the screening devices in play in cases such as these.

Hirsch gives a telling example to illustrate his theses that the terms of positional competition are set by the combined effects of historically prior inequality and the mechanism of cumulative advantage. It involves exclusive suburban land. People seeking an ideal lifestyle mix of comfort, educational opportunity, and exclusivity in a suburb are subject to a market failure process. They find themselves in a suburb they come to view as non-exclusive—as soon as they have arrived. They could "leap frog" to a new suburb—repeat the process again—but with more social waste.

The alternative is collective action, through the law, and the introduction of zoning. This immediately impacts on inequality:

> In practice, however, destructive effects within the suburb itself can be checked in a variety of ways, notably through planning and zoning restrictions. . . . To the extent that such restrictions preserve the quality of suburban living by limiting the number of newcomers, existing suburban locations will then reap capitalization gains; and excess demand will be contained by price. This is the auction process of matching positional goods to increasing demand that was discussed previously. (Hirsch 1976, p.40)

In other words, this solution to crowding—"screening"—*interacts* with the auction process. It compounds inequality via capitalization and subsequent rent generation that drives up the auction prices. Land zoning produces unearned rents just as the licensing requirements to limit desirable positions of advantage produce rents.

It would be historically naive not to observe that such unearned premiums on property values generate local coalitions of the affluent very concerned with who moves in to their neighbourhood. Add in the specific policy that local services are funded by taxation on local property values and one aspect of American racial injustice is explained: the contrast between the urban ghetto (with a downward spiral of collapsing property prices, deteriorating services and schooling, increased social problems) and the wealthy suburb to which many Black Americans cannot gain access as they have no access to credit (Wilson 2012).[3]

[3] Zoning laws are a form of local legislation, and the state and municipalities are involved in drawing up such categories. You may have reduced access to credit, if you are a Black American, because your current property value is so low and it is low because you live in a neighbourhood that has

The parallel with Gomberg's and Fishkin's critique of the current organization of work is obvious: with a limited number of positions of advantage, but many competitors, those positions must be protected via a sequence of screening devices, or "bottlenecks", including licensing or credentialling.[4] The latter works to increase the rental value of the limited set of occupations. Increasingly, they are used by the already advantaged to lock that in place and install entry barriers.[5]

Exclusivity, via legally generated barriers, generates a windfall capital gain to those already in place as controllers of a scarce resource. In Hirsch's example the entry level cost to join this suburban community rises as it is being "auctioned off". As property is a durable—and bequeathable—good, there are three kinds of inequality in play: first movers receive a windfall, only those who can pay have access to the good at its rapidly inflating price, and the accrued capital gains produce unearned benefits to both groups which are, furthermore, transferable to descendants. One might add that at every stage of this process there is a role for a fee-taking intermediary. If that fee is expressed as a percentage of the value of the asset, then those intermediaries have an interest in driving up asset values, too.[6]

First mover advantage is crucial to these explanations; Hirsch illustrates the point, once again, with land. The original owners enjoy "windfall gains" on its capitalized value when land valued solely for agricultural purposes becomes valuable for leisure purposes:

> [T]he result of the auction process of matching growing demand with static supply . . . is an increase in relative price and an associated capitalization of the underlying asset, which can be expected to accrue to old wealth and

been "redlined"—explicitly demarcated for Black Americans by a municipality, in a classic "Catch-22" (Rothstein 2017).

4 As we noted above, one of the primary uses to which Gomberg wishes to put his analysis is at the service of a theory of racial justice.

5 "The cities we live in are zoned to protect our wealth, but deter the unskilled from sharing in it. Professional licensing policy and an immigration policy tilted toward the low-skilled shield us from the intense market competition faced by those in nonprofessional occupations" (Reeves 2017, p.4). (Reeves says of his use of the term "we"—"I am writing about my own class. . . . This is a book about me and, likely, you too" (Reeves 2017, p.5).) See also (Baker 2016).

6 There is a tradition, stemming back to Mill and Henry George, of egalitarian suspicion of land as a classical "factor of production". A strand of asset-centred egalitarianism argues on "Georgist" grounds that there is a compelling prima facie case that all non-developed land should be held in collective ownership to generate a social dividend for all (Kerr 2017).

> thereby, in itself, to increase the concentration of wealth holding. (Hirsch 1976, p.35)

Hirsch notes that only some positional goods are "durable" and hence "capitalisable" (Hirsch 1976, p.36). For this class of goods he further notes that:

> The old rich make capital gains on positional assets they acquired early, and these gains make it harder for the new rich to rise on the relative wealth scale. . . . A head start in this competition for relative ascendancy accrues to those who acquired such assets in earlier, less expensive auctions. At the limit, the only people who can now afford to buy at auction will be those who have similar assets to sell. (Hirsch 1976, p.36)

In other words, "at the limit" auctions involve the rich selling to other rich people. This is the dynamic of steady, relentless, capital accumulation by wealthy elites that Thomas Piketty identifies in the actual history of his three, representative, "neo-proprietarian" societies of France, the United Kingdom and Sweden in *Capital and Ideology* up to the first world war (Piketty 2020, chapters 3–5).

Hirsch also pioneers the treatment of that which Daniel Halliday and Keith Hankins have recently theorized as "upstream agency" (Halliday and Hankins 2020). They mean by this "the actions and position of parties who are able to shape the competition for a positional good without themselves participating in the competition" (Halliday and Hankins 2020, p.280). They do this in two ways: "by supplying the positional goods for which downstream agents compete, and by conferring positional value on the goods in question" (Halliday and Hankins 2020, p.28).

Usually, as Halliday and Hankins note, the goods supplier is not in competition to consume it. There may be more than one interested party shaping this framing of the competition, and there are some cases where a party who is "upstream" in one competition may be "downstream" in another. Supply, and value conferral, may come apart and be supplied by different agents. Examples might be the "credentialling" role of educational institutions, or systems of ranking or rating, or the framing supplied by auction houses and dealers for the "very best" art (Brown 2019). We take such upstream agency to be endemic in capitalism and vital to the reproduction and spread of positional goods. Once again, the subject is intermediation and, in a society dominated by rent-seeking activity, the important role played by such intermediaries, for example, in the legal encoding of assets (Pistor 2019). Positionality involves market signalling and numerous agents have an interest in "signal boosting" the exclusivity of positional goods. When a property developer surrounds a "high-end" hotel with boutiques selling luxury items they are signal boosting the status of the hotel, allowing it to position itself in the market as liable to attract the kind of customer who shops in luxury boutiques.

We want to emphasize, for our purposes, that throughout his discussion Hirsch's conclusion is disjunctive: the challenge that a widespread market in positional goods poses is either we tolerate social waste, or we put in place measures to eliminate it only at the cost of exacerbating prior inequality. Furthermore, in the case of durable, capitalizable, goods there is a first mover advantage, accumulated (cumulative) historical advantage, and the systematic advantaging of "old money" if inherited estates can be kept intact.

Different legal systems treat that issue differently: French inheritance law, for example, explicitly attempts to secure the goal of capital dispersal, while in the United Kingdom and the United States inheritance taxation have become politically contentious. In US politics the fiscal measures framed by the Right as "death taxes" are virtually defunct. This is important, because as we will discuss in our Conclusion any attempt to address current levels of inequality needs to take into account that there is no stepping into the same river twice: we cannot simply go back to the comparatively inclusive growth of 1945–1980. The attempt to restore more inclusive growth cannot ignore the successful rent extraction that has taken place. Piketty's books are not warnings about a patrimonial capitalism to come; rather descriptions of a patrimonial capitalism that is already here. Without effective inheritance or wealth taxes these unjust accumulations of wealth are themselves an obstacle to progressive alternatives.

Hirsch wanted to generalize over all three cases—auctions, relieved crowding, and unrelieved crowding—as three tokens of one type of market failure: taken together, they "disturb the harmony of expectation and outcome on which the smooth and efficient working of a decentralized market economy depends" (Hirsch 1976, p.32). But had his concern been with inequality, Hirsch could equally well have concluded that he is describing mechanisms that either are socially wasteful, or exacerbate inequality, or typically do both.

9.2 Opportunity Hoarding

Our overall explanation of inequality has focused on rent seeking and shifts away from "blaming the 1%". We are not arguing that the very top end of the income and wealth distribution is not an egalitarian problem—far from it. They play a crucial role in maintaining the "deflationary bloc". But the problem of inequality in our own societies is so hard to deal with, politically, because it is so entrenched and ranges more widely than the activities of the ultra-rich. The rentier capitalism of the last forty years has built a broad base of social and political support even if that is largely determined along class lines (Stewart 2018a). The topic of opportunity hoarding, once again, in our view helpfully moves the focus away from a small group of dominators.

The insight of Charles Tilly's account of opportunity hoarding is that it is an activity tolerated by the narrow class of dominators, yet carried out by a broader segment of society (Tilly 1998). We will argue, as has Richard V. Reeves, that it is endemic to our form of rentier capitalism (Christophers 2020; Reeves 2017). As Reeves insightfully points out, when it comes to the shaping of public opinion around the issue of inequality, the members of the upper 20% of US society work in education and the media and have a considerable voice when it comes to shifting blame to those above them, namely, the 1% (Reeves 2017, p.8). Indeed, it is the strongly held meritocratic convictions of the upper 20% that help to channel their anger "upwards" towards the "undeserving rich" while the privilege of their own class is, perhaps unsurprisingly, something of a blind spot.

Tilly was the first to name this phenomenon (Tilly 1998). His examples of everyday opportunity hoarding spanned topics from inheritance to particular instances of immigrant communities in the United States establishing local monopolies of niche trades. He viewed exploitation and opportunity hoarding as two strategies that organizations use to solve functional, organizational, problems by either creating or importing categorical distinctions such as male/female, black/white, or other ascriptive categories from social life generally into economic life. They produce long-term patterns of established inequality:

> Bounded categories deserve special attention because they provide clearer evidence for the operation of durable inequality, because their boundaries do crucial organizational work, and because categorical differences actually

> account for much what ordinary observers take to be results of variation in individual talent and effort. (Tilly 1998, p.6)

Exploitation is the more extensively studied phenomenon: disproportionate value is actually extracted from a common enterprise by exploiters at the expense of the exploited. When it comes to the justification of such unfair returns, Tilly believes that exploiters very often take advantage of ascriptive categories to justify their rewards:

> Durable inequality among categories arises because people who control access to value producing resources solve pressing organizational problems by means of categorical distinctions. Multiple parties—not all of them powerful, some of them even victims of exploitation—then acquire stakes in those solutions. (Tilly 1998, pp.7–8)

By contrast, if exploitation is primarily the preserve of the powerful, then Tilly believes that opportunity hoarding is a case where the less powerful engage in inequality-producing behaviour that is tolerated by the more powerful.

This is an aspect of his more general insight that even the victims of past exploitation can "acquire a stake" in new forms of durable inequality where they join the ranks of the past perpetrators. This has the implication that, in the specific case of opportunity hoarding, if it is a less common phenomenon than exploitation, it might, for all that, be very extensive in its social effects because of its pervasiveness:

> *Opportunity Hoarding*: which operates when members of a categorically bounded network acquire access to a resource which is valuable, renewable, subject to monopoly, supportive of network activities, and enhanced by the network's modus operandi. (Tilly 1998, p.10)

Our hypothesis throughout has been that the extensive patterns of inequality in the affluent societies of the West are in significant part explained by the way in which the domain of the positional has expanded to the goods of social mobility. That is because these goods are particularly prone to opportunity hoarding by those who seek to maintain their local control of positional goods (Reeves 2017, chapter 6).

The most obvious examples can be drawn from a society in which the goods of education and healthcare are to a significant extent determined by private market provision, namely, the United States. However, beyond the American experience the widening inequality in other societies is partly explained by the inequality in the provision of the goods of social mobility.

This is markedly so, as we have noted, in the case of the value of property, especially housing assets, where it can be indirectly connected to access to publicly funded schooling and hence to differential educational outcomes. European societies that can take pride in their egalitarian ethos and high-quality publicly funded education may, nevertheless, also have a parallel system of elite private education. Alternatively, state-funded schooling in certain areas can attract a reputation for high-quality outcomes that creates property price bubbles in the local catchment area. Property prices here function as a proxy for elite access.

We are here moving away from outright domination by the wealthy to the more subtle process of opportunity hoarding by the better off and thus to the bourgeois activity of driving up the costs of the goods of social mobility (Reeves 2017). This can happen either directly, via high healthcare insurance or educational costs, or indirectly, such as being able to afford to live in the "right" area.

This helpfully moves us away from a focus on the malfeasance of the "1%". We share Temin's view that the spectacular success of the American 1% in predatory value extraction is exemplary of something deeper (Temin 2017). That deeper feature is the structural advantage of America's upper 20% of citizens and not all of those people are "dominators" (Stewart 2018a). America is putatively a classless society even though that has never, in fact, been the case. It does explain a certain discomfort with the language of class-based distinction, but when Matthew Stewart writes without irony of America's new aristocracy of the 9.9% he is correctly identifying an intensified form of class identification based on intensified class competition (Stewart 2018a).[7] It is the logic of competition itself that forces these citizens into competition with each other—by "pitting people against each other". We are dealing here with opportunity hoarders and not dominators.

[7] Richard Reeves notes the political distortions of members of the upper 20% becoming very angry with the 1%, noting both that "all the inequality action is above that line" (i.e. between the line demarcating the upper 20% from the lower 80%) and, yet, "more than a third of the demonstrators on the May Day 'Occupy' march in 2011 had annual earnings of more than $100, 000" (Reeves 2017, p.6, p.7).

That explains our further claim that we cannot hope to dispel the socially damaging effects of positional competition by treating it as socially optional—as confined to competition for brands of champagne, or wrist watches, or luxury hotels where the wealthy can engage in ultimately futile competition with each other over socially irrational expenditure. (At least this consumption has a multiplier effect and generates indirect benefits to others.) Tilly's insight is that, as the dynamics of inequality evolve, the scope of the positional expands to include the goods of social mobility. Positionality, social structure, and political action work together in an entrenching cycle of ever-deepening inequality.

Fishkin makes the helpful point that, in the domain of the positional, it might seem that everyone is drawn into a zero-sum game hoping to be a winner (Fishkin 2014, pp.138–9). However, he notes the pervasiveness of the desire not to be conspicuously a loser. Perhaps your goal is not the largest house in your neighbourhood, but simply not conspicuously to occupy the smallest, the shabbiest, or the one that bespeaks of your comparative lack of advantage. We think Fishkin's insight helps to explain the pervasive extent of positional competition. "Fear of downward mobility", as he puts it, can be a powerful motive. In a society where the actions of others have made an instrumental good such as money very important, aspiring to be in the middle of the pack can be as expensive as aiming to be wealthy and hence distinguished in Smith's sense (Fishkin 2014, p.201). This further complicates an experimental finding we will discuss in the next chapter, namely, that in societies that are very "gappy" in their distributions, status seeking can come to seem pointless. However, there is nevertheless a distinction between trying to emulate the Joneses and trying, instead, to avoid the shame of social stigmatization.

9.3 Positionality and Cultural Legislation

Our interpretation of an important paper by Corey Robin is that his argument establishes that empirical facts about the actual history of capitalism further develop the connections between inequality, positionality and class implicit in Hirsch's and Tilly's arguments (Robin 2013). These mutually reinforcing arguments substantiate our claim that weakly egalitarian societies will, through time, find it structurally impossible to meet the sufficientarian standard that a citizen can appear in public without shame.

These societies will be unable to avoid class stratification that will, in turn, harden to become obstructions to social mobility such that those in poverty will be inescapably locked into a "shameful condition".

We use the word "condition" because not everyone in this position will feel shame and, indeed, they ought not to do so. The pressure from capitalism's emotional regime on the poor to feel ashamed of their situation is real but unjust. In fact, there is no shame in losing a competition that is rigged against you. Some will react with anger. Some will react by developing counter-cultural norms that undercut the dominant attitudes that condemn them. Yet some will, indeed, endorse the very norms that make their condition shameful and not only feel that their own shame is justified, but also extend that attitude to others.

Our thesis is that once positionality encompasses the non-positional, and once opportunities are inter-generationally hoarded, weakly egalitarian societies will evolve a rigid three-part structure. One class is constituted by the historical beneficiaries of past inequality, another is constituted by those with the resources to compete for the positional, and a third is constituted by those locked out of such competition and unable to transfer any positional advantage to their children. It is this last position of fixed poverty with no possibility of mobility—the situation of the chronically dominated—that is, we will show, particularly damaging to a person's well-being. This is particularly the case in a society with a false ideology of meritocracy.

We will draw on Robin's argument for a specific reason: as we have noted, when Hirsch distinguishes democratic and oligarchic wealth we think that has an unfortunate connotation. If we can isolate these two forms of wealth, then this suggests that an individual could settle, simply, for the enjoyment of her appropriate share of democratic wealth and leave the pursuit of oligarchic wealth to those irrational enough to persist even when they have learned of the logic of Hirsch's arguments.

One might, for example, simply accept the new affluence in material goods and benefit from the comparatively low level of consumption inequality compared to inequality generally. A person in our affluent societies can take advantage of cheap clothes, cell phones, and televisions and withdraw from status competition. Indeed, they may well be living an ethically more admirable life were they do so. When Luther Vandross and Janet Jackson sing "the best things in life are free" one can call to mind Adam Smith's remark that the truest source of happiness was feeling beloved. Love of family and friends; enjoyment of nature; free music recitals, and public libraries—is there not enough there to live a happy life? Perhaps Carol Graham's "happy peasants" have good reason to be happy, finding happiness and well-being in everyday manifestations of love, friendship, affection, and religious consolation.

This is, indeed, one response from current defenders of inequality in very unequal societies, such as the United States. They admit that the logic of capitalism does, indeed, produce a socially stratified society; but the very same processes also drive down the costs of production and make consumption inequality less problematic than income and wealth inequality. Poor people in the United States today have cell phones, refrigerators, televisions, and access to public goods that previous generations never enjoyed. You do not need to be a particularly wealthy person to fly in a plane—the exclusive preserve of the very wealthy in the 1950s.

We have multiple responses to this argument. The first is to note, as Hirsch does at the very outset of his argument, that the mere existence of positional goods problematizes how we think about public goods and private goods on the commercial market. Many positional goods are technically private—supplied by the market—but his main point is that they are also "social". To the extent that positional goods are social, it is not up to the individual to retreat from positional competition without retreating from society. Whether or not you can appear in society without shame is not solely a matter of individual decision and doing what is required to tag along in positional competition is a defensive necessity. Marketization brings more things on to the market, but it also expands the social power of those most able to afford them. That is why what Hirsch calls the "commercialization effect" is one expression of the market power of the wealthy. When it comes to the goods of social mobility a level playing field is not in their interests.

Secondly, the Timothy Leary formula ignores the extent to which positionality intersects with political domination. On the market, to use Marx's formulation, we are playthings of alien forces. One's quality of life also depends on public goods—from food safety regulation to street lighting. The sociality of these goods is constitutive and there is no avoiding the actions of others when it comes to their hoarding, or sequestration, or manipulation. Our lives and well-being all depend on public goods; escaping or opting out is not a genuine possibility.

Hirsch explained how one of the rational responses to crowding or congestion in the provision of goods is screening. Screening wastes resources by making today's university degree necessary for a job that used to require only graduation from high school. By this logic, university fees become another example of Hirsch's "defensive necessity". Marketization turns the goods of healthcare and education into markers of class-based advantage. Those who already enjoy disproportionate power in this domain also seek to consolidate that advantage.

Those who "opt out" from status competition, then, opt out from social mobility both for themselves and, importantly, for their children. We think these are all important arguments with considerable cumulative force, but Robin develops the point a crucial stage further. We have emphasized the importance of history and stratification in Hirsch's original account. One aspect of this is first mover advantage. This, in turn, explains the "cheaper" auctions of the past and hence how advantage in durable, capitalizable, goods can be transferred inter-generationally. Cumulative advantage generates over centuries and interacts with another important theme. That which Robin adds to this account is the role of the market as the location of heroic action and the generator of an aesthetic of value production.

Robin argues that, for the key precursor of the Austrian School—Nietzsche—the economy is associated with the mass democracy of modernization where the "lowering" of value leads inevitable to its eventual elimination as a category. The creation of value—true value—is dependent on a shameful origin in labouring work that it must deny, just as perfectionist values depend for their social realization on the material labour of "lower" types of people.

For Nietzsche, once the lower types were perceived as coming to political power in the late nineteenth century, nihilism becomes a live social possibility. That is because the very conditions of true value are being eliminated. Robin controversially argues that, in response, Schumpeter and Hayek offer a counter-narrative where heroic, martial, individual values can be realized in the marketplace itself. Schumpeter connects the heroic figure of the entrepreneur to the role of founder while Hayek has a cultural theory of the wealthy as legislators for taste.

This offers a deeper answer to the question of why the consumer-citizen cannot simply turn her back on positional goods and make do with "democratic wealth" instead. For Nietzsche, democratic wealth is a contradiction; the mass market destroys the very condition of true value. Hayek's (and Schumpeter's) responses were different:

> Hayek offered an alternative account of the market as the proving ground of aristocratic action. . . . Schumpeter invoked a half-century of social

> thought . . . to emphasize not only "the importance of the extra-rational and irrational element in our behavior," *but also the power of capital to shape the preference of the consumer.* (Robin 2013, emphasis ours)

This point, we argue, allows one to address the lacuna that we identified in Hirsch's argument. The problem is not simply the disconnection between the micro-motivations of the consumer and total social states, but also the top-down determination of those micro-motives by systemic influences from the culture of capitalism itself. We mean, quite literally, the cultural vindication of economic values in Robin's sense:

> Hayek developed this notion into a full-blown theory of the wealthy and the well-born as an avant-garde of taste, as makers of new horizons of value from which the rest of humanity took its bearings. Instead of the market of consumers dictating the actions of capital, it would be capital that would determine the market of consumption—and beyond that, the deepest beliefs and aspirations of a people. (Robin 2013)

The connection that Robin sees between Nietzsche and Hayek is that liberty is the precondition for "the emergence of a heroic legislator of value", but in very different circumstances.

In Hayek's account it is the fact that we do not know which, among all of us, will be able to imagine such new horizons that implies a policy of giving liberty for all. We guarantee it to the select few by dint of guaranteeing it to all. This is so even though, for most people, such liberty is not needed. Once again, the aesthetic image of an "avant-garde" is put to use—a metaphor drawn from the military:

> Only from an advanced position does the next range of desires and possibilities become visible, so that the selection of new goals and the effort toward their achievement will begin long before the majority can strive for them. (Hayek 1960)

The wealthy are the reconnaissance party for our culture. This cultural account supplements the workings of Hirsch's systemic account: for Nietzsche, the only wealth worthy of the name must asymmetrically depend on the work-labour of others. Hayek's narrative is liberating, because by transposing heroic self-legislation into the market in one sense it democratizes it, while in another sense it re-introduces—indeed, celebrates—the asymmetric dependence of "democratic wealth" on "oligarchic wealth". Hayek is offering his own explanation of Harrod's "vector view": the main body of the army must always lag behind the reconnaissance elite troops of the avant-garde.

As Robin notes, Hayek celebrates the fact that patrimonial capitalism will allow avant-garde creators of value to determine for us what we actually want in virtue of their very great wealth:

> More interesting is how explicit and insistent Hayek is about linking the legislation of new values to the possession of vast amounts of wealth and capital, even—or especially—wealth that has been inherited. . . . Thanks to their patronage, producers will find cheaper ways of making and delivering these products—cheap enough, that is, for the majority to enjoy them. What was before a luxury of the idle rich—stockings, automobiles, piano lessons, the university—is now an item of mass consumption. (Robin 2013)

Inherited wealth puts in place a patrimonial class who make a disproportionate contribution to the common good (from Hayek's perspective) because they are liberated from material need. This is another twist on Veblen's lament that social waste was the point.

Accumulated wealth introduces a distinction between these refined arbiters of taste and the nouveaux riches who must follow their lead in matters of taste. Capitalism, then, finds the means to reproduce within itself the cultural role of the aristocrat in the guise of the true legislator of taste. Distinction, now, attaches not to inheriting an aristocratic title, but playing the role of a cultural ephor. Robin concludes: "The men of capital, in other words, are best understood not as economic magnates but as cultural legislators" (Robin 2013).

This pressurizes the putatively reassuring distinction between democratic and oligarchic wealth. If oligarchic wealth dictates the terms of value, then mass democratic taste is left with nothing other than nihilism. It is reduced to nothing, because of the pressure of the oligarchic determination of the terms of taste. If the marketplace can be the location of heroic action, then appearing in public in a cheap pair of trainers is, indeed, a source of shame—an archaic notion if ever there was one (Williams 2002). This valorization of competition—the battlefield is, above all, a place where people are pitted against each other for the highest stakes—forms part of the meritocratic ethos we will examine below. We have already noted Keynes's sardonic comment that diverting people's energies into market competition at least kept them away from the more literally dangerous forms of conflict.

It would be reassuring to think that in our own affluent societies positional competition was, for at least some of us, merely optional. However, if Robin's more ambitious thesis is correct, we have already abandoned the category of the "merely material". Counter-cultural abnegation runs the risk of being another kind of status good, particularly in a context of "inconspicuous consumption". In a recent television series, British artist Grayson Perry took delight in explaining the workings of a high-end delicatessen in Brooklyn where affluent New York professionals took on the artisanal roles of running the store. With no apparent irony, wealthy professionals spent several hours a week dispensing artisanal cheese and craft beer in a way Perry neatly satirized with the phrase "performative egalitarianism" (Barrow et al. 2020). Cos-playing the lives of shop attendants as a form of hobby is another example of deliberately concealing one's wealth and liberty to enter, and leave, the work of the service worker at will. The merely material life of the service worker has here become a subject of irony to those who do not have to do it—the oligarchically wealthy. As Hegel insightfully observed, the rich rabble stand in an incorrect relationship to work—one that is not emancipatory—when it is labour they do not have to do. For these Brooklyn professionals, artisanal work is actually a form of ironic play.

This example reflects deep shifts in social norms around the oligarchic and the democratic. We will discuss meritocracy in some detail in chapter 12; we would be the first to acknowledge that while we have been influenced by Veblen there has been a major shift in social norms around work from his time. His critique of conspicuous consumption formed part of his broader critique of American mores of the Gilded Age. Our own equivalent to Veblen, sociologist Elizabeth Currid-Halkett, notes the ironic inversion of how America's affluent people communicate their wealth. Whereas a wealthy person in earlier centuries would not dream of breastfeeding their child or eating organic vegetables that look as "authentic" as possible, the new aspirational class seeks, above all, cultural authenticity as that Protean term is defined by, well, people like them.

Affluence means that they can leverage their wealth into cultural capital but, above all, the new aspirational class seeks inconspicuousness in consumption—the very opposite of Veblen's leisured class. Veblen correctly identified consumption behaviour as driven by emulation and imitation (Currid-Halkett 2017, p.4). Yet Currid-Halkett also notes that

Veblen's critique of the leisure class was not solely conceptualized in terms of "conspicuousness":

> Veblen's over-arching thesis is that the recognition of social division and stratification is central to understanding modern society. . . . Ironically, the demonstration of high social position (through consumption, leisure and nonpecuniary practices) often manifested itself through the uselessness of objects and activity. (Currid-Halkett 2017, p.5)

This puts Hirsch's concern with socially wasteful expenditure in a new light.

For Veblen, writing for the society of his time, participation in elite sports showed that one has time to waste; having "too many" servants for the domestic tasks available shows one has money to waste. Both are signs of social status. For Currid-Halkett, as our societies have changed so "new forms of consumption and behavior have emerged to reveal social position" (Currid-Halkett 2017, p.5). The signs that now signal social distinction are more subtle, and the modern meritocrat, above all, wants to stress her work ethic and the "impossible" amount of time she has to spend working. We take this as a transformation in the cultural expression of oligarchic wealth, but not the elimination of it as a key explanatory category. The modern oligarch is an heroic martyr to the market.

As Boltanski and Chiapello explained, it is hard to escape the toils of capitalism: it is adept at taking anti-capitalist critique and folding its values into itself. Turning one's back on status and renouncing the values of the positional is another form of low-key status signalling. There is no escape: being unbranded is itself a brand. Cool capitalists such as Steve Jobs spend time on an ashram and return, bare-footed and vegan, to attach counter-cultural values to a mass consumer product that charges premium prices.

The "war of position", as Gramsci put it, that sees America's wealthiest citizens detaching themselves from the project of solidaristic social provisioning involves a process of the class-based framing of publicly provided goods as shabby, inferior and "declassé". How can a person be poor if they have a cell phone? Perhaps it does make a difference whether it is a $20 phone from the drugstore or a high-end $1,500 smartphone. For a core of life goods there is a spreading influence of the positional from which one cannot opt out and for which one must, under duress, compete.

9.4 Positionality, De-Marketization, and Public Goods

We would now like to bring out the connection between positionality and the rent-seeking hypothesis. On one, direct, interpretation those who hoard opportunities aim to preserve their economic advantages. They do so primarily, in this case, by passing it on to their children. Liberals, such as ourselves, are resigned to the continued existence of the family (while noting its pluriform nature) even if in some respects it frustrates the aims of justice. That is because it reflects other values and, like Rawls, who formulated the issue in this canonical way, normative pluralism means that there is no reason grounded in justice alone for its abolition. Combined with the right to make gifts, it seems we cannot object to people seeking to advantage their children. Opportunity hoarding, then, is part and parcel of the reasonable partiality that parents show their children.

However, we think that quietism would be too quick. Samuel Freeman's point, that we noted earlier, is that there is no right to join an unjust association or, for that matter, to participate in unjust practices. The right to make gifts is not interfered with if, following Mill's suggestion, we amend the right to inherit on the part of the recipients of those gifts. The ethical motive of partiality to one's nearest and dearest, including family members, is ethically admirable. Tainted partialism, by contrast, is a vice of character. Opportunity hoarders have no right to participate in unfair practices.

De-marketization education and healthcare are of crucial importance to our argument.[8] Public provisioning has a role to play here; against the claim that state action inevitably "crowds out" private investment, de-marketization of key life goods simply makes private provision redundant. Firstly, public collective provision reduces the stakes of positional competition as Hussain rightly notes.[9]

Secondly, one respect in which people live much better lives than in previous centuries is not simply that they have more material goods of far higher quality through the market. It is equally significant that the administrative state and its regulations have produced safe workplaces, safe transportation, and clean air and water. Public parks, public libraries, and public museums

[8] It is worth noting that the cases of education and healthcare are importantly different. It is one thing to lavish gifts on one's children foreseeing that this will also confer educational advantage; it is another thing to steal healthcare from other people's children so that your child will survive at the cost of another child dying, as noted in (Runciman 2009).

[9] As did Hirsch, who makes the same proposal (Hirsch 1976, p.187).

open to all enhance the quality of life for everyone. The shared commons of an unspoiled natural environment or a shared public culture accessible to all through a high standard of education all make significant, non-market based, contributions to shared well-being.

Thirdly, universal basic services provided by the state of sufficiently high quality put pressure on their private alternatives. If the marginal advantage to your children of expensive private tuition is so low, given the quality of their public education, then why pay for it?

Fourthly, paradoxically it is the high level of social protections that makes Scandinavians far more likely than Americans to take risks, even the commercial risks of enterprise. The twist to that particular narrative is that Scandinavians are far more likely than Americans to attribute success in life to luck.

This lead on to the key question: how will we pay for it? We will discuss this question in our final chapter: for now, we note that the Scandinavian welfare state model builds a stable electoral coalition by providing basic services of such high quality the middle class is not embarrassed to use them. But these benefits are partially taxed back by progressive taxation.

As Hussain further points out, if an enthusiast for marketization thinks this spending is "wasteful", then it is a question of where social waste is located. If we educate "too many" young people for positions of social advantage this can seem like a waste. But positional competition for limited places is also wasteful. There is greater societal advantage to having a large number of well-educated citizens—a public good par excellence—than wasteful spending on violin lessons or "educative" trips to foreign cities whose sole point is to game an admissions process to an elite institution.

There is more to opportunity hoarding, in any case, than its direct connection to the transmission of socio-economic advantage. Opportunity hoarders also hoard emotional capital. We mean by this that they view themselves as the appropriate focus of admiration and envy. They act from a strong sense of entitlement. It is this theme in particular that we will develop further in chapters 11 and 12.

We have reached a turning point in our analysis. The arguments we have presented in this and the previous chapter against capitalist market societies are not novel, but we agree with Scanlon that their assessment requires empirical evidence. The egalitarian ought to appeal to the highest quality empirical evidence to hand, as the relevant empirical sciences develop. Our contribution in this book is to consider the arguments to this point in the light of the evidence supplied by the new science of happiness. The assessment of that evidence is undertaken in our pivotal next chapter. In this chapter, we turn attention from the institutional mechanisms that characterize capitalist market societies and that generate, exacerbate, and entrench inequalities—such as opportunity hoarding and the stratification that comes with it—and look more closely at their impact on well-being.

10

The Science of Happiness, Inequality, and Well-Being

Propositional Summary

1. While caution is needed when employing empirical data from the new science of happiness, this chapter analyses what we can learn from it when assessing the impact inequality has on our lives.
2. Well-being—how well your life is going for you—is a complex notion with many different conceptualizations. While hedonists reduce it to having pleasurable experiences and desire satisfaction theorists to having one's desires met, objective list theorists argue that well-being—or "flourishing", according to eudaemonists—is independent from such subjective attitudes. Each of these philosophical theories has its strengths and weaknesses and has different counterparts in psychological measurements.
3. We defend an ecumenical approach to well-being that has a broad appeal and integrates key aspects of well-being on which different theories agree. Combining elements from eudaimonism and Robert Boyd's notion of a "cluster property", our approach views well-being as being able to exercise one's distinctive capacities and realize one's values so as to make life go well for oneself.
4. Our ecumenical, yet committal, approach provides generic truths about well-being, while embracing the pluralism that characterizes the constructs, methodologies, and measurements at play in the new science of happiness. We discuss the normative relevance of our approach by connecting well-being to justice. In addition, we stress the care with which to derive policy implications from the context-specific claims provided by the science of happiness.
5. The emotions that the emotional regime of capitalism expects from and instils in people—frustration and anxiety about status competition,

Extravagance and Misery. Alan Thomas, Alfred Archer, and Bart Engelen, Oxford University Press.
 DOI: 10.1093/oso/9780197781722.003.0011

shame for being poor, and envy for the rich—are detrimental to their well-being, on multiple understandings of the latter.

6. We discuss available empirical evidence to what extent money buys you happiness. As Easterlin discovered, the rich in developed countries are on average happier than the poor, but rising material wealth over time is typically not correlated with rising happiness. When a country grows richer, people adapt as their—and others'—material desires increase.
7. In light of mixed evidence for the claim that inequality is detrimental to well-being, we stress the importance of people's perceptions of inequality. If increasing inequality is taken as a sign of social mobility—as they often are in developing economies—it can increase happiness. When perceived as an unfair outcome of a rigged game, however, inequality predictably reduces lower well-being.
8. We summarize what we have learned from the science of happiness, when properly contextualized. In capitalist societies, where social mobility is frustrated, wealth is concentrated and inequalities become entrenched, the well-being is reduced for those forced on (or off) the treadmill for money, status, and education.

Introduction

Our aim in this book is to analyse the extent to which our capitalist societies live up to the ideal that market societies set themselves: to bring about the public good in a way that expresses a founding ideal of liberty with equality for all. One of our innovations is that we draw on a new resource to do this: the inter-disciplinary synthesis of work in philosophy, psychology, and economics known colloquially as "the science of happiness". In this chapter then, we shift our attention from the workings of capitalist societies to their impact on the people whose lives they govern. We will analyse the current state of knowledge about the impact that wealth and income inequalities, generated and entrenched in capitalist societies, have on happiness and well-being. We will first explain what we mean by the latter terms before investigating the empirical evidence for their links with inequality.

This discussion furthers our aim of critically investigating capitalism's emotional regime for three reasons. First, as happiness is widely considered one of the basic emotions, it can be expected to play a central part in capitalism's emotional regime. Secondly, the broader term—well-being—also features in the promise of capitalist societies to make us all better off. Thirdly, the other politically relevant emotions that we discuss in the next chapter—shame, admiration, and envy—are plausibly linked to well-being. Inequalities that trigger and aggravate shame and envy are concerning because they undermine people's well-being. To see how that works, we first need to understand what well-being is and how it is connected to both of these emotions.

However, we will begin by addressing scepticism about the very idea of a science of happiness, voiced in works such as William Davies's *The Happiness Industry* (Davies 2015). Davies fears that the very idea of such a science shifts the authority about one's mental life from the first person to the third person, granting psychologists more authoritative knowledge of a key aspect of human psychology: subjective well-being. Davies argues that this change in the location of authority facilitates the use of psychological knowledge for administrative and technocratic purposes. In our words, his concern is that capitalism first makes us miserable and then inaugurates a new science that repairs our psychological health via such fads as mindfulness or other "productivity hacks".

While we do not wish to minimize these concerns, Davies paints with a broad brush and treats some parts the science of happiness with more seriousness than it deserves. As Horowitz (2017) makes clear in his compelling history, the rise of the "science of happiness" has had many boosters. Some, but not all of these are over-ambitious academics making too much of their results. In our view, none of the science we draw upon here is guilty of such boosterism, nor, for that matter, does it represent a threat to first-personal authority.

First-personal authority, as we understand it, is constitutively incapable of being replaced by a third-personal perspective captured by psychology. Writing from our liberal-republican perspective, with our attention directed to forms of domination, we acknowledge it would be a concern if a scientific enterprise masked dominating manipulation. However, we do not share Davies's complete scepticism towards there being a robust body of psychological knowledge that bears on egalitarianism. In fact, we believe that such knowledge should be incorporated in the kind of normative reflection that Rawls described as "wide reflective equilibrium". Such reflection is informed by a broader psychological and social scientific understanding of individuals and social structures (Rawls 1971/1999). Whether the new science of happiness can help in this respect and what we can learn from it when assessing the impact of inequality on our lives is our topic in this chapter. We take the lesson of Davies's book to be "proceed with caution" and we will do so when we apply empirical results to the critique of capitalist societies.

10.1 Why (Not) Use Empirical Evidence About Happiness and Well-Being?

If inequality is a bad thing, one might reasonably suppose that increasing inequality correlates with increasingly bad effects both on societies and individuals.[1] In identifying these, the effects of inequality on well-being seem to be central. What could be more important, in justifying egalitarian schemes, than whether or not they enable people to lead lives that go well for them? If one can show that inequality is harmful to well-being (because it causes harms or at least is correlated with such harms), then we have additional reasons for setting ourselves the aim of reducing inequality. That is, potentially, an important political role for the new science of happiness, which purports to measure subjective well-being and provide scientific evidence about the factors that make people better off or happier.

This makes our task appear simple: we can merely check the evidence to see whether inequality correlates with reduced well-being. It is then a short step to assume that there is a causal connection: inequality causes reduced well-being. The policy solutions seem to follow equally straightforwardly. This is, in a nutshell, the central narrative of Wilkinson and Pickett's work summarized by the subtitle of their second book *The Inner Level: How More Equal Societies Reduce Stress, Restore Sanity and Improve Everyone's Well-being* (Wilkinson and Pickett 2018).

However, our task is not that easy, for several connected reasons. First, as we will show in this chapter, "well-being" is an essentially contested concept (Gallie 1955/6). Psychologists, philosophers, and others fundamentally disagree on its nature and how to measure it. In this chapter, we aim to develop and defend an ecumenical approach that has broad appeal and can function as the basis for political diagnosis and action. Secondly, the empirical evidence is often mixed in its results and sometimes seemingly contradictory.

[1] Tammy Harel Ben-Shahar (2018) helpfully distinguishes "cardinal positional goods" in this respect. In contrast, with ordinal positional goods, where only winning and losing matters, cardinal positional goods, such as money, are different. Here, the size of the gap between winners and losers or the extent of the inequality matters: the farther you are behind, i.e. the bigger the gap, the bigger the harm to your well-being will be.

Thirdly, generating normative claims from the science of happiness is, as we noted above, rarely straightforward. Improving well-being is pro tanto good, but it is easy to generate counter-examples of obviously problematic ways of improving well-being. Throughout this book, we have kept in mind Carol Graham's caution as to whether policy prescriptions follow directly from claims about well-being.

Take someone who, motivated by malicious envy, destroys something that another person values to restore a prior equality between them. If this person's malicious delight is larger than the pain of the deprived person, the restoration of equality has improved overall well-being, but not in ways of which anyone would approve (apart from the malicious person him- or herself). This is the basic motivation for the levelling-down critique against the claim that inequality is inherently bad.

Or take the finding that inequality and well-being can be problematically disconnected. Mexico, for example, has one of the highest levels of self-reported happiness globally, but is also one of the world's most unequal societies. This is worrying for egalitarians, as high levels of inequality can turn out to be compatible with high levels of happiness, for example in societies that are stratified into non-comparing groups of people.

Note the implication for those who value equality merely instrumentally, that is, as conducive to overall well-being. Such instrumental egalitarians might, in trying to bring about a happier society, use such data to encourage residential sorting where people from the same social strata live and socialize together, or assortative mating, where people from the same social spheres marry each other. When Thomas Piketty (2014) deplores the rise of a patrimonial capitalism where your life prospects are determined by accident of birth or whom you marry, instrumental egalitarians may retort: at least that mitigates the otherwise detrimental impact of inequality on well-being.

Those who—like Wilkinson and Pickett—rely on empirical evidence that equality improves well-being claim that both are tightly connected and reduce worries about inequality to worries about well-being. This strategy risks losing the fight with non-egalitarians for two reasons. First, the empirical evidence might turn out to be equivocal. Secondly, it might suggest unjust ways of promoting well-being. Egalitarians should oppose residential sorting, assortative mating or any other strategy that encourage people only to engage with people from their own social strata, even if these are robust ways of (individual and overall) protecting aggregate levels of well-being.

Alternatively, those who argue that inequality is intrinsically bad may be forced to pay a price in terms of overall happiness if they secure their goal of reducing it. They might put the point about social stratification to a different use: to explain how radically unequal societies stabilize themselves, in spite of their intrinsic injustice, by minimizing social discontent and giving each social class its appropriate peer group for comparison. Class stratification is the safety valve that prevents inequality producing significantly impaired well-being in socially destabilizing ways. This identifies a social mechanism without justifying it. In chapter 13, we show how a just society does not need such a mechanism and that justice and well-being can go hand in hand without it.

Adaptation is another psychological mechanism that complicates the inference from (in)equality to (un)happiness. While poor people often remarkably adapt their preferences and accept their lot, people who lifted themselves from poverty in a poor society can be plagued by the insecurity of losing precarious gains and be unhappier than those who remained in poverty (Graham 2009, pp.17–8). In addition, when countries develop rapidly:

> It is upwardly mobile, lower middle income respondents rather than the poor who are made unhappy by inequality or economic insecurity, due to higher levels of awareness and loss aversion. (Graham 2009, p.131)

This claim extends to affluent societies, with a study in Germany from the 1980s showing how rising inequality came with financial anxiety for both the poor and middle-class, but leaving especially the latter group more dissatisfied with their lives than before (Roth, Hahn, and Spinath 2017). Again, such evidence should not lead egalitarians to conclude that it would have been better if the material situation of these people had not been improved at all.

Cases like these suggest the numerous pitfalls that egalitarians need to avoid when drawing on the science of happiness. There is no one-dimensional argument relating (in)equality to well-being, but a multi-dimensional argument with several, distinct, well-grounded empirical generalizations all of which are hedged by "ceteris paribus" clauses. Getting from evidence that helps identify relevant considerations to making all things considered claims and proposing policy fixes is the task of the critically engaged social scientist and political philosopher.

In this chapter and the next we argue that egalitarians can still rely on the science of happiness provided care is taken over the context-specificity of its claims. We think philosophers such as ourselves can contribute to this task by clarifying what well-being is and by bridging the existing gap between philosophical analyses of its meaning and its use in the science of happiness literature. Typically, the intellectual division of labour works as follows: economists and psychologists focus on measuring, quantifying, and relating well-being to other things, while philosophers make conceptual distinctions between being and feeling happy, well-being, flourishing, and other related concepts. This results in a disciplinary disconnect between scientific (economic and psychological) approaches and philosophical (conceptual and normative) approaches. We aim to bridge that gap, respecting the plurality of methodologies of the science of happiness and connecting their evidence to broader conceptual and normative issues.

10.2 General and Specific Conceptions of Well-Being

In general terms, people say they are well off when things are going well *for* them. Well-being, often treated as synonymous to "welfare" and "flourishing", relates to the quality of one's life. As Dan Haybron puts it, well-being is:

> [W]hat benefits a person, is good for her, makes her better off, serves her interests, or is desirable for her for her sake. To be high in well-being is to be faring well, doing well. (Haybron 2011)

Well-being refers to "the extent to which a life is not so much good overall but good for the person living it" (Haybron forthcoming, p.41) or, in other words, "how well a person's life is going for that person" (Crisp 2015). As such, any conception of well-being needs to provide a plausible account of "what makes a life or some part of it good for one" (Alexandrova 2017, p.xxx). Health, for example, is undoubtedly one of many constituents of well-being. Your well-being is constituted by the things that are intrinsically good *for you* (Heathwood 2010). It typically depends on things you care about. For example, your well-being is typically negatively affected when you or your child becomes ill. These things make your life go less well for you.

The claim that someone's well-being matters is uncontroversial. It matters to that person and to the people who care about her. At the societal level, well-being is a value that policy makers take into account when designing policies. Ceteris paribus (but note the multiple pitfalls we pointed out earlier on), the more well-being experienced by the members of a society, the better. This does not imply that we agree with welfarists, who claim that well-being is the *only* thing that matters (value monism) or that well-being is the only aspect that makes something good. Even if we will not try to answer what other values should matter when it comes leading a good live, as Haybron (forthcoming) does, or which role exactly well-being should play in ethics and political philosophy, we will say something about its normative relevance below. Even if it is only one of many values—as value pluralists like ourselves claim—we should be concerned when some factor, like wealth or income inequality, turns out to be detrimental to well-being. Of course, economic inequality can be morally bad for multiple reasons, not all of which are related to well-being: it may be unjust, violate people's rights, and infringe on citizens' liberty and autonomy. In this chapter then, we limit our argument to focus on how exactly inequalities can be said to have a worryingly detrimental impact on well-being.

Different conceptions of well-being offer different views of what it is that is good for you. A good conception or theory of well-being captures those goods that we think of as being good *for* a person and that we should promote if we want to benefit that person (Tiberius 2015). Some conceptions have long lists of such prudential goods or constituents of well-being while others argue there are only a few or even only one.

In search of a more detailed conceptualization, one can distinguish between five approaches in the literature (Crisp 2007, 2015; Haybron 2011; Heathwood 2010; Tiberius 2015). These are: first, objective list theory; second, hedonism; third, (neo-Aristotelian) eudaimonism; fourth, preferentism; fifth, hybrid conceptions of well-being. Other categorizations are possible as well. We follow the simpler, more traditional categorization of the "Big Three" (Parfit 1984; see also: Alexandrova 2017): first, objective list; second, mental-state and; third, desire satisfaction theories. This threefold distinction can help get a better grasp of the multifarious meanings that have been attributed to well-being and to happiness.[2]

On the first approach, defended by, inter alia, Sir David Ross (1930/2002), John Finnis (2011), and Martha Nussbaum (1992, 2000), constituents

[2] While the crucial disagreement concerns which theory best captures what exactly well-being means and why it is relevant, note that this categorization itself is also subject to debate (Alexandrova 2017; Dolan and White 2007). Take hedonism: is this a mental-state theory ("well-being consists in a subjective experience of pleasure") or an objective list theory (with pleasure being the only thing on the list that matters for well-being)? Or consider (neo-Aristotelian) eudaimonism, a view that understands well-being as flourishing. Is this an objective or subjective theory?

of well-being are objective: what makes them good for the person is independent from whether the latter likes, enjoys, or values them (Finnis 2011; Parfit 1984). If a person fails to appreciate these prudentially good things, she is simply making a mistake.

Plausible candidates on this objective list are "happiness, knowledge, friendship, freedom, rational activity, creative activity, and being respected" (Heathwood 2010, p.645). One might plausibly add achievement, self-respect, autonomy, virtue, health, and love (we noted in chapter 6 Adam Smith's view that being loved is the highest good) (Fletcher 2013). According to Nussbaum, the ten "central human capabilities" are life; bodily health; bodily integrity; the capacities of the senses; imagination and thought; emotions; practical reason; affiliation; a positive connection to other species; play; and control over one's environment (Nussbaum 2006, pp.76–8). Amongst psychological approaches, Martin Seligman defends an objective list conception: "well-being is a combination of feeling good as well as actually having meaning, good relationships and accomplishment" (Seligman 2002, p.25). Amongst contemporary philosophers, Martha Nussbaum (2008) has most prominently reinterpreted the classic Aristotelean and Millian idea that happiness is a complex and multi-faceted concept that cannot be reduced to pleasure. What matters for one's life to go well is not (only) how one experiences things but how one does things and what things one does.

The underlying rationale here is Aristotelian. Furthermore, according to Aristotle, human flourishing is possible only within a just society. If we live in a society that is clearly unjust, the eudaimonist argues, we are all worse off:

> To the extent that privileged groups live a charmed life and insulate themselves from the sufferings of the poor, everyone is missing out on happiness, since they are all living in a bad, unjust, world. (Nussbaum 2008, p.S98)

Nussbaum is here building on Rousseau's argument that we discussed in chapter 6: that a radically unequal society is detrimental to fundamental human capacities such as the ability to sympathize with others. (We also noted Smith's more optimistic take that commercial society creates the threat of corruption of moral sentiments, but a threat that can be contained by moral education.) Nussbaum also echoes Hegel's argument about social exclusion: the poor have no choice but to be excluded, while the rich exclude themselves. The people Hegel includes in his "rabble" can be living lives either of extravagance or misery: in both cases they do not share the lives of most of their fellow citizens. For Hegel, the only way truly to realize freedom—via meaningful work—is denied to rich and poor alike. This social dimension distinguishes eudaimonism from more individualist approaches such as hedonism and desire satisfaction views.

Despite their plausibility, objective list theories of well-being face challenges (Heathwood 2010). First, proponents need to explain how the different items on the list relate to each other and to the overall concept of well-being (Haybron forthcoming, p.172). Secondly, why are these things on the list and not others? According to critics, objective list theories are defective if they simply enumerate rather than explain the things on the list (Tiberius 2015). To know whether a list is complete, we need a principle in virtue of which certain things *are* indeed good for us.

The third challenge concerns the objective nature of the goods on the list and asks: what if people have no interest in the goods on the list? Why should we believe that social, creative and healthy activities would be better for someone who just wants to be a solitary, pizza-eating, couch potato? Is an objective list account not necessarily perfectionist in nature, violating the liberal principle that people have the right and freedom to develop their own conceptions of the good life? Subjectivists—such as hedonists and desire satisfaction theorists—insist that well-being is "subject-relative": something can be said to contribute to someone's well-being *only if* it relates to what that person cares about, which is why they typically refer to the oft-used notion of "subjective well-being". According to Fletcher, subjective pro-attitudes like endorsing, desiring, experiencing, and feeling affected are necessary components of each and every good on his objective list: achievement, friendship, happiness, pleasure, self-respect, and virtue (Fletcher 2013, p.216). Below, we address these concerns by offering a grounding explanation pioneered by Richard Boyd (Boyd 1988, 2003).

From both an historical and political perspective, the most influential rival of objective list theories is hedonism, which understands well-being in the subjective terms of pleasure and pain. On this account, well-being is a mental state characterized by experiences of pleasure (and the absence of experiences of displeasure) or satisfaction (and the absence of experiences of dissatisfaction).

However, despite its seeming simplicity, hedonists have conflicting ideas about the nature of pleasure (Tiberius 2015). "Sensationalists" like Jeremy Bentham (1843) and Roger Crisp (2006) argue that it is a sensation shared by pleasurable or enjoyable experiences: "that what makes accomplishment, enjoyable experiences, or whatever good for people is *their being enjoyable*, and that this is the only "*good-for*-making property there is" (Crisp 2006, p.623). By contrast, "attitudinalists" like Fred Feldman (2004; 2010) argue that pleasure is a pro-attitude and that happiness arises when a person takes (attitudinal) pleasure *in* something.

Historically speaking, the most influential hedonist was Bentham (1843), according to whom pleasure is a sensation that can vary only in intensity and duration. Mill (1863/1998, p.10, p.16) agreed with Bentham that happiness boils down to "pleasure, and the absence of pain" but stressed the qualitative differences between "higher" and "lower" pleasures (Crisp 2006, pp.112–5). While most philosophers agree that Mill's account is conceptually and phenomenologically more accurate than Bentham's, most contemporary psychologists still take a largely Benthamite line. Daniel Kahneman, for example, explicitly traces his "hedonic flow" account back to Bentham: his account focuses on "total experienced utility", an aggregation of one's moment-based experiences. The idea is that it is desirable for individuals to spend as much time as possible on the "pleasurable" side of the "affective space" (Kahneman 2000). In line with Bentham (1843), Kahneman argues that this kind of utility can be usefully measured, aggregated, and compared across individuals.

The implications for empirical studies of well-being are clear. If well-being consists in pleasure, and pleasure is rightly understood as a hedonic state along one quantitative dimension, then we can measure well-being simply by adding numbers. If, however, Mill—or Aristotle for that matter—is correct, such a methodology fails to capture the complexity of well-being. The fact that hedonism makes well-being measurable does not necessarily turn it into a plausible account of well-being.

In the so-called science of happiness, two ways of measuring happiness dominate (Layard 2011). First, subjects can be asked to state their current feelings, moods, and emotions. Simply aggregating such hedonic states fits a rather crude, quantitative approach à la Bentham. Second, subjects can be asked to reflect on their feelings and judge how happy or satisfied they are with their lives. Such "life satisfaction" measures understand happiness not as an experience or sensation but as a more stable evaluative judgement about one's quality of life. In contrast to the more experiential focus of the first measurements ("how happy do you feel?"), this has a more evaluative focus ("how happy are you with your life?"). While the first amounts to a "feeling conception", the second involves a "judgement conception" of happiness

(Nussbaum 2008). Obviously, both can generate different responses. For example, a "weekend effect", where people are happier in weekends than on weekdays, arises with the former but not the latter (Ryan, Bernstein, and Brown 2010).

There are different ways of relating these measurement techniques to the philosophical conceptions. One can say that the first (experiential) approach measures pleasure and thus fits hedonism, while the second (life satisfaction) approach measures something more complex and thus fits eudaimonism. Others argue that this tracks the "distinction between happiness (which can be momentary and short-lived) and well-being (most likely more enduring and related to life satisfaction)" (Helliwell, Layard, and Sachs 2015, p.89). In our view, this actually constitutes a move not only away from a hedonist conception of well-being but also away from a conception of well-being in terms of happiness. We follow Kahneman in arguing that both techniques measure subjective well-being, both of which can also be called "happiness" (Kahneman 2000). Both one's momentary experiences and one's more global evaluative judgements are, after all, through and through subjective appraisals.

Note that other measurements are available. A third asks subjects not how happy they are with their lives, but how they would place themselves on Hadley Cantril's "ladder of life" (Cantril 1965). It asks subjects to compare their actual life to the best possible life they can imagine for themselves (Graham 2009, pp.29–30; 2011, p.6). People who feel satisfied with their lives (despite the poverty they live in, for example) may nevertheless place themselves low on the Cantril ladder. Afghans, for example, are on average quite happy when they think of their own lives. However, invoking the Cantril ladder and asking Afghans to imagine lives they could have lived leads to lower levels of well-being (Graham 2009, p.35; 2011, p.20). Interestingly, well-being on this account correlates "more closely with income than do either happiness or life satisfaction questions, as most respondents compare their lives to a national or international reference norm" (Graham 2011, p.6).

Perhaps the best-known *philosophical* objection to hedonism is also the most damaging (Crisp 2006, p.99). Nozick's thought experiment of an experience machine shows that what matters to people cannot be reduced to the hedonist concern for having as many pleasurable experiences as possible (Nozick 1974, pp.42–45). Most of us, Nozick convincingly argues, "want to do certain things, and not just have the experience of doing them" (Nozick 1974, p.43). Since most people prefer truth over (deceptive) pleasure, hedonism does not track what people themselves take to be in their own good. In spite of its seemingly subjective character, it actually turns out to be an objective list account with one item on the list: pleasure (whether you like it or not). The objection then is not so much that it boils down to an objective list theory but that this list is too short and fails to explain why people think that other things besides pleasure are good for them. We think this is a decisive reason to reject hedonistic theories of well-being.

The last of the Big Three theories of well-being is the one dominant in social sciences and (welfare) economics: preferentist or desire-based conceptions (Crisp 2015; Heathwood 2016). Here, well-being consists in having one's preferences satisfied or one's desires fulfilled.

A contemporary preferentist conception focuses on "decision utility", which is inferred from observed preferences and not from "life satisfaction" or "experienced utility" measurements (Kahneman 2000). Rather than trying to measure subjective feelings or judgements, this approach assesses the extent to which people are able to satisfy their preferences. Focusing on observed preferences, this approach aims to avoid the issue of how to make inter-personal comparisons of utility.

A first objection to preferentism is that satisfying some preferences—like misguided preferences and preferences to harm oneself—seems an unlikely constituent of well-being. Other preferences, such as sexist or racist preferences, raise obvious ethical issues. Indeed, more nuanced preferentist conceptions argue that only the satisfaction of suitably "laundered" or filtered preferences contribute to well-being. While Brandt (1979) argues that desires need to be "rational", Griffin (1986) claims that they need to be "informed" and Harsanyi filters out "all clearly anti-social preferences, such as sadism, envy, resentment and malice" (Harsanyi 1982, p.56). On these views, the satisfaction of irrational, uninformed, and/or anti-social preferences does not add to well-being. Of course, the challenge here is to implement this in a way that is neither ad hoc nor circular in its justification. According to Fletcher, the problem lies in the assumption that one's desires ground, rather than merely track what is good for someone (Fletcher 2013, pp.216–17). An objective list conception, like Fletcher's or ours, can avoid that criticism by taking "what someone desires" to be merely indicative of "what is good for someone".

A second problem arises when considering empirical research that reveals how people's preferences are inconsistent, unstable and influenced by seemingly irrelevant features. When framing effects cause preferences to reverse, which of their incoherent preferences are to be satisfied if their well-being is to be improved? If people form preferences on the fly, should we not dig deeper and ask what people value and care about, what their ultimate goals in life are? A related conception then understands well-being as the achievement of aims worth pursuing or the realization of values (Raibley 2012; Scanlon 1998, pp.118–23). One's well-being here depends on the extent to which one's goals and values in life are achieved.

Such an "aims achievementist" conception has both a subjective and an objective component. The subjective component lies in the conative and evaluative aspect: each person is to set her own goals in life and to determine what values to hold dear. This aligns with the liberal principle of enabling persons to devise and revise their own conceptions of the good (rather than having those imposed by another). The objective component lies in the focus on the achievement of aims, not on the extent to which one is aware of or enjoys it. The well-being of someone who aims to lead a long and healthy life is diminished if she has a life-threatening brain tumour, even if she does not know or feel it. Or think of someone with a cheating fiancé: even if she is blissfully aware, her well-being is diminished if she values having a trustful relationship with a partner. Focusing on achieving fundamental aims and cares instead of satisfying rather trivial preferences, the idea is that the latter (such as the scratching of an itch), does not add as much to one's well-being as the former (such as the birth of one's long-awaited child) (Raibley 2012, p.1119).

Now that we have set out the main philosophical conceptions of well-being, we defend our own, ecumenical approach which is, nonetheless, committal about some of the issues described. Our strategy is to identify a core conception of well-being, supported by most—but not all—of the arguments that we have considered for each of the conceptions we have outlined.

10.3 Our Approach: Ecumenical Yet Committed

A first way out of the stalemate between competing conceptions of well-being and towards an ecumenical approach lies in appreciating the multiple hybrid conceptions, which incorporate different aspects of these competing conceptions. Sumner, for example, claims that something contributes to one's well-being, if one finds it satisfying or prefers it (subjective) *and* if it is independently valuable (objective) (Sumner 1996, pp.163–4). Alternatively,

Millian utilitarianism, Aristotelian eudaimonism, laundered preferentism, and aim achievementism equally stress both more subjective and objective elements.

A particularly interesting hybrid approach is that of Carol Graham, who argues that well-being has two complementary "dimensions": "pleasure and meaning" or "hedonic utility and life evaluation" (Graham 2011, p.35)[3]. This matches up to two aspects of the folk psychological concept; people themselves sort their own activities under these two dimensions (Graham 2011, p.36; White and Dolan 2009). Answers to life satisfaction questions or the Cantril ladder of life questions are "more sensitive to socioeconomic status" than responses that measure pleasure or hedonic utility because the former involve "means, capacity and agency" (Graham 2011, p.37).[4]

> [B]oth dimensions of happiness matter . . . which dimension matters is, at least in part, determined by an individual's capacity to pursue a purposeful and fulfilling life. (Graham 2011, p.38)

If this basic capacity is impaired through poverty, you will likely adapt and focus less on long-term investments in projects like work or health (Graham 2011, p.38). But if there is social and institutional support for your life projects, they become more ambitious. That does not mean that the rich necessarily score well on both meaning and happiness: "the rich are notorious for jumping onto a hedonic treadmill in search of more money and losing sight of the importance of leisure time and companionship" (Graham 2011, p.39). We have discussed Adam Smith's explanation of this fact in chapter 6: the desire for wealth is the desire for distinction—even amongst the wealthy. That is why positional concerns intensify with wealth instead of diminishing. Highly unequal societies give the wealthy more prominence as a class but intensifies competition within that class for comparative "distinction".

[3] On occasion, Graham's account is ambivalent between the concepts of well-being and happiness. For example, she claims that "people's conceptualizations of happiness (. . .) are to a large extent determined by their agency" and that "the absence of agency severely limits well-being, broadly defined as the capacity to lead a fulfilling life, even if respondents who lack agency report being happy" (Graham 2011, p.31). We think those claims are true and insightful, but form part of a theory of what happiness and well-being are from the perspective of the respondents—they are not claims about conceptions.

[4] She cites, in support of this thesis, papers on the connection between happiness and income such as (Diener et al. 2010; Kahneman and Deaton 2010).

Emphasising the difference between "well-being" and "happiness" provides a second way into our ecumenical approach. While well-being more generally refers to "the good for a person", happiness is arguably a more psychological term, closer to a mental state, "which could include life satisfaction, domain satisfaction, positive affect, positive emotional condition" (Haybron and Tiberius 2015, p.714). These two related conceptions often get conflated—especially in empirical research. The empirical data gathered by the science of happiness might well track happiness well but arguably fail to amount to an adequate account of well-being (Haybron 2007, 2008). Psychological measurements of both (positive) affect and life satisfaction arguably capture only some aspects of well-being, but not all.

Take the "aim achievementist" conception of well-being, which refers to the things a person cares about. These typically include mental states like pleasure and happiness but also being in good health, having good relations with family and friends and having a meaningful job, each of which contributes to well-being because one cares about them. Happiness then refers to a subset of those things: the mental states that provide us with positive experiences. As Nozick already stressed, we may care about happiness but also about other things. If happiness and well-being do not coincide, as we claim here, something can decrease one's well-being without making one less happy. Blissfully unaware of a disease or a cheating partner, one's happiness arguably remains intact, while one's well-being is decreased. As Graham explains, the reverse is true as well: increasing social mobility makes people's lives better off and thus arguably increases well-being, but can also make them less happy (Graham 2009, p.17).

Our ecumenical approach then is still committal as it defends a combined focus on eudaimonia and what people care about. This, we argue, is a way of incorporating the most plausible elements of well-being without ending up in the academic trenches of the philosophical well-being literature.

Let us first quickly provide four reasons for our refusal to get bogged down in discussion on well-being's exact definition. First, not much hinges on it for our purposes in this book. As we will stress throughout the book, we firmly believe that our claims about the relation between well-being, inequality, and emotions such as shame and envy hold regardless of one's favoured conception of well-being. The second reason relates to you, our readers. Our aim is to appeal to an audience as broad as possible, precisely because we are convinced that our analysis of the political psychology of economic inequality in market societies yields interesting insights for everyone living under capitalism's emotional regime. Given our focus on inequality and the psychology that underlies its impact, we do not wish to alienate anyone particularly invested in one specific conception of well-being.

Thirdly, not only empirical research but also social scientific and philosophical claims about the relations between inequality, emotions, and well-being rely on different conceptions of well-being. Here too, we want to be inclusive and make use of these insights, regardless of their specific conception of well-being at play.

The fourth relates to policy making. In their pluralistic "pragmatic subjectivism", Dan Haybron and Valerie Tiberius argue that policies should be justified on the basis of the multiple conceptions of well-being that citizens themselves hold: "Well-being policy, then, must focus on well-being as people themselves see it" (Haybron and Tiberius 2015, p.723). If you value being in trustful relationships, policies promote your well-being if they engender social trust. But for those who value living it up in Paris, policies should try and promote that hedonistic aspect of their lives.

This connects to Rawls's principle of reasonable pluralism and the liberal idea that, within the bounds of the reasonable, persons should be free to develop and revise their conceptions of the good. Our ecumenical approach with respect to well-being fits this liberal commitment best and is thus "person-respecting" (Haybron and Tiberius 2015, p.716).[5] However, we also place emphasis on the importance, to Rawls, of living under an institutional regime that educates individuals to develop conceptions of the good that presuppose justice. His focus on stability and the threat posed to stability by the "special attitudes" were central to his later work and are important here (Rawls 2001). The aim is the convergence of reasonable conceptions of the good life with justice. That is also why Nussbaum stresses that people lead less good lives in unjust societies than in just ones.

While we are serious in our aim to keep as many readers on board as possible, let us explain why we think eudaimonism has the most plausible story to tell about well-being. An important reason is that it is the most inclusive view with the broadest scope of explanation. It can accommodate the data appealed to by hedonist and preferentist accounts, while the converse does not hold.

[5] Note that existing measurement methods, such as "life satisfaction", are not perfectionist. As Carol Graham notes, "one feature of happiness surveys that makes them a powerful research tool . . . is their open-ended nature. In other words, we do not define happiness for the respondent; each respondent defines happiness for him- or her self" (Graham 2011, p.28).

Let us first explain how we take eudaimonia, or human flourishing, to relate to objective list theories. We see the human mind as a bundle of rational capacities with mental states holistically related to inputs, output and other mental states (Putnam 1975). When it comes to how well a life goes for a specific person, an objective list enumerates the properties whose instantiation in that person's life makes it go well. While objective lists have been criticized for merely enumerating seemingly unrelated properties, eudaimonists do more as they stress mutual relations amongst these properties in a way that grounds their goodness. We focus, in particular, on Richard Boyd's version which emphasizes the functional underpinning of the co-occurrence of these properties (Boyd 1999), which—clustered together—identify goodness for a person (Fine 2012). What it is for a person to be eudaimon is that, in the exercise of her distinctive capacities, she realizes these values in her life in such a way as to make that life go well for her. As Haybron (forthcoming, pp.69–70) explains, eudaimonists have a "nature-fulfillment" theory of well-being, which connects well-being to facts about human nature: "to flourish, on this sort of approach, is to live in accordance with the sort of being one is".[6]

When it comes to "goodness for" a person, well-being then is the co-occurrence of a cluster of properties that do more than merely co-occur. What Boyd calls a "homeostatic cluster property" (Boyd 1999; see also: Rubin 2008) dynamically integrates the items that other objective list theorists merely list. "Goodness for a person" consists in a property cluster, together with the mechanisms that hold the cluster together and give it its distinctive unity.

Importantly not all relevant properties need to be present as long as the cluster includes the "important" ones. (We are dealing here with a true generic statement about a kind, just as a three-legged horse still belongs in the species kind "equus caballus".) It is the goal of well-being theorists to determine the central features of the cluster that constitutes well-being for the human species. Boyd himself enumerates the following properties: "being educated, being physically healthy, sharing friendship, sharing love, enjoying leisure, engaging in physical recreation, engaging in cooperative efforts,

[6] Note that Haybron (forthcoming, p.119) himself does not ultimately endorse an Aristotelian understanding of well-being, arguing that this fails to provide "a minimally believable account of the one datum theories of well-being most need to get right—the badness of suffering." Instead, he prefers a Millian hybrid theory in which well-being has two aspects: (1) flourishing, or self-fulfilment (eudaimonic well-being)—which encompasses both psychic flourishing or happiness and agential flourishing or value-fulfilment, and (2) pleasure (hedonic well-being) (Haybron forthcoming, pp.172–5).

creating and appreciating art and being autonomous" (Boyd 1988, p.203). We share Boyd's view that this is the right kind of cluster, because the co-presence of these properties is mutually supporting (Boyd 1988, p.203) and involves the support of broader social structures (which we will explain later on). This is unsurprising given Boyd's political commitment to Marxism (Boyd 1988, p.203).[7]

Formulating the correct objective list, and deciding which properties are crucial to it, is not an easy task. However, if successful, it will invoke (homeostatic) property clusters and exhibit the mechanisms, both intra- and inter-individual, underlying their co-occurrence. Interestingly, empirical data suggest that a couple of simple but robust patterns exist: "What is most remarkable is how stable the standard determinants of happiness are in countries worldwide, regardless of their levels of development . . . some very simple patterns hold" (Graham 2011, p.13).

> [A] stable marriage, good health, and enough (but not too much) income are good for happiness. Unemployment, divorce and economic instability are terrible for happiness—everywhere that happiness is studied. (Graham 2011, p.13)

We think that Boyd's account can be put to use so as to formulate some generic truths about prudential value: goodness for a person. Crucially, this is to be combined with a principle of equal respect for persons applied equally to those who choose to lead atypical lives. This is, as Haybron explains, a key feature of Aristotelian versions of eudamonist theories of well-being.

> well-being is grounded in species or kind norms—what is distinctively or characteristically human. What's good for you, then, depends partly on what human beings are characteristically like. This is not to say that all people should live the same way. The theory allows plenty of room for individual difference, and might even deem individuality among our characteristically human qualities. Human excellence has many faces. At the same time, certain things do seem important for well-being, no matter who you are. We are a social species, for instance, so that a psychopath with no capacity for normal human relationships is worse off for it: he is missing out

[7] Note that we are not endorsing all of Boyd's views, which include being consequentialist about the right (Boyd 2003; see also: Rubin 2008). Our interest is solely in Boyd's theory of value, that we have interpreted restrictively as a theory of value for a person.

on an important element of a full life for a human being. (Haybron, forthcoming, p.79)

In addition, Julia Annas helpfully distinguishes between the living of one's life and the circumstances of one's life (Annas 2012, p.17). Education and other circumstances of a person's life can lead her to soldiering, war experience, and a certain set of virtues. A different life might have set her on a path to the scholarly virtues. It seems to us that there is a difference of degree, not of kind, between those lives and those of a person whose life's circumstances involve disabilities of one form or another. What a person is "able" to do is partly a function of technology and, hence, of the kind of society they live in. As physicist Stephen Hawking adapted himself to motor neurone disease this undoubtedly altered his capacities (again, relative to technology) but did not prevent him leading a life of achievement, meaning, and worth. He adapted his life plans to his circumstances—just as the scholar and the soldier do. Each of these atypical lives deserve equal respect and a Boyd-inspired eudaimonism is not in conflict with this point.

10.4 Well-Being: Methodological and Normative Issues

Now that we have discussed the philosophy of well-being, we will rely on Anna Alexandrova's work to relate it to the science of well-being, which measures and studies it empirically (Alexandrova 2017). Alexandrova crucially distinguishes between theories, constructs, and measures, which can create conceptual confusion when not categorized properly. While "psychological hedonism" (a theory) is about "affect" (a construct) and is measured by "subjective happiness scales" (a measure), "economic subjectivism" (a theory) is about "preference satisfaction" (a construct) and is measured by, for example, consumption (a measure).

Theories of well-being are typically philosophical in nature and purport to adequately capture the one true meaning of well-being.[8] In contrast to the dominant view in philosophy that there actually is one such theory ("invariantism"), most scientists of well-being make use of different theories

[8] At the level of high theory, Alexandrova distinguishes the "Big Three" that we analysed before. For an overview of all the theories, constructs, and measure that Alexandrova distinguishes, see her introduction (Alexandrova 2017, pp.xxxvi–xxxvii) and her Appendix A (Alexandrova 2017, pp.157–61).

for different purposes ("variantism") (Alexandrova 2017, p.27). Given our commitment to Boyd's view, we will offer our own take on her distinction.

According to Alexandrova, philosophical debates typically move forward by formulating counterexamples to a specific theory, which are then countered by either, first, biting the bullet; secondly, going hybrid; or, thirdly, making the theory more intricate (Alexandrova 2017, pp.28–31). Take the objection against hedonism: things other than pleasurable sensations seem to matter for well-being as well. Hedonists who bite the bullet deny this, for example by arguing that people who prefer reality over Nozick's experience machine are mistaken or motivated by values other than well-being. Another response would be to go hybrid and combine hedonism with other aspects. Finally, one can make the theory more intricate by adding complexities and modifications to avoid the objection.

The problem here is that this misguided project of trying to rescue one's preferred theory increases the distance between theories and measures of well-being (Alexandrova 2017, pp.32–7). While philosophers are going ever more principled, hybrid, or intricate, psychologists largely ignore those debates and go on measuring. They simply take whatever they can use in their scientific toolbox.

In her explanation and justification of what scientists of well-being are doing, Alexandrova argues for a number of inter-connected claims: variantism, theory diversity, construct pluralism, and contextualism. These help to clarify our ecumenical approach. First of all, according to Alexandrova's "well-being variantism", there is no "all-purpose" concept or theory of well-being. Because such a "master theory of well-being is not forthcoming nor indeed needed", we are justified in using many measures and constructs (Alexandrova 2017, p.xxxviii). Alexandrova advises well-being researchers to tolerate different standards for, conceptions of, and measurements related to well-being, which fits the complexity and multifaceted nature of well-being itself. When someone asks you how you are doing, she can be asking about your physical comfort (when they saw you trip), about your life satisfaction or flourishing (when your best friend uses that significant tone of voice), or about objective aspects of your quality of life (when a social worker comes over). All of these aspects plausibly relate to your well-being.

We want to meet Alexandrova half-way here. We do, in fact, think there is a truth about well-being and think Boyd's homeostatic property cluster account captures that well. But we also think that what it claims to be generically good for the human kind allows multiple counter-instances, which differentiates it from the project of finding a "master theory" that "defines" well-being by stipulating necessary and sufficient conditions. Any account in terms of generic truths does not work in terms of necessary and sufficient conditions, but in terms of a "core" versus "periphery" model.

That is why we can agree with Alexandrova's further claim that there are multiple mid-level theories which specify different "kinds" of well-being and are situated in between what she calls "high theories" and specific "measures" of well-being (Alexandrova 2017, pp.117–9). This reflects the context dependence of explanation and the need, in context, for supplementary hypotheses to capture the complexity of particular cases. Following the methodological lead of Nancy Cartwright and Jon Elster, we agree that the science of happiness is made up of a patchwork of lower-level, context-specific generalizations as well as high -level generalizations such as Boyd's claims about well-being.

Our commitment to Boyd's view as a high-level generic truth about well-being does not preclude us from ecumenically embracing both "construct pluralism" and "measure pluralism". We do not think it is our job as philosophers to police the practices of scientists that use different constructs and measures, often for pragmatic and experimental reasons. While psychologists mostly talk about mental states, economists usually refer to preference satisfaction and development theorists and medical researchers tend to talk about objective quality of life (Alexandrova 2017, p.3). The new science of happiness exhibits numerous robust, but context-specific, claims that vary greatly in their methodological assumptions and ceteris paribus conditions. It is an emerging, multi-disciplinary science with an inherent plurality of approaches and is none the worse for that. Our work in the philosophical vineyard fortunately allows us to avoid the complexity of operationalizing sound experimental approaches to well-being.

Another methodological issue we need to address concerns well-being's normative relevance. Given the normative claims we want to make—about the detrimental impact on well-being of the extensive levels of inequality in capitalist societies—it is important for us to show that the theories, constructs, and measures we refer to have normative and thus ethical and political relevance. In fact, we consider it a desideratum for any conception of well-being if it also shows why one should promote it (Tiberius 2015). Well-being, in and of itself, is obviously valuable—it is part of what makes our lives worthwhile—and attempts to theorize and measure it should not ignore its normative aspect (Alexandrova 2017, pp.xxi–xxiii).

Well-being and happiness are increasingly acknowledged as important in both academic circles and amongst policy makers. They have even arguably replaced the previously narrow-minded focus on economic indicators. For example in 2010, the then prime minister of the United Kingdom, David Cameron, claimed "it's time we focused not just on GDP but on GWB—general wellbeing" (Stratton 2010).[9] Following the example of Bhutan, several Western countries have pledged to focus more on (the impact of policies on) well-being. While the Human Development Index (HDI), inspired by Amartya Sen's work on capabilities, encompasses wealth, health, and education, the Gross National Happiness Index (GNHI) covers not only living standards (like household income, housing quality), health (like disability, mental health), and education (like literacy, knowledge, and values) but also psychological well-being (like life satisfaction, emotional balance), culture (like sociocultural skills and participation), time use (like working and sleeping hours), good governance (like political participation, freedom and performance), community (like social support and relationships), and ecological aspects (like pollution and wildlife) (Studies 2012). All these seem to be plausible ingredients of well-being on any understanding. Even if it is controversial, it is an ecumenical approach in action.

Despite our focus on well-being, we do not claim that well-being is the foundational concept of ethics or the only value to be promoted. We share Rawls's assumption that the right is prior to the good, and even if well-being is very important for social policy there are certainly numerous constraints on how this valuable end is to be brought about. Freedom, justice, human rights, and poverty reduction are worthwhile goals of social policy, even if they do not impact people's well-being.

So what are the implications for the conceptions of well-being we discussed? As will become clear, things like relationships, health, freedom, and autonomy are widely acknowledged to be good for persons and thus conducive to well-being on almost any account. As such, these things can easily be included in our ecumenical understanding of well-being. To analyse the

[9] While we have expressed some doubts about William Davies's wide-ranging scepticism, we do agree with his criticism of the rather opportunistic interest in well-being theory by politicians like Cameron, who never enacted meaningful policy responses to, for example, increasing levels of inequality despite the empirical evidence that this would promote well-being overall. Aspiration is one thing; policy another.

normative relevance of each of the conceptions, we first discuss which role they can play in guiding, justifying, and evaluating the impact of policies on well-being. Next, we address the normative worries each of them raises.

First, let us take objective list and eudaimonist views such as our own. They are relevant, paradoxically, because most policy makers disregard conceptual issues and simply focus on improving objective circumstances, such as the income, education, and health of citizens (Sen 1999). Measures like the Human Development Index (HDI) that monitor these objective circumstances align well with objective list accounts. They enable policy makers to develop and implement practical social changes that improve the plight of people without getting lost in conceptual work (the task of philosophers) or measurement issues (the task of scientists). The rationale here is simple but plausible: the richer, healthier, and better educated people are, the better off they are. This idea has moved the policy focus from economic growth and material wealth to a more inclusive set of policy goals and indicators.

Normative worries surrounding objective list and eudaimonist conceptions focus on their potentially perfectionist and paternalist implications. Now, given that most policy makers focus on capabilities and thus on providing citizens with freedoms, opportunities, and abilities to be and do what they deem valuable, they allow for people to make their own choices based on their own priorities or values. Policies should aim to further conditions that enrich people's opportunities to flourish and enable them to achieve well-being, understood as doing or being whatever they have reason to value (Robeyns 2016). The capability approach rightly stresses both the plurality of aspects that matter to well-being and the different weights people give to these aspects. While some value highly the capability to lead a long and healthy life, others may have a different view of what constitutes *their* well-being. The extent to which people are willing, for example, to forego hedonist benefits in exchange for more health differs from person to person, and liberal policies can and should respect this, even when based on eudaimonist considerations.

Secondly, what about the normative relevance of hedonistic and mental state conceptions of well-being? This reveals itself in the simple question: why remain obsessed with economic growth and increasing people's material wealth, if this does not make people (feel) happier (Frank 1999/2010)? Policy makers also have an obvious duty to eliminate the kinds of suffering brought about by hunger, disease, avoidable death, violence, or sexual abuse, all of which are clearly detrimental to well-being on this account. According to Dolan and White, happiness research data can be relevant for policy makers by helping assess costs and benefits that would otherwise be hard to quantify (such as psychological costs of air pollution, unemployment, or crime) and by providing a unit of measurement that enables comparisons of different sets of policies (Dolan and White 2007, p.78).

In addition, this notion of well-being has gained political traction, with more and more countries increasingly focusing on experienced happiness as one of their policy goals. Consider the influential "Sarkozy Report" authored by Joseph Stiglitz, Amartya Sen, and Jean-Paul Fitoussi, which recommends the use of subjective measures of well-being such as life satisfaction for designing public policies and assessing social progress (Stiglitz, Sen, and Fitoussi 2009). As the World Happiness Report (2015) notes, this focus has spread across OECD countries and the rest of the globe (Helliwell, Layard, and Sachs 2015, p.4). In a sense, the United States already had happiness as a policy goal since Thomas Jefferson listed "the pursuit of happiness" as one of people's inalienable rights in his original draft of the US Declaration of Independence. In 1809, he stated that "the care of human life and happiness (. . .) is the only legitimate object of good government". So much for the good news — the extent to which (the science of) happiness is already having a positive impact on social policy. What about the problems?

First, hedonist and mental-state conceptions suffer from the obvious problem that people may take pleasure in really bad things. Conversely, painful experiences and unpleasant emotions are not by definition bad in themselves—the pain of a marathon runner contributes to her later sense of achievement as an obstacle overcome. As we will argue in the next chapter, envy, anger, and shame, for example, can be appropriate emotional responses to a situation, spurring people to (morally) desirable behaviour, even if it does not make them feel good. Virtuous behaviour can be painstakingly hard. Here, eudaimonists have the upper hand as they can accommodate the insight that even unpleasurable things can be good for people (Nussbaum 2008, S97).

Secondly, a minority of sceptics claim that policy can influence social and environmental factors that impact individual happiness, but will hardly impact happiness itself. Take research into the extent to which people's personality traits, such as "cheerfulness", are genetically inherent, which shows that "genetic variation explains about 33% of the variance in individual happiness" (Neve et al. 2012, p.207). In a similar vein, Easterlin holds that each person has an inherent level of happiness to which she tends to revert after short-term fluctuations (Easterlin 2003). If the goal is to make people happier, policies aimed at improving people's conditions in terms of income, health, and education risk having only a small impact on their hedonic mental states. However, this argument remains philosophically controversial. We have already endorsed, in chapter 3, Fishkin's countervailing claim that nature and nurture both contribute no less than 100%! Alternatively, one might also think that policies that had the potential to impact 67% of the variation in any given individual's happiness still has plenty to work with.

Thirdly and relatedly, mental state accounts are confronted with the problem of adaptation and the "hedonic treadmill effect" (Brickman and Campbell 1971; Diener, Lucas, and Scollon 2006). This refers to people's tendency to adapt to changes in health, material wealth, living conditions, et cetera (Easterlin 1974). People in miserable conditions or living in crime-ridden and corrupt societies nonetheless often report reasonable degrees of happiness (Graham 2011, p.ix). The problem is that adaptation can cause societies to get "stuck" in dysfunctional equilibria with people adapting to circumstances they have good reasons to reject (Graham 2009, p.211). Such adaptation may be beneficial for individual happiness, but leads to the collective acceptance of conditions that should be rejected. The worry, then, is that real problems may not be addressed by well-being policies if we rely exclusively on mental-state conceptions of well-being. After all, unjust inequalities, discrimination, and human rights violations do not necessarily make victims feel bad if they have adapted to being treated this way. This problem provides a serious obstacle to drawing normative or policy implications from the robust yet context-sensitive results from the science of happiness.

It is worth recalling at this point Carol Graham's two "dimensions" of happiness: pleasure and meaning. While expanding everyone's capacity for agency would improve "meaning", it would also decrease "pleasure", i.e. happiness as a hedonic mental state. Graham uses the example of obesity, which carries a social stigma in the United States and is associated with lower happiness and lower income. While losing weight is a difficult long-term commitment, an obese person can make himself happier in the short run—and thus adapt to her situation—by socializing with other obese people (Graham 2011, p.44).[10] So obese people can easily get trapped in suboptimal equilibria by socializing only with other obese Americans to avoid social stigma.

[10] "Obesity is much more the norm among people in low-skilled professions than those in high skilled ones. . . . We also found a negative link between obesity and upward income mobility. The

Obesity-reducing policies may promote people's freedom and autonomy in the long run but produce short-term unhappiness (Graham 2011, p.46, p.52). On the basis of a republican understanding of liberty as non-domination, the primary goal has to be making people freer in their range of choices and thus removing the stigma from obesity. If costs to happiness are incurred along the way—so be it.

All too narrow conceptions of well-being as experienced happiness thus risk ignoring major problems and justifying the wrong kind of "solutions". The upside here is that people themselves do not only care about leading pleasurable lives. Often, they make appropriate investments in the future of themselves and the people they care about (Graham 2011, p.43). In line with Graham's point about the psychology of investment, we will argue that market societies typically put better off people in a position where their enhanced opportunity set makes them psychologically pre-disposed to make long-term investments in their own future and—importantly—in their children's future. Conversely, these societies trap the worst off in suboptimal equilibria that reduce their capabilities to escape those situations.[11] Their capacity for the kind of long-term investments (that eudaimonist aspects of human flourishing require) is diminished: "if choices and opportunities . . . are lacking, then individuals may select into happiness" (Graham 2011, p.45). This selection into (experienced, short-run) happiness, however, deflects from more important structural changes in the (objective, long-run) determinants of well-being.

In sum, the idea of "happy slaves" turns out to be very real, and not a hypothetical thought experiment (Sen 1985b, p.188). Members of oppressed groups adapt to their plight and many people are perfectly satisfied with their lives, even though they are less well off than they should be. People who are objectively far worse off than others still report life satisfaction levels that are roughly similar to others (Riis et al. 2005). While real, however, adaptation is often not complete: "there is very strong evidence of continuing well-being effects from major disabilities and unemployment" (Helliwell, Layard, and Sachs 2015, p.16).

implications are that if a person is obese and works at Wal-Mart, he or she is less likely to move on to a better job and also has less incentive to reduce his or her weight. Thus poor health norms may contribute to creating poverty traps as well as health traps" (Graham 2011, pp.100–101).

[11] "The same traits that allow people to adapt to adversity and remain happy may also result in greater tolerance for a bad equilibrium, not least because there is no immediately obvious way to change that equilibrium from the perspective of the average individual" (Graham 2011, p.50).

So what about the normative relevance of the third, i.e. preferentist conception of well-being? As it provides the basis for normative welfare economics and the policy prescriptions that follow from it, preferentism has obvious normative relevance. In short, the questions here are what people prefer and what enables them to do more of the things they prefer. A lot of the cost benefit analyses that guide policy making are all about which policies and other institutional setups maximize aggregate welfare, assuming that well-being (or "welfare" in economic lingo) can be equated with preference satisfaction and measured in terms of willingness-to-pay. Even if you think that preference satisfaction is a mistaken theory of well-being, you can still hold on to the main results of welfare economics if you take preferences only as indicative and not constitutive of what is good for people (Hausman and McPherson 2009).

Which problems do preferentists face? The first and perhaps biggest relates to the adaptation mechanism discussed before. Next to the "hedonic treadmill effect" we analysed (which poses normative issues for hedonism), research has found evidence for a distinct "satisfaction treadmill effect" (Kahneman 2000). This refers to the fact that people's preferences change as their income increases. More specifically, people's reference point—whatever they consider "satisfactory"—adapts and rises when they become wealthier. As people's preferences change when they grow richer, their gains in wealth do not automatically result in gains in preference satisfaction. On this account, the policies aimed at increasing incomes will not increase well-being. The problem here is that justice does not align with well-being understood in terms of preference satisfaction. Injustices should worry us, even if they do not inhibit the preference satisfaction of people adapting to them (Nussbaum 2008, S100).

The second problem relates to the fact that most measurements of preference satisfaction rely on revealed preferences in market exchanges (one's preferences are expressed in one's willingness to pay for something) or on stated preferences in surveys. However, simply asking people how much they would be willing to pay obviously leads to biases because of pre-existing inequality. If I am poorer than you, your (revealed or stated) willingness to pay for something is likely higher than mine, but that does not mean you have a stronger preference for it. Something's value can be hard or even impossible to express in monetary terms.

In conclusion, let us return to the normative implications of our ecumenical, yet committed approach, with its preferred conception of well-being: the homeostatic property cluster account of prudential goodness. First of all, we want to note that it is compatible with acknowledging the normative relevance of other conceptions. Public policies typically are justified in multiple ways and, given the often partially overlapping conceptions of well-being, policies that improve well-being on one account are likely to improve it on our account as well. Happiness, measured in terms of life satisfaction, for instance, is interrelated with other, more objective aspects of well-being, such as health or job satisfaction (Dolan and White 2007). Conversely, people suffering from depression are also more likely to suffer from other diseases (Dolan and White 2007, p.76).

Our preferred theory of well-being—a version of eudaimonism that we hope includes insights from the capability approach—then constitutes our "thick theory of the good", as Rawls terms it. Such a single, schematic view of the good life is compatible with the methodological pluralism characteristic of the science of happiness. So what are its implications for the debate between consequentialist approaches (that aim to promote happiness or well-being), capability approaches (that stress the importance of *enabling* people to achieve well-being), and Rawls (who criticizes both)? Actually, we think the gap here is less extensive than it appears. When Rawls uses the original position, parties are assumed to not know their own identities and so cannot make choices based on their own preferences. Hence Rawls's list of primary goods is justified as "what you would want if you wanted anything" (Rawls 1971/1999, p.230). But this is Rawls's "thin" theory of the good designed for the original position. Later in his *A Theory of Justice*, this restriction is lifted and Rawls's develops a "thick" theory of the good that includes a distinctly Aristotelian moral psychology.

We do not deny there is a genuine dispute here. Rawls criticizes consequentialists and strongly consequentialist capability theorists like Amartya Sen for justifying principles of justice on the basis of consequences for well-being (consequentialists) or on variable conversion rates of resources into well-being (capability theorists). According to Rawls, this approach violates the publicity condition that he thought was essential to any conception of justice. Yet Rawls also remarks that one does not need to be a consequentialist to be interested in consequences (Rawls 1971/1999, p.26). Many aspects of his overall view draw on theories in psychology and sociology. A rapprochement between a Rawlsian view about justice and a broader philosophical and psychological account of well-being thus puts in a position to address issues such as the stability of justice, or the congruence of justice with an individual's conception of the good.

10.5 Well-Being and Emotional Regimes

In anticipation of the following chapters, we need to answer two questions: what role do emotions play in different conceptions of well-being and how does well-being relate to our notion of "emotional regimes"? The main claim that we have defended throughout the book is that capitalism is institutionally underpinned by an emotional regime that expects, and instils, emotions in people that are arguably detrimental to their well-being, such as shame, anxiety, and envy.

In light of our understanding of an emotional regime, it is crucial to see the close and bidirectional interplay between social, institutional, and political structures on the one hand and the mental and emotional lives of the people governed by those structures on the other. The institutional and emotional aspects of life in the specific kind of societies we are currently living are closely intertwined. In capitalist market societies, the norms that govern emotional responses have an obvious impact on how people feel, and which kinds of lives and activities they consider admirable, dignifying, stressful, painful, and shameful. In the next chapter, each of these emotions and their role in market societies will be scrutinized in more detail. Here, we stress their obvious connections to well-being and why evidence from the science of happiness proves insightful when it comes to analysing the emotional regime of capitalism.

Two examples serve to illustrate the idea of emotional regimes as involving the complex entwinement of institutional and emotional factors. A first example here is the Rousseauian views of amour-propre that we discussed in chapter 6 (Kolodny 2010; Neuhouser 2013). Under the right social and political conditions, institutions will shape this emotion into a justified and proper sense of self-regard. Under the wrong conditions, however, amour-propre becomes "inflamed" and detrimental to well-being (on multiple understandings of this term). This is paradigmatic of the kind of explanation that concerns us in this book. The claim is not the causal, unidirectional one that defective institutions—such as private property—cause bad emotions to arise or that emotions inherent to human nature inevitably lead to specific institutional setups. Instead, the interplay matters: specific institutions have emotional corollaries (and vice versa) that support their continued existence. The inauguration of private property increases the emotionally charged desire for social status and people's focus on outward appearances to signal how well they are doing, in turn aggravating status competition through consumption. The institutional and emotional aspects mutually reinforce each other.

Rousseau's philosophical insights about people's desires for recognition and status have recently been confirmed by psychological research. It has been shown that the desire for status—defined as the "respect, admiration, and voluntary deference individuals are afforded by others"—is a distinct and crucial motive across cultures, personalities, gender, and age. (Anderson, Hildreth, and Howland 2015, p.574). Status turns out to be key to well-being.

> People's subjective well-being, self-esteem, and mental and physical health appear to depend on the level of status they are accorded by others. (Anderson, Hildreth, and Howland 2015, p.574)

As Rousseau already claimed, status is borne out of social comparison, which gets amplified in unequal societies. People in unequal societies "are more likely to fear being looked down upon by others" which in turn negatively impacts their well-being (Anderson, Hildreth, and Howland 2015, p.574).

In a second example, Boyd argues that the human good becomes "fragmented" (Boyd 2003, pp.34–8) under capitalist institutions, inhibiting people from living better lives (Boyd 1999). Boyd's picture revolves around the interplay between human minds—clusters of co-occurring mental properties—and the mechanisms supporting this co-occurrence, such as the social structures in which those minds are embedded.

> [T]here are in addition psychological and social mechanisms which when, and the extent to which, they are present contribute to the homeostasis. They probably include cultivated attitudes of mutual respect, political democracy, egalitarian social relations, (...) etc. (Boyd 1988, p.203)

Good-making features, and the mechanisms underlying them, can operate at both the individual and the institutional level. This is in line with our claim that the factors that influence a person's well-being can extend beyond the individual, such as good governance, strong social capital, or extensive public goods, and the empirical literature vindicates that claim (Helliwell, Huang, and Harris 2009; Helliwell and Putnam 2004). For example, evidence suggests that democratic participation itself has positive impact on happiness (Frey and Stutzer 2002).[12] The social and institutional mechanisms underpinning well-being then, can either encourage and diffuse it, or serve to frustrate it.

As a Marxist, Boyd argues that capitalist social conditions thwart, instead of facilitate people leading good lives. Capitalism is an inhospitable place for happy lives, either intra- or inter-individually. Indeed, it may actually be "designed" to be obstructive in this way (Boyd 2003, p.36). This book develops this point further. We will see the direct bearing of this claim in the next section, where we cite comparisons of well-being in different countries dealing with the presence, or absence, of institutional factors such as the rule of law, crime, and corruption. As mentioned, this story is complicated by the psychological mechanism of adaptation that has individuals reconcile themselves to living, for example, in an unjust society (Graham 2009, p.206).

So what role do emotions play in all this? In line with our ecumenical approach, we will argue that our claims about the emotions at stake—negative ones like shame, anxiety, frustration, and envy and positive ones like happiness and a sense of self-esteem—tend to hold for different conceptions of well-being. Take shame and its correlate of low self-esteem.

First, on objective list conceptions of well-being, shame is obviously detrimental to well-being as it impedes the realization of many plausible items on such a list, such as happiness, relationships, freedom, and being respected. Shame tends to make people unhappy, withdraw from social life, and engage in fewer social relationships. When people are ashamed, they are in a sense unfree given that they fail Pettit's "eyeball test". Unlike the free citizen, or *liber*, the person suffering from shame cannot look others in the eye as political equals. In addition, shame is a social emotion that results from a threat to self-esteem and self-respect, which in turn results from or is reinforced by a lack of esteem and respect by others. Whatever is deemed objectively good for a person, leading a life in shame impairs it.

In her *Hiding from Humanity*, Martha Nussbaum discusses the nefarious character of shame from an eudaimonist perspective (Nussbaum 2004). Since a rich emotional life is part and parcel of a good life and a healthy

[12] Although Graham notes the direction of causation problem: does being more satisfied with your life cause you to be more politically involved, or does political involvement cause you to be more satisfied with your life—or both (Graham, 2011, p.93)?

personality, Nussbaum argues that people surrendering to shame are "hiding from humanity" and thus leading emptier lives. Shame is typically experienced by people struggling with their own existence (Nussbaum 2004, pp.93–4). It dismisses, rejects, and degrades persons and it denies their personhood and equal dignity (Nussbaum 2004, pp.230–9). Since eudaimonist conceptions of well-being revolve around self-realization, self-development, and human flourishing, shame is clearly antithetical to it (Nussbaum 2008, S92–3).

Secondly, on hedonist conceptions of well-being, shame is once again obviously bad for the person experiencing it. In contrast with emotions like joy or love, which contribute to well-being, emotions like shame have a negative impact on well-being simply because they feel bad. Shame clearly has an unpleasant experiential aspect to it. When people experience shame—sometimes called "high level" shame in contrast with "low level" shame that refers to a more enduring (and hence more tolerable) state—they experience stings of embarrassment, they feel small and shrink in the eyes of another. Shame essentially involves a negative evaluation of or threat to one's social self in its entirety (Kemeny, Grunewald, and Dickerson 2004). This also helps explain why people experiencing shame desire and tend to withdraw, to hide, and to disappear from view (Williams 1993, pp.89–90).

Thirdly, on preferentist conceptions of well-being, shame will be detrimental as well, both because people prefer to avoid shame and because shame inhibits satisfying other preferences (such as engaging in social relations). Even "low level" shame typically isolates people from others, as they attempt to avoid shameful situations. This in turns inhibits them from doing what they, in the absence of shame, would value doing. Since shame is bad for the person at hand, whatever conception of well-being one defends, it is clearly detrimental to well-being on our ecumenical approach.

The same analysis can be carried out for the other emotions that we will be focusing on in the next chapter. We will argue that each is a crucial part of the emotional regimes of capitalist societies: status anxiety, envy, and admiration for the rich. In each case, different conceptions prove compatible as they deliver convergent verdicts about the bearing of these emotions on well-being. Instead of becoming mired in conceptual arguments over which theory of well-being best captures what makes people's lives go well and why, our ecumenical approach stresses that they have a lot in common and single out different aspects of the multi-faceted phenomenon we call "well-being".

As our aim is to develop a political psychology of economic inequality, we believe that such an ecumenical approach enables us to make broad use of empirical evidence about the relationship between inequality, emotional responses, and well-being. Nobody would deny, for example, that being able to experience pleasure and avoid suffering is at least *one* facet of one's life going well. The same goes for being in good health, having stable relationships, having a sense of self-esteem and self-respect, and being able to live in a society that does not structurally induce feelings of shame, envy, anxiety, and frustration.

10.6 Income, Wealth, and Well-Being

While our goal in the rest of this chapter is to investigate what the science of happiness tells us about the link between well-being and economic inequality (a relative concept), we focus first on the link between well-being and income and wealth (absolute concepts). If income turns out to be positively correlated with well-being, this means that income inequalities translate into well-being inequalities. That is arguably problematic in and of itself without the need to introduce comparative dimensions.

Despite the truism that money can't buy happiness, it is reasonable to expect that they are correlated. Does the data support that hypothesis? While there is extensive disagreement on the tentative correlation between *inequality* and happiness, "there is much less debate about the relationship between income and happiness within countries. Income matters to happiness" (Graham 2009, p.14). In this section then, we discuss empirical findings on this relationship between money and well-being, before doing the same for the relationship between economic *inequality* and well-being in the next section.

Since wealth enables people to satisfy more needs and desires, it makes sense to assume that it makes them better off, regardless whether this is understood in eudaimonist, hedonist, or preferentist terms. More wealth will likely make one happier, facilitate flourishing, and enable one to satisfy more preferences. Within a country or society, the empirical evidence indeed suggests that the rich are on average happier than the poor (Frank 2007, p.24). Happiness, here measured in terms of "life evaluation", has been found to be correlated both with income and changes in income (Diener, Tay, and Oishi 2013, pp.273–4).

As mentioned, this conclusion is "ceteris paribus" and does not necessarily imply that getting rich always buys you happiness. It depends on your initial situation and whether people around you are getting richer as well. In most developed countries, the extensive economic growth over the last four decades has not led to comparable increases in average subjective well-being. Hence the Easterlin paradox: while the rich within developed countries are on average happier than the poor, rising average income over time is typically not correlated with rising average happiness for most people (Easterlin 1974, 2017; Easterlin et al. 2010). In both the United States and western European countries, consistent increases in GDP over the last few decades were not accompanied by increases in happiness (Easterlin 1995).

Therefore, despite the positive correlation between income and happiness levels *within* a country, such a relationship is weak at best *across* countries and over time (Easterlin 1974; Graham 2009, chapters 2, 6). Although increases in income can produce short-term increases in subjective well-being, it appears that over time people adapt as their material desires increase. This same paradoxical relation holds between income and health:

> Richer people tend, on average, to be healthier and happier than poorer people in the same society. But when comparing rich countries, it makes no difference whether on average people in one society are almost twice as rich as people in another . . . differences in average income or living standards between whole populations or countries don't matter at all, but income differences within those same populations matter very much indeed. (Wilkinson and Pickett 2009, p.13)

When comparing country averages, material wealth does matter for well-being but its significance decreases as countries get richer:

> In poorer countries, economic development continues to be very important for human wellbeing. Increases in their material living standards result in substantial improvements both in objective measures of wellbeing like life expectancy, and in subjective ones like happiness. But as nations join the ranks of the affluent developed countries, further rises in income count for less and less. (Wilkinson and Pickett 2009, p.8)

It follows that economists and policy makers in developed countries who aim to promote well-being by further increasing material welfare overemphasize the extent to which buying commodities makes people happy. Equally, they underestimate the importance of goods that cannot be bought, such as friendships or communal ties (Dolan and White 2007, p.81).

Easterlin's initial findings were not fine-grained; they simply correlated countries' GDP with averages of reported happiness. More fine-grained and recent research focuses on differences within states and between states (Diener et al. 2010; Diener, Tay, and Oishi 2013). The cross-national differences in mean and average happiness can be predicted reasonably well from characteristics like wealth. According to the 2015 World Happiness Report, which compares average national life satisfaction across countries, differences in GDP per capita explain one-third of the differences in happiness (Helliwell, Layard, and Sachs 2015, p.29).

Several factors explain this complex evidence. First, different results can be due to different measures: average GDP per capita (Easterlin 1974) is something very different from household income (Diener, Tay, and Oishi 2013). If increases in material wealth over time, due to rising GDP, are unequally distributed and economic benefits go almost exclusively to the rich, most people are not becoming happier for obvious reasons. Seeing other groups prosper may well detract from one's happiness. The larger these disparities, the less changes in GDP per capita can be expected to change most people's actual living standards. As such, Diener, Tay, and Oishi's more recent work provides a refined version of the Easterlin hypothesis of interest for intra-societal distributional questions.

Our scenario of the gains of economic growth being unequally distributed, with the rich capturing most of them is not a hypothetical one (Diener, Tay, and Oishi 2013, p.274). Consider the data we provided in chapter 1 about inequality in the United States. Recall how "the top 1% captured 95% of the income gains" from 2009 to 2012 (Saez and Zucman 2016). On a larger time frame, from 1993 to 2015, average income has risen 25.7% with the top 1% incomes growing by 94.5% and the bottom 99% by only 14.3% (Saez and Zucman 2016). Nicholas Buttrick, Samantha Heintzelman, and Shigehiro Oishi explain why these facts, in themselves, provide a plausible explanation for the refined version of the Easterlin paradox:

> In countries in which these gains are distributed more equally, economic growth does, in fact, lead to increased happiness as one might expect. It is only when increases in income are concentrated among fewer beneficiaries (and thus where status gaps are likely larger and more salient) that growth

> does not lead to increases in national happiness. Introducing a psychological perspective demystifies the outcomes stemming from inequality. (Buttrick, Heintzelman, and Oishi 2017, p.15)

The controversy surrounding the Easterlin paradox dissolves as soon as one factors in intra-societal inequality. This helps explain why the Easterlin paradox holds in some societies but not others. In societies where internal distributions are fair, there will be a reliable correlation between increased economic growth and increased well-being. In societies where aggregate growth is unfairly distributed, status issues come to the fore (in two ways we will distinguish below), and the "gappier" the distribution the more such inequalities frustrate any positive impact of economic growth on well-being. We have already described, in chapter 8, Goldin's conception of "greedy jobs" where rising inequality and the dominance of a money ethos raise the competitive stakes (Goldin 2014, pp.10–3). The connection between the treadmill of ever-increasing hours at work and diminished well-being is evident.

People who get richer tend to set themselves and their peers higher standards, which in turn causes a disconnect between (rising) material wealth and (stagnating) subjective well-being. As we will see in chapter 12 on the dominant meritocratic ideology of the United States and the United Kingdom this is particularly so when it comes to hours spent working. Wealthy people in these societies may favour inconspicuous rather than conspicuous displays of wealth; however, they are keen to advertise how extraordinarily hard they work (particularly in the United States). This finding connects with two of the philosophical issues already canvased: social stratification (which can exacerbate the pains of positional competition amongst the highest strata of "competitors", as we discussed in chapter 9) and adaptation (discussed above in this chapter).

The refined Easterlin paradox is consonant with the claim from chapter 6 on which Rousseau, Smith, and Hegel converged: the wealthy do not seek wealth for its own sake but instrumentally for the sake of social distinction. The desire for wealth is part of the competition for attention and this intensifies amongst the already rich. Status competition between the wealthy triggers competition more widely, but these wider competitions are not for the high-end artworks, boats, and jewellery for which the rich compete. The real problem, we have argued, is when the wealthy start to annex for themselves the key goods of education and healthcare. While one can shrug one's shoulders about the difference between your $30 wristwatch and the $30,000 wristwatch of the very wealthy, the story is different when the wealthy monopolize access to educational opportunities and social networks.

Social comparison and adaptation to changing wealth levels and increasing consumption norms lead to an "escalation of material aspirations with economic growth" (Easterlin et al. 2010, p.22467). As Graham explains, this again goes some way to explaining the Easterlin paradox of "happy peasants and miserable millionaires":

> The intuition is that until basic needs are met, people are not concerned about relative differences, and the relationship between happiness and income resembles a linear one. At higher levels, however, it curves off and resembles a logarithmic function.[13] (Graham 2009, p.158)

Adaptive preference formation processes matter crucially in understanding the Easterlin paradox. As people (and the countries they live in) become wealthier, their desires, goals, and aspirations change accordingly:

> Lasting happiness is again unlikely because any improvement is overhauled by a rise in aspirations. (Veenhoven 1991, p.6)

As noted in chapter 6, Adam Smith already understood this point that the societal standards that people are expected to meet increase as societies get richer. What is the empirical evidence for Smith's claim when applied to our societies—far more affluent than the societies of his time?

These claims are empirically vindicated in the work of Diener, Tay, and Oishi, who find that rising income generally does make people happier but only if it is not accompanied by rising aspirations and expectations (Diener, Tay, and Oishi 2013). People become happier when they make more money, but not when they are expecting to make even more money. The "hedonic adaptation" or "hedonic treadmill" effect turns out to be key (Diener, Tay, and Oishi 2013, p.268). As mentioned, changes in wealth have a short-lived impact on happiness, which remains at remarkably stable levels in the long run as people adapt to changing circumstances.

What matters here is whether people compare themselves with their own past selves or with others. With social comparison, one's reference point not

[13] Graham adds, however, that "concerns for relative income differences arise at surprisingly low levels of income" (Graham 2009, p.158). Graham cites (Ravallion and Lokshin 2005).

only changes as others become richer (or poorer for that matter). If we compare our income with others, then the positive effect of higher income will be offset by the negative effect of higher consumption norms (Easterlin 1995, p.36). This would, importantly, reveal that people are concerned and worried about the inequalities in their own societies, from which they draw the materials for inter-group comparisons.

Crucially, the science of happiness confirms the fact that the comparisons that matter to well-being are to one's reference group (Diener, Tay, and Oishi 2013, p.268). How well one is doing individually is "anchored" by perceptions of how one's peers are faring. Measuring happiness as life satisfaction, Ada Ferrer-i-Carbonell found that "individual happiness and welfare depend not only on the material achievements and income in absolute terms but also on one's relative position income wise" (Ferrer-i-Carbonell 2005, p.1001). Michael McBride found a positive relation between subjective well-being and income, but also discovered that one's subjective well-being decreases as others earn more and one's perceived relative income decreases (McBride 2001, p.276). Such relative-income effects are stronger at higher income levels, implying again that absolute income levels matter more to the poor. This again supports the refined version of the Easterlin paradox and the idea that inter-group comparison particularly impacts the middle class: acute peer group sensitivity is a luxury that very poor people cannot afford. Diener, Tay and Oishi find support for both local and global comparisons (Diener, Tay, and Oishi 2013, p.267), which depend on people's use of media (Becchetti et al. 2013).

But what about objective list approaches to well-being; how do they relate to income and/or wealth? Broadly speaking, three things seem objectively to matter to people's well-being: physical and mental health; the ability to meaningfully engage with others, and autonomy, achievement, and self-respect. When analysing the relation between income and wealth on the one hand and these factors on the other, three strategies arise.

First, one can provide conceptual arguments for why money buys things that contribute to these objective aspects of well-being. In general, money can buy things that predictably lead to longer, healthier lives, to less (status) anxiety, and to opportunities to spend more time with loved ones. As such, the rich are freer to pursue meaningful activities (both in work and in leisure) and enjoy higher social prestige. In contrast, the poor typically lead unhealthier lifestyles, are more stressed about paying their bills, are less free and autonomous, and typically do not enjoy the social prestige of their wealthier counterparts. As we have already noted, in market societies like ours, it is the wealthy who can, and do, make strategic investments to protect themselves from risks of all kinds.

Secondly, one can look for empirical support for correlations between income/wealth and these objective ingredients of well-being. Starting with health, this correlation with well-being has been repeatedly established. A study of the US healthcare system revealed that the richest 1% live up to 10 years (women) or even 15 years (men) longer than the poorest 1%, with 33% of Americans delaying seeing a doctor for medical problems because of the costs (Saad, 2019; Dickman, Himmelstein, and Woolhandler 2017, p.1432). Poverty continually causes ill health, not only by restricting ongoing access to quality healthcare but also because parental socio-economic status has an impact on early brain development and on educational levels, which are correlated with (un)healthy lifestyles. An extensive study with 1.7 million participants concluded that socio-economic status in itself significantly impacted life expectancy, only to be surpassed by smoking and physical inactivity (Stringhini et al. 2017).

The empirical evidence for a correlation with social ties and relationships is less clear. In general, the rich spend *less* time with others, in part because the poor have to rely more on others for all kinds of needs. A recent study found that the rich do indeed spend less time socializing, but also spend *more* time with friends, whereas the poor spend more time with families and neighbours. Because "money frees people to be socially connected with those they choose rather than those who can provide resources", it arguably promotes meaningful (rather than necessitated) interactions or at least provides the liberty to choose with whom to interact (Bianchi and Vohs 2016, p.480). This connects to the issue that money promotes autonomy and helps achieve self-esteem and self-respect. The rich can be claimed to be more autonomous because they are "deliberate architects of their social worlds" (Bianchi and Vohs 2016, p.485). This comes with a considerable downside: the insulation of the rich from the rest of society as they live in and only socialize with their own social circle.

A third strategy connects empirical findings on subjective and objective well-being into a single account. On the basis of Veenhoven's findings, for example, one can draw the rather unsurprising conclusion that those who live in hardship tend to be less happy than those who meet a minimal standard of material wealth (Veenhoven 1991). Money buys things—food, healthcare, education, consumer goods—that make people both subjectively and objectively better off. As mentioned, happiness studies suggest that income, like good mental and physical health, a decent job, and good relationships, contribute significantly to people's life satisfaction.

On the basis of a longitudinal study, Dolan and White argue that "the most important domains for global life satisfaction were satisfaction with finances, health, and work, followed by leisure, housing, and the environment, in that order" (Dolan and White 2007, p.79).[14] Helliwell, Layard, and Sachs find that six variables explain almost three-quarters of international differences in happiness scores: social support, GDP per capita, health, freedom, generosity, and the absence of corruption (Helliwell, Layard, and Sachs 2015, p.24).

Even though the causal relationships are not entirely clear, numerous studies show a high correlation between health and happiness (Graham 2009, chapter 5). In addition, long-term relationships have been shown to matter. Only a few life events have a lasting impact on subjective well-being. While getting married is not one of those, getting a divorce, becoming a widow(er) and getting fired from work are (Diener, Lucas, and Scollon 2006, p.309). In these cases, people's remarkable ability to adapt to new circumstances was not complete and the reduction in objective well-being is clearly consequential.

10.7 Income and Wealth Inequality and Its Relation to Well-Being

We now turn from correlations between income/wealth and well-being to the relationship between income/wealth *inequalities* and well-being. Does living in an unequal society in itself has a negative impact on well-being? That answer is not entirely clear. Reviewing the available "evidence on the impact of income inequality on well-being", Dolan, Peasgood, and White conclude that it is "mixed" (Dolan, Peasgood, and White 2008, p.108). Others call it "inconclusive" (Rözer and Kraaykamp 2013, p.1011).

Several studies confirm the existence of so-called inequality averse preferences: "inequality correlates negatively with happiness in Western societies" (Ferrer-i-Carbonell and Ramos 2014, p.1019). This study found

[14] Dolan and White are summarizing the main conclusions of (Praag, Frijters, and Ferrer-i-Carbonell 2003).

that "the richer the individuals' reference group is, the unhappier individuals are" and that there is both "a negative effect of overall inequality and a positive effect of being at the top of the income distribution of own reference group". Moreover, not only does inequality matter (people do not like it) but also its extent matters (Ferrer-i-Carbonell 2005, p.997).

Another study of happiness levels in twenty-nine European countries found little or no correlation between inequality and subjective well-being amongst those with the highest incomes but found a negative correlation amongst those with the lowest incomes (van de Werfhorst 2014, p.123). While the rich score around 8.1 on a happiness scale, regardless whether they live in equal or unequal countries, the poor score an average of 7.9 in equal countries and 7.2 in unequal countries. The impact of inequality—the gaps between the rich and the poor—on well-being thus arguably depends on which sides of the gaps one finds oneself.

However, we are not convinced that these empirical studies are asking the right question. More helpful to the egalitarian, and hence to our project, are findings about *perceptions* of inequality and their impact on well-being (Oshio and Urakawa 2014; Buttrick, Heintzelman, and Oishi 2017). That, recall, was one of the crucial lessons we took from Rousseau in chapter 6, who inaugurated the whole modern discussion of "false needs". When it comes to inequality, false perception of its origins and effects is as potent as the truth.

Focusing on such perceptions, Carol Graham claims that inequality can lead to both rising and falling levels of happiness (Graham 2009, chapter 6). If inequality is perceived to provide persistent advantage to the rich and disadvantage to the poor (as, for example, in highly unequal Latin American countries), then it has a negative effect. In countries where inequality is perceived as a sign of opportunity, it can have either a negative or a positive effect: "inequality can be a signal of future opportunity and mobility as much as it can be a sign of injustice"[15] (Graham 2009, p.17). This reinforces our point that the impact of societal inequality is mediated by what can only be called an ideology: a societal narrative about the point of inequality. To understand this, empirical evidence about inequality's perceptions should be combined with its normative justifications and associated emotional regime.

In some cases, for example, inequality is taken as relatively limited, related to market merits, and unlikely to harden into the kind of class hierarchy that diminishes social mobility. In other cases, it is taken as the product of a rigged

[15] Graham is citing Alesina and Glaeser (2004) here.

system, as reinforcing class hierarchy, and as shutting down social mobility. These different frames shape individual perceptions of what it means to live in an unequal society.

For example, Graham distinguishes between "frustrated" and "non-frustrated achievers" in the same comparison group (Graham 2009, p.152)[16]. The former are generally dissatisfied with their lives, fear unemployment, and are "more concerned about relative income differences" (Graham 2009, p.153). The main cause of their unhappiness is the insecurity of their new circumstances and the fear of losing recent (often hard-won) gains. By contrast, the absolutely poor often adjust to their precariousness and, sadly, have little to lose. Graham concludes that:

> [S]lightly raised expectations in the context of rapid economic change may result in more frustration and risk aversion than do static poverty levels. (Graham 2009, p.154)

Graham thus endorses the fine-grained version of the Easterlin paradox that cites inter-group comparison as a key explanatory factor:

> [W]hile wealthier people are happier than less wealthy ones on average, people of similar income levels are less happy when the incomes of those in a relevant reference group, ranging from neighbors to professional cohorts, to towns and cities, are higher. (Graham 2009, p.158; Luttmer 2005)[17]

In other words, assessing the impact of inequality on well-being can only be done by specifying other parameters: the overall level of income and wealth, whether a distributive pattern is viewed as justified or not, and whether social mobility remains possible.

When discussing Jon Elster's mechanistic approach to social explanations, we stressed that social scientific findings demand contextualization to determine which mechanism causally explains a pattern. In the case at hand, inequality that is perceived as unjustified and as being a product of (and reinforcing) prior relations of advantage and disadvantage makes the

[16] Graham notes that recent migrants, in particular, may find themselves in this category (Graham 2011, p.x).

[17] Graham argues, as we did above, that in an increasingly mediatized and inter-connected world, people may no longer restrict themselves to comparisons within their own society, further complicating the role of relative comparisons (Graham 2009, p.165).

disadvantaged even less happy. Inequality that is associated with a promise of social mobility in an expanding economy where everyone's life opportunities are growing together can have the opposite effect. What is the empirical evidence for both these mechanisms?

A particularly interesting study is that of Buttrick, Heintzelman, and Oishi (2017), as it investigates the psychological mechanisms underlying the negative correlation between income inequality and well-being, as for example observed by Wilkinson and Pickett. Next to adaptation, they show that any supposed impact of inequality on well-being depends on how it is perceived. They concluded that: "When perceived as unimportant, legitimate, surmountable, beneficial, fair, or part of God's plan, for example, inequality matters less for well-being" (Buttrick, Heintzelman, and Oishi 2017, p.16). It depends on the extent to which people optimistically associate inequality with social mobility and increased opportunities or pessimistically with entrenched hierarchies that only work well for the rich.

Unfortunately, over the next two chapters, we will argue that the pessimistic view is the more realistic one when it comes to the inequalities in capitalist market societies like the United States and United Kingdom. It is important to quote Buttrick, Heintzelman, and Oishi at greater length here.

> In many developing societies, especially those transitioning from more equal planned economies to more unequal free-market regimes, an increase in inequality is interpretable as an opportunity to climb the social ladder (. . .). [This] may explain the relationship between inequality and well-being in China, where those in the countryside are a bit more optimistic about their future prospects, and thus happier as inequality increases, than those living in the cities, and may also explain relationships between inequality and happiness across other developing countries. Importantly, when perceptions of inequality change, so too does its relationship with well-being. When inequality loses its association with hope and instead becomes interpreted as a signal of a rigged society, higher inequality relates to lower well-being. (Buttrick, Heintzelman, and Oishi 2017, p.16)

This contextualization is key to a sophisticated understanding of the relation between inequality and well-being. Instead of claiming that the former decreases the latter across the board, as Wilkinson and Pickett do, we claim this only occurs when inequalities are perceived as unfair outcomes of the structural and institutional mechanisms that govern our capitalist societies.

This conclusion builds on the earlier thesis of Oishi, Kesebir, and Diener that inequality contributes to unhappiness via what they took to be two mediating factors: trust and a sense of fairness (Oishi, Kesebir, and Diener 2011). We see those two factors as closely connected: we mistrust our fellow citizens when they persistently benefit from, and work to support, a system that treats the rest of us systematically unfairly.

An additional way in which increased inequality can be expected to decrease happiness is that it shifts people's focus from what matters to things that do not substantially contribute to happiness. According to Frank, inequality, in combination with social comparison, means that we increasingly prioritize positional goods over non-positional goods (Frank 2007, pp.87–94). The more we do so, the evidence suggests, the lower our well-being will be. Focusing on earning more money to fund status competition means longer working hours, longer commutes, and less quality time for leisure and friends, all of which demonstrably reduce happiness: "the evidence suggests that subjective well-being will be higher in the society with a greater balance of nonpositional consumption. And yet in each case the actual trend in U.S. consumption patterns has been in the reverse direction" (Frank 2007, p.90). Instead of collectively cutting back on positional consumption to free up time for quality relationships or meaningful non-comparative activities, we seem to remain stuck in the (increasingly) suboptimal outcomes generated by positional competition. Once again, we want to add the important rider that when it comes to key competitions derived from the marketization of healthcare and education, there are serious costs to opting out.

Again, we conclude this section with a focus on the objective ingredients of well-being—health, education, meaningful activities and relationships, autonomy, self-esteem, and self-respect—and ask how those relate to (income and wealth) inequality.

The relationship between inequality and health has been well documented. Wilkinson and Pickett, in their 2009 book *The Spirit Level: Why Equality Is Better for Everyone* (Wilkinson and Pickett 2009), provide empirical evidence to support the broad claim that income inequality is correlated negatively to things objectively good for people, like health (for example, life expectancy, infant mortality, obesity), the quality of social relations (for example, trust, rate of homicides, rate of imprisonment) and educational performance (for example, children's literacy). Their data from twenty-three developed countries (and across states of the United States) lead them to conclude that developed countries can make progress, not by increasing their overall wealth, but by distributing it more fairly and equally.

Their most striking result, as we noted in chapter 4, is that such progress would improve the lot not only of the worst-off in society but also of the best-off. When it comes to safety, trust, community, and education, it is better to be rich in a more equal society than to be rich in a less equal society (Wilkinson and Pickett 2009, p.109). So not only are rich people on average healthier and better off than poor people in the same society, but both richer and poorer do better in less unequal societies. Robert Frank's example of the millionaire driving their Ferrari on public roads riddled with potholes (Frank 2011, p.220) provides a suggestive metaphor for how public goods—infrastructure and education, but also intangibles as safety, trust, and public health—trump individual wealth as determinants for well-being.

In addition, Wilkinson and Pickett show how most objective ingredients of well-being have a social gradient, which means that richer people get more of it than poorer people and that inequality exacerbates this: "only the health and social problems which have strong social class gradients—becoming more common further down the social hierarchy—are more common in more unequal societies" (Wilkinson and Pickett 2009: 27). While problems without social gradients—like breast cancer—are not more prevalent in less equal societies, the latter deal with disproportionately higher rates of infant mortality, AIDS, teenage births, and depression. Each of these health issues is more prevalent in unequal societies, such as the United States, the United Kingdom, and Portugal, compared with, for example, Japan or the Nordic countries (Wilkinson and Pickett 2009, p.82). The same holds when comparing less equal US states such as Alabama, California, or Mississippi with more equal states like Alaska, New Hampshire, or Utah (Wilkinson and Pickett 2009, p.83).

According to Wilkinson and Pickett, the most plausible underlying mechanisms at work here are inequality's impact on status competition and social capital (see also: Layte 2012). We explore these in greater detail in chapter 12 on meritocracy—the ideology that ties the different elements of our emotional regime together.

When it comes to health, other researchers corroborate the findings of Wilkinson and Pickett. A meta-analysis of studies with over 60 million participants found a negative correlation between income inequality and longevity (Kondo et al. 2009, p.7). Growing inequality, with most of the wealth gains going to the top rather than the bottom, has only widened this gap in health (Dickman et al. 2017; Chetty et al. 2016).

Yet this overall account has also been contested. Pop, Ingen, and Oorschot stress that evidence for Wilkinson and Pickett's "income inequality thesis" is mixed, contradictory, and inconclusive (Pop, Ingen, and Oorschot 2013). They found that life expectancy in most countries actually increased in periods in which economic inequality rose substantially (1987–2008) and argue that tentative correlations between health and well-being depend on the selection of country and how both concepts are operationalized and measured. Especially when moving from correlation to causation, more and more fine-grained (individual, multi-level, and longitudinal) data is needed. Wilkinson and Pickett, the criticism goes, rely mostly on macro-level data to back up their micro-level story that increased inequality leads people to suffer from heightened social evaluative stress and anxiety caused by inflamed status competitions.

Let us examine their causal claims in more detail and introduce a further distinction that vindicates their conclusions. Wilkinson and Pickett present a number of narrative explanations that render plausible a causal interpretation of the data, with inequality *causing* health and social issues because they heighten stress, insecurity, and anxiety when comparing with others. In their words, inequality "gets under the skin" (Wilkinson and Pickett 2009, chapter 3). In *The Inner Level: How More Equal Societies Reduce Stress and Improve Everyone's Well-Being*, they stress this point further, noting how "worries about how we are seen and judged by others—what psychologists call 'the social evaluative threat'—are one of the most serious burdens on the quality and experience of life in rich developed countries" (Wilkinson and Pickett 2018, p.4).

This is the claim, then, that evaluative stress and anxiety are exacerbated by inequality, especially when combined with a meritocratic ideology of social mobility, where the rich are admired (as they have made it) and the poor stigmatized (as they could have made it if they tried). Such anxiety is exacerbated by increased focus on social status and positional goods in more unequal societies (Wilkinson and Pickett 2009, p.43). In sum, inequality combined with upward social comparisons induces anxiety, stress, and shame.

Interestingly, Paskov and co-authors differentiate between two hypotheses, both of which are compatible with Wilkinson and Pickett's account. The first is that "the larger the gap between income groups in a society, the greater the need to keep up with the striv[-ing] for status" (Paskov, Gërxhani, and Werfhorst 2013, p.114). When inequality widens, the distance between the steps on the social ladder grows larger, the benefits of getting to the top become greater, and "there is more to gain in terms of money and status from moving up in the hierarchy" (Paskov, Gërxhani, and Werfhorst 2013, p.114).

This hypothesis supports our case for strong egalitarianism, where the relations between different socio-economic groups in a distribution are so "close knit" and "chain connected" that the distance between any pair cannot be excessively "gappy" (Rawls 1971/1999, pp.70–2; Thomas 2017, pp.41–6). Not only does Rawls permit only those inequalities that maximally benefit the worst off but also the whole distributive pattern has to have a certain profile. The kind of "gappy" distributions that Paskov et al. think are particularly damaging to well-being are also those that Rawls rules out as unjust(ified).

The second, alternative hypothesis that Paskov et al. discuss is that increased inequality *diminishes* status competition simply because moving up the socio-economic ladder becomes more difficult. People might actually give up "because they do not believe they can move upwards due to low social mobility" (Paskov, Gërxhani, and Werfhorst 2013, p.114). Some empirical evidence interestingly supports the second hypothesis: "Income inequality is negatively associated with status-seeking" (Paskov, Gërxhani, and Werfhorst 2013, p.114). If you believe that the game is rigged, you may simply elect not to play, and pay the costs of not doing so. As we will note in our discussion of meritocracy, even those who lose out in the meritocratic "big sort" may retain a commitment to the ideology of meritocracy if they believe they would have done better in a contest that was not rigged from the outset. Meritocracy, as we will see, is a flexible view that can be embraced by its "winners" and "losers" alike—both of whom might be equally miserable but committed to the view that society's goods must go to its winners. While the winners feel entitled, the losers simply believe that they were cheated—they are counterfactual meritocrats.

In our view, both of these mechanisms are likely at play in our own societies. Which one is more dominant depends in part on the prevailing ideology and the perception of inequality we highlighted before. When people no longer believe the meritocratic discourse of social mobility and come to see the growing distance between the socioeconomic ladder's steps as increasingly harder to climb, they may opt out of the status competition, either with resigned acceptance or with frustration and anger. If winners indeed take all, as they do in specific markets, such as for executive compensation, then inequality grows so disproportionate that "keeping up with the Joneses" becomes pointless and opting out of status competition can improve individual well-being in these circumstances, even if it means acquiescing in injustice (Frank and Cook 1996).

Again, whether inequalities are perceived as a sign of social mobility or of entrenched privilege turns out to be crucial to their impact on well-being. Buttrick, Heintzelman, and Oishi (2017, p.15) stress how "perceptions of inequality matter as much as objective measures for wellbeing" and how "the more objective correlates of inequality—greater levels of illness and mortality, neighbourhoods with fewer services for residents, weaker, less responsive government, and a diminution of opportunities for the future all negatively impact people's well-being". Psychological and social mechanisms at play here interact with each other and mediate between inequality and well-being, as perceptions of inequality change how members of a society relate to each other and themselves.

Amongst the psychological mechanisms are habituation, adaptation, and salience (Buttrick, Heintzelman, and Oishi 2017, p.16). Social mechanisms include increased status competition that salient inequalities tend to trigger and that predictably lead to status anxiety, conflicts, and distrust. In their study of thirty thousand European citizens, Delhey and Dragolov examine this in "Why Inequality Makes Europeans Less Happy: The Role of Distrust, Status Anxiety, and Perceived Conflict" (Delhey and Dragolov 2014). The mechanisms mediating between inequality and well-being, they argue against Wilkinson and Pickett, vary across different kinds of societies. While generalized mistrust matters more in already affluent societies, they argue, developing societies are more likely to take inequality to negatively impact well-being via status anxiety.

Note how the negative impact of inequality on well-being need not operate via increased status-seeking. Even if people in deeply unequal societies engage in less status-seeking behaviour—perhaps because they have given up because they view it as futile—the inequalities themselves can harm their well-being. In his book *Falling Behind: How Rising Inequality Harms the Middle Class*, Frank shows how the disproportionate growth of wealth amongst the (super-)rich puts ever more pressure on people lower on the socio-economic ladder (Frank 2007). The (super-)rich spending ever more money on luxury goods (mansions, cars, planes, expensive watches, shoes, and barbecues) increases consumption norms for those just below. Given local standards for comparison, this rise in consumption standards runs from top to bottom. In order to not "fall behind", everyone has to spend more and more, which explains why working hours, commuting times, and indebtedness have all gone up (Frank 2007). Again, all this arguably harms objective aspects of well-being. The rider we would add here is that it is the ethos of competitiveness that negatively impacts well-being, even if those ranked lower are competing for cheaper goods. Such competition is even more detrimental when it comes to goods of social mobility—education and healthcare—where all are forced to compete on the same playing field.

The works of Frank, and Wilkinson and Pickett, basically provide empirical support for Rousseau's insight, central to chapter 6, into people's tendency to see themselves through the eyes of others and compare with those others when judging their self-worth (*amour-propre*) (Rousseau 1753).[18] As Rousseau and Smith already knew, our self-esteem and self-respect, important psychological bases for well-being, depend heavily on the esteem and respect we receive from others. As socio-economic status becomes increasingly important as a signal and source of such social evaluation, as it does in capitalist societies, growing inequality has increasingly detrimental effects on well-being. Rousseau already knew how our desire for recognition and status can become inflamed, turning into a desire to win the status competition (Kolodny 2010). Even if we are equals, we seek to be "first amongst equals".

When inequality and status competition run amok, a cohesive social fabric and trust disintegrate (Wilkinson and Pickett 2009, 2018). Robert D. Putnam demonstrated how economic equality and high levels of social capital are inter-related (Putnam 2000). Rising inequality in the United States over the last few decades is reflected in key social indicators such as the incidence of violent crime, homicide, and, again particularly noticeable in the United States, the size of its prison population (Temin 2017, p.37, pp.101–5). Again, all this is obviously bad news for people's well-being, objectively understood, given that community, trust, and security are plausible ingredients of well-being.

Of course, the United States has specific characteristics, such as racial inequality, lax gun regulations, and the "war on drugs" that help explain the mass incarceration of Black men and this casts doubt over the role of inequality

[18] Frank also notes that some positional influence would operate via framing effects without the mediation of "peer influences . . . would be just as strong in a world completely free of jealousy and envy" (Frank 2016, p.112). Perceptions of reasonable spending are shaped by the frame of what others are spending and what counts in context as an "acceptable" standard (Frank 1997, pp.165–6).

in this respect (Alexander 2010). It is a special confounding factor whereby racial inequality and socio-economic inequality intersect. Socio-economic class and race intersect in a specific way in a US context. Yet this is not to overlook the socio-economic devastation imposed on Black communities by mass incarceration: families are broken up, single mothers are placed at a competitive disadvantage in a market structured around the norm of the "typical" worker (Goldin 2014, 2021). That said, it is telling that, even within the United States, the most unequal states do worst in this regard (Wilkinson and Pickett 2009, chapters 10–11).

Other research reveals how social capital mediates between income losses and well-being. While the 2008 economic crisis, for example, did not result in loss of well-being in countries with high social capital (like Iceland), countries with low social capital (like Greece) experienced a further erosion of trust and corresponding levels of well-being (Helliwell, Layard, and Sachs 2015, pp.33–5). If the social fabric is strong, it can help "sustain, or even improve subjective well-being in the face of natural disasters or economic shocks" (Helliwell, Layard, and Sachs 2015, p.6).

10.8 Using the Science of Happiness

While the science of happiness is, qua science, still in its early stages, we believe that it provides some well-grounded generalizations for egalitarians like us. We have argued how a degree of healthy scepticism does not undermine the nuanced version of the Easterlin paradox that we have canvased in this chapter.[19] We have noted Elster's methodological point that contextualization is needed to determine the operation of each (seemingly contradictory) social scientific mechanism. We have shown how such contextualization can provide support for distinct conclusions, depending on whether one focuses on aggregate inequality, how income and wealth are internally distributed, how "gappy" those distributions are and how the resulting inequalities are perceived. In highly unfair and unequal societies with gappy distributions, the well-being of many citizens is negatively impacted by the treadmill of

[19] According to Graham, "The relationship between happiness and income is mediated by a range of factors that can alter its slope/functional form. These include the particular questions that are used to measure happiness; the selection of countries that are included in the survey sample; the specification of the income variables (log or linear); the rate of change in economic conditions in addition to absolute levels; and changing aspirations as countries go from the ranks of developing to developed countries" (Graham 2009, p.14).

ever increasing competition for money and status, while for other citizens their well-being is negatively impacted as they are forced to give up on competing in any realistic way. In sum, we think Graham is right: "divergent conclusions may each be correct" (Graham 2009, p.14). When suitably contextualized, there is no inconsistency: the Easterlin paradox is actually the name of a family of paradoxes.

Let us conclude this chapter by relating our explanations back to our analysis of positional goods in the previous chapter. We can explain the basis of the Easterlin paradox in the terms reformulated by Buttrick, Heintzelman, and Oishi for highly unequal societies (Buttrick, Heintzelman, and Oishi 2017). Easterlin's original explanation of his paradox was that individuals anchor their expectations relatively, not absolutely. Poorer people are not just receiving less, they also crucially receive less than they believe ought to be their due. The rich are aware that they have more than is due to them. As such, the former are aggrieved, the latter contented, and rising average standards do not change those relative perceptions. What it is to be a fully participating member of society costs more as average standards increase. People are more concerned with the relative position on the steps of the escalator than with the fact that it is moving upwards. A rising general standard intensifies these relative effects. Buttrick, Heintzelman, and Oishi's point is that these effects are further intensified if you feel you are being cheated.

In our attempt to better understand the many ways in which inequality can harm well-being, we add two important elements to Wilkinson and Pickett's account. First, we limit ourselves to capitalist societies, where institutional mechanisms frustrate social mobility, concentrate wealth at the top, and entrench inequalities. This provides much needed contextualization to analyse the causal mechanisms at play. Instead of assembling large-scale, multi-country comparisons to defend general claims about inequality and well-being, as Wilkinson and Pickett do, we aim to identify the structural mechanisms at play in specifically capitalist societies.

Secondly, we analyse these societies' emotional regimes, focusing on the role that envy, shame, and anxiety play in upholding those structural mechanisms. These emotions figure not only in empirical research on inequality and well-being but also in the work of political philosophers writing about (in)equality and (in)justice.

We thus interpret the empirical evidence reviewed in this chapter as calling for more rather than less philosophy. As the science of happiness develops and tentatively answers important empirical questions, philosophy can help to refine concepts—like "well-being"—necessary to gather and interpret empirical data, build plausible normative models of just societies, and combine those with a thorough understanding of the emotions at play. We undertake that task in the next chapter leading up to our discussion of meritocracy in chapter 12. This chapter, then, forms merely a prolegomenon to our analysis in the next chapter of how inequalities in capitalist societies impact well-being via three key emotions: shame for being poor and admiration for and envy of those who are rich. We will now focus on the disciplinary role played in capitalist societies by discourses that tell people to feel such emotions when considering their place within their society.

11

Inequality, Shame, Envy, and Admiration

A Smithian Perspective

Propositional Summary

1. Adam Smith suggests that being unable to acquire the goods needed to appear in public without shame means that one is living in poverty. We show the continued relevance of this idea for contemporary definitions of poverty and argue that the shame of poverty is an important part of the nature of poverty, as it is both an inevitable part of stratified capitalist societies and actively promoted through cultural portrayals of poverty.
2. We argue that those who wish to promote well-being have good reason to accept the link between shame and poverty considered above. Shame is a painful emotion concerned with the failure to achieve certain standards which motivates social withdrawal and often leads to isolation and depression. Poverty-related shame is a key factor in the experience of poverty and leads people to withdraw from public life, avoid engaging with public officials and pretend to be better off than they really are. These are negative impacts on well-being, regardless of what theory of well-being we subscribe to. The shame of poverty help stabilize the capitalist system by serving as a barrier to attempts to challenge and protest this system.
3. We consider and respond to several objections that might be raised against the idea that we should take the shame of poverty into account in political theorizing.
4. We explain Adam Smith's argument that people have a natural tendency to admire the rich which leads them to emulate them and defer to them. We provide philosophical and psychological support for Smith's claims about admiration and argue that this tendency has a negative effect on

Extravagance and Misery. Alan Thomas, Alfred Archer, and Bart Engelen, Oxford University Press.
 DOI: 10.1093/oso/9780197781722.003.0012

well-being and will likely be greater in societies with higher levels of economic inequality.

5. We examine Veblen's account of how market societies are characterized by admiration and envy for the rich which leads to a desire to emulate the rich. Admiration and envy for the rich is especially likely to generate a desire to emulate the rich in market societies given that these societies promise the possibility of social mobility which suggests that emulation is a genuine possibility, that the poor really could become rich and also that the rich deserve their wealth.
6. We will argue that envy and admiration are not merely incidental features of market societies, rather they form key components of their emotional regimes which are actively promoted through media representations of the rich.
7. We consider and respond to the idea that egalitarian concerns are motivated by irrational envy and so should be disregarded from political theorizing. In response, we argue that envy for the rich is rational in capitalist societies. Moreover, the fact that envy plays an important role in the emotional regime of capitalist societies means that those who support the capitalist system are in no position to claim that envy has no role to play in politics. The attempt to dismiss egalitarian concerns as motivated by the politics of envy is an attempt to enforce this emotional regime and to dismiss criticism of this system. Malicious envy for the rich in capitalist societies can be understood as an outlaw emotion. Paying close attention to this emotion can bring help make the feeling rules of capitalist societies clearer and enable new ways of perceiving the world.

Introduction

The troubling conclusion of chapter 9 was that, above a certain level of material well-being, capitalist societies are dominated by positional concerns in the way foreshadowed by both Rousseau and Veblen. In the previous chapter, we drew on recent findings from the science of happiness to consider how inequalities impact well-being in capitalist societies that are characterized by an increased concern for, and scope of, positionality. We tried to disentangle various claims that, together, fall under the heading of the famous "Easterlin paradox". Viewed from the perspective of social theory, both Veblen and Hirsch connect these positional concerns to social stratification.

In their narrative, an historical logic to capitalism sees the emergence of a generic division into three classes: a patrimonial class, who originally determined the terms of taste and are now exemplary consumers and objects for emulation; an aspiring class, forced into competition for status goods as a matter of defensive necessity; finally, the residual class. The lives of the latter are dominated by material goods alone—what one might term merely material goods. In this chapter, we further justify our claim that, even if material wealth has increased for this class, their well-being has not. We turn our attention to those emotions that play a crucial role in capitalist societies and that harm the well-being of the residual class and—to a lesser extent—the middle class. Shame, admiration and envy all play key roles in the emotional regimes of capitalist societies, or so we will argue.

There is no doubt that the worst off, in the affluent welfare state societies of our world, live at a standard far above that of the worst off in the past or in poor societies of our own time. However, this class lives in a society driven by positional concerns with no realistic material prospect of being able to compete for such positional goods. In the light of Piketty's recent history of the evolution of inequality regimes, ironically history seems to have repeated itself as his narrative begins with societies split trifunctionally between clergy, nobility, and workers (Piketty 2020). The social classes are now different, but the trifunctionality has returned in our capitalist societies, albeit without the legitimating narrative that the good order of society depends on everyone respecting their place in this tripartite arrangement. (Although we will discover an echo of this justificatory thesis in the meritocratic ideology that we will evaluate in the following chapter.)

We are developing the thesis, then, that social stratification is endemic to capitalist modes of economic organization and there will always, functionally, be an "underclass". It exists to play a disciplinary role, just as Kalecki claimed (Kalecki 1943). Even as average standards in society rise, there will be an "overclass" of those who are the inheritors of cumulative advantage and whose emulation drives consumerism. This social stratification presents a basic challenge to capitalist societies. In such a system, some people struggle to meet their basic needs while others will revel in luxury: Hegel's extravagance and misery. How is a society to ensure that the majority remain content with such a hugely unequal economic order rather than seeking to overthrow it? How to ensure that the rich do not feel uneasy about possessing so much wealth when others are struggling to survive?

Corey Robin is, in our view, correct in his diagnosis: the wealthy are exemplary economic magnates and cultural legislators. With no apparent irony, French speakers refer to these figures as "Mycénes": comparable to the wealthy and leisured class of ancient Mycenae as memorialized in Homer's *Illiad*. Historically, in the United States—although this social norm is weakening—the very wealthy were expected to be philanthropists and patrons of the arts.

At the other end of the scale, Hegel feared that the worst off would be gripped by these false needs as strongly as anyone but be permanently alienated from any way of satisfying them. This is the very class that was the focus of Adam Smith's optimism about commercial society: the new opportunities for the working poor decisively tipped the balance for his positive assessment of commercial society's prospects.

From our perspective, it is the situation of the worst off that is the focal point of comparison between political liberalism and Roman republicanism. For the Rawlsian political liberal, committed to justice as fairness, her primary concern must be with the fate of the worst off relative to any given nation-state and its level of material circumstances. The shame that the poor are expected to experience is arguably, like envy for the rich, one of the factors that is both detrimental to well-being and one of the special attitudes that threatens the stabilization of a just society in ways that would have been familiar to Rousseau, Smith, and Hegel. As for Roman republicanism, Pettit's consequentialist perspective is also particularly concerned with that class of people for whom further resources would disproportionately benefit their well-being.

In this chapter we examine Smith's diagnosis of the way in which inequality in market societies influences people's emotional lives and the damaging impact that this has on their well-being. We begin by examining Smith's "sufficientarian" standard for the worst off: that the representative worst-off person should be able to appear in public without shame. This criterion, as interpreted by sociologist Peter Townsend and economist Amartya Sen, continues to be relevant in the light of the findings of the new science of happiness and empirical research on the connection between shame and poverty. We will then turn to the other key emotional phenomena that Smith (along with Thorsten Veblen) identified in market societies: admiration and envy for the rich. We will argue that both the shame experienced by the poor and the envy and admiration directed towards the rich form key parts of the emotional regime of capitalist societies that are supported by the promises and myths of such societies. Moreover, these problems will be particularly acute in market societies that exhibit the kind of radical economic disparities evident in the New Inequality. While these emotions help to keep the economic regime of capitalism in place, they also have a significantly damaging impact on the well-being of those living in capitalist societies.

11.1 The Inevitability of Shame in Stratified Societies

Schematically, our argument is this: inherited structures of inequality—produced by the very same historical processes that have shaped the cultural logic of capitalist societies—place the worst off in a situation with these features. First, they are excluded from the auctions for positional goods; secondly, they are excluded from access to the goods of social mobility; thirdly, they are placed in a situation where "opting out" is not an option. The explanation that we have canvased is that the category of oligarchic wealth has subsumed that of democratic wealth (to use Harrod's terminology) and, therefore, these citizens cannot appear in public without shame. Smith may have had grounds for optimism for the emergent capitalist society with which he was familiar, but stratified capitalist societies dominated by positional concerns make it impossible for the worst off to meet Smith's criterion. He would have been the first to acknowledge this: it is a corollary of his own view as one of his pessimistic scenarios for the development of commercial society.

The psychological literature on shame is clear: societies in which poverty is construed as a social failure—for example, a failure to compete in meritocratic terms—makes the shame of poverty in the eyes of the poor even more psychologically damaging. Given that highly unequal societies in our world may, in some cases, legitimate the structural sources of inequality via a narrative of past or present merit, then poverty is not just inevitable. It is, in a meritocracy, also shameful and therefore socially stigmatizing. Simply put, an unequal society needs a legitimating narrative to present to those at the bottom end of the income and wealth distribution to justify their comparative position. Meritocracy is one such conception: you were given a fair chance to compete, but you lost.

Given our central concern with tracing out the connections between inequality, well-being, and key justifying emotions, it is important that we consider one prominent way of connecting these three issues. Several recent views that we would classify as weakly egalitarian diagnose what is wrong with poverty by using Smith's test. The emotion of shame can play a justificatory role in explaining our intuitions about which forms of inequality are permissible and which are not. An unequal distribution is damaging to well-being if it causes a certain kind of shame. Therefore, all and only those unequal distributions must be ruled out; as a corollary, we have a criterion for the acceptability of a prima facie unequal distribution.

One reason that shame has an important justificatory role when it comes to justifying the distribution of resources is that shame is particularly damaging to an individual's well-being. Based on the empirical and theoretical literature on shame, we will argue that it is, indeed, prima facie plausible to claim that a society must ensure that people have sufficient resources to appear in public without shame. This is an important standard that a society must meet to protect the well-being of its citizens.

This is also going to be crucial to our take on the debate between weak and strong egalitarians. The weak egalitarian may well embrace a sufficientarian standard like Smith's. Combined with Paretianism, this can give a veto to the worst off on departures from equality, but a veto that is lost when they meet a sufficient standard. The idea is that the better off, and best off, can continue to improve their absolute positions at no absolute cost to the worst off provided the latter have met a sufficient standard. However, if "sufficiency" is read relatively, as Smith's criterion implies, then as the average level of affluence in a society rises the standard of sufficiency rises too. If the weak egalitarian is also a consequentialist, then there is a case for capping the well-being of the best off which must not be permitted to rise beyond a certain threshold (if the Easterlin paradox is true) and for resourcing the worst off.

The prospect, then, is of weak egalitarianism tying together the prospects of all socio-economic classes in a way that the strong egalitarian does *ab initio*. Rawls always maintained that his goal was a society that was just throughout, and it seems crucial to the defensibility of his overall view that the interests of all the social groups be close knit and chain connected. Any change to the prospects of one group ramifies throughout the prospects of all others. The weak egalitarian does not explicitly adopt those commitments, but if she is prepared to connect the top end and the bottom end of any distribution using the shame criterion, then weak egalitarianism approximates to Rawls's result. Can the weak egalitarian rest the fundamental justification of her outlook on Smith's sufficientarianism? It follows that this issue of the defensibility—or otherwise—of Smith's sufficientarian criterion is very important for our overall argument and the choice between strong and weak egalitarianism.

The context of Smith's originating discussion concerns the taxation of consumable commodities in *The Wealth of Nations.* He divides them into "necessaries" and "luxuries" before examining the effects of taxation on these two kinds of commodity. The details of Smith's fiscal policy need not concern us here. What is of interest for the purposes of our discussion is that Smith claims that necessary commodities involve both "the commodities which are indispensably necessary for the support of life" such as food, water, and housing, and "whatever the custom of the country renders it indecent for creditable people, even of the lowest order, to be without" (Smith 1776/1981, V.2.II.4). As Smith goes on to explain, these goods will vary between different societies and also within the same society at different periods of history:

> A linen shirt, for example, is, strictly speaking, not a necessary of life. The Greeks and Romans lived, I suppose, very comfortably though they had no linen. But in the present times, through the greater part of Europe, a creditable day labourer would be ashamed to appear in public without a linen shirt, the want of which would be supposed to denote that disgraceful degree of poverty which, it is presumed, nobody can well fall into without extreme bad conduct. (Smith 1776/1981, V.2.II.4)

For Smith, those goods that are needed to appear in public without shame are to be counted among the basic necessities of life. He further argues that taxing these goods is inadvisable, as a rise in the price of these commodities will either lead to a rise in wages or make it harder for people to bring up their families and so reduce the supply of useful labour. Taxing luxuries on the other hand, is acceptable, as this would not be likely to lead to a rise in wages nor would it make it harder for people to bring up a family.

Smith's criterion resonates to the present day. It plays a prominent role in sociologist Peter Townsend's "relativized" conception of poverty. Townsend argues that poverty should be understood as an inability to secure the basic necessities of life and that any adequate understanding of what these basic necessities are will have to be society relative. This means that any account of human necessities must be made in reference to a particular society and a particular time. This is even true for such obvious necessities as nutrition, as the amount of calories people need will depend in part on the work they do, the amount of energy they need to expend in travelling each day, and the leisure activities they engage in (Townsend 1979b, p.51). All these factors will be determined, to a large extent, by the society he or she lives in.

Beyond this, the time and place one lives in also influences the consumer norms of that society. Townsend gives the example of tea drinking in the United Kingdom (Townsend 1962/2010, p.92). Drinking tea is by no means essential from a nutritional point of view. However, it is an almost essential ingredient of social life in the United Kingdom, not least as a result of government policy. Tea (of low quality) was universally provided, albeit rationed, in World War II and the price was capped by rationing well into the 1950s. Given this, someone who is unable to buy tea will face challenges in developing and maintaining social relationships: the ethos of tea drinking is that it is a social "leveller". In other countries though, it would not be tea that would be needed to sustain these relationships but coffee, wine, or something else entirely. Similarly, at a different point in British history (prior to the eighteenth and nineteenth centuries, when tea's popularity spread to the middle and working classes), tea was not a basic necessity in the United Kingdom. As Townsend notes, a society's norms of expected consumption will tend to rise in line with its level of wealth (Townsend 1962/2010, p.99). As a society becomes wealthier, its members will be encouraged to view an increasing number of goods as necessities.

Amartya Sen's account of poverty was also influenced by Smith's criterion. Sen attempted to develop an "objective" conception of poverty that accommodates Adam Smith's criterion, by arguing that the ability to appear in public without shame should be considered an important part of how poverty is understood (Sen 1983, 2009). He argued that we should judge how well-off people are in terms of their abilities to do things that they have reason to value. Conversely, poverty should be understood in terms of capability deprivation (Sen 2009, pp.254–7). The ability to appear in public without shame is a centrally important capability amongst a person's bundle of such capabilities (Sen 1983, p.159; 2000, p.4; 2009, p.256). Only those with this capability count as not impoverished. Possessing this capability will involve the ability to secure the commodities that are deemed necessary to be considered "decent". What these commodities are, and what is needed to secure them will, as both Smith and Townsend have pointed out, vary between different societies and historical periods. Nevertheless, the ability to appear in public without shame remains an important capability across societies and historical periods, though the resources needed to possess the capability will vary. This approach is absolutist, then, as poverty is defined in terms of a lack of capabilities. Nevertheless, it captures the core of Smith's insight, as the level of resources required to meet this standard will vary between different societies and different points in history.

Though Townsend and Sen disagree on whether poverty should be viewed in a relative or absolute way, both agree that people can be considered free from poverty only if they have sufficient resources to secure the goods that one's society deems it shameful to be without and that the level of resources needed to secure these goods will be higher in countries where the average income is higher. This shame criterion has proved influential beyond the academy. For example, the influence of this criterion is evident in this observation made by the director of the UK think tank The Institute for Public Policy Research, Nick Pearce, who in 2013 claimed that "individuals require a sufficient income to live free of stigma or shame" and that any inequalities that exist in society need to be "within ranges constrained by these factors" (Pearce 2013). An important part of how poverty should be understood, then, is as lacking the goods that a society deems necessary to have to appear in public without shame.

The shame attached to poverty is not only something that tends to arise in stratified market societies. It is also heavily promoted and reinforced through cultural portrayals of poverty and through specific kinds of government policies. In her study of media framings of socio-economic class in the United States, Diana Kendall states how stories of people in poverty are typically framed in a negative way that suggests the poor are to blame for their poverty (Kendall 2011, pp.99–109). A particularly clear example of this is the framings of stories of poor mothers which stereotypes these women as "childlike, hyperfertile, lazy, and bad mothers" (Kelly 2010, p.76; cited in Kendall 2011, p.101).

Similarly, Elaine Chase and Robert Walker studied the discursive truths about people in poverty prevailing in the United Kingdom by conducting a discourse analysis of media reports on poverty and focus group discussions. They found that poor people were generally viewed as being unwilling to work, having limited talents, being dysfunctional, and lacking ambition (Chase and Walker 2015b, p.260). These views fitted neatly with the way poor people were portrayed in the media, which played "a key role in demonizing those who are not working and in receipt of benefits" (Chase and Walker

2015b, p.267). Those in poverty are presented by the media as "shameful, immoral, depraved, irresponsible, and indolent" (Chase and Walker 2015b, p.268). This narrative is further entrenched by the stigmatizing effect of means-testing anti-poverty policies where those in poverty must publicly confess failure before being eligible for benefits (Walker and Chase 2015, p.11).

The idea that poverty is shameful is promoted most directly through the capitalist logic that ties worthiness to wealth. However, this is not the only feature of the emotional regime of capitalist societies that promotes a link between shame and poverty. As the historian Katie Barclay (2022) argues, the rise of capitalism was accompanied by a rising association of well-being and comfort with material goods. In her work on changing approaches to comfort in Scotland, Barclay found that in eighteenth-century Scotland, comfort was associated with a feeling of belonging in a particular place. This became replaced in the nineteenth century with a view of comfort as something that could be achieved through purchasing material goods such as ornaments, expensive fabrics and crockery, and all the other components of a middle-class home (Barclay 2022). Home ownership itself was increasingly viewed as important for achieving feelings of security. The rise of capitalism was also accompanied by a growing understanding of consumption as closely linked to identity. Buying certain brands of clothes or certain kinds of computers or cars "not only communicated who they were to others" but also "allowed people to 'become' their fullest selves" (Barclay 2022, p.449). Being able to purchase certain goods became essential for the membership of certain emotional communities. To be a dandy, for example, one needed to be able to dress like one (Barclay 2022, p.451). This, then, can be seen as further source of shame associated with poverty. Not only is a lack of wealth shameful in itself, the inability to purchase comfort and security for oneself and one's family is a further source of shame. Underpinning Barclay's historical arguments is a structural one, which we highlighted before: one dimension of the social power of the wealthy is their ability to determine and shape the terms of taste. What counts as the kind of item that one cannot be seen without is determined by the rich, not the poor.

The shame of poverty, then, has an important role to play in how we should understand poverty, as it is both an inevitable part of stratified capitalist societies and actively promoted through cultural portrayals of poverty. We turn now to examine the impact of the shame of poverty both on well-being and on the stability of capitalist societies.

11.2 The Moral Psychological Impact of the Shame of Poverty

Is there good reason, from the point of view of well-being, to care whether or not people are able to appear in public without shame? In this section we will argue that those who wish to promote well-being do have good reason to care about Smith's test. We will first explain the nature of shame and stress three of its commonly accepted features. First, that shame is a painful emotion. Secondly, that shame is concerned with the failure to achieve certain standards. Thirdly, that shame motivates social withdrawal. Having highlighted these three features of the nature of shame, we will then investigate the effects of shame, emphasizing two important effects shame has been found to have: withdrawal leading to isolation and hence depression.

We will then focus on the more specific connection between shame and poverty. We will argue that there is good reason to think that shame and poverty are connected and then point to some specific effects that this specific form of shame has been found to have: social withdrawal, refusal to engage with public officials, and social pretence. We will then argue that on *all* of the major theories of well-being that we discussed in our previous chapter, if poverty is shameful then this will have a serious negative impact on well-being. This provides *prima facie* justification for thinking that the shame test is a relevant way of assessing levels of poverty in society. In addition, this psychological impact of the shame of poverty plays a key role in the emotional regime of capitalist societies by playing a disciplinary function and creating an obstacle in the way of those experiencing poverty from engaging in successful moral address towards others.

It is worth recalling a methodological issue we noted earlier; several philosophers have argued that it is a mistake to think that we can discover all the interesting aspects of different emotions by providing necessary and sufficient conditions for emotional categories. Rather, we should categorize emotions according to the degree of similarity to prototypical instances of the emotion. In the following discussion of shame, we will follow this approach by outlining features that we take to be part of prototypical instances of shame without claiming that these features are either necessary or sufficient for shame.

We begin by examining the nature of shame. A paradigmatic feature of shame is that it is a painful emotion that involves the *failure to meet certain standards.* Heidi Maibom, for example, claims that shame is a "painful emotion concerned with the failure to live up to certain standards, norms, and ideals" (Maibom 2010, p.566). Similarly, Deonna et al. claim: "In shame, we apprehend a trait or action of ours that we take to exemplify the polar opposite of a self-relevant value as indicating our incapacity to exemplify this self-relevant value even to a minimal degree" (Deonna, Rodogno, and Teroni 2011, p.102).[1] This feature of shame might also be characterized as involving a *loss of self-respect*. For example, Rawls describes shame as, "the emotion evoked by shocks to our self-respect" (Rawls 1971/1999, p.388).

More needs to be said about the kind of evaluation involved, especially because guilt is also generally taken to involve a failure to comply with norms. One popular way to explain the difference is to say that shame takes the whole person as its object, while guilt targets particular actions. As Martha Nussbaum puts the point, shame focuses on "the very being of the person who feels it" while guilt focuses only on an action or desire and "need not extend to the entirety of the agent" (Nussbaum 2004, p.207).[2] The fact that shame involves a global evaluation of the person helps to explain one of its characteristic motivational responses, namely, withdrawal from the social and the gaze of others, as the global negative evaluation leads to a desire to hide the whole self (Wicker, Payne, and Morgan 1983, p.36; Williams 1993, pp.93–4; Ben-Ze'ev 2004, p.115).

If that is the nature of shame, what are the physical and psychological effects of experiencing it? In recent years there has been a surge of research into the physical and psychological effects of experiencing shame. This literature has highlighted links between shame and several ramified negative psychological effects such as aggression,[3] eating disorders,[4] negative effects on the immune system,[5] and post-traumatic stress syndrome[6]. It has been characterized as an emotion that is both physically and emotionally painful.[7] For our purposes, we will focus on two effects of shame that we take to be particularly relevant to well-being: social withdrawal and depression.

A study conducted by Marcela Matos and colleagues found that people's memories of experiencing shame correlated with experiencing higher levels

[1] See also (Galligan 2016, p.65) and (Ben-Ze'ev 2000, p.512).

[2] Others who endorse the claim that shame is a globalist emotion while guilt is not include (Ben-Ze'ev 2000; Piers and Singer 1953, chapters 1–2; Tangney and Dearing 2002; Taylor 1985, chapter 4).

[3] See (Elison et al. 2014; Velotti et al. 2014; Gilligan 2001).

[4] See (Burney and Irwin 2000; Frank 1991; Kelly et al. 2013; Kelly and Carter 2013; Sanftner et al. 1995; Swan and Andrews 2003; Troop et al. 2008).

[5] See (Dickerson and Kemeny 2004; Dickerson et al. 2004).

[6] See (Andrews et al. 2000; La Bash and Papa 2014).

[7] See (Dickerson et al. 2009; Eisenberger 2011; MacDonald and Leary 2005).

of social anxiety (Matos, Pinto-Gouveia, and Gilbert 2013). Similarly, a study led by Thomas A. Fergus et al. (2010) found a link between shame and social anxiety that was not present for guilt. These findings are supported by subsequent studies that linked shame, but not guilt, to social anxiety.[8] Shame has also been found to increase pro-inflammatory cytokine activity leading to social withdrawal suggesting that shame leads people to withdraw from social situations (Dickerson and Kemeny 2004; Dickerson et al. 2004).

Shame is also linked with depression. Across several studies, Bernice Andrews and her colleagues found evidence that shame "plays a significant role in the onset and course of depression" (Andrews et al. 2000, p.37). Bodily shame, for example, was found to play a mediating role between sexual or physical abuse and chronic depression (Andrews 1995). These findings were replicated in subsequent studies that also found a link between shame more generally and the onset of depression (Andrews and Hunter 1997; Andrews, Qian, and Valentine 2002; Nussbaum 2004). The association of shame and guilt suggested by these studies was supported by a meta-analysis which both supported the link between the two and found shame to be more strongly linked to depression than guilt (Kim, Thibodeau, and Jorgensen 2011).

Turning to the more specific issue of the link between shame and poverty, shame has been found to be a key factor in the experience of poverty. In Townsend's extensive study of poverty in the United Kingdom he noted both "the social shame of those with little money," and the desire "to avoid the shame of pleading poverty" (Townsend 1979b, pp.241, 841). Beyond this cultural context, Robert Walker led a wide-ranging study of the experiences of those living in poverty in a diverse range of countries including China, India, Norway, Pakistan, South Korea, Uganda, and the United Kingdom. One key finding of this extensive body of research was that shame was a central feature of how people experience poverty and of cultural portrayals of poverty. While respondents in the very different national and cultural settings covered in this volume were not asked to rank the negative aspects of poverty, shame was, with subtle variations, certainly a very important component of their life experience (Walker 2014, p.183).

Similarly, the Oxford Poverty and Human Development Initiative (OPHI) claims that

[8] See (Hedman et al. 2013; Levinson, Byrne, and Rodebaugh 2016).

> Poor people and communities today continue to cite direct experiences of indignity, shame and humiliation as painful components of their deprivation, meaning that shame and humiliation also play a profound role in the daily lives of people living in poverty. (OPHI 2017)

Given that shame is a core part of the experience of poverty, what effects does this shame have on people?[9]

One important effect of the shame of poverty is that it leads people to withdraw from public life. Walker describes how respondents from across the seven countries in his study reacted to the shame of poverty by declining invitations to social occasions (Walker 2014, pp.124–5). A single father from Britain described how he "Shut the curtains and hid away," while a respondent from Beijing said, "I dare not meet the neighbours. When I see them far away, I hide myself" (Walker 2014, p.125). Respondents from Uganda, meanwhile, stopped participating in village meetings in order to avoid being humiliated (Walker 2014, p.125). These responses should be unsurprising given what we have said about the link between shame and social withdrawal. It is also a vindication of Smith's original insight: if you cannot meet his criterion of appearing in public without shame, then you withdraw instead.

One, particularly damaging, form that this takes is withdrawing from engagement with public officials. As a UN report on poverty notes:

> Stigmatization and prejudicial attitudes generate a sense of shame, discouraging persons living in poverty from approaching public officials and seeking the support that they need. Not wishing to expose themselves to even greater social discrimination by accessing services that are stigmatized by society, persons living in poverty may refrain from claiming entitlements such as food vouchers or subsidies, accessing public housing or attending free health clinics. (Sepúlveda Carmona 2011, p.5)

Tragically, then, it seems that the shame and stigma directed to those in poverty leads not only to social withdrawal but also to a failure to claim welfare benefits which people are entitled to.

[9] For further evidence of cross-cultural links between shame and poverty see (Chase and Walker 2013; Walker et al. 2013; Gubrium and Lødemel 2013; Narayan et al. 2000; Yongmie 2013).

Another response to the shame of poverty is pretence. Chase and Walker's study of poverty in the United Kingdom found that people experiencing poverty often pretended not to be poor (Chase and Walker 2013). One respondent described how she pretended that her volunteer work was paid employment saying:

> I don't like people knowing I am on benefits. If I didn't know you, I'd tell you I worked. I class this as a proper job (working as a volunteer), that's why I wear the identity badge that way (back to front) so no one sees that I'm volunteering . . . so it looks like I'm doing a proper job. (Chase and Walker 2013, p.748)

Another reported pretending to still be in his previous job saying:

> On the rare occasions that I go out, if I meet someone and I'm chatting to them and that, I don't really say, "I'm on the dole", I just parrot fashion my last job. I just say, "Yeah I work in the factory". It's a pretty faceless job anyway. So yeah, I suppose there's probably a little bit of shame in there somewhere. (Chase and Walker 2013, p.748)

Through forms of pretence, people in poverty try to mask the shame that accompanies poverty.

According to virtually every theory of well-being we canvased in chapter 10, poverty damages well-being. The hedonist will note shame is both physically and emotionally painful. Moreover, it is linked with social anxiety, depression, pretence, and withdrawal from public life, conditions which are either painful in themselves or likely to lead to further painful experiences. Given that hedonists claim that we should judge a person's well-being in terms of the balance of pleasurable experiences over painful ones, the hedonist assessment of the shame caused by poverty seems clear. Shame is painful in itself and leads to further painful experiences, so the shame caused by poverty has a negative effect on well-being.

The same verdict emerges from preferentism: people prefer not to feel shame, as can be seen from the strategies, such as withdrawal and pretense, that people employ to avoid being shamed by others. Not only is shame undesirable—people prefer to lead their lives not having to feel ashamed—but it also leads to other undesirable consequences. People generally prefer not to be depressed, face social anxiety, or to deceive those around them.

Given that preferentists judge well-being in terms of whether someone's preferences are being fulfilled, they should also accept that the shame of poverty has a negative effect on well-being.

In chapter 10, we endorsed a version of objective list theory. Again, if the shame of poverty is both painful in itself and leads to further painful experiences, then an objective list theorist would rule that at least in this regard, the shame of poverty is bad for well-being. However, objective list theorists have more resources available to criticize the shame of poverty than do hedonists or preferentists.

First, objective list theorists typically list "achievement" as one of the components on the list of things that contribute to well-being (Fletcher 2013, p.214; Heathwood 2010, p.645). The shame of poverty is linked to depression, social withdrawal, and social anxiety, and these in turn are likely to limit what people can achieve. The objective list theorist then would class the shame of poverty as having a negative effect on well-being according to this component as well. Furthermore, both Fletcher and Heathwood list friendship as another component that is typically included on the list of things that contribute to well-being. Given the links between poverty-induced shame and social withdrawal and pretence, there seems good reason to think that it has a negative impact on this component of well-being too. A more complex theory can identify a more complex range of harms.

The shame of poverty not only has a negative effect on the well-being of the poor but also plays a key role in stabilizing the capitalist economic system. First, by focusing attention to the perceived failures of the self, shame is not a response that is likely to lead people to challenge the system that made them poor. If it is the problems of the self that have led to poverty—remember the key role of personal responsibility in the emotional regime of capitalist societies—then people in poverty should focus on self-critique and self-development rather than system-critique and campaigning for a better economic system. The response to poverty encouraged by shame is to work harder, to develop existing skills or to retrain. After all, the poor have no reason to complain or protest about their own situation, as it is their own fault that they do not have more resources. As Barclay notes, this is exactly the kind of response that is promoted by the precarious nature of work in late capitalist societies (Barclay 2022, p.448).

The shame of poverty also serves as a barrier to the poor's ability to successfully engage in moral address. To understand this point we first need to understand the way social factors can impact upon moral address. As

Vanessa Carbonell argues, social factors like oppression and marginalization can constrain who is able to successfully engage in moral address with others (Carbonell 2019). According to a popular view of moral responsibility, responsible moral agents are those who can legitimately be targeted with reactive attitudes such as resentment and gratitude because they are fellow members of the moral community (Strawson 1962). To be an appropriate target of this kind of attitude, the person being targeted must recognize the other person's authority to make this kind of address and the person making the address must recognize the person they are addressing as an appropriate target (Darwall 2006, 75).

For example, for blame to be successful the person being blamed must recognize the authority of the person doing the blaming to demand that she stop acting that way, which involves recognizing the blamer as having equal standing as a member of the moral community. In addition, the person making the address must also believe that the person being addressed will recognize their authority. Social factors may impede successful moral address in two ways. First, they may act as a barrier to those being addressed recognizing the equal moral standing of the person addressing them. Secondly, the person who would make the moral claim may believe that their equal moral standing would not be recognized and so engage in self-silencing (Carbonell 2019, p.177).

An emotional logic of capitalism which holds that poverty indicates a shameful lack of worth may create both kinds of obstacle. A society full of messages and narratives that one's worth is determined by one's wealth is not conducive to the wealthier members of society recognizing the equal moral standing of the poor. In such a society, even if those in poverty succeed in making moral demands for a more egalitarian distribution of wealth, they will likely be dismissed on the grounds that they lack standing to make them.

From the perspective of society's "winners", such ungrounded complaints from the poor stem from the very same fault that causes the poverty: a refusal to accept personal responsibility for one's economic fate. Such complaints from those who are seen as lacking in worth for their greater share of the productive surplus can be viewed by the rich as the illegitimate complaints from the envious, lazy, and untalented. In this way, whatever anger or outrage is expressed by the poor against the concentration of wealth and against income inequality will be viewed as indicating a problem with the person expressing that anger or outrage, rather than indicating that the state of the world is somehow reprehensible. The moral address of the rich by the poor, then, will often fail, as the rich will not recognize the poor as having the appropriate standing to address them.[10]

Similarly, the prevalence of the message that poverty indicates a lack of worth may give the poor good reason to believe that they are not viewed by the rich as possessing the moral standing needed to make authoritative moral claims. This belief may arise from experience of being treated with disrespect or from internalizing the message that the poor deserve less respect than the rich. Either way, the belief that their moral authority will not be recognized is likely to discourage the poor from engaging in moral address.[11]

The case of poverty-related shame also points towards a third obstacle to moral address. As we have seen, the shame of poverty often leads people to hide their poverty, either by withdrawing from public life or by masking their poverty from others. This is a further obstacle to moral address, as making one's poverty visible to others is an important part of morally protesting that poverty. As the journalist Jeremy Seabrook points out, the hiding of poverty is a way in which people in poverty are pressured to "collude with the denial that they even exist" (Seabrook 2013, p.171). This invisibility and the masking that accompanies it may also have a wide range of psychological effects. Many moral psychological problems may arise from this masking behaviour. The need to constantly mask one's struggles seems likely to create problems for authenticity, integrity, and feeling at ease in the world.

This moral psychological impact of the shame of poverty in capitalist societies functions to protect the stability of the capitalist system. One of the key challenges to the stability of capitalism is finding a way of keeping the majority of people content in a system in which wealth and control are in the hands of a minority. The self-directed nature of shame encourages the poor to focus their attention on what is lacking in themselves rather than on challenging the system that made them poor. Another challenge to the stability of

[10] This may be seen as a moral analogue of what Kristie Dotson calls "testimonial quieting", where a member of an oppressed group is not taken seriously as an epistemic agent because they are not valued as a knower (Dotson 2011, p.242).

[11] The fact that the poor may be blamed and shamed for their poverty suggests that the rich do in fact view the poor as members of the moral community. On Darwall's view, blaming someone assumes that the blamed is an equal member of the moral community and has the ability to recognize the authority of the blamer. On this view, the rich appear to be conceptually confused, as they both are and are not treating the poor as members of the moral community. There are several ways to respond to this puzzle. One response is to say that the rich are indeed conceptually confused about the nature of blame and this shows the contradictions that lurk in the emotional logic of capitalism. Alternatively, we might think that the rich are attributing a form of what Carbonell calls "second-class moral citizenship" to the poor, in which they can be appropriately blamed but have no authority to blame others in return (2019, p.167). Thanks to Yvette Driessen for pressing us on this point.

capitalism lies in ensuring that the rich feel comfortable with the highly unequal levels of power and wealth that they benefit from. The shame of poverty and the invisibility it engenders also address this issue by acting as barriers to the poor from successfully morally addressing the rich (and from teaming up with others to protest the harms and injustices inflicted on them). This helps to protect the rich from moral objections to this unequal system of power and wealth.

11.3 Shame, Stigmatization, and Rationality

There are several ways to object to our claim that Smith's shame test should be considered part of our understanding of poverty that we will now consider.

First, it might be argued that the shame of poverty plays a socially useful role. Robert Walker summarizes the rationale behind this idea in the following: "The threat of shame is used to encourage effort commensurate with the work ethic and shame is applied to those who fail economically, as judged by their poverty status, and especially to those who claim welfare benefits" (Walker 2014, p.189). The shame people feel when they are in poverty will motivate them to find a job to ensure they do not remain poor and the threat of shame will encourage others to work hard to ensure they do not become impoverished. This encourages people to do all they can to ensure they do not become poor and so have to rely on state assistance, i.e. be or become one of what Mitt Romney derogatorily called society's "takers".

We have already expressed our scepticism towards the claim that the main cause of recent inequality in the United States is skill-biased technological change. This is an explanation favoured by economists, partly because in this case inequality is a correct market signal. Those who are losing out need to make themselves better adjusted to the changing demands on human productivity. It would be a natural extension of this approach to find a positive role for being ashamed for having failed to adjust to these market signals. The signals were there: if you choose to ignore them, then you are shamefully at fault.

However, as Walker's investigation into the connection between shame and poverty makes clear, the empirical evidence provides no support for this justification of the shame of poverty (Walker 2014). Modern sociology and social psychology demonstrate that the model is based on false premises that condemn it to failure—failure that is demonstrated empirically through the life experiences of the people in poverty cited in this volume. It presumes that the benefits to society outweigh the costs to individuals threatened with shame since the latter will come to work harder contribute more to economic growth and cost society less by making fewer claims on welfare.

> The scientific evidence [. . .] demonstrates that behaviour is seldom if ever changed by the threat of shame and that once shame is imposed, a person is excluded socially and potentially becomes a free agent unfettered and uncontrollable by the imposition of social norms and expectations. (Walker 2014, p.190)

There is, then, no empirical support for this justification of the shame of poverty. However, this argument opens the door to an alternative challenge. If we accept that shame is not a fitting response to poverty, then we might be tempted to think that the shame experienced by those in poverty is irrational. This may in turn lead us to think that these irrational feelings ought not to influence how society seeks to distribute its resources. As discussed above, shame is commonly characterized as an emotion that is a response to a failure to meet certain standards. However, there is a disagreement in the literature concerning whether the relevant standards must be endorsed by the person experiencing shame. We do not intend to adjudicate between these different views here. Either view might be used to support the claim that the shame of poverty is irrational.

According to many theorists of shame, the standards that shame responds to are those held by other people. For example, according to the anthropologist, Ruth Benedict, shame is, "a reaction to other's criticisms" (Benedict 1946, p.222ff). Many philosophers writing about shame endorse similar views (Blackburn 1998, p.17; Galligan 2016; Taylor 1985, chapter 3). According to these accounts, shame is not a response to a failure to live up to one's own values. Rather, it is a response to the failure to live up to other people's standards, which may or may not be shared by the subject themselves. As Anthony O'Hear points out, feelings of shame come apart from the public expressions designed to cause shame (O'Hear 1977, p.77). It is possible to be the victim of public shaming without feeling any shame whatsoever. O'Hear concludes from this that shame is an appropriate response to being shamed by others when the target judges that the standards she is being held to are reasonable (O'Hear 1977, p.78). If we accept this view of shame then we might think that those experiencing the shame of poverty can avoid their shame by simply rejecting the false idea that poverty is a legitimate source of shame.

However, there remains a clear reason for people to feel shame in response to poverty, even if they reject the idea that poverty is inherently shameful. As Deonna et al. argue in their defence of an account of shame as a response to a person's *own* values, it is possible for such an account to accommodate the relevance of the shaming behaviour of others (Deonna, Rodogno, and Teroni 2011). According to their account, the feeling of shame requires a person to feel that something she values is threatened (Deonna, Rodogno, and Teroni 2011, p.130). However, this feeling may well be an appropriate reaction to the shaming behaviour of others, even when the target does not endorse the standards she is being held against, as this shaming behaviour is likely to impact on other things she does care about, such as her social standing, public image, or reputation (Deonna, Rodogno, and Teroni 2011, p.130). People in poverty then may reasonably react with shame in response to attempts to publicly shame them, even if they do not see poverty as a legitimate source of shame.

This worry about the shaming behaviour of others impacting on social standing is not a mere theoretical possibility. As Walker makes clear in his sociological analysis of shame and poverty, people in poverty have to face humiliation, contempt and disdain from their more affluent fellow citizens (Walker 2014, p.154). Owen Jones's *Chavs: The Demonization of the Working Class* shows in detail the many ways in which the public expressions of contempt from British middle-class people demonize the British working class (Jones 2011). Those living in poverty then, have good reason to be concerned about being publicly shamed by others, even if they do not share the values of those doing the shaming.

According to Bernard Williams's defence of the moral value of shame, a mature moral agent should only feel shame in response to failing to live up to the standards of people who are worthy of respect (Williams 1993, chapter 4). While the opinions of those we have no respect for should not have the power to shame us, it can be appropriate to feel shame in response to those whom we respect, even if we do not share their opinions. It is valuable to be sensitive to these judgements, as it encourages people to take the moral judgements of others into account when engaging in their own ethical judgements. Given that no one is a perfect moral judge, it is epistemically useful to allow the judgements of others to play a role in determining when we should reconsider our own judgements. The upshot of this account is that those who reject the shamefulness of poverty may nevertheless have reason to feel shame in response to the judgements of those they respect.

Cheshire Calhoun provides a more far-reaching defence of experiencing shame in the face of judgements one does not share. Calhoun argues that the two previous approaches to feeling shame for failing to live up to norms that one rejects encourage us to locate the problem in the wrong place. They do so by encouraging us to see those who are being shamed as irrational for feeling shame in the face of norms they reject. At worst, this could involve chastising "the subordinated for feeling ashamed" (Calhoun 2004, pp.136–7). Instead, Calhoun argues that shame is a rational response to the contempt of others, even when we do not share the evaluation that is involved in this contempt.

The reason for this is that morality is a social practice people should take their fellow members of this practice seriously. As we noted in chapter 7, when we discussed Pettit and Brennan's "economy of esteem", we should be suspicious of people who attach no importance at all to what others think of them. Unlike Williams, Calhoun does not think that the benefits here are purely *epistemic*. For Calhoun, the primary importance of shame is its *practical* weight. This means that shame does not simply make us rethink our own judgements. It also functions to show to us how we are viewed by those with whom we are engaged in the shared social practice of morality (Calhoun 2004, p.143). Calhoun argues that, given that our identities are in a large part socially constructed, the viewpoints of those with whom we share our social practices help to determine our identities. Those who refuse to pay attention to shaming criticisms, then, fail to take the social practice of morality seriously.

11.4 Smith and Admiration for the Rich

So far we have argued that the link that Smith draws between poverty and shame deserves to be taken seriously. The shame of poverty is both an inevitable part of stratified societies and something that is actively promoted through cultural portrayals of poverty. This shame has a significant negative impact on the well-being of the poor and plays a key role in the emotional regime of capitalist societies by serving as an obstacle to moral address for those living in poverty.

We turn now to another important insight from Smith about our emotional responses to economic inequality which concerns the admiration we feel towards the wealthy. Throughout this book we have focused on this puzzle: in societies that are putatively liberal democracies, where the views of the average voter ought to hold sway, extensive inequalities have emerged and become deeply entrenched. We have endorsed one explanation of the extent and persistence of such inequalities in chapter 2. They are the product of extractive rent seeking whereby the upper 20% of the income distribution gain at the expense of everyone else. Why, then, is this tolerated? We have already noted the general importance of an ideology of meritocracy that will be our focus in the next chapter. Here we focus on a more specific aspect of the emotional regime of market societies: that it seems wrong to critique the rich because their wealth is admirable independently of its having been meritoriously earned.

Both Smith and Veblen described the importance in market societies of admiration for, and the emulation of, the rich. In this chapter we will assess both of their explanations: for Smith, this desire comes from our admiration of the rich, while for Veblen it involves emulation. Having exposited these accounts, we will then explain why there is good reason to think that the problems identified by Smith and Veblen will be particularly acute in market societies that exhibit the kind of radical economic disparities evident in the New Inequality. We think Smith and Veblen were correct that the admiration and envy that people feel for the rich is a crucial part of the emotional regime of capitalist market societies. Not only are these emotions plausibly triggered in such societies (and exacerbated by the inequalities these societies generate), they help sustain them. It is the admiration for the rich that motivates many people to join schemes in which they are pitted against each other, not merely for wealth, but also in a competition for distinction—just as Smith claimed in his inaugurating discussion.

As we outlined in chapter 6, in *The Theory of Moral Sentiments*, Smith outlined a view of morality based on sympathy (Smith 1759/1982). Sympathy, as he understands it, is based on imagining what we would feel were we in another person's situation. According to Smith, we have a natural tendency to engage in this imaginative projection. When we observe another person's action, we imagine what we would feel in their situation and compare it to what the agent is actually feeling. If our imagined feelings are similar to the actual feelings of the agent, then we are sympathizing with them. Sympathy then, consists of approval of an agent's feelings as appropriate for the situation (Smith 1759/1982, I.i.3.2).

Sympathy plays an important role in thinking about how we should feel in a particular situation, as we have a desire to be approved of by others. The approval by others of our actions or emotional responses provides us with an incentive to act or feel in this way. However, Smith claims that we not only desire to be approved of by other people; we also desire to be *worthy* of that approval. Smith explains what it is to be worthy of a given emotional reaction in terms of the reaction a well-informed and impartial spectator would have to our actions and emotional responses (Smith 1759/1982, III).

Our concern is not Smith's account of sympathy and the moral sentiments but rather with a particular way in which Smith claims these moral sentiments can be corrupted. This account has implications for how we think of both consumerism and inequality. According to Smith, we find it easier to feel sympathy with joy than with sorrow (Smith 1759/1982, I.iii.1.5). One reason for this is that it is pleasant to share in another's happiness, whereas sharing in another's pain is unpleasant. Note here the element of replication, or mirroring, in Smith's account of sympathy. According to Smith, this disposition to sympathize more with another's joy than with their sorrow makes it attractive for people to display their wealth. As Smith explains:

> The rich man glories in his riches, because he feels that they naturally draw upon him the attention of the world, and that mankind are disposed to go along with him in all those agreeable emotions with which the advantages of his situation so readily inspire in him. (Smith 1759/1982, I.III.2.i)

The rich flaunt their wealth, at least partly because of the expected emotional responses, such as admiration, of others. Moreover, according to Smith, the attention and admiration that the wealthy receive for their riches is the primary benefit that they gain from their wealth.[12] The rich man, says Smith, "is fonder of his wealth, upon this account, than for all the other advantages it procures him" (Smith 1759/1982, I.III.2.i).

Together with the shame experienced by those in poverty, we have here the two limiting cases of an economy of spectacle, or attention, structured around publicity. The rich receive attention and admiration while the poor are either ignored or viewed with contempt. In both cases people's lives in capitalist market societies are inextricably linked to the positions they occupy

[12] Smith claims that wealth is not the only source of social distinction and admiration but it is by far the most important (Smith 1776/1981, V.I.b.11; Rasmussen 2016, pp.347–8).

in its stratified and highly unequal structure. The emotions connected to these social positions are both sustained and reinforced by the mechanisms that perpetuate this inequality.

What does the emotion of admiration involve? According to Smith, admiration involves "Approbation heightened by wonder and surprise" (Smith 1759/1982, I.i.4.3). The first element of Smith's account of admiration is "approbation". That admiration involves a positive judgement or approval should be uncontroversial. As Ben-Ze'ev puts the point, admiration involves, "a highly positive evaluation of someone" (Ben-Ze'ev 2000, p.56). Similarly, William Lyons claims that admiration involves: "a pro-evaluation or approval" (Lyons 1980, p.90). As yet this does not tell us a great deal, as many emotions involve a positive evaluation of some sort. Respect, for example, also involves a positive evaluation but is not the same emotion as admiration (Archer and Matheson 2019, p.248).

According to Smith, the distinctive feature of the positive appraisal involved in admiration is that it involves a sense of *wonder* or *surprise*. Smith is not alone in making this claim. Charles Darwin (1872/1998, p.269) makes a similar point when he claims that admiration is, "surprise associated with some pleasure and a sense of approval." Relatedly, the admiration has been claimed to involve a judgement that the object of admiration possesses a value that is rare (Forrester 1982, p.102), extraordinary (Chappell 2019, p.15), or superior to the subject (Schindler et al. 2013, p.89).

Admiration is also, according to Smith, an important form of support for those who receive it. First, admiration provides what André Grahle terms "epistemic support" (Grahle 2019, p.152). When people praise and admire us this strengthens our confidence in our own praiseworthiness. As Smith puts the point, "Their approbation necessarily confirms our own self-approbation. Their praise necessarily confirms our own sense of our own praiseworthiness" (Smith 1759/1982, III.2.3). This implies that receiving the admiration and esteem of others gives us good reason to feel more confident in our own praiseworthiness and so boosts our self-esteem. Admiration from others also helps to facilitate the appropriate positive emotional response in ourselves, something Grahle terms "innervative support"(Grahle 2019, p.152). When we witness someone else's admiration we can, through sympathy, be brought to experience a similar feeling and gain a feeling of pride in our behaviour (Grahle 2019, p.153).[13]

[13] Grahle claims that admiration also supports the target through providing her with petitionary reasons to continue acting as they are (Grahle 2019, p.154).

Having examined the nature of admiration we are now able to consider why Smith thinks our admiration for the rich is damaging. First, the admiration for the rich leads those with fewer resources to feel deference towards those with more and to attempt to emulate them.[14] This follows because "Their dress is the fashionable dress; the language of their conversation, the fashionable style; their air and deportment, the fashionable behaviour" (Smith 1759/1982, I.iii.2.3). It is not just such dress choices and mannerisms that people seek to imitate but also their foolish or immoral behaviour. As Smith continues, "Even their vices and follies are fashionable; and the greater part of men are proud to imitate and resemble them in the very qualities which dishonour and degrade them" (Smith 1759/1982, I.iii.3.7). To make matters worse, Smith thinks that most people are more inclined to admire "wealth and greatness" than "wisdom and virtue" (Smith 1759/1982, I.iii.3.2). This is why Smith claims that the "disposition to admire, and almost worship, the rich and the powerful, and to despise, or, at least, to neglect persons of poor and mean condition," is "the great and most universal cause of the corruption of our moral sentiments" (Smith 1759/1982, I.iii.3.1).

Thus, two centuries before Hayek, Smith explained the psychological mechanisms that will allow Hayek to identify the role of the wealthy in our society as arbiters of taste in the way we discussed in chapter 9. The behaviours they engage in are reflected, via our consumerized economy of attention, in the tastes of the many who seek to emulate them. Smith's claims that our admiration for the rich leads to deference and emulation are supported by work in philosophy and psychology on the motivational effects of admiration.

First, several philosophers endorse the view that admiration leads to a desire to emulate. Moses Mendelssohn, for example, has argued that admiring someone's virtues brings about a desire "to be equally capable of such a sublime disposition" or in other words, a "desire to emulate" (Lessing and Mendelssohn 1972, p.168). More recently, Linda Zagzebski has argued that admiration "gives rise to the motive to emulate the admired person in the way she is admired" (Zagzebski 2017, p.43). A similar view is held by Mark Schroeder, who claims that admiration "is the kind of state to motivate you to emulate the people you admire, insofar as you are able" (Schroeder 2010, p.42).

[14] Smith claims this is a more frequent cause of deference towards the rich than the expectation that they will repay our deference with some benefit (Smith 1759/1982, I.iii.2.3). David Hume makes a similar point in his *Treatise of Human Nature* II.iii.5.

While philosophers may disagree about how exactly to characterize the connection between admiration and emulation, the existence of some kind of connection is well supported by empirical evidence.[15] Studies by Immordino-Yang and colleagues, for example, exposed participants to stories about people acting virtuously (Immordino-Yang et al. 2009; Immordino-Yang and Sylvan 2010). Those who read these stories spontaneously mentioned the desire to become a morally better person who would perform virtuous actions in the subsequent discussion, leading the authors to conclude that admiration is a "profoundly motivating" emotion (Immordino-Yang and Sylvan 2010, p.110). Similarly, in a series of studies conducted by Algoe and Haidt, participants were first asked to report their experiences of admiration and then questioned about the motivational impact that this emotion had on them (Algoe and Haidt 2009). The experimenters found a positive relationship between admiration and a desire to emulate.[16]

Admiration also appears to be linked to deference in the way Smith assumes. David Velleman suggests that admiring someone disposes us, "to defer to him and to approve of his words and actions" (Velleman 2009, p.42). While there is less empirical work on the link between admiration and deference, several studies have investigated related questions. Algoe and Haidt found admiration to motivate people to praise and enhance the reputation of the admired person (Algoe and Haidt 2009). Relatedly, Onu et al. found that admiring someone motivated people to seek out the guidance of the admired person (Onu, Smith, and Kessler 2015). Admiration for more powerful people has also been found to be associated with hierarchy-maintaining behaviour (Sweetman et al. 2013). Finally, Cuddy et al. (2007) found that admiration is linked to a desire to associate and cooperate with those being admired (Cuddy, Fiske, and Glick 2007). This is far from conclusive but does support Smith's claim that admiration is connected with deferential behaviour. The philosophical and psychological literature, then, supports Smith's claims about admiration. There is strong empirical support for the claim that admiration leads to a desire to emulate and some support, albeit weaker and more speculative, for the claim that admiration promotes deferential behaviour.

[15] According to one of the current authors, the desire to emulate should be seen as part of a general connection between admiration and motivation to promote the value that is judged to be present in the object of admiration (Archer 2019). For an amendment to this view see also (Cawston 2019).

[16] For further empirical support for this connection see (Aquino, McFerran, and Laven 2011; Cox 2010; Freeman, Aquino, and McFerran 2009; Landis et al. 2009; Schnall, Roper, and Fessler 2010; Thrash and Elliot 2004; Vianello, Galliani, and Haidt 2010).

According to Smith, this deference to and desire to emulate the rich is a particularly worrying problem because the rich display a greater degree of vice than those with less money. Those without wealth must earn the approval of others through good conduct. The rich however, will be admired anyway due to their wealth and so do not need to earn the admiration of others through good conduct (Rasmussen 2016, p.349; Smith 1759/1982, I.iii.2.4–2.5). This means they have less incentive to act virtuously, as they will be admired regardless.

There is an exact parallelism here, as we noted in chapter 6, between Smith's account and Hegel's: the "middling sort of person" can be emancipated through the right kind of emancipatory relation to work and the recognition of others. It is those at the extremes of extravagance and misery that Hegel feared would be cut off from this realization of freedom. In Smith, too, it is the rich who are exempted from the constraint of requiring others to take an interest in one's own interest without flattery or subservience. They can act with a flagrant disregard for social norms, while those with fewer resources are dependent on the good opinion of others and so cannot ignore these norms.

As we saw earlier, admiration provides support for people that encourages them to continue acting in the same way. The wealthy, then, are encouraged by the admiration they receive to continue acting in the way that they are. To make matters worse, those without wealth will often be led away from the path of virtue by their imitation of the rich. They are enticed to act viciously by the hope that if they can achieve the same position as the rich then they too will not have to worry about acting decently in order to receive the admiration of others (Rasmussen 2016, p.347; Smith 1759/1982, I.iii.3.8). According to Smith, this process is, "the cause of all the tumult and bustle, all the rapine and injustice, which avarice and ambition have introduced into this world" (Rasmussen 2016, p.347; Smith 1759/1982, I.iii.2.8).

In addition to negatively impacting moral behaviour, Smith also claims that this distortion is harmful for well-being. As we saw in chapter 6, according to Smith, "happiness consists in tranquillity and enjoyment" but "without tranquillity there can be no enjoyment" (Rasmussen 2016, p.349; Smith 1759/1982, III.3.30). Beyond a basic level, wealth and material possessions do not make a great contribution to happiness. Instead, Smith thinks the poor are more likely to attain happiness, as they have open to them every source of happiness apart from "the frivolous pleasures of vanity and superiority" pleasures that for Smith are often in conflict with tranquillity

(Rasmussen 2016, p.350; Smith 1759/1982, III.3.31). Despite happiness being available to those lacking wealth, they often fail to achieve it because they mistakenly believe that they will be happier if they achieve a superior position to the one that they currently occupy. This leads people to spend their lives labouring hard to achieve material possessions—i.e. emulate the rich—that do little to increase their happiness. As we discussed in chapter 6, Smith describes an example of a poor man's son whose admiration for the rich leads him to devote his life to becoming wealthy in the following way:

> Through the whole of his life he pursues the idea of a certain artificial and elegant repose which he may never arrive at, for which he sacrifices a real tranquillity that is at all times in his power, and which, if in the extremity of old age he should at last attain it, he will find to be in no respect preferable to that humble security and contentment which he had abandoned for it. It is then, in the last dregs of life [. . .] that he begins at last to find that wealth and greatness are mere trinkets of frivolous utility. (Smith 1759/1982, IV.1.8)

The distortion, then, that causes us to admire and sympathize with the rich leads people to devote their lives to attaining wealth that will make little contribution to their well-being. Attempts to emulate the rich, even when successful, do not provide the kinds of positive effects that are being promised.

Smith thinks that most of us are capable of understanding that the pursuit of wealth and prosperity does not make us happier (Smith 1759/1982, IV.1.9) However, we tend not to come to this understanding. Instead, we are naturally disposed to view wealth as desirable and admirable and to spend our lives striving to obtain it. This should be no surprise as Smith holds that we also have a natural tendency to try to improve our position (Smith 1776/1981, II.iii). Although this tendency is not conducive to happiness at the individual level, Smith nevertheless believes that it has a useful role to play as it promotes economic development (Smith 1759/1982, IV.1.10). Those who pursue their own wealth, "are led by an invisible hand to [. . .] without intending it, without knowing it, advance the interest of our society, and afford means to the multiplication of the species" (Smith 1759/1982, IV.1.10). So while our natural tendency to mistakenly think that the pursuit of wealth will bring us happiness is mistaken with regards to individuals, Smith thinks that it is an important driver of economic and social development.[17]

[17] The claim that the pursuit of wealth is an individual vice that brings collective benefits was outlined thirty years earlier by Bernard Mandeville (Mandeville 1742 [1970], p.68).

As we noted in chapter 6, Dennis Rasmussen has pointed out that the link Smith makes between our admiration for the rich and the corruption of our moral sentiments is closely linked to the existence of economic inequality (Rasmussen 2016, p.347). While Smith does not make this link explicit, Rasmussen stresses that Smith's argument here presupposes a link to economic inequality: "without *any* economic inequality there would *be* no rich and poor to sympathize with to differing degrees, and presumably the more economic inequality there is in a given society, the more this distortion will be present." (Rasmussen 2016, p.347). While some degree of inequality is needed for there to be rich people and poor people, this by itself shows that greater economic inequality would make this problem worse. The answer, can be found by looking at what Smith takes the rich to be admired for:

> If we examine, however, why the spectator distinguishes with such admiration the condition of the rich and the great, we shall find that it is not so much upon account of the superior ease or pleasure which they are supposed to enjoy, as of the numberless artificial and elegant contrivances for promoting this ease or pleasure. He does not even imagine that they are really happier than other people: but he imagines that they possess more means of happiness. And it is the ingenious and artful adjustment of those means to the end for which they are intended, that is the principle source of his admiration. (Smith 1759/1982, IV.1.8)

The rich are admired because they possess greater means for achieving happiness than other people. This makes it clear why greater inequality would exacerbate this corruption of our moral sentiments. The greater the difference between the rich and the poor, the greater the difference between the means of happiness available to the poor and those available to the rich. Smith is not only committed to inequality having an essential role to play in this corruption of the moral sentiments, but also to thinking that the problem will be worse the greater the inequality (Rasmussen 2016). An important question to raise against Smith's claim is whether there is good reason to think that people really do admire the rich in the way he suggests. We will return to this question later in the chapter. First, we consider a related argument developed by Thorstein Veblen.

11.5 Veblen and Emulation of the Rich in Market Societies

Smith takes our tendency to desire wealth and to seek to become wealthy to be a natural one, rather than one that is particular to market societies. There are, though, several reasons to think that capitalist market societies will be particularly likely to encourage the development of this tendency. In what follows, we discuss reasons why admiration for the rich plays a crucial role in the emotional regime of such market societies. Not only do they generate feelings of admiration for the rich but also these feelings help sustain, and thus reinforce, the continued existence of these market societies and their mechanisms to generate and exacerbate inequality.

The first reason to think admiration plays a central role in the emotional regime of market societies is suggested in Veblen's study of the leisure class. Veblen claims the leisure class arose from the same economic forces as property ownership (Veblen 1899/2009, p.33). Property, for Veblen, entails competition for resources: "Wherever the institution of private property is found, even in a slightly developed form, the economic process bears the character of a struggle between men for the possession of goods" (Veblen 1899/2009, p.34). While classical economists tend to characterize the aim of this struggle as being the consumption of resources accumulated, Veblen claims that the real aim is to secure the honour and status that possessing these goods will bring:

> The motive that lies at the root of ownership is emulation; and the same motive of emulation continues active in the further development of the institution to which it has given rise and in the development of all of those features of the social structure which this institution of ownership touches. The possession of wealth confers honor; it is an invidious distinction. (Veblen 1899/2009, p.35)

Veblen claims that in what he calls "primitive communal" societies, people would have been more concerned with inter-group comparisons, with comparing the superiority of their group compared to their enemies (Veblen 1899/2009, p.36). As private ownership develops, intra-group comparisons become more significant, as people seek to display their superiority to others. These social comparisons become increasingly based on property, as societies industrialize, because this is how people show they have power and authority over others. Whereas reputation can be quite established and recognized in smaller communities, current market societies are so much bigger and, in a sense, anonymous. To signal their superiority to others, people make use of expensive status symbols (such as fancy suits, cars and houses) to signal and even flaunt their wealth. Eventually, wealth begins to be seen as a signal of esteem in its own right:

> The possession of wealth, which was at the outset valued simply as an evidence of efficiency, becomes, in popular apprehension, itself a meritorious act. Wealth is now itself intrinsically honorable and confers honor on its possessor. (Veblen 1899/2009, p.37)

Wealth begins as a signal that someone is worthy of esteem because they are powerful, but over time transforms into being admired for its own sake.

This leads to the development of what Veblen calls "pecuniary emulation", in which people are motivated by a "desire to excel in pecuniary standing and so gain the esteem and envy of one's fellowman" (Veblen 1899/2009, p.39). People attempt to equal, or surpass, the wealth of others in order to be deemed worthy of honour, admiration, or envy. Of course, to actually receive the esteem of others, it is not enough for people to simply possess more wealth than others, they must also display it. As Veblen explains, "The wealth or power must be put in evidence, for esteem is awarded only on evidence" (Veblen 1899/2009, p.42) This, according to Veblen (1899 [1953], chapter 3), explains why people engage in what he calls "conspicuous consumption"—another of his innovations (Veblen 1899/2009, chapter 3). They want to show others how wealthy they are and so provide evidence that they are fitting targets of esteem and envy. Because wealth is likely to become an important source of esteem and status in capitalist market societies, there is reason to worry that our tendency to admire the rich will be particularly prevalent in such societies.

To make matters worse, the promise of equality in capitalist market societies encourages a form of admiration for the rich that is likely to provoke a desire to emulate. As we have seen, both philosophical analysis and empirical psychological investigations into the nature of admiration suggest that there is a link between admiring someone and desiring to emulate them. However, a detailed examination of this work shows that this is subject to important restrictions. Zagzebski restricts the connection to admiration for "acquired human excellences" which can be imitated and does not think that it holds for "natural talents", which cannot (Zagzebski 2017, p.43).

Admiration, then, is only likely to provoke a desire to emulate when emulation is possible (Zagzebski 2015, p.254). Similarly, drawing on a review of the empirical literature on admiration, Onu et al. claim that a likely moderator of the connection between admiration and emulation is, "the feasibility of imitation" (Onu, Kessler, and Smith 2016, p.228). Admiration, then, seems much more likely to lead to a desire to emulate if the admirer believes that emulation is feasible.

Combining this insight into the nature of admiration with the promised equality of market societies enables us to see why such societies are especially likely to encourage a desire to emulate the rich. Market societies are supposed to be free of the rigid hierarchies of previous forms of society. The promise of social mobility says that even the poor can become rich if they are sufficiently talented and hard-working, which would not have been possible in feudal societies. The promise of social mobility, then, encourages the form of admiration that is linked to a desire to emulate. This means that people's admiration for the rich will be especially likely to make themselves worse off by spending their lives in a struggle for wealth that is unlikely to be successful and that would be unlikely to improve their well-being even if it were successful. While admiration for the rich may be a problem in other kinds of societies as well, there is good reason to think that this will be especially problematic in capitalist market societies.

Like Smith, Veblen thought that the rich become objects of admiration and that one of the primary motives to become rich was to secure the admiration of others. However, Veblen provides a wider account of the emotional reactions that people may be seeking to provoke through their wealth, as the rich seek not just the admiration of others but also their envy. To understand the role that envy may play in the moral psychology of market societies, we will first explain how we understand the nature of envy.

Like admiration, envy is an emotion that involves a judgement of positive value. Feeling envy for another person involves viewing that person as having something, or being someone, of value. Envy, though, more clearly involves a comparative judgement than admiration, as envy involves the judgement that someone has something the envier lacks but wants (Ben-Ze'ev 2000, p.282; Morgan-Knapp 2014; Protasi 2016, p.536). Envy is also an unpleasant emotion to experience, while admiration is a pleasant emotion (Protasi 2019, p.50). The unpleasantness of envy is emphasized in Aristotle's

(*Rhetoric*, Bk II, Chapter 10) definition of envy as, "pain at the good fortune of others," and also Kant's (*Metaphysics of Morals* 6:459) claim that envy is, "a propensity to view the well-being of others with distress". Envy also involves a counterfactual comparison. As Aristotle (*Rhetoric* 1388a) claims, "we envy those who are near us in time, place, age, or reputation." Similarly, Ben-Ze'ev claims that, "in envy, our attention is focused on those perceived to be immediately above us," while Elster claims that envy involves the thought that "it could have been me" (Ben-Ze'ev 1992, p.556; Elster 1999, p.70).

This connection is supported by empirical studies conducted by Niels van de Ven and Marcel Zeelenberg in which participants recalled an autobiographical episode in which someone did better than them at something they (the participant) found important for themselves (van de Ven and Zeelenberg 2015). Participants were then asked to rate the extent to which they felt that it could have been they who had obtained the achievement and the extent to which they felt envious of the person who had in fact obtained it. The more participants thought that they could have been the ones to gain the achievement, the more likely they were to feel envy.

In a complementary study, participants were prompted to imagine a scenario designed to elicit envy. A control group was given one version of the scenario while another group was given a version manipulated to alter how close the participants felt to the desired outcome. Again, those who felt closest to the counterfactual scenario felt the most envy. Moreover, those in the group with the manipulated scenario were more likely to engage in counterfactual thinking and experienced stronger feelings of envy. The authors concluded that "the counterfactual thought 'it could have been me' is clearly associated with the experience of envy" (van de Ven and Zeelenberg 2015, p.966).

To fully understand the nature of envy, it is important also to distinguish between two different kinds of envy.[18] Aristotle distinguished *phthonos*, an emotion directed at the good fortune of others, "not with the idea of getting something for ourselves, but because other people have it" and *zêlos*, which "*is felt* not because others have these goods, but because we have not got them ourselves" (*Rhetoric* 1387b). Following roughly this distinction, psychologists commonly distinguish between *benign envy*, which involves a desire to improve one's own position, and *malicious envy*, which involves

[18] Protasi (2016) distinguishes between four kinds of envy that she calls: emulative, inert, spiteful, and aggressive. For our purposes, it is sufficient to make the distinction between benign and malicious envy.

a desire to bring the envied person down to the same position as the envier (van de Ven 2016).[19] This distinction can be found in several languages including Dutch, Thai, Polish, and Arabic (Protasi 2016, p.536).

There are important differences between these two forms of envy. First, they have important different motivational profiles. Benign envy motivates self-improvement and malicious envy motivates people to damage the position of the envied person (van de Ven, Zeelenberg, and Pieters 2009). Secondly, they appear to have different eliciting conditions. The two most important differences here concern deservingness and perceived control (van de Ven 2016, p.340). When the envier judges the success of the envied person to be deserved, they are more likely to experience benign envy and, conversely, if the envied person's success is judged to be undeserved then it is more likely that the envy will be malicious (van de Ven, Zeelenberg, and Pieters 2012). Similarly, when enviers feel that they had some control over their situation, meaning that they too could achieve the envied person's success, they are more likely to feel benign envy towards the envied person. Conversely, when enviers judge themselves to have less control over obtaining the desired outcome, they are more likely to experience malicious envy (van de Ven, Zeelenberg, and Pieters 2012).

We can now explain why envy of the rich and the connected desire to emulate them are likely to be especially problematic in capitalist forms of market society. First, the promise of equality in such societies promotes the kind of counterfactual thinking associated with envy. Envy involves a counterfactual comparison in which the envier judges that they could have been the one in the position of the envied person. The equality promised by capitalist societies encourages people to believe that they too could be in the position of the rich, if they only work hard enough. The dual promise of such societies is the truth of meritocracy and, hence, merit-based social mobility. These are societies of "aspiration". As such, capitalist market societies encourage people to make the kind of counterfactual judgement that is involved in experiencing envy. In contrast, a society in which people did not believe in the possibility of social mobility would be one in which this kind of counterfactual judgement would be much less likely. Much more about the world would need to change for a poor person to become rich in a feudal society than in a market society. We should, then, expect envy of the rich to be more

[19] Rawls (1971, p.532) also distinguishes between "emulative envy" (close to benign envy) and "envy proper" (close to malicious envy).

prevalent in capitalist market societies than in societies that do not promise social mobility.

Secondly, the promise of social mobility in capitalist market societies encourages people to believe that getting into the position of the admired person is achievable through a combination of talent and hard work. This encourages the belief that the rich deserve their wealth, as it was achieved through talent and hard work. Given that benign envy is more likely to be elicited when the envier judges first that they have some control over their situation and second that the envied person is judged to be deserving of their success, the promise of social mobility encourages benign rather than malicious envy towards the rich. This is important, as benign envy is more likely to lead to a desire to emulate. Much as Smith anticipated, the envy for the rich that occurs in capitalist market societies is likely to promote the desire to emulate the rich.

11.6 Admiration, Emulation, and Envy in Capitalist Market Societies

Having examined Smith and Veblen's arguments about the role that admiration and envy play in bringing about a desire to emulate the rich and argued that the promises of capitalist market societies mean that this desire is likely to be especially strong in these societies, we can now connect this to the concept of an emotional regime. We will argue that envy and admiration are not merely incidental features of market societies, rather they form key components of their emotional regimes.

Our starting point is that emotions of envy and admiration towards the rich tend to be endorsed and indeed promoted as legitimate emotional experiences in market societies. A key means through which these emotions are encouraged is through media representations of the rich, which encourage people to emulate the wealthy. As Diana Kendall explains in her book *Framing Class: Media Representations of Wealth and Poverty in America*, an important means by which the media promote desires to emulate the rich is by encouraging people to identify with them:

> In a mass-mediated culture such as ours, the media do not simply mirror society; rather, they help to shape it and to create cultural perceptions. . . . Television shows, magazines, and newspapers sell the idea that the only way

> to get ahead is to identify with the rich and powerful and to live vicariously through them.... Constantly bombarded by stories about the lifestyles of the rich and famous, viewers feel a sense of intimacy with elites, with whom they have little or no contact in their daily lives. (Kendall 2011, p.211)

Kendall explains various ways in which the framing of class in the media encourages this desire to emulate. First, consensus framing encourages people to see the wealthy as like everyone else by downplaying or obscuring differences in wealth between different social classes (Kendall 2011, pp.29–34). Secondly, admiration framing shows the rich as morally virtuous people who are willing to help those less fortunate than themselves (Kendall 2011, pp.34–9). Thirdly, emulation framing focuses on the achievable nature of the wealthy's achievements by emphasizing their humble origins and encourages others to aspire to the same (Kendall 2011, pp.39–42). Finally, price tag framing focuses on the cost of the items bought by the wealthy (Kendall 2011, pp.42–9) This encourages a view, "according to which a person's worth is measured by what he or she owns" (Kendall 2011, p.212).

All four ways of presenting wealth encourage people to view the pursuit of wealth as valuable and worthwhile. Kendall's work builds on earlier arguments by bell hooks, who argued that television has had a special role to play in fostering a sympathetic attitude towards the rich and encouraging people to emulate them. It does so by reinforcing the message that capitalist market societies promise both equality and social mobility. Because everyone has an equal right to purchase anything, the poor can hope to become rich themselves and purchase the same consumer goods enjoyed by the rich (hooks 2000, p.71). Television also encourages people to admire the rich by presenting them as heroic and through fostering a sense of identity with the rich, even amongst those from radically different class backgrounds (hooks 2000, p.73).

For hooks, the ideology of consumerism is key to this sense of identity, as the rich are depicted as being, "like everyone else in that they live to consume" (hooks 2000, p.72). Support for hooks's claims about the effects of television can be found from an extensive study of over 300 American children into the effects of television viewing on consumerist attitudes and mental health (Schor 2004). Children who spent more time watching television were found to be more involved in consumer culture, meaning that they were less content with what they had, were more oriented towards possessions and money and cared more deeply about brands and products (Schor 2004, chapter 8).

Media framing of wealth creates, maintains, and reinforces the desire to emulate the rich. This does not mean however, that media companies deliberately conspire to create this desire. As Gregory Mantsios points out, the way in which the media frame the wealthy is a straightforward expression of the ideological outlook of those who run the media and entertainment industry:

> Those who own and direct the mass media are themselves part of the upper class, and neither they nor the ruling class in general have to conspire to manipulate public opinion. Their interest is in preserving the status quo, and their view of society as fair and equitable comes naturally to them. (Mantsios 2000, pp.95–6)

The presentation of the rich as worthy of emulation may simply reflect the class outlook of those who work in the media industry and take decisions about its content.

This research suggests that the envy and admiration that is felt towards the rich is not simply the result—as Smith claimed—of a natural tendency. While such a natural tendency may exist, these emotional reactions are likely to be particularly strong in capitalist market societies because of their legitimating ideology. The ideologies of consumerism and meritocracy encourage people to value material possessions and to envy and admire those who acquire and possess more than them. This encourages people to try to emulate those who have more than them and so to spend their lives labouring hard to achieve material possessions that do little to increase their well-being.

11.7 Ought We to Disregard Envy and Admiration for the Rich?

We have argued that envy and admiration for the rich are a core part of the emotional regime of market societies. Furthermore, these emotions encourage a desire to emulate the rich that has a predictably negative impact on well-being. That desire is culturally reinforced. However, this does not tell us how we should respond to this situation. In fact, it is common for egalitarian concerns to be dismissed as being motivated by envy. For example,

Margaret Thatcher, the former Prime Minister of the United Kingdom and Conservative Party leader, dismissed egalitarianism as "the politics of envy, the incitement of people to regard all success as if it were something discreditable" (Thatcher 1974). This critique is not only found in the rhetoric of politicians. Several philosophers and economists also dismiss egalitarian concerns for this reason.

For example, Hayek claims: "When we inquire into the justification of these demands [for equality], we find that they rest on the discontent that the success of some people often produces in those that are less successful, or to put it bluntly, on envy" (Hayek 1960, p.93).[20] Similarly, Anne Hendershott describes egalitarian proposals to redistribute wealth and reorganize the economy as "the ultimate act of envious revenge" (Hendershott 2020, ch.6). Underlying this and similar dismissals of egalitarianism is the thought that people's envy for the rich is not relevant for political theorizing. We will now consider and respond to the most developed version of this argument presented by Christopher Morgan-Knapp.

Morgan-Knapp argues that envy for the rich is irrational (Morgan-Knapp 2014). Given this we might think that we should not pay it much attention in our political theorizing. The starting point of this argument is the following characterization of envy:

> Envy's characteristic presentation is of the subject lacking some good that her rival possesses, of this difference between them being bad for the subject, of this difference reflecting poorly on the subject's worth, and of the difference being underserved. (Morgan-Knapp 2014, p.118)

Morgan-Knapp then argues that no distribution of material possessions can possibly satisfy all these features. Differences in material possessions between two people can be bad for the person who has less but only when it involves their access to positional and positionally distributed goods (Morgan-Knapp 2014, pp.120–1). It is only in the case of these goods that someone possessing more than another will prevent the other from acquiring something or diminish the value of what the other possesses.

[20] See (Nozick 1974, chapter 8) In an earlier work one of the present authors discussed Harvard economist Martin Feldstein's view that only a "spiteful egalitarian" would reject Pareto improvements in a distribution (Feldstein 2005; Thomas 2017, p.38).

However, Morgan-Knapp argues that this difference cannot fulfil the remaining two criteria. When someone else's possession of a good is undeserved it does not reflect poorly on the worth of the envier. On the other hand, when the difference does reflect poorly on the subject's worth this is because the difference is deserved in some way. This means that these two criteria cannot be met simultaneously. This means that economic envy will always be misrepresenting the situation and so is never a fitting response to differences in material possessions. The envy people feel towards the rich should not influence our political theorizing, then, as this emotion is not fitting and misrepresents the situation.

However, there is good reason to think that economic envy can be excusable and that excusable economic envy is relevant for political theorizing (Bankovsky 2018). Miriam Bankovsky defends this position by drawing on Rawls's distinction between particular and general envy (Bankovsky 2018, p.63; Rawls 1971/1999, p.531). Particular envy is directed at someone for a particular object or status that the other possesses. For example, envying another because the other has a place in an elite sports team that the envier was hoping would be theirs (Bankovsky 2018, p.263). General envy, on the other hand, involves a comparison between, "the *general situation* and *kinds of goods* that are enjoyed by two different *groups*" (Bankovsky 2018, p.263, emphasis in original). A cricketer from a poor school that lacks the advanced cricket facilities possessed by a wealthier school may feel this kind of envy when someone from the wealthy school gets a place in an elite team ahead of him. Here the envy is not directed at the player but at the competitive advantage that the members of the group of privileged cricketers have over him.

In such cases, the envied person may not deserve their success and yet that success still reflects badly on the worth of the envier (Bankovsky 2018). The poorer cricketer's failure is deserved in the sense that he is a weaker cricketer than the richer cricketer, but underserved in the sense that an unjust social structure is largely responsible for his comparative weakness. Bankovsky describes this as a situation where, "Personal desert is combined ambivalently with undeserved social injustice, and the blow to self-esteem is entangled with the sense that it is *undeserved*" (Bankovsky 2018, p.264). This means that an envier could meet all Morgan-Knapp's criteria for envy without misrepresenting the situation.

It might be objected that it would not be rational for the poorer cricketer to base his self-esteem on cricketing success, if he knows that the social structure is set up such that he is likely to fail to make elite teams. However, as

Bankovsky rightly points out, this response would ignore the fact that the process of establishing what one takes as the basis of their self-esteem is not wholly under their control but rather is, "an intersubjective and recognitive process" (Bankovsky 2018, p.266). As Rawls made clear, our bases of self-esteem are informed by the social world we are a part of. If achieving success in cricket is especially valued in the cricketer's social world, then it makes sense for him to make this a basis of his self-esteem.[21]

Applying this consideration back to the issue of economic envy shows why envy makes sense in the context of capitalist societies. Because the social world involves an emotional regime that encourages envy and admiration for the rich, it makes sense that people will blamelessly see a failure to achieve wealth as reflecting badly on their self-esteem. Those who dismiss people's envy for the rich as irrelevant for political theorizing are ignoring the emotional regime that promotes and encourages this envy and the fact that this emotional regime is a legitimate target of political criticism.

Importantly, the role of envy in the emotional regime of capitalism shows that supporters of capitalist societies are themselves endorsing a politics of envy, as they are endorsing a political and economic system in which the promotion of envy for the rich is integral to its stability and continued existence. As such, they are in no position to criticize and dismiss egalitarians for endorsing a "politics of envy", as envy also has a key role to play in the very system and legitimating discourse that they promote.

It might be objected that there is an important difference between the envy for the rich that egalitarians are accused of and the kind of envy for the rich promoted under capitalism. As we discussed, there is a difference between benign envy, which aims at improving the position of the envier, and malicious envy, which aims at bringing the envied person down to the same level as the envier. The envy for the rich that features in the emotional regime of capitalism arguably involves a desire to become more like the person being envied. It is not a desire to bring the envied person down to the same position as the envier. Those wishing to defend capitalism then, may point out that the benign form of envy for the rich that features in capitalism's emotional regime is not the same as the destructive form of malicious envy that they claim is motivating egalitarians.

[21] Another way to respond is to argue that egalitarians are motivated by resentment rather than envy and so are not vulnerable to the criticisms made of the envious (Young 1987).

This distinction matters because benign envy is argued to be a morally permissible and perhaps even virtuous emotion, while malicious envy is generally viewed as a morally bad emotion (Protasi 2016, 2021, chapter 3). Sara Protasi, for example, argues that those who experience certain forms of benign envy provide a model for how to engage in fair competition with others and will be motivated to improve both themselves and others (Protasi 2021, p.80). Malicious envy, though, is "radically vicious", as it is bad both for the envier and for others (Protasi 2021, p.93). The envy endorsed by defenders of capitalism, then, is less morally objectionable (and may even be morally desirable) than the envy they claim motivates egalitarians.

One reply here is that, however plausible it may be, it still involves conceding that those who endorse free market capitalism are also engaging in the politics of envy. This seems to take away much of the force from the criticism of egalitarians. "You are engaging in the politics of envy" on closer inspection is revealed to include the caveat "and so are we but in a different way", undermining some of the strength of the conservative's dismissal of egalitarianism. The more important point, though, is that this reveals the true nature of the criticism, namely that egalitarians feel the wrong kind of envy towards the rich. Instead of feeling malicious envy, they should be feeling benign envy towards the rich. Putting the criticism in these terms reveals that it is functioning to enforce capitalism's emotional regime. This emotional regime mandates that the rich should be admired, envied benignly, and emulated. The concerns of egalitarian critics are dismissed precisely because they do not comply with these feeling rules.

The significance of this point becomes clear when we consider the different eliciting conditions of benign and malicious envy. Several psychological studies have found that malicious envy is more likely to occur than benign envy when the envier judges that the envied person's success is undeserved (Lange and Crusius 2015; Lange, Crusius, and Hagemeyer 2016; van de Ven 2016; van de Ven, Zeelenberg, and Pieters 2012).[22] This suggests a connection between the thesis that benign envy is key to capitalism and the controversial thesis that market entitlements are deserved. Egalitarians are likely to view the wealth of the rich as undeserved and may, as a result, feel malicious envy. Dismissing these concerns as a politics of envy is simply a convenient way to avoid engaging with the claim that this wealth is undeserved.

[22] However, other studies did not find this (Lange and Crusius 2015; Lange, Crusius, and Hagemeyer 2016). For further discussion, see (Protasi 2021, pp.36–7).

The conservative dismissal of malicious envy is a way of changing the subject from whether the rich deserve the wealth to the emotional states of those claiming they do not.

We noted in chapter 2 how Dean Baker remarks that the average worker finds it hard to see the connection between curtailing very high incomes and a generalized benefit for the incomes of all. Such a person may, indeed, view this proposal as "vindictive" (Baker 2016, p.20). Defenders of inequality, of course, want most citizens to frame this issue as the vindictive punishment of society's "winners". We think that Alison Jaggar's concept of "outlaw emotions" can help us understand the nature of this move (Jaggar 1989).

Outlaw emotions are those that contravene a society's emotional rules (Jaggar 1989, p.166). For example, in a society that demands gratitude from welfare recipients some people may instead feel resentment when they receive their welfare payment. In the same way, feelings of malicious envy towards the rich can be viewed as an outlaw emotion that is prohibited by the emotional regime underpinning capitalist societies in which admiration and benign envy towards the rich are mandated. Outlaw emotions are more likely to be experienced by those in subordinate positions who do not benefit from the existing social structures. While they are often confusing and disorienting, Jaggar argues that these emotions can also be epistemically valuable, as they enable and motivate new ways of seeing the world (Jaggar 1989, p.167).

The clash between the resentment felt by the welfare recipient and the gratitude they are supposed to feel can be the first step towards taking a critical stance to the dominant values present in society and to a welfare system that stigmatizes recipients. Similarly, the clash between feeling malicious envy towards the rich and the socially prescribed feelings of admiration and benign envy can prompt an investigation into the causes of economic inequality and capitalist exploitation.[23] This does not mean that we should always encourage such feelings or accept them uncritically. Rather, we should attend to outlaw emotions carefully and seriously instead of dismissing, suppressing, or condemning them from the start (Jaggar 1989, p.169).

Attending to the outlaw emotion of malicious envy encourages us to question the extent to which the rich really are deserving of our admiration and benign envy. The rags to riches entrepreneur who achieves wealth through

[23] Compare this claim to the claim that envy for the rich can play a useful role in triggering reflection on one's social situation and so help raise awareness of injustice (Frye 2016, pp.522–3).

the exercise of qualities of character such as ingenuity and hard work and determination may be worthy of admiration and benign envy. However, in other cases, admiring the rich as wealth creators, risk takers, and suppliers of enterprise to the productive process is simply mistaken, as it misrepresents the way in which contemporary political institutions favour not the heroic figure of the entrepreneur, but rather the "insider" figure of the rent seeker. As addressed at length in previous chapters, the many mechanisms that cause undeserved wealth concentration at the top and growing economic inequalities can be summarized as a form of "rentier capitalism" (Christophers 2020), which is marked by a hugely "unfair distribution of the benefits and costs of economic production" (Scanlon 2018, p.152) The rent seeking that many of the rich are engaged in turns economic competition from win-win, to win-lose, as the rent seeker gains at the expense of her fellow citizens via her insider status in economic (and other) institutions.

While many wealthy people in capitalist societies have strong work ethics, this does not justify the gaps between what they and others earn. Many people, rich and poor alike, work very long hours: the differentiating factor is not the effort they put in but the structure of our economic institutions that sees, for example, American CEOs paid more than their median worker by a factor of 1,000 (Leder 2021). The idea that the wealthy are worthy targets of admiration and benign envy and that the rest should therefore try to emulate them assumes a highly idealized—and indeed mostly fictional—view of wealth accumulation that mistakes insider rent seekers on corporate boards for heroic entrepreneurs. While benign envy for the rich may be unobjectionable in those cases where it is fitting, we are sceptical that this applies for most of the rich in our own highly unequal capitalist societies. We saw, in chapter 9, the importance of an heroic framing of the market as akin to a field of battle—a place of shame and honour. That explains the prominence of cultural tropes such as the heroic entrepreneur, which some astute captains of industry seek to cultivate. However, that does not mean that we ought to take this self-description at face value. As we have noted at several points in this narrative, those actually subjected to high levels of risk in our societies are the poor, not the rich—not that they have any say in the matter.

When the personal qualities of the rich are not admirable qualities such as strategic foresight and determination, but rather the capacity to exploit rent-extracting niches, then malicious envy might well be an appropriate response. If the superior status of the rich has been derived from opportunity hoarding and the unfair exploitation of prior advantage, such that they enjoy goods that you would have received under an alternative and fair institutional set-up, then an attitude of malicious envy is appropriate. If restitution or redress is unavailable, we see no objection to seeing the unfair gains of the rent seeker confiscated even if they cannot be redistributed. The malicious envy we feel towards the rent seekers enables us to view levelling down as a justifiable option in this case.

Does this mean that egalitarians ought to always express their malicious envy and perhaps even promote it in others? Not necessarily. As Amia Srinivasan has argued, victims of oppression often find themselves in situations where they must choose between a fitting emotional response to injustice and the emotional response that best advances their cause (Srinivasan 2018).[24] Malicious envy may well be a fitting but counterproductive response to the rent-seeking rich that is unlikely to advance the egalitarian cause.

That said, one can also argue the egalitarian cause would indeed be advanced by promoting malicious envy. According to contemporary neo-Machiavellians, our politics needs to be less civil, more agonistic, and more open to the channelling of emotions such as envy, rancour, outrage, and anger against socio-economic elites (Green 2016; McCormick 2011). A conception of political civility that dismisses such outlaw emotions can be interpreted as obstructing the needed development of fairer political and economic institutions. Outlaw emotions such as malicious envy can trigger scepticism as to whether the wealthy deserve their status as role models, innovators, and cultural legislators. The policing of emotions that occurs when benign envy is legitimized and promoted and malicious envy is dismissed is clearly not a neutral activity. Discrediting or banishing envy, animosity, and rancour from politics serves to reinforce an unfair institutional structure that systematically advantages those who can extract rents (insiders) at the cost of those are unable to do so (outsiders).

Conclusion

In summary, we have examined Smith's account of the ways in which inequality in market societies influences people's emotional lives and the damaging impact that this has on their well-being. We began by looking at Smith's claim that to be free from poverty one must possess sufficient resources to

[24] For further discussion, see (Archer and Mills 2019).

acquire the goods that are needed to appear in public without shame. We argued that there is good reason to include such a standard in our understanding of poverty, given the damaging impact that the shame of poverty has on well-being. This shame, though, is not simply an unfortunate by-product of capitalist societies but rather is a key part of the emotional regime of such societies.

While those in poverty experience shame as a result, the rich receive admiration and envy from others. We have examined the explanations given by Smith and Veblen and explored how these emotional responses give rise to a desire to emulate the rich. We then explored the various ways in which capitalist societies promote this desire: through identifying wealth as a source of esteem and through promoting the promises of equality and social mobility. Again, envy and admiration for the wealthy are not merely incidental features of market societies but rather key components of the emotional regimes of such societies supported by the ideologies of meritocracy and consumerism which are promoted heavily in the media.

We concluded this chapter by responding to those who argue that economic envy does not have a legitimate role to play in political theorizing. We have argued that inducing envy for the rich plays a key role in the emotional regime underpinning and stabilizing capitalist societies. Given that the promotion of envy for the rich is integral to the stability of the capitalist societies, those who endorse capitalism are in no position to criticize egalitarians for endorsing a "politics of envy". Against critics of egalitarianism, who argue that we should feel benign, not malicious, envy towards the rich, we have argued that this reveals the true nature of this criticism of egalitarians: it serves to enforce the emotional regime underpinning capitalist society by dismissing the concerns of those who violate its feeling rules. Malicious envy for the rich, then, is aptly understood as an outlaw emotion in capitalist societies. Given the potential for outlaw emotions to motivate new investigations and enable new ways of perceiving the world, we should attend carefully to such feelings rather than dismissing them. Like anger and outrage, malicious envy can trigger critical investigations into how capitalist institutions unfairly favour rent seekers and the extent to which the rich really are really deserving of our admiration.

One challenge remains to our discussion of admiration and envy for the rich in market societies. Earlier in the book, we argued that market societies promise a society in which social mobility is possible and where people will be rewarded for their talents. However, the reality of such societies is quite different as the ability of the rich to gain first mover advantage in the competition for positional goods and their willingness to engage in opportunity hoarding means the promised social mobility never arrives. Although market societies promise to deliver a situation in which rewards are distributed according to merit, they do not deliver on this promise.

Given this situation, it seems odd that people continue to feel admiration and benign envy towards the rich. As we have already seen, benign envy tends to be elicited when the envier judges that they are capable of achieving what the envied person has achieved and where they judge the envied person deserving of her success. Similarly, a study by Onu et al. suggests that group-based admiration is elicited by groups of higher status only when their high position in a status hierarchy is judged to be deserved (Onu, Smith, and Kessler 2015).[25] This suggests an instability in the emotional regime of capitalist market societies. People are encouraged to feel admiration and benign envy for the rich. However, these emotions involve a judgement that they deserve their success and the reality of market societies provides little basis for this judgement. There is a danger that when people realize the true nature of the system that they will no longer feel this admiration and benign envy. In the next chapter, we analyse the role played by the ideology of meritocracy in ensuring that the emotional regime of market societies prevents people from coming to the conclusion that the game has been rigged all along.

[25] For similar results, see also (Sweetman et al. 2013; van de Ven, Zeelenberg, and Pieters 2011).

12

The False Promise of Meritocracy and Its Emotional Regime

Propositional Summary

1. Meritocracy is governance by the few: an oligarchy, but selected on the basis of merit and not wealth. The social meaning of the value of employment has changed such that we think that jobs ought to facilitate "careers open to talents". We trace the evolution of the concept of meritocracy, via the works of proponents such as Daniel Bell and critics such as Michael Young, before identifying a plausible meritocratic claim that the desert base for allocating socially valuable roles ought to be personal merits.
2. The strongest objections to meritocracy come from the Right: Nozick's procedural theory of justice concerns entitlements, not desert, and their role is to respect rights with no adjustment of the market system to meet an external goal (such as rewarding merit). Similarly, Hayek argues that it is a misunderstanding of a market to think that price information can incorporate individual labour burdens. There is, then, no coherent way in which a market can be adjusted to individual merits.
3. Amartya Sen argues that the idea of production as an output from several divisible components commits a fallacy of decomposition: at the level of theory, we might seek to identify a marginal contribution made by a factor. In practice, outputs are the product of all factors of production operating together. The identification of an individual's marginal productive contribution is a chimera. The relevant counterfactual judgements are not available. We consider Iris Marion Young's complementary argument that, given the inscrutability of these judgements, they will be wholly based on comparative power. We further consider the extensive evidence that outcomes attributed to merit are better explained as substantially determined by luck.

Extravagance and Misery. Alan Thomas, Alfred Archer, and Bart Engelen, Oxford University Press.
 DOI: 10.1093/oso/9780197781722.003.0013

4. The winners in a meritocracy, even if the ideal were feasible, have strong affective motivations generationally to transmit their own advantages to their children. Sociological evidence suggests that this takes the form of restructuring the field of opportunities so that those advantaged under current arrangements rig the outcome for the next generation. This destabilizes the very conditions of their own (putative) merit-based success. We consider examples from education.
5. Those who have benefitted from the New Inequality of the last forty years cannot give a plausible differential explanation of why merit plays the role that does in justifying extensive levels of inequality in the United States given that winner takes all markets, globalization, and skills-biased technological change are trans-national phenomena. We focus, in particular, on US executive remuneration.
6. We compare several explanations of the puzzle that the more unequal a society the less its citizens seem concerned about inequality. Furthermore, extensive inequality sees increased, not decreased, belief in the ideology of meritocracy even though it seems a "hard sell" to those who lose out. We consider the explanation that many citizens are actually ignorant of the extent of inequality. We canvas the explanation that meritocracy is endorsed not only by its self-certified winners but also by its losers as reflecting belief in a fundamentally just world.
7. The meritocratic myth plays an important role in the ideology of capitalism by mandating certain positive affective responses towards the wealthy and the poor alike. We consider the important role of the mass media in framing these responses to both classes of people.
8. The putatively meritocratic justification for inequality would, if true, constitute a form of social Darwinism. Unfortunately, for that version of the view to be true the sorting process and the outcome would need to be independent. Wilkinson and Pickett have demonstrated that they are not. Such justifications have a damaging effect on the well-being on the worst off who are mandated to feel shame at occupying their merited place in the social order.
9. The emotional reactions mandated by a meritocratic justification of inequality constitute a form of affective injustice. The legitimate anger of the poor is directed back against them: they are told, instead to feel ashamed.

Introduction

In his magisterial history of inequality regimes, Thomas Piketty isolates a specific aspect of the legitimation narrative of our current system: it "celebrates winners and denigrates losers more aggressively than any earlier regime" (Piketty 2020, p.172). This aspect of our societies that has also come in for relentless criticism in recent philosophical work on meritocracy (Frank 2016; Littler 2017; Markovits 2019; Piketty 2014, 2020; Putnam 2016; Sandel 2020; Scanlon 2018). In this chapter we offer our own interpretation of the resilience of this meritocratic narrative: it is resilient because of its centrality to the emotional logic of capitalist societies and its key role in ensuring their stability. Drawing on the work of Jonathan Mijs, we will show that the strongly ingrained meritocratic narrative has this unique property: not only would we continue to believe if it were false but also it is more widely believed the more obviously false it is (Mijs 2021).[1]

Our aim is to offer a distinct perspective to this substantial literature that criticizes meritocracy by examining the role that meritocracy plays in the emotional regime of capitalist societies. Societies that are believed to be meritocracies are no longer committed to a belief in natural hierarchies, although a residuum of that belief persists in the claim that achievement has a "bedrock" in natural talent (perhaps genetically determined). Hierarchies are, then, not "natural" but the product of social processes of differentiation. The meritocrat justifies those processes by adjusting differentiation to individual merit.

According to this view, wealth is evidence of personal distinction: evidence for the successful exercise of market-relevant virtues. Poverty is evidence of the opposite; evidence of personal failure and something of which a person ought to be ashamed. The latter makes sense if people were, indeed, given equal opportunity to access the market and the economic losers failed to cultivate their market-relevant virtues or to work hard enough. Those

[1] This is our interpretation of Mijs's data, not his claim. He restricts himself to the facts that in highly unequal societies there is more widespread belief in meritocracy. We add the supplementary assumption that meritocrats must believe that their own society is approximately fair so the degree of inequality ought to be relatively constrained in the way Smith originally envisaged. (This was, recall, Deborah Boucoyannis's reconstruction of a Smithian view that we discussed in chapter 6 (Boucoyannis 2013).) The meritocrat, confronted by the New Inequality, is in the odd position of having to reconcile the proper working of the sorting mechanism with highly unequal results that ought not, by her own lights, to be its appropriate outcome.

judgements are comparative: this is a competitive context where people are "pitted against each other".[2]

There are vestiges, here, of the Smithian ideal discussed in chapter 6 and it is why those committed to this ideal might take issue with our explanation of the source of inequality in this book. The first, deep, source of agreement is that we have endorsed Smith's own critique of the rent seeker. However, the recent Smithian trying to explain the New Inequality may claim that it is an empirical question how much inequality is explained in this way. He or she may further argue that we have not paid sufficient attention to how much inequality arises from the exceptional productive contributions of the most hard-working, efficient, well-trained, or intelligent workers in the economy. Much recent inequality in the United States is, after all, technically to be classified as income from labour (Baker 2016). We are talking about the recent past, and for this critic, Piketty's long-run data about the tendency of returns to capital to outstrip returns to labour is not the best explanation of the relatively short run of thirty years of data in the United States (as we discussed in chapters 1 and 2).

The best explanation, our putative critic continues, is that globalization, the free movement of capital and labour, and the development of technology has empowered the most productive among us—from a global pool of talent—to receive what are, in fact, merited rewards on the labour market. These markets have, recently, tended towards a "winner takes all" logic where the very best performers in a domain are rewarded far more even than those immediately below them in the distribution.

The meritocrat whose views we evaluate in this chapter says: don't shoot the messenger! Winner takes all markets are, indeed, truth tellers—sometimes cruelly so. Some superstar individuals do make a decisive difference to the bottom line of organizations and so deserve their extra rewards—and not just in elite sports or in the star system of Hollywood. Furthermore, we have just lived through another industrial revolution—the digital revolution—and that has both transformed the fortunes of those

[2] We do not mean to deny that many employees work within firms. Internally to those firms, many people are organized into teams, and work with others on the basis of cooperation and mutual trust. They therefore compete indirectly—they compete with other teams in other firms (also made up of "teams of teams"). However, this relocates the issue to whether or not people are pulling their weight on the team—it is an unusual firm where remuneration is averaged across work teams. Furthermore, teamwork is a feature of better-quality work—Boltanski and Chiapello's "project based" work in which many workers do not engage (Boltanski and Chiapello, 2005). The more fundamental issue is the competition simply to be employed at all.

involved in building these distinctive kinds of capital goods, those putting them to use in various forms of intermediation (some productive, some not), and those professionals smart enough to integrate these new technologies into their own professions (such as finance and medicine).[3]

On this view, inequality is performing its economic function of sending out a market signal to those who need to upgrade their skills to become competitive in a new globalized market dominated by symbolic analysts or knowledge workers who "add value" to the high-end production process. This was the conception of the post-industrial society formulated by sociologist Daniel Bell in his widely influential 1973 book *The Coming of Post-Industrial Society* with the revealing subtitle *A Venture in Social Forecasting* (Bell 1973).

Even so-called progressives in the United States echo this theme when they are, as James Galbraith put it, "stuck on the supply side" with their mantra of "research, infrastructure, and education" (Galbraith 1998, chapter 12). Former presidential candidate Hillary Clinton's tone-deaf observation that economically devastated regions of the United States required better broadband connections—presumably to allow its inhabitants to upgrade their skills to compete with the country's coastal elites—was representative of the aspirational meritocracy of the New Democrats (Clinton 2017, p.272). The New Democrats in the United States and their counterpart in the United Kingdom (New Labour) felt compelled to accept the so-called facts of globalization. Those facts determined where workers in the affluent West could realistically view themselves in a globalized economic order (Cebul 2019).[4]

For this meritocratic critic, we are not giving credit where credit is due, namely to citizens who work hard—in some cases, very hard—against a background context of having educated themselves to have the right skill set. The Smithian ideal sees the wise legislator adjust social outcomes to individual virtues. Prominent amongst those virtues now is what Americans laud as a

[3] Productive intermediation might be the use of technology in the rebirth of "merchant capitalism", where a market intermediary exerts (technologically enhanced) power over both producers and consumers driving down pay and employment standards (Lichtenstein 2012). We have noted Herman Mark Schwartz's general model of a franchise economy, which Big Tech not only represents in a paradigmatic form; its products enable the technological intermediation used by other firms of this type (Schwartz 2021).

[4] However, it is worth keeping in mind that these New Democrat and New Labour policies were, historically, prefigured by the "turns to austerity" taken by socialists. François Mitterrand's "tournant de la rigueur" dated from 1983; James Callaghan's issues dated from the sterling crisis of 1976 and the acceptance by his then-chancellor, Denis Healey, of the terms of a bailout package from the International Monetary Fund, where a \$3.9 billion loan was extended on the basis of a £2.5bn in cuts to public spending.

"work ethic". Veblen emphasized that the rich of his day tried to emulate what they imagined to be aristocratic indolence. The aim was to be so wealthy as to place oneself in the very situation that Hegel thought was the predicament of his "rich rabble": to be cut off from work as a source of freedom and to be limited to corrupting leisure and consumption. For the rich rabble, work was no longer a necessity. For Veblen, that was the very fact that the wealthy sought to publicize as they emulated the lifestyle of the rentier aristocrat.

However, today's wealthy people are the very opposite, they take every opportunity to emphasize how hard they work while also, in their manner and deportment, trying to conceal how wealthy they are. Management professor Morten Hansen cites the following data:

> In a 2009 survey by Harvard Business School professor Leslie Perlow and research associate Jessica Porter, 94 percent of the 1,000 professionals surveyed reported working 50 hours or more a week, and a staggering 50 percent of them said they worked more than 65 hours a week. The latter figure translated into 13 hours per day, five days a week. Ouch! In a study of high earners, management writers Sylvia Ann Hewlett and Carolyn Buck Luce found that a full 35 percent worked more than 60 hours a week, and 10 percent worked more than 80 hours a week. A job with the traditional 40-hour workweek seems like a part-time gig. (Hansen 2018, pp.45–6)

Hansen's goal is to convince us all that this is not the way to be productive—but he does not address the underlying ideological question of why people want to signal to others that they work extremely long hours at the cost of their own health, happiness, and social relationships. (In "high-end" services in the United States, such as law and finance, the hours are even longer than 65 hours a week, particularly in the early career stages.)

We have already noted Goldin's argument that elite jobs are now "greedy" jobs—greedy of an employee's time. We have repeatedly noted the importance of privatized healthcare in creating job locks whereby employers can assume that employees will not leave no matter what time demands are placed on them. In the background are the routine demands of Galbraith's "debt peonage": the paying off of mortgages and other forms of debt, increasingly, now, educational debt. More damagingly, employers organize production on the assumption that the "exemplary employee" is on hand to work evenings, weekends, or in the case of junior employees at investment banks, to work at any time of the day or night (as needed) for an average total of 105 hours of work every week for an extended period (Kimathi 2021). Employees, in this approach, are expected to accommodate employer demands—and not vice versa. With every employee set against each other it is in no one's individual interest to try to change this system, especially not in companies that grade each employee vis-à-vis each other and routinely fire the worst performers—so-called rank and yank systems pioneered by GE executive Jack Welch.

For Adam Smith, life's central value is feeling beloved—this value does not fit comfortably into a busy work schedule with thirteen hours in the office every day. This description resembles far more closely his cautionary tale of the son of the poor man, in *The Theory of Moral Sentiments*, who emulates the wealthy at the expense of his own happiness and well-being. In our societies one primary way to emulate our exemplars of businesspeople, whom we assume are wealthy, successful, and happy, is to imitate their "work ethic". Media representations, once again, depict workplaces as glamorous places where one would want to spend thirteen hours a day—not simply places of personal achievement, but also of meaning, emotional satisfaction, and the location of one's "second family", whose relationships might prove easier to negotiate than those of one's time-and-attention starved actual family.

We have, throughout this book, emphasized our indebtedness to Smith as much as to Rawls: for the former, the effect on character of commercial society tends towards the general good. At the level of individual character, commercial society cultivates self-control, prudence, and a spirit of energetic enterprise compared to the predicament of the feudal serf or the eighteenth-century rural labourer. If we can ameliorate the pathologies of commercial society, the virtues it cultivates in people will be in their interests in the long run. Hegel also thought freedom came through work in the right kind of institutional setting, the corporations, that also supplied the terms of social recognition and hence freedom. In our own societies, the governing ideology of meritocracy praises prudence and frugality, but particularly industry. For meritocrats, inequalities in affluent societies are justified by the merits of those at the top (with the distortion of rent seeking set aside).

This chapter investigates the role of meritocracy in the emotional regime of capitalist societies. We will begin by explaining the rise to prominence of the ideal of meritocracy in the late twentieth century. We will then try to give the ideal a reasonable and defensible interpretation. Having done this, we will argue that this ideal is incoherent, unfeasible, and instable. Moreover, meritocratic discourse deploys false narratives, plays a functional role in supporting social hierarchy and has particularly damaging effects on well-being.

12.1 A Short History of Meritocracy

We will begin our discussion with Hannah Arendt's claim that meritocracy constitutes an "oligarchy" though this oligarchy is "not of wealth or birth, but of talent" (Arendt 1961/2006, pp.176–7). Meritocracy as a principle of governance is a special instance of oligarchic governance—the governance of the many by the few. In a genuine meritocracy, the few, however, have achieved that standing in a free and open competition with positions of advantage open to all. This idea contrasts with the practice, in various cultures and times, of making valuable social offices goods that can themselves be purchased. Jobs are distributed via the labour market, but our understanding of their social meaning is that they are to be distributed according to a person's qualifications and not solely their ability to pay. The latter we now usually regard as a form of corruption.[5]

Meritocracy reserves the right to rule for those who possess the necessary skill set to do so. This holds not just in the political domain but also to a much broader category of offices, or positions of advantage, in economic institutions. These institutions tend to be internally hierarchical, with a pyramidal structure where rewards increase as workers progress through its ranks. In a meritocracy, the rewards of rising in the hierarchy will go to those who deserve them and any difference in economic rewards will reflect differing levels of contribution.

Whether in governance or commerce, these internal hierarchies will be influenced by workers' position in the originating hierarchy—the education system. These multiple, iterated, sets of bottlenecks structure the field of opportunities (Fishkin 2014; Gomberg 2007). As the individual progresses through an education system into the workplace, they find access to hierarchy funnelled through these bottlenecks that thin the number of candidates at every stage. Furthermore, these facts are commonly known, and the understanding of this field of opportunities informs the strategies and rational life

[5] We concede there are borderline cases: if a small grocery store is run by one family and that family wants to create a new job, can that legitimately be a form of gift exchange to another family member? Or must they publicly advertise the post?

plans of citizens, particularly parental planning on behalf of their children and the latter's understanding of the opportunities realistically open to them.

The meritocrat believes that this structure of opportunities can and should be so organized as to ensure that the system "sorts" people according to their merits, where process and product are suitably independent of each other. Those who occupy positions of advantage are the beneficiaries of multiple, bundled, forms of reward: their work does not require close monitoring, is intellectually challenging, carries high social status and is highly remunerated (Gomberg 2007). Those who occupy societies' worst positions are, at least, employed.[6] But work for the worst off will likely involve meaningless work with no intrinsic rewards, which is closely supervised and intellectually stultifying (Gomberg 2007). It not only carries low social status but may even carry stigma. It is poorly remunerated, in some cases to the point where a person can be poor while in work and depend on either supplementary state benefits or private charity to survive. Nevertheless, if the system as a whole sorts people to where they ought to be—then, according to meritocrats, it is functioning properly.

There is a direct connection between these meritocratic ideas and the emotional regime of capitalism that we have been describing. On this view, wealth is a marker of success and desert, and so the rich may reasonably feel pride in their achievements, while the poor should feel ashamed at their comparatively minimal productive contribution. The meritocratic narrative explains and justifies the mutual reinforcement of emotional attitudes and institutional structures. In capitalist market societies, meritocratic narratives play the social role of making poverty shameful and the poor naturally feel compelled to withdraw from social interactions with others. The rich, by contrast, are to be admired while between these two strata are the middle-class experiencing frustration and status anxiety—we have left it open whether those two emotions are also problems for the wealthy.

One would expect, then, to see the ideal of meritocracy widely denounced by those who are not rich. However, it is a staple of conservative rhetoric to the point where, in 2016, then conservative leader Theresa May envisioned the United Kingdom as "the world's great meritocracy" (May 2016). Clearly, only the positive, emancipatory aspect of meritocracy was on her mind when she extolled a vision of the United Kingdom as a place where "everyone has a

[6] We grant this point to the meritocrat for a fair assessment of her view of "working well"; we do not withdraw our claim that involuntary unemployment is a capitalist market society's primary disciplinary device with a particular impact on the worst off.

chance to go as far as their talent and hard work will allow". The sociologist Jo Littler has aptly called meritocracy "one of the prevalent social and cultural tropes of our time" (Littler 2017, p.1). This an ironic inversion of the use the term when it first came into use as part of a socialist critique of inequality.

The term was coined in 1956 by Alan Fox in an article called "Class and Equality" for the UK-based socialist magazine *Socialist Commentary*.[7] Fox's article criticized the assumption that higher occupational status must be linked both to higher education and to higher income (1956, p.13). Fox argued that inequality would persist as long as this assumption remains unchallenged, since "our society [will] be divisible into the blessed and the unblessed—those who get the best and the most of everything and those who get the poorest and the least" (1956, p.13). This would allow those deemed to be meritorious to dominate the lives of the others and secure more than their fair share of society's resources as their reward (Fox 1956, p.13). Fox objects, as does Gomberg, to "bundling": the compounding of interesting work, status, and high remuneration at one end of the job scale and meaningless work, stigma, and low pay at the other.

While Fox led the way, by far the most famous work on meritocracy was published shortly after by the utopian socialist, politician, and social reformer Michael Young. His satirical novel *The Rise of the Meritocracy* was first published in 1958 (Young 1958/1994). Its putative narrator is a fictional character who shares the name "Michael Young" with the book's author and who presents a sociological "study" of the transformation of British society at the close of the twentieth century and leading into the twenty-first. The ironic perspective in this satirical work turned out to be easily misunderstood. The work describes the transformation of Britain from a society in which social position was determined by social class into a society where positions of power and influence were distributed according to the merit principle. According to this principle, merit determined by the combination of intelligence and effort (Young 1958/1994, p.84).

Yet, this study also "documents" a pushback in the year 2034 when a populist movement, combining members of the lower class with a leadership made up of high-status women, has rebelled. The basis of this rebellion is a call for an egalitarian and classless society allowing for the appreciation

[7] While Michael Young is generally credited for having coined the term, David Kynaston noted that the term was used two years previously by Fox (Kynaston 2014, loc 3666). For further discussion see (Littler 2017, pp.32–4).

of a broad range of values. The rebels' manifesto envisages a society in which: "Every human being would then have equal opportunity [...] to develop his own special capacities for leading a rich life" (Young 1958/1994, p.159). This resembles the normative perspective defended fifty years later by both Gomberg and Fishkin which we will discuss in more detail in our concluding chapter 13 (Fishkin 2014; Gomberg 2007).

Young intended his satire to capture what was attractive about meritocracy, but also "how sad and fragile" it could be (Young 1958/1994, p.xvi). In the introduction for the second edition of his book in 1994, he noted with concern that the book's ironies had been lost on many of its readers. who had taken Young to be endorsing meritocracy rather than satirizing it (Young 1958/1994, p.xv). Reflecting later on the flawed reception of his book Young commented that while "it is good sense to appoint individual people to jobs on their merit" this becomes a problem when the meritorious "harden into a social class without room in it for others" (Young 2001). This point was, indeed, lost as Young's popularization of the term coincided with its positive valence as expressing a political ideal to which we ought collectively to aspire.

Philosopher Thomas Mulligan has presented an extended, recent defence of this ideal (Mulligan 2017). It is based on the premise that "people should get what they deserve" (Mulligan 2017, p.8). More concretely, his vision of meritocracy combines an ideal of equality of opportunity with an ethic of personal responsibility (Mulligan 2017, p.4). On this view, it is a realistically utopian project to secure equal opportunities for all to achieve success in life, most importantly when it comes to the outcomes where there are different distributions of power, money, and status. If we can secure that framework, then an ethic of personal responsibility that sees people's different ambitions and choices will lead to responsibility-sensitive outcomes, in which talent and effort are rewarded.

Mulligan does not put his framework to use in explaining the New Inequality, but Harvard economics professor Greg Mankiw has appealed to meritocratic ideology in this context: the reason that the 1% are paid so highly, he avers, is that in a globalized market for labour, these top CEOs are indeed the highest performers—as they claim to be (Mankiw 2013). In this case, the personal merit of these Pikettyan "supermanagers" is their individual productive contribution to the performance of their firm. Multi-national corporations draw on large pools of talent across many countries: to have the "edge" in these internal competitions, or in lateral hiring, the executives concerned must be exceptionally deserving—or so Mankiw argues.

It is certainly true that distributing positions of advantage by merit is preferable to alternative methods of distribution, such as selling such to the highest bidder. Employments under the control of the state have, historically, always been important sinecures in the patronage systems of machine politics. Jobs "in the gift" of the state are an invitation to corruption unless openly accessible via transparent criteria. Some public sector jobs, surprisingly, are still open to purchase (Piketty 2020, p.159).

The principle that careers should be allocated according to talent has played a historical role in breaking down rigid caste structures by affording people with low caste status avenues to economic advancement and social mobility. When an upper class, reproduced by birth and inheritance, monopolizes positions of advantage there is no possibility of social mobility, which stifles opportunities. The result, as Young points out, is that "human tragedy was also social waste" (Young 1958/1994, p.15). The social waste, refers to the fact that talents are not made use of in an economically efficient way (Young 1958/1994, p.4). The social tragedy here is that this form of domination is an obstruction of people's liberty interests (Young 1958/1994, p.4). People who ought to be free to lead many different kinds of valuable life, are dominated by having their life choices reduced by the limitations of the system itself. They are cut off from the intrinsic and extrinsic rewards of better work for which they are well-suited. This cuts them off not just from better remuneration, but also from the associational goods and status that come from different kinds of employment. Hierarchical societies are not only less efficient, they are also less free.

A crucial document in translating Young's object of dystopian satire into a positive ideal was Daniel Bell's "Meritocracy and Equality". Bell argued—unsurprisingly—that the justifying logic of the forthcoming post-industrial society would be meritocratic (Bell 1972, p.30). He was explicit that this would be involve only a starting gate conception of equality of opportunity—certainly not equality of outcomes. Again, his rhetorical contrast was with a rigid class system in which positions are allocated by nepotism or patronage rather than through "fair competition open equally to talent and ambition" (Bell 1972, p.41). Unlike Young, Bell was wholly in favour of meritocracy.

For Bell, sufficientarian justice should be met first—"a basic set of services and income which provides him with adequate medical care, housing and the like" (Bell 1972, p.65). Any further inequality of income and status should go to "those who have an *earned* status or have achieved positions of rational authority or competence" (Bell 1972, p.65). Worried about the psychological effects on the worst off, Bell adds that everyone is entitled to fundamental respect, but entitlement to praise attaches to those who have performed excellently in some domain. The aim is that society will be run by "those worthy of praise" (Bell 1972, p.66).

In his articulation of the philosophical rationale for meritocracy, Thomas Mulligan takes it to be desert based. As he points out, the idea that people should get what they deserve and what they deserve is determined by their merits is a view with a long philosophical history and can be found in the works of Plato, Aristotle, Confucius, and even in the Bible (Mulligan 2017, pp.9–10). He re-iterates the justification in terms of outcomes: meritocratic systems are the most economically efficient. An alternative justification is Aristotle's: "All agree that the just in distributions must accord with some sort of merit." (350 BC [2002]: 1131a). This is an intrinsic justification in terms of fairness. The best candidate is the right person for the job not because he or she will be better at it but because it is only fair that the best candidate gets the job.

The central claim of those who take the meritocratic idea as a principle of justice is that whosoever is in some way deserving should receive rewards, while those who lack desert should not. Desert claims involve a three-place relation: (1) a desert subject (the people at hand), (2) a desert object (the treatment that those people are said to deserve), and (3) a desert base (the grounds on which the desert subject is said to deserve the desert object). So when it comes to the economically unequal societies we have discussed in this book, in which some are poor and some are rich, a possible desert claim—and in fact one that is often made in dominant meritocratic narratives—is that both the rich and the poor (the desert subjects) deserve to have the income and wealth that they actually have (the desert object), because the rich work hard and the poor do not (desert base).

Besides "working hard", another possible desert base, which is the one that Young refers to and we will be mostly relying on here, is some kind of "achievement", "performance", or "productive contribution", which is typically thought of as being the combined product of both hard work and talent (a broader notion than intelligence). Meritocrats believe that the inequality between ordinary people and the likes of Bill Gates and Steve Jobs is just as the latter make extremely productive contributions and hence are justified in receiving the monetary rewards bestowed on them. Similarly, if you slack and fail to produce anything of value, you deserve to remain poor.

This approach has several appealing features. First, it fits with the desert-based intuitions that many people have. Mulligan illustrates the appeal of meritocracy with an example of a race in which the timings for all Black runners are automatically increased by one minute. In this race, William, a White runner, takes 30 seconds more to go round the track than Brian, a Black runner. Under the rules of the race, a minute is added to Brian's time, and so William wins the race. As Mulligan argues, there is something unjust about this state of affairs. A meritocratic approach to justice can justify and explain this thought by saying that the problem here is that the competitors are not being rewarded in line with their merits. To get what they deserve, people need an equal opportunity to succeed, which was not the case in this race (Mulligan 2017, p.71).

As well as explaining such intuitions, the meritocratic ideal also provides a diagnosis as to why various forms of disadvantage constitute injustices. If someone faces barriers to success because of racism, sexism, classism, ableism, or another form of prejudice or discrimination, then this is unjust because justice requires equality of opportunity. Factors like the colour of one's skin, one's gender, or one's socio-economic background do not in themselves make one more or less deserving and thus should not in themselves play a role in the distribution of advantages and disadvantages.

Finally, meritocracy places an emphasis on personal responsibility which many find attractive. The meritocratic ideal rewards talent and hard work and so encourages people to take responsibility for working hard and developing their talents. If you know that the right person will get the job, you will be motivated to do your best to become that person. It is, according to Mulligan, only in a society where rewards and success are determined by merit that people can be fully responsible for how their life is going, as only in such societies will someone's "successes and failures turn on his merits alone" (Mulligan 2017, p.6).

In summary, at the core of the meritocratic political ideal is the concept of desert. People's position in the social hierarchy should be allocated according to their merits. To make this the case, it is essential that people are given equal opportunities to succeed in life. This is a positive political ideal that emphasizes the importance of personal responsibility and aligns considerations of fairness with considerations of efficiency.

12.2 Meritocracy as an Incoherent Ideal

We will begin our assessment of the ideal of meritocracy in a surprising place: the most stringent critiques of the ideal come not from the progressive Left, but the libertarian Right. The best case we have made for the ideal to this point is that the Smithian legislator, whom we can assume to be the constitutional and institutional designer, will adjust economic institutions to ensure that the market virtues are rewarded. This is a justification of market institutions in terms of outcomes and, as Amartya Sen points out, that runs counter to the fundamental approach of Robert Nozick (Sen 1985a, p.4).

The only question about a chess position is whether the pieces were initially placed on the board correctly and whether the current position is the outcome of legal moves of the pieces. Similarly, for Nozick's ideal social process view of justice, the only question about the current pattern in the distribution of resources across economic agents is whether they were justly acquired and then justly transferred by gift or contractual exchange (Nozick 1974). There is no other criterion for a just distribution. Entitlements, protected by rights, permit certain kinds of "changes in the normative landscape" of requirements and entitlements, but Nozick is not a consequentialist about rights. This system is autonomous—it is not "for" anything, although it may be combined with other assumptions to produce "Left" as opposed to "Right" libertarianism. Asking whether this normative structure rewards virtuous character traits to economic outcomes is like asking whether the number seven is green: the question does not make any sense. The point of the system is to protect and respect liberty, not to promote the goal of economic efficiency or reward merit. That marks one extreme position here: Nozick thinks it is a categorical confusion to "adjust" the market to personal merits (or any other patterned justice principle for that matter).

Another convincing source of scepticism comes from none other than Hayek, who notes that the function of rewards in a market society is not to reward meritorious behaviour (as economists like Mankiw and many laypeople think) but to encourage productive behaviour. The role that prices (on the labour market in the form of salaries) play in a market society is not to reward those with merit but to provide information about the demand and supply for certain goods and services.[8] The price nexus is not there to reward the individual merits of those who engage in the production process: it

[8] For further discussion of Hayek's ideas here, see (Anderson 2005).

cannot be a measure of their individual labour burdens. The craftsperson making a violin in her workshop markets it at the price the market will support whether or not her craft skills come to her easily or as a result of laborious effort. The price of the violin is determined by and reflects supply (willingness to accept) and demand (willingness to pay), not personal merit. Moreover, these goods and services will be rewarded equally regardless of whether they were acquired through merit or through luck. This is how it should be, according to Hayek, if we want markets to continue to serve their function of informing people of how much certain goods and services are valued by others (Hayek 1960, p.160). The market nexus discards this information about individual labour burdens, and it must do so to do the job we assign it.

The importance of Hayek's observation for our discussion is that it shows that, even by the lights of those who defend them, the function of markets is not to reward people in line with their merit. Not only is this not the role markets are supposed to play but if markets rewarded people in line with their merit, they could no longer play the informational role for which we actually value them. This is not to say that a society could not in principle seek to eliminate luck from the distribution of resources. It does show though, that the ideal of meritocracy does not provide support for market societies in the way that proponents of meritocracy claims that it does. Meritocracy, then, if applied to the economic system we actually have, would be radically revisionary utopian proposal applied to the market. Markets play the same role in Rawls's system as it does for Hayek. As Paul Smith insightfully observes:

> For Rawls, just as competitive markets establish an objective and public valuation of heterogeneous products, so, presumably, a fair and competitive labor market would establish an objective and public valuation of heterogeneous jobs and thus the income (and other benefits) socially necessary to compensate any particular labor burden. (Smith 1998, p.210)

It would be mistake, Rawls famously argued, to confuse the idea of an intra-institutional entitlement with the idea of pre-institutional sense of desert that constitutes the foundational justification for the basic structure of society (Rawls 1971/1999). The role of markets within that structure is to respect the structure of market entitlements—not to track personal merit.

12.3 Meritocracy as an Unrealizable Ideal

The next family of sceptical arguments do not view the ideal as incoherent, but as simply not feasible. If there is a theoretical task of identifying the productive contribution of an individual, at the margin, to the value of an overall product then the problem is that this task cannot be completed. Attempts to complete this task are inevitably politicized in a problematic way. Furthermore, the individual's ability to make such a contribution reflects the effect of luck and the operation of background resources of social capital.

The first kind of scepticism attaches to the very idea that one can identify an individual productive contribution at all. Amartya Sen discusses this issue in his famous paper "The Moral Standing of the Market", upon which we have previously drawn in our argument (Sen 1985a). There is a parallel between this argument and Joseph Fishkin's argument over the identification of the respective contributions of nature and nurture to talent: we will call it the "factorial fallacy" (Fishkin 2014). As Fishkin explains the idea, the contribution of nature and nurture is always 100% of each: we are not identifying separate causal contributions or vectors that can be combined. Without any of these "contributions" there is no output. Sen's version of the argument is applied to the idea of an individual productive contribution—the "personal production view" (Sen 1982). That it cannot explain the basis of individual reward rests on two fundamental economic facts: "owned impersonal resources" and "interdependent production".

We have already drawn upon the former—our example was taken from Scanlon and Sen—the case of a landowner permitting a company to use their land as a shortcut with greatly increased profitability for the latter (Sen 1982; Scanlon, p132, fn. 16). The company makes a rental payment to the landowner: that is a contribution to production, but not in any active sense—it is a paradigmatic form of rentier fee extraction. Here we focus on the latter, interdependent production problem:

> If production is an interdependent process, involving the joint use of different resources, it is not generally possible to separate out which resource has produced how much of the total output [. . .]. Marginal accounting, when consistent, has an important function in decision making regarding the use of resources [. . .] to read in that counter-factual marginal story one of "actual production" [. . .] is to take the marginal calculus well beyond its logical limits. (Sen 1985a, pp.15–6)

Marginal calculation might identify different factors of production, and their "weighting", without any implication that "any of these [. . .] factors could produce their respective shares unaided by the others" (Sen 1985a, p.16). Furthermore, Sen continues:

> [T]he apportioning is not even one that is done by adding together the marginal contribution of all the respective units one after another, but rather goes by weighting the entire amount of the resource input by the marginal valuation of the counterfactual additional contribution of that resource at the point of equilibrium [. . .]. The personal production adds to this real use a spurious interpretation as to whom has produced what. This comes, as it were, from nowhere, and it is essentially a fiction. It might, of course, be seen as a "convenient fiction", but that fiction is a whole lot more convenient for some than for others. (Sen 1985a)

There is simply no way of reverse engineering from the prices of products and services on the market to the contribution of factors of production to argue that a specific individual contributed his or her "share" of the composite result. An additional problem is in justifying the ownership of that factor of production. Counterfactuals about what an individual contributes to the overall product from a complex process are impossible to establish.

Iris Marion Young offers a similar critique of meritocracy (though her critique could also be classified as the claim that meritocracy is, as Arendt claimed, one version of oligarchic domination).[9] I. Young's point is that it is naive in the extreme to assume that the determination of what counts as an individual productive contribution in a complex organization is not, itself, going to be a politically determined judgement based on who has power over whom. Her critique then amounts to this: even if it were feasible to determine an individual's deservingness, this will not be done in a just way and will inevitably involve political decisions that will be contestable (Young 1990/2011).

She starts her argument against meritocracy by outlining several criteria that would need to be met in order for a meritocratic system to be just (Young 1990/2011, p.201). First, there would need to be a way of defining skills and competencies that was neutral with respect to differing cultural

[9] To avoid confusion between Michael Young and Iris Marion Young, who both feature in this chapter, we will from this point refer to "M. Young" and "I. Young".

values. Secondly, these skills would have to be entirely job-related, such that they serve as a reliable predictor of who will perform well in the job. Thirdly, it must be possible to judge levels of performance and merit on an individual basis (as opposed to at an organizational or team level). Finally, the way in which merit is measured must be neutral with regard to cultural values.[10]

While proponents assume that these conditions can all be met without difficulty—for example, in James Fishkin's *Justice, Equal Opportunity and the Family*—I. Young argues that there are four significant obstacles to the possibility of a neutral assessment of merit (Fishkin 1983; Young 1990/2011, p.202). First, most jobs involve the performance of a complex array of tasks that make straightforward performance measurement difficult. Secondly, the structure of many organizations makes it difficult to identify and measure an individual's contribution to a team's performance. Thirdly, many jobs require those performing them to use their judgement and discretion in how to do their work. This again makes neutral evaluation difficult. Finally, in large, modern, hierarchical organizations those performing the assessments often have no experience of doing the work that they are evaluating, making them badly positioned to make competent performance assessments of that work.

While these are general problems, all four obstacles are particularly problematic in professional and managerial work due to the complexity of the work, the dependence on others, and the levels of discretion involved. Together, these barriers give us strong reason to doubt that a neutral assessment of merit is possible, especially in those jobs for which competition is strongest (Young 1990/2011, p.205). This is the practical paradox that performance measures are hardest to establish for the jobs carrying the most prestige and remuneration. The meritocratic explanation fails, then, where its proponents most need it: to justify the very high salaries paid and rents extracted at the "top end" of the distribution.

Given these barriers to impartial, culturally neutral, measures of merit, I. Young claims that managers unavoidably evaluate merit on the basis of subjective and value-laden judgements (Young 1990/2011, p.205). This fact alone need not be problematic. However, when these judgments are made by those occupying privileged positions in an unequal society she argues that:

[10] Once again, Michael Young anticipated this point, arguing that in his meritocratic dystopia the measurement of merit would have been placed on an objective, scientific, basis.

> Their criteria of evaluation often emphasize norms of conformity which contribute to the smooth maintenance and reproduction of the existing relations of privilege, hierarchy, and subordination, rather than neutrally evaluating only technical competence and performance. (Young 1990/2011, p.205)

Achieving a position of status within an organizational hierarchy, then, depends on pleasing those in power. The result is that "the system of performance evaluation within such a hierarchy supports and reproduces relations of domination" (Young 1990/2011, p.212). Given the lack of any culturally neutral criteria to evaluate merit, assessors of merit judge people according to culturally informed value judgements that serve to reinforce existing hierarchies, which constitutes a form of domination of those below them in the hierarchy.

The argument of one Young can be helpfully supplemented with a point made by the other Young we have discussed in this chapter. Michael Young (1958/1994) noted, presciently, that one role of the emerging meritocratic class was to "cream off" the elite leadership of the working class. This is prescient given that we have noted how a striking aspect of the politics of the last forty years has been the decline—often as a result of explicit policy—of the institutional supports of countervailing power, notably trade unions and political parties. The meritocratic ethos is inherently individualistic and opposed to the politics of class solidarity. I. Young's analysis of the self-perpetuating nature of elite hierarchies within the firm seems to exemplify, in microcosm, a more general process at the level of society as a whole. Conformity with elite norms can help a person to be elevated into its "aspirational classes", leaving their working-class background behind. Robert H. Frank offers a different ground for scepticism about the idea of an individual productive contribution: the whole idea is vitiated not by politics, but by luck. Frank's claim is that no such contribution can be identified in a way that excludes the operation of constitutive luck. He argues in his book *Success and Luck: Good Fortune and the Myth of Meritocracy* that meritocracy mis-identifies effects that are, in fact, the product of luck (Frank 2016). According to Frank the view that we live in a society in which success results from merit is a harmful myth. What is ignored in this view of society is the extensive role of luck in determining who is successful.

Frank begins by pointing to the crucial role that luck has played in the careers of many successful people. For example, in some contexts, the role of luck in determining success can be seen by looking at the role that the time of year in which a person is born has in influencing what they will achieve in life. A study of professional hockey players in the United States and Canada found that 40% were born between January and March while only 10% were born between October and December (Baker and Logan 2007). The reason appears to be that players are typically grouped together in teams based upon the year on which they were born. Players born earlier in that year then will tend to be more physically and mentally developed than players born at the end of the year and as a result will be more likely to be stand-out performers for their teams. This means they are more likely to be selected for elite-level teams with the best coaching and training programs, which makes them more likely to have further success. Older children in school classes have a similar advantage over their younger classmates, as they are more likely to perform better in tests (Sprietsma 2010), take on leadership roles (Dhuey and Lipscomb 2008), and eventually become a CEO (Du, Gao, and Levi 2012).

What these studies show is the significant impact that chance events can have in influencing your future success. So even if rewards go to those with the best performances, these performances are influenced by much more than only talent and effort. Luck plays a major role in constituting and becoming who we are and what we are good at. This is, once again, the working of the mechanism of cumulative advantage. Initial luck that takes a person through the first "bottleneck" then compounds its effects and helps them through further bottlenecks.

A more relevant example for our purposes is the fact that the socioeconomic status of one's parents is a major determinant of one's own socioeconomic status. As a comparative analysis of Denmark, Finland, Norway, the United Kingdom, and the United States found that the children of parents in the top 20% of earners were more than twice as likely to end up in the top 20% themselves than those born to parents in the bottom 20% (Jäntti et al. 2006). The lack of social mobility was particularly stark in the United States, where someone born into the bottom 20% is more than three times more likely to themselves be in the bottom 20% of earners than someone born into the top 20% (Chetty et al. 2014). Given that the socioeconomic position that one is born into is not something one can have any control over, this evidence provides us with compelling reason to accept that luck has a major influence over one's socio-economic position.

Wilkinson and Pickett further develop this insight by pointing out that the role of luck is not simply a matter of determining which talented people become successful but also in determining who becomes talented (Wilkinson and Pickett 2018 p.166). They support this claim by appealing to several studies investigating the effects of poverty on cognitive development. In the first study, based on data from the United Kingdom's Millennium Cohort Study, children who live in poverty were found to have lower levels of cognitive development at ages three, five, and seven and the effects were worse when children had lived in poverty for longer periods of time (Dickerson and Popli 2016). Similar results were found in large-scale studies of children in the United States (Brooks-Gunn and Duncan 1997; Korenman et al. 1995). Indeed, in a particularly noteworthy study of children in the United Kingdom, poverty was found to be a stronger determinant of children's cognitive development by age three than either maternal depression or the marital or living arrangements of the parents (Kiernan and Mensah 2009). These statistics give us good reason to accept the claim that luck plays a major role not just in determining how far our talents take us but also in determining what talents we develop in the first place (Wilkinson and Pickett 2018, p.167). As a consequence, it is not so much talent and effort that are rewarded but being born in the right kind of circumstances, which is not something for which one can be deserving.

Poverty not only influences mental development; it also influences how a child's educational abilities are evaluated by educators (Wilkinson and Pickett 2018, p.167). In a systematic review of the empirical literature on the gap in the United States between the educational achievements of white children compared to Black children, Ronald Ferguson concludes that while the evidence is inconclusive, "teachers' perceptions, expectations, and behaviours probably do help to sustain, and perhaps even to expand, the Black-White test score gap" (Ferguson 2003, p.495). More conclusively, a study conducted by Simon Burgess and Ellen Greaves investigated the difference between the grades that pupils receive from a teacher who knows who they are and the grades they receive in anonymized assessments (Burgess and Greaves 2013). They found that 12.4% of white students received higher grades in the anonymous assessment compared with 20.2% of Pakistani students, 18.3% of Black African students and 18.1% of Bangladeshi students. Similarly, poorer students (those eligible for free school meals) were more likely to receive higher grades in the anonymized assessment in all their subjects. They argued that this data was best explained by appealing to the unconscious stereotypes of their teachers. When these factors are at play in the real world, they thwart the meritocratic principle that people should get what they deserve.

A whole range of factors beyond people's control have a major influence on determining their socioeconomic position. Systematic forms of oppression and disadvantage play a significant role in determining one's socioeconomic status. Gender is one factor that has a significant influence on socioeconomic position. In the European Union for example, the average gender pay gap is 16.2% with a rate of 21.5% in Germany, the Eurozone's largest and most successful economy (Eurostat 2018). The gender pay gap is 21% in the United Kingdom while in the United States earnings of women in full-time employment were 81.8% of the equivalent figures for men (Bureau of Labor Statistics 2018). Another significant factor is race. In 2017, the median income was $68,145 for white households, $50,486 for Hispanic households and $40,258 for Black households. Again, these statistics highlight the major role that luck has in determining one's socioeconomic position (Fontenot et al. 2018). Those born into disadvantaged groups are significantly less likely to achieve a high socio-economic status than those born into privileged groups.

Cumulatively, these arguments show that the meritocrat faces serious and principled difficulties in identifying and establishing their core idea of merit as they have to discount too many confounding variables. We turn now to a problem that would arise if the problems of identifying and establishing what merit is and how to measure it could somehow be overcome—that of instability.

12.4 Meritocracy as an Unstable Ideal

We noted Bannerjee and Bercuson's blunt observation that, for Rawls, whether a conception is just and whether it is stable are not identical questions, but they nearly are (Bannerjee and Bercuson 2015). We ought not to consider for implementation conceptions of justice that cannot stabilize themselves. We turn from attacks on the coherence and feasibility of the ideal of meritocracy to its stability.

The argument is, to a certain degree, sociological: that Fishkin and Gomberg are correct that there is a feedback loop between how a society structures the field of opportunities and the strategies that economic actors adopt to negotiate it. If, to take a pertinent example, a society puts in place a sequence of bottlenecks that, in every case, limit the number who can pass through them to generate a socio-economic elite, then it makes sense to focus energy and resources on the early bottlenecks. When it comes to human capital, it is noteworthy that some of our most admired egalitarian societies, such as Sweden and Germany, have "elite" education systems that offer very different parallel educational tracks for different classes of young people.[11]

This is how, for example, we can make sense of the intensity of the competition for access to Manhattan's "elite" kindergartens! Risk analyst turned financial regulator, Richard Bookstaber describes the dark comedy of access to Manhattan's most exclusive kindergartens:

> [T]he quid pro quo for [Jack] Grubman helping with his boss's boardroom infighting was for [Sandy] Weill to take a million bucks from the coffers of the world's largest financial corporation to give Grubman's twin two-year-olds a leg up getting into nursery school. And not just any nursery school.... The 92nd Street Y, a bastion of privilege in New York's Upper East Side.... The competitive nursery school phenomenon is a New York singularity that is difficult for normal folk to fathom. (Bookstaber 2007, p.131)

As Bookstaber notes, "No one seriously thinks that a three-hour playgroup can be transformed into a singular educational experience, no matter how much money and culturally aware parentage is thrown at it," rather, parents are "paying $20,000 or more a year to connect to the high-society play date underground" (Bookstaber 2007, p.132).

The concern, then, is not with education but with status and social capital. It may be an extreme case—possibly America's most extreme case—but many parents will share Grubman's sentiment that there are "no bounds for what you do for your children" (Bookstaber 2007, quoted on p.132). The point is equally well made by Fishkin: given that opportunity bottlenecks are sequenced, what we see in action is what we would call cumulative advantage. For that reason, the temporally early bottlenecks become crucially important—and campaigns amongst the super-rich for kindergarten places for their toddlers become explicable (Fishkin 2014, p.72, fn.138).

[11] Fishkin discusses how the German Gymnasium system forms a secondary education bottleneck for university access and notes the evolution of a complementary system of alternative routes to other vocations via an equally well-developed apprenticeship system. But the streaming happens early in the educational process (Fishkin 2014, pp.146–7, p.210).

Our point is that once it is commonly known that the field of opportunity is structured in this way, one can reasonably expect more and more candidates to "up their game" over time.[12] The structure of the field of opportunities can stay in place, but the extent of the whole field must expand. If it does not, two things will happen: an inflation in standards, combined with an increased salience of "non-merit-based" factors in determining who gets the valued positions, or there is an elite reproduction problem. Both outcomes would destabilize the meritocratic narrative. Far from being abstract possibilities, both sociological trends are evident in the recent history of the United States.

If you choose, in Waheed Hussain's phrase, to "pit people against each other", and if your society seems to be divided into "insiders and outsiders" while the dominant myth is that these statuses can be earned by merit, then people's behaviour will change. Once the stakes of the competition go up, it makes sense to increase the resources put into winning. Hence the very different lives of the three classes of children in Robert D. Putnam's *Our Kids* with its diagnosis of an emerging "class based" apartheid in America (Putnam 2016). One of the most striking aspects of the book is how many resources wealthy parents are willing to put into advantaging their children. The mismatch between resources expended, achievements unlocked, and the difficulty of achieving insider status shows that other factors are in play that the meritocrat fails to take into account—social capital, networking, and cronyism featuring prominently amongst them. That is one source of "angrynomics"—the rage of the frustrated meritocrat who discovers that the meritocratic narrative is false after the considerable expenditure of time and resources in the belief that it is true.

A complementary argument is Christopher Hayes's claim that meritocracy is fatally unstable as an ideal beyond a single generation—a point implicit in Michael Young's discussion. He appeals to the very idea about opportunity hoarding that we presented in chapter 9, above. In his radical critique of the possibility of creating a genuinely meritocratic society, he argues that meritocracy's acceptance of differences in power, status, and wealth is in tension with its claim to bring about social mobility. Hayes calls this "The

[12] Hayes notes the decline of the meritocratic impact of America's twentieth-century standardized educational testing regimes due to the rise of "The test prep industry", which allows parents with more money to better prepare their children for the test (Hayes 2012, p.38).

Iron Law of Meritocracy", adapted from Michel's "Iron Law of Oligarchy", and describes it in the following way, "Eventually the inequality produced by a meritocratic system will grow large enough to subvert the mechanisms of mobility" (Hayes 2012, p.57; Michels 1962).

The reason for this, according to Hayes, is that those who reach the positions of power, status, and wealth will use their position to make sure that they, and those they care about, stay in that position (Hayes 2012, p.59). So while equal opportunity and social mobility are a necessary condition for any meritocracy, implementing the latter inevitably leads to inequalities that hamper equal opportunity and social mobility and thus undermine its own preconditions. While the idea is that one can climb the socio-economic ladder, the inequalities that we have been discussing cause the different steps of the ladder to come too far apart to actually be climbed. In Keith Payne's words, the ladder of social mobility is "broken"; our point, and Hayes's, is that those who have already climbed the ladder break it after their ascent (Payne 2017). (This is why we have focused on opportunity hoarding.) Once again, emotions feature in this explanation: the special affection that people have for their own children and their desire generationally to transmit advantage to them.

One of the primary mechanisms by which inequalities thwart social mobility is the transmission of privilege via education. Drawing on data from over 30 million college students in the United States between 1999 and 2003, Chetty et al. find that a child of a parent in the top 1% of earners is 77 times more likely to attend an Ivy League college than a student whose parents are in the bottom 20% of earners (Chetty et al. 2017). The most straightforward way in which this privilege is passed on is through the rich investing in their child's education from an early age by spending money on tuition fees for private schools or private tutors as well as enriching extra-curricular activities such as sport music and foreign travel (Deresiewicz 2014).

This is not the only way in which wealthy parents are able to secure their child a place at an elite college. Other processes by which the children of American elites are able to secure their children a place in elite American colleges are well-documented in Daniel Golden's *The Price of Admission* (Golden 2006). He explains how the admission politics of elite colleges, "channel the children of the privileged into premier colleges, paving the way into leadership positions in business and government" (Golden 2006, p.1). There are several ways in which these procedures favour those from wealthy families. First, the children of former students at an elite university are far more likely to gain admission to that university than other children, with alumni children typically making up 10% to 25% of the student body at elite colleges (Golden 2006, p.6). At Harvard, one-third of alumni children are admitted, which is nearly four times higher than its overall admissions rate (Golden 2006, p.27). Harvard's then Dean of admissions, William Fitzsimmons, admits that being the child of alumni does give applicants an admissions boost and that is used as a tie-breaker to decide between comparable candidates (Golden 2006, p.27).

In addition, children of major donors are also more likely to be admitted at elite colleges. At Harvard for example, applicants whose parents are members of the Committee of University Resources, a group of just over four hundred members consisting of the University's biggest donors, are far more likely to be admitted than other children. While less than one in ten undergraduate applications are successful at Harvard, more than half of the committee have had at least one child at Harvard (Golden 2006, p.25). It is not only the children of donors who appear to receive a boost in the admissions process, applications from the children of people judged to be potential donors are also more likely to be accepted. Students whose parents are wealthy enough to be judged as potential future donors to the university are labelled as "development cases". These cases make up 2%–5% of those attending elite colleges (Golden 2006, p.6). The admission criteria for elite universities then are weighted in favour of wealthy applicants, which supports Hayes's hypothesis that those in positions of power and privilege will try and ensure that their children will inherit this power and privilege.

America's ruling elite currently faces an elite reproduction problem (Turchin 2023): its ruling ideology, meritocracy, combined with an ideology of continual growth, suggests that as more and more people achieve higher standards of excellence, both the field of opportunity and the extent of remuneration ought to expand. Yet the opposite is happening: artificial bottlenecks are being generated via the opportunity hoarding we described in chapter 9 and the extraction of rent is confined to those with insider status where the chance to break into this circle is not dependent on merit. The meritocrat's focus on individual human capital and its development is trumped, in practice, by social capital—social networks, status, and the class status of one's parents.

12.5 The Falsity of the Meritocratic Explanation of the New Inequality

Ironically, the part of the argument in which we establish that the meritocratic explanation of the New Inequality is false can be shortest because the basic point, once made, is obvious. The recent meritocrat places great importance on the forces of globalization. As large economies such as China, India, Brazil, and Russia further developed and millions of upskilled workers joined the global labour market, the affluent economies of the West had to (allegedly) "re-think" their role. This suggests an expansion of the global pool of talent for all jobs, including, presumably, the roles of senior executives in large multi-national corporations. We would expect to see free trade drive down the salaries of such executives as this talent pool widened. Other factors cited as explanations for the New Inequality, such as skills-biased technical change, should also have had an international impact.

Yet the data show that the New Inequality is concentrated in the United States with a paler imitation of some of its features in the United Kingdom. It is in the United States that remuneration for executives, shareholders, high-end advisers in law and finance, financial services, and other industries with high levels of intellectual property rights protection (pharmaceuticals, computing, law) has exploded, also since globalization. When the same global forces produce one result in the United States, but quite different results in France, Germany, Japan, or South Korea, one has to suspect they are not the whole explanation and that there is something about the political culture of the United States that explains this level of inequality.

It is difficult to see how the meritocrat can generate such a differential explanation. Standards of education and a work ethic are also prevalent in these other comparator countries. What is it about the American wealthy that makes them work so much harder and smarter? If that explanation is elusive, the competing rent-seeking explanation is much better placed to explain the New Inequality: indeed, as we noted in chapter 2, we can actually put a numerical figure on it.

The belief that CEO remuneration in the United States is explained by the exceptionally high performance of the individuals concerned seems oddly detached from the actual practice in these industries. Corporate executives are supposed to inherit the intellectual mantle of the heroic entrepreneur, but that misdescribes their role. They enter the scene in the established firm as a manager, not an entrepreneur, and in many cases the first risk they eliminate at the high end of this market is the risk to their own remuneration package. The performance-related aspect of their remuneration turns them not into professional managers, but into financial technicians. We have noted the methods by which such managers are able to manipulate the conditions of their own remuneration—in particular through the company share price (Lazonick and Shin 2019).

There is no empirical evidence that CEO remuneration tracks overall corporate performance in a way that would explain their differential pay as a reflection of merit. It is hard to understand what that could mean in an American company like Chipotle Mexican Grill, whose CEO, in 2001, earned 3,000 times its median employee salary. (The company employs 76,000 people.) And Chipotle is only ninth on the list of the top ten US companies with the largest CE-to-median-worker pay differentials in the Russell 3000 stock index. These figures have emerged after the data has been massaged, for example, by excluding low-paid employees working overseas in countries such as India. It is hard even to comprehend how a CEO can be three or five thousand times more meritorious than their employee earning the median wage.

As markets do not reward merit, it should be no surprise to see that the most extensive economic inequalities do not reflect differences in deservingness. Whatever one's preferred desert base—hard work, talent, performance as the combination of hard work and talent, contribution to a firm or to society, or even other oft-heard criteria such as responsibility—wealth and deservingness simply do not match at all (Moriarty 2005, p.263). The case obviously holds *a fortiori* for rentier capitalists and others whose wealth is either inherited or extracted.

Given that we do not live in the kinds of meritocratic societies that the dominant ideology wants us to believe, we might actually be stuck in the worst of both worlds. Not only do the poor and middle class lack the kinds of access to the goods of social mobility that the wealthy have, the myth of meritocracy nonetheless holds them responsible for the fact that they end up lower on the socio-economic ladder. This fits with our overall claim: the obvious injustice of the unequal opportunities that result from pre-existing and self-reinforcing inequalities is aggravated by the damaging message that tells people it's their own fault. Instead of feeling outraged or angry at the injustice of rent extraction and opportunity hoarding, they should feel ashamed of their own lack of effort. We analyse the impact of meritocracy's myth in more detail further on in this chapter.

12.6 The Functional Role of Meritocratic Beliefs

Any explanation of the New Inequality in meritocratic terms that explains it as the market appropriately rewarding exceptional personal merit is false. The question, then, is why this legitimating narrative persists despite the intellectual onslaught against it in recent philosophical and popular commentary. Our explanation is that the ideology of meritocracy plays an important role in the emotional regime of market societies.

We might expect that this narrative would be a particularly "hard sell" to those living in societies characterized by great inequality. After all, the greater the inequality, the higher our beliefs would have to be in the differences between the comparative merits of the rich and the poor to allow us to believe that wealth is allocated according to merit. Moreover, given the ways in which the wealthy in market societies use their wealth to ensure that the system is rigged in their favour, we can expect that these processes will be worse in less equal societies and so generate more discontent.

However, a significant body of research suggests that this is not the case. The increase in inequality in Western societies has not been accompanied by a growth in popular concern about inequality (Alesina and Glaeser 2004; Lübker 2007; Kenworthy and McCall 2008; Kuziemko et al. 2015; McCall 2013). Similarly, people living in less equal societies do not express more concern about inequality than those living in more equal societies (Bucca 2016; McCall 2013; Paskov and Dewilde 2012; Wietzke 2016). What explains these puzzling phenomena?

One explanation is that there is widespread ignorance about the extent of inequality. Citizens in Europe, the United States, and Latin America have all been found to significantly underestimate the extent of economic inequality in their countries (Bucca 2016; Cruces et al. 2013; Norton and Ariely 2011; Osberg and Smeeding 2006). Dan Ariely calls this the "knowledge gap between what we have and what we think we have" (Ariely 2015). This may be thought to explain why societies with higher levels of inequality do not have higher levels of concern for inequality. If people are unaware of the extent of inequality in their society, then it is perhaps unsurprising that higher levels of inequality do not lead to greater concerns about inequality.

However, as Jonathan Mijs argues, this explanation appears to be too simplistic (Mijs 2021). If we accept this explanation, then we should expect that people's concerns about the inequality in their society would increase as they receive information about it. However, the empirical evidence about how people in fact respond to such information provides a more complicated picture. Both Kuziemko et al. and Alesina et al. found that providing information about inequality to participants from France, Italy, Sweden, the United States, and the United Kingdom increased their levels of concern about inequality (Kuziemko et al. 2015; Alesina, Stantcheva, and Tesa 2018). However, Kuziemko et al. also found that this did not have a significant impact on policy preferences (Kuziemko et al. 2015). On the other hand, Cruces et al. found that providing poor people with information about other people's income increased their support for redistributing wealth (Cruces et al. 2013).

Perhaps the most surprising results are from Trump, who asked participants from Sweden and the United States to estimate the levels of inequality in their societies (Trump 2017). As expected, almost all participants underestimated the extent of inequality in their society. Those in the treatment group were then informed about the actual levels of inequality while those in the control group were not. Participants were then asked what they thought levels of income inequality *ought* to be. Those in the treatment group, who had been informed that inequality was higher than they had thought, were found to recommend levels of inequality around 50% higher than those in the control group. It seems then that people increased the levels of inequality they were willing to accept as they discovered that the levels of inequality in their own society were higher than they had thought. Mijs argues that taking all these results together suggests that people's lack of awareness of the extent of inequality cannot fully explain their lack of concern for inequality (Mijs 2021).

Instead, Mijs offers an alternative explanation, that people living in more unequal societies will be more likely to view inequality as resulting from a meritocratic process (Mijs 2021). Greater socio-economic inequality produces less political resistance, rather than more resistance, because higher socio-economic inequality correlates more strongly with meritocratic beliefs—notably, a belief in the importance of "hard work" (Mijs 2021, p.12). In more egalitarian societies, on the other hand, people are more likely to view inequality as resulting from structural forces (Mijs 2021, p.12). Mijs is careful to note that these are correlations and he is not making any causal claims: perhaps meritocratic beliefs facilitate high inequality rather than the latter causing the former (Mijs 2021; Janmaat 2013; Schröder 2017). Regardless how the causal story actually goes, we think Mijs's data gives us insight into Bossuet's paradox that increasing inequality, and an avowed concern about it, produces no political action.

A noteworthy finding is that, in his survey of attitudes, Mijs identifies the most unequal societies as least concerned with inequality (Janmaat 2013).[13] In the most unequal societies, "citizens . . . are more likely to explain success in terms of meritocratic factors and less likely to believe in structural inequality" (Mijs 2021, p.8). Mijs's explanation is that this is an adaptation mechanism: people would prefer to believe that they live in a fair world than to believe that they live in an unfair one (Mijs 2021, p.11, citing inter alia Bénabou and Tirole 2006). Moreover, those in powerful positions have a strong incentive to believe this narrative and to propagate it to others. As Mijs explains:

> We can think of the American Dream as such a cultural narrative, or repertoire, that elites draw from and reproduce in order to justify their privileges—a cultural solution or coping mechanism for exceptionally high levels of inequality characterizing the US. (Mijs 2021, p.11)

A key determinant of reactions to inequality, in his view, is "their exposure to and interactions with people across economic fault lines", something that is positively discouraged when socio-economic inequality develops into a status hierarchy via background meritocratic beliefs (Mijs 2021, p.8).

We would go further: if you are one of society's "winners", then you obviously want to claim your advantages have been earned by your personal merits. Successful meritocrats have a high degree of confirmation bias (Hayes 2012, p.31). However, if you are one of society's "losers" then you want to believe in meritocracy for one of two reasons. First, you want to believe that the option of doing better is still open to you (the "audacity of hope"). We want to believe in social mobility, even if it is largely an illusion. Alternatively, you may want to believe that you would have done better had the contest not been rigged. The counterfactual meritocrat argues that, had she been given a level playing field, chances are that she would have won the competition, but the odds were unfairly stacked against her. That is still a commitment to meritocracy, as it views one's own failures as stemming from

[13] While there is a global trend, the United States, once again, stands out: "At least two thirds of citizens in all countries—and as much as 95% of Americans—attribute success to meritocratic factors" (Mijs 2019, p.3).

specific forms of unfairness present in the particular competition they were involved in rather than a recognition that society as a whole is not meritocratic. As Hayes puts it, "like the lottery, the meritocracy allows everyone to imagine the possibility of deliverance, to readily conjure the image of a lavish and wildly successful future" (Hayes 2012, p.47).

12.7 Merit's Role in the Emotional Regime of Capitalism

We have argued that extensive and unjust inequality locks itself in place via its creation of the artificial bottlenecks we have described in this book. The advantaged, who restrict their associational connections with the less advantaged, lack empathy for the latter and view their own comparative advantage as reflecting their own merits and the situation of the worse off as reflecting their lack of merit. Unequal societies are also likely to involve greater social distance between the rich and the poor, leading to widespread ignorance about the extent of inequality and the causes behind it (Mijs 2021). People may be aware of abstract statistics about inequality but these lack the emotional pull of the concrete experience of other people's circumstances and so the emotional gap persists even if people are made aware of these facts (Mijs 2021).`

Scanlon notes that "in unjust societies, with high levels of economic inequality, the tendency to form non-comparing groups can foster the development of unjustified ideas of desert and entitlement" (Scanlon 2018, p.39). He also notes that a sense of superiority, combined with the false evaluative belief that some people are simply "worth more" than others, cuts people off from associational goods. People who could be your friends and neighbours are simply not to be associated with in a way that leads to losses to all. It is not so much that the non-snobbish have much to lose from associating with snobs, but that the latter have lost an opportunity to change their false evaluative beliefs to the ultimate advantage of all.

Yet, in what Bill Bishop calls "the big sort", Americans increasingly isolate themselves not only in "super zip codes" of affluence, but literally withdraw into gated communities with "people like us" (Bishop 2008). That is why reassuring data on America's undoubted demographic changes leading to progressive social change are so misleading: a whole society may become more diverse while its micro-communities become increasingly homogeneous in terms of wealth and class. Relatedly, Scanlon notes that high levels of socio-economic inequality, mediated via meritocratic attitudes, leads to associational "sorting" and failures of sympathy and what one might call "political irresponsibility" (Scanlon 2018, p.39).[14] In other words, inequality is self-reinforcing: amongst its bad social effects is its effective removal of any political opposition to its own entrenchment.

In the absence of non-comparing groups, the meritocratic mindset goes unchallenged. This is the mindset well described by Silicon Valley philanthropy adviser Emmett Carson who stopped using the phrase "social justice" when speaking to his wealthy clients to avoid alienating them. He switched to "fairness" instead, to accommodate his clients' view that:

> I'm being targeted because I've been successful, I've worked hard, I made it; and because I made it, I am now the target, that you think *you deserve some of my success that you haven't earned.* (quoted in Giridharadas 2018, p.52, emphasis added)

Note the passive aggression in the last sentence we have emphasized: resentment and anger at the "takers" defrauding the makers. The best off can take an interest—or convincingly feign an interest—in addressing inequality (Giridharadas 2018). However, given their entrenched meritocratic beliefs, this cannot be on terms that threaten their own status: they dictate the relevant terms, so philanthropy is the answer.[15]

Philanthropy redistributes without addressing structural questions about the source of inequality and it reinforces the meritocratic narrative: the privately wealthy ought to control redistributive policies, not the state, because they are more intelligent and efficient than any public employee (Giridharadas 2018, pp.5–6).[16] The fact that they are wealthy is evidence of how smart they are (where familiarity with the fallacy of begging the question falls outside the scope of being smart in this sense). In Giridharadas's

[14] We should emphasize that this is our term, not Scanlon's: he thinks that the better off, cut off from association with others, will become "moralisers" towards others, less committed to fair equality of opportunity, less committed to equality of concern, and less responsible "as public officials and as citizens and voters" (Scanlon 2018, p. 39).

[15] A darker interpretation here is that elites' positioning themselves as the leaders of social change not only fails to create positive change but actively "serves to keep things as they are" (Giridharadas 2018, p.8).

[16] The social power to shape the mediatized framing of who ought to act to address social problems—whether the democratic state or concerted groups of the privately wealthy—can lead to private initiatives either complementing or undermining democracy (Horvath and Powell 2016). In the latter case, the elite private actor does not discount public opinion, but seeks to re-mould it in favour of (private) elite interests (Giridharadas 2018, p.234).

analysis of the extensive industry of philanthropy, it is premised on the success of a market society substantially to enrich the few. This is justified, by the few, on meritocratic grounds. They are also then justified in "giving back" in ways that do not challenge the market mechanism and legitimates placing them in control of redistribution using methods legitimated by market activity. The culture of philanthropy is now dominated by those with a background in the private sector or at least inculcated into its methods. One aspect of this approach is a paternalism that never sees fit to involve the beneficiaries of charitable giving in decision making.

As we explained in chapter 5, we understand emotional regimes to consist of feeling rules and guidelines that prescribe and prohibit certain emotions in certain contexts and that are supported by a range of rituals, practices, narratives, myths, and emotives that express and inculcate them. These emotional regimes are a key underpinning of any stable political regime (Reddy 2001) and will tend to serve the interests of those in a position of power and dominance (Jaggar 1989). We will now explain the role that the myth of meritocracy plays in the emotional regime of market societies. By doing so we aim to provide a more unified understanding of the role that this myth plays in supporting unequal market societies, together with a more complete understanding of the harmful effects of this myth.

First, the myth of meritocracy promotes a set of emotional responses towards the wealthy. According to this myth, the wealthy have achieved their wealth through a combination of talent and hard work and so can legitimately feel proud of their wealth. They are also worthy targets of the admiration and emulation of others. We have already discussed, in chapter 11, Adam Smith's claim that the rich tend to be admired and emulated by others. However, Smith argued that this is a corruption of our moral sentiments and stems from our tendency to find it easier to sympathize with joy than sorrow. According to Smith, then, our admiration of the rich and desire to emulate them are misguided and unfitting, though also useful for economic development.

The myth of meritocracy promotes the view that our admiration, benign envy, and emulation of the rich are not misguided but rather fitting responses to their merits. Because wealth is a sign of talent and hard work, we should admire the rich, as their wealth is an indication of their merit. Moreover, because those who are talented and who work hard will become wealthy, it makes sense for people to try to emulate the rich, as they too can become wealthy if they are sufficiently gifted and industrious.

There are various ways in which the emotional response of admiration towards the rich is mobilized in market societies. One important method are the stories that are told about the wealthy in the media. According to Jo Littler, media representation of the wealthy tends to be framed in ways that draw on and support the myth of meritocracy (Littler 2017, p.120). Littler identifies three recurring tropes in media representation of the rich that help to mobilize feelings of admiration and emulation towards them by utilizing and reinforcing the myth of meritocracy.

The first trope is that of the "normcore plutocrat" (Littler 2017, p.120). This term is used to identify, "how the plutocrat—whose power is gained to an extensive degree through wealth—can attempt to maintain and increase their power and wealth by 'performing ordinariness'" (Littler 2017, p.120). This involves representing the wealthy as people who are no different from ordinary people.

The second trope is that of the kind parent. This is the term Littler gives for media representations of the wealthy as kindly, "paternalistic custodians of society" (Littler 2017, p.129). Littler argues that this trope plays a key role in media representations of wealthy philanthropists, such as Bill and Melinda Gates, who are presented as loving, good-hearted benefactors who selflessly give their wealth to help the less fortunate.[17] This way of representing the wealthy sends the message that their power is legitimate, as it is based on their kindness and expertise (Littler 2017, p.133). Similarly, Gregory Mantsios describes media representations of the rich as portraying them as, "people of special talent and skill, who even their victims (workers and consumers) can admire" (Mantsios 2000, p.93). This media trope then mobilizes the emotion of admiration which helps to reinforce the power of the rich by promoting deference towards them.

The final trope Littler identifies is that of the luxury-flaunters in which wealthy people are represented as, "living lives of outlandish or admirable glamour and luxury" (Littler 2017, p.133). We can find such presentations in luxury advertisements and television shows such as *Lifestyles of the Rich and Famous, Rich Kids of Instagram* and *Keeping Up with the Kardashians.* Similarly, the British magazine *Hello!* is filled with photos of the lavish lifestyles, homes, and interior decorations of the wealthy that "encourage us to be cowed yet pointlessly aspirational at the spectacle of their wealth"

[17] As Littler points out, such media representations serve to mask Philanthrocapitalism, a form of philanthropy in which the charitable serve to promote private business interests (Littler 2017, p.132).

(Littler 2017, p.133).[18] This form of framing is frequently presented alongside "the neoliberal meritocratic trope of hard work" (Littler 2017, p.134). The message being sent, then, is that the rich should be celebrated for owning possessions which are far out of reach for ordinary people, but they possess such goods because they are exceptionally hard working. If others were willing to work as hard, then they too could achieve such luxury. Again, then, people are encouraged not just to admire the rich but also to emulate them.

In addition to the emotions that the myth of meritocracy promotes towards the wealthy, it also promotes emotional responses towards the poor. As detailed in chapter 11, shame is encouraged as a fitting response to poverty for those experiencing it, while others are encouraged to look down contemptuously on the poor. We have already seen that shame for poverty is a core part of the emotional regime of market societies and that there is reason to be especially concerned about the link between shame and poverty in unequal market societies. The myth of meritocracy adds a new dimension to the existing shame of poverty.[19] According to this myth, poverty is not only shameful because it involves lacking certain possessions but also because of the message it sends about the talents and character of those in poverty. If wealth is allocated on the basis of talent and hard work then those who lack wealth must either be talentless, lazy, or both. The societal stigma of the poor as lazy good-for-nothings easily translates into widespread feelings of shame for being in that position.

The emotions that the myth of meritocracy promotes towards the poor are also supported by the ways in which the media represents the lives of those in poverty. Heather Bullock and her colleagues summarize media representations of the poor in the United States in the following: "the poor are either rendered invisible or portrayed in terms of characterological deficiencies and moral failings" (Bullock, Wyche, and Williams 2001). According to a report by the Joseph Rowntree foundation into the way that poverty is reported by the media in the United Kingdom, "coverage of poverty is peripheral in mainstream UK media" and "the causes of poverty and the consequences of poverty were rarely explored" (McKendrick et al. 2008).

[18] Littler's discussion of luxury-flaunters is closely related to Diana Kendall's account of "price-tag framing" discussed in chapter 11 (Kendall 2011, pp.42–9).

[19] Alain de Botton makes a very similar point when he claims that, "To the injury of poverty, a meritocratic system now added the insult of shame" (Botton 2005, p.164). However, this way of putting the point suggests that shame and poverty are in no way linked prior to the rise of meritocratic discourse. We do not wish to make this suggestion and so put the point in terms of the exacerbation of the existing link between shame and poverty.

In more than forty hours of non-news television broadcasts (excluding documentaries specifically concerning poverty) analysed by the authors of the report between 2005 and 2007 the term "poverty" featured on two occasions and the subject of poverty was regarded by editors and journalists as "possessing little news value" (McKendrick et al. 2008).

When poor people *are* represented in the media, the focus tends to be on individual causes of poverty rather than structural or societal causes. As Kendall argues:

> By using framing that focuses on the lives of individuals, media reports may point a spotlight on the negative attributes of poor people believed to be welfare dependent. Such framing may predispose media audiences to think of the issue primarily in terms of welfare dependency and to ignore larger societal conditions (structural constraints) that contribute to poverty initially. (Kendall 2011, p.101)

This is in line with what we discussed previously: the extent to which the role of luck and circumstances is undervalued in societies with a strong meritocratic discourse. The focus on individual rather than structural factors encourages the poor to feel ashamed of their poverty and others to feel contempt towards them.

We can also look to the kinds of program in which poor people are most likely to appear on television. As Bullock et al. point out, low-income people are far more likely to feature on daytime talk shows and real-life crime shows than as characters in television dramas (Bullock, Wyche, and Williams 2001). These shows promote a judgemental attitude towards low-income people. The talk shows focus on "dysfunctional relationships, infidelity, and unruly, promiscuous teenage girls," which "support negative stereotypes about low-income people" (Bullock, Wyche, and Williams 2001, p.232). While the real-life crime shows "reinforce the stereotype that low-income men, particularly poor men of color, are involved with drugs," despite this not accurately representing the typical drug consumer or dealer (Bullock, Wyche, and Williams 2001, p.232). Again, the recurrence of these stereotypes reinforces the view that the poor are morally deficient and responsible for their own poverty, encouraging the idea that poverty is merited and, hence, shameful.

Media representations of poverty also contribute to promoting the meritocratic view that poverty is shameful through a process of othering directed against welfare recipients. In an analysis of articles in the American magazine *Newsweek* concerning welfare and poverty between 1993 and 1995, Marieke de Goede found that welfare recipients were "strongly defined as an outgroup" (Goede 1996, p.335). According to de Goede, these stories sent the following message: "Welfare recipients thus live by different moral standards than 'we' do" (Goede 1996, p.335) Similarly, in their study of the UK media, McKendrick et al. found that even compassionate coverage of poverty tended to present those living in poverty as an outgroup and "as lacking initiative, unproductive and a burden on 'us'" (McKendrick et al. 2008). One way this othering process is achieved is through the use of language that sets the poor apart from the rest of society. For example, the term "underclass" began to be used to refer to the poor in the 1970s and became a key part of discussions of poverty in the 1980s and 1990s (Katz 1995, 1989). The use of this term in media discourses around poverty promotes the idea that those experiencing poverty are different from other people, that they do not share society's moral values and that they pose a threat (Katz 1995; Lister 2004). This reinforces the idea that those living in poverty lack merit and so reinforces the shame of poverty.

It is not just traditional media that presents poverty as shameful. In an analysis of a hundred Facebook memes about welfare, Dobson and Knezevic found that these memes stigmatize the poor in a way that appeals to and reinforces the myth of meritocracy (Dobson and Knezevic 2017). The five main themes they found in these memes were that those on benefits are, "frauds; that they are lazy; that they are undeserving; that they need to be punished; and finally, that the larger economic system is to blame" (Dobson and Knezevic 2017, p.791). As Dobson and Knevevic point out, all but the last of these trends contribute to the stigmatization of the poor by sending the message that the poor are immoral and deserving of their poverty (Dobson and Knezevic 2017, p.791).

Another common trope in media representations of poverty is as something to rise above or escape from. As Kendell points out, a recurring narrative in relation to poverty is of people who have lifted themselves out of poverty (Kendall 2011, p.109). For example, the film *Homeless to Harvard: The Liz Murray Story* tells the story of a woman who grew up in poverty with drug-addicted parents, sleeping rough, and frequently going without food, who managed to work hard at school and get a place at Harvard (Kendall 2011, p.109). Stories like these are designed to be both heartwarming and inspirational, to promote admiration for those who have worked hard to get out of a position of poverty and encourage others to do the same. However, they ignore the typical experience of those facing poverty and promote an individualistic view of poverty in which poverty can be solved by individual resourcefulness rather than structural changes. Again, this narrative sends the message that the poor are responsible for their own plight.

To sum up, the myth of meritocracy plays a key role in the mobilizing of the emotions of admiration and envy towards the rich and shame and contempt for poverty. In doing so it plays a key role in reinforcing the power of the dominant in society. Admiration and envy lead to deference towards the rich and a desire to emulate them, making it harder for their position in society to be challenged. Similarly, the promotion of the shamefulness of poverty reinforces the view that the poor do not deserve any more than they have and so undermines attempts to object to inequality. While this is bad enough, we will see in the next section that the picture looks even worse when we consider the role that inequality plays in people's beliefs about meritocracy alongside the impact of meritocratic beliefs on well-being.

12.8 The Impact of Meritocratic Beliefs on Well-Being

We have discussed Mijs's argument that the more unequal a society, the stronger the correlation with meritocratic beliefs. It would be unfortunate, then, if such beliefs also correlated with reduced levels of well-being. Yet in making the positive case for meritocracy, we noted that the meritocrat had to make a crucial assumption: the independence of the sorting mechanism from its outcome. Unfortunately, as Wilkinson and Pickett have demonstrated, that claim of independence is false (Wilkinson and Pickett 2018).

The most clear-eyed defenders of meritocracy take the market to be a truth teller and not always a kind one. If we allow it do its job—measure individual merit—then we would be forced to acknowledge that it is a form of social Darwinism. It may not be palatable to hear this, but the truth about meritocracy is that in this form of social Darwinism, the socially "fit" rise, and those less able to cope cluster at the base of the social order. That would explain the steep drop-off in the social gradients of well-being that Wilkinson and Pickett document (Wilkinson and Pickett 2018). Again, don't shoot the messenger: the message that the market is sending is that those at the bottom end of the distribution need to change their market-relevant virtues (or acquire them).

Wilkinson and Pickett show that the data does not even support this disenchanted view. People are not being "sorted" by some property (such as resilience, or merit) such that the relative proportion of people with and without that property is independent of the sorting process itself. Rather, as they explain, "the effect of changing inequality in a society is precisely to change the overall burden of almost all the problems with social gradients. (Wilkinson and Pickett 2018, p.xxii). The rise in the overall burden of ill effects that goes with higher levels of inequality can be explained only if the sorting process itself exacerbates them: "these problems are driven by the stress of social status differences themselves" (Wilkinson and Pickett, p.xxii).

We have tried to be fair to the normative vision of the meritocrat, but this seems to us a serious problem even for idealized versions of the view (if social Darwinism is your ideal). The sorting process and the sorting product (outcome) are not independent: income and wealth inequality exacerbate status competition, whose bad effects are magnified at the bottom end of each social gradient.

Michael Young was certainly aware of the damage that the myth of meritocracy did to the powerless in his political dystopia. Young describes their situation in the following:

> As for the lower classes, their situation is different too. Today all persons, however, humble, know they have had every chance. They are tested again and again. If on one occasion they are off-colour, they have a second, a third, and fourth opportunity to demonstrate their ability. But if they have been labelled "dunce" repeatedly they cannot any longer pretend; their image of themselves is more nearly a true, unflattering reflection. Are they not bound to recognize that they have an inferior status—not as in the past because they were denied opportunity; but because they *are* inferior? For the first time in human history the inferior man has no ready buttress for his self-regard. (Young 1994, pp.97–8)

Young's point is that a society in which status is allocated solely on the basis of economic success—which the meritocratic narrative interprets as indicative of merit—will be one that has a damaging influence on the self-respect of those at the bottom of the social scale. While a rigid class or caste society allows those at the bottom to console themselves with the thought that their place in society does not reflect their abilities, a society that people believe to be meritocratic offers no such consolation. In such a society, those at the bottom of the social scale will be forced to confront the fact that they are lacking in merit, at least according to their society's standards. Apparently, the fact that they fail to succeed means that they do not deserve to succeed. This can be expected to have a damaging impact on their self-respect. Michael Sandel, in his latest book, *The Tyranny of Merit*, makes this point, claiming that the meritocratic narrative "congratulates the winners but denigrates the losers, even in their own eyes" as those at the bottom of the hierarchy will find it "hard to escape the demoralizing thought that their failure is their own doing, that they simply lack the talent and drive to succeed" (Sandel 2020, pp.24–5). The blame and shame (and of course the lack of esteem and respect) directed at the poor can become internalized, with the predictable result that people's self-esteem and self-respect drop.

Richard Sennett and Jonathan Cobb reached a similar conclusion in their investigation of the ways in which class impacted on self-esteem in a study conducted in the United States in the 1970s (Sennett and Cobb 1973). Through 150 in-depth interviews with manual workers in Boston they sought to understand the way in which being working class impacted on people's sense of dignity and self-respect. In their conclusion, they comment on the damaging effects that the myth of meritocracy has on those occupying lower levels of the social hierarchy:

> If all men start on some basis of equal potential ability, then the inequalities they experience in their lives are *not* arbitrary, they are the logical consequence of different personal drives to use those powers—in other words, social differences can now appear as questions of character, of moral resolve, will and competence. (Sennett and Cobb 1973, p.256)

If societal hierarchies are believed to be determined by merit (regardless whether they actually are) and I am at the bottom of the hierarchy then this must be, so the discourse and people's reasoning goes, because I am lacking in merit.

12.9 Meritocracy, Oppression, and Affective Injustice

Meritocracy plays a key role in the emotional regime of market societies. It reinforces the power of the dominant in society by encouraging people to feel admiration and envy towards them, while at the same time promoting emotions of shame and contempt towards the poor. To make matters worse, these narratives are more likely to be accepted in societies with higher levels of inequality.

However, the problems with the myth of meritocracy do not end here. This myth not only helps to reinforce the position of the dominant within (increasingly) unequal societies but, does so in a way that causes distinctly emotional damage, harming people's well-being. In this section we will argue that these emotional harms constitute distinctly emotional forms of injustice. We will develop this argument by appealing to the concept of *affective injustice*, as outlined by both Amia Srinivasan and Shiloh Whitney (Srinivasan 2018; Whitney 2018).

To begin, let's consider how Srinivasan uses the term. Srinivasan argues that the victims of oppression often find themselves in situations where anger would be a fitting response to their situation but also a response that would harm their interests (Srinivasan 2018, p.127). For example, anger is typically an appropriate emotion for victims of racist oppression to feel in response to their oppression. However, in some situations they may find that expressing anger will radicalize their opponents and alienate potential allies and play into social stereotypes others hold of them. In such cases, Srinivasan claims that, in addition to the original injustice of racist oppression, there is also a secondary *affective* injustice (Srinivasan 2018, p.135). This is the injustice of having to manage the psychological and normative conflict between one's legitimate feelings of anger and the need to avoid feeling and expressing anger in order not to bring about further harm.[20]

Similarly, Whitney uses the term "affective injustice" to refer to cases in which the emotional experiences of oppressed groups are denied uptake (Whitney 2018). For example, a man who responds to a woman's anger by treating her as acting "hysterically" treats her anger as revealing something about her own mental instability rather than as a response to something happening in the world (Whitney 2018, p.49; see also Frye 1983). In this example, the man refuses to grant the woman's anger what Whitney calls "affective weight": he does not let the woman's anger emotionally move him. Rather he treats it as an indication that something is wrong with her. Whitney compares this affective injustice to Miranda Fricker's (2007) account of *epistemic* injustice (Fricker 2007). Just as negative stereotypes may mean that victims of oppression are not seen to be as credible as other people, equally

[20] See (Archer and Mills 2019) for further discussion.

they may undermine "the weight afforded one's feelings" (Whitney 2018, p.495).

The emotional regime of meritocracy leads to a similar form of affective injustice being inflicted upon the poor. It would be fitting for the poor to feel anger at the ways in which market societies are rigged in favour of the rich. However, the narrative of meritocracy places the responsibility for poverty squarely with the poor. This makes it harder for the anger of the poor to receive uptake, as people are encouraged to think that the poor have no one but themselves to blame for their poverty. This then makes it unlikely that these appropriate feelings of anger will receive uptake. More generally, the stigmatization of the poor discourages other people from feeling sympathy towards them. As we have already discussed, terms like "underclass" and consistent media representations of the poor as an outgroup discourage people from feeling sympathy or compassion towards the poor. This lack of sympathy means that the emotional responses of the poor are likely to be either ignored or dismissed.

However, the problem is not only one of a lack of uptake. By the meritocratic logic, any negative feelings the poor have about their condition should be directed at themselves. This encourages the poor to feel ashamed of themselves rather than feeling anger towards the social and economic forces keeping them in poverty. While we have already discussed the harmful effects of shame, the point we wish to make now concerns the *injustice* of the promotion of these feelings of shame (which is a key aspect of the emotional regime of market societies), given the fact that the system is rigged in favour of the rich (which is a key aspect of our capitalist societies).

The poor are, in effect, being told to participate in a competition that is rigged against them from the start and then told to feel ashamed for failing to succeed in this competition. In this case, the meritocratic aspect of the emotional regime is systematically promoting unfitting negative attitudes towards a particular group of people in society. We take it that the systematic imposition of unfitting negative attitudes on a particular group of people should be seen as a particular form of affective injustice. As Archer and Matheson point out, at the most general level, an affective injustice is, "a wrong done to someone specifically in their capacity as an affective being" (Archer and Matheson 2022, p.768).[21] The systematic imposition of unfitting negative

[21] This characterization adapts Fricker's characterization of epistemic injustice, which she describes as cases, "in which someone is wronged specifically in their capacity as a knower", to the

attitudes towards a particular group is not a form of affective injustice in the sense explored by Srinivasan or Whitney. However, it does fit with the characterization of affective injustice provided by Archer and Matheson, as it is a wrong done to someone in their role as a subject of affective experiences.

A more substantive general account of the nature of affective injustice is provided by Francisco Gallegos, who argues that an affective injustice is, "a state in which individuals or groups are deprived of 'affective goods' which are owed to them" (Gallegos 2022, p.186). He identities two fundamental affective goods that people may be owed. First, subjective well-being. While people are not owed subjective well-being directly, they can be entitled to the subsidiary goods that make subjective well-being possible. Similarly, while not all experiences that are harmful to subjective well-being constitute an affective injustice, Gallegos argues that where someone is frequently subjected to negative emotional experiences that are harmful to their subjective well-being, this can constitute an injustice. For example, someone who is forced to endure extreme emotional distress due to long periods of financial precarity may be said to be subject to an affective injustice (Gallegos 2022, p191). The many arguments in this book about capitalism's institutional mechanisms that generate, perpetuate, and exacerbate inequality and the emotional regime that accompanies and reinforces it, can thus be said to be a continual sources of affective injustice. The second fundamental affective good is emotional aptness. While people do not have a right to have apt emotional responses, they can be wronged when they are subject to severe social costs for their apt emotional responses. Thus a meritocratic ideology deprives people of both kinds of fundamental goods: it promotes the idea that the poor should experience shame in response to their poverty, an emotional response which is both negative and inapt. In these multiple ways the narrative of meritocracy interacts with other oppressive images and narratives that exist in market societies such as, amongst others, sexist, racist, homophobic, and ableist narratives.

Of course, we cannot hope to cover the range of different oppressive narratives that can be found in market societies. Nor should we assume that these various forms of oppression will take the same shape across different societies or within the same society at different times. It would be a mistake, for example, to think we can neatly draw on understandings of

case of affective injustice (Fricker 2007, p.1). For some possible interpretations of this claim, see (Thomas 2018).

racism in the United States to help us understand the nature of racism in the United Kingdom or the Netherlands. As Paul Gilroy points out: "'Race' has to be socially and politically constructed and elaborate ideological work is done to secure and maintain the different forms of 'racialization' which have characterized capitalist development" (Gilroy 1987/2002, p.35). This ideological work will always take place in interaction with other features of society and culture.

With these caveats in mind, we wish to make one general observation about the way in which meritocracy will interact with other, existing forms of oppression. Our starting point is a specific observation made by Patricia Hill Collins about the way in which various myths about Black American women in the United States serve to divert attention away from the fact the disadvantages and injustices that Black Americans face in the United States. First, the image of the "mammy" depicts Black American women as "the faithful, obedient domestic servant" (Collins 2009, p.80). This image helps to mask the fact that many Black American women are forced by economic circumstances to accept positions as domestic workers by presenting this as a job they are naturally disposed to be suited to and enjoy.

Secondly, the very different image of the matriarch, referring to "overly aggressive, unfeminine women" who scare away the fathers of their children and are unwilling to spend time nurturing their children (Collins 2009, p.83). According to Collins, this image, "allows White men and women to blame Black women for their children's failures at school and with the law, as well as Black children's subsequent poverty" (Collins 2009, p.84). The problems facing Black children and young people then, can be blamed on the matriarch's shortcomings as a mother. As Collins points out, by placing the blame here, this myth, "diverts attention from political and economic inequalities that increasingly characterize global capitalism" (Collins 2009, p.84). In doing so it presents a "sanitized view of American society," in which "those African-Americans who remain poor cause their own victimization" (Collins 2009, p.84).

These images are likely to have arisen from the specific circumstances in which racism developed in the United States. Nevertheless, it is worth examining the role that these two narratives play in relation to the racial inequality in the United States. In the absence of such narratives and images, the claim that American society is meritocratic would be very hard for people to accept. If the United States were truly meritocratic then there would need to be some explanation as to why Black people are over-represented in the ranks of the poor. These images either distract attention away from the problem (in the case of the mammy) or provide an explanation for this over-representation (in the case of the matriarch). In doing so they serve to bolster the narrative of meritocracy by helping it avoid or respond to the otherwise awkward fact of disadvantage facing Black people. In addition, the narrative of meritocracy also helps to reinforce these narratives, by providing supposed evidence to those who believe in the lesser merits of Black Americans. The narrative of meritocracy and these existing oppressive images and narratives are then likely to be mutually reinforcing.

The case we have considered is specific to a particular context but the logic underpinning it is one that is likely to apply more generally. In societies with little social mobility and marked by various forms of disadvantage and oppression, the narrative of meritocracy is likely to be repeatedly challenged by the fact that society is not, in fact, meritocratic. The general lesson to take away from this specific case then, is that existing oppressive narratives and images can serve to bolster the narrative of meritocracy against what would otherwise be clear evidence that meritocracy is a myth. In turn, the myth of meritocracy is likely to bolster these existing oppressive narratives.

Conclusion

In summary, we have argued that meritocracy is a myth, but a myth that plays a major role in market societies. While others have criticized meritocracy for damaging the self-respect of the poor and for promoting the domination of one group over another, we have sought to extend these critiques by arguing that meritocracy plays a key role in the emotional regime of market societies. The narrative plays a consistent role in media framing of the lives of both the rich and the poor, endorsing the emotions of admiration and (benign) envy towards the rich and contempt and shame towards the poor. In doing so it helps to reinforce the position of the powerful in society and undermine the position of the powerless.

To make matters worse, belief in meritocracy appears to be stronger in less equal societies, meaning that societies in which inequality is highest tend to be ones in which people care least about it. The problem with the myth of meritocracy, though, is not just that it serves to reinforce the position of the powerful and to legitimize inequality but also the way in which it does this. As we argued, the myth of meritocracy not only damages well-being but also constitutes at least two forms of affective injustice against the poor. First, it discourages affective uptake of the fitting emotions of the poor. Secondly, it promotes unfitting negative attitudes towards them. The problem then is not just that the myth of meritocracy serves to reinforce a form of society that is damaging to society but also that the way in which it does so is unjust. We concluded by exploring ways in which the myth of meritocracy draws on existing narratives and images of oppression in ways that are mutually reinforcing.

13

Liberal and Republican Emotional Regimes Revisited

Propositional Summary

1. The distinction between strong and weak egalitarianism is clarified. The connection Rawls makes between this distinction and his political psychology is further clarified. It is explained how this distinction explains both the nature of welfare state capitalism and anti-capitalist alternatives to it.
2. Taking Pettit's republicanism and Rawlsian liberalism as representative of weak and strong egalitarianism, we describe how political psychology allows us to make the case for the latter vis-à-vis the former by appealing to the symbolism of mutual investments. Pettit presupposes the virtue of boldness; our Rawlsian proposal connects it to investments in each other that ground a sense of self-worth. Public affirmation of mutually assured principles of justice is an act of mutual recognition.
3. We describe the rationale for a jobs guarantee by the state. It would express the consistent use of the state's monopoly powers; it would decommodify labour; it would have significant well-being effects.
4. Fishkin's anti-bottleneck principle is set out; the goal is to implement fair equality of opportunity by restructuring the field of opportunity. Asset base egalitarianism achieves this while also reconceiving the boundaries of work. Those capitalized by the state can directly access productive opportunity.
5. Demarketization of goods vulnerable to positional competition and the provision of public goods are essential complements to our proposals. Public goods as a general category have a disproportionate impact on both social trust and well-being.

Extravagance and Misery. Alan Thomas, Alfred Archer, and Bart Engelen, Oxford University Press.
 DOI: 10.1093/oso/9780197781722.003.0014

6. We interpret Rawls's associationalism as a strategy for re-channelling positional competition in a society where the previous strategies for controlling it have been implemented. Associationalism reinforces a distinct political principle identified by Hussain as a principle of solidarity.
7. A conception of public financing in which the state appears as a financial intermediary is contested. Monetarily sovereign states establish what counts as money for political purposes. If they choose to run a deficit they conventionally issue matching debt instruments but this is not revenue raising. Giving every citizen a bank account at the central bank as of right reflects our democratic values and that finance can always be put to positive social ends.
8. We have tackled the pressing issues of gender and global justice via our prioritarian focus. In the actual circumstances of our world to be concerned with the worst off is to be concerned, disproportionately, with the groups who are in fact the most discriminated against, marginalized, and whose prospects would be most improved if we pursue the goal of justice as a whole.

Introduction

Our argument is drawing to a close. As Marion Fourcade and Kieran Healy noted over a decade ago, critiques of capitalism, in works spanning philosophy, economics, sociology, geography and psychology, now form an extensive body of work (Fourcade and Healy 2007). Four claims have set our treatment apart:

First, instead of critiquing capitalism as a whole, we have focused on the unstable, rent-extracting, de-legitimating capitalism that has generated the New Inequality of the last forty years.

Secondly, we have focused on the consequences of this inequality for well-being by drawing on the resources of the new science of happiness, which has further developed since Fourcade and Healy's survey.

Thirdly, we have employed the notion of "emotional regimes" to analyse specifically, the role that emotions play in the interplay between the social and institutional mechanisms in capitalism generating, perpetuating and exacerbating inequality on the one hand and the impact on well-being on the other.

Fourthly, we want to move beyond diagnosis to solutions: we think we have some of the necessary answers to these problems even if only in a schematic form. The schematic form is necessary for two reasons: we have addressed some of this in earlier work and diagnosis was our primary task here (Thomas 2017). Nevertheless, in this chapter we hope to set out a relatively optimistic view of our collective future.

13.1 Strong and Weak Egalitarianism and Social Stability

In previous work one of the current authors has defended, as a realistically utopian ideal, a conception of a property-owning democracy (Thomas 2017). It is a pre-distributive, asset-focused form of egalitarianism that argues that every citizen ought to receive a basic allocation of capital as of right. For our argument here we will also take it to be exemplary of strong egalitarianism. What qualifies a view as strongly egalitarian? To explain what we mean by this we will cite this well-known paragraph in Rawls:

> Yet sometimes the circumstances evoking envy are so compelling that given human beings as they are, no one can reasonably be asked to overcome his rancorous feelings. A person's lesser position as measured by his index of objective primary goods may be so great as to wound his self-respect: and given his situation we may sympathize with his sense of loss. Indeed, we can resent being made envious, for society may permit such large disparities in these goods that under existing social conditions these differences cannot help but cause a loss of self-esteem. . . . Since self-respect is the main primary good, the parties would not agree, I shall assume, to count this sort of subjective loss as irrelevant .(Rawls 1971/1999, p.467)

This is Rawls's most explicit framing of his conception of justice in terms of the emotions: reasonable envy, rancour, and self-respect (and its loss). It evokes both Rousseau and Hegel: the former in the phrase "given human beings as they are"; the latter in the phrase "existing social conditions". Existing social conditions will be "overcome" through the practical task of changing our institutions and social structures via the creation of institutions that reinforce each citizens' self-respect.

Rawls envisages a classless society that is "just throughout" and where the interests of each socio-economic group is, in his terminology, both close-knit and chain-connected (Rawls 1971/1999, p.71; Thomas 2017, pp.41–2). This implies that any change in the prospects for one group ramifies throughout the structure impacting every group. This is a salient point of contrast with the perspective of the weak egalitarian, who has no objection to a distributional change that makes a better off person even better off, provided that the least advantaged person is made no worse off. Rawls is, then, a strong egalitarian in the following sense:

> [T]he difference principle is a strongly egalitarian conception in the sense that unless there is a distribution that makes both (the more advantaged and the less advantaged) person better off . . . an equal distribution is to be preferred. (Rawls 1971/1999, pp.65–6)

According to this conception of justice, the "ceiling" and "floor" of a distribution move together. In Samuel Freeman's words:

> [T]he difference principle . . . justifies measures that mitigate inequality by reducing the wealth of the most advantaged in ways that maximally benefit the least advantaged. (Freeman 2020, p.186)

There is a fundamental contrast between Rawls's Rousseauian republic of equals, in which every citizen's interests are systematically interconnected with those of all other citizens, and those consequentialist distributions which permit "gappy" distributions across different groups.

That feature carries over from consequentialism to the most notorious target of Rawls's critique, namely, welfare state capitalism. Given the success of Nordic social democracy, most egalitarians are unsympathetic to Rawls's claim that all forms of welfare state capitalism are unjust (Rawls 2001).

This point about gappy distributions helps to explain the grounds of Rawls's critique: welfare state capitalism does not rule out substantial gaps in the chain linking the prospects of different groups individuated by their socio-economic status. Furthermore, if the role of incentives is to grow the pie for everyone, then the top end of the distribution must arguably be uncapped under certain forms of welfare state capitalism.

Adopting a sufficientarian perspective, for example: he or she can argue that if the least advantaged person has achieved a satisfactory level of well-being, then further increases in her well-being are no longer mandatory. The better off may blamelessly seek further to improve their position at no absolute cost to the most disadvantaged. This is particularly so if the additional well-being to the better off functions as an economic incentive—in the textbook sense—where such incentives increase aggregate utility overall. In this defence of inequality, they lead to overall growth, without it being "hamstrung"—as the critic sees it—by the veto Rawls gives to the worst off even if they are living at a sufficient standard.

In the background here are two other issues. The first is the structural dependence of the redistributivist state on private capitalists if you assume that redistribution works via tax and transfer. How can ambitious social programs be afforded if there are not wealthy individuals carrying a disproportionate degree of the tax burden in absolute terms?

Second, and in tension with this first thought, there is the problematic role played in welfare state capitalism by positional goods. Here, as we have seen (and as Scanlon, Swift, and Brighouse have all argued), we cannot justify inequalities in positional goods to the individual by arguing that this is "growing the pie" for all. Positional competition is zero-sum.

Welfare state capitalism, then, contains multiple implicit tensions. First, the funding of social programs seems to require an uncapped top end of wealthy people to carry a significant part of the tax burden and to "pay for" redistribution. Second, as we have argued in chapter 11, the least advantaged must be living at a decent sufficient standard where sufficiency includes social inclusion. Inclusion seems to involve positional goods. Third, as we discussed in chapter 9, it assumes that the wealthy are cultural legislators who drive up the standard for what counts as social inclusion in the domain of the positional. While Adam Smith's time required linen shirts, now social inclusion requires a smartphone with a broadband connection.

Against this rival, weakly egalitarian, conception—as expressed by welfare state capitalism—we argue that impermissible inequality arises when the "top end" of any distribution is unconstrained, even when the worst off in that distribution are living at some sufficient standard of decency. The existence of the very rich leads to multiple forms of domination: domination by the rentier class and the many forms of opportunity hoarding.

Rather than resolve these tensions, the welfare state capitalist lives with them by assuming continual economic growth. The wealthy supposedly drive this growth; their wealth trickles down to fund an ever rising "sufficient" standard; the middle class benefit from a reduction in consumption inequality. Proponents of this view might counter our critique by claiming that a properly designed welfare state capitalism will de-marketize key goods. It will thereby prevent the domain of the positional encroaching on the goods of social mobility, such as education and healthcare. (Even if such societies tolerate separate, private, provision of education and medical treatment to run alongside the public option.) Second, carrying the tax burden for social programs needs to be re-located to an affluent middle class—hence the need for very high rates of progressive taxation at the top end of the distribution. This actually used to be a signal form of tax policy in the United States: very high levels of personal progressive taxation of income. Admittedly, on this conception, positional competition will always be with us, as will the "relatively poor". But it will be contained, limited to domains that do not impact upon social mobility, and in that sense made "optional".

Clearly, for many progressives, such an idealized form of Nordic welfare state capitalism represents an ideal social system. Both Thomas Piketty and T.M. Scanlon seem drawn to a social democratic ideal of this kind. This kind of view is explicitly endorsed by Robert S. Taylor, an influential recent theorist of republicanism, and it is implicit in Pettit's work (Taylor 2017; Pettit 2012, 2014). Some property-owning democrats, such as Martin O'Neill, hold a view of this kind (O'Neill 2020).

Within this cluster of views there is a self-aware form of welfare state capitalism that does not shy away from the reality of class conflict. In his updating of the Smithian ideal that we have discussed throughout this book, Joshua Preiss is open in his adaptation of a core strategy inspired by Adam Smith. Preiss's "just work" view hopes to restore rapid and inclusive growth with the state intervening to strengthen the bargaining power of labour using a variety of pro-worker policies (Preiss 2021). The point is that even if the rentier-investor class seeks to dominate the ordinary worker, the scale and rapidity of growth and worker prosperity will frustrate that goal. There is a virtuous spiral of the market virtues being translated into a middle-class quality of life that reinforces those very virtues and spreads them further.[1] If there is going to be a comparatively wealthy capitalist class—and welfare state capitalism explicitly permits this—it needs to be recruited into a social consensus that brings essentially conflicting class interests into a mutually satisfactory alignment with the state acting as "honest broker".

[1] In Preiss's account, his "Smithian well ordered society" produces "not only greater equality but also greater opportunity, tolerance of diversity, social mobility, and a commitment to fairness" (Preiss 2021, p.61).

We argue that, as a matter of historical record, even in the case of egalitarian paradigms like the Nordic countries, its wealthiest citizens will draw the line at some stage in the process that O'Neill and Preiss envisage. In Sweden, this line was drawn at the "Meidner Plan", where corporate profit taxes were intended to purchase shares in major Swedish companies that would be transferred, step-by-step, to funds under the control of labour unions.[2] It was a plan for the democratization of the economy. The success of broader economic policies, Keynesian in inspiration, were leading to high profits for the very small number of private capitalists who dominated the Swedish economy (Viktorsson and Gowan 2017). Wage restraint by workers was producing super-profits for employers. The Meidner Plan, which aimed at the gradual transformation of firms into majority ownership by wage-earner funds, produced a powerful political backlash from both Sweden's wealthiest families and middle class and died in the Swedish elections of 1976 (Viktorsson and Gowan 2017).

We are sceptical, then, about the long-run success of social democratic policies to control this class-based conflict as welfare state capitalism tries to balance conflicting social forces. In addition, there is the problem of path-dependency: once oligarchic pressure has significantly eroded democratic control, it is very hard to recover it. As one of the authors of this book has argued before, inequality of income may be suppressed for a time, but the long-term accumulation of capital inequality has destabilizing effects (Thomas 2017).

Thomas Piketty's history of the development of capitalism notes the steady and uninterrupted accumulation of massive levels of capital inequality over the nineteenth century up to the First World War. The success of social democratic inequality in restricting this inequality in the mid-twentieth century was comparatively brief. Since then, income compression has been undone by a background of capital inequality, the drift to oligarchy as large-scale controllers of capital acquire undue influence on the political process, all against a background of class division.

Class division impacts even on educational and healthcare systems insulated from the positional: via "dual track" systems of public and private provision side by side, or by public provision undermined via the

[2] In Piketty's comprehensive history of inequality regimes, Sweden in 1980 tops the chart as "one of the most egalitarian [societies] ever seen in terms of income distribution.... The top decile's share of total income was less than 25 percent, compared with 35 percent for Western Europe and around 50 percent for the United States in 2018" (Piketty 2020, p.260).

comparative advantage of the affluent. (More so in the case of education than healthcare.) Positional competition can easily be displaced horizontally: for example, if a successful state-funded school has places that cannot literally be bought and sold, then this competition will be displaced to the property prices of housing near to that school.

We have our doubts, then, about the long-term stability of a sufficientarian welfare state that is forced to reconcile its internal tensions by committing itself to continual growth. This is the crux of the Easterlin paradox: "sufficiency" is an elusive goal in a society that legitimates inequality via such class-based hierarchies. We have framed our doubts in this book on this issue of stability through the lens of the emotional regime of capitalist societies. Welfare state capitalist societies, even in Scanlon and Piketty's idealized forms, are still capitalist societies. They recruit the emotional logic that we have described here to maintain their social and institutional structures. They inevitably evolve into the rent-seeking societies we criticized in our opening chapters as the social advantaged seek to lock in their advantages and pass them on to their offspring.

We have traced how capitalist societies are structured around a range of class-based social mechanisms that are disciplinary in nature. Class-based hierarchy puts in place a series of artificial bottlenecks artificially to constrain the supply of key life goods. Note how the capitalism that we target here is not the capitalism of the Industrial Revolution to which Marx and Engels reacted. The issue is not the social power of a small group of monopolistic capitalists; rather the domination of most citizens by a rentier-investor class who exploit their comparative advantage to create, and benefit from, the numerous forms of rent extraction we have documented in this book.

Artificial bottlenecks, such as those in employment (access to jobs) or education (access to positions of advantage), are appropriately conceptualized as rent-extracting opportunities. By failing to address the issue of the underlying holding of capital, capitalist societies, even with a welfare state, fail to address these structural issues, while emotionally appealing to many of their citizens, promising social mobility and emancipation through work.

There is a deeper problem here. We have noted Tooze's claim that corporate actors in the contemporary United States face no major countervailing power at all (Tooze 2021a).[3] There is a significant academic literature on the decline of mass participation and the technocratic hollowing out of

[3] We have already noted the complementary arguments of (Rendueles 2017).

politics, but our current point is that the effect of this is asymmetric. The organized interests of capital are impacted less by these evolutions than the interests of trade unions, progressive parties, and the civil society organizations that once underpinned them. The abstract debates between strong and weak egalitarianism, then, can be transposed into a broader discussion of the specific implementation of the Rawlsian "choice of a social system". But that takes us back to our originating question: specifically from the perspective of human well-being, what gives strong egalitarianism the advantage?

13.2 Self-Respect, Confidence, and Mutual Investment

How does the general contrast between strong and weak egalitarianism play out in the choice between Rawlsian political liberalism and Roman republicanism? From the plethora of conceptions of justice we have not denied that we view only these two conceptions—or a synthesis between them—to be the most defensible options (Thomas 2017). The issue is complicated because, on the one hand, Pettit is a defender of a sophisticated version of welfare state capitalism on a consequentialist basis (Pettit 2012, 2014). On the other hand, he is also a relational egalitarian, stressing the ideal of an achieved status, that of the Roman *liber*, or free person, just as Rawls's Rousseauian view is structured around the ideal of the citizen. We think that there is an important way to distinguish the two views, namely, the symbolic importance of mutual investment in the material basis of the self-respect of other citizens in the context of mutual recognition.

The recognitional component of Pettit's view lies in his endorsement of Smith's criterion: the ability to appear in public without shame. This is both an example of the politics of recognition and expresses the republican ideal of not being dominated by another. As we noted in the previous chapter, Elizabeth Anderson observes that "Smith depicts market relations as egalitarian: the parties to exchange interact on terms of equal authority, esteem and standing" (Anderson 2017, p.4). Both Smith's and Rousseau's views thus have a recognitional component. That said, we will argue that strong egalitarianism succeeds where weak egalitarianism fails in substantiating this claim.

The difference is this: if Smith's criterion captures the reasonable demand for mutual recognition by the payment of a decent social minimum that facilitates full membership in society, then further inequalities that do not reduce this minimum level are permissible. The Smith criterion seems compatible with the Paretian reading of—or surrogate for—the difference principle.[4] The Rousseau-Rawls argument, by contrast, connects the desire for recognition directly to a strongly egalitarian restriction on inequality of income and wealth.[5]

Our focus here is on one way in which the contrast between these two views plays out. We can reconstruct from Pettit's work a political psychology of domination: those who are dominated are craven, deferential, and themselves manipulative towards those upon whom they depend for the satisfaction of their own interests. According to Pettit, the undominated must possess a certain boldness or self-confidence. It is one thing to secure the status of the *liber*, or free person, and another thing to assure that a person who enjoys this status will boldly assert his or her projects:

> The eyeball test does not require that people should be able to look one another in the eye, regardless of their personal lack of nerve. It requires that they have this capacity in the absence of what would count, even by the most demanding standards of their society, as mere timidity or cowardice. The reference to timidity is essential, since *no public safeguards can compensate for differences between individual personalities and for variations in people's capacity to deal with the overbearing assumptions of others.* (Pettit 2012, pp.84–5, emphasis added).

Pettit suggests here that if citizens lack this kind of boldness, or confidence, to stand up to the would-be dominator, then it is difficult to see how state action in a republican polity can bring it about.

This is a problem for any theory which explains how to move from the kinds of unjust societies in which we currently live to a more just republican polity. If democratic action, channelled via our collective agency of the democratic state, does indeed succeed in making our society more just what are we to do when faced with those who do not advance their legitimate claims?

[4] As Samuel Freeman notes, on this interpretation the difference principle itself is "perfectly compatible with the vast inequalities typical of welfare state capitalist economies, so long as they benefit the least advantaged members of society" (Freeman 2020, p.176).

[5] Freeman also points out that when Rawls presented his final conception of (domestic) justice, the difference principle has some distinctive work to do as expressive of what he calls "reciprocity at the deepest level" that is also, for Rawls, "essential to democratic equality" (Rawls 2001, p.126, p.133). If the difference principle were merely a Paretian principle that did not restrict any inequality, no matter how extensive it was (provided it benefitted the worst off), Rawls would not think that the principle had these implications for this ideal of democratic citizenship.

Recent work on epistemic injustice has focused on this kind of case: where repeated silencing, or interruption, leads to people silencing themselves (Fricker 2007). Our own view is that the general category of epistemic injustices covers a broad range of cases, but certainly it includes the phenomenon that Karen Jones describes as a loss of confidence, or in her terms, a lack of "intellectual self-trust" (Jones 2012). Repeated treatment of this kind results in people silencing themselves, in the absence of the immediate presence of a dominator: people like me are just not listened to, so why speak? This kind of treatment has been called, by Kristie Dotson, a form of "testimonial smothering" (Dotson 2011).[6]

The idea of lacking confidence in one's own standing as able to advance projects both goes beyond epistemology and is not merely an issue in transitional justice. We think it is helpful to examine how Rawls addresses the problem. In his critique of welfare state capitalism, Rawls focuses on the psychology of what it is like to be dominated. He contrasted two kinds of cases.

> In the first way we become sullen and resentful, and we are ready on the occasion to take violent action in protest against our condition. . . . The least advantaged are bitter; they reject society's conception of justice and see themselves as oppressed. (Rawls 2001, p.128)

Rawls surmises that the payment of a decent social minimum may forestall this first reaction of bitterness and violence. However, such an approach would fail to address the second type amongst the dominated:

> *If they are not withdrawn from their public world* but rather to consider themselves full members of it, the social minimum, whatever it may provide beyond essential human needs, must derive from an idea of reciprocity. (Rawls 2001, p.130, emphasis added)

On this second understanding, people who are dominated do not become violent. We can assume that the politics of redress that underpins their welfare state societies entitles them to a decent social minimum. But they do not determine its level; it falls below that to which they are entitled if they were bound to their fellow citizens by ties of reciprocity. Their reaction to their standing in the eyes of others is not violence, but withdrawal.

[6] See also (Abramson 2014).

Mutual recognition implies full membership; full membership, Rawls argues, involves relations of reciprocity. We interpret that requirement as the view that relating to each other as equals involves recognizing the expressive significance of mutual investment in each other's psychological capacities. It matters not only that we resource each other's projects but also how we do so—in a way expressive of the value of mutual reciprocity.[7]

Those who are marginalized withdraw from society not because those who seek to dominate them seek to marginalize and exclude them. We can assume, under welfare state capitalism, that the democratic majority possesses a benign collective intent. The problem is that those who are marginalized under these arrangements seek to exclude *themselves*. They do so because they lack confidence in their own self-worth—a point that Rawls returns to repeatedly. Hence the reference, in the passage quoted, to "withdrawal" and cynicism. Equally, when Rawls mentions the psychology of the dominator, he explicitly connects the psychology of the dominator to that of the dominated: the citizens of a well-ordered society will

> acquire a sufficiently strong and effective sense of justice so that they normally comply with just arrangements and are not moved to act otherwise, say, by social envy and spite, or by a will to dominate or a *tendency to submit.* (Rawls 2001, p.181, emphasis added)

This is not to blame the victim for complicity with their domination; rather, Rawls's argument is that the dominator may instil in others a propensity to be dominated under certain social conditions. Rawls is as concerned with the resiliency of those who may be subject to domination as the anxiety-driven motivations of those who seek to dominate. One of our core arguments in this book is that we need to expand our focus beyond dominating individuals to dominating practices that dominators tolerate on the part of a broader class of citizens.

Rawls connects this lack of confidence in one's own self-worth to lack of recognition from others. His point is not that the worst off have not benefitted from a decent social minimum. Rather, the underlying point is psychological: that there is a difference between supplying the material basis of a citizen's self-worth and doing so in such a way that gives them confidence in that self-worth. Self-worth is in the eye of the beholder—the person

[7] For a similar argument, see (late) Nozick (1989, pp.286–91).

whom we have resourced to give them confidence in their own projects. But to realize that goal it is not enough to say: we have adequately funded your projects, why are you timid in putting them forward? The vice of excessive timidity ought to be our concern, too, as confidence comes from the mutual recognition bound up with reciprocal social relations.

The material bases of self-respect are distributed with a view to *expressing* the ideal of democratic citizenship, where each of us can, as a *liber*, look any of our fellow citizens in the eye with neither deference nor timidity. The public affirmation of mutually assured principles of justice is such an act of mutual recognition. In a society well-ordered by justice you can have confidence in your self-worth because your fellow citizens have confidence in you as expressed by your joint commitment to the ideal of reciprocity. Our focus is on this key line in Rawls: that "self-respect is secured by the public affirmation of the status of equal citizenship for all" (Rawls 1971/1999, pp.544–6, pp.477–9).

This public affirmation is achieved by the mutual investment in each other that reflects the confidence of the collective "We" in each of us, its constituent members. Each of us ought to have confidence in our projects, and therefore be able to value them, precisely because collectively those of us who have chosen to regulate our social co-ordination together via publicly known principles of justice have that confidence in each other.

The idea, then, is that resourcing every citizen's basic standing in the eyes of others requires making an investment in them and in the confidence in their self-worth. Rawls believes that this confidence is a fragile phenomenon and that the institutions of civil society play an important role in sustaining it:

> The account of *self-respect as perhaps the main primary good has stressed the great significance of how we think others value us.* But in a well-ordered society the need for status is met by the public recognition of just institutions, together with the *full and diverse internal life of the free communities of interest* that the equal liberties allow. . . . Having chosen a conception of justice *that seeks to eliminate the significance of relative economic and social advantages as supports for men's self-confidence,* it is essential that the priority of liberty be firmly maintained. (Rawls 1971/1999, pp.477–8, emphases added)

This passage also attaches significance to the "full and diverse internal life" of "free communities of interest". While the reciprocal affirmation of justice has removed our ability to compete with each other by taking income and wealth as markers of social status, the only social status that matters is that of citizen. However, even with that issue resolved, the fragile social resource of confidence in one's own self-worth is something that can be fostered and protected by the very same institutions to which the republican democrat, such as Pettit, appeals on different grounds, that is, as avenues of contestation in a republican polity.

Our argument is that if one shares the goal of a republican polity not only to ensure the material basis of self-respect but also to promote the psychological conditions necessary for that material basis to play its role, then our aim should be to implement strong egalitarianism. Only attention to the social supports for confidence will allow the republican polity to realize its ideals. This is another respect in which it seems to us that a liberal-republican view is stronger than either justice as fairness or republicanism taken as self-sufficient, stand-alone views. While this provides the schematic form of the solution, we need to set out, step by step, the concrete policy proposals that follow from it. That is our task for the remainder of this chapter.

13.3 Full Employment and the De-Commodification of Labour

We have focused, specifically, on how the transition from the ideals of a market society to the failings of its capitalist variant begin from the monopoly power of the wealthy over the means of production, but expand into a range of forms of domination. We have, following Kalecki, placed particular importance on the disciplinary role of unemployment. In so far as Pettit's weak egalitarianism disposes him to welfare state capitalism, the issue remains to what extent full employment is mandated in a view of this kind.

We have noted that Rawls's political liberalism was committed both to full employment and to the related proposal that the state function as the employer of last resort (Thomas 2020b). While we will not reproduce here arguments why one of the current authors claims that this represents the de-commodification of labour (Hockett 2019; Thomas 2020b), we do believe that this is what this commitment represents and that we can explain it, using our current vocabulary, as an issue of mutual respect.

In the opening chapter we noted Joan Robinson's and Hyman Minsky's diagnoses that, under the auspices of a "Keynesianism", the monopoly powers of the state were put to use solely to underwrite corporate profits in the aggregate (as described by the Levy-Kalecki profits equation (Levy, Farnham, and Rajan 2008). In so far as the state's monopoly in the creation of money was concerned, the legislative state outsourced central banking to an autonomous central bank mandated to ensure both price stability and full employment (in the representative case of the US Federal Reserve) (Dietsch, Claveau, and Fontan 2018; Thomas 2023). Yet, in practice, price stability—inflation control—received priority over the maintenance of full employment. Apart from a renegade like Hyman Minsky, the idea of the state functioning as guarantor of full employment has been a policy dead letter for the last forty years (Minsky 2013; Tcherneva 2020; Thomas 2020b).

In a monetarily sovereign state, central banking has a dual mandate to maintain price stability and full employment (Baker, Rawlins, and Stein 2017). This reflects Keynes's simple point that employment is a monetary phenomenon: an unemployed person cannot find work at a wage she is prepared to accept. However, in our monetarily sovereign states the central bank has, once again, learned to be helpless. One of these goals has, in practice, taken priority over the other. Motivated by a dubious piece of economic ideology, central banks have managed a putative "trade off" between their goals; yet they have done so heavily in favour of inflation control and not full employment.

Having encouraged the spread of market-based finance, the state, via its agent the central bank, has been drawn in to what Mark Blyth has called a "moral hazard distortion game" with the major financial institutions that are famously "too big to fail" as an entire group (Blyth 2020). The state views the infrastructural power of finance as too important to allow market disruption, in a crisis, to be resolved by market means such as extensive institutional bankruptcies. We noted Minsky's argument in chapter 1 that bailouts are, of their nature, inflationary—a central bank takes assets with no market value and treats them as though they had viable market prices. The financial system has benefitted from this state insurance again and again, even as austerity politics cut public services elsewhere.

Citizens as a whole might reasonably construe this policy as placing the sovereign power of money creation at the service of the rentier-investor class alone. A significant contribution to the wealth inequality that has seen affluent citizens pull away from the rest has been falling interest rates over the past 35 years (including the notorious "Greenspan put") that has inflated asset prices and hence capital gains (Taylor and Ömer 2020, p.53).[8] All of these outcomes are a direct result of central bank policy.[9]

We do not deny that central bankers are well intentioned public servants who try to act for the public good. They might reasonably retort that it is the democratic failures of fiscal (tax) policy that have created pressure for central banks to pursue goals that are outside their actual remit as technocratic institutions (Thomas 2023). They did not create the moral hazard game they must play, nor the timidity of states in taxing the rich, nor negligence in cracking down on tax evasion by individuals and corporations. These are all reasonable points: we need to re-imagine the institutional role of such banks (Thomas 2023). Yet they have undoubtedly contributed to the underlying logic we described in our opening chapter: inequality produces macro-economic instability that produces financial crises which, in turn, force central bank interventions that support the market, thereby valorizing the risky practices that produce the next crisis—and cause more inequality.[10]

We noted, in chapter 6, the prescience of Fichte's derivation of the conclusion that his ideal of republican non-domination required the state to function as employer of last resort, just as there is a direct line from Rawls's relational egalitarianism to the same conclusion (Moriarty 2009). Thomas Fazi and Bill Mitchell contrast state employment of residual labour as a form of "pump priming" of the labour market with the separable idea that this guarantee is issued by the state. The former, as traditionally conceived, "maintains full capacity by hiring 'off the top'—that is, by competing for resources at market prices and relying on so-called spending multipliers to generate the extra jobs necessary to achieve full employment" (Fazi and Mitchell 2017, p.232). Mitchell and Fazi agree with Hegel that this policy is, indeed, potentially inflationary with the state competing with private employers in this way for resources.

That is not, however, how the public jobs guarantee which they favour works. By contrast, it is not inflationary because: "the government's unconditional job offer is at a fixed wage (the fixed price rule) and the buffer stock

[8] "[B]eginning in the 1980s, the Federal Reserve cut interest rates after every stock market wobble. . . . In Wall Street jargon, the Fed's Governor Alan Greenspan planted an interest rate 'put' to shore up the stock market and aggregate demand. His successors Ben Bernanke, Janet Yellen and Jerome Powell continued the practice" (Taylor and Ömer 2020, p.52).

[9] The underlying cause is Taylor and Ömer's primary explanatory factor: wage suppression. Suppressed wages have put no upward pressure on prices, so high interest rates have not been required to suppress inflation (Taylor and Ömer 2020, p.57).

[10] Following Minsky's pioneering work (Minsky 1986/2008) the working of these "Minskyan cycles" and "supercycles" is well understood (Dafermos, Gabor, and Michell 2020; Palley 2011).

of jobs fluctuates in accordance with the strength of non-government sector spending (a floating quantity)" (Fazi and Mitchell 2017, p.231). Proponents of the guarantee note that it is politically uncontroversial for a central bank to underwrite the rental price of money (the interest rate) or to underwrite the price of key commodities (such as stockpiling grain or oil).[11] Yet it seems controversy begins at the mere suggestion of putting a floor under the cost of labour (Hockett 2019; Tcherneva 2020, p.50).

The proposal, then, is for a public option of employment for any citizen who wants to be employed.[12] We propose that it differ from the payment of an unconditional basic income because the alternative to being employed is to receive, instead, Rawls's decent civic minimum—an amount calculated to cover only basic needs, topped up by an appropriate level of unemployment benefit (Thomas 2020b). One can only reasonably presume that the kind of unconditional basic income proponents of that view have in mind would be far higher than this alternative payment under already existing capitalism.[13]

The jobs that the state offers will be of meaningful work paying a living wage. It goes beyond minimum wage policy as it functions now because, as Pavlina Tcherneva acerbically comments, the wage of an unemployed person who cannot secure a minimum wage job "is, in fact, zero" (Tcherneva 2020, p.47). The state already engages in the large-scale employment of many citizens for many different public purposes.[14] We simply lack the imagination, as a society, to think about those employed via a jobs guarantee could be tasked to do. Given the dominance in our thinking of the private sector option, it is natural to think of the public option as representing a second grade safety net, for employment—particularly for work on infrastructure.[15] But if a person who turns down a lucrative job at a software company to work as a social worker values things other than pecuniary reward, given the incentive

[11] Tcherneva notes the important disanalogies: a commodity stock does not lose its resale value. As we have seen, the private labour market de-values the long-term unemployed; people who want to be in work want to be in work continually to develop their trained abilities (Tcherneva 2020, p.51). Most importantly, unemployment is a harm to those who suffer it (ibid).

[12] The word "voluntary" is important: this is not the return of the Victorian workhouse. Those who do not want to work, even if they can, *also* receive the decent civic minimum.

[13] The contrast between the policy of the state acting as employer of last resort and Van Parijs's original, groundbreaking, arguments for an unconditional basic income (as his answer to the question of "what, if anything, justifies capitalism) is the focus of (Thomas 2020b; Van Parijs 1995).

[14] Tcherneva notes that currently 20% of employment in the United States serves one or other form of public service (Tcherneva 2020, p.22).

[15] Hockett also argues that "The jobs that would come of these efforts would have every reason to come to be seen as high prestige, not make-work vocations" (Hockett 2019, p.123). This directly addresses Hegel's concern that this work would indeed merely be "make work".

to taking risks in a property-owning democracy might that same person not join a software collective generating free software for the public commons? We lack imagination when it comes to the jobs of the future. Fazi and Mitchell similarly argue that:

> A new employment paradigm where community development and other non-traditional jobs would become valued . . . public debate and education can help broaden the concept of valuable work until activities which we might construe today as being leisure would become considered to be "gainful employment". (Fazi and Mitchell 2017, p.245)

It is important to note that this policy is part of a package of proposals—as it was in Rawls's work—that bring about a larger transformation of the economy into either a property-owning democracy or liberal market socialism.

When we assess this policy in context we are presupposing that all the principles of justice as fairness will have been fully implemented. That is why, in this chapter, we focus on the idea of a realistically utopian transformation of work that also, after the kind of macro-level radical restructuring Rawls and Mill have in mind, redraws the lines of what counts as "work".

In particular, in the non-capitalist proposals we are defending here, all work incentives will be compensatory alone (Smith 1998). Furthermore, all work will be meaningful, because no employer will be able to find a citizen willing to do work that is meaningless or degrading. It is in this context that the policy of the state acting as employer of last resort will deal with two aspects of current economic insecurity: unemployment itself and both precarity and low pay in work (Tcherneva 2020).[16]

As an extension of the state's monopoly powers, a jobs guarantee would be a critical macroeconomic stabilization mechanism. It would, therefore, be justified by its role in stabilizing productive efficiency alone. However, from Fichte, to Rawls and on to the work of Hockett and others, the fundamental case for a state backed jobs guarantee is, as we have argued, normative: it represents the fundamental de-commodification of human labour (Hockett 2019; Thomas 2020b).

[16] For example, Tcherneva notes that in the United States in 2018 "there were 6.9 million working people earning below the official poverty level" (Tcherneva 2020, p.16).

Our particular focus here is on the impact of a policy of full employment on well-being. The vagaries of a financialized business cycle determined primarily by private investment decisions sees a significant number of people involuntarily (structurally) unemployed through no fault of their own (Tcherneva 2020, p.28).[17] If that is unfair, the unfairness is compounded when private sector employers discriminate, in employment, against the long-term unemployed whom they view as de-skilled and expensive (as they require retraining) (p.29). Tcherneva notes that this is the fertile breeding ground for other, more obviously noxious, direct forms of discrimination (p.30).

The impact on well-being of long-term unemployment is severe, from reduced health, higher levels of suicide, to alcoholism, depression, and anxiety (Linn, Sandifer, and Stein 1985; Paul and Moser 2009). The social withdrawal that is correlated with long-term unemployment makes it even less likely that a person will be hired into the private sector (Tcherneva 2020, p.36).

State-backed full employment is an extension of its role as insurer of last resort: in insuring the productive employment of human capital, this policy encourages, instead of discourages, risk taking. Enterprise and productive efficiency are more likely to develop when all citizens are empowered to take productive risks without the threat of dropping into the "industrial reserve army" of the structurally unemployed. As we have argued throughout this book, despite their image of heroic wealth creators, it is the wealthy in our societies who take the fewest risks while the poor are exposed to the greatest risks. For all these reasons, we think that Rawls (and Fichte) are right that relational egalitarianism demands the state act as employer of last resort. It forms part of the realistically utopian restructuring of work that is the inevitable consequence of a transition to either a property-owning democracy or to liberal market socialism.

[17] On the neo-Keynesian diagnosis we set out in chapters 1 and 2, the state has facilitated the normalization of continual financial crises as part of a financialized business cycle. It is the employees of non-financial firms who primarily pay the price in terms of unemployment as these shocks are transmitted to the "real" economy.

13.4 Realistic Utopianism About Work: Eliminating Bottlenecks

The issue of full employment has an indirect bearing on our next topic: the elimination of bottlenecks as part of the full implementation of fair equality of opportunity. We have noted, at various points in this book, the role played in the frustration of the aims of fair equality of opportunity by the creation of artificial bottlenecks or the intensification of those bottlenecks that are unavoidable.

We think it is helpful to view the creation of involuntary unemployment as itself one form of artificial bottleneck: a person has to manoeuvre through it even to get a job. We noted the operation of Paul Gomberg's "socialization principle": that a society that has no intention of offering fair access to positions of advantage to all, and yet is putatively committed to an ethos of meritocracy, has to find various ways of narrowing channels of access to jobs (Gomberg 2007). Gomberg noted that, under actually existing capitalism, it is viewed as socially wasteful to educate people for jobs "beyond their station" and that jobs are streamed by social class in a way that correlates, in some cases, with ethnicity or citizenship status (Gomberg 2007). We can add this point to Tilly's taxonomy of "durable inequalities".

Fishkin has argued that any given society's opportunity structure is a vast and complex network of institutions and relations (Fishkin 2014, p.130). We cannot map entirely, but we do not have to do so to reform it. We simply need to identify access to key social goods, such as those necessary on any conception of the good life, and ask whether access to such goods has been regimented into what Fishkin calls "zero sum competitions for fixed numbers of scarce opportunities" (Fishkin 2014, p.130). We have argued that the goods of social mobility are of crucial importance here—the goods of education and healthcare.

The question is what it takes to eliminate bottlenecks of that specific kind. What would it be fully to implement fair, and not merely formal, equality of opportunity? Our view, once again, is that the pre-distributive and asset-focused strategies of an on-going wealth tax, inheritance tax, and the payment of a citizens' dividend in the form of demogrants will be supplemented by a wider account of the role of the state in removing Fishkin's "bottlenecks".[18]

[18] There are details of policy that we will not go into here: whether such demogrants are one-off payments or recurring, whether they are timed to be payable at critical life stages, who qualifies,

For example, Thomas Piketty has recently proposed a demogrant that includes a lifetime educational allowance—also part of Bruce Ackerman and Anne Alstot's original proposal inspired by Thomas Paine's *Agrarian Justice* (Ackerman and Alstot 1999; Piketty 2020).[19] Life-long access to a capital grant for the re-training of one's own human capital is a core aspect of an asset-based egalitarianism (Thomas 2017).

More generally: as Fishkin points out, if there is an artificial bottleneck you either put more people through it or you create a way around it (Fishkin 2014, p.171). Asset-based egalitarianism facilitates both strategies, directly and indirectly. Directly, demogrants facilitate life-long retraining opportunities with multiple "on ramps" to new productive opportunities. Fishkin's helpful metaphor of an "on ramp" is of a later opportunity to access a position of advantage after a person has missed out because they did not pass through a crucial bottleneck earlier in life. But we also envisage an indirect effect through the realistically utopian transformation in the nature of work proposed by both Rawls and Mill.

We cannot develop the full account here, but we will set out how we see this proposal as working. We will begin with Fishkin, who, perfectly reasonably in our view, objects to Rawls's postulation of the very idea of a natural lottery of talents; on Fishkin's republican conception, the developmental process is reciprocally shaped by the idea of an accessible set of opportunities that reconceptualizes the idea of a natural endowment.[20] As people interact with their environment, their sense of what possibilities are open to them shape the capacities that they develop from their underlying traits (Fishkin 2014, pp.105–6 ff). They will make extraordinary efforts to achieve specific goals with which they are deeply identified (and that may be the most rewarding for them.) The social environment can be enabling or disabling, depending on how the space of possibilities has been politically determined.

Fishkin's examples include the child who shows particular ability in one domain and whose efforts are nurtured, or the child who cannot behave

and the ultimate source of funding—whether a Georgist land tax or a society-wide unit trust, for example.

[19] Similarly, George Sher has proposed that the worst off in the labour market be resourced so as to "provide each with access to a package of resources and opportunities that affords him a reasonable chance of succeeding if he does try" (Sher 2014, p.50).

[20] He acknowledges the influence on his views of Ronald Dworkin and John Dewey (Dewey 1916, pp.50–1; Dworkin 2000, p.91). We call his view republican, however, because of the equally detectable influence of Walzer's *Spheres of Justice* (Fishkin 2014, p.159, fn. 55; Walzer 1983).

"appropriately" in a classroom whose developmental opportunities are foreclosed going forward.[21] Fishkin concludes that the extent to which constitutive luck is involved problematizes the thought that individuals can make choices for which they can be held individually responsible (Fishkin 2014, p.56 ff). Scanlon draws the conclusion that for individuals to form life plans in circumstances against which they can raise no reasonable complaint, we need to ensure that a sufficient range of options is available to him or her (Scanlon 2018).

As Fishkin notes, the life of an egalitarian planner would be a lot simpler in what Bernard Williams called the Big Test society in his famous paper "The Idea of Equality" (Williams 1973b). Williams's fable is of a society divided into two hereditary castes of warriors and non-warriors. On meritocratic grounds, the non-warriors demand a Big Test to allow their children to compete for a place as a warrior; the children of the warriors, better fed, trained, and prepared their whole life for the Test, pass it while all the children of non-warriors fail. This merely formal sense of equal opportunity is seriously deficient, as Williams pointed out, because it does not look at the opportunity-rich background structure within which people develop.

Fishkin's observes that a single test makes it easy to identify the core capacities people need to develop (in the case of the warriors, physical strength and stamina). But in a morally pluralistic society where we seek to enrich the social scripts from which people choose, such "unitary opportunity structures", as Fishkin calls them, must be dismantled (Fishkin 2014, p.128). People must be educated into a much wider range of capacities with fewer counting as a limited "core" of essential capacities.

Forming a direct link to our discussion in chapter 10 at the core of Fishkin's approach is his understanding of well-being, influenced by Joseph Raz's account in *The Morality of Freedom*, where a person's autonomy is internal to his or her well-being (where, again, the antecedent here is Mill) (Raz 1986; Fishkin 2014, pp.196–7). What matters to the individual is internal to their conception of the good life; they may have taken their aims from the list of social scripts that their social context affords them. Perhaps their goals are the mundane ones of being a good parent or carer rather than joining billionaires in a space safari to the planet Mars. What matters to their

[21] In his complementary analysis, Gomberg follows through on that thought: the child who has failed to develop classroom discipline is channelled along a path where close supervision is the norm, leading on to closely supervised, unrewarding, and menial labour when he or she leaves the education system at the earliest feasible stage.

prudential good is not whether their aim is commonplace, but their identification with it as authors of their own fate (Raz 1986, pp.289–90).

It is this morally pluralistic outlook that we seek to implement through the fair equality of opportunity principle. Its full implementation will bring about a radical reshaping of the space of possibilities within which people develop their capacities. As Robert Taylor argued, the rational revision of one's life plans involves not just the re-shaping of the raw material of desires, but the broader question of the management of all our inner resources—including, more fundamentally, who we want to be. The nature of our desires follows on from that prior question.

The idea of a schematic social form such as a property-owing democracy may seem far too abstract to have an impact on the task of rationality as Robert Taylor conceives of it:

> Rationality's task of designing and implementing a plan of life requires the utilization of external resources, including especially the generic, liquid, form of such resources—money. But there is a middle term, so as to speak, between a plan of life and the external resources needed for its realization: *internal* resources, including skills, drive and self-discipline . . . as Jon Elster has noted, akrasia, myopia, and extreme risk-aversion can act as barriers to the development of internal resources. (Taylor 2004, p.344)

However, we see a direct connection between Rawls's non-capitalist social system, the idea of symbolically expressive mutual investment in the capacities of citizens, and a space of human flourishing in which rationality achieves its task.[22] This investment forms the link between the external resource of capital and the internal resources that enable the development of the individual. It is the obstacles to the latter that the science of happiness teaches us are as widely mal-distributed, under actually existing capitalism, as the external resources themselves.

Fair equality of opportunity requires the implementation of what Fishkin (2014, chapter 3) calls the values of an opportunity pluralist society that reflects four field defining principles, not all of which for reasons of scope can be discussed here. The four principles are pluralism about values and aims, the minimizing of positional goods and competitive roles, pathway

[22] As Fishkin notes, "the opportunity structure shapes the pattern of human capital development" (Fishkin 2014, p.182).

pluralism (i.e. the anti-bottleneck principle) and a plurality of qualified "gatekeepers". However, of these four it is Fishkin's anti-bottleneck principle that is the most important and we will discuss that proposal in more detail.

Fishkin's commitment to evaluative pluralism is to a world where not everyone agrees—or is forced to agree—on what the most valuable social opportunities are. That is because of an underlying pluralism of values and aims. The stock of social scripts is, indeed, a case of the shared "commons". But Fishkin shares Mill's concern that this stock of scripts might be too restricted a basis for creating a variety of patterns of the good life (Fishkin 2014). This first way of conceptualizing a plural opportunity society attaches importance to avoiding Tilly's forms of durable inequality: the partitioning of available choices so that a wider range of options are available depending on one's gender, or race.

Clearly, Fishkin's concern with limiting both positionality and competition together overlaps strongly with our goals in this book. He shares our view that a good can be framed in a person's practical reasoning as positional or not—that you want a large SUV because you like the space in the cabin, or because you want an SUV that is larger than your neighbour's SUV (Fishkin 2014, p.138). Society's valued roles should be, as much as possible, non-competitive and not bundled together, as in a Jane Austen novel, where whom you marry is bundled together with both wealth and social class (Fishkin 2014, p.140). Conceptualizing the opportunity structure this way is also to assess the value of the stakes of competition. The more positionality and zero-sum competitions there are in a society, the more the distinction between "absolute and relative advantage" collapses: "they turn any person's advantage into someone else's disadvantage" (Fishkin 2014, p.141).[23] Bottlenecks vary in their severity and their pervasiveness: as the social theorist starts to generalize over them, patterns emerge—as in Tilly's identification of opportunity hoarding.

The anti-bottleneck principle, as its name implies, is a form of resistance: resistance to the collapsing of a plurality of reasons into a narrow set. For example, amongst the class of parents, motivations will be diverse in their attitudes to their children's education; but if they find themselves in a social context not of their own making structured as a "Big Test" society,

[23] "[T]he problem of merit presupposes—and arises only in the context of—zero-sum competition for scarce roles and educational opportunities. Whenever a valued good or role falls outside these zero sum competitions, this marginally decreases the stakes of the problem of merit" (Fishkin 2014, p.141).

that diversity is narrowed (Fishkin 2014, p.145). All of them will have been drawn into the domain of Hirsch's defensive necessity: non-competitive and non-positional reasons are forced into the mould of competitive and positional ones. The liberal problems of the familial transmission of advantage, the pervasiveness of meritocratic values, and identifying an elusive "fair starting gate" are all exacerbated in a society structured and dominated by key bottlenecks.

Fishkin's anti-bottleneck principle puts in place a form of pathway pluralism to match the underlying value pluralism (Fishkin 2014, p.146). Education is paradigmatic but, as Fishkin notes, "bottlenecks can be found in every corner of the opportunity structure" (Fishkin 2014, p.150). Presciently, given the evolution of American inequality, he cites a geographical example of a contrast between "Opportunityland" and "Povertyland" where the geography of opportunity is divided.[24] Whether the contrast is mapped onto coastal elites versus left behind flyover states, from inner cities to suburbs to exurbs and the rural, the geography of America's opportunity structure is a complex patchwork of inequality along lines of race and class.

Given his Deweyan inspiration, Fishkin also endorses a meta-principle on the question of who guards the guardians—who has the authority to put in place, reinforce, and perpetuate bottlenecks in the opportunity structure? Fishkin calls for "multiple, competing sources of authority—which do not all agree" as the arbiters of the multiple developmental paths open to citizens (Fishkin 2014, p.152). In policy terms, those multiple sources of authority may be the spur to pluralism about the manifold nature of meritorious achievement. However, the deeper aim, as Brighouse, Swift, and Fishkin all note, is that by lowering the stakes of competition via merit we free up people to seek developmental opportunities for their own sake. These are, as Fishkin notes, ultimately Mill's "experiments in living" (Fishkin 2014, p.154).[25]

This takes us back to the ideal of the free market we discussed in chapter 8: the Arrow-Debreu paradigm in which every agent is equally powerless when it comes to price setting. If monopolistic and anti-competitive practices—the practices endemic to capitalism according to Veblen's analysis that we discussed in chapter 8—are bottlenecks in the domain of price, is there a mutually reinforcing connection between free markets and developmental opportunities? Once again, a property-owning democracy allows

[24] Fishkin's schematic example fits uncannily well on to the United Kingdom's actual North/South divide as described in (Dorling 2011).

[25] See also (Anderson 1991).

any agent to go "directly" on to the market in order to shape the space of productive opportunity.[26] In a society structured around meaningful work for all, this expansion of the space of opportunities works for the common good.

The ultimate aim, as both Gomberg and Fishkin emphasize, is an ideal whereby we re-organize the nature of work and re-draw the boundary of what counts as "work". That re-organization emerges as Mill suggested it would: from the free choices of a highly educated workforce whose full potential has been realized via investment in human capital. Gomberg tends to associate the very idea of fixed, top-down, organization of positions of opportunity with "liberal egalitarianism", but we obviously view that as a limiting perspective in his critique. Liberal egalitarians from Mill to Rawls are concerned not just with "bottom-up" fair competition within a space of opportunity that is fixed—fixed, perhaps, by artificial bottlenecks. They are equally concerned with the organization of positions of advantage themselves.

Scanlon's discussion is exemplary in this regard: the justification for the existence of any positions of advantage is that this is a necessity of production that maximally advantages the worst off.[27] Furthermore, justice, and not simply productive efficiency, can be a decisive reason for re-organizing the nature of work:

> If an institution is organized in a way that requires those occupying a certain role to have a certain ability, but could serve its purposes equally well if it were organized in a different way that did not require this ability, then equality requires that it make this change, because giving preference to candidates who have this ability is unjustified. . . . [T]he values that are relevant for institutional justification . . . are not limited to what might be called values of output efficiency, but *also include the value, for individuals, of the opportunities for productive work that an institution provides.*[28] (Scanlon 2018, p.46, emphasis added)

[26] As Scanlon notes, the children of the wealthy have a comparative advantage in marketing their ideas when they can rely on their family for start-up funding (Scanlon 2018). The same applies, as we have noted, to the gatekeeping bottlenecks of internships, apprenticeships, or work experience when all of these are unpaid (or radically underpaid). A property-owning democracy is one form of unblocking what Fishkin calls "a credit bottleneck" (Fishkin 2014, p.223).

[27] See, for example, (Scanlon 2018).

[28] Fishkin also notes that "ameliorating bottlenecks sometimes has efficiency costs. Such costs need to be balanced against the values of promoting opportunity pluralism, and there is no simple formula for doing so" (Fishkin 2014, p.179). Yet he notes the crucial distinction between a practice that might be cheap, efficient, and micro-rational for an individual agent (such as an employer) while at the macro-level its widespread adoption would "tend to impair the productive use and development of human capital" (Fishkin 2014, p.181). He sees a role for the state here as, clearly, does our disjunctive proposal for a property-owning democracy or liberal market socialism.

What we take to be the core insight of Gomberg's argument is that the way in which we currently organize work violates Scanlon's principles. We would align his critique with our analysis of rent seeking: jobs in our societies are clusters of roles, opportunities, powers, status, and remuneration that generate rent from positions of advantage while also creating what you might reasonably call positions of disadvantage. Gomberg's particular focus is on the sharing of menial labour, but we think that does not capture his deeper point that we need to re-conceptualize how work is organized in terms of specific roles.[29]

His example is the way functional roles might be individuated in a hospital:

> *People should not do things for which they are untrained or unqualified*. . . . "Positions" could be broken down into specific abilities that have been mastered and hence could be contributed. Most important, each person who previously did only routine labor would have the opportunity to acquire new abilities.[30] (Gomberg 2007, pp.76–7, emphasis added)

You need not fear, then, checking into a hospital to be operated on by a hospital porter. But under the imagined re-organization of work, how much menial labour will have been eliminated, and how will job tasks currently clustered in job roles be redistributed across a complex team of individuals and, for that matter, people complemented by automation?[31] If it is a necessity of production that we divide labour, does it have to be bundled into our current sets of jobs, or can breaking it down into tasks spread across a more highly educated workforce ensure that all work remains meaningful—for all?

[29] In the background here is Fishkin's deeper point that in our folk psychological explanations we tend to bundle capacities together often in a way tied together by social stereotypes (Fishkin 2014, p.110). That blinds us to alternative taxonomies of how capacities can be bundled together. Stereotypes are crucial to Tilly's theory of durable inequality, for example, employment opportunities being sorted into "men's work" and "women's work".

[30] Fishkin expresses the goal as follows: "[R]estructure opportunities in ways that increase the range of opportunities open to people, at all stages in life, to pursue different paths that lead to forms of human flourishing. In doing this, we ought to give particular priority to those whose current range of opportunities is relatively narrow" (Fishkin 2014, p.1). As we note below in the text, Rawls makes the same point.

[31] Our view is that Gomberg's proposal is a necessary, but not sufficient, condition for breaking down the (gendered) "ideal worker norm" identified by Joan Williams (Williams 1999). We have historically inherited workplaces where the ideal (male) worker norm correlates significantly with the most desirable positions of advantage. See also (Fishkin 2014, p.226).

Under the full realization of fair equality of opportunity, every citizen's opportunity for self-realization through work will develop via this realistically utopian transformation in work. It will produce the dismantling of internal hierarchies of the workplace that represent yet another form of bottleneck—an intra-firm bottleneck constraining access to positions of advantage. Each person will seek out those opportunities that realize the distinctive capacities they have sought to realize with, at the social level, the mutual complementarity of those projects characteristic of the Humboldtian social union of social unions described by Rawls in Part Three of *A Theory of Justice*:[32]

> The division of labour is overcome . . . by willing and meaningful work within a just union of social unions in which all can freely participate as they so incline. (Rawls 1971/1999, p.464)

Rawls's theory of the moral sentiments, like Smith's, aims to overcome the psychologically damaging impact of the division of labour.

The aim is not, ultimately, to rehabilitate an ideal of meritocracy established on a "fairer" basis. The whole of section 17 of *A Theory of Justice* is devoted to defending the fair equality of opportunity principle from the claim that it leads to a "callous meritocratic society" (Rawls 1971/1999, p.100). On the contrary, a society well-ordered by justice will move away from "social efficiency and technocratic values" (p.101). This is an emphasis that increases as society develops and the difference principle "transforms the aims of society in fundamental respects" (p.107).[33] The implementation of all three parts of both of Rawls's justice principles will "gradually reshape the social structure so that market forces also shift" in a way that sees the market drive down the "premium" earned by the "better endowed" (p.307). (Drive it down, that is, to elimination given that in a property-owning democracy all incentives are compensatory.)

Over time, the supply of better-educated workers in a context where all jobs are equally attractive levels down income inequality. Attractive jobs will attract qualified workers; unattractive jobs will require greater remuneration (or will cease to exist). Equal treatment requires "more attention to those with

[32] Paul Smith comments: "People tend to prefer to do what they are good at and to be socially useful, because of the intrinsic rewards, and tend to be most useful doing what they are good at. So individual preference among socially equal jobs tends to coincide with social utility" (Smith 1998, p.213).

[33] This Rawlsian phrase is strikingly similar to Fazi and Mitchell's description of a state-backed jobs guarantee as "a longer term force for historical change" (Fazi and Mitchell 2017, p.246).

fewer native assets and to those born into the less favorable social positions" (Rawls 1971/1999, p.100). Rawls's perspective, like Mill's, is that the progress of society sees educational resources being directed less to returns on "trained productive abilities" and more on "their worth in enriching the personal and social life of citizens, including the less favored" (Rawls 1971/1999, p.107). This is a natural complement to his associationalism that we will discuss below.

13.5 De-Marketization, Public Goods, and the Commons

We have argued that it is a limitation of our imagination to take those employed via the jobs guarantee to be put to work solely on infrastructural projects. That point must be handled with care: we do not want to deny that the looming climate crisis will create extensive jobs to deal with our survival as a species in anything like our current circumstances. It will take many workers to make our entire energy supply electrical, or make our housing and land use sustainable. However, we do want to connect the idea of the public guarantee to a broader renewal of the commons. We inherit a common stock of culture and technology from the past that is, as a collective achievement, free. If it is not free, then it has been successfully "enclosed" by private parties as much by intellectual property law as by a physical fence. The regeneration of our shared commons is an important task for those working under the jobs guarantee.

A shared commons does not feature in GDP statistics any more than do public parks, clean air and water, or the safety of everyday transportation, but they do contribute to our shared well-being. The same is true of our shared stock of social capital. If there is a perverse and vicious cycle running from inequality over a decrease in trust and social capital to increasing inequality, this can be broken either by creating more equality or by increasing social capital. Our goals are, of course, to bring about both via asset-based egalitarianism.

The World Happiness Report 2015 shows that "social and economic equality is associated with higher levels of social capital and generalized trust" (Helliwell, Layard, and Sachs 2015, p.9). When countries lack social capital and are characterized by a generalized distrust and perception of corruption, the tendency not to contribute to the provision of public goods increases. High social capital, on the other hand, raises well-being both directly and indirectly, "by promoting social support systems, generosity and voluntarism, and honesty in public administration, and by reducing the costs of doing business" (Helliwell, Layard, and Sachs 2015, p.9). Chapter 9 of the World Happiness Report 2015 discusses how investments in education, the public sanctioning of free riders, but also the reduction of inequality can increase social capital and thus contribute to well-being both directly and indirectly.

Furthermore, if taxation policies are perceived as fair and as providing public goods, potentially negative effects of relative income comparisons on well-being are reduced (Helliwell, Huang, and Harris 2009; Helliwell and Putnam 2004).[34] To use Waheed Hussain's helpful metaphor, this is a way of "lowering the stakes" of the competition between citizens (Hussain 2020). The more goods are de-marketized and made public, crucially the goods of social advancement such as education and healthcare, the less citizens need feel anxiety over being pitted against each other in a zero-sum competition. On the basis of the data we have mustered in chapter 10, one can only hypothesize that the introduction of de-marketized, high-quality, public education and healthcare systems in the United States would have ramified positive effects on well-being.

Breaking the vicious cycle between inequality, community, and well-being can even result in a virtuous cycle. People who are happier are more likely to do volunteering work, which in turn increases their well-being (Thoits and Hewitt 2001). Volunteering does not only contribute to people's own but also others' well-being. According to Dolan and White, this shows that policy makers who are "interested in promoting certain prosocial behaviors and discouraging harmful behaviors, such as suicide, may want to directly influence SWB [subjective well-being]" (Dolan and White 2007, p.77). By making people happier, they are likely to generate spillover effects and increase well-being overall.

The question, however, is which form of a just society is more likely to achieve this. Our argument is that a society that is committed to a predistributive conception such as justice as fairness will do better than its welfare state counterpart. The fair value of a universal right to access to capital would see a significant flattening out of wage differentials in a fair overall distribution. The state as employer of last resort completes this vision (Thomas

[34] "Concerns for relative income differences are mediated by perceptions about what inequality signals, as well as the availability (or not) of public goods" (Graham 2009, pp.165–6).

2020b). Only this non-capitalist society will allow market societies to achieve Adam Smith's emancipatory promise and to live up to the very principles that they advertise themselves as honouring. We have tracked through the effects of inequality on social class, social structure, and ultimately the well-being of citizens for whom further material gains seem to diminish, and not to enhance, their happiness.

We see three issues that we have raised in this book as complementary: the erosion of the associational basis of countervailing power, the jobs guarantee, and the realistically utopian transformation of work. We have noted the way in which the interests of the rentier-investor class seem "naturally" self-organizing while the social basis of countervailing power has been eroded, in some cases by explicit political action. In particular, the social basis of mass-based political parties has been undermined. However, proponents of the job guarantee, as we have seen, envisage it changing the boundaries between economic society and associations. Pavlina Tcherneva, in particular, has focused on the way in which local forms of associations might be put to use to implement the guarantee via "social enterprise" (Tcherneva 2012). For that reason, then, we also think it is important to explain and defend Rawls's associationalism as an important component of his strongly egalitarian vision.

13.6 Rawlsian Associationalism: Putting Positionality in Its Place

A challenge that we can foresee is this: even under our two non-capitalist social systems, will positional competition not persist? Will people not continue to engage in status evaluations of each other? It is hard to envisage a fundamental transformation in people's psychologies where this propensity will simply go away—even if we agree with Rousseau that such a transformation would be no loss to us all. Rawls seems resigned to limiting, not eliminating, such comparisons—but is his appeal to the safety valve of plural associational groups an evasion, not a solution, of the basic problem of the persistence of positionality as Thomas Scanlon at one point suggests (Scanlon 2018, p.3)? In this section we will explain why we think not.

As we have noted throughout this book, positional goods can only come within the scope of Rawls's conception of the theory of stability in *Justice as Fairness* when he explicitly considers the destabilizing special attitudes.

This is not a concern even representable in the original position that assumes the mutual disinterestedness of its parties. The problems that positional goods pose can arise only once we have taken an interest in other people's interests—whether or not that is caused by our own anxiety. This contrasts, then, with the original position's restriction on the parties' "not try[-ing] to gain relative to one another" (Rawls 1971/1999, p.125).

Our view is that Rawls's associationalism needs to be viewed from three perspectives. The first—Joshua Cohen's perspective—is that securing the values of citizenship eliminates the most fundamental domain of status evaluative conflict. The second perspective is Fishkin's conception of an opportunity pluralistic society. The third perspective is the distinction that Waheed Hussain drew between reasons of justice and reasons of solidarity. We will discuss each in turn.

The first approach, then, is that originally developed (in a Rousseauian vein) in Joshua Cohen's original paper "The Natural Goodness of Humanity" (Cohen 1997). Rawls's primary strategy for the suppression of positional competition is to offer us a guarantee with respect to our most fundamental status, namely, our status as a citizen. Our mutually secured status as citizens is secured in a society well-ordered by justice. It is not, then, subject to the anxiety that, as we have seen, Rawls believed was the primary motive for positional competition. We have added to this basic idea a further suggestion that the symbolic and expressive importance of how we secure this status via mutual investment in the material basis of each other's self-respect also matters.

The Rawlsian solution—and here we draw on the work of Joshua Cohen and Frederick Neuhouser—guarantees not merely formal civic equality, but also its fair value. That, in our proposal, is addressed only in a property-owning democracy that forestalls both the accumulation of wealth and the "drift to oligarchy".

Further, Rawls attempts to re-channel positional competition. We blunt the force of our desire to feel superior to one another by making this relative comparison: we compare ourselves to our fellow citizens and find that we have equal basic worth. We therefore agree with Joshua Cohen and Frederick Neuhouser—and disagree with Nico Kolodny—that this comparative judgement that finds us to be on a par with others makes sense. What, then, is this Rawlsian "re-channelling" of positional competition? In this book, we have emphasized the importance to Rawls of freedom to associate in multiple, non-comparing groups.

Why is this appeal to non-comparing groups important? In a helpful discussion, Thomas Scanlon frankly expresses the concern that this move on Rawls's part is "evasive" (Scanlon 2018, p.36). Scanlon's concern is this: even in a society with only fair inequalities, Rawls is committed to his fundamental principle of human well-being, namely, the Aristotelian principle. That principle obviously values human achievement. How can we not, then, be drawn into thinking some stubbornly meritocratic thoughts? Further, the connection between such thoughts and status attribution is an uncomfortably close one. For example, if there are some core human attributes that we all have reason to value, then will there not be some desirable jobs that constitute a recognition that a person has achieved, relative to those attributes, to a high degree (Scanlon 2018, p.33)?

Scanlon sets aside the Rousseauian argument that people seek desirable jobs only to feel superior to others. In his case—to make things as tricky as possible for those sympathetic to Rawls—a person is socially rewarded with pay and status for a job that, in turn, is expressive of some admirable human capabilities we all have reason to value.[35] Even in a society well-ordered by justice, there will be those who receive less because their job is less socially valued even if that inequality is justified—as Scanlon insists it must be—as a necessity of the productive process that benefits the worst off to the maximal degree.

This is the orthodox response that Scanlon presents on Rawls's behalf—the one he views as evasive—that appeals to the existence of a plurality of non-competing groups:

> [T]here should be for each person at least one community of shared interests to which he belongs and where he finds his endeavors confirmed by his associates. (Rawls 1971/1999, p.388)

Later Rawls expands on the point:

> [T]he plurality of associations in a well-ordered society, each with its secure internal life, tends to reduce the visibility, or at least the painful visibility, of variations in men's prospects. For we tend to compare our circumstances

[35] Similarly, Joseph Fishkin concludes that "in any society with at least a somewhat specialised division of labor . . . there are some limits . . . on the number of people likely to be needed in any given profession. As long as more people want to pursue those roles than are needed, the roles cannot help but be at least somewhat competitive, whatever the method of allocation" (Fishkin 2014, p.141).

> with those of others in our group, or in positions we regard as relevant to our aspirations.(Rawls 1971/1999, p.470)

At this juncture to address Scanlon's concern we think it is helpful to reiterate three points. First, that in a property-owning democracy there are no envy-generating special incentives (Smith 1998, pp.215–6). Second, we think that a property-owning democracy, or the Millian alternative of liberal market socialism, will press the issue of the re-organization of work beyond simply alleviating Fishkin's "bottlenecks". We think Paul Gomberg is right that, with the issue of status hierarchy resolved, we can approach the functional individuation of jobs as a bundle of tasks in a utopian way. In the present context, that may undermine one presupposition of Scanlon's argument, namely, the individuation of jobs into those that confer market-based merit on specific kinds of admirable achievement by individuals.

This issue segues into another, which is Fishkin's conception of an opportunity pluralist society. If Scanlon is right that there are subtle social pressures to re-define merit as the kinds of merit rewarded on the market, then the diversity of associations helps to remove this pressure.

> Rawls may be talking about differences in income and wealth, but his main concern, and my concern here, is with individual's sense of failure at turning out to be less good than they have reason to want to be at things that are worth striving for. The shielding effect of non-comparing groups seems less controversial as a way of dealing with the latter problem than with unhappiness due to economic differences. (Scanlon 2018, p.36)

The diversity of associational life is one way in which we can control and redress the narrow interpretation of merit as market-favouring merit alone. If you restore classic cars, and join a local group of classic car enthusiasts, then their admiration of your project is what matters to you and not your "book smarts". If your Ramblers' Club admires your knowledge of the local walking routes and your stamina, once again your self-respect is sustained without reference to those forms of merit that are tailored to the market.

We think it is worth repeating here another Scanlonian insight that, if prevailing social attitudes convert socio-economic inequality into a status hierarchy of social superiors and inferiors, then the putatively "inferior" are unfairly denied associational goods, too. That would further imply that the plurality of associations compensates for the way in which the social union of social unions operates in the economic sphere by giving everyone social support for their self-respect in distinct associational groups. The bank manager and the bank clerk can both go walking in the Ramblers' Club and associate with each other on the basis of a shared interest in the countryside, even if the manager thinks she is the intellectual superior to the clerk (because her pay check tells her so).

This point, then, evolves directly into the second perspective on Rawlsian associationalism: Fishkin's conception of an opportunity pluralistic society that we described in the previous section. We have interpreted his thesis through the lens of our republican commitments: that liberty depends on the individual having a wide range of possible options and developmental paths open to him or her. In the complex structure of a society's field of opportunities, some pathways are structured and linear with clearly defined gatekeepers; others are not. As we have noted, the egalitarian planner needs to take note of which forms of access attach to which goods and if those are essential life goods that are the component of any person's conception of the good life. Changing the structure of opportunities can exacerbate, or reduce, the problems of familial inter-generational transmission of advantage, the problem of meritocracy, the challenge of critical early life "starting gates" and the fate of our ethical aspiration to individuality (Fishkin 2014, p.131). What this also achieves is Rawls's associational pluralism: a plurality of aims is sustained by the social recognition of such aims and this, in turn, demands a rich ecosystem of free associations.

The third perspective on Rawlsian associationalism that we will consider focuses on a special class of reasons for being concerned with the protection of associational liberties: reasons of solidarity. In "Pitting People Against Each Other", Waheed Hussain criticized the same kinds of disciplinary devices we have also focused on in this book (Hussain 2020). He also draws out the connection between this issue of social discipline and the privatization of healthcare and education. In the latter two cases, he notes, competition has been introduced where it is not appropriate. The privatization of these domains makes them, in his terminology, "rivalry defining arrangements" where people are "pitted against each other" not simply for a job, but for that which a prestigious and highly paid job entails. It entails better healthcare and greater opportunity to advantage one's children in the rivalrous arrangements of access to elite educational institutions. The stakes, then, of such competitions are very high: this is not just marketization, but bundling. The high status, high pay job is also the gateway to top end educational and healthcare provision.

Hussain argued that a concern for justice and liberty does not exhaust the principles to which the egalitarian is committed because we can make sense of a distinct third commitment to solidarity. Neighbourly solidarity, for example, is to treat the wildfire approaching your neighbour's house as if it were approaching your own (Hussain 2020, p.95). Solidarity motivates you to react with the same actions and emotions (to run for a garden hose, to feel relief if the wind blows the wildfire away from your neighbour's house). From his Hegelian perspective, our "station and its duties" makes us part of multiple such solidaristic associations. But the most fundamental of such associations is our shared political society where, assuming the Rawlsian simplification that a single society has no entry and exit conditions and is not a voluntary association, it would be unconscionable to pit people against each other for access to life's most basic goods.

Hussain argues that, when it comes to the common good, which he understands as the collection of Rawlsian primary social goods, we ought not to permit the operation of rivalrous or competitive arrangements (Hussain 2020, p.99). But the solidaristic commitment not only attaches to keeping some goods off the market, but also to constraining how we marketize those goods that are appropriate for the market. When he goes on to consider how we might permit rivalrous arrangements in some contexts—including in economic life—Hussain suggests that we ought only be permitted to do so, in such contexts, if we also "lower the stakes" (Hussain 2020, p.106).

If we are going to compete, then the gains from winning ought to be capped—Hussain talks of introducing a "ceiling" or upper limit—and the losses from losing underwritten—here Hussain invokes a complementary "floor" or minimum level of provision of goods (2020, p.106). Clearly, that is a functional specification that matches on to the aims of a property-owning democracy. We are co-opting Hussain to supply yet another argument in the over-determined case for such a non-capitalist form of social organization: one grounded on his distinct class of reasons of solidarity. This is, as Fishkin notes, not to envisage a society that has banned competition: given the circumstances of justice, there will be scarcity, a productive surplus to be contended for, and a lot to occupy those who freely choose to enter tooth and nail competition because it is to their taste. But that is the point: "opportunity pluralism aims to lower some of the stakes . . . to shatter others so that they are not one competition but many, and to encourage people to value a mix of roles and goods that are not as competitive or positional" (Fishkin 2014, p.185).

Hussain adds to our overall argument the solidaristic reasons for an extensive domain of public goods, including access to high-quality and free public education and healthcare over and above reasons grounded in the fair equality of opportunity principle itself. In addition to reasons of justice, there are reasons of solidarity. Reduce the stakes of positional competition matters, also for the latter class of reasons. In terms of policy, Hussain's proposal is shared with Robert Frank's approach—one that we have also drawn upon throughout this book.

Frank has long argued that the solution to positional competition is the imposition of a "steeply progressive consumption tax" targeted at high earners (Frank 2016, chapter 7, section 5, see also pp.158–71). It is another example of an economic "free lunch" because the tax eliminates the waste generated by positional competition: the money saved goes back into consumption and investment:

> The tax rate would start out low and would then rise steadily as taxable consumption increased. Under the current income tax, rates can't rise too high without choking off savings and investment. But higher marginal rates on consumption would actually encourage savings and investment. (Frank 2016, p.118)

If such a tax were instated, there would be no loss of utility—even to the wealthy.[36] In fact, they are benefitting the most from the elimination of wasteful positional spending.

This benefit is both direct and indirect. Directly, their positional goods generate the same preference satisfaction with reduced expense. Indirectly, a higher level of public goods supported by higher investment is good for everyone, therefore including the rich, with Frank's highly pertinent example being that the purchasers of high-performance sports cars will not have to endure crumbling roads dotted with potholes (Frank 2016, p.119). Frank concludes:

[36] Compare Greg Mankiw's assertion that, "As far as I know, no one has proposed any credible policy intervention to deal with rising inequality that will make everyone, including those at the very top, better off" (Mankiw 2013, pp.22–3).

> Therein lies the fiscal alchemy inherent in the progressive consumption tax. By inhibiting a collection of largely unproductive expenditure cascades, it would effectively create new resources out of thin air. (Frank 2016, p.121)

Frank's arguments can be seen as a consolidation of a broader argument, proposed by Nicholas Kaldor and endorsed by Rawls, that fairness requires an expenditure tax which exempts from taxation that part of the tax base intended for saving (Kaldor 1956).

Noting that the details of tax policy are "not part of the theory of justice", Rawls suggests nonetheless that the default for the tax system ought to be Kaldor's proportional tax on a person's spending. Rawls endorses Kaldor's rationale: if one's income is fairly earned in a society well-ordered by justice, one's spending makes a claim on the "common store of goods" and this need not interfere with the propensity to save. The role of progressive taxation is to "forestall accumulations of property and power" (Rawls 1971/1999, p.279). It is, then, part of a response to the fact of domination. The rationale for progressive taxation in this light is stability, not raising revenue—so we can infer that Rawls believed stabilization was the basic aim of the tax system. Frank's supplementary proposal can be seen as deepening this rationale of using the fiscal policy of the state to stabilize by damping down the fire of positional competition to everyone's benefit.

In their ground-breaking paper, Harry Brighouse and Adam Swift also noted that reducing the stakes in positional competition gives greater salience to other, non-positional, reasons for valuing a good (Brighouse and Swift 2006). In our world of highly credentialed rent seekers, fierce competition to pass through sequential bottlenecks consumes people's time and attention; but suppose we had brought about a wider set of societal reforms? Suppose some socially valued positions were assigned by lottery; or the great majority of workers were paid the kind of "solidaristic wages" paid in 1970s Sweden, or job tasks had been broken down and shared amongst more workers? Then the value of educational credentialling would go down and the non-positional value of being educated would, comparatively, go up (Brighouse and Swift 2006, pp.488–9). Clearly, our advocacy of our two non-capitalist alternatives falls within the spirit of their general proposals. The different parts of the opportunity structure are connected and strategic changes ramify widely through it.

This leads on to further issues given that, as our critique of rent seeking throughout this book has made clear, our problem in our affluent societies is not a lack of savings. On the contrary—glut, excess, abundance—however it is described, our problem is that the productive use of capital is being suffocated by its unproductive use under rentier capitalism. That leads, perversely, to the question of "how we can afford" the egalitarian policies we are defending here—even in the presence of this abundance of capital. It is to that issue that we now turn.

13.7 A People's Money

If there is an overall aim to this chapter, it is to argue that we need to overcome our collective learned helplessness in the face of the claims that there is no alternative to our current actually existing capitalism. We have realistically utopian options—more than one might think. Our target in this section is the rhetorical strategy that stifles all utopian ambitions—"how will we pay for it?".

We have set out a large-scale contrast between two non-capitalist alternative social systems (a property-owning democracy and liberal market socialism) and welfare state capitalism. We think the most sophisticated defenders of welfare state capitalism ground it on agonistic class relations and we have isolated one key reason for this.

The welfare state capitalist thinks that all banking is intermediation, and the state functions like a bank in this sense: it is a redistributive intermediary. Just as banks intermediate between savers and borrowers, so states intermediate between wealthy private capitalists and the recipients of the tax and transfer resource allocation of the state. The difference in this case is that the state literally sequesters the income of the wealthy and transfers it to the worst off via the taxation system. It seems a reasonable assumption, then, that the more ambitious the social programs of the redistributive state, the more it ought to tolerate the drivers of economic growth—not just the wealth creators, but their presumptive right to the full "product of their labour" at least ex ante. That wealth is then redistributed ex post. What if that conception of the structural dependence of the welfare state on a private capitalist class were false?

Underpinning our utopian proposals in this chapter is this larger issue: where the burden of social costs lies. Do arguments from market efficiency count against the kind of systematic reforms that we have in mind? One's starting assumptions matter a great deal in this argument. Our discussion of full employment was premised on the idea of the monetarily sovereign state. What we are opposed to, essentially, is the idea that the monetarily sovereign nation-state must engage in various misplaced self-binding strategies.

For our opponent, the structural dependence of the state on private capitalists involves a curious indirection in how such states engage in their monetary, fiscal, and employment policies. They must never "crowd out" the capital of the wealthy private investor who must be induced to save by an attractive rate of return. The whole direction of a society's investment must be left in private hands. The state plays a reduced role: putting in place compensation for market failures, Pigouvian taxes for negative externalities such as pollution, supplying public goods on grounds of efficiency, and trying to "steer" monetary policy by setting a key price in the economy—the rental price which banks pay for money at the central bank. This is not the place for full consideration of why we dissent from this picture. However, as we noted in the case of full employment, earlier on in this chapter, we see no reason why the state should not make the full use of all of its monopoly powers for the general good and not just for sectional interests. What it does, in the "self-limiting" strategy we have described, is exercise some of its monopoly powers but not others in a way that advantages some social interests over others.

Our point is that, in the interests of consistency, the monetarily sovereign state can put all of its resources, both monetary and fiscal, towards desirable social ends. Abba Lerner's idea of "functional finance" does exactly this (Lerner 1936). This implies that we can abandon the idea that the monetarily sovereign state is structurally dependent on a class of wealthy private capitalists who must be placated if the state is to pursue its social goals. If the aim of taxation is not, then, to raise revenue—what is it for?

We take ourselves to be defending an orthodox view of the nature of money first expressed by John Maynard Keynes in his work *A Treatise on Money*, but in recent years this view has attracted what we regard as misplaced controversy in its guise as modern monetary theory (or "MMT"). We do not intend to enter into those controversies here: it seems to us uncontroversial that a monetarily sovereign state does not need to "raise revenue" via taxation. As the ultimate monopolist of money, the state tries to ensure there is enough money to sustain economic activity at the level of the economy's actual real resources and tries to navigate an upper and lower bound in so doing. Too much money beyond the upper bound is potentially inflationary; too little money below the lower bound is a brake on economic activity and potentially deflationary. As Keynes pointed out, for "four thousand years" states have declared what *counts as* money for its purposes—notably, the payment of taxes. That is not how the *value of* money is established. Money is an enabler of economic activity: it is the activity—in which of course the state may be engaged as participant—that determines this value. In Mike Beggs's phrase, that which gives value to money is "countless price-setting decisions by mainly private firms, reacting strategically to the structure of costs and the demands that they face, in competition with other firms" (Beggs 2012).

Money is one form of promissory obligation—an IOU—and the state has no need for IOUs written to itself (Hockett and James 2020). When the state issues financial instruments that themselves pay interest (unlike the bank notes in your wallet) that is not the cost of its "borrowing". If the state spends more than it taxes away from an economy (setting aside interaction with the rest of the world for now) then it runs a deficit. State deficits are in an accounting identity with private wealth: together they sum to zero. The sale and purchase of state debt instruments follows the convention that the state issues interest-paying debt instruments equivalent to the deficit (Kelton 2020). It is not the raising of revenue by, in effect, borrowing from wealthy people and institutions. These issues have been enshrouded by a politically generated fog about whether or not it is "good" or "bad" for states to be in surplus or deficit, which is not, in our view, a well-posed question (Kelton 2020).

Our interest is a limited one: what, in this discussion, is the role of fiscal (tax) policy and can we put it to use to promote social ends, as Abba Lerner insisted that we could for both fiscal and monetary policy? One canard in this debate is that if the state can issue money, then it does not need to tax at all. That ridiculous view ignores the fact that, as a political theory of money, Keynesian monetary theory wants all obligations to the state paid in the state currency to give citizens a motivation to use it—rather than, for example to use cryptocurrencies. For our purposes all we need to establish the corollary that fiscal policy, freed from being "revenue raising", is an exercise in stabilization. To that end, we can use fiscal policy to target the goods involved in positional competition and we can be creative in imagining how to do this.

Faced with challenges of the scale we now face, it is perhaps helpful that even governments that are conservative in orientation are being more open about their own capacities when it comes to "overt monetary financing" as the obfuscatory jargon calls it. Faced with the need to bail out the international financial system to the value of some $15 trillion, or to furlough millions of workers when a global pandemic brought the world economy to a halt, it seems the money was there (all along, you might say) (Tooze 2021a, 2018). This has inspired various proposals to fully democratize a people's money.

Robert Hockett, the author of a detailed proposal for a "people's quantitative easing", sees a direct connection between the relationship between the public and the private options when it comes to employment and when it comes to money (in a book co-authored with Aaron James):

> What we'd no longer have is indefinitely extended, monetized public full faith and credit flowing or gushing toward artfully inflated secondary and tertiary markets.... Instead public full faith and credit will run only toward primary markets and only to those further markets—like those for home mortgage, higher education, small businesses and public utility loans—that really legitimately require government support. (Hockett and James 2020)

In our current institutional division of labour, banking can be understood on a franchise model where private banks dispense the "full faith and credit" of the state because they are supposed to have an epistemic advantage over a central bank (Hockett and Omarova 2017). Genuine money creators in their own right, not intermediaries, private banks are supposed to have detailed knowledge of individual client's circumstances that allow them to assess whether they are a good credit risk or not. However, having outsourced this capacity to issue "IOUs" that are vertically integrated into the state's sovereign authority to create money, the risk of "over-promising" at the macro-level is omnipresent.

At the micro-level of any given bank, detailed knowledge of the credit worthiness of the customer becomes unimportant with the rise of securitized products and the model of "originate to distribute" where, for example, a mortgage issuer sells the asset on immediately. Further, as we saw in chapter 8, the financial system as a whole is more than a key public infrastructure: it has produced the secondary and tertiary markets in which the rentier-investor class speculate, as opposed to making genuine productive investments. Hockett writes of those markets:

> Meanwhile, speculative markets, where public credit-money flows are now far larger than any real need for liquidity or hedging could ever justify, will become private affairs. For that reason, those markets will shrink and pose much lower risks to the larger economy. (Hockett 2020b, p.106)

That is a reversal of our current priorities, where we have argued that Minsky was right that we have normalized both financial crises and the central bank "put"—the pre-commitment to put a floor under asset prices—that means that the investment banks and hedge funds that operate in this casino of secondary and tertiary markets (as Keynes called it) have their potential downside risks insured which, of course, means they can afford to be more reckless.

In a people's quantitative easing, every citizen would be given access to an account opened for them at the central bank thereby ending the problem of the unbanked at a stroke. "Helicopter money" is simply credited to these interest-bearing accounts, with the central bank able to restrict access to such deposits as a means of modulating access to credit (in addition to its initial allocation). This innovation bypasses private intermediaries, reduces their influence and importance, offers more flexible policy options (such as "dated" money supplied on a "use it or lose it" basis) and transforms the financial sector as we know it. How do we pay for it? As we always pay for it:

> How do we pay for it all? By deciding to make the payments and *spending the dollars into existence....* The government creates money *in the very act of spending it.* The very act of keystroking dollar credits into bank accounts *creates money.* (Hockett and James 2020)

If inflation is the product of a mismatch between the amount of such public IOUs—money—and real resources in the economy, then democratic control of both have to proceed hand in hand. That is why, for example, Keynes believed that two-thirds of investment in a modern economy should be steered, not controlled, by the state as he explained in a government report in 1928 (*Britain's Industrial Future, Being the Report of the Liberal Industrial Inquiry of 1928*). It is implicit in this view that the idea that state investment "crowds out" private investment is empirically false; state-directed investment crowds private investment in (Hockett 2020b). This is particularly in the case of strategically key markets where private actors wait for the state to issue its profit-underwriting guarantee before entering it (Janeway 2018).

Our proposal, then, is that overt monetary financing—the use of the sovereign power of the state to create money—be put at the service of the common good, not sectional ends (Turner 2015). Either a property-owning democracy or liberal market socialism will incorporate state investment planning and a genuinely democratized central bank serving the common good. We are not inventing "a people's money": via a democratic state, in a monetarily sovereign state our money has always been ours.

13.8 Priorities Without Prioritarianism

It may seem late in our argument to consider issues that, for many of our readers, are the most pressing issues of our time—particularly at the global level. Where, they will ask, are the discussion of race, gender, and the environment? Where is the issue of global justice that deals with the claims of the world's most vulnerable people?

Our position is, once again, aligned with that of Scanlon. In discussing prioritarianism, Scanlon argues that it is a false dichotomy to suggest that we have to choose between egalitarianism and a concern with prioritarianism (Scanlon 2018).[37] Our concern with the worst off is an egalitarian concern but its direction and focus has to be shaped by the contingencies of our actual world. For example, egalitarian reasons are strongest in the case of the poor, but not restricted to the poor. In our actual world they take "priority", but not for prioritarian reasons; rather, for egalitarian ones:

> The cumulative effect of these overlapping reasons for objecting to inequality is a form of priority for the worst off. The forms of inequality that there is strongest reason to object to, and to eliminate if possible, are the forms affecting the poor, especially those who are both poor and subject to discrimination. But this does not make what I have offered a prioritarian as opposed to egalitarian view. This is because most of the reasons supporting this priority, including the particular objections to unequal status, violations of equal concern, and lack of fairness in political and economic institutions, are themselves egalitarian in character. (Scanlon 2018, p.154)

Our argument echoes Scanlon's: the marginalized, excluded, and poorest people in our own societies tend to be women, people with disabilities, members of ethnic minorities or recent migrants. If we ask who in our world is the worst off, then people living in absolute poverty are clearly the worst off.

[37] Where by the latter we mean the view that "[B]enefiting people matters more the worse off these people are" (Parfit 1997, p.213).

One can go further: there are vast sectoral inequalities in our societies. Over the last forty years, remuneration in some key parts of the "high-end" service sectors such as financial services, law, and accounting has exploded at the top end while austerity policies have penalized the worst off—most dependent on public services. These high-end employments look like paradigms of "winner takes all" markets where, for example, the very best tax advisors when it comes to "minimizing your tax burden" are remunerated far in excess of the next tier down. However, it is here that the representation of women is low, and the aggregate contribution of this fact to overall inequality data is disproportionately high.

But an egalitarian is not primarily concerned with the inequality between male and female investment bankers (absent overt discrimination), but with the relation between returns in that industry to inequality overall. The key point is that outside these key sectors, as Joshua Preiss puts it, "in occupations where pay is linear, reflecting differences in human capital and hours worked, the within-occupation hourly wage gap between men and women largely disappears" (Preiss 2021, p.11).[38] The focus, then, should be on the kind of sectoral inequalities that we discussed in the opening two chapters (Galbraith 1998). This fact suggests to us that we are correct to focus on priorities without prioritarianism: to aim at justice as a whole will, in fact, disproportionately benefit women and ethnic minorities as they currently suffer the most from injustice.[39]

However, we would add that in redressing the injustices that they suffer, we simply need justice, not gender or racial or global justice, unless the issue is the specific payment of remedies for past wrongs—the domain of rectificatory justice which we have explicitly set aside here. We have drawn on the critiques of Paul Gomberg and Joseph Fishkin in our accounts of equality of opportunity and the deeper question of how we organize work. The issues that they raise have a particular salience for issues of class and race.

[38] "[I]ndustries where the majority of workers are women tend to pay less than industries where the majority of workers are men" (Preiss 2021, p.113). More generally, the fact that "winner-takes-all markets exacerbate the effects of our gendered division of labor on gender wage inequality" is the focus of (Preiss 2021, p.11, chapter 5). We have noted that this book has been written during the coronavirus pandemic that started in late 2019: for various reasons, including social norms around childcare and the differential impact of the pandemic on the services sector, it has disproportionately impacted on the economic prospects of women (Tooze 2021b, p.101).

[39] To take a representative example, Preiss notes that "the majority of the 'immiserated proletariat' in American society are women, who remain more likely than their male counterparts to find low-wage, insecure, 'dead-end' employment in the service industries. Women represent 63% of minimum wage workers" (Preiss 2021, p.117).

Charles Tilly also noted that amongst the most durable forms of inequality is gender inequality. In the case of racial justice it was Dr Martin Luther King Jr.; his widow, Coretta Scott King; and Sadie Alexander who emphasized the centrality of full employment via a state jobs guarantee to securing its goals (Alexander 1945; King 2000; Sommers, Hegland, and Delices, 2018).

Therefore, we do take ourselves to have addressed the issues of gender, racial, and global justice in setting our compass towards justice as a whole as a comprehensive ideal—even if we do not claim that our proposals will suffice to eliminate all these problems in their entirety. When we advance the aims of justice as a whole, we thereby advance the aims of gender and racial justice because, in fact, the category of the worst off tends to be weighted more heavily towards women, members of ethnic minorities, and other socio-economically vulnerable groups.

We can go beyond the statement of an aspiration: we have proposed policies that will give every citizen access to opportunities under reasonable conditions of choice. There will be employment for anyone who wants to work that is secure, not meaningless work, and at least paid at the level of a generous minimum wage. For those who choose not to work there will be a decent civic minimum, supplemented by restricted purpose demogrants for life-long education, or to fund a business start-up, or (at the limit) to fund an annuity. Those demogrants will be funded by the social dividend on land, including sovereign wealth, or on a long-term market tracking unit trust fund administered for all citizens by the state. At the macro-level full employment reflects a commitment by the state for a higher degree of macro-management to smooth out business cycles, direct national investment, co-operate with other nation-states to end systematic tax evasion by corporations, and to reform all state-mandated restricted licensing (whether for intellectual property, or licensed occupations) in the public interest.

The upshot will be a realistically utopian transformation of education and work that, in particular, uses tax policy and the provision of public goods to control positional competition. The goods of social mobility will be accessible to all and Frank's progressive consumption tax will dampen down asset price inflation that will also be targeted by the activist central bank (under democratic control). This will create the option for what both Mill and Rawls envisioned as a "stationary state" that, faced with exogenous environmental constraints, no longer seeks economic growth but a fairer distribution of the prosperity that already exists.

Conclusion

Throughout this book we have contrasted a publicly affirmed ideology of market fundamentalism with an actually existing neo-liberalism as a political practice. The latter, we have argued, is equivalent to corporatist socialism (Hayek's "syndicalism"). The destabilizing events of the past decade and a half, from the global financial crisis to the pandemic that began in late 2019, have made it more difficult to maintain that actual practice is legitimated by the ideal of market fundamentalism. There have, of course, been massive policy successes from the perspective of this ruling ideology such as the liberalization of global capital flows, the assault on organized labour, and the erosion of the associational and solidaristic class basis of progressive politics. But this process of marketization has been achieved not by rolling back the state, but by co-opting it. From our perspective, the "new" statism that emerged during the global pandemic ought not to have surprised anyone: it was a reflection of an unchanged underlying reality. It is noteworthy how quickly, here in the affluent West, the wholly explicable inflationary surge caused by supply chain shocks was taken as a pretext for a return of the politics of austerity.

What we have called for here, underpinned by the new research of the science of happiness, is a progressive and statist politics that uses the full range of the monopoly powers of the state—a state that never went away. The state, instead, went into abeyance and retreated into its learned helplessness when faced with the organized interest of capital. We have not dissented from the verdict that our current problems are the paradoxical product of decades of success. The Cold War ended, defence spending was retrenched, and until the global pandemic the affluent West saw increasing prosperity (punctuated by crises) and inter-societal inequality narrowed. But the engine of decay—the coordination of intra-societal elites—saw the substantial increase in intra-societal inequality characteristic of rentier capitalism that produced the logic we have described here. This logic is one of deepening inequality, instability, financial crises, and the entrenchment of the "rich get richer" dynamic.

Extravagance and Misery. Alan Thomas, Alfred Archer, and Bart Engelen, Oxford University Press.
 DOI: 10.1093/oso/9780197781722.003.0015

We have aligned ourselves in this book with the perspective of the neo-Keynesians who sought Keynes's goal of the euthanasia of the rentier class. We have expressed that aim as the goal of maximizing the ratio of productive to unproductive use of capital. However, our society has gone so far in the other direction that we noted, in passing, Javier Moreno Zacarés's recent essay on the "euphoria" of the rentier (Zacarés 2021). Zacarés surveys a recent body of literature suggesting that we may have historically moved past capitalism to something worse: an economy centred on extractive rent seeking.

We can envisage a powerful challenge to our argument here from the critic who responds that rent-seeking activity is a regrettable aspect of capitalism but also that it is an emergent, yet essentially supervenient feature of the system—like the corruption to which it is closely connected—which the system can survive. We are not that optimistic: excessive rent seeking is stifling the productive employment of capital. In the process, whatever its impact on productive efficiency, rent-extractive capitalism is making a mockery of any legitimating ideal of justice, and that, we have argued, explains the price we are paying in terms of human well-being.

We may well have reached, in the affluent West, the point of exogenous limits to growth. The historical misfortune of a crisis within capitalism that saw extensive unemployment, deepened poverty, and the loss of people's savings, homes, and aspirations may well have created a moment of political opportunity. That opportunity would be politically to manage expectations so that a more productive, de-financialized, and more humane economic system can see us collectively within our ecological constraints. That will require political action, motivated by a sense of justice. While we are not politicians, it is in casting light on the demands of justice that we have made some contribution to new policies for a fairer future.

List of Works Cited

Abramson, Kate. 2014. 'Turning Up the Lights on Gaslighting', *Philosophical Perspectives*, 28: 1–30.

Abu-Lughod, Lila. 1990. 'Shifting Politics in Bedouin Love Poetry', in Catherine Lutz and Lila Abu-Lughod (eds.), *Language and the Politics of Emotion* (Cambridge University Press), pp. 24–45.

Ackerman, Bruce, and Anne Alstot. 1999. *The Stakeholder Society* (Yale University Press).

Ackerman, Seth. 2012. 'The Red and the Black', *Jacobin*, December 20. https://jacobinmag.com/2012/12/the-red-and-the-black [Accessed 30/11/23].

Adams, John. 1790/1973. *Discourses on Davila* (Da Capo).

Ahmed, Sara. 2004a. 'Affective Economies', *Social Text*, 22: 117–39.

Ahmed, Sara. 2004b. *The Cultural Politics of Emotion* (Edinburgh University Press).

Alesina, Alberto, and Edward Glaeser. 2004. *Fighting Poverty in the USA and Europe: A World of Difference* (Oxford University Press).

Alesina, Alberto, Stefanie Stantcheva, and Edorado Tesa. 2018. 'Intergenerational Mobility and Preferences for Redistribution', *American Economic Review*, 108: 521–4.

Alexander, Michelle. 2010. *The New Jim Crow: Mass Incarceration in the Age of Colorblindness* (The New Press).

Alexander, Sadie T. M. 1945. 'The Role of Negro Woman in the Economic Life of the Postwar South', *STMA*, Box 71, FF80 University of Pennsylvania Archives.

Alexandrova, Anna. 2017. *A Philosophy for the Science of Well-Being* (Oxford University Press).

Algoe, Sara B., and Jonathan Haidt. 2009. 'Witnessing Excellence in Action: The "Other-Praising" Emotions of Elevation, Gratitude, and Admiration', *Journal of Positive Psychology*, 4(2): 105–27.

Alichi, Ali, Kory Kantenga, and Juan Solé. 2016. 'Income Polarization in the United States', IMF Working Paper. https://www.imf.org/external/pubs/ft/wp/2016/wp16121.pdf [Accessed 30/11/2023].

Anderson, Cameron, John Angus D. Hildreth, and Laura Howland. 2015. 'Is the Desire for Status a Fundamental Human Motive?', *Psychological Bulletin*, 131: 574–601.

Anderson, Elizabeth. 1991. 'John Stuart Mill and Experiments in Living', *Ethics*, 102: 4–26.

Anderson, Elizabeth. 2005. 'How Not to Complain About Taxes (III): "I Deserve My Pretax Income"', *Left2Right*, January 26. https://left2right.typepad.com/main/2005/01/how_not_to_comp_1.html [Accessed 30/11/23].

Anderson, Elizabeth. 2015. 'Liberty, Equality and Private Government', *The Tanner Lectures on Human Values*. https://tannerlectures.utah.edu/_resources/documents/a-to-z/a/Anderson%20manuscript.pdf [Accessed 30/10/23].

Anderson, Elizabeth. 2017. *Private Government: How Employers Rule Our Lives (and Why We Don't Talk About It)* (Princeton University Press).

Andrews, Bernice. 1995. 'Bodily Shame as a Mediator Between Abusive Experiences and Depression', *Journal of Abnormal Psychology*, 104: 277–85.

Andrews, Bernice, Chris R. Brewin, Suzanna Rose, and Marilyn Kirk. 2000. 'Predicting PTSD Symptoms in Victims of Violent Crime: The Role of Shame, Anger, and Childhood Abuse', *Journal of Abnormal Psychology*, 109: 69–73.

Andrews, Bernice, and Elaine Hunter. 1997. 'Shame, Early Abuse, and Course of Depression in a Clinical Sample: A Preliminary Study', *Cognition and Emotion*, 11: 373–81.

Andrews, Bernice, Mingyi Qian, and John D. Valentine. 2002. 'Predicting Depressive Symptoms with a New Measure of Shame: The Experience of Shame Scale', *British Journal of Psychology*, 41(1): 29–42.

Annas, Julia. 2012. *Intelligent Virtue* (Oxford University Press).

Aquino, Karl, Brent McFerran, and Marjorie Laven. 2011. 'Moral Identity and the Experience of Moral Elevation in Response to Acts of Uncommon Goodness', *Journal of Personality and Social Psychology*, 100(4): 703–18.

Archer, Alfred. 2019. 'Admiration and Motivation', *Emotion Review*, 11(2): 140–50.

Archer, Alfred, and Benjamin Matheson. 2019. 'When Artists Fail: Honoring and Admiring the Immoral', *Journal of the American Philosophical Association*, 5: 246–65.

Archer, Alfred, and Benjamin Matheson. 2022. 'Commemoration and Emotional Imperialism', *Journal of Applied Philosophy*, 39(5): 761–77.

Archer, Alfred, and Georgina Mills. 2019. 'Anger, Affective Injustice, and Emotion Regulation', *Philosophical Topics*, 47: 75–94.

Arendt, Hannah. 2006. *Between Past and Future: Eight Exercises in Political Thought* (Penguin Books).

Ariely, Dan. 2015. 'How Equal Do We Want the World To Be? You'd Be Surprised', *TED Talk March 2015*. https://www.ted.com/talks/dan_ariely_how_equal_do_we_want_the_world_to_be_you_d_be_surprised [Accessed 30/11/23].

Aristotle. 350 BC/2002. *Nicomachean Ethics*. Translated and edited by Sarah Broadie and Cristopher Rowe (Oxford University Press).

Arneson, Richard. 1999. 'Against Rawlsian Equality of Opportunity', *Philosophical Studies*, 93: 77–112.

Arrow, Kenneth J., and Gerard Debreu. 1954. 'Existence of an Equilibrium for a Competitive Economy', *Econometrica*, 22: 265–90.

ATD Fourth World Conference. 2013. 'Ending the Violence of Extreme Poverty—A Must for Sustainable Societies'. https://www.atd-fourthworld.org/eradicating-extreme-poverty-a-must/ [Accessed 30/11/23].

Atkinson, Anthony. 2015. *Inequality: What Can Be Done?* (Harvard University Press).

Austin, John L. 1962. *How to Do Things with Words* (Clarendon Press).

Baker, Dean. 2016. *Rigged: How Globalization and the Rules of the Modern Economy Were Structured to Make the Rich Richer* (Center for Economic and Policy Research).

Baker, Dean, Sarah Rawlins, and David Stein. 2017. 'The Full Employment Mandate of the Federal Reserve: Its Origins and Importance', Center for Economic and Policy Research. https://cepr.net/report/full-employment-mandate-of-the-fed/ [Accessed 30/11/23].

Baker, Joseph, and A. Jane Logan. 2007. 'Developmental Contexts and Sporting Success: Birthdate and Birthplace Effects in National Hockey League Draftees 2000–2005', *British Journal of Sports Medicine*, 41(8): 515–7.

Bankovsky, Miriam. 2018. 'Excusing Economic Envy: On Injustice and Impotence', *Journal of Applied Philosophy*, 35(2): 257–79.

Bannerjee, Kiran, and Jeffrey Bercuson. 2015. 'Rawls on the Embedded Self: Liberalism as an Affective Regime', *European Journal of Political Theory*, 14: 209–28.

Barker, Tim. 2020. 'From Keynes to the Keynesians: Socialised Investment and the Spectre of Full Employment', in *Verso Blog*. https://www.versobooks.com/blogs/4936-from-keynes-to-the-keynesians-socialised-investment-and-the-spectre-of-full-employment [Accessed 30/11/23].

Barclay, Katie. 2022. 'Capitalism and Consumption', in K. Barclay and P. N. Stearns (eds.), *The Routledge History of Emotions in the Modern World* (London: Routledge), pp.440–59.

Barrett, Lisa Feldman. 2017. *How Emotions are Made: The Secret Life of the Brain* (Houghton Mifflin Harcourt).

Barrow, Flo, Neil Crombie, Marian Edusei, Joe Evans, Fran Rowlett-McCormick, and Adam Simons (Executive Producers). 2020. 'Grayson Perry's Big American Road Trip', TV Program, Channel 4, UK.

Baumol, William. 1974. 'The Transformation of Values: What Marx "Really" Meant (An Interpretation)', *Journal of Economic Literature*, 12: 51–62.

Baumol, William. 1986. *Superfairness* (MIT Press).

BBC. 2011. Why Is Chav Still Controversial? *BBC.com/news*, June 3. https://www.bbc.com/news/magazine-13626046 [Accessed 30/11/23].

Becchetti, Leonardo, Stefano Castriota, Luisa Corrado, and Elena Giachin Ricca. 2013. 'Beyond the Joneses: Inter-Country Comparisons and Happiness', *Journal of Socio-Economics*, 45: 187–95.

Mike Beggs. 2012. 'Debt: The First 500 Pages', *Jacobin*, August 27 https://jacobin.com/2012/08/debt-the-first-500-pages [Accessed 30/11/23].

Beggs, Mike. 2018. 'The Minsky Millennium', *Jacobin*, November 27. https://jacobin.com/2018/11/the-minsky-millennium [Accessed 30/11/23].

Bell, Daniel. 1972. 'Meritocracy and Equality', *Public Interest*, 29: 29–68.

Bell, Daniel. 1973. *The Coming of Post-Industrial Society: A Venture in Social Forecasting* (Basic Books).

Bénabou, Roland, and Jean Tirole. 2006. 'Incentives and Prosocial Behavior', *American Economic Review*, 96(5): 1652–78.

Benedict, Ruth. 1946. *The Chrysanthemum and the Sword: Patterns of Japanese Culture* (Houghton Mifflin Harcourt).

Bentham, Jeremy. 1843. *The Works of Jeremy Bentham* (vol. 8). Edited by J. Bentham (Bowring, Tait).

Ben-Ze'ev, Aaron. 1992. 'Envy and Inequality', *Journal of Philosophy*, 89: 551–81.

Ben-Ze'ev, Aaron. 2000. *The Subtlety of Emotions* (MIT Press).

Ben-Ze'ev, Aaron. 2004. *Love Online: Emotions on the Internet* (Cambridge University Press).

Bercuson, Jeffrey. 2014. *John Rawls and the History of Political Thought: The Rousseauvian and Hegelian Heritage of Justice as Fairness* (Routledge).

Bianchi, Emily C., and Kathleen D. Vohs. 2016. 'Social Class and Social Worlds: Income Predicts the Frequency and Nature of Social Contact', *Social Psychological and Personality Science*, 7: 479–86.

Bishop, Bill. 2008. *The Big Sort: Why the Cluster of Like-Minded America Is Tearing Us Apart* (Houghton Mifflin Harcourt).

Blackburn, Simon. 1998. *Ruling Passions: A Theory of Practical Reasoning* (Oxford University Press).

Blinder, Alan S. 1982. 'The Anatomy of Double Digit Inflation in the 1970s', in Robert E. Hall (ed.), *Inflation: Causes and Effects* (University of Chicago Press), pp. 261–82.

Blyth, Mark. 2015. 'Ending the Creditor's Paradise', *Jacobin*, February 27. https://www.jacobinmag.com/2015/02/germany-austerity-blyth-speech-spd [Accessed 30/11/23].

Blyth, Mark. 2020. 'Fed. Defends the "Creditors Paradise"', *theanalysis.news*, edited and presented by Paul Jay. https://theanalysis.news/fed-defends-the-creditors-paradise-mark-blyth/ [Accessed 30/11/23].

Blyth, Mark. 2023. 'Maybe a Fiscal Crisis Is What You Make of It?' *Renewal*, October 4. https://renewal.org.uk/maybe-a-fiscal-crisis-is-what-you-make-of-it-two-cheers-for-colin-hays-the-new-orleans-effect/ [Accessed 30/11/23].

Boltanski, Luc, and Ève Chiapello. 2005. *The New Spirit of Capitalism* (Verso).

Bookstaber, Richard. 2007. *A Demon of Our Own Design: Markets, Hedge Funds, and the Perils of Financial Innovation* (John Wiley).

Bork, Robert. 1978/1993. *The Antitrust Paradox* (The Free Press).

Botton, Alain de. 2005. *Status Anxiety* (Penguin).

Boucoyannis, Deborah. 2013. 'The Equalizing Hand: Why Adam Smith Thought the Market Should Produce Wealth Without Steep Inequality', *Perspectives on Politics*, 11: 1051–70.

Bourdieu, Pierre. 1985. *Distinction: A Social Critique of the Judgement of Taste* (Harvard University Press).

Bourdieu, Pierre. 1990. *The Logic of Practice* (Stanford University Press).

Bourguignon, François. 2012. *The Globalization of Inequality* (Princeton University Press).

Boyd, Richard. 1988. 'How to Be a Moral Realist', in Geoffrey Sayre-McCord (ed.), *Essays on Moral Realism* (Cornell University Press), pp. 181–228.

Boyd, Richard. 1999. 'Homeostasis, Species and Higher Taxa', in Robert Wilson (ed.), *Species: New Interdisciplinary Essays* (MIT Press), pp. 141–86.

Boyd, Richard. 2003. 'Finite Beings, Finite Goods: The Semantics, Metaphysics and Ethics of Naturalist Consequentialism, Part II', *Philosophy and Phenomenological Research*, 67: 24–47.

Brandt, Richard B. 1979. *A Theory of the Good and the Right* (Clarendon Press).

Braun, Benjamin. 2020. 'Central Banking and the Infrastructural Power of Finance: The Case of ECB Support for Repo and Securitization Markets', *Socio-Economic Review*, 18: 395–418.

Braun, Benjamin. 2021. 'Asset Manager Capitalism as a Corporate Governance Regime', in Jacob S. Hacker, Alexander Hertel-Fernandez, Paul Pierson, and Kathleen Thelen (eds.), *American Political Economy: Politics, Markets and Power* (Cambridge University Press), pp. 270–94.

Brennan, Geoffrey, and Philip Pettit. 2004. *The Economy of Esteem: An Essay on Civil and Political Society* (Oxford University Press).

Brentano, Franz. 1874/1995. *Psychology from an Empirical Standpoint* (Routledge).

Brickman, Philip, and Donald T. Campbell. 1971. 'Hedonic Relativism and Planning the Good Society', in Mortimer H. Appley (ed.), *Adaptation Level Theory: A Symposium* (Academic Press), pp. 287–305.

Brighouse, Harry, and Adam Swift. 2006. 'Equality, Priority and Positional Goods', *Ethics*, 116: 471–97.

Britain's Industrial Future, Being the Report of the Liberal Industrial Inquiry of 1928. 1928. (Ernest Benn Limited). (Primary author John Maynard Keynes).

Brooks-Gunn, Jeanne, and Greg J. Duncan. 1997. 'The Effects of Poverty on Children', *Future of Children*, 7(2): 55–71.

Brown, Kathryn. 2019. 'Private Influence, Public Goods and the Future of Art History', *Journal for Art Market Studies*, 3: 1–17.

Bryan, Alexander. 2019. 'The Dominating Effect of Economic Crises', *Critical Review of International Social and Political Philosophy*, 24(6): 1–25.

Bucca, Mauricio. 2016. 'Merit and Blame in Unequal Societies: Explaining Latin Americans' Beliefs About Wealth and Poverty', *Research in Social Stratification and Mobility*, 44: 98–112.

Buchanan, James. 1965. 'An Economic Theory of Clubs', *Economica*, 32: 1–14.

Bullock, Heather E., Karen Fraser Wyche, and Wendy R. Williams. 2001. 'Media Images of the Poor', *Journal of Social Issues*, 57: 229–46.

Bureau of Labor Statistics. 2018. 'Table 39: Median Weekly Earnings of Full-Time Wage and Salary Workers by Detailed Occupation and Sex', *Current Population Survey 2018*. https://www.bls.gov/cps/cpsaat39.htm [Accessed 30/11/23].

Burgess, Simon, and Ellen Greaves. 2013. 'Test Scores, Subjective Assessment, and Stereotyping of Ethnic Minorities', *Journal of Labor Economics*, 31(3): 535–76.

Burkitt, Ian. 2018. 'Decentring Emotion Regulation: From Emotion Regulation to Relational Emotion', *Emotion Review*, 10(2): 167–73.

Burney, John, and Harvey Irwin. 2000. 'Shame and Guilt in Women with Eating Disorder Symptomatology', *Journal of Clinical Psychology*, 56(1): 51–61.

Buttrick, Nicholas R., Samantha J. Heintzelman, and Shigehiro Oishi. 2017. 'Inequality and Well-Being', *Current Opinion in Psychology*, 18: 15–20.

Calhoun, Cheshire. 2004. 'An Apology for Moral Shame', *Journal of Political Philosophy*, 12: 127–46.

Campbell, Sue. 1997. *Interpreting the Personal: Expression and the Formation of Feelings* (Cornell University Press).

Cantril, Hadley. 1965. *The Pattern of Human Concerns* (Rutgers University Press).

Carbonell, Vanessa. 2019. 'Social Constraints on Moral Address', *Philosophy and Phenomenological Research*, 98(1): 167–89.
Cartwright, Nancy. 1980. 'The Truth Doesn't Explain Very Much', *American Philosophical Quarterly*, 17: 159–63.
Cartwright, Nancy. 1983. *How the Laws of Physics Lie* (Clarendon Press).
Cartwright, Nancy. 2007. 'Are RCTs the Gold Standard?', *Biosocieties*, 2: 11–20.
Cawston, Amanda. 2019. 'Admiring Animals', in Alfred Archer and Andre Grahle (eds.), *The Moral Psychology of Admiration* (Rowman and Littlefield), pp. 165–78.
Cebul, Brent. 2019. 'Supply Side Liberalism: Fiscal Crisis, Post-Industrial Policy, and the Rise of the New Democrats', *Modern American History*, 2(2): 139–64.
Chandler, Alfred D. 1962. *Strategy and Structure: Chapters in the History of Industrial Enterprise* (MIT Press).
Chang, Ha-Joon. 2007. *Bad Samaritans: The Myth of Free Trade and the Secret History of Capitalism* (Bloomsbury).
Chappell, Sophie-Grace. 2019. 'No More Heroes Any More?', in Alfred Archer and Andre Grahle (eds.), *The Moral Psychology of Admiration* (Rowman and Littlefield), pp. 11–28.
Chase, Elaine, and Robert Walker. 2013. 'The Co-construction of Shame in the Context of Poverty: Beyond a Threat to the Social Bond', *Sociology*, 47: 739–54.
Chase, Elaine, and Robert Walker. 2015a. 'Constructing Reality? The "discursive truth" of Poverty in Britain and How It Frames the Experience of Shame', in E. Chase and G. Bantebya-Kyomuhendo (eds.), *Poverty and Shame: Global Experiences* (Oxford University Press), pp.256–69.
Chase, Elaine, and Robert Walker. 2015b. 'The "Shame" of Shame: Experiences of People Living in Poverty in Poverty', in Elaine Chase and Grace Bantebya-Kyomuhendo (eds.), *Poverty and Shame: Global Experiences* (Oxford University Press), pp. 161–74.
Chetty, Raj, David Grusky, Maximilian Hell, Nathaniel Hendren, Robert Manduca, and Jimmy Narang. 2017. 'The Fading American Dream: Trends in Absolute Income Mobility Since 1940', *Science*, 356: 398–406.
Chetty, Raj, Nathaniel Hendren, Patrick Kline, and Emmanuel Saez. 2014. 'Where Is the Land of Opportunity? The Geography of Intergenerational Mobility in the United States', *Quarterly Journal of Economics*, 129: 1553–623.
Chetty, Raj, Michael Stepner, Sarah Abraham, Shelby Lin, Benjamin Scuderi, Nicholas Turner, Augustin Bergeron, and David Cutler. 2016. 'The Association Between Income and Life Expectancy in the United States, 2001–14', *Journal of the American Medical Association*, 315: 1750–66.
Christophers, Brett. 2020. *Rentier Capitalism: Who Owns the Economy, and Who Pays for It?* (Verso).
Church, Jeffrey. 2010. 'The Freedom of Desire: Hegel's Response to Rousseau on the Problem of Civil Society', *American Journal of Political Science*, 54: 125–39.
Ci, Jiwei. 2013. 'Agency and Other Stakes of Poverty', *Journal of Political Philosophy*, 21: 125–50.
Clark, Margaret S. 1989. 'Historical Emotionology: From a Social Psychologist's Perspective', in Andrew E. Barnes and Peter N. Stearns (eds.), *Social History and Issues in Human Consciousness: Some Interdisciplinary Connections* (New York University Press), pp. 262–6.
Clinton, Hilary. 2017. *What Happened* (Simon & Schuster).
Cohen, Gerry A. 2008. *Rescuing Justice and Equality* (Harvard University Press).
Cohen, Gerry A. 2009. *Why Not Socialism?* (Princeton University Press).
Cohen, Joshua. 1997. 'The Natural Goodness of Humanity', in Andrews Reath, Barbara Herman, and Christine M Korsgaard (eds.), *Reclaiming the History of Ethics: Essays for John Rawls* (Cambridge University Press), pp. 102–39.
Cohen, Joshua. 2010. *Rousseau* (Oxford University Press).
Collins, Patricia Hill. 2009. *Black Feminist Thought: Knowledge Consciousness and the Politics of Empowerment* (Routledge).

Condorcet, Nicolas de. 1794. *Esquisse d'un tableau historique des progrés de l'esprit humain* (Chez Agasse).

Cox, Keith S. 2010. 'Elevation Predicts Domain-Specific Volunteerism 3 Months Later', *Journal of Positive Psychology*, 5(5): 333–41.

Crisp, Roger. 2006. *Reasons and the Good* (Oxford University Press).

Crisp, Roger. 2007. 'Ethics Without Reasons', *Journal of Moral Philosophy*, 4: 40–49.

Crisp, Roger. 2015. 'Well-Being', in Edward N. Zalta (ed.), *The Stanford Encylopedia of Philosophy* (Winter 2021 Edition). https://plato.stanford.edu/archives/win2021/entries/well-being/ [Accessed 30/11/23].

Crouch, Colin. 2011. *The Strange Non-Death of Neoliberalism* (Polity).

Cruces, Guillermo, Ricardo Perez-Truglia, and Martin Tetaz. 2013. 'Biased Perceptions of Income Distribution and Preferences for Redistribution: Evidence from a Survey Experiment', *Journal of Public Economics*, 98: 100–112.

Csikszentmihalyi, Mihaly. 1991. *Flow: The Psychology of Optimal Experience* (Harper Collins).

Cuddy, Amy J. C., Susan T. Fiske, and Peter Glick. 2007. 'The BIAS Map: Behaviors from Intergroup Affect and Stereotypes', *Journal of Personality and Social Psychology*, 92(4): 631–48.

Currid-Halkett, Elizabeth. 2017. *The Sum of Small Things: A Theory of the Aspirational Class* (Princeton University Press).

Dafermos, Yannis, Daniela Gabor, and Jo Michell. 2020. 'Institutional Supercycles: An Institutional Macro-Finance Approach', *National Institute of Economic and Social Research*. https://www.rebuildingmacroeconomics.ac.uk/post/institutional-supercycles-an-evolutionary-macro-finance-approach [Accessed 30/11/23].

Dagger, Richard. 1997. *Civic Virtues: Rights, Citizenship and Republican Liberalism* (Oxford University Press).

Dancy, Jonathan. 1993. *Moral Reasons* (Blackwell Publishers).

Darwall, Stephen. 2004. 'Equal Dignity in Adam Smith', *Adam Smith Review*, 1: 129–34.

Darwall, Stephen. 2006. *The Second-Person Standpoint: Morality, Respect, and Accountability* (Harvard University Press).

Darwall, Stephen. 2010. 'Smith's Ambivalence About Honour', in Vivienne Brown and Samuel Fleischacker (eds.), *The Philosophy of Adam Smith: The Adam Smith Review, 5: Essays Commemorating the 250th Anniversary of The Theory of Moral Sentiments* (Routledge), pp. 30–49.

Darwin, Charles. 1872/1998. *The Expression* of *the Emotions in Man and Animals*. 3rd Edition (Oxford University Press).

Davies, William. 2015. *The Happiness Industry: How the Government and Business Sold Us Well-Being* (Verso).

Dawtry, Rael J., Robbie M. Sutton, and Chris G. Sibley. 2015. 'Why Wealthier People Think People Are Wealthier, and Why It Matters: From Social Sampling to Attitudes to Redistribution', *Psychological Science*, 26: 1389–400.

Delhey, Jan, and Georgi Dragolov. 2014. 'Why Inequality Makes Europeans Less Happy: The Role of Distrust, Status Anxiety, and Perceived Conflict', *European Sociological Review*, 30: 151–65.

Deonna, Julien A., Raffaele Rodogno, and Fabrice Teroni. 2011. *In Defense of Shame: The Faces of an Emotion* (Oxford University Press).

Deresiewicz, William. 2014. 'Don't Send Your Kid to the Ivy League: The Nation's Top Colleges Are Turning Our Kids into Zombies', *New Republic*, July 22. https://newrepublic.com/article/118747/ivy-league-schools-are-overrated-send-your-kids-elsewhere [Accessed 30/11/23].

Deutschmann, Christoph. 2012. 'Limits to Financialisation', *European Journal of Sociology*, 52: 347–89.

Dewey, John. 1916. *Democracy and Education* (The Macmillan Company).

Dhuey, Elizabeth, and Stephen Lipscomb. 2008. 'What Makes a Leader? Relative Age and High School Leadership', *Economics of Education Review*, 27(2): 173–83.
Dickerson, Andrew, and Gurleen K. Popli. 2016. 'Persistent Poverty and Children's Cognitive Development: Evidence from the UK Millennium Cohort Study', *Journal of the Royal Statistical Society: Series A (Statistics in Society)*, 179(2): 535–58.
Dickerson, Sally S., Tara L. Gruenewald, T. L., and Margaret E. Kemeny. 2009. 'Psychobiological Responses to Social Self Threat: Functional or Detrimental?', *Self and Identity* 8(2–3): 270–85.
Dickerson, Sally S., and Margaret E. Kemeny. 2004. 'Acute Stressors and Cortisol Responses: A Theoretical Integration and Synthesis of Laboratory Research', *Psychological Bulletin*, 130: 355–91.
Dickerson, Sally S., Margaret E. Kemeny, Najib Aziz, Kevin H. Kim, and John L. Fahey. 2004. 'Immunological Effects of Induced Shame and Guilt', *Psychosomatic Medicine*, 66: 124–31.
Dickman, Samuel L., David U. Himmelstein, and Steffie Woolhandler. 2017. 'Inequality and the Health-Care System in the USA', *Lancet*, 389(10077): 1431–41.
Diener, Ed, Richard E. Lucas, and Christie Napa Scollon. 2006. 'Beyond the Hedonic Treadmill: Revising the Adaptation Theory of Well-Being', *American Psychologist*, 61: 305–14.
Diener, Ed, Weiting Ng, James Harter, and Raksha Arora. 2010. 'Wealth and Happiness Across the World: Material Prosperity Predicts Life Evaluation, Whereas Psychosocial Prosperity Predicts Positive Feeling', *Journal of Personality and Social Psychology*, 99: 52–61.
Diener, Ed, Louis Tay, and Shigehiro Oishi. 2013. 'Rising Income and the Subjective Well-Being of Nations', *Journal of Personality and Social Psychology*, 104: 267–76.
Dietsch, Peter, François Claveau, and Clément Fontan. 2018. *Do Central Banks Serve the People?* (Polity).
Dobson, Kathy, and Irena Knezevic. 2017. '"Liking and Sharing" the Stigmatization of Poverty and Social Welfare: Representations of Poverty and Welfare Through Internet Memes on Social Media', *tripleC: Communication, Capitalism and Critique. Open Access Journal for a Global Sustainable Information Society*, 15(2): 777–95.
Dobzhansky, Theodosius. 1955. *Evolution, Genetics and Man* (Wiley).
Dolan, Paul, Tessa Peasgood, and Mathew White. 2008. 'Do We Really Know What Makes Us Happy? A Review of the Economic Literature on the Factors Associated with Subjective Well-Being', *Journal of Economic Psychology*, 29: 94–122.
Dolan, Paul, and Matthew P. White. 2007. 'How Can Measures of Subjective Well-Being Be Used to Inform Public Policy?', *Perspectives on Psychological Science*, 2: 71–85.
Dorling, Danny. 2011. *So You Think You Know About Britain?* (Constable).
Dotson, Kristie. 2011. 'Tracking Epistemic Violence, Tracking Practices of Silencing', *Hypatia*, 26(2): 236–57.
Drennan, Matthew P. 2015. *Income Inequality: Why It Matters and Why Most Economists Didn't Notice* (Yale University Press).
Du, Qianqian, Huasheng Gao, and Maurice David Levi. 2012. 'The Relative-Age Effect and Career Success: Evidence from Corporate CEOs', *Economics Letters*, 117(3): 660–2.
Dworkin, Ronald. 2000. *Sovereign Virtue: The Theory and Practice of Equality* (Harvard University Press).
Dymski, Gary. 2010. 'From Financial Exploitation to Global Banking Instability: Two Overlooked Roots of the Subprime Crisis', in Martijn Konings (ed.), *The Great Credit Crash* (Verso), pp. 72–102.
Easterlin, Richard A. 1974. 'Does Economic Growth Improve the Human Lot? Some Empirical Evidence', in Paul A. David and Melvin W. Reder (eds.), *Nations and Households in Economic Growth: Essays in Honor of Moses Abramowitz* (Academic Press), pp. 89–125.
Easterlin, Richard A. 1995. 'Will Raising the Incomes of All Increase the Happiness of All?', *Journal of Economic Behavior and Organization* 27: 35–47.

Easterlin, Richard A. 2003. 'Explaining Happiness', *Proceedings of the National Academy of Sciences of the United States of America*, 100: 11176–83.

Easterlin, Richard A. 2005a. 'Building a Better Theory of Well-Being', in Luigino Bruni and Pier Luigi Porta (eds.), *Economics and Happiness* (Oxford University Press), pp. 29–64.

Easterlin, Richard A. 2005b. 'Feeding the Illusion of Growth and Happiness: A Reply to Hagerty and Veenhoven', *Social Indicators Research*, 74: 429–43.

Easterlin, Richard A. 2017. 'Paradox Lost?', *Review of Behavioral Economics*, 4: 311–39.

Easterlin, Richard A., Laura Angelescu McVey, Malgorzata Switek, Onnicha Sawangfa, and Jacqueline Smith Zweig. 2010. 'The Happiness-Income Paradox Revisited', *Proceedings of the National Academy of Sciences of the United States of America*, 107: 22463–8.

Edmundson, William A. 2017. *John Rawls: Reticent Socialist* (Cambridge University Press).

Eichengreen, Barry. 2011. *Exorbitant Privilege: The Rise and Fall of the Dollar and the Future of the International Monetary System* (Oxford University Press).

Eisenberger, Naomi I. 2011. 'Why Rejection Hurts: What Social Neuroscience Has Revealed About the Brain's Response to Social Rejection', in J. Decety and J. Cacioppo (eds.), *The Handbook of Social Neuroscience* (Oxford University Press), pp. 109–27.

Ekman, Paul. 1992. 'An Argument for Basic Emotions', *Cognition and Emotion*, 6: 169–200.

Ekman, Paul. 1994. 'All Emotions are Basic', in Paul Ekman and Richard Davidson (eds.), *The Nature of Emotion: Fundamental Questions* (Oxford University Press), pp. 15–9.

Elison, Jeff, Carlo Garofalo, and Patrizia Velotti. 2014. 'Shame and Aggression: Theoretical Considerations', *Aggression and Violent Behavior* 19(4): 447–53.

Ellsworth, Phoebe C. 1994. 'Levels of Thought and Levels of Emotion', in P. Ekman and R. J. Davidson (eds.), *The Nature of Emotions: Fundamental Questions* (Oxford University Press), pp. 192–6.

Elster, Jon. 1983. *Sour Grapes* (Cambridge University Press).

Elster, Jon. 1999. *Alchemies of the Mind: Rationality and the Emotions* (Cambridge University Press).

Eurostat. 2018. 'Gender Paygap in Unadjusted Form', *Eurostat Statistics Explained*. https://ec.europa.eu/eurostat/statistics-explained/index.php/Gender_pay_gap_statistics [Accessed 30/11/23].

Fazi, Thomas, and William Mitchell. 2017. *Reclaiming the State: A Progressive Vision of Sovereignty for a Post-Neoliberal World* (Pluto Press).

Feldman, Fred. 2004. *Pleasure and the Good Life: Concerning the Nature, Varieties and Plausibility of Hedonism* (Oxford University Press).

Feldman, Fred. 2010. *What Is This Thing Called Happiness?* (Oxford University Press).

Feldstein, Martin. 2005. 'Rethinking Social Insurance', *American Economic Review*, 91: 1–24.

Fergus, Thomas, David P. Valentiner, Patrick B. McGrath, and Simon Jencius. 2010. 'Shame- and Guilt- Proneness: Relationships with Anxiety Syndrome Symptoms in a Clinical Sample', *Journal of Anxiety Disorders*, 24(8): 811–15.

Ferguson, Ronald F. 2003. 'Teachers' Perceptions and Expectations and the Black-White Test Score Gap', *Urban Education* 38(4): 460–507.

Ferrer-i-Carbonell, Ada. 2005. 'Income and Well-Being: An Empirical Analysis of the Comparison Income Effect', *Journal of Public Economics*, 89: 997–1019.

Ferrer-i-Carbonell, Ada, and Xavier Ramos. 2014. 'Inequality and Happiness', *Journal of Economic Surveys*, 28: 1016–27.

Feygin, Yakov. 2021. 'The Deflationary Bloc', *Phenomenal World*. New York. https://www.phenomenalworld.org/analysis/deflation-inflation/ [Accessed 30/11/2023].

Fichte, J. G. 1800/2012. *The Closed Commercial State*. Translated and with an Introduction by Anthony Curtis Adler (State University of New York Press).

Fine, Kit. 2012. 'Guide to Ground', in Fabrice Correia and Benjamin Schnieder (eds.), *Metaphysical Grounding: Understanding the Structure of Reality* (Cambridge University Press), pp. 37–80.

Finnis, John. 2011. *Natural Law and Natural Rights* (Oxford University Press).

Fisher, Mark. 2009. *Capitalist Realism* (Zero Books).
Fishkin, James. 1983. *Justice, Equality of Opportunity, and the Family* (Yale University Press).
Fishkin, Joseph. 2014. *Bottlenecks: A New Theory of Equal Opportunity* (Oxford University Press).
Fleischacker, Samuel. 2004. *On Adam Smith's Wealth of Nations: A Philosophical Companion* (Princeton University Press).
Fletcher, Guy. 2013. 'A Fresh Start for the Objective-List Theory of Well-Being', *Utilitas*, 25: 206–20.
Flynn, James R. 1987. 'Massive IQ Gains in 14 Nations: What IQ Tests Really Measure', *Psychological Bulletin*, 101: 171–91.
Fontenot, Kayla, Jessica Semega, and Melissa Kolla. 2018. 'Income and Poverty in the United States 2017 United States Census Bureau Report No. P60-263'. https://www.census.gov/library/publications/2018/demo/p60-263.html [Accessed 30/11/23].
Formisano, Ronald P. 2015. *Plutocracy in America: Increasing Inequality Destroys the Middle Class and Exploits the Poor* (Johns Hopkins University Press).
Formisano, Ronald P. 2017. *American Oligarchy: The Permanent Political Class* (University of Illinois Press).
Forrester, Mary Gore. 1982. *Moral Language* (University of Wisconsin Press).
Fourcade, Marion, and Kieran Healy. 2007. 'Moral Views of Market Society', *Annual Review of Sociology*, 33: 285–311.
Fox, Alan. 1956. 'Class and Equality' *Socialist Commentary* (May): 11–3.
Frank, Emily S. 1991. 'Shame and Guilt in Eating Disorders', *American Journal of Orthopsychiatry*, 61(2): 303–6.
Frank, Robert H. 1985. *Choosing the Right Pond: Human Behavior and the Quest for Status* (Oxford University Press).
Frank, Robert H. 1997. 'The Frame of Reference as a Public Good', *Economic Journal*, 107: 1832–47.
Frank, Robert H. 1999/2010. *Luxury Fever: Weighing the Cost of Excess* (Princeton University Press).
Frank, Robert H. 2007. *Falling Behind: How Rising Inequality Harms the Middle Class* (University of California Press).
Frank, Robert H. 2011. *The Darwin Economy: Liberty, Competition and the Common Good* (Princeton University Press).
Frank, Robert H. 2016. *Success and Luck: Good Fortune and the Myth of Meritocracy* (Princeton University Press).#)
Frank, Robert H., and Philip J. Cook. 1996. *The Winner-Take-All Society: Why the Few at the Top Get So Much More Than the Rest of Us* (Penguin).
Frank, Thomas. 2005. *What's the Matter with Kansas?* (Henry Holt).
Frankfurt, Harry. 2015. *On Inequality* (Princeton University Press).
Fraser, Nancy. 2014. 'Behind Marx's Hidden Abode', *New Left Review*, 86.
Fraser, Nancy. 2016. 'Contradictions of Capitalism and Care', *New Left Review*, 100.
Freeman, Dan, Karl Aquino, and Brent McFerran. 2009. 'Overcoming Beneficiary Race as an Impediment to Charitable Donations: Social Dominance Orientation, the Experience of Moral Elevation, and Donation Behavior', *Personality and Social Psychology Bulletin*, 4: 72–84.
Freeman, Richard B. 1996. 'Solving the New Inequality', *Boston Review*. 21(6): 3–10.
Freeman, Samuel. 2013. 'Property-Owning Democracy and the Difference Principle', *Analyse and Kritik*, 35: 9–36.
Freeman, Samuel. 2020. 'Replies to Critics', *Philosophy and Public Issues*, 10: 173–345.
Fricker, Miranda. 2007. *Epistemic Injustice: Power and the Ethics of Knowing* (Oxford University Press).
Friedman, Milton. 2002. *Capitalism and Freedom: 40th Anniversary Edition* (Chicago University Press).

Frey, Bruno S., and Alois Stutzer. 2002. *Happiness and Economics* (Princeton University Press).
Fromm, Erich. 1973. *The Anatomy of Human Destructiveness* (Henry Holt).
Frye, Harrison P. 2016. 'The Relation of Envy to Distributive Justice', *Social Theory and Practice*, 42(3): 501–24.
Frye, Marilyn. 1983. 'A Note on Anger', in *The Politics of Reality: Essays in Feminist Theory* (Crossing Press), pp. 84–94.
Furman, Jason, and Peter Orszag. 2018. 'A Firm-Level Perspective on the Role of Rents in the Rise of Inequality', in Martin Guzman (ed.), *Toward a Just Society: Joseph Stiglitz and Twenty-First Century Economics* (Columbia University Press), pp. 19–47.
Gabor, Daniela. 2020. 'Critical Macro-Finance: A Theoretical Lens', *Finance and Society*, 6: 45–55.
Galbraith, James K. 1998. *Created Unequal: The Crisis in American Pay* (A Twentieth Century Fund Book).
Galbraith, James K. 2008. *The Predator State: How Conservatives Abandoned the Free Market and Why Liberals Should Too* (The Free Press).
Galbraith, James K. 2012. *Inequality and Instability: A Study of the World Economy Just Before the Great Crisis* (Oxford University Press).
Galbraith, James K. 2014. *The End of Normal: The Great Crisis and the Future of Growth* (Simon & Schuster).
Galbraith, John Kenneth. 1967/2007. *The New Industrial State* (Princeton University Press).
Gallegos, Francisco. 2022. 'Affective Injustice and Fundamental Affective Goods', *Journal of Social Philosophy*, 53: 185–201.
Galligan, Philip. 2016. 'Shame, Publicity and Self-Esteem', *Ratio*, 29: 57–72.
Gamble, Andrew. 2014. *Crisis Without End: The Unravelling of Western Prosperity* (Macmillan).
Gammon, Earl. 2008. 'Affect and the Rise of the Self-Regulating Market', *Millennium: Journal of International Studies*, 37: 251–78.
Gilens, Martin. 2012. *Affluence and Influence: Economic Inequality and Political Power in America* (Princeton University Press).
Gilens, Martin, and Larry Page. 2014. 'Testing Theories of American Politics: Elites, Interest Groups and Average Citizens', *Perspectives on Politics*, 12: 73–9.
Gilligan, James. 1996. *Violence: Our Deadly Epidemic and Its Causes* (GP Putnam).
Gilligan, James. 2001. *Preventing Violence* (Thames & Hudson).
Gilliom, J. 2001. *Overseers of the Poor: Surveillance, Resistance, and the Limits of Privacy* (University of Chicago Press).
Gilroy, Paul. 1987/2002. *There Ain't No Black in the Union Jack* (Routledge).
Giridharadas, Anand. 2018. *Winners Take All: The Elite Charade of Changing the World* (Alfred A. Knopf).
Goede, Marieke de. 1996. 'Ideology in the US Welfare Debate: Neo-liberal Representations of Poverty', *Discourse and Society*, 7: 317–57.
Golden, Daniel. 2006. *The Price of Admission: How America's Ruling Class Buys Its Way into Elite Colleges and Who Gets Left Outside the Gates* (Crown Publishers).
Golden, Lester. 2020. 'How to Stop the Plutocracy Game: Index the Top 1%'s Tax Rates to Decreasing Inequality', *Medium.com*. https://medium.com/the-national-discussion/how-to-stop-the-plutocracy-game-index-the-top-1-s-tax-rates-to-decreasing-inequality-a3a19f42cd97 [Accessed 30/11/23].
Goldin, Claudia. 2014. 'A Grand Gender Convergence: Its Last Chapter', *American Economic Review*, 104(4): 1091–119.
Goldin, Claudia. 2021. *Career & Faimly: Women's Century-Long Journey Towards Equity* (Princeton University Press).
Gomberg, Paul. 2007. *How to Make Opportunity Equal: Race and Contributive Justice* (Blackwell Publishing).
Gowan, Peter. 2010. 'The Crisis in the Heartland', in Martijn Konings (ed.), *The Great Credit Crash* (Verso), pp. 47–71.

Graham, Carol. 2009. *Happiness Around the World: The Paradox of Happy Peasants and Miserable Millionaires* (Oxford University Press).

Graham, Carol. 2011. *The Pursuit of Happiness: An Economy of Well-Being* (Oxford University Press).

Graham, Carol. 2017. *Happiness for All? Unequal Hopes and Lives in Pursuit of the American Dream* (Princeton University Press).

Graham, Carol, and Sergio Pinto. 2018. 'Unequal Hopes and Lives in the USA: Optimism, Race, Place, and Premature Mortality', *Journal of Population Economics*, 32: 665–733.

Graham, Carol, and Peter Young. 2003. 'Ignorance Fills the Income Gulf', *Boston Globe*, June 23.

Grahle, Andre. 2019. 'Admiration as Normative Support', in Alfred Archer and Andre Grahle (eds.), *The Moral Psychology of Admiration* (Rowman and Littlefield), pp.149–64.

Green, Jeffrey Edward. 2016. *The Shadow of Unfairness: A Plebeian Theory of Liberal Democracy* (Oxford University Press).

Greenspan, Patricia. 1988. *Emotions and Reasons: An Inquiry into Emotional Justification* (Routledge).

Griffin, James. 1986. *Well-Being: Its Meaning, Measurement and Moral Importance* (Oxford University Press).

Grima, Benedicte. 1992. *The Performance of Emotion Among Paxtun Women* (University of Texas Press).

Griswold, Charles L. 1999. *Adam Smith and the Virtues of Enlightenment* (Cambridge University Press).

Gross, James J. 1998. 'The Emerging Field of Emotion Regulation: An Integrative Review', *Review of General Psychology*, 2(3): 271.

Gubrium, Erika, and Ivar Lødemel. 2013. '"Not Good Enough": Social Assistance and Shaming in Norway', in Erika Gubrium, Sony Pellissery, and Ivar Lødemel (eds.), *The Shame of It: Global Perspectives on Anti-Poverty Policies* (Policy Press), n.p.

Hacker, Jacob S. 2006. *The Great Risk Shift: The New Economic Insecurity and the Decline of the American Dream* (Oxford University Press).

Hacker, Jacob S. 2011. 'The Institutional Foundations of Middle Class Democracy', *Policy Network*, 6: 33–7.

Halliday, Daniel, and Keith Hankins. 2020. 'Positional Goods and Upstream Agency', *Australasian Journal of Philosophy*, 98: 279–93.

Hansen, Morten. 2018. *Great at Work: How Top Performers Do Less, Work Better, and Achieve More* (Simon & Schuster).

Harman, Gilbert. 1986. *Change in View: Principles of Reasoning* (MIT Press).

Harel Ben Shahar, Tammy. 2018. 'Positional Goods and the Size of Inequality', *The Journal of Political Philosophy* 26(1): 103–20.

Harbin, Ami. 2014. 'Mentorship in Method: Philosophy and Experienced Agency', *Hypatia*, 29(2): 476–92.

Harrod, Roy Forbes. 1958. 'The Possibility of Economic Satiety—Use of Economic Growth for Improving the Quality of Education and Leisure', in The Committee for Economic Development (ed.), *Problems of United States Economic Development* (Literary Licensing), pp. 207–14.

Harsanyi, John C. 1982. 'Morality and the Theory of Rational Behaviour', in Amartya Sen and Bernard Williams (eds.), *Utilitarianism and Beyond* (Cambridge University Press), pp. 39–62.

Hausman, Daniel M., and Michael S. McPherson. 2009. 'Preference Satisfaction and Welfare Economics', *Economics and Philosophy*, 25(1): 1–25.

Haybron, Dan. 2007. 'Life Satisfaction, Ethical Reflection and the Science of Happiness', *Journal of Happiness Studies*, 8: 99–138.

Haybron, Dan. 2008. *The Pursuit of Unhappiness: The Elusive Psychology of Well-Being* (Oxford University Press).

Haybron, Dan. 2011. 'Happiness', in Edward N. Zalta (ed.), *The Stanford Encyclopedia of Philosophy* (Summer 2020 Edition). https://plato.stanford.edu/archives/sum2020/entries/happiness/ [Accessed 30/11/23].

Haybron, Dan. forthcoming. *The Lives We Should Want* (Oxford University Press).

Haybron, Dan, and Valerie Tiberius. 2015. 'Well-Being Policy: What Standard of Well-Being?', *Journal of the American Philosophical Association*, 1: 712–33.

Hayek, Friedrich. 1945. 'The Use of Knowledge in Society', *American Economic Review*, 35: 519–30.

Hayek, Friedrich. 1945/2007. *The Road to Serfdom* (University of Chicago Press).

Hayek, Friedrich. 1960. *The Constitution of Liberty* (University of Chicago Press).

Hayek, Friedrich. 2012. *Law, Legislation and Liberty: A New Statement of the Principles of Justice and Political Economy* (Routledge Classics).

Hayes, Christopher. 2012. *Twilight of the Elites: America After Meritocracy* (Crown Publishers).

Heathwood, Christopher. 2006. 'Desire Satisfactionism and Hedonism', *Philosophical Studies*, 128: 539–63.

Heathwood, Christopher. 2010. 'Welfare', in John Skorupski (ed.), *The Routledge Companion to Ethics* (Routledge), pp. 645–55.

Heathwood, Christopher. 2016. 'Desire-Fulfilment Theory', in Guy Fletcher (ed.), *The Routledge Handbook of the Philosophy of Well-Being* (Routledge), pp. 135–147.

Hedman, Erik, Peter Ström, Angela Stünkel, and Ewa Mörtberg. 2013. 'Shame and Guilt in Social Anxiety Disorder: Effects of Cognitive Behavior Therapy and Association with Social Anxiety and Depressive Symptoms', *PLoS One*, 8: e61713.

Hegel, Gottfried Wilhelm Friedrich. 1820/1991. *Elements of the Philosophy of Right* (Cambridge University Press).

Helliwell, John F., Haifang Huang, and Anthony Harris. 2009. 'International Differences in the Determinants of Life Satisfaction', in Bhaskar Dutta, Tridip Ray, and E. Somanathan (eds.), *New and Enduring Themes in Development Economics* (World Scientific Publishing), pp. 3–40.

Helliwell, John F., Richard Layard, and Jeffrey Sachs (eds.). 2015. 'World Happiness Report 2015', Sustainable Development Solutions Network.

Helliwell, John F., and Robert D. Putnam. 2004. 'The Social Context of Well-Being', *Philosophical Transactions of the Royal Society*, 359: 1435–46.

Hendershott, Anne. 2020. *The Politics of Envy* (Crisis Publications).

Henrich, Joseph. 2020. *The Weirdest People in the World: How the West Became Psychologically Peculiar and Particularly Prosperous* (Farrar, Strauss and Giroux).

Herzog, Lisa. 2013. *Inventing the Market: Smith, Hegel and Political Theory* (Oxford University Press).

Hill, Christopher, and Brian P. McLaughlin. 1999. 'There Are Fewer Things in Reality Than Are Dreamt of in Chalmers's Philosophy', *Philosophy and Phenomenological Research*, 59: 445–54.

Hirsch, Fred. 1976. *Social Limits to Growth* (Harvard University Press).

Hirschman, Albert. 1985. 'Reflection on the Latin American Experience', in Leo Lindberg and Charles S. Maier (eds.), *The Politics of Inflation and Economic Stagnation* (Brookings Institution Press), pp. 53–77.

Hobson, John. 1902. *Imperialism: A Study* (James Nisbet).

Hochschild, Arie Russell. 1983. *The Managed Heart* (University of California Press).

Hochschild, Arlie Russell. 1979. 'Emotion Work, Feeling Rules, and Social Structure', *American Journal of Sociology*, 85: 551–75.

Hockett, Robert. 2014. 'Real Arrow-Securities for All: Just and Efficient Insurance Through Macro-Hedging', *Review of Banking and Financial Law*, 34: 609–54.

Hockett, Robert. 2019. 'Open Labor Market Operations', *Challenge*, 62(2): 113–27.

Hockett, Robert. 2020a. 'The Capital Commons, Part 1: Why We Must Separate Public and Private Capital Management', *Law and Political Economy Project*. https://lpeproject.org/

blog/the-capital-commons-part-1-why-we-must-separate-public-and-private-capital-management/.
Hockett, Robert. 2020b. *Financing the Green New Deal: A Plan of Action and Renewal* (Palgrave Macmillan).
Hockett, Robert. 2021. 'Labor's Capital: Why and How to Put Public Capital at the Service of Labor', *New Labor Forum*, January. https://newlaborforum.cuny.edu/2021/01/08/labors-capital-why-and-how-to-put-public-capital-at-the-service-of-labor/ [Accessed 30/11/2023].
Hockett, Robert, and Daniel Dillon. 2019a. 'Income Inequality and Market Fragility: A Model and Some Empirics in the Political Economy of Finance, Part II', *Challenge*, 62: 427–52.
Hockett, Robert, and Daniel Dillon. 2019b. 'Income Inequality and Market Fragility: Some Empirics in the Political Economy of Finance, Part I', *Challenge*, 62: 354–74.
Hockett, Robert, and Aaron James. 2020. *Money from Nothing: Or, Why We Should Stop Worrying About Debt and Learn to Love the Federal Reserve* (Melville House).
Hockett, Robert, and Saule Omarova. 2017. 'The Finance Franchise', *Cornell Law Review*, 102: 1143–218.
Hodgson, Geoffrey M. 2017. 'Karl Polanyi on Economy and Society: A Critical Analysis of Core Concepts', *Review of Social Economy* 75(1): 1–25.
hooks, bell. 2000. *Where We Stand: Class Matters* (Routledge).
Hornsby, Jennifer. 2008. 'A Disjunctive Conception of Acting for Reasons', in Adrian Haddock and Fiona Macpherson (eds.), *Disjunctivism: Perception, Action, Knowledge* (Oxford University Press), pp. 244–61.
Horowitz, Daniel. 2017. *Happier? The History of a Cultural Movement That Aspired to Transform America* (Oxford University Press).
Horvath, Aaron and Walter W. Powel. 2016. 'Contributory or Disruptive: Do New Forms of Philanthropy Erode Democracy?', in Rob Reich, Chiara Cordelli, and Lucy Bernholz (eds.), *Philanthropy in Democratic Societies* (University of Chicago Press), pp. 87–122.
Hussain, Waheed. 2020. 'Pitting People Against Each Other', *Philosophy and Public Affairs*, 48: 79–113.
Hussain, Waheed. 2023. *Living with the Invisible Hand: Markets, Corporations and Human Freedom* (Oxford University Press).
Illouz, Eva. 1997. *Consuming the Romantic Utopia: Love and the Cultural Contradictions of Capitalism* (University of California Press).
Illouz, Eva. 2007. *Cold Intimacies: The Making of Emotional Capitalism* (Polity Press).
Immordino-Yang, Mary Helen, Andrea McColl, Hanna Damasio, and Antonio Damasio. 2009. 'Neural Correlates of Admiration and Compassion', *Proceedings of the National Academy of Sciences*, 106(19): 8021–6.
Immordino-Yang, Mary Helen, and Lesley Sylvan. 2010. 'Admiration for Virtue: Neuroscientific Perspectives on a Motivating Emotion', *Contemporary Educational Psychology*, 35(2): 110–5.
Irwin, Sarah. 2018. 'Lay Perceptions of Inequality and Social Structure', *British Journal of Sociology*, 52: 211–27.
Jaggar, Alison M. 1989. 'Love and Knowledge: Emotion in Feminist Epistemology', *Inquiry*, 32: 151–76.
Jan, Tracy. 2017. White People Are Really Confident That Things Are Getting Better for Black People. *Washington Post*, September 18, 2017, https://www.washingtonpost.com/news/wonk/wp/2017/09/18/white-people-are-really-confident-things-are-getting-better-for-black-people/ [Accessed 30/11/23].
Janeway, Williams. 2018. *Doing Capitalism in the Innovation Economy: Markets, Speculation and the State*, second edition (Cambridge University Press).
Janmaat, Jan Germen. 2013. 'Subjective Inequality: A Review of International Comparative Studies on People's Views about Inequality', *European Journal of Sociology*, 54: 357–89.
Jäntti, Markus, Bernt Bratsberg, Knut Røed, Oddbjørn Raaum, Robin Naylor, Eva Österbacka, and Tor Eriksson. 2006. 'American Exceptionalism in a New Light: A Comparison of

Intergenerational Earnings Mobility in the Nordic Countries, the United Kingdom and the United States', IZA Discussion Paper No. 1938. http://ftp.iza.org/dp1938.pdf [Accessed 30/11/23].

Jensen, Michael C., and William H. Meckling. 1976. 'Theory of the Firm: Managerial Behavior, Agency Costs and Ownership Structure', *Journal of Financial Economics*, 3: 305–60.

Jensen, Michael C., and Kevin J. Murphy. 1990. 'CEO Incentives—It's Not How Much You Pay, But How', *Harvard Business Review*: 138–49.

Jones, Karen. 2012. 'The Politics of Intellectual Self-Trust', *Social Epistemology*, 26: 237–51.

Jones, Owen. 2011. *Chavs: The Demonization of the Working Class* (Verso).

Kagan, Jerome. 1984. 'The Idea of Emotion in Human Development', in C. E. Izard, J. Kagan, and R. B. Zajonic (eds.), *Emotions, Cognition, and Behavior* (Cambridge University Press), pp. 38–72.

Kahneman, Daniel. 2000. 'Experienced Utility and Objective Happiness: A Moment Based Approach', in Daniel Kahneman and Amos Tversky (eds.), *Choices, Values and Frames* (Cambridge University Press), pp. 673–92.

Kahneman, Daniel, and Angus Deaton. 2010. 'High Income Improves Evaluation of Life but Not Emotional Well-Being', *Proceedings of the National Academy of Sciences of the United States of America*, 107: 16489–93.

Kaldor, Nicholas. 1956. *An Expenditure Tax* (George Allen and Unwin).

Kalecki, Michael. 1943. 'Political Aspects of Full Employment', *Political Quarterly*, 14: 322–31.

Katz, Michael B. 1989. *The Undeserving Poor: From the War on Poverty to the War on Welfare* (Pantheon Books).

Katz, Michael B. 1995. *Improving Poor People: The Welfare State, the 'Underclass', and Urban Schools as History* (Princeton University Press).

Kelly, Maura. 2010. 'Regulating the Reproduction and Mothering of Poor Women: The Controlling Image of the Welfare Mother in Television News Coverage of Welfare Reform', *Journal of Poverty*, 14(1): 76–96.

Kelly, Alison C., and Jacqueline C. Carter. 2013. 'Why Self-Critical Patients Present with More Severe Eating Disorder Pathology: The Mediating Role of Shame', *British Journal of Clinical Psychology*, 52(2): 148–61.

Kelly, Alison C., Jacqueline C. Carter, David C. Zuroff, and Sahar Borairi. 2013. 'Self-Compassion and Fear of Self-Compassion Interact to Predict Response to Eating Disorders Treatment: A Preliminary Investigation', *Psychotherapy Research*, 23(3): 252–64.

Kelton, Stephanie. 2020. *The Deficit Myth: Modern Monetary Theory and the Birth of the People's Economy* (Public Affairs).

Kemeny, Margaret E., Tara L. Grunewald, and Sally S. Dickerson. 2004. 'Shame as the Emotional Response to Threat to the Social Self: Implications for Behavior, Physiology, and Health', *Psychological Inquiry*, 15: 153–60.

Kendall, Diana Elizabeth. 2011. *Framing Class: Media Representations of Wealth and Poverty in America* (Rowman and Littlefield).

Kenworthy, Lane, and Leslie McCall. 2008. 'Inequality, Public Opinion and Redistribution', *Socio-Economic Review*, 6(1): 35–68.

Kerr, Gavin. 2017. *The Property-Owning Democracy* (Routledge).

Keynes, John Maynard. 1923. *A Tract on Monetary Reform* (Macmillan).

Keynes, John Maynard. 1930. *A Treatise on Money: Vol I: The Pure Theory of Money* (Macmillan).

Keynes, John Maynard. 1930/1932. 'Economic Possibilities for our Grandchildren', *Essays in Persuasion* (Harcourt Brace), pp. 358–73.

Keynes, John Maynard. 1936/1964. *A General Theory of Employment, Interest and Money* (First Harvest/Harcourt).

Khan, Lina. 2017. 'Amazon's Antitrust Paradox', *Yale Law Journal*, 126(3): 710–805.

Kiernan, Kathleen E., and Fiona K. Mensah. 2009. 'Poverty, Maternal Depression, Family Status and Children's Cognitive and Behavioural Development in Early Childhood: A Longitudinal Study', *Journal of Social Policy*, 38(4): 569–88.

Kimathi, Sharon. 2021. 'Goldman Sachs Analysts Reveal Abusive Working Conditions in Leaked Survey', *Fintechfutures.com*, March 19. https://www.fintechfutures.com/2021/03/goldman-sachs-analysts-reveal-abusive-working-conditions-in-leaked-survey/ [Accessed 20/07/2024].

Kim, Sangmoon, Ryan Thibodeau, and Randall S. Jorgensen. 2011. 'Shame, Guilt, and Depressive Symptoms: A Meta-Analytic Review', *Psychological Bulletin* 137: 68–96.

King, Martin Luther. 2000. *Why We Can't Wait* (Signet Classics).

King, Stephen. 2000. *On Writing: A Memoir of the Craft* (Charles Scribner and Sons).

Klein, Ezra. 2012. 'Romney's Theory of the "Taker Class" and Why It Matters', *Washington Post*, September 18.

Klein, Matthew C., and Michael Pettis. 2020. *Trade Wars Are Class Wars: How Rising Inequality Distorts the Global Economy and Threatens International Peace* (Yale University Press).

Kolodny, Niko. 2010. 'The Explanation of Amour-Propre', *Philosophical Review*, 119: 165–200.

Kondo, Naoki, Grace Sembajwe, Ichiro Kawachi, Rob M. van Dam, S. V. Subramanian, and Zentaro Yamagata. 2009. 'Income Inequality, Mortality and Self-Rated Health: Meta-Analysis of Multilevel Studies', *British Medical Journal*, 339: 1178–81.

Konings, Martijn. 2015. *The Emotional Logic of Capitalism: What Progressives Have Missed* (Stanford University Press).

Korenman, Sanders, Jane E. Miller, and John E. Sjaastad. 1995. 'Long-Term Poverty and Child Development in the United States: Results from the NlSY', *Children and Youth Services Review*, 17(1–2): 127–55.

Krause, Sharon R. 2008. *Civil Passions: Moral Sentiment and Democratic Deliberation* (Princeton University Press).

Krueger, Alan B. 2012. 'The Rise and Consequences of Inequality in the United States'. https://obamawhitehouse.archives.gov/sites/default/files/krueger_cap_speech_final_remarks.pdf [Accessed 30/11/23].

Kuhn, Moritz, Moritz Schularick, and Ulrike I. Steins. 2020. 'Income and Wealth Inequality in America 1949–2016', *Journal of Political Economy*, 128: 3469–519.

Kuziemko, Ilyana, Michael I. Norton, Emmanuel Saez, and Stefanie Stantcheva. 2015. 'How Elastic Are Preferences for Redistribution? Evidence from Randomized Survey Experiments', *American Economic Review*, 105(4): 1478–508.

Kynaston, David. 2014. *Modernity Britain: 1957–1962* (Bloomsbury Publishing USA).

Landis, Shauna K., Martin F. Sherman, Ralph L. Piedmont, Matthew W. Kirkhart, Edward M. Rapp, and Denise H. Bike. 2009. 'The Relation between Elevation and Self-Reported Prosocial Behavior: Incremental Validity over the Five-Factor Model of Personality', *The Journal of Positive Psychology*, 4(1): 71–84.

Lange, Jens, and Jan Crusius. 2015. 'Dispositional Envy Revisited: Unravelling the Motivational Dynamics of Benign and Malicious Envy', *Personality and Social Psychology Bulletin*, 41: 284–94.

Lange, Jens, Jan Crusius, and Birk Hagemeyer. 2016. 'The Evil Queen's Dilemma: Linking Narcissistic Admiration and Rivalry to Benign and Malicious Envy', *European Journal of Personality*, 30: 168–88.

Larmore, Charles. 2004. 'Liberal and Republican Conceptions of Freedom', in Daniel Weinstock and Christian Nadeau (eds.), *Republicanism: History, Theory and Practice* (Frank Cass), pp. 96–119.

Lasch, Christopher. 1995. *The Revolt of the Elites and the Betrayal of Democracy* (W. W. Norton and Company).

Layard, Richard A. 2011. *Happiness: Lessons from a New Science* (Penguin Books).

Layte, Richard. 2012. 'The Association Between Income Inequality and Mental Health: Testing Status Anxiety, Social Capital, and Neo-Materialist Explanations', *European Journal of Sociology*, 28: 498–511.

Lazonick, William. 2014. 'Profits Without Prosperity: How Stock Buybacks Manipulate the Market and Leave Most Americans Worse Off', *Harvard Business Review* (September): 46–55.

Lazonick, William, and Jang-Sup Shin. 2019. *Predatory Value Extraction: How the Looting of the Business Corporation Became the US Norm and How Sustainable Prosperity Can Be Restored* (Oxford University Press).

Leder, Michelle. 2021. 'Is a CEO Worth 1000 Times the Average Worker?', *Bloomberg.com*, June 1. https://www.bloomberg.com/opinion/articles/2021-06-01/is-a-ceo-worth-1-000-times-the-median-worker [Accessed 18/7/2024].

Lerner, Abba. 1936. 'A Note on Socialist Economics', *Review of Economic Studies*, 4(1): 72–76.

Lerner, Abba. 1943. 'Functional Finance and Federal Debt', *Social Research*, 10: 38–51.

Lessing, Gotthold E., Moses Mendelssohn, and Friedrich Nicolai. 1972. *Briefwechsel über das Trauerspiel* [*Correspondence on tragedy*]. J. Schulte-Sasse (ed.). Munich, Germany: Winkler.

Levinson, Cheri A., Meghan Byrne, and Thomas L. Rodebaugh. 2016. 'Shame and Guilt as Shared Vulnerability Factors: Shame, but Not Guilt, Prospectively Predicts Both Social Anxiety and Bulimic Symptoms', *Eating Behaviors*, 22: 188–93.

Levy, David A., Martin P. Farnham, and Samira Rajan. 2008. 'Where Profits Come From: Answering the Critical Question that Few Ever Ask', Jerome Levy Forecasting Center. https://www.levyforecast.com/profits-perspective/.

Levy, Jonathan. 2021. *Ages of American Capitalism* (Random House).

Lewis, Arthur. 1954. 'Economic Development with Unlimited Supplies of Labour', *Manchester School*, 22(2): 139–91.

Lichtenstein, Nelson. 2012. 'The Return of Merchant Capitalism', *International Labor and Working-Class History*, 81: 8–27.

Lind, Michael. 2020. *The New Class War: Saving America from the Managerial Elite* (Portfolio).

Lindsey, Brink, and Steven Teles. 2017. *The Captured Economy: How the Powerful Enrich Themselves, Slow Down Growth, and Increase Inequality* (Oxford University Press).

Linn, Margaret W., Richard Sandifer, and Shayna Stein. 1985. 'Effects of Unemployment on Mental and Physical Health', *American Journal of Public Health*, 75: 502–6.

Lister, Ruth. 2004. *Poverty* (Polity Press).

Littler, Jo. 2017. *Against Meritocracy: Culture, Power and Myths of Mobility* (Routledge).

Lockwood, David. 1966. 'Sources of Variation in Working Class Images of Society', *Sociological Review*, 14: 249–67.

Lonergan, Eric, and Mark Blyth. 2020. *Angrynomics* (Agenda Publishing).

Longino, Helen. 2001. *The Fate of Knowledge* (Princeton University Press).

Lübker, Malte. 2007. 'Inequality and the Demand for Redistribution: Are the Assumptions of the New Growth Theory Valid?', *Socio-Economic Review*, 5(1): 117–48.

Luttmer, Erzo F. P. 2005. 'Neighbors as Negatives: Relative Earnings and Well-Being', *Quarterly Journal of Economics*, 120: 963–1002.

Lyons, William E. 1980. *Emotion* (Cambridge University Press).

MacDonald, Geoff, and Mark R. Leary. 2005. 'Why Does Social Exclusion Hurt? The Relationship Between Social and Physical Pain', *Psychological Bulletin* 131(2): 202–23.

Mackenzie, Donald. 2006. *An Engine, Not a Camera: How Financial Models Shape Markets* (MIT Press).

Maibom, Heidi. 2010. 'The Descent of Shame', *Philosophy and Phenomenological Research*, 80: 566–94.

Malacrino, Davide. 2020. 'How the Rich Get Richer', *IMFBlog*. IMF. https://blogs.imf.org/2020/11/30/how-the-rich-get-richer/ [Accessed 30/11/23].

Mankiw, Gregory. 2013. 'Defending the One Percent', *Journal of Economic Perspectives*, 27: 21–34.

Mantsios, Gregory. 2000. 'Media Magic: Making Class Invisible', in T. Ore (ed.), *The Social Construction of Difference and Inequality: Race, Class, Gender and Sexuality* (Mayfield), pp. 88–96.

Markovits, Daniel. 2019. *The Meritocracy Trap: How America's Foundational Myth Feeds Inequality, Dismantles the Middle Class, and Devours the Elite* (Penguin).

Marx, Karl. 1994. 'On the Jewish Question', in Joseph J O'Malley and Richard A. Davis (eds.), *Marx: Early Political Writings* (Cambridge University Press), pp. 28–56.

Marx, Karl and Friedrich Engels. 1848/2011. *The Communist Manifesto*. Translated by Samuel Moore, introduction by : Marshall Berman (Penguin).

Matos, Marcella, José Pinto-Gouveia, Paul Gilbert. 2013. 'The Effect of Shame and Shame Memories on Paranoid Ideation and Social Anxiety', *Clinical Psychology and Psychotherapy*, 20(4): 334–49.

May, Theresa. 2016. 'Britain, the Great Meritocracy: Prime Minister's Speech', September 9. https://www.gov.uk/government/speeches/britain-the-great-meritocracy-prime-ministers-speech [Accessed 30/11/23].

Mayer, Jane. 2017. *Dark Money: The Hidden History of the Billionaires Behind the Rise of the Radical Right* (Anchor Books Imprint).

McBride, Michael. 2001. 'Relative-Income Effects on Subjective Well-Being in the Cross-Section', *Journal of Economic Behavior and Organization*, 45: 251–78.

McCall, Leslie. 2013. *The Undeserving Rich: American Beliefs About Inequality, Opportunity and Redistribution* (Cambridge University Press).

McCloskey, Deirdre Nansen. 2016. *Bourgeois Equality: How Ideas, Not Capital nor Institutions, Enriched the World* (University of Chicago Press).

McCormick, John P. 2011. *Machiavellian Democracy* (Cambridge University Press).

McDowell, John. 1982. 'Reason and Action—III', *Philosophical Explorations*, 5(4): 301–5.

McKendrick, John H., Stephen Sinclair, Anthea Irwin, Hugh O'Donnell, Gill Scott, and Louise Dobbie. 2008. 'The Media, Poverty and Public Opinion in the UK', Joseph Rowntree Foundation Report, September 10. https://www.jrf.org.uk/report/media-poverty-and-public-opinion-uk [Accessed 30/11/23].

Meade, James. 1964. *Efficiency, Equality and the Ownership of Property* (Allen & Unwin).

Meshelski, Kristina. 2019. 'Rawls's Socialism and Pure Procedural Justice', *Ethical Perspectives*, 26: 343–7.

Mesquita, Batja, Jozefien De Leersnyder, and Dustin Albert. 2014. 'The Cultural Regulation of Emotions', in James J. Gross (ed.), *Handbook of Emotion Regulation*, Second edition (The Guilford Press), pp. 284–301.

Michels, Robert. 1962. *Political Parties: A Sociological Study of the Oligarchic Tendencies of Modern Democracy* (The Free Press).

Mijs, Jonathan B. 2021. 'The Paradox of Inequality: Income Inequality and Belief in Meritocracy Go Hand in Hand', *Socio-Economic Review*, 19(1): 7–35.

Milanović, Branko. 2016. *Global Inequality: A New Approach for the Age of Globalization* (Harvard University Press).

Milanović, Branko. 2019. *Capitalism Alone: The Future of the System that Rules the World* (Harvard University Press).

Mill, John Stuart. 1863/1998. *Utilitarianism*. Edited by Roger Crisp (Oxford University Press).

Mill, John Stuart. 1869/2006. *On Liberty and the Subjection of Women* (Penguin Classics).

Mill, John Stuart. 1871/1909. *Principles of Political Economy* (Hackett).

Miller, David. 1996. 'Two Cheers for Meritocracy', *Journal of Political Philosophy*, 4(4): 277–301.

Minkoff, Scott L., and Jeffrey Lyons. 2019. 'Living with Inequality: Neighborhood Income Diversity and Perceptions of the Income Gap', *American Politics Research*, 47: 329–61.

Minsky, Hyman. 1975. *John Maynard Keynes* (Columbia University Press).

Minsky, Hyman. 1986b. 'Keynesian Socialism', in *Hyman P Minsky Archive*, edited by Levy Institute of Bard College, pp. 1–5.

Minsky, Hyman. 1986/2008. *Stabilizing an Unstable Economy* (McGraw Hill).
Minsky, Hyman. 2013. *Ending Poverty: Jobs Not Welfare* (Levy Economics Institute of Bard College).
Mitnik, Pablo, Erin Cumberworth, and David Grusky. 2016. 'Social Mobility in a High-Inequality Regime', *Annals of the American Academy of Political and Social Sciences*, 663: 140–84. https://www.vox.com/recode/22651953/americans-gig-independent-workers-benefits-vacation-health-care-inequality [Accessed 30/11/23].
Montgomerie, Johnna. 2009. 'The Pursuit of (Past) Happiness? Middle Class Indebtedness and American Financialisation', *New Political Economy*, 14: 1–24.
Montgomerie, Johnna. 2010. 'Neoliberalism and the Making of Subprime Borrowers', in Martijn Konings (ed.), *The Great Credit Crash* (Verso), pp. 103–18.
Morgan-Knapp, Christopher. 2014. 'Economic Envy', *Journal of Applied Philosophy*, 31(2): 113–26.
Moriarty, Jeff. 2005. 'Do CEOs Get Paid Too Much?', *Business Ethics Quarterly*, 15: 257–81.
Moriarty, Jeff. 2009. 'Rawls, Self-Respect, and the Opportunity for Meaningful Work', *Social Theory and Practice*, 35: 441–59.
Mulligan, Thomas. 2017. *Justice and the Meritocratic State* (Routledge).
Nagel, Thomas. 1970. *The Possibility of Altruism* (Oxford University Press).
Narayan, Deepa, Robert Chambers, Meera K. Shah, and Patti Petesch. 2000. *Voices of the Poor: Crying Out for Change* (Oxford University Press for the World Bank).
Neuhouser, Frederick. 2008. *Rousseau's Theodicy of Self-Love: Evil, Rationality and the Drive for Recognition* (Cambridge University Press).
Neuhouser, Frederick. 2013. 'Rousseau's Critique of Economic Inequality', *Philosophy and Public Affairs*, 41: 193–225.
Neuteleers, Stijn, and Bart Engelen. 2014. 'Talking Money: How Market-Based Valuation Can Undermine Environmental Protection', *Ecological Economics*, 177: 253–60.
Neve, Jan-Emmanuel De, Nicholas A. Christakis, James H. Fowler, and Bruno S. Frey. 2012. 'Genes, Economics and Happiness', *Journal of Neuroscience, Psychology and Economics*, 5: 193–211.
Norman, Richard. 2001. 'Practical Reasons and the Redundancy of Motives', *Ethical Theory and Moral Practice*, 4: 3–22.
Norton, Michael I., and Dan Ariely. 2011. 'Building a Better America—One Wealth Quintile at a Time', *Perspectives on Psychological Science*, 6(1): 9–12.
Nozick, Robert. 1974. *Anarchy, State and Utopia* (Basic Books).
Nozick, Robert. 1989. *The Examined Life: Philosophical Meditations* (Simon and Schuster).
Nussbaum, Martha C. 1992. 'Human Functioning and Social Justice: In Defense of Aristotelian Essentialism', *Political Theory*, 20: 202–46.
Nussbaum, Martha C. 2000. *Women and Human Development* (Cambridge University Press).
Nussbaum, Martha C. 2004. *Hiding from Humanity: Disgust, Shame, and the Law* (Princeton University Press).
Nussbaum, Martha C. 2006. *Frontiers of Justice: Disability, Nationality, Species Membership* (Harvard University Press).
Nussbaum, Martha C. 2008. 'Who Is the Happy Warrior? Philosophy Poses Questions to Psychology', *Journal of Legal Studies*, 37: S81–S113.
Nussbaum, Martha C. 2015. *Political Emotions: Why Love Matters for Justice* (Harvard University Press).
OECD. 2014. 'Focus on Inequality and Growth: Does Income Inequality Hurt Economic Growth?' https://www.oecd.org/els/soc/Focus-Inequality-and-Growth-2014.pdf [Accessed 30/11/23].
O'Hear, Anthony. 1977. 'VI—Guilt and Shame as Moral Concepts', *Proceedings of the Aristotelian Society*, 77(1): 73–86.
Oishi, Shigehiro, Selin Kesebir, and Ed Diener. 2011. 'Income Inequality and Happiness', *Psychological Science*, 22: 1095–1100.

Okun, Arthur M. 1973. 'Upward Mobility in a High-Pressure Economy', *Brookings Papers on Economic Activity*, 4(1): 207–62.

O'Neill, Martin. 2020. 'Social Justice and Economic Systems: On Rawls, Democratic Socialism, and Alternatives to Capitalism', *Philosophical Topics*, 48(2): 159–201.

Onu, Diana, Thomas Kessler, and Joanne R. Smith. 2016. 'Admiration: A Conceptual Review', *Emotion Review*, 8: 218–30.

Onu, Diana, Joanne R. Smith, and Thomas Kessler. 2015. 'Intergroup Emulation: An Improvement Strategy for Lower-Status Groups', *Group Processes and Intergroup Relations*, 18(2): 210–24.

Osberg, Lars, and Timothy Smeeding. 2006. '"Fair" Inequality? Attitudes Toward Pay Differentials: The United States in Comparative Perspective', *American Sociological Review*, 71(3): 450–73.

Oshio, Takashi, and Urakawa, Kunio. 2014. 'The Association Between Perceived Income Inequality and Subjective Well-being: Evidence from a Social Survey in Japan', *Social Indicators Research: An International and Interdisciplinary Journal for Quality-of-Life Measurement*, 116(3): 755–70.

Oxfam. 2016. 'An Economy for the 1%: How Privilege and Power in the Economy Drive Extreme Inequality and How This Can Be Stopped'. https://policy-practice.oxfam.org/resources/an-economy-for-the-1-how-privilege-and-power-in-the-economy-drive-extreme-inequ-592643/ [Accessed 30/11/23].

Oxfam. 2017. 'An Economy for the 99%'. https://www.oxfam.org/en/research/economy-99 [Accessed 30/11/23].

Oxford Poverty and Human Development Initiative (OPHI). 2017. 'Missing dimensions & data gaps' Available at: https://ophi.org.uk/research/missing-dimensions-and-data-gaps [Accessed 18/7/2024].

Page, Benjamin I., Larry M. Bartels, and Jason Seawright. 2013. 'Democracy and the Policy Preferences of Wealthy Americans', *Perspectives on Politics*, 11: 51–73.

Page, Benjamin I., and Martin Gilens. 2017. *Democracy in America? What Has Gone Wrong and What We Can Do About It* (University of Chicago Press).

Palley, Thomas. 2011. 'A Theory of Minsky Super-Cycles and Financial Crises', *Contributions to Political Economy*, 30: 31–46.

Palley, Thomas. 2012. *From Financial Crisis to Stagnation: The Destruction of Shared Prosperity and the Role of Economics* (Cambridge University Press).

Palley, Thomas. 2013. *Financialization: The Economics of Finance Capital Domination* (Palgrave Macmillan).

Parfit, Derek. 1984. *Reasons and Persons* (Clarendon Press).

Parfit, Derek. 1991. 'Equality or Priority?', in *Lindley Lectures Delivered at the University of Kansas* (Lawrence, Kansas), pp. 1–42.

Parfit, Derek. 1997. 'Equality and Priority', *Ratio*, 10(3): 202–21.

Parvin, Phil. 2017. 'Democracy, Capital, and the Rise of the New Inequality', *Political Theory*, 45: 863–76.

Paskov, Marii, and Caroline Dewilde. 2012. 'Income Inequality and Solidarity in Europe', *Research in Social Stratification and Mobility*, 30(4): 415–32.

Paskov, Marii, Klarita Gërxhani, and Herman G. Van de Werfhorst. 2013. 'Income Inequality and Status Anxiety', GINI Discussion paper 90. Amsterdam: AIAS.

Paskov, Marii, Klarita Gërxhani, and Herman G. van de Werfhorst. 2017. 'Giving Up on the Joneses? The Relationship Between Income Inequality and Status-Seeking', *European Sociological Review*, 33: 112–23.

Paul, Karsten I., and Klaus Moser. 2009. 'Unemployment Impairs Mental Health: Meta-Analyses', *Journal of Vocational Behavior*, 74: 264–82.

Payne, Keith. 2017. *The Broken Ladder: How Inequality Affects the Way We Think, Live and Die* (Viking).

Pearce, Nick. 2013. 'What Should Social Democrats Believe?', *Juncture*. IPPR. https://www.ippr.org/juncture/what-should-social-democrats-believe [Accessed 30/11/23].

Pettis, Michael. 2001. *The Volatility Machine: Emerging Economics and the Threat of Financial Collapse* (Oxford University Press).

Pettit, Philip. 1997. *Republicanism: A Theory of Freedom and Government* (Oxford University Press).

Pettit, Philip. 2012. *On the People's Terms: A Republican Theory and Model of Democracy* (Cambridge University Press).

Pettit, Philip. 2014. *Just Freedom: A Moral Compass for a Complex World* (W. W. Norton and Company).

Philippon, Thomas. 2015. 'Has the US Finance Industry Become Less Efficient? On the Theory and Measurement of Financial Intermediation', *American Economic Review*, 105: 1408–38.

Philippon, Thomas. 2019. *The Great Reversal: How America Gave Up on Free Markets* (Harvard University Press).

Piers, Gerhart, and Milton B. Singer. 1953. *Shame and Guilt: A Psychoanalytic and Cultural Study* (Charles C. Thomas).

Piketty, Thomas. 2014. *Capital in the 21st Century* (Harvard University Press).

Piketty, Thomas. 2020. *Capital and Ideology* (Harvard University Press).

Piketty, Thomas, and Emmanuel Saez. 2014. 'Inequality in the Long Run', *Science*, 344: 838–43.

Pippin, Robert B. 2020. 'Did Hegel Comprehend His Own Time in Thought? The Market in *The Philosophy of Right*', *estetica. studi e ricerche*, X(2): 571–88.

Pistor, Katharina. 2019. *The Code of Capital: How the Law Creates Wealth and Inequality* (Princeton University Press).

Plamper, Jan. 2012. *The History of Emotions: An Introduction* (Oxford University Press).

Polanyi, Karl. 1944. *The Great Transformation: The Political and Economic Origins of Our Time* (Beacon Press).

Pop, Ioana Andreea, Erik van Ingen, and Wim van Oorschot. 2013. 'Inequality, Wealth and Health: Is Decreasing Income Inequality the Key to Create Healthier Societies?', *Social Indicators Research*, 113: 1025–43.

Posner, Eric, and Glen Weyl. 2018. *Radical Markets: Uprooting Capitalism and Democracy for a Just Society* (Princeton University Press).

Praag, Bernard van, Paul Frijters, and Ada Ferrer-i-Carbonell. 2003. 'The Anatomy of Subjective Well-being', *Journal of Economic Behavior and Organization*, 51: 29–49.

Prasad, Monica. 2006. *The Politics of Free Markets: The Rise of Neoliberal Economic Policies in Britain, France, Germany and the United States* (University of Chicago Press).

Preiss, Johsua. 2021. *Just Work for All: The American Dream in the 21st Century* (Routledge).

Price, Carter C., and Kathryn A. Edwards. 2020. 'Trends in Income From 1975 to 2018', *Rand Corporation Working Paper*. RAND Corporation.

Protasi, Sara. 2016. 'Varieties of Envy', *Philosophical Psychology*, 29(4): 535–49.

Protasi, Sara. 2019. 'Happy Self-Surrender and Unhappy Self-Assertion', in Alfred Archer and Andre Grahle (eds.), *The Moral Psychology of Admiration* (Rowman and Littlefield), pp. 45–60.

Protasi, Sara. 2021. *The Philosophy of Envy* (Cambridge University Press).

Putnam, Hilary. 1975. 'Philosophy and Our Mental Life', in *Philosophical Papers Volume 2: Mind, Language, and Reality* (Cambridge University Press), pp. 291–303.

Putnam, Robert D. 2000. *Bowling Alone: The Collapse and Revival of American Community* (Simon & Schuster).

Putnam, Robert D. 2016. *Our Kids: The American Dream in Crisis* (Simon & Schuster).

Raibley, Jason R. 2012. 'Happiness Is Not Well-Being', *Journal of Happiness Studies*, 13: 1105–29.

Railton, Peter. 1986. 'Facts and Values', *Philosophical Topics*, 14: 5–31.

Rasmussen, Dennis C. 2008. *The Problems and Promise of Commercial Society: Adam Smith's Response to Rousseau* (Pennsylvania State University Press).

Rasmussen, Dennis C. 2013. 'Adam Smith and Rousseau: Enlightenment and Counter-Enlightenment', in Christopher J. Berry, Maria Pia Paganelli, and Craig Smith (eds.), *The Oxford Handbook of Adam Smith* (Oxford Handbooks Online), pp. 54–76.

Rasmussen, Dennis C. 2016. 'Adam Smith on What Is Wrong with Economic Inequality', *American Political Science Review*, 110: 342–52.

Rasmussen, Dennis C. 2018. 'Smith, Rousseau and the True Spirit of a Republican', in Dennis C. Rasmussen, Maria Pia Paganelli, and Craig Smith (eds.), *Adam Smith and Rousseau* (Edinburgh University Press), pp. 241–59.

Ravallion, Martin, and Michael Lokshin. 2005. 'Who Cares About Relative Deprivation?', *Policy Research Working Paper*. Washington, DC: World Bank.

Rawls, John. 1971/1999. *A Theory of Justice* (Belknap Press).

Rawls, John. 1993. *Political Liberalism* (Columbia University Press).

Rawls, John. 1999a. *Collected Papers* (Harvard University Press).

Rawls, John. 1999b. *The Law of Peoples* (Harvard University Press).

Rawls, John. 2001. *Justice as Fairness: A Restatement* (Harvard University Press).

Rawls, John. 2007. *Lectures on the History of Political Philosophy* (Harvard University Press).

Rawls, John. 2009. *A Brief Inquiry into the Meaning of Sin and Faith: With 'On My Religion'* (Harvard University Press).

Raz, Joseph. 1986. *The Morality of Freedom* (Oxford University Press).

Reddy, William. 2001: *The Navigation of Feeling: A Framework for the History of Emotions* (Cambridge University Press).

Reeves, Richard. 2017. *Dream Hoarders: How the American Upper Middle Class Is Leaving Everyone Else in the Dust, Why That Is a Problem, and What to Do About It* (Brookings Institution Press).

Rendueles, César. 2017. 'From Global Regression to Post-Capitalist Counter-Movements', in Heinrich Geiselberger (ed.), *The Great Regression* (Polity Press), chapter 12.

Riesman, David. 1950. *The Lonely Crowd* (Yale University Press).

Riis, Jason, George Loewenstein, Jonathan Baron, Christopher Jepson, Angela Fagerlin, and Peter A. Ubel. 2005. 'Ignorance of Hedonic Adaptation to Hemo-Dialysis: A Study Using Ecological Momentary Assessment', *Journal of Experimental Psychology: General* 134: 3–9.

Roberts, Carys, and Matthew Lawrence. 2017. 'Wealth in the Twenty-First Century: Inequalities and Drivers', Institute for Public Policy Research. https://www.ippr.org/publications/wealth-in-the-twenty-first-century [Accessed 30/11/23].

Robeyns, Ingrid. 2016. 'The Capability Approach', in Edward N. Zalta (ed.), *The Stanford Encyclopedia of Philosophy*.

Robin, Corey. 2013. 'Nietzsche's Marginal Children: On Friedrich Hayek', *Nation*, May 7. https://www.thenation.com/article/archive/nietzsches-marginal-children-friedrich-hayek/ [Accessed 30/11/23].

Robinson, Joan. 1972. 'The Second Crisis of Economic Theory', *American Economic Review*, 62: 1–10.

Robinson, Joan. 1966. *An Essay on Marxian Economics* (Macmillan).

Robinson, Joan. 1976. 'The Age of Growth', *Challenge*, 19: 4–9.

Robinson, Joan. 1977. 'What Are the Questions?', *Journal of Economic Literature*, 15: 1318–39.

Rodrik, Dani. 2011. *The Globalization Paradox: Why Global Markets, States, and Democracy Can't Coexist* (Oxford University Press).

Rosaldo, Michelle Z. 1980. *Knowledge and Passion: Llongot Notions of Self and Social Life* (Cambridge University Press).

Rosaldo, Michelle Z. 1984. 'Toward an Anthropology of Self and Feeling', in Richard A. Schweder and Robert A. LeVine (eds.), *Culture Theory: Essays on Mind, Self, and Emotion* (Cambridge University Press), pp. 137–57.

Rosanvallon, Pierre. 2013. *The Society of Equals* (Harvard University Press).

Ross, W. D. 1930/2002. *The Right and the Good* (Oxford University Press).

Roth, Bettina, Elisabeth Hahn, and Frank M. Spinath. 2017. 'Income Inequality, Life Satisfaction and Economic Worries', *Social Psychological and Personality Science*, 8: 133–41.
Rothstein, Richard. 2017. *The Color of Law: A Forgotten History of How Our Government Segregated America* (Liveright Publishing Corporation).
Rousseau, Jean-Jacques. 1762/1964. *Du contrat social ou, principes du droit politique. Oeuvres Complètes III* (Gallimard).
Rözer, Jesper, and Gerbert Kraaykamp. 2013. 'Income Inequality and Subjective Well-Being: A Cross-National Study on the Conditional Effects of Individual and National Characteristics', *Social Indicators Research*, 113: 1009–23.
Rubin, Michael. 2008. 'Is Goodness a Homeostatic Property Cluster?', *Ethics*, 118: 496–528.
Runciman, David. 2009. 'How Messy It All Is', *London Review of Books*. October 22. https://www.lrb.co.uk/the-paper/v31/n20/david-runciman/how-messy-it-all-is [Accessed 30/11/23].
Ryan, Richard M., Jessey H. Bernstein, and Kirk Warren Brown. 2010. 'Weekends, Work, and Well-Being: Psychological Need Satisfactions and Day of the Week Effects on Mood, Vitality, and Physical Symptoms', *Journal of Social and Clinical Psychology* 29: 95–122.
Ryle, Gilbert. 1949/2000. *The Concept of Mind* (Penguin Classics).
Ryle, Gilbert. 1954. 'Pleasure', *Aristotelian Society Supplementary Volume*, 28: 135–64.
Saad, Lydia. 2019. 'More Americans Delaying Treatment Due to Cost', *Gallup*, December 9. https://news.gallup.com/poll/269138/americans-delaying-medical-treatment-due-cost.aspx [Accessed 20/07/2024]
Saez, Emmanuel, and Gabriel Zucman. 2016. 'Wealth Inequality in the United States Since 1913: Evidence from Capitalized Income Tax Data', *Quarterly Journal of Economics*, 131: 519–78.
Salganik, Matthew J., Peter Sheridan Dodds, and Duncan J. Watts. 2006. 'Experimental Study of Inequality and Unpredictability in an Artificial Cultural Market', *Science*, 311: 854–6.
Sandel, Michael. 2020. *The Tyranny of Merit: What's Become of the Common Good?* (Farrar, Straus and Giroux).
Sanftner McGraw, Jennifer, Debora Hill Barlow, Donna E. Marschall, and June P. Tangney. 1995. 'The Relation of Shame and Guilt to Eating Disorder Symptomology', *Journal of Social and Clinical Psychology*, 14(4): 315–24.
Satz, Debra. 2010. *Why Some Things Should Not Be for Sale: The Moral Limits of Markets* (Oxford University Press).
Scanlon, Thomas. 1998. *What We Owe to Each Other* (Belknap Press).
Scanlon, Thomas. 2003. 'The Diversity of Objections to Inequality', in *The Difficulty of Tolerance* (Cambridge University Press), pp. 202–18.
Scanlon, Thomas. 2018. *Why Does Inequality Matter?* (Oxford University Press).
Scheer, Monique. 2012. 'Are Emotions a Kind of Practice (and Is That What Makes Them Have a History)? A Bourdieuian Approach to Understanding Emotion', *History and Theory*, 51: 193–220.
Scheman, Naomi. 1980. 'Anger and the Politics of Naming', in S. McConnell-Ginet, R. Borker, and N. Furmen (eds.), *Women and Language in Literature and Society* (Praeger Publishers), pp. 174–87.
Schiller, Robert. 1993. *Macro Markets: Creating Institutions for Managing Society's Largest Economic Risks* (Clarendon Press).
Schindler, I., V. Zink, J. Windrich, and W. Menninghaus. 2013. 'Admiration and Adoration: Their Different Ways of Showing and Shaping Who We Are', *Cognition and Emotion*, 27: 85–118.
Schnall, Simone, Jean Roper, and Daniel M. T. Fessler. 2010. 'Elevation Leads to Altruistic Behavior', *Psychological Science*, 21: 315–20.
Schor, Juliet B. 2004. *Born to Buy: The Commercialized Child and the New Consumer Culture* (Scribner).

Schroeder, Mark. 2010. 'Value and the Wrong Kind of Reason', *Oxford Studies in Metaethics* 5: 25–55.
Schröder, Martin. 2017. 'Is Income Inequality Related to Tolerance for Inequality?', *Social Justice Research*, 30, 23–47.
Schumpeter, Joseph. 1942. *Capitalism, Socialism and Democracy* (Harper Perennial).
Schwartz, Herman Mark. 2017. 'Club Goods, Intellectual Property Rights, and Profitability in the Information Economy', *Business and Politics*, 19(2): 191–214.
Schwartz, Herman Mark. 2019. 'American Hegemony: Intellectual Property Rights, Dollar Centrality, and Infrastructural Power', *Review of International Political Economy*, 26(3): 490–519.
Schwartz, Herman Mark. 2021. 'Mo' Patents, Mo' Problems: Corporate Strategy, Structure and Profitability in America's Political Economy', in Jacob S. Hacker et al. (eds.), *The American Political Economy: Politics, Markets and Power* (Cambridge University Press), pp. 247–69.
Schwarze, Michelle A., and John T. Scott. 2019. 'Mutual Sympathy and the Moral Economy: Adam Smith Reviews Rousseau', *Journal of Politics*, 81: 66–80.
Seabrook, Jeremy. 2013. *Pauperland: Poverty and the Poor in Britain* (Hurst Publishers).
Seligman, Martin. 2002. *Authentic Happiness: Using the New Positive Psychology to Realize Your Potential for Lasting Fulfilment* (Free Press).
Sen, Amartya. 1982. 'Just Desert', *New York Review of Books*, March 4.
Sen, Amartya. 1983. 'Poor, Relatively Speaking', *Oxford Economic Papers*, 35: 153–69.
Sen, Amartya. 1985a. 'The Moral Standing of the Market', *Social Philosophy and Policy*, 2: 1–19.
Sen, Amartya 1985b. *Commodities and Capabilities* (Oxford University Press).
Sen, Amartya. 1999. *Development as Freedom* (Oxford University Press).
Sen, Amartya. 2004. 'Capabilities, Lists, and Public Reason: Continuing the Conversation', *Feminist Economics*, 10: 77–80.
Sen, Amartya. 2009. *The Idea of Justice* (Belknap Press).
Sennett, Richard, and Jonathan Cobb. 1973. *The Hidden Injuries of Class* (Norton).
Sepulveda Carmona, Magdalena. 2011. 'Report of the Special Rapporteur on Extreme Poverty and Human Rights: Penalization of People Living in Poverty and Human Rights' SSRN 2437813.
Shapiro, Ian. 2016. *Politics Against Domination* (Belknap Press).
Shaxson, Nicholas. 2011. *Treasure Islands: Uncovering the Damage of Offshore Banking and Tax Havens* (St. Martin's Press).
Sher, George. 2014. *Equality for Inegalitarians* (Cambridge University Press).
Sherman, Gary D., Jooa J. Lee, Amy J. C. Cuddy, Jonathan Renshon, Christopher Ovels, James J. Gross, and Jennifer S. Lerner. 2012. 'Leadership Is Associated with Lower Levels of Stress', *Proceedings of the National Academy of Sciences of the United States of America*, 109: 17903–7.
Slobodian, Quinn. 2019. 'The False Promise of Enlightenment', *Boston Review*, May 29. https://bostonreview.net/articles/quinn-slobodian-drain-darkness/ [Accessed 30/11/23].
Smith, Adam. 1776/1981. *An Inquiry into the Nature and Causes of the Wealth of Nations* (Liberty Fund).
Smith, Paul. 1998. 'Incentives and Justice: G. A. Cohen's Egalitarian Critique of Rawls', *Social Theory and Practice*, 24: 205–35.
Soederberg, Susanne. 2013. 'The US Debtfare State and the Credit Card Industry: Forging Spaces of Dispossession', *Antipode*, 45: 493–512.
Solow, Robert M. 2014. 'Thomas Piketty Is Right', *New Republic*, April 23. https://newrepublic.com/article/117429/capital-twenty-first-century-thomas-piketty-reviewed [Accessed 30/11/23].
Sommers, Jeffrey, Rachel Hegland, and Patrick Delices. 2018. 'American Public Policy and Full Employment: The Imperative of Martin Luther King's Political Economy in the 21st Century', *Journal of Black Studies*, 8.

Sonti, Samir. 2018. 'The World Paul Volcker Made', *Jacobin*, December 20. https://jacobinmag.com/2018/12/paul-volcker-federal-reserve-central-bank [Accessed 30/11/23].

Soros, George. 1998. *The Crisis of Global Capitalism* (Public Affairs).

Spelman, Elizabeth V. 1989. 'Anger and Insubordination', in Ann Garry and Marilyn Pearsall (eds.), *Women, Knowledge, and Reality: Explorations in Feminist Philosophy* (Unwin Hyman), pp. 263–73.

Sprietsma, Maresa. 2010. 'Effect of Relative Age in the First Grade of Primary School on Long-Term Scholastic Results: International Comparative Evidence Using PISA 2003', *Education Economics*, 18(1): 1–32.

Srinivasan, Amia. 2018. 'The Aptness of Anger', *Journal of Political Philosophy* 26(2): 123–44.

Standing, Guy. 2011. *The Precariat: The New Dangerous Class* (Bloomsbury).

Stein, Ben. 2006. 'In Class Warfare, Guess Which Class Is Winning', *New York Times*, November 26.

Stewart, Matthew. 2018a. 'The Birth of the New American Aristocracy', *Atlantic*. https://www.theatlantic.com/magazine/archive/2018/06/the-birth-of-a-new-american-aristocracy/559130/ [Accessed 30/11/23].

Stewart, Matthew. 2018b. 'The 9.9 Percent Is the New American Aristocracy', *Atlantic*. https://www.theatlantic.com/magazine/archive/2018/06/the-birth-of-a-new-american-aristocracy/559130/ [Accessed 30/11/23].

Stiglitz, Joseph E. 2012. *The Price of Inequality: How Today's Divided Society Endangers Our Future* (W. W. Norton & Company).

Stiglitz, Joseph E., Amartya Sen, and Jean-Paul Fitoussi. 2009. 'Report of the Commission on the Measurement of Economic Performance and Social Progress'. https://www.researchgate.net/publication/258260767_Report_of_the_Commission_on_the_Measurement_of_Economic_Performance_and_Social_Progress_CMEPSP [Accessed 30/11/23].

Storm, Servaas. 2017a. 'The New Normal: Demand, Secular Stagnation and the Vanishing Middle-Class'. https://www.ineteconomics.org/research/experts/sstorm [Accessed 30/11/23].

Storm, Servaas. 2017b. 'What Mainstream Economists Get Wrong About Secular Stagnation'. https://www.ineteconomics.org/perspectives/blog/what-mainstream-economists-get-wrong-about-secular-stagnation [Accessed 30/11/23].

Stout, Lynn. 2012. *The Shareholder Value Myth: How Putting Shareholders First Harms Investors, Corporations, and the Public* (Berrett-Koehler Publishers).

Stratton, Allegra. 2010. 'David Cameron Aims to Make Happiness the New GDP', *Guardian*, November 14.

Strawson, Peter. 1962. 'Freedom and Resentment', *Proceedings of the British Academy*, 48: 187–211.

AStringhini, Silvia, et al. 2017. 'Socioeconomic Status and the 25 × 25 Risk Factors as Determinants of Premature Mortality: A Multicohort Study and Meta-Analysis of 1 7 Million Men and Women', *Lancet*, 389: 1229–37.

Stropoli, Rebecca. 2021. 'How the 1 Percent's Savings Buried the Middle Class in Debt', *Chicago Booth Review*, May 15.

Sugden, Robert. 2018. *The Community of Advantage: A Behavioral Economist's Defence of the Market* (Oxford University Press).

Sumner, L. Wayne. 1996. *Welfare, Happiness and Ethics* (Oxford University Press).

Swan, Sarah, and Bernice Andrews. 2003. 'The Relationship Between Shame, Eating Disorders and Disclosure in Treatment', *British Journal of Clinical Psychology*, 42(4): 367–78.

Sweetman, Joseph, Russell Spears, Andrew G. Livingstone, and Anthony S. R. Manstead, 2013. 'Admiration Regulates Social Hierarchy: Antecedents, Dispositions, and Effects on Intergroup Behavior', *Journal of Experimental Social Psychology*,49(3): 1078–91.

Tangney, June Price, and Ronda L. Dearing. 2002. *Shame and Guilt* (The Guilford Press).

Taplin, Jonathan. 2017. *Move Fast and Break Things: How Facebook, Google, and Amazon Have Cornered Culture and What It Means for All of Us* (Macmillan).

Taylor, Gabrielle. 1985. *Pride, Shame and Guilt: Emotions of Self-Assessment* (Oxford University Press).

Taylor, Lance, and Özlem Ömer. 2020. *Macroeconomic Inequality from Reagan to Trump: Market Power, Wage Repression, Asset Price Inflation, and Industrial Decline (Studies in New Economic Thinking)* (Cambridge University Press).

Taylor, Robert S. 2004. 'Self-Realization and the Priority of Fair Equality of Opportunity', *Journal of Moral Philosophy*, 1: 333–47.

Taylor, Robert S. 2017. *Exit Left: Markets and Mobility in Republican Thought* (Oxford University Press).

Tcherneva, Pavlina. 2012. 'Full Employment Through Social Entrepreneurship: The Nonprofit Model for Implementing a Job Guarantee', Levy Economics Institute of Bard College.

Tcherneva, Pavlina. 2013. 'The Job Guarantee: Delivering the Benefits That Basic Income Only Promises—A Reply to Guy Standing', *Basic Income Studies*, 7: 66–87.

Tcherneva, Pavlina. 2014. 'Growth for Whom?', *One Pagers* (Levy Economics Institute).

Tcherneva, Pavlina. 2015. 'When a Rising Tide Sinks Most Boats: Trends in US Income Inequality', *Policy Note* (Levy Economics Institute).

Tcherneva, Pavlina. 2017. 'Inequality Update: Who Gains When Income Grows?', *Policy Note* (Levy Economics Institute).

Tcherneva, Pavlina. 2020. *The Case for a Job Guarantee* (Polity Press).

Temin, Peter. 2017. *The Vanishing Middle Class: Prejudice and Power in a Dual Economy* (MIT Press).

Thatcher, Margaret. 1974. 'Britain Can Win', *News of the World*, September 22.

Therborn, Göran. 2017. 'Dynamics of Inequality', *New Left Review*, 103, Jan/Feb.

Thoits, Peggy A., and Lyndi N. Hewitt. 2001. 'Volunteer Work and Well-Being', *Journal of Health and Social Behavior*, 42(2): 115–31.

Thomas, Alan. 2006. *Value and Context: The Nature of Moral and Political Knowledge* (Clarendon Press).

Thomas, Alan. 2008. *Thomas Nagel* (Routledge).

Thomas, Alan. 2010. 'Alienation, Objectification and the Primacy of Virtue', in Jonathan Webber (ed.), *Reading Sartre: On Phenomenology and Existentialism* (Routledge), pp. 161–79.

Thomas, Alan. 2011. 'Cohen's Critique of Rawls: A Double Counting Objection', *Mind*, 120: 1099–141.

Thomas, Alan. 2015. 'Rawls and Political Realism: Realistic Utopianism or Judgement in Bad Faith?', *European Journal of Political Theory*, 16: 304–24.

Thomas, Alan. 2017. *Republic of Equals: Pre-Distribution and Property-Owning Democracy* (Oxford University Press).

Thomas, Alan. 2018. 'Should Epistemic Injustices Be Redressed by the "Corrective Virtues"?', in Mark LeBar (ed.), *Justice: The Virtues* (Oxford University Press), pp. 209–36.

Thomas, Alan. 2019. 'Edmundson on Neo-Liberalism: Towards a "Left-Rawlsian" Political Economy', *Ethical Perspectives*, 26: 352–8.

Thomas, Alan. 2020a. 'Freeman on Property-Owning Democracy', *Philosophy and Public Issues*, 10: 45–68.

Thomas, Alan. 2020b. 'Full Employment, Unconditional Basic Income and the Keynesian Critique of Rentier Capitalism', *Basic Income Studies*, 15(1): 1–38.

Thomas, Alan. 2020c. 'Rawls on Economic Liberty and the Choice of Systems of Social Cooperation', in John Mandle and Sarah Roberts-Cady (eds.), *John Rawls: Debating the Major Questions* (Oxford University Press), pp. 109–21.

Thomas, Alan. 2021. 'Market Socialism, Labour Market Domination, and the State as Employer of Last Resort', *Review of Social Economy*,79(3): 528–53.

Thomas, Alan. 2023. 'Is the Democratisation of Central Banking a Technocratic Problem?', SSRN preprint. https://papers.ssrn.com/sol3/papers.cfm?abstract_id=4455087 [Accessed 30/11/23].

Thompson, Don. 2018. *The Orange Balloon Dog: Bubbles, Turmoil and Avarice in the Contemporary Art Market* (Aurum Press).

Thompson, Douglas I. 2019. 'Review of Kevin Vallier, *Must Politics Be War? Restoring Our Trust in the Open Society*', *Notre Dame Philosophical Reviews.* https://ndpr.nd.edu/reviews/must-politics-be-war-restoring-our-trust-in-the-open-society/.

Thrash, Todd M., and Andrew J. Elliot. 2004. 'Inspiration: Core Characteristics, Component Processes, Antecedents, and Function', *Journal of Personality and Social Psychology*, 87(6): 957.

Tiberius, Valerie. 2015. 'Prudential Value', in Iwao Hirose and Jonas Olson (eds.), *The Oxford Handbook of Value Theory* (Oxford University Press), pp. 158–74.

Tilly, Charles. 1998. *Durable Inequality* (University of California Press).

Tomasi, John. 2012. *Free Market Fairness* (Princeton University Press).

Tooze, Adam. 2018. *Crashed: How a Decade of Financial Crises Changed the World* (Allen Lane).

Tooze, Adam. 2021a. 'The Gatekeeper', *London Review of Books.* April 22.

Tooze, Adam. 2021b. *Shutdown: How Covid Shook the World's Economy* (Allen Lane).

Townsend, Peter. 1962/2010. 'The Meaning of Poverty', *British Journal of Sociology*, 13: 210–27.

Townsend, Peter. 1979. *Poverty in the United Kingdom* (Allen Lane).

Troop, Nicholas A., Steven Allan, Lucy Serpell, Janet L. Treasure. 2008. Shame in Women with a History of Eating Disorders: European Eating Disorders Review: *Professional Journal of the Eating Disorders Association*, 16(6): 480–8.

Trump, Kris-Stella. 2017. 'Income Inequality Influences Perceptions of Legitimate Income Differences', *British Journal of Political Science*, 48: 929–52.

Turchin, Peter. 2023. *End-Times: Elites, Counter-Elites, and the Path of Political Disintegration* (Penguin).

Turner, Adair. 2015. 'The Case for Monetary Finance: An Essentially Political Issue', *16th Jacques Polak Annual Research Conference, IMF.* Washington, DC.

Van de Ven, Niels. 2016. 'Envy and Its Consequences: Why It Is Useful to Distinguish Between Benign and Malicious Envy', *Social and Personality Psychology Compass*, 10(6): 337–49.

Van de Ven, Niels, Alfred Archer, and Bart Engelen. 2019. 'More Important and Surprising Actions of a Moral Exemplar Trigger Stronger Admiration and Inspiration', *Journal of Social Psychology*, 159(4): 383–97.

Van de Ven, Niels, and Marcel Zeelenberg. 2015. 'On the Counterfactual Nature of Envy: "It Could Have Been Me"', *Cognition and Emotion*, 29(6): 954–71.

Van de Ven, Niels, Marcel Zeelenberg, and Rik Pieters. 2009. 'Levelling Up and Down: The Experiences of Benign and Malicious Envy', *Emotion*, 9(3): 419.

Van de Ven, Niels, Marcel Zeelenberg, and Rik Pieters. 2011. 'Why Envy Outperforms Admiration', *Personality and Social Psychology Bulletin*, 37(6): 784–95.

Van de Ven, Niels, Marcel Zeelenberg, and Rik Pieters. 2012. 'Appraisal Patterns of Envy and Related Emotions', *Motivation and Emotion*, 36(2): 195–204.

van de Werfhorst, Herman G. 2014. 'Changing Societies and Four Tasks of Schooling: Challenges for Strongly Differentiated Educational Systems', *International Review of Education*, 60(1): 123–44.

Van Parijs, Philippe. 1995. *Real Freedom for All: What (If Anything) Can Justify Capitalism?* (Oxford University Press).

Van Sickle, John V., and Benjamin A. Rogge. 1954. *Introduction to Economics* (Van Nostrand).

Varian, Hal R. 1976. 'Two Problems in the Theory of Fairness', *Journal of Public Economics*, 5: 249–60.

Varoufakis, Yanis. 2011. *The Global Minotaur: America, the True Origins of the Financial Crisis and the Future of the World Economy* (Zed Books).

Veblen, Thorstein. 1899/2009. *The Theory of the Leisure Class* (Oxford World's Classics).

Veblen, Thorstein. 1921/2019. *The Engineers and the Price System* (E-Artnow Reprint Editions).

Veenhoven, Ruut. 1991. 'Is Happiness Relative?', *Social Indicators Research*, 24: 1–34.
Velleman, David. 2009. *How We Get Along* (Cambridge University Press).
Velotti, Patrizia, Jeff Elison, and Carlo Garofalo. 2014. 'Shame and Aggression: Different Trajectories and Implications', *Aggression and Violent Behavior*, 19(4): 454–61.
Vergara, Camila. 2020. 'Populism as Plebeian Politics: Inequality, Domination and Popular Empowerment', *Journal of Political Philosophy*, 28: 222–46.
Vetter, Barbara. 2013. 'Multi-Track Dispositions', *Philosophical Quarterly*, 63: 330–52.
Vianello, M., E. M. Galliani, and J. Haidt. 2010. 'Elevation at Work: The Effects of Leaders' Moral Excellence', *Journal of Positive Psychology*, 5(5): 390–411.
Vickrey, William. 1960. 'Utility, Strategy and Social Decision Rules', *Quarterly Journal of Economics*, 74: 507–35.
Viktorsson, Mio Tastas, and Saoirse Gowan. 2017. 'Revisiting the Meidner Plan', *Jacobin* August 22. https://www.jacobinmag.com/2017/08/sweden-social-democracy-meidner-plan-capital [Accessed 30/11/23].
Walker, Robert. 2014. *The Shame of Poverty* (Oxford University Press).
Walker, Robert, and Elaine Chase. 2015. Adding to the Shame of Poverty: The Public, Politicians and the Media. *Child Poverty Action Group*, 148: 9–13
Walker, Robert, Grace Bantebya Kyomuhendo, Elaine Chase, et al. 2013. 'Poverty in Global Perspective: Is Shame a Common Denominator?', *Journal of Social Policy*, 42: 215–33.
Walzer, Michael. 1983. *Spheres of Justice: A Defense of Pluralism and Equality* (Basic Books).
Weinstein, Jack Russell. 2019. 'Adam Smith on Slavery', https://www.adamsmithworks.org/documents/adam-smith-on-slavery [Accessed 18/07/24].
Welpinghus, Anna. 2018. 'Is the Appropriateness of Emotions Culture-Dependent? The Relevance of Social Meaning', *Journal of Social Ontology*, 4: 67–92.
Werhane, Patricia. 1991. *Adam Smith and His Legacy for Modern Capitalism* (Oxford University Press).
White, Matthew, and Paul Dolan. 2009. 'Accounting for the Richness of Daily Activities', *Psychological Science*, 20: 1000–8.
Whitney, Shiloh. 2018. 'Affective Intentionality and Affective Injustice: Merleau-Ponty and Fanon on the Body Schema as a Theory of Affect', *Southern Journal of Philosophy* 56(4): 488–515.
Wicker, Frank W., Glen C. Payne, and Randall D. Morgan. 1983. 'Participant Descriptions of Guilt and Shame', *Motivation and Emotion*, 7: 25–39.
Wietzke, Frank-Borge. 2016. Kicking Away the Ladder? Poverty Reduction and Public Support for Redistribution in Emerging Economies. *Socio-Economic Review*, 14(3): 419–42.
Wilkinson, Richard, and Kate Pickett. 2009. *The Spirit Level: Why Equality Is Better for Everyone* (Allen Lane).
Wilkinson, Richard, and Kate Pickett. 2018. *The Inner Level: How More Equal Societies Reduce Stress, Restore Sanity and Improve Everyone's Well-Being* (Allen Lane).
Williams, Bernard. 1973a. 'Deciding to Believe', in *Problems of the Self: Philosophical Papers 1956–1972* (Cambridge University Press), pp. 136–51.
Williams, Bernard. 1973b. 'The Idea of Equality', in *Problems of the Self: Philosophical Papers 1956–1972* (Cambridge University Press), pp. 230–49.
Williams, Bernard. 1993. *Shame and Necessity* (University of California Press).
Williams, Bernard. 2002. *Truth and Truthfulness: An Essay in Genealogy* (Princeton University Press).
Williams, Joan. 1999. *Unbending Gender: Why Family and Work Conflict and What to Do About It* (Oxford University Press).
Wilson, William Julius. 2012. *The Truly Disadvantaged: The Inner City, the Underclass, and Public Policy* (University of Chicago Press).
Winters, Jeffrey. 2011. *Oligarchy* (Cambridge University Press).
Wittgenstein, Ludwig. 1979. *Notebooks 1914–16* (Blackwell).

World Economic Forum. 2017. *The Global Risks Report 2017.* http://www3.weforum.org/docs/GRR17_Report_web.pdf [Accessed 30/11/23].

Wu, Tim. 2020. *The Curse of Bigness: How Corporate Giants Came to Rule the World* (Atlantic Press).

Yack, Bernard. 1986. *The Longing for Total Revolution: Philosophic Sources of Social Discontent from Rousseau to Marx and Nietzsche* (Princeton University Press).

Yongmie, Nicola Joe. 2013. 'The Psychosocial Dimensions of Poverty: When Poverty Becomes Shameful', *Critical Social Policy*, 33: 514–31.

Young, Iris M. 1990/2011. *Justice and the Politics of Difference* (Princeton University Press).

Young, Michael. 1958/1994. *The Rise of the Meritocracy* (Transaction Books).

Young, Michael. 2001. 'Down with Meritocracy', *Guardian*, June 29. https://www.theguardian.com/politics/2001/jun/29/comment [Accessed 30/11/23].

Zacarés, Javier Moreno. 2021. 'Euphoria of the Rentier?', *New Left Review*, 129. https://newleftreview.org/issues/ii129/articles/javier-moreno-zacares-euphoria-of-the-rentier [Accessed 30/11/23].

Zagzebski, Linda T. 2015. 'Exemplarism and Admiration', in Christian Miller, R. Michael Furr, Angela Knobel, and William Fleeson (eds.), *Character: New Directions from Philosophy, Psychology, and Theology* (Oxford University Press), pp. 251–68.

Zagzebski, Linda T. 2017. *Exemplarist Moral Theory* (Oxford University Press).

Zelizer, Valerie A. 1979. *Morals and Markets: The Development of Life Insurance in the United States* (Columbia University Press).

Zucman, Gabriel. 2015. *The Hidden Wealth of Nations: The Scourge of Tax Havens* (University of Chicago Press).

Index of Names

For the benefit of digital users, indexed terms that span two pages (e.g., 52–53) may, on occasion, appear on only one of those pages.

Index of Terms

For the benefit of digital users, indexed terms that span two pages (e.g., 52–53) may, on occasion, appear on only one of those pages.

Tables are indicated by an italic *t* following the page number.